Upper West Side

Central Park

Upper East Side

Upper Midtown

Morningside Heights and Harlem

Lower Midtown

East River

Morningside Heights and Harlem
Pages 222–33

Upper Midtown
Pages 168–83

Lower Midtown
Pages 152–67

Upper West Side
Pages 212–21

Gramercy and the Flatiron District
Pages 124–31

Upper East Side
Pages 184–205

Central Park
Pages 206–11

East Village
Pages 118–23

0 kilometers   2

0 miles   1

Books should be returned or renewed by
above. Renew by phone **08458 247 200**
www.kent.gov.uk/libs

braries & Archives

EYEWITNESS TRAVEL

NEW YORK CITY

Main Contributor **Eleanor Berman**

LONDON, NEW YORK,
MELBOURNE, MUNICH AND DELHI
www.dk.com

Project Editor Fay Franklin

Art Editor Tony Foo

Editors Donna Dailey, Ellen Dupont, Esther Labi

Designers Steve Bere, Louise Parsons, Mark Stevens

Editorial Assistant Fiona Morgan

Contributors

Lester Brooks, Patricia Brooks, Susan Farewell

Photographers

Max Alexander, Dave King, Michael Moran

Illustrators

Richard Draper, Robbie Polley, Hamish Simpson

This book was produced with the assistance of
Websters International Publishers.

Printed and bound by L.Rex Printing Co. Ltd, China.

First published in Great Britain in 1993
by Dorling Kindersley Limited
80 Strand, London WC2R 0RL

14 15 16 17 10 9 8 7 6 5 4 3 2 1

Reprinted with revisions 1994, 1995 (twice), 1997, 1999, 2000, 2001, 2002,
2003, 2004, 2005, 2006, 2007, 2008, 2009, 2010, 2011, 2012, 2013, 2014

Copyright 1993, 2014 © Dorling Kindersley Limited, London

A Penguin Random House Company

A CIP catalogue record is available from the British Library.

ISBN: 978-1-40932-687-8

Throughout this book, floors are referred to in accordance with
American usage, ie the "first floor" is at ground level.

MIX
Paper from
responsible sources
FSC™ C018179
www.fsc.org

Front cover main image: Chrysler Building

◀ Towering skyscrapers in central New York

Contents

How to use this Guide 6

New York
Yankees Baseball
star Babe Ruth
(1895–1948)

Introducing
New York City

Great Days in
New York City 10

Putting New York City
on the Map 14

Iconic yellow taxis in New York City

The History of
New York City 18

New York City
at a Glance 36

New York City
Through the Year 52

The Manhattan
Skyline 56

Fresh produce for sale in Chinatown

Authentic New York dining at the Oyster Bar in Grand Central Terminal

The New York City Ballet

Solomon R. Guggenheim Museum, Upper East Side

HOW TO USE THIS GUIDE

This Eyewitness Travel Guide helps you get the most from your stay in New York with the minimum of practical difficulty. The opening section, *Introducing New York*, locates the city geographically, sets modern New York in its historical context and describes the highlights of the year. *New York at a Glance* is an overview of the city's attractions. Section two, *New York Area by Area*, guides you through the city's sightseeing areas. It describes all the main

sights with maps, photographs and detailed illustrations. In addition, seven planned walks take you step-by-step through special areas.

Well-researched tips on where to stay, eat, shop, and on sports and entertainment are in section three, *Travelers' Needs*. Children's New York lists highlights for young visitors, and section four, *Survival Guide*, shows you how to do everything from mailing a letter to using the subway.

New York City Area by Area

Manhattan has been divided into 15 sightseeing areas, each described separately. Each area opens with a portrait, summing up the area's character and

history and listing all the sights to be covered. Sights are numbered and clearly located on an *Area Map*. After this comes a large-scale *Street-by-Street Map* focusing on the most interesting

part of the area. Finding your way around each area is made simple by the numbering system. This refers to the order in which sights are described on the pages that follows.

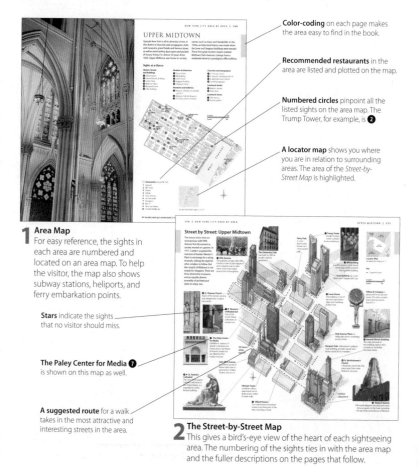

Color-coding on each page makes the area easy to find in the book.

Recommended restaurants in the area are listed and plotted on the map.

Numbered circles pinpoint all the listed sights on the area map. The Trump Tower, for example, is ❷

A locator map shows you where you are in relation to surrounding areas. The area of the *Street-by-Street Map* is highlighted.

1 Area Map
For easy reference, the sights in each area are numbered and located on an area map. To help the visitor, the map also shows subway stations, heliports, and ferry embarkation points.

Stars indicate the sights that no visitor should miss.

The Paley Center for Media ❼ is shown on this map as well.

A suggested route for a walk takes in the most attractive and interesting streets in the area.

2 The Street-by-Street Map
This gives a bird's-eye view of the heart of each sightseeing area. The numbering of the sights ties in with the area map and the fuller descriptions on the pages that follow.

New York City at a Glance

Each map in this section concentrates on a specific theme: *Museums, Architecture, Multicultural New York,* and *Celebrated New Yorkers*. The top sights are shown on the map; other sights are described on the following two pages.

Each sightseeing area is color-coded.

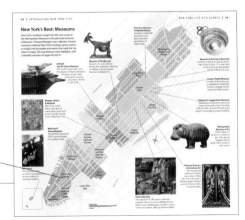

Practical Information lists all the information you need to visit every sight, including a map reference to the Street Finder at the back of the book.

Numbers refer to each sight's position on the area map and its place in the chapter.

3 **Detailed information on each sight**
All important sights in each area are described in depth in this section. They are listed in order, following the numbering on the *Area Map*. Practical information on opening hours, telephone numbers, websites, admission charges and facilities available is given for each sight. The key to the symbols used can be found on the back flap.

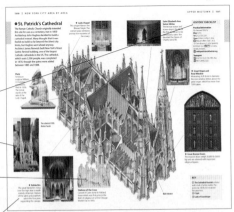

The Visitors' Checklist provides the practical information you will need to plan your visit.

The facade of each major sight is shown to help you spot it quickly.

Stars indicate the most interesting architectural details of the building, and the most important works of art or exhibits on view inside.

Numbered circles point out key features of the sight listed in a key.

4 **New York's major sights**
These are given two or more full pages in the sightseeing area in which they are found. Notable buildings are dissected to reveal their interiors; and museums and galleries have color-coded floor plans to help you find particular exhibits.

INTRODUCING
NEW YORK
CITY

GREAT DAYS IN NEW YORK CITY

New York is a city packed with treasures of things to see and do. Whether here for several days, or just wanting a flavor of this great city, you need to make the most of your time. Over the following pages, you'll find itineraries for some of the best attractions New York has to offer, arranged first by theme and then by length of stay. There's a mix of activities, and the schedules are not meant to be rigid – you'll find ample time to explore places that catch your fancy. Price guides on pages 10–11 show the cost for two adults or for a family of two adults and two children including lunch.

City Landmarks

Two adults
allow at least $140

- A tour of the UN
- Modern, Art Deco, and Beaux Arts edifices
- Lights of Times Square
- Empire State Building

Morning
Start at the East River with a guided tour of the **United Nations headquarters** *(see pp162–5)*, with its striking modern architecture. Then head to 42nd Street, detouring into the unique residential enclave of **Tudor City** *(see p160)*, and dropping in to admire the Art Deco interior of the **Chrysler Building** *(see p157)*. Next is **Grand Central Terminal**, a great Beaux Art landmark *(see pp158–9)*. Admire the Main Concourse and explore the shopping gallery, colorful food market, and a food court with everything from sushi to Southern barbecue to New York cheesecake. Another lunchtime option is chowder or a platter of Long Island oysters at the **Grand Central Oyster Bar** *(see p299)*.

Afternoon
Back on 42nd Street is another Beaux Arts creation, the **New York Public Library** *(see p148; free one-hour tours at 11am and 2pm Tue–Thu)*. The marble halls, stairways, Main Reading Room and Periodicals Room are highlights. Check your e-mail for free in the Bill Blass Public Catalog Room. Look out also for current exhibits. Behind the library is **Bryant Park** *(see p147)*, a welcome oasis of green in midtown. Ahead is New York's most famous crossroads, **Times Square** *(see p149)*, gateway to the glittering neon of Broadway. Just beyond is 42nd Street, now a bright avenue of restored theaters, giant movie palaces, and Madame Tussaud's Wax Museum, with many true-to-life celebrities. Hail a cab to the **Empire State Building** *(see pp138–9)* and end the day with a fine twilight view of the city from the 86th-floor observatory.

Glistening Prometheus Statue and Lower Plaza at Rockefeller Center

Art and Shopping

Two adults
allow at least $135

- A morning of modern art
- Lunch at Rockefeller Center
- Fifth Avenue shopping
- Tea at The Pierre

Morning
The spectacular **Museum of Modern Art** (MoMA) *(see pp174–7)* will easily fill your morning with its wonderful art. Allow a couple of hours to enjoy its great works, including Van Gogh's *The Starry Night* and Claude Monet's *Water Lilies*, as well as Picasso's *Les Demoiselles d'Avignon*, to name just a few. Don't miss the design exhibits on floor three; one of MoMA's best-known facets. Leave the museum and stroll over to the **Rockefeller Center** *(see p146)* for lunch at the Rock Center Café, where you can watch the ice skaters in winter. In summer the rink is transformed into a leafy garden, where you can dine at the Rink Bar.

The neon lights of Times Square, the city's famous crossroads

◀ Aerial view of the tip of Manhattan in 1942

Afternoon

After lunch head for **St. Patrick's Cathedral** *(see pp180–81)*, the largest Catholic cathedral in the US and one of the city's finest places of worship. Then continue along **Fifth Avenue** for an afternoon of upscale shopping. Saks Fifth Avenue is just across the street from St. Patrick's at 50th Street. Heading uptown, the temptations include a dizzying variety of glitzy shops, such as Cartier (52nd St), Henri Bendel (55–56th sts), Prada, Tiffany (57th St), and Bergdorf Goodman (57–58 sts). End the day on Lexington Avenue with a final splurge – enjoy a drink at **Whiskey Blue** *(see p308)*.

Historic New York

Two adults
allow at least $120

- **A boat trip to Ellis Island and the Statue of Liberty**
- **Lunch at Fraunces Tavern**
- **A tour of Old New York**

Morning

At Battery Park, board the ferry to the **Statue of Liberty** *(see pp76–7)* and on to **Ellis Island** *(see pp80–81)*, the point of arrival for many immigrants (round trip includes both stops). On your return, exit the park at **Bowling Green**, the city's oldest park *(see p75)*. Walk to the **Fraunces Tavern Block Historic District** *(see p78)*, New York's last block of 18th-century commercial buildings. The recreated Tavern includes a museum of the revolutionary period and a restaurant that is the perfect choice for an atmospheric lunch.

Afternoon

A block away is Stone Street Historic District, rebuilt after a fire in 1835. Look for **India House** *(see p58)*, once the New York Cotton Exchange, now **Harry's Café**. Take William Street to Wall Street and **Federal Hall** *(see p70)*, with exhibits on the US Constitution. Nearby is the **New York Stock Exchange** *(see pp72–3)* and **Trinity Church** *(see p70)*, built in 1839. Go up Broadway to **St. Paul's Chapel** *(see p93)*, miraculously unscathed after the World Trade Center fell behind it. Ahead is **City Hall** *(see p92)*. Finally, head for the **South Street Seaport Historic District**, heart of the 19th-century port *(see pp84–5)*, with a view of the awesome **Brooklyn Bridge** *(see pp88–91)*.

A Family Fun Day

Family of four allow at least $225

- **A morning in Central Park**
- **Lunch at the Boathouse**
- **Dinosaurs at the American Museum of Natural History**

Morning

Central Park *(see pp207–11)* was made for family fun. Ride the vintage Carousel, watch model boats in action at Conservatory Pond, visit the Zoo, then watch the animal parade on the Delacorte clock on the half hour. There are themed playgrounds to please all ages: Safari at West 91st Street (2–5 years); Adventure at West 67th Street (6–12 years). The Swedish Cottage

Central Park, a vast area of fun rides, animals, and places to play

Marionette Theater, at West 79th, presents classic fairy tales at 10:30am and noon Tue–Fri (Wed also 2:30pm) and 1pm Sat; book ahead. Rent bikes or take a boat out on the lake, then lunch at the Boat House, which has a view of the lake. In winter, you can ice skate at the Wollman rink.

Afternoon

Depending on ages and interests, choose between the interactive **Children's Museum** *(see p221)*, or the famous dinosaurs and dioramas at the **American Museum of Natural History** *(see pp218–19)*. Finish up on West 73rd Street for a "wee tea" at Alice's Tea Cup.

Ellis Island, the view greeting early immigrants to New York

View uptown over the vast expanse of Central Park

2 days in New York City

- Marvel at the masterpieces in the Met
- Ascend the Empire State Building for iconic views
- Take a boat to the Statue of Liberty and Ellis Island

Day 1
Morning Start with a one-hour guided tour of the city's vast **Metropolitan Museum of Art** (pp192–9), known as the Met, daily at 10:15am. Follow this with a walk through neighboring **Central Park** (pp206–211), with views of the lake and the skyline beyond.

Afternoon Hop on the Fifth Avenue bus to 59th Street and Grand Army Plaza, then walk on down **Fifth Avenue** (p172) to the **Rockefeller Center** (p146) at 49th Street, passing shopping meccas such as Bergdorf Goodman, Tiffany, Trump Tower, and Saks Fifth Avenue, as well as the striking **St. Patrick's Cathedral** (pp180–81). Visit the 89th-floor observatory at the **Empire State Building** (pp138–9) for the legendary panorama of the city. For souvenir shopping, the "world's largest store," **Macy's** (pp136–7), is a block west. After dark, enjoy the bright lights of **Times Square** (p149), and take in a **Broadway** (p336) show. Check the TKTS booth on Times Square for discount seats.

Day 2
Morning To avoid long lines head to **Battery Park** (p79) early to catch the boat to the **Statue of Liberty** (pp76–7) and **Ellis Island** (pp80–81), the symbol of America's immigrant heritage. There will be time on your return to visit the moving **National September 11 Memorial** (p74), in Lower Manhattan. Book in advance.

Afternoon Stroll down Wall Street, taking in the monumental Neo-Classical facade of the **New York Stock Exchange** (pp72–3) on the corner of Broad Street. Next,

head to historic **South Street Seaport** (p86), once the hub of New York's seafaring activity. Spend a couple of hours wandering this cobblestone neighborhood, now home to historic ships, museums, food stalls, and shops. End the day with a sunset walk across **Brooklyn Bridge** (pp88–91).

3 days in New York City

- Enjoy modern art at MoMA
- Visit the National September 11 Memorial
- See a show on Broadway

Day 1
Morning Take in city views from the top of the **Empire State Building** (pp138–9), then stroll up **Fifth Avenue** (p172) with its luxury stores. Detour along 42nd Street to see the beautiful interiors of the **Grand Central Terminal** (pp158–9), then continue on to the **Rockefeller Center** (p146) for an exploratory wander. **St. Patrick's Cathedral** (pp180–81) is across the street.

Afternoon See masterpieces at the **Museum of Modern Art** (pp174–7) and shop for souvenirs at the MoMA store or **Macy's** (pp136–7). At night, the bright lights of **Broadway** (p336) beckon.

Day 2
Morning After a stroll through Central Park (pp206–211), visit the **Metropolitan Museum of Art** (pp192–9). Step into the lobby

of Frank Lloyd Wright's **Solomon R. Guggenheim Museum** (pp190–91) to admire the amazing architecture, and linger to see some modern art.

Afternoon Take a walk on the **High Line** (p140), the city's park in the sky, then stroll around the leafy lanes of trendy **Greenwich Village** (pp110–17) and browse its many book, clothes, and music stores. At night, sample the lively cafés of **SoHo** (pp102–109), or opt for a show at the **Lincoln Center for the Performing Arts** (p216).

Day 3
Morning Start with the city's symbol of freedom, the **Statue of Liberty** (pp76–7), and a visit to the fascinating **Ellis Island** (pp80–81); arrive early at **Battery Park** (p79) for shorter lines for the boat ride. Afterward, take time to visit the **National September 11 Memorial** (p74).

The spiral rotunda of Frank Lloyd Wright's Solomon R. Guggenheim Museum

Afternoon Visit the fascinating **Museum of Jewish Heritage** *(p79)*, then wander down Wall Street to see the grand **New York Stock Exchange** *(pp72–3)*. End the day with a stroll and an early dinner in **South Street Seaport** *(p86)*, from where there are also great views of **Brooklyn Bridge** *(pp88–91)*.

5 days in New York City

- Take a walk in Central Park
- Explore Greenwich Village, SoHo, and Chelsea
- View the city from across beautiful Brooklyn Bridge

Day 1

Morning Head to **Fifth Avenue** *(p172)* to browse its famous stores and nearby sights including **St. Patrick's Cathedral** *(pp180–81)* and the **Rockefeller Center** *(p146)* with its Art Deco skyscrapers and beautiful gardens.

Afternoon Enjoy the open spaces of **Central Park** *(pp206–211)*, the masterpieces at the **Metropolitan Museum of Art** *(pp192–9)*, and great views from atop the **Empire State Building** *(pp138–9)*. In the evening, take in the lights of **Broadway** *(p336)*.

Day 2

Morning The boat ride to the **Statue of Liberty** *(pp76–7)* and **Ellis Island** *(pp80–1)* is a thrill, offering remarkable photo opportunities. Take the boat back late morning and visit the **National September 11 Memorial** *(p74)*, a very poignant experience.

Afternoon Visit the vibrant **Museum of Jewish Heritage** *(p79)*, then make your way to Wall Street for a stroll through the skyscraper canyons and to see the **New York Stock Exchange** *(pp72–3)*. Look out for the **Federal Hall** *(p70)* along the way. Next, spend a couple of hours exploring **South Street Seaport** *(p86)*, the city's old maritime center and now a lively complex with museums, shops, and restaurants.

Day 3

Morning Spend the morning exploring two major museums, the **Museum of Modern Art** *(pp174–7)* and Frank Lloyd Wright's **Solomon R. Guggenheim Museum** *(pp190–91)*, both with exciting modern art collections.

Afternoon Explore Manhattan's neighborhoods: the quaint, historic streets and lively cafés of **Greenwich Village** *(pp110–117)*, the shops and classic cast-iron buildings of **SoHo** *(pp106–107)*, or peruse a few of the many art galleries in **Chelsea** *(pp132–41)*. Take a walk along the city's most unusual park, the **High Line** *(p140)*, ending with the upscale boutiques on 14th Street in the trendy **Meat Packing District** *(pp115–16)*.

Day 4

Morning Explore the **Upper West Side** *(pp212–21)*, walking down to **Columbus Circle** *(p217)*. Take a tour of the **United Nations** *(pp162–5)* headquarters, then explore the **Lower East Side** *(pp94–103)*, where the **Lower East Side Tenement Museum** *(p99)* tells the tale of life in the city's old tenements. **Orchard Street** *(p100)*, a mix of bargain stores and hip boutiques, serves the newest generation of residents.

Afternoon Check out some big-name stores, such as **Lord and Taylor** *(p311)* and **Bloomingdales** *(p183)*, or take in at least one more museum. The **Frick Collection** *(pp204–205)*,

The Immigration Museum on Ellis Island, where 12 million US immigrants arrived

housed in a palatial gilded age mansion, has an outstanding collection of Old Masters. Alternatively, visit the **Whitney Museum** *(pp202–203)*, home to the entire range of 20th-century American art. In the evening, head to **Harlem** *(pp274–5)* for a jazz club or to see a show at the famous **Apollo Theater** *(p275)*.

Day 5

Morning Walk across **Brooklyn Bridge** *(pp88–91)* to **Brooklyn Heights Promenade** *(p269)* for views of Manhattan. A subway ride leads to Brooklyn's impressive **Grand Army Plaza** *(p250)* and the world-class **Brooklyn Museum** *(pp252–5)*.

Afternoon Spend some time admiring the lovely **Brooklyn Botanic Garden** *(p251)*, famous for its Japanese Garden, and **Prospect Park** *(pp250–51)*, laid out by Central Park's designers. Visit the **Brooklyn Academy of Music** *(p250)* for avant-garde theater and dance.

Elevated walkway on the Brooklyn Bridge, the world's first steel-wire suspension bridge

Putting New York City on the Map

New York is a city of eight million people, covering
301 sq miles (780 sq km). The city gives its name to
the state of New York, the capital of which is Albany,
156 miles (251 km) to the north. New York is also
a good base from which to visit the historic towns
of Boston and Philadelphia, as well as the
nation's capital, Washington, DC.

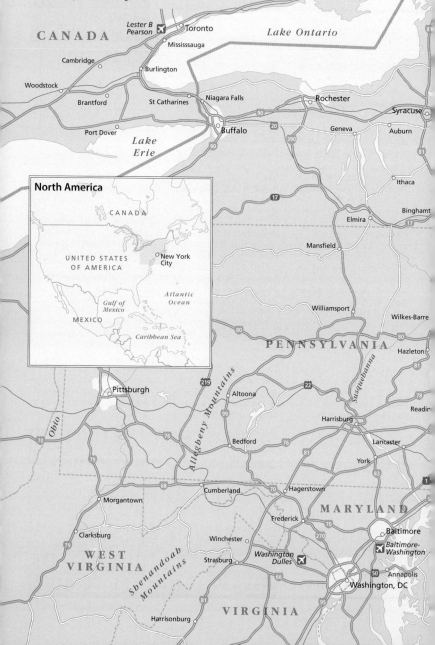

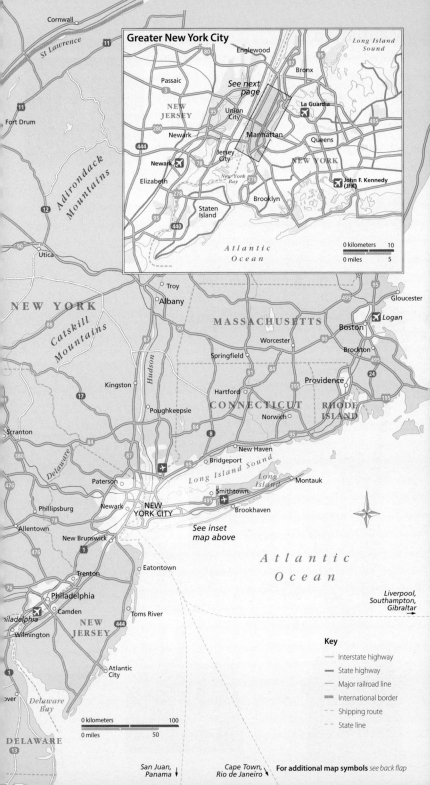

Greater New York City

Englewood

Bronx

Passaic

See next page

NEW
JERSEY

Union
City

La Guardia

Newark

Manhattan

Queens

Jersey
City

NEW
YORK

Newark

New York
Bay

John F. Kennedy
(JFK)

Elizabeth

Brooklyn

Staten
Island

*Atlantic
Ocean*

0 kilometers   10

0 miles   5

Cornwall

St Lawrence

Fort Drum

*Adirondack
Mountains*

Utica

Troy

Albany

MASSACHUSETTS

Gloucester

Logan

Boston

NEW YORK

*Catskill
Mountains*

Worcester

Brockton

Springfield

Hudson

Kingston

Hartford

Providence

Poughkeepsie

CONNECTICUT

RHODE
ISLAND

Scranton

Delaware

Norwich

New Haven

Paterson

Bridgeport

Long Island Sound

*Long
Island*

Montauk

Phillipsburg

Newark

NEW
YORK CITY

Smithtown

Allentown

Brookhaven

New Brunswick

*See inset
map above*

Trenton

Eatontown

*Atlantic
Ocean*

Philadelphia

Camden

Toms River

*Liverpool,
Southampton,
Gibraltar*

hiladelphia

Wilmington

NEW
JERSEY

Atlantic
City

Key

Interstate highway

State highway

Major railroad line

International border

Shipping route

State line

*Delaware
Bay*

DELAWARE

0 kilometers   100

0 miles   50

*San Juan,
Panama*

*Cape Town,
Rio de Janeiro*

For additional map symbols *see back flap*

Manhattan

This guide divides Manhattan into 15 areas, each with its own chapter. Many of New York's oldest and newest buildings rub shoulders in Lower Manhattan. It is from here, too, that you can take the Staten Island ferry, for breathtaking views of the city's famous skyline and the Statue of Liberty. Midtown includes the Theater District and Fifth Avenue's glittering shops. Museum Mile, alongside Central Park on Upper East Side, is a cultural paradise. To the north lies Harlem, America's most famous black community.

Grand Central Terminal
This Beaux Arts station has been a gateway to the city since 1913. Its concourse is a vast pedestrian area with a high-vaulted roof (see pp158–9).

Morgan Library & Museum
One of the world's finest collections of rare manuscripts, prints, and books is on display in this palazzo-style building (see pp166–7).

Statue of Liberty
Presented as a gift from the French to the American people in 1886, this towering statue has become a symbol of freedom throughout the world (see pp76–7).

Ellis
Island

Statue of
Liberty

48TH STREET
42ND STREET
34TH
THEATER
DISTRICT
Rockefeller
Center
TIMES
SQUARE
AMS

TENTH AVENUE
NINTH AVENUE
EIGHTH AVENUE
SEVENTH AVENUE
SIXTH AVENUE
AVENUE

CHELSEA
Empire State
Building
Pierpont
Morgan
Library

14TH STREET
GREENWICH
VILLAGE
WASHINGTON
SQUARE
GRAMERCY
PARK
23RD ST
AVENUE

Hudson River

WEST ST
CANAL ST
VARICK ST
SOHO
HOUSTON
THIRD
SECOND
FIRST
EAST
VILLAGE

TRIBECA
BROADWAY
DELANCEY ST
LOWER
EAST SIDE
EAST BROADWAY
BOWERY

WEST ST
CHURCH ST
BROADWAY
CIVIC
CENTER

LOWER
MANHATTAN
SOUTH STREET
VIADUCT
Brooklyn
Bridge

East River

**Cathedral of
St. John the Divine**
When it is finished, at some time after the mid-21st century, this great cathedral will be the largest in the world. It is also a theater and music venue (see pp228–9).

United Nations
New York is the headquarters of the global organization set up to preserve world peace and security (*see pp162–5*).

Empire State Building
This is one of America's tallest buildings and a symbol of New York City. Built in the 1930s, it has since attracted more than 110 million visitors (*see pp138–9*).

Metropolitan Museum of Art
With a stunning collection of artifacts dating from prehistoric times to the present, this is one of the world's greatest museums (*see pp192–99*).

Brooklyn Bridge
This bridge spans the East River between Manhattan and Brooklyn. Built in 1883, it was the largest suspension bridge and the first to be constructed of steel (*see pp88–91*).

Solomon R. Guggenheim Museum
A masterpiece of architecture by Frank Lloyd Wright, this unique building contains a fine collection of 19th- and 20th-century painting (*see pp190–91*).

THE HISTORY OF NEW YORK CITY

From its first sighting almost 500 years ago by Giovanni da Verrazano, New York's harbor was the prize that all of Europe wanted to capture. The Dutch first sent fur traders to the area in 1621, but they lost the colony they called New Amsterdam to the English in 1664. The settlement was re-christened New York and the name stayed, even after the English lost the colony in 1783, at the end of the Revolutionary War.

The Growing City

In the 19th century, New York grew rapidly and became a major port. Ease of shipping spawned manufacturing, commerce was king and great fortunes were made. In 1898, Manhattan was joined with the four outer boroughs to form the world's second-largest city. From 1800 to 1900, the population grew from 79,000 to 3 million people. New York City became the country's cultural and entertainment mecca as well as its business center.

The Melting Pot

The city continued to grow as thousands of immigrants came seeking a better life. Overpopulation meant that many at first lived in slums. Today, the mix of cultures has enriched the city and become its defining quality. Its eight million inhabitants speak some 100 languages.

Manhattan's skyline took shape as the city grew skyward to make space for its ever-increasing population. Throughout its history, the city has experienced alternating periods of economic decline and growth, but it remains one of the world's most vital cities.

The following pages illustrate significant periods in New York's history.

A deed signed by New Amsterdam's last Dutch governor, Peter Stuyvesant, in 1664

◀ The southern half of Manhattan and part of Brooklyn in 1767

Early New York City

Manhattan was a forested land populated by Algonquian-speaking Natives when the Dutch West India Company established a fur trading post called New Amsterdam in 1625. The first settlers built houses helter-skelter, so even today the streets of Lower Manhattan still twist. Broadway, then called by the Dutch name *Breede Wegh*, began as an Indian trail known as the Weekquaesgeek Trail. Harlem has also kept its Dutch name. The town was unruly until Peter Stuyvesant arrived to bring order. But the colony did not produce the expected revenues, and in 1664 the Dutch let it fall to the English, who renamed it New York.

Growth of the Metropolis

▨ 1664   ▨ Today

Seal of New Netherland
The beaver pelt and wampum (Indian shell beads) on the seal were the currency of the colony of New Netherland.

The First New Yorkers
Algonquian-speaking Natives were the first inhabitants of Manhattan.

Dutch ships

Iroquois Pot
Iroquois Indians were frequent visitors to early Manhattan.

Indian Village
Some Algonquians lived in longhouses on Manhattan before the Dutch arrived.

Native canoe

First View Of Manhattan (1626)
The southern tip of Manhattan resembled a Dutch town, down to the windmill. Although shown here, the fort had not yet been built.

1524 Giovanni da Verrazano sails into New York harbor

1626 Peter Minuit buys Manhattan from the Natives

1625 Dutch establish first permanent trading post

1653 Wall is built for protection from attack; adjacent street is called Wall Street

1600	1620	1640

1609 Henry Hudson sails up the Hudson River in search of the Northwest Passage

1625 First black slaves brought from Africa

1643–45 Indian skirmishes end with temporary peace treaty

1654 First Jewish settlers arrive

1647 Peter Stuyvesant becomes colonial governor

Dutch Delftware
Colonists brought
this popular tinglazed
earthenware pottery
from Holland.

Tiger timbers

Where to see
Dutch New York

Dug up by workmen in 1916, these
remnants of a Dutch ship, the *Tiger*, which
burned in 1613, are the earliest artifacts of
the period and are now in the Museum of
the City of New York *(see p201)*. Rooms in
this museum, as well as in the Morris-Jumel
Mansion *(see p237)* and the Van Cortlandt
House Museum *(see p242)*, display Dutch
pottery, tiles and furniture.

Manhattan Skyline
The Strand, now Whitehall
Street, was the site of the
city's first brick house.

Fort
Amsterdam

Purchase of Manhattan
Peter Minuit bought the island
from the Natives in 1626 for
$24 worth of trinkets.

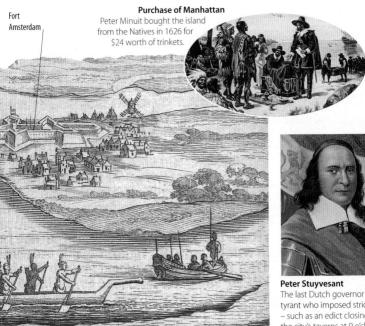

Peter Stuyvesant
The last Dutch governor was a
tyrant who imposed strict laws
– such as an edict closing all
the city's taverns at 9 o'clock.

1660 First city hospital established

1664 British forces oust Dutch
without a fight and change
name to New York

1676 Great
Dock built on
East River

1698 Trinity Church
dedicated

1660

1680

1700

*The surrender of New
Amsterdam to the British*

1683 First New York
city charter established

1693 Ninety-two cannons
installed for protection; area
becomes known as the Battery

1680s Bolting Laws give
New York exclusive right
to process and ship grain

1689 Merchant Jacob Leisler
leads revolt against taxes and
takes over the city for two years

1691 Leisler sentenced to
death for treason

Colonial New York City

Under British rule, New York prospered and the population grew rapidly. The bolting of flour (grinding grain) was the main commercial enterprise. Shipbuilding also flourished. As the city prospered, an elite emerged that could afford a more refined way of life, and fine furniture and household silver were made for use in their homes during the Colonial period. During more than a century of governing New York, Britain proved more interested in profit than in the welfare of the colony. The Crown imposed hated taxes, and the spirit of rebellion grew, although loyalties were divided, especially in New York. On the eve of Revolution, New York was the second-largest city in the 13 colonies, with 20,000 citizens.

Growth of the Metropolis

1760   Today

Colonial currency
This early paper money was based on the British pound.

Bedroom

Colonial Street
Pigs and dogs roamed free on the streets of Colonial New York.

Dining room

Shipping
Trade with the West Indies and Britain helped New York prosper. In some years, 200 or more vessels visited the port.

Kas
This Dutch-style pine wardrobe was made in New York's Hudson River valley around 1720.

1702 Lord Cornbury appointed Colonial governor; he often wore women's clothes

1711 Slave market set up at the foot of Wall Street

1734 John Peter Zenger's libel trial upholds freedom of the press

1720 First shipyard opens

1700

1710

1720

1730

1710 Iroquois chief Hendrick visits England

1725 New York Gazette, city's first newspaper, is established

1732 First city theater opens

1733 Bowling Green becomes first city park; first ferries to Brooklyn

Captain Kidd

The Scottish pirate William Kidd was a respected citizen, lending a block and tackle to help build Trinity Church *(see p70)*.

Van Cortlandt House

Frederick Van Cortlandt built this Georgian-style house in 1748 on a wheat plantation in what is now the Bronx. Today a museum (see p242), it shows how a well-to-do Dutch-English family once lived.

West parlor

Where to see Colonial New York

Colonial buildings are open to the public at Historic Richmond Town on Staten Island *(see p256)*. Fine examples of Colonial silver and furniture are on display at the Museum of the City of New York *(see p201)*.

Richmond Town General Store

Colonial Kitchen

Plain white cheese, called "white meat," was often served in place of meat. Waffles, introduced by the Dutch, were popular. Fresh fruit was rare, but preserved fruits were eaten.

Pewter baby bottle

Cheese mold

Waffle iron

Sucket fork, for eating preserved fruits

Decorative Carvings
A face carved in stone peers over each of the front windows.

1741 Slave uprising creates hysteria; 31 slaves are executed, 150 imprisoned

1754 French and Indian War begins; King's College (now Columbia University) founded

British soldier

1759 First jail built

1740	1750	1760

King's College

1762 First paid police force

1763 War ends; British gain control of North America

Revolutionary New York City

Dug up into trenches for defense, heavily shelled by British troops, and scarred by recurring fires, New York suffered during the American Revolution. But despite the hardships, many continued to enjoy cricket games, horse races, balls, and boxing matches. After the British took the city in 1776, it became their headquarters. The Continental army did not return to Manhattan until November 25, 1783, two years after the fighting ended.

Growth of the Metropolis

▦ 1776   ▦ Today

Battle Dress
The Continental (Patriot) army wore blue uniforms, while the British wore red.

British soldier

Soldier's Haversack
American soldiers in the War of Independence carried their supplies in haversacks.

American soldier

Toppling The King

New Yorkers tore down the statue of King George III in Bowling Green and melted it down to make ammunition.

Battle of Harlem Heights
Washington won this battle on September 16, 1776. But he did not have enough troops to hold New York so retreated, leaving it to the British.

Patriot

Death of a Patriot
While working behind British lines in 1776, Nathan Hale was captured and hanged by the British without trial for spying.

1765 British pass Stamp Act; New Yorkers protest; Sons of Liberty formed

1767 New duties imposed with Townshend Act; after protests, the act is repealed

1770 Sons of Liberty fight British in the "Battle of Golden Hill"

1774 Rebels dump tea in New York harbor to protest taxes

1760

1770

178

St. Paul's Chapel

1766 St. Paul's Chapel completed; Stamp Act repealed; Statue of George III erected on Bowling Green

General William Howe, commander in chief of the British troops

1776 War begins; 500 ships under General Howe assemble in New York harbor

Fire Fighters

Fires had long threatened the city, but during the war a series of fires nearly destroyed it. In the wake of the patriot retreat, on September 21, 1776, a devastating fire razed Trinity Church and 1,000 houses.

Leather fire bucket

Flags of the Revolution

Washington's army flew the Continental colors, with a stripe for each of the 13 colonies and a Union Jack in the corner. The Stars and Stripes became the official flag in 1777.

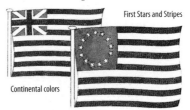

First Stars and Stripes

Continental colors

General Washington Returns

Washington received a hero's welcome when he reentered New York on November 25, 1783, after the British withdrawal.

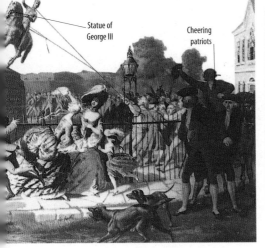

Statue of George III

Cheering patriots

Where to see the Revolutionary City

In 1776, George Washington used the Morris-Jumel Mansion in upper Manhattan as a headquarters *(see p237)*. He also slept at the Van Cortlandt House *(see p23 and p242)*. After the war he bade farewell to his officers at Fraunces Tavern *(see p78)*.

Morris-Jumel mansion

1783 Treaty of Paris signed, US wins independence; British evacuate New York

1789 George Washington inaugurated as first president at Federal Hall

1790 US capital is moved to Philadelphia

1801 *New York Post* founded by Alexander Hamilton

1794 Bellevue Hospital opens on the East River

1790

1800

1785 New York named US capital

1792 Tontine Coffee House built – first home of the Stock Exchange

1804 Vice President Aaron Burr kills political rival Alexander Hamilton in a duel

1784 Bank of New York chartered

1791 New York Hospital, city's oldest, opens

Washington's inauguration

New York City in the 19th Century

Firmly established as the nation's largest city and preeminent seaport, New York grew increasingly wealthy. Manufacturing increased due to the ease of shipping; tycoons like John Jacob Astor made millions. The rich moved uptown; public transportation followed. With rapid growth came fires, epidemics and financial panics. Immigrants from Ireland, Germany, and other nations arrived. Some found prosperity; others crowded into slums in Lower Manhattan.

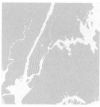

Growth of the Metropolis
▨ 1840   ▨ Today

Sheet Music
The Stephen Foster ballad *Jeanie With the Light Brown Hair was* popular at this time.

Croton Distributing Reservoir was built in 1842. Until then, New Yorkers had no fresh drinking water – they relied on deliveries of bottled water.

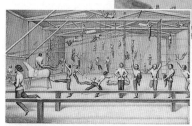

Keeping Fit
Gymnasiums such as Dr. Rich's Institute for Physical Education were established in New York in the 1830s and 1840s.

Omnibus
The horse-drawn omnibus was introduced for public transportation in 1832 and remained on New York streets until World War I.

1805 First free state schools established in New York

1811 Randel Plan divides Manhattan into grid pattern above 14th Street

1812–14 War of 1812; British blockade New York harbor

The Constitution, most famous ship in War of 1812

1835 Much of old New York razed in city's worst fire

1810

1820

1830

1807 Robert Fulton launches first steamboat, on the Hudson River

1822 Yellow fever epidemic; people evacuate to Greenwich Village

1827 New York abolishes slavery

1823 New York surpasses Boston and Philadelphia to become nation's largest city

1837 New Yorker Samuel Morse sends first telegraph message

The Brownstone
Many brownstone row houses were built in the first half of the century. The raised stoop allowed separate entry to the parlor and ground-floor servants' quarters.

Crystal Palace was an iron and glass exhibition hall erected for the 1853 World's Fair.

The Port of New York

New York's importance as a port city grew by leaps and bounds in the early 19th century. Robert Fulton launched his first steam-boat, the *Clermont*, in 1807. Steamboats made travel much quicker – it now took 72 hours to reach Albany, which was both the state capital and the gateway to the West. Trade with the West by steamboat and canal boat, and with the rest of the world by clipper ship, made the fortunes of many New Yorkers.

The steamboat *Clermont*

New York in 1855
Looking south from 42nd Street, Crystal Palace and the Croton Distributing Reservoir stood where the main public library and Bryant Park are today.

Crystal Palace in Flames
On October 5, 1858, New York's Crystal Palace exhibition hall burned to the ground, just as its predecessor in London did.

Grand Canal Celebration
Ships in New York harbor lined up to celebrate the 1825 Erie Canal opening. In connecting the Great Lakes with Albany, the state capital, on the Hudson River, the canal opened a water link between the Midwest and the Port of New York. New York realized huge profits.

1849 Astor Place riots; ships set sail for California Gold Rush

1851 *New York Times* first published

1861 Civil War begins

1863 Draft riots last four days, many die

1853 New York hosts World's Fair

1857 Financial panic and depression

1865 Abraham Lincoln lies in state in City Hall

1840

1850

1860

Early baseball player

1845 New York Knickerbockers, first organized baseball team chartered

Clipper ship card

FOR SAN FRANCISCO

1858 Vaux and Olmsted design Central Park; Macy's founded

Crowds in Central Park

1842 Croton Reservoir built

FREE TRADE

The Age of Extravagance

As New York's merchant princes grew ever wealthier, the city entered a gilded era during which many of its most opulent buildings went up. Millions were lavished on the arts with the founding of the Metropolitan Museum, Public Library and Carnegie Hall. Luxury hotels like the Plaza and the original Waldorf-Astoria were built, and elegant department stores arose to serve the wealthy. Such figures as William "Boss" Tweed, political strongman and king of corruption, and circus man Phineas T. Barnum were also larger than life.

Growth of the Metropolis
▨ 1890 ▨ Today

Overlooking the Park
The Dakota (1880) was the first grand luxury apartment house on the Upper West Side (see p220).

Palatial Living
Mansions lined Fifth Avenue. When it was built in 1882, W.K. Vanderbilt's Italianate palace at 660 Fifth Avenue, was one of the farthest north.

Fashion City
Lord & Taylor built a new store on Broadway's Ladies' Mile; 6th Avenue between 14th and 23rd streets was known as Fashion Row.

The Elevated Railroad
By the mid-1870s, elevated railroads or "Els" ran along 2nd, 3rd, 6th and 9th avenues. They made travel faster, but left noise, grime and pollution in their wake.

1867 Brooklyn's Prospect Park completed

1868 First elevated railroad built on Greenwich Street

1870 J.D. Rockefeller founds Standard Oil

1871 The first Grand Central Depot opens on 42nd St.; "Boss" Tweed is arrested and imprisoned

1877 A.G. Bell demonstrates the telephone in New York

1865

1870

1875

1869 First apartment house built on 18th Street; Black Friday financial crisis hits Wall Street

The interior of the Stock Exchange

1873 Banks fail: Stock Exchange panics

1872 Bloomingdale's opens

Mark Twain's Birthday
Mark Twain, whose 1873 novel *The Gilded Age* portrayed the decadent lifestyle of New Yorkers, celebrated his birthday at Delmonico's.

Where to see the Age of Extravagance

The Gold Room in the Henry Villard Houses *(see p178)* is a good place to experience the city's past. Formerly the Music Room, it is now an upscale bar called Gilt. The Museum of the City of New York also has period rooms *(p201)*.

Elevated train

Streetcar

Bowery

The Tweed Ring
William "Boss" Tweed led Tammany Hall, which dominated city government. He stole millions in city funds.

Nast's cartoon of "Boss" Tweed

Rural Fifth Avenue
This painting by Ralph Blakelock shows a shanty-town at 86th Street. Today it is one of New York's most expensive addresses.

Tammany Tiger
The Museum of the City of New York has "Boss" Tweed's cane, which sports a gold Tammany Tiger mascot on its handle.

1880 Canned fruits and meats first appear in stores; Metropolitan Museum of Art opens; streets lit by electricity

1883 Metropolitan Opera opens on Broadway; Brooklyn Bridge completed

1886 Statue of Liberty unveiled

1891 Carnegie Hall opens

1880

1885

1890

1879 St. Patrick's Cathedral completed; first city telephone exchange opened on Nassau Street

1888 Great Blizzard dumps 22 in (56 cm) of snow

Grand display of fireworks over Brooklyn Bridge, 1883

1890 First moving picture shows appear in New York

1892 Cathedral of St. John the Divine begun; Ellis Island opens

New York City at the Turn of the Century

By 1900, New York was a hub of American industry: seventy per cent of the country's corporations were based there, and the port handled two-thirds of all imported goods. The rich got richer, while in the crowded slums, disease spread. Even so, immigrants kept their rich traditions alive, and political and social reform emerged. In 1900, the International Ladies' Garment Workers' Union was founded to battle for the rights of the women and children who toiled in dangerous factories for low wages. The Triangle Shirtwaist Factory fire in 1911 also hastened reform.

Growth of the Metropolis
▨ 1914   ▨ Today

Gateway to America
Almost five times as crowded as the rest of New York, the Lower East Side was the most densely populated place in the world.

Crowded Conditions
Tenements were unhealthy and overcrowded. They often lacked windows, air shafts or proper sanitary facilities.

Where to see Turn-of-the-Century New York

The Lower East Side Tenement Museum *(see p99)* has exhibits on tenement life.

Tailor's scissors

Hip bath

Inside a Sweatshop
Workers toiled long hours for low wages in the overcrowded sweatshops of the garment district. This view of Moe Levy's shop was taken in 1912.

Streetcars on Broadway

1895 Olympia Theater is first to open in the Broadway area

1895

1896 First bagel served in a Clinton Street bakery

1897 Waldorf-Astoria Hotel opens: the largest hotel in the world

1898 Five boroughs merge to form world's second-largest city

1900 Mayor Robert Van Wyck breaks ground for city's first subway with silver shovel

1901 Macy's opens Broadway department store

1900

1903 Lyceum Theater opens – oldest Broadway house still in use

Flatiron Building

Overlooking Madison Square where Broadway, Fifth Avenue and 23rd Street meet, the 21-story tower was one of the city's first skyscrapers (1902). Triangle-shaped, it was dubbed the Flatiron Building (see p129).

Underlying steel structure

Elaborate limestone facade

Only 6 ft (185 cm) wide at apex of triangle

Supper in the Saddle
Decadent parties were all the rage. C.K.G. Billings's horseback dinner at Sherry's restaurant in 1903 was the talk of all New York.

Plaza Promenade
The section of Fifth Avenue in front of the Plaza Hotel was considered the most elegant in the city.

Ventilated hairpiece

High Fashion
In 1900 styles were stiff, with wire hoops and bustles worn beneath ornate dresses. Later, clothes became softer and more practical.

Long bustle

Wire hoops

1906 Architect Stanford White shot at Madison Square Garden, which he had built in 1890

1909 Wilbur Wright flies first plane over New York

1910 Pennsylvania Station opens

1913 Woolworth Building is world's tallest; new Grand Central Terminal opens; Harlem's Apollo Theater opens

1905

1910

1905 First crossing of the Staten Island Ferry

1907 First metered taxicabs; first Ziegfeld Follies

1911 Triangle Shirtwaist Factory fire kills 146 sweatshop workers; New York Public Library completed

Woolworth Building

New York City Between the Wars

The 1920s were a time of high living for many New Yorkers. Mayor Jimmy Walker set the pace, whether squiring chorus girls, drinking in speakeasies or watching the Yankees. But the good times ended with the 1929 stock market crash. By 1932, Walker had resigned, charged with corruption, and one-quarter of New Yorkers were unemployed. With Mayor Fiorello La Guardia's 1933 election, New York began to recover and thrive.

Growth of the Metropolis
▨ 1933   ▨ Today

Exotic Costumes
Chorus girls were a major Cotton Club attraction.

The Cotton Club
This Harlem nightclub was host to the best jazz in town, as first Duke Ellington and then Cab Calloway led the band. People flocked from all over the city to hear them.

Defying Prohibition
Although alcohol was outlawed, speakeasies – semi-secret illegal drinking dens – still sold it.

Home-Run Hitter
In 1927, baseball star Babe Ruth hit a record 60 home runs for the Yankees. Yankee Stadium *(see p243)* became known as "the house that Ruth built."

Sawed-off shotgun concealed in violin case

Gangsters
Dutch Schultz was the kingpin of an illegal booze racket.

1918 End of World War I
1919 18th Amendment bans alcohol, launches Prohibition Era
1920 US women get the vote

Opening of the Holland Tunnel

1926 Jimmy Walker becomes mayor

1931 Empire State Building becomes world's tallest

1920

THE NEW YORKER

1925

1930

1924 Novelist James Baldwin is born in Harlem

1925 *The New Yorker* magazine is launched

1927 Lindbergh flies across the Atlantic; first talking movie, *The Jazz Singer*, opens; Holland Tunnel opens

1929 Stock market crash; Great Depression begins

1930 Chrysler Building completed

Big Band Leaders
Banned from many downtown clubs, black artists like Cab Calloway starred at the Cotton Club.

Broadway Melodies
The 1920s were the heyday of the Broadway musical, with a record number of plays opening.

The Great Depression

The Roaring Twenties ended with the stock market crash of October 29, 1929, which set off the Depression. New York was hard hit: squatters' shacks sprang up in Central Park and thousands were out of work. But art flourished as artists went to work for the Works Projects Administration (WPA), creating outstanding murals and artworks throughout the city.

Waiting to receive benefits in 1931

Lindbergh's plane, *Spirit of St. Louis*

Breakfast menu

Lindbergh's Flight
New Yorkers celebrated Lindbergh's nonstop solo flight across the Atlantic in 1927 in a variety of ways, including a breakfast in his honor.

Rockefeller Center
Millionaire John D. Rockefeller drives the final rivet to celebrate the opening of Rockefeller Center on May 1, 1939.

Mass Event
Forty-five million people visited the 1939 World's Fair in New York.

1933 Prohibition ends; Fiorello LaGuardia begins three terms as mayor

1935

1936 Parks Department headed by Robert Moses; new parks created

1939 Rockefeller Center is completed

1940 Queens-Midtown Tunnel opens

1940

1941 US enters World War II

1942 Times Square blacked out during World War II; Idlewild International Airport (now JFK) opens

1945

1944 Black leader Adam Clayton Powell elected to Congress

Postwar New York City

Since World War II, New York has seen both the best of times and the worst. Although established as the financial capital of the world, the city itself almost went bankrupt in the 1970s. In 2008 the collapse of the Wall Street bank Lehman Brothers precipitated the worst financial crisis since 1929. Since the early 1990s, New York has seen a dramatic drop in the crime rate and an increase in the restoration of such landmarks as Grand Central Terminal and the "new" Times Square. This constant rebuilding is emblematic of the city's position as the cultural and financial hub of the United States.

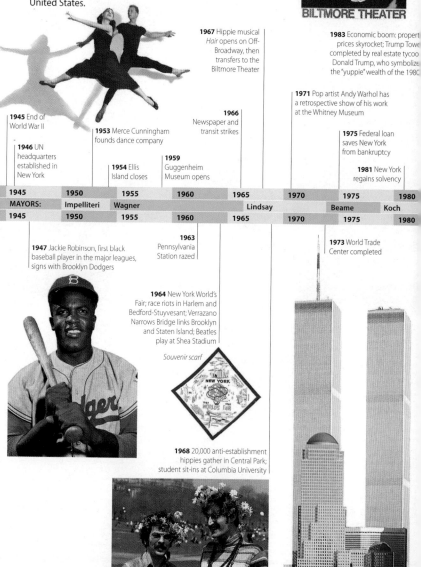

BILTMORE THEATER

1967 Hippie musical *Hair* opens on Off-Broadway, then transfers to the Biltmore Theater

1983 Economic boom: propert prices skyrocket; Trump Towe completed by real estate tyco Donald Trump, who symboliz the "yuppie" wealth of the 198C

1971 Pop artist Andy Warhol has a retrospective show of his work at the Whitney Museum

1966 Newspaper and transit strikes

1945 End of World War II

1953 Merce Cunningham founds dance company

1975 Federal loan saves New York from bankruptcy

1946 UN headquarters established in New York

1954 Ellis Island closes

1959 Guggenheim Museum opens

1981 New York regains solvency

1945	1950	1955	1960	1965	1970	1975	1980
MAYORS:	Impelliteri	Wagner			Lindsay	Beame	Koch
1945	1950	1955	1960	1965	1970	1975	1980

1947 Jackie Robinson, first black baseball player in the major leagues, signs with Brooklyn Dodgers

1963 Pennsylvania Station razed

1973 World Trade Center completed

1964 New York World's Fair; race riots in Harlem and Bedford-Stuyvesant; Verrazano Narrows Bridge links Brooklyn and Staten Island; Beatles play at Shea Stadium

Souvenir scarf

1968 20,000 anti-establishment hippies gather in Central Park; student sit-ins at Columbia University

Andy Warhol with actresses Candy Darling and Ultra Violet

1988 Twenty-five percent of New Yorkers live below the poverty line

2001 Terrorist attack on the World Trade Center; Mayor Giuliani is a great support to the people of New York. President George W. Bush declares war on terrorism

1990 David Dinkins, New York's first black mayor, takes office; Ellis Island reopens as an immigration museum

2003 A major power outage on August 14 leaves 50 million people in the North East (including New York City), mid-West, and ports of Canada, blacked out for up to 24 hours

2012 Hurricane Sandy hits New York City, causing wide-spread flooding, damage, and power outage across the city

1987 Stock market crash

1994 Rudolph Giuliani takes office as mayor

1985	1990	1995	2000	2005	2010	2015	2020
	Dinkins	Giuliani		Bloomberg			
1985	1990	1995	2000	2005	2010	2015	2020

1986 Shock of corruption scandals rock Mayor Koch's administration; Centennial of Statue of Liberty

2000 Population reaches just over 8 million

2009 US Airways flight 1549 crash-lands in the Hudson River. All 155 passengers survive

2013 One World Trade Center (formerly Freedom Tower) opens

2002 The lights go on in a regenerated 42nd Street, which crosses Broadway at Times Square. The area remains one of the city's liveliest and most congested

1995 The neglected Chelsea Piers are renovated and open as a mammoth sports and entertainment complex (see p140)

NEW YORK CITY AT A GLANCE

There are almost 300 places of interest described in the Area by Area section of this book. They range from the bustling New York Stock Exchange *(see pp72–3)* to Central Park's peaceful Strawberry Fields *(see p210)*, and from historic synagogues to dazzling skyscrapers. The following 14 pages provide a time-saving guide to New York's most noteworthy sights. Museums and architecture each have a section, and there are guides to the people and cultures that have given the city its unique character. Each sight is cross-referenced to its own full entry. Below are the top ten tourist attractions to start you off.

New York's Top Ten Tourist Attractions

Ellis Island
See pp80–81

Empire State Building
See pp138–9

Fifth Avenue
See p172

Rockefeller Center
See p146

Museum of Modern Art
See pp174–7

Statue of Liberty
See pp76–7

Central Park
See pp206–11

Metropolitan Museum of Art
See pp192–9

Brooklyn Bridge
See pp88–91

Chinatown
See pp98–9

◄ Iconic Chrysler Building, illuminated at night

New York's Best: Museums

New York's museums range from the vast scope of the Metropolitan Museum to the personal treasures of financier J. Pierpont Morgan's own collection. Several museums celebrate New York's heritage, giving visitors an insight into the people and events that made the city what it is today. This map features some highlights, with a detailed overview on pages 40 and 41.

Museum of Modern Art
Picasso's *She-Goat* (1950) is among the impressive collection on display in the renovated Museum of Modern Art.

Intrepid
Sea-Air-Space Museum
This military and maritime history museum also traces the progress of flight exploration. It is housed in a large aircraft carrier situated at Pier 86.

Morgan Library & Museum
One of the world's finest collections of manuscripts, prints and books includes this rare French Bible from 1230.

Merchant's House Museum
This perfectly preserved 1832 house belonged to a wealthy trader.

Ellis Island
This museum vividly re-creates the experiences of many millions of immigrant families.

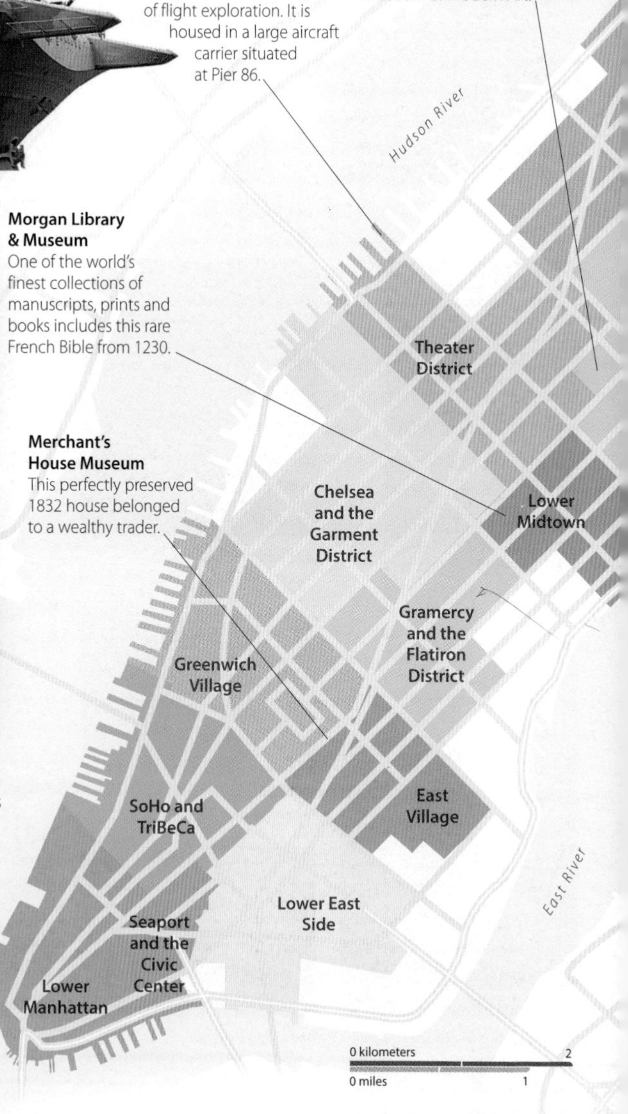

Hudson River

Theater District

Chelsea and the Garment District

Lower Midtown

Gramercy and the Flatiron District

Greenwich Village

East Village

SoHo and TriBeCa

Lower East Side

Seaport and the Civic Center

Lower Manhattan

East River

0 kilometers 2
0 miles 1

American Museum of Natural History
Dinosaurs, meteorites and much more have fascinated generations of visitors here.

Morningside Heights and Harlem

Museum of the City of New York
Costumes, works of art and household objects (such as this 1725 silver dish) create an intricate and detailed picture of New York's past.

Upper West Side

Cooper-Hewitt Museum
A wealth of decorative arts is displayed in industrialist Andrew Carnegie's former Upper East Side mansion.

Central Park

Solomon R. Guggenheim Museum
Painting and sculpture by almost all major avant-garde artists of the late 19th and 20th centuries fill Frank Lloyd Wright's stunningly renovated building.

Upper East Side

Metropolitan Museum of Art
Of the millions of works in its collection, this 12th-dynasty Egyptian faïence hippo is the museum's own mascot.

Upper Midtown

Whitney Museum of American Art
This exceptional collection includes many views of New York. One of the best is *Brooklyn Bridge: Variation on an Old Theme* (1939), by Joseph Stella.

Frick Collection
The collection of 19th-century rail-road magnate Henry Clay Frick is displayed in his former home. Masterpieces include *St. Francis in the Desert* (about 1480) by Giovanni Bellini.

Exploring New York's Museums

You could devote an entire month to New York's museums and still not do them justice. There are more than 60 museums in Manhattan alone, and half as many again in the other boroughs. The wealth of art and the huge variety of offerings – from Old Masters to old fire engines, dinosaurs to dolls, Tibetan tapestries to African masks – is equal to that of any city in the world. Some museums close on Monday, as well as on another day. Many stay open late one or two evenings a week, and some have one evening when entry is free. Most museums charge for admission; for some, this is a suggested donation rather than a mandatory fee.

Painting and Sculpture

New York is best known for its art museums. The **Metropolitan Museum of Art** houses an extensive collection of American art, as well as world-famous masterpieces. **The Cloisters**, a branch of the "Met" in Upper Manhattan, is a treasury of medieval art and architecture. The **Frick Collection** has a superb display of Old Masters. In contrast, the **Museum of Modern Art (MoMA)** houses Impressionist and modern paintings. **The Whitney Museum of American Art** and the **Solomon R. Guggenheim Museum** also specialize in modern art, the Whitney's biennial show being the foremost display of work by living artists. Today's cutting-edge art is at the **New Museum of Contemporary Art**, while the work of craft artists can be seen at the **American Folk Art Museum**. The **National Academy Museum** displays a collection of 19th- and 20th-century art, donated by academy members. In Harlem, the **Studio Museum** shows the work of black artists.

Crafts and Design

If you are interested in textiles, porcelain and glass, embroideries and laces, wallpaper, and prints, visit the **Cooper-Hewitt Museum**, the decorative arts out-post of Washington's Smithsonian Institution. The design collections at **MoMA** trace the history of design from clocks to couches. The **Museum of Arts and Design** offers the finest work of today's skilled artisans in mediums from furniture to pottery, and the **American Folk Art Museum** presents folk forms, from quilts to canes. Silver collections are notable at the **Museum of the City of New York**. The fine displays of native art at the **National Museum of the American Indian** include jewelry, rugs and pottery.

Prints and Photography

The **International Center of Photography** is the only museum in New York that is totally devoted to this medium. Collections can also be seen at the **Metropolitan Museum of Art** and **MoMA**, and there are many examples of early photography at the **Museum of the City of New York** and **Ellis Island**.

Prints and drawings by such great book illustrators as Kate Greenaway and Sir John Tenniel are featured at the **Morgan Library & Museum**. The **Cooper-Hewitt Museum** has examples of the use of prints in the decorative arts.

Corn husk doll, American Museum of Natural History

Furniture and Costumes

The annual exhibition of the Costume Institute at the **Metropolitan Museum of Art** is always worth a visit. Also impressive is the American Wing, with its 24 rooms of original furnishings tracing life from 1640 to the 20th century. Period rooms depicting New York in various settings, beginning with the 17th-century Dutch, are on display at the **Museum of the City of New York**.

There are also some house museums that give a realistic picture of life and furnishings in old New York. The **Merchant's House Museum**, a preserved residence from 1832, was occupied by the same family for 98 years. **Gracie Mansion** was the residence of mayor Archibald Gracie, who bought it in 1798 from a shipping merchant, and it is open periodically for public tours. The **Theodore Roosevelt Birthplace** is the brownstone where the 26th president of the United States grew up, and the **Mount Vernon Hotel Museum** was an early 19th-century resort.

The Peaceable Kingdom (c.1840–45) by Edward Hicks, at the Brooklyn Museum

Palm pistol at the New
York City Police Museum

History

American history unfolds at **Federal Hall**, the United States' first capitol, where George Washington took his oath as America's first president on the balcony in April 1789.

Visit the **Fraunces Tavern Museum** for a glimpse of colonial New York. **Ellis Island** and **Lower East Side Tenement Museum** re-create the hardships faced by immigrants. The **Museum of Jewish Heritage** in Battery City is a living memorial to the Holocaust. The **New York City Fire Museum** and the **New York City Police Museum** chronicle heroism and tragedy, while the **South Street Seaport Museum** recreates early maritime history.

Technology and Natural History

Forest-dwelling bonga, American Museum
of Natural History

Science museums hold exhibitions from nature to space-age technology. The **American Museum of Natural History** has vast collections covering flora, fauna and cultures from around the world. Its Rose Center/Hayden Planetarium offers a unique view of space. The **Intrepid Sea-Air-Space Museum** is a repository of technology that

chronicles military progress. It is based on the decks of an aircraft carrier. If you missed a classic Lucille Ball sitcom or footage of the first man on the moon, the place to visit is the **The Paley Center for Media**, which holds these and many other classics of TV and radio.

Art from other Cultures

Artwork of other nations is the focus of several special collections. Oriental art is the specialty of the **Asia Society** and the **Japan Society**. The **Jewish Museum** features major collections of Judaica and has changing exhibitions of various aspects of Jewish life. **El Museo del Barrio** is dedicated to the arts of Puerto Rico, including many Pre-Columbian Taino artifacts.

Egyptian
mummy,
Brooklyn
Museum

For an impressive review of African-American art and history, visit the **Schomburg Center for Research in Black Culture**. Finally, the **Metropolitan Museum of Art** excels in its multicultural displays, ranging from the art of ancient Egypt to that of contemporary Africa.

Libraries

New York's notable libraries, such as the **Morgan Library & Museum**, offer superb art collections as well as a chance to view pages from ancient manuscripts and rare books. The **New York Public Library's** collection includes historic documents and manuscripts of many famous works.

Beyond Manhattan

Other museums worth a visit include the **Brooklyn Museum of Art**, with a huge collection of artifacts from across the world and over one million

paintings. The **Museum of the Moving Image** in Queens has a unique collection of motion-picture history. The **Jacques Marchais Museum of Tibetan Art** is a rare find on Staten Island as is **Historic Richmond Town**, a well-restored village dating from the 1600s.

New York's Best: Architecture

Even when following world trends, New York has given its own twist to the turns of architectural fashion, the style of its buildings influenced by both geography and economy. An island city, with space at a premium, must look upward to grow. This trend was reflected early on with tall, narrow town houses and later with the city's apartment buildings and skyscrapers. Building materials such as cast-iron and brownstone were chosen for their local availability and useful appeal. The result is a city that has developed by finding flamboyant answers to practical needs. A more detailed overview of New York's architecture is on pages 44–5.

Apartment Buildings
The Majestic is one of five Art Deco twin-towered apartment buildings on Central Park West.

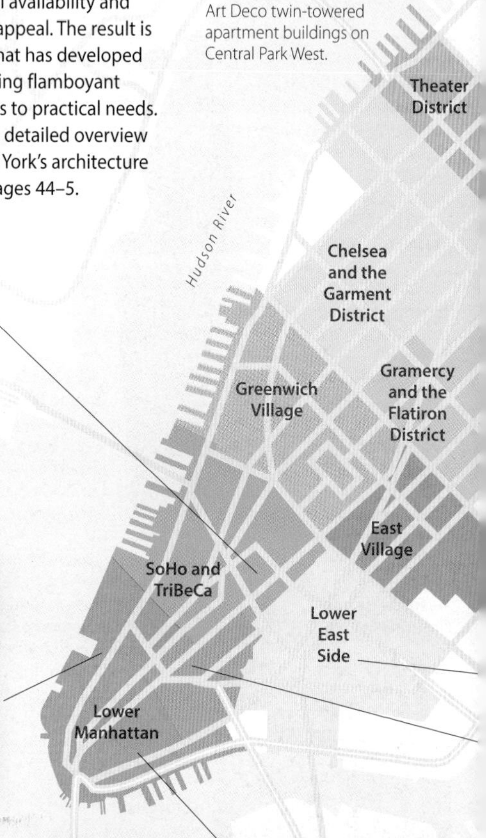

Cast-Iron Architecture
Mass-produced cast iron was often used for building facades. SoHo has many of the best examples, such as this building at 28–30 Greene Street.

Post-Modernism
The quirky, yet elegant, shapes of buildings like the World Financial Center, built in 1985 *(see p71)* mark a bold departure from the sleek steel-and-glass boxes of the 1950s and 1960s.

Brownstones
Built from local sandstone, brownstones were favored by the 19th-century middle classes. India House, built in a Florentine palazzo style on Wall Street is typical of many brownstone commercial buildings.

Theater District

Hudson River

Chelsea and the Garment District

Greenwich Village

Gramercy and the Flatiron District

East Village

SoHo and TriBeCa

Lower East Side

Lower Manhattan

Morningside Heights and Harlem

Upper West Side

Central Park

Upper East Side

Upper Midtown

Lower Midtown

East River

19th-Century Mansions
The Jewish Museum *(see p188)*, formerly the home of Felix M. Warburg, is a fine example of the French Renaissance style that typified these mansions.

Beaux Arts
Opulent style, created for the richest of owners, is exemplified by the Beaux Arts grandeur of the Frick mansion.

Modernism
The Seagram Building's sleek bronze-and-glass walls, scant decoration and monumental scale typify postwar architecture *(see p179)*.

The Skyscraper
The glory of New York architecture, these buildings expressed a perfect blend of practical engineering skill and fabulous decoration, such as this gargoyle on the Chrysler Building.

0 kilometers		2
0 miles	1	

Federal Architecture
Federal style was popular in civic architecture of the 19th century; City Hall combines it with French Renaissance influences.

Tenements
Constructed as an economic form of housing, for many these buildings were a stark introduction to new lives. Mainly built on the Lower East Side, the apartments were hopelessly over-crowded. In addition, the buildings' design, with inadequate air shafts, resulted in apartments with little or no ventilation.

Exploring New York's Architecture

During its first 200 years, New York, like all of America, looked to Europe for architectural inspiration. None of the buildings from the Dutch colonial period survive in Manhattan today; most were lost in the great fire of 1776 or torn down to make way for new developments in the early 1800s. Throughout the 18th and 19th centuries, the city's major architectural trends followed those of Europe. With the advent of cast-iron architecture in the 1850s, the Art Deco period and the ever-higher rise of the skyscraper, New York's architecture came into its own.

Federal Architecture

This American adaptation of the Neoclassical Adam style flowered in the early decades of the new nation, featuring square buildings two or three stories tall, with low hipped roofs, balustrades and decorative elements – all carefully balanced. **City Hall** (1811, John McComb, Jr. and Joseph François Mangin) is a blend of Federal and French Renaissance influences. The restored warehouses of **Schermerhorn Row** (c. 1812) in the Seaport district are also in Federal style.

Brownstones

Plentiful and cheap, the brown sandstone found in the nearby Connecticut River Valley and along the banks of the Hackensack River in New Jersey was the most common building material in the 1800s. It is found all over the city's residential neighborhoods, used for small homes or small apartments – some of the best examples of brownstone can be found in **Chelsea**. Because street space was limited, these buildings were very narrow in width, but also very deep. A typical brownstone has a flight of steps, called a stoop, leading up to the living floors. Separate stairs lead down to the basement, which was originally the servants' quarters.

Tenements

Tenements were built to house the huge influx of immigrants who arrived from the 1840s up to World War I. The six-story blocks, 100 ft (30 m) long and 25 ft (8 m) wide, offered very little light and air except from tiny sidewall air shafts and windows at each end, leaving the middle rooms in darkness. The tiny apartments were called railroad flats after their similarity to railroad cars. Later designs had air shafts between buildings, but these helped the spread of fire. The **Lower East Side Tenement Museum** has scale models of the old tenements.

Cast-iron Architecture

An American architectural innovation of the 19th century, cast iron was cheaper than stone or brick and allowed ornate features to be prefabricated in foundries from molds and used as building facades. Today, New York has the world's largest concentration of full and partial cast-iron facades. The best, built in the 1870s, are in the **SoHo Cast-Iron Historic District**.

The original cast-iron facade of 72–76 Greene Street, SoHo

Beaux-Arts

This French school of architecture dominated the design of public buildings and wealthy residential properties during New York's gilded age. This era (from 1880 to about 1920) produced many of the city's most prominent architects, including Richard Morris Hunt (**Carnegie Hall**, 1891; **Metropolitan Museum of Art**, 1895), who in 1845 was the first American architect to study in Paris; Cass Gilbert (**Custom House**, 1907; **New York Life Insurance Building**, 1928; the

A typical brownstone with stoop leading up to the main entrance

Architectural Disguises

Some of the most fanciful forms on the New York skyline were devised by clever architects to disguise the city's essential but utilitarian – and rather unattractive – rooftop water tanks. Look skyward to discover the ornate cupolas, spires and domes that transform the most mundane of features into veritable castles in the air. Examples that are easy to spot are atop two neighboring Fifth Avenue hotels: the Sherry Netherland at 60th Street and the Pierre at 61st Street.

Standard water tower

The Dakota Apartments, built in 1884, on the Upper West Side across from Central Park

US Courthouse

US Courthouse, 1936); the teams of Warren & Wetmore (**Grand Central Terminal**, 1913; **Helmsley Building**, 1929; Carrère & Hastings (**New York Public Library**, 1911; **Frick Mansion**, 1914); and McKim, Mead & White, the city's most famous firm of architects (**Villard Houses**, 1884; **United States General Post Office**, 1913; **Municipal Building**, 1914).

Apartment Buildings

As the city's population grew and space became ever more precious, family homes in Manhattan became much too expensive for most New Yorkers, and even the wealthy joined the trend toward communal living. In 1884 Henry Hardenbergh's Dakota *(see p220)*, one of the first luxury apartment buildings, started a spate of turn-of-the-century construction on the Upper West Side. Many of the buildings resembled castles and

châteaux, and were built around courtyards not visible from the street. Favorite landmarks are the five **Twin Towers** on Central Park West, the San Remo, Eldorado, Century, the Beresford, and the Majestic. Built during the peak of Art Deco (1929 to 1931), they create the distinctive skyline seen from the park.

Skyscrapers

In 1902 Daniel Burnham, a Chicago architect, built the **Flatiron Building**, so tall at 300 ft (91 m) that skeptics said it would collapse. By 1913, the **Woolworth Building** had risen to 792 ft (241 m). New zoning laws demanded that skyscrapers be built in such a way as to allow light to reach street level. This suited the Art Deco style. The **Chrysler Building** (1930) was the world's tallest until the **Empire State Building** (1931) was completed. Both are Art Deco classics, but it was Raymond Hood's **Group**

Art Deco arched pattern on the spire of the Chrysler Building

Health Insurance Building that represented New York in 1932 in the *International Style* architectural survey.

The World Trade Center was New York's tallest building until September 2001 *(see p56)*. It represented the Modernist style, now superseded by the Post-Modern style, such as the **Citigroup Center** (1977). In 2013, One World Trade Center became the western world's tallest building, reaching 1,776 ft (541 m), a reference to the year of American Independence.

DIRECTORY

Where to find the Buildings

245 Fifth Avenue
(Apartment Building)

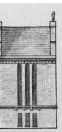

60 Gramercy Park North
(Brownstone)

The Pierre
(Beaux Arts)

Sherry Netherland
Hotel (Beaux Arts)

Multicultural New York City

Wherever you go in New York, even in pockets of the hectic high-rise downtown, you will find evidence of the richly ethnic flavor of the city. A bus ride can take you from Madras to Moscow, Hong Kong to Haiti. Immigrants are still coming to New York, though numbers are fewer than in the peak years from 1880 to 1910, when 17 million people arrived. In the 1980s, a million newcomers, largely from Caribbean countries and Asia, arrived and found their own special corner of the city. Throughout the year you will encounter crowds celebrating one of many festivals. To find out more about national celebrations and parades, see pages 52 to 55.

Hell's Kitchen
For a while called "Clinton" to reflect a new neighborhood mix, this was the first home of early Irish immigrants.

Little Korea
Not far from Herald Square is a small Korean enclave with a variety of restaurants.

Little Ukraine
Services are held at T. Shevchenko Place as part of the May 17 festivities to mark the Ukrainians' conversion to Christianity.

Theater District

Chelsea and the Garment District

Greenwich Village

Gramercy and the Flatiron District

Little Italy
For eleven days in September, the Italian community gathers around the Mulberry Street area, and the streets are taken over by the celebrations of the Festa di San Gennaro.

SoHo and TriBeCa

East Village

Lower East Side

Lower Manhattan

Seaport and the Civic Center

0 kilometers   2
0 miles   1

Chinatown
Every year, in January or February, Mott Street is packed as residents celebrate the Chinese New Year.

The Lower East Side
The synagogues around Rivington and Eldridge streets reflect the religious traditions of this old Jewish area.

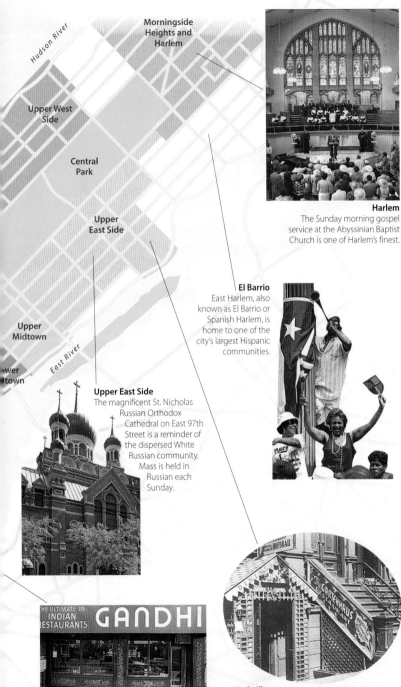

Morningside Heights and Harlem

Hudson River

Upper West Side

Central Park

Upper East Side

Upper Midtown

wer
town

East River

Harlem
The Sunday morning gospel service at the Abyssinian Baptist Church is one of Harlem's finest.

El Barrio
East Harlem, also known as El Barrio or Spanish Harlem, is home to one of the city's largest Hispanic communities.

Upper East Side
The magnificent St. Nicholas Russian Orthodox Cathedral on East 97th Street is a reminder of the dispersed White Russian community. Mass is held in Russian each Sunday.

Little India
The restaurants of East 6th Street offer Eastern atmosphere at affordable prices.

Yorkville
Only a few cafés and bierkellers remain to keep the flavor of this former uptown German district. The Steuben Day Parade is still held here each September.

Exploring New York's Many Cultures

Even "native" New Yorkers have ancestral roots in other countries. Throughout the 17th century, the Dutch and English settled here, establishing trade colonies in the New World. Soon America became a symbol of hope for the downtrodden elsewhere in Europe. Many flocked across the ocean, some penniless and with little knowledge of the language. The potato famine of the 1840s led to the first wave of Irish immigrants, followed by German and other European workers displaced by political unrest and the Industrial Revolution. Immigrants continue to enrich New York in countless ways, and today an estimated 100 languages are spoken.

1940s, they were the city's fastest-growing and most upwardly mobile ethnic group, extending the old boundaries of Chinatown and establishing new neighborhoods in parts of Brooklyn and Queens. Once a closed community, Chinatown now bustles with tourists exploring the streets and markets, and sampling the creative cuisine.

Hispanic religious carving at El Museo del Barrio *(see p233)*

The Hispanic Americans

Puerto Ricans were in New York as early as 1838, but it was not until after World War II that they arrived in large numbers in search of work. Most live in El Barrio, formerly known as Spanish Harlem. Professionals who fled Fidel Castro's Cuba have moved out of the city itself but are still influential in Hispanic commerce and culture. Parts of Washington Heights have large Dominican and Colombian communities.

The Germans

The Germans began to settle in New York in the 18th century. From John Peter Zenger onward *(see p23)*, the city's German community has championed the freedom to express ideas and opinions. It has also produced giants of industry, such as John Jacob Astor, the city's first millionaire.

The Italians

Italians first came to New York in the 1830s and 1840s. Many came from northern Italy to escape the failing revolution at home. In the 1870s, poverty in southern Italy drove many more Italians across the ocean. In time, Italians became a potent political force in the city, exemplified by Fiorello La Guardia, one of New York's finest mayors.

The Chinese

The Chinese were late arrivals to New York. In 1880, the population of the Mott Street district was a mere 700. By the

The Irish

The Irish, who first arrived in New York in the 1840s, had to overcome harsh odds. Starving and with barely a penny to their names, they labored hard to escape the slums of Five Points and Hell's Kitchen, helping to build the modern city in the process. Many joined the police and fire-fighting forces, rising to high rank through dedication to duty. Others set up successful businesses, such as the Irish bars that act as a focus for the now-scattered New York Irish community.

Turkish immigrants arriving at former Idlewild Airport in 1963

The Jews

There has been a Jewish community in New York since 1654. The city's first synagogue, Shearith Israel, was established by refugees from a Dutch colony in Brazil and is still active today. These first settlers, Sephardic Jews of Spanish descent, included such prominent families as the Baruchs. They were followed by the German Jews, who set up successful retailing enterprises, like the Straus brothers at Macy's. Russian persecution led to the mass immigration that began in the late 1800s. By the start of World War I, 600,000 Jews were living on the Lower East Side. Today, this area is more Hispanic and Asian than Jewish, but it holds reminders of its role as a place of refuge and new beginnings.

Eastern States Buddhist Temple, in central Chinatown *(see pp98–9)*

The African Americans

Perhaps the best-known black inner-city community in the Western world, Harlem is noted for the Harlem Renaissance of writing *(see pp32–3)* as much as it is for great entertainment, gospel music and soul food. The move of black African Americans from the South to the North began with emancipation in the 1860s and increased markedly in the 1920s, when Harlem's black population rose from 83,000 to 204,000. Today Harlem is undergoing revitalization in many areas. The African American population has also dispersed throughout the city.

The Melting Pot

Other New York cultures are not distinctly defined but are still easily found. Ukrainians gather in the East Village, around St. George's Ukrainian Catholic Church on East 7th Street. Little India can be spotted by the restaurants along East 6th Street. Koreans own many of the small grocery stores in Manhattan, but most tend to live in the Flushing area of Queens. The religious diversity of New York can be seen in the Islamic Center on Riverside Drive; the Islamic Cultural Center on 96th

A woman celebrating at the Greek Independence Day parade

Street – Manhattan's first major mosque; and the Russian Orthodox Cathedral on East 97th Street *(see p201)*.

The Outer Boroughs

Brooklyn is by far the most international borough of New York. Caribbean newcomers from Jamaica and Haiti are one of the fastest-growing

The New York police, a haven for Irish Americans

immigrant groups. West Indians tend to cluster along Eastern Parkway between Grand Army Plaza and Utica Avenue, the route of the lavish, exotically costumed West Indian Day Parade in September. Recently arrived Russian Jewish immigrants have turned Brighton Beach into "Little Odessa by the Sea," and the Scandinavians and Lebanese have settled in Bay Ridge and the Finns in Sunset Park. Borough Park and Williamsburg are home to Orthodox Jews, and Midwood has an Israeli-Middle East accent. Italians live in the Bensonhurst area. Greenpoint is little Poland, and Atlantic Avenue is home to the largest Arab community in America.

The Irish were among the earliest groups to cross the Harlem River into the Bronx. Japanese executives favor the more exclusive Riverdale area. One of the most distinctive ethnic areas is Astoria, Queens, which has the largest Greek population outside the mother-land. Jackson Heights is home to a large Latin American quarter, including 300,000 Colombians. Indians also favor this area and neighboring Flushing. But it is the Asians who have transformed Flushing, so much so that the local train is popularly known as "The Orient Express."

Newcomers who made their mark *see also pp50–51.*

The dates mark the year these immigrants entered the US via New York.

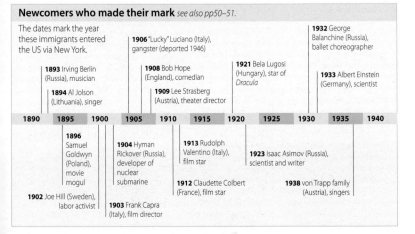

1893 Irving Berlin (Russia), musician
1894 Al Jolson (Lithuania), singer
1896 Samuel Goldwyn (Poland), movie mogul
1902 Joe Hill (Sweden), labor activist
1903 Frank Capra (Italy), film director
1904 Hyman Rickover (Russia), developer of nuclear submarine
1906 "Lucky" Luciano (Italy), gangster (deported 1946)
1908 Bob Hope (England), comedian
1909 Lee Strasberg (Austria), theater director
1912 Claudette Colbert (France), film star
1913 Rudolph Valentino (Italy), film star
1921 Bela Lugosi (Hungary), star of *Dracula*
1923 Isaac Asimov (Russia), scientist and writer
1932 George Balanchine (Russia), ballet choreographer
1933 Albert Einstein (Germany), scientist
1938 von Trapp family (Austria), singers

1890	1895	1900	1905	1910	1915	1920	1925	1930	1935	1940

Remarkable New Yorkers

New York has nourished some of the best creative talents since the beginning of the 20th century. Pop Art began here, and Manhattan is still the world center for modern art. The alternative writers of the 1950s and '60s – known as the Beat Generation – took inspiration from the city's jazz clubs. And as it is the financial capital, many leading world financiers have made New York their home.

Pop artist Andy Warhol

Novelist James Baldwin

Writers

Much great American literature was created in New York. *Charlotte Temple, A Tale of Truth*, first published in 1791 by Susanna Rowson (c. 1762–1824), was a tale of seduction in the city and a best-seller for 50 years.

America's first professional author was Charles Brockden Brown (1771–1810), who came to New York in 1791. The novels of Edgar Allan Poe (1809–49), the pioneer of the modern detective story, expanded the thriller genre. Henry James (1843–1916) published *The Bostonians* (1886) and became the master of the psychological novel, and his friend Edith Wharton (1861–1937) became known for her satirical novels about American society.

American literature finally won international recognition with Washington Irving's (1783–1859) satire, *A History of New York* (1809). It earned him $2,000. Irving coined the names "Gotham" for New York and "Knickerbockers" for New Yorkers. He and James Fenimore Cooper (1789–1851), whose books gave birth to the "Western" novel,

formed the Knickerbocker group of US writers. Greenwich Village has always attracted writers, including Herman Melville (1819–91) whose masterpiece, *Moby Dick* (1851), was very poorly received at first.

Jack Kerouac (1922–69), Allen Ginsberg, and William Burroughs all went to Columbia University and drank at the San Remo Café in Greenwich Village. Dylan Thomas (1914–53) lived at the Chelsea Hotel *(see p141)*. Novelist Nathanael West (1902–40) worked in the Gramercy Park Hotel, and Dashiell Hammett (1894–1961) wrote *The Maltese Falcon* while living there. James Baldwin (1924–87), born in Harlem, wrote *Another Country* (1963) on his return to New York from Europe.

Artists

The New York School of Abstract Expressionists founded the first influential American art movement. It was launched by Hans Hofmann (1880–1966) with Franz Kline and Willem de Kooning, whose first job in America was as a housepainter. Adolph Gottlieb, Mark Rothko (1903–70), and Jackson Pollock (1912–56) went on to popularize this style. Pollock, Kline and de Kooning all had their studios on the Lower East Side.

Pop Art began in New York in

the 1960s with Roy Lichtenstein and Andy Warhol (1926–87), who made some of his cult films at 33 Union Square. Keith Haring (1958–90) was a very prolific graffiti artist who gained fame for his Pop Art murals and sculptures.

Robert Mapplethorpe (1946–89) acquired notoriety for his homoerotic photos of men. Jeff Koons was part of the Neo-Pop or Post-Pop movement of the 80s.

The illusionistic murals by Richard Haas enliven many walls throughout the city.

Actors

In 1849 the British actor Charles Macready started a riot by saying Americans were vulgar. A mob stormed the Astor Place Opera House, where Macready was playing Macbeth, police opened fire, and 22 rioters were killed. In 1927 Mae West (1893–1980) spent 10 days in a workhouse on Roosevelt Island and was fined $500 for giving a lewd performance in her Broadway show *Sex*. Marc Blitzstein's radical pro-labor opera *The Cradle Will Rock* produced by Orson Welles (1915–85) and John Houseman (1902–88), was immediately banned and the show had

Vaudeville actress Mae West

to move to another theater. The actors managed to get around the ban by buying tickets and singing their roles from the audience.

The musical has been New York's special contribution to the theater. Florenz Ziegfeld's (1869–1932) *Follies* ran from 1907 to 1931. The opening of *Oklahoma!* on Broadway in 1943 began the age of musicals by the famous duo Richard Rodgers (1902–79) and Oscar Hammerstein, Jr. (1895–1960).

Off Broadway, the Provincetown Players at 33 MacDougal Street were the first to produce Eugene O'Neill's (1888–1953) *Beyond the Horizon* (1920). His successor as the major innovative force in US theater was Edward Albee, author of *Who's Afraid of Virginia Woolf?* (1962).

Musicians and Dancers

Leonard Bernstein (1918–90) followed a long line of great conductors at the New York Philharmonic, including Bruno Walter (1876–1962), Arturo Toscanini (1867–1957) and Leopold Stokowski (1882–1977). Maria Callas (1923–77) was born in New York but moved to Europe.

Carnegie Hall *(see p150)* has featured Enrico Caruso (1873–1921), Bob Dylan and the Beatles. A record concert attendance was set in 1991 when Paul Simon drew a million people for his free concert in Central Park.

The legendary swinging jazz clubs of the 1930s and 1940s are now gone from 52nd Street. Plaques on "Jazz Walk" outside the CBS building

Josephine Baker

honor such famous performers as Charlie Parker (1920–55) and Josephine Baker (1906–75).

Between 1940 and 1965, New York became a world dance capital, with the establishment of George Balanchine's (1904–83) New York City Ballet and the American Ballet Theater. In 1958, choreographer Alvin Ailey (1931–89) set up the American Dance Theater, and Bob Fosse (1927–87) changed the course of musicals.

Tycoon Cornelius Vanderbilt

Industrialists and Entrepreneurs

The rags-to-riches story is an American dream. Andrew Carnegie (1835–1919), "the steel baron with a heart of gold," started with nothing and died having given away $350 million. His beneficiaries included public libraries and universities throughout America. Many other foundations are the legacies of wealthy philanthropists. Some, like Cornelius Vanderbilt (1794–1877), tried to shake off their rough beginnings by patronizing the arts. In business, New York's "robber barons" did what they liked with apparent

impunity. Financiers Jay Gould (1836–92) and James Fisk (1834–72) beat Vanderbilt in the war for the Erie Railroad by manipulating stock. In September 1869 they caused Wall Street's first "Black Friday" when they tried to corner the gold market, but fled when their fraud was discovered. Gould died a happy billionaire, while Fisk was killed in a fight over a woman.

Modern entrepreneurs include Donald Trump *(see p35)*, owner of Trump Tower, and the late Leona and Harry Helmsley. After Leona passed away in August 2007, the bulk of the Helmsley's $4-billion estate was left to a charitable trust.

Architects

Cass Gilbert (1858–1934), who built such Neo-Gothic skyscrapers as the Woolworth Building of 1913 *(see p93)* was one of the men who literally shaped the city. His caricature can be seen in the lobby, clutching a model of his masterpiece. Stanford White (1853–1906) was as well known for his scandalous private life as for his fine Beaux Arts buildings, such as the Players Club *(p130)*. For most of his life, Frank Lloyd Wright (1867–1959) spurned city architecture. When he was persuaded to leave his mark on the city, it was in the form of the Guggenheim Museum *(pp190–91)*. German-born Ludwig Mies van der Rohe (1886–1969), who built the Seagram Building *(p179)*, did not believe in "inventing a new architecture every Monday morning," although some might argue that this is just what New York has always done best.

Musical producer Florenz Ziegfeld

NEW YORK CITY THROUGH THE YEAR

Springtime in New York sees Park Avenue filled with blooms, while Fifth Avenue goes green for St. Patrick's Day, the first of the year's many big parades. Summer in the city is hot and humid, but it is worth forsaking an air-conditioned interior to step outside, where parks and squares are the setting for free open-air music and theater. The first Monday in September marks Labor Day and the advent of the orange-red colors of autumn. Then, as Christmas nears, the shops and streets begin to sparkle with dazzling window displays.

Dates of the events on the following pages may vary. For details, consult the listings magazines *(see p369)*. NYC & Co., part of the New York Convention and Visitors Bureau *(see p363)*, issues a useful quarterly free calendar of events.

Spring

Every season in New York brings its own tempo and temptations. In spring, the city shakes off the winter with tulips and cherry blossoms in the parks and spring fashions in the stores. Everyone window shops and gallery hops. The hugely popular St. Patrick's Day Parade draws the crowds, and thousands don their finery for the Easter Parade down Fifth Avenue.

Inventive Easter bonnets in New York's Easter Parade

March

St. Patrick's Day Parade *(Mar 17)*, Fifth Ave, from 44th to 86th St. Green clothes, beer and flowers, plus bagpipes.
Greek Independence Day Parade *(Mar 25)*, Fifth Ave, from 49th to 59th St. Greek dancing and food.

Easter

Easter Flower Show *(week before Easter)*, Macy's department store. Annual floral extravaganza with a different theme each year *(pp136–7)*.

Yellow tulips and cabs shine on Park Avenue

Easter Parade *(Easter Sun)*, Fifth Ave, from 44th to 59th St. Paraders in costumes and outrageous millinery gather around St. Patrick's Cathedral.

April

Cherry Blossom Festival *(late Mar–Apr)*, Brooklyn Botanic Garden. Famous for Japanese cherry trees and beautifully laid out ornamental gardens.
TriBeCa Film Festival *(Apr)*. Celebrates film, music, and culture with more than 100 films from around the world *(p340)*.
Earth Day Festival Activities *(varies)*.
Baseball *(Apr–late Sep/early Oct)*. Major league season starts for Yankees and Mets *(p352)*.
New York City Ballet Spring Season *(Apr–Jun)*, New York State Theater and Metropolitan Opera House in Lincoln Center *(p216)*.

May

Five Boro Bike Tour *(first Sun)*, a 42-mile (68-km) ride ending with a festival with live music, food and exhibitions.
Cuban Day Parade *(first Sun)*, a carnival on Sixth Ave, between 44th St and Central Park South.

Parading in national costume on Greek Independence Day

Ninth Avenue International Food Festival *(mid-May)*, from W 37th to W 57th St. Ethnic foods, music, and dance.
Washington Square Outdoor Art Exhibit *(usually last two weekends May; also Sep)*.
Memorial Day Activities *(last weekend)*. A parade down Fifth Ave, festivities at South Street Seaport.

Average Daily Hours of Sunshine

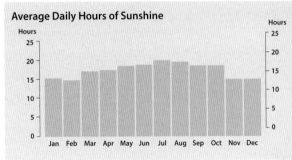

Hours

Days of Sunshine
New York enjoys long hours of summer sun from June to August, with July the month of greatest sunshine. The winter days are much shorter, but many are clear and bright. Autumn has more sunshine than spring, although both are sunny.

Summer

New Yorkers escape the hot city streets when possible, for picnics, boat rides, and the beaches. Macy's fireworks light up the Fourth of July skies, and more sparks fly when the New York Yankees and Mets baseball teams are in town. Summer also brings street fairs, outdoor concerts, and free Shakespeare and opera in Central Park.

Policeman dancing in the Puerto Rican Day Parade

June

Puerto Rican Day Parade
(early Jun), Fifth Ave, from 44th to 86th St. Floats and marching bands celebrate people of Puerto Rican descent living in the US.

Museum Mile Festival *(second Tue)*, Fifth Ave, from 82nd to 105th St. Free entry (usually 6–9pm) to the several museums located along this stretch of Fifth Ave.

Central Park Summerstage *(Jun–Aug)*, Central Park. Music and dance of every variety, almost daily, rain or shine.

Metropolitan Opera Parks Concerts. Free evening concerts in parks throughout the city *(pp342–3)*.

Shakespeare in the Park *(Jun–Sep)*. Star actors take on the Bard at Delacorte Theater, Central Park *(p339)*.

NYC Pride March *(late Jun)*. The annual parade sets off from 36th St and goes along Fifth Ave to Christopher St past the Stonewall Inn *(p347)*.

July

Macy's Firework Display *(Jul 4)*, usually the East River. This is the undisputed high point of the city's Independence Day celebrations, featuring the best fireworks in town.

American Crafts Festival *(mid-Jun–early Jul)*, Lincoln Center *(p216)*. Displays of high quality crafts.

Mostly Mozart Festival *(end Jul–end Aug)*, Avery Fisher Hall, Lincoln Center *(pp342–3)*.

NY Philharmonic Parks Concerts *(late Jul–early Aug)*. Free concerts in parks throughout the city *(p343)*.

Lincoln Center Festival *(Jul)*.

Festivities at a summer street fair in Greenwich Village

Dance, opera, and other performing arts from around the world.

August

Harlem Week *(mid-Aug)*. Films, art, music, dance, fashion, sports, and tours.

Out-of-Doors Festival *(Aug)*, Lincoln Center. Free dance and theater performances *(p338)*.

US Open Tennis Championships *(late Aug–early Sep)*, Flushing Meadows *(p352)*.

Crowds of spectators flock to the US Open Tennis Championships

Average Monthly Temperature

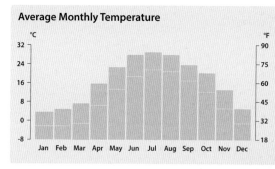

Temperature
The chart shows the average minimum and maximum temperatures for each month in New York. With top temperatures averaging 84° F (29° C), the city can become hot and humid. In contrast, the months of winter, although rarely below freezing, can seem bitterly cold.

Autumn

Labor Day marks the end of the summer. The Giants and the Jets kick off the football season, the Broadway season begins and the Festa di San Gennaro in Little Italy is the high point in a succession of fun neighborhood fairs. Macy's Thanksgiving Day Parade is the nation's symbol that the holiday season has arrived.

September

Richmond County Fair *(Labor Day weekend)*, in the grounds of Historic Richmond Town, Staten Island *(p256)*. New York's only authentic county fair.
West Indian Carnival *(Labor Day weekend)*, Brooklyn. Parade, floats, music, dancing, and food.
Brazilian Festival *(early Sep)*, E 46th St, between Times Sq and Madison Ave. Brazilian music, food, and crafts.

Exotic Caribbean carnival costume in the streets of Brooklyn

New York is Book Country *(mid–late Sep)*, Fifth Ave, from 48th to 59th Sts. Book fair.
Festa di San Gennaro *(third week)*, Little Italy *(p98)*. Ten days of festivities and processions.
New York Film Festival *(mid-Sep–early Oct)*, Lincoln Center *(p216)*. American films and international art films.
Von Steuben Day Parade *(third week)*, Upper Fifth Ave. German-American celebrations.
American Football *(season begins)*, MetLife Stadium, home to the Giants and the Jets *(pp352–3)*.

October

Columbus Day Parade *(2nd Mon)*, Fifth Ave, from 44th to 86th Sts. Parades and music to celebrate Columbus's first sighting of America.
Pulaski Day Parade *(Sun closest to Oct 5)*, Fifth Ave, from 26th to 52nd Sts. Celebrations for Polish-American hero Casimir Pulaski.
Rockefeller Center Ice Skating Rink *(Oct–Mar)*. Skate beneath the famous Christmas Tree.
Halloween Parade *(Oct 31)*, Sixth Avenue, Greenwich Village. Brilliant event with fantastic costumes.
Big Apple Circus *(Oct–Jan)*, Damrosch Park, Lincoln Center. Special themes are presented each year *(p357)*.
Basketball *(season begins)*, Madison Square Garden. Local team is the Knicks *(pp352–3)*.

Huge Superman balloon floating above Macy's Thanksgiving Day Parade

November

New York City Marathon *(first Sun)*. From Staten Island through all the city boroughs.
Macy's Thanksgiving Day Parade *(fourth Thu)*, from Central Park West and W 79th St to Broadway and W 34th St. A joy for children, this famous parade features floats, huge balloons, and even an appearance from Santa.
Christmas Spectacular *(Nov–Dec)*, Radio City Music Hall. Variety show, with the Rockettes.

Revelers in Greenwich Village's Halloween Parade

Average Monthly Rainfall

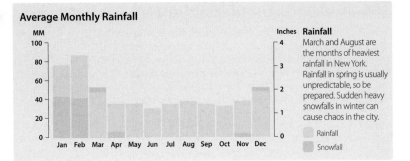

Rainfall
March and August are the months of heaviest rainfall in New York. Rainfall in spring is usually unpredictable, so be prepared. Sudden heavy snowfalls in winter can cause chaos in the city.

Rainfall

Snowfall

Winter

New York is a magical place at Christmas – even the stone lions at the Public Library don wreaths for the occasion, and shops become works of art. From Times Square to Chinatown, New Year celebrations punctuate the season, and Central Park becomes a winter sports arena.

Statue of Alice in Wonderland in Central Park

December

Tree-Lighting Ceremony
(early Dec), Rockefeller Center *(p146)*. Lighting of the giant Christmas tree in front of the RCA Building.
Messiah Sing-In *(mid-Dec)*, Lincoln Center *(p214)*. The audience rehearses and performs under the guidance of various conductors.
Hanukkah Menorah *(mid–late Dec)*, Grand Army Plaza, Brooklyn. Lighting of the huge menorah (candelabra) every night during the eight-day Festival of Lights.
New Year's Eve. Fireworks display in Central Park *(pp208–9)*; festivities in Times Square *(p149)*; 5-mile (8-km) run in Central Park; poetry reading in St. Mark's Church.

January

National Boat Show
(Jan), Jacob K. Javits Convention Center *(p140)*.
Chinese New Year *(late Jan/Feb)*, Chinatown *(pp98–9)*. Dragons, fireworks, and food.
Winter Antiques Show *(Jan)*, Seventh Regiment Armory *(p189)*. NYC's most prestigious antiques fair.

February

Black History Month. African-American events take place throughout the city.
Empire State Building Run-Up *(early Feb)*. Runners race to the 102nd floor *(pp138–9)*.
Lincoln and Washington Birthday Sales *(Feb 12–22)* Big department stores sales throughout the city.
Westminster Kennel Club Dog Show *(mid-Feb)*, Madison Square Garden *(p137)*. Major dog show.

Chinese New Year celebrations in Chinatown

PUBLIC HOLIDAYS

New Year's Day (Jan 1)
Martin Luther King Jr. Day (3rd Mon, Jan)
Presidents' Day (3rd Mon, Feb)
Memorial Day (last Mon, May)
Independence Day (Jul 4)
Labor Day (1st Mon, Sep)
Columbus Day (2nd Mon, Oct)
Election Day (1st Tue, Nov)
Veterans Day (Nov 11)
Thanksgiving Day (4th Thu, Nov)
Christmas Day (Dec 25)

The giant Christmas tree and decorations at Rockefeller Center

The Southern Tip of Manhattan

Lower Manhattan, as seen from the Hudson River, encompasses some of the most striking modern additions to the city skyline, such as the distinctively topped quartet of the World Financial Center. You will also catch glimpses of earlier Manhattan: Castle Clinton set against the green space of Battery Park and, behind it, Custom House. From 1973 until September 2001 the area also boasted the World Trade Center. Its landmark towers were destroyed in a terrorist attack on the city. The One World Trade Center building (formerly known as Freedom Tower), on the northwest corner of the National September 11 Memorial, was completed in 2013.

Locator Map
The Southern Tip

National September 11 Memorial
Built on the site of the former World Trade Center, the National September 11 Memorial is a tribute to the nearly 2,977 people who died in a terrorist attack on the city.

The Upper Room
This walk-around sculpture by Ned Smyth is one of many works of art in Battery Park City (see p74).

Detail from The *Upper Room*

An Earlier View
This 1898 photograph shows a skyline now changed beyond recognition.

KEY

① **World Financial Center** has at the heart of its complex the Winter Garden – a place to shop, dine, be entertained, plus great views of the Hudson River *(see p71)*.

② **One World Trade Center** was completed in 2013. Numerous other skyscrapers are still being built on the complex.

③ **Liberty View**

④ **Liberty Plaza**

⑤ **Bank of New York**

⑥ **East Coast War Memorial** in Battery Park, features a huge bronze eagle by Albino Manca in honor of the dead of World War II.

⑦ **26 Broadway**

⑧ **17 State Street**

⑨ **Castle Clinton**

⑩ **US Custom House**

26 Broadway
The tower of the former Standard Oil Building resembles an oil lamp. The interior is still decorated with company symbols.

East Coast War Memorial
In Battery Park, a huge bronze eagle by Albino Manca honors the dead of World War II.

American Merchant Mariners' Memorial *(1991)*
This sculpture by Marisol is on Pier A, the last of Manhattan's old piers. The pier also has a clock tower that chimes the hours on ships' bells.

Shrine of Mother Seton
The first US-born saint lived here *(see p78)*.

Lower Manhattan from the East River

At first sight, this stretch of East River shoreline, running up from the tip of Manhattan Island, is a seamless array of 20th-century office buildings. But from sea level, streets and slips are still visible, offering glimpses of old New York and the Financial District to the west. On the skyline itself, a few of the district's early skyscrapers still proudly display their ornate crowns above their more anonymous modern counterparts.

Locator Map
⬜ East River View

Vietnam Veterans' Plaza
An engraved green-glass memorial dominates the former Coenties Slip, a wharf filled in to make a park in the late 19th century *(see p78)*.

Hanover Square
A statue of one of the Dutch mayors, Abraham De Peyster, sits near the house where he was born in 1657.

India House
The handsome brownstone at One Hanover Square is one of the finest of its kind.

Battery Maritime Building
This historic ferry terminal serves only Governors Island *(see p79)*.

Downtown Heliport
Air-Sea Rescue and sightseeing flights operate from here.

Delmonico's
This upscale steakhouse draws many carnivores.

New York Stock Exchange
Although hidden from view by more modern edifices, this is still the hub of the hectic Financial District *(see pp72–3)*.

KEY

① One New York Plaza
② 55 Water Street
③ Barclay's Bank Building
④ 1 Financial Square
⑤ New York Stock Exchange
⑥ Citibank Building
⑦ Chase Manhattan Bank Tower
⑧ 120 Wall Street

40 Wall Street
In the 1940s, the pyramid-topped tower of the former Bank of Manhattan was hit by a light aircraft.

Bank of New York
This serene 1928 interior is part of the bank set up in 1784 by Alexander Hamilton *(see p25)*.

70 Pine Street
Replicas of this elegant Gothic-style tower can be seen near the Pine and Cedar Street entrances.

100 Old Slip
Now in the shadow of One Financial Square, the small palazzo-style First Precinct Police Department was the city's most modern police station when it was built in 1911.

Carved medallion, 100 Old Slip

***Queen Elizabeth* Monument**
The ocean liner that sank in 1972 is remembered here.

South Street Seaport

Where the Financial District ends, the skyline, as seen from the East River or Brooklyn, changes dramatically. The corporate headquarters are replaced by the piers, low-rise streets and warehouses of the old seaport area, now restored as the South Street Seaport *(see pp84–5)*. The Civic Center lies not far inland, and a few of its monumental buildings can be seen. The Brooklyn Bridge marks the end of this stretch of skyline. Between here and midtown, apartment blocks make up the majority of riverside features.

Locator Map
☐ South Street Area

Stonework on the Woolworth Building

Pier 17
A focal point of the Seaport, this leisure pier is undergoing renovations which are due to be completed in 2015.

Woolworth Building
The handsomely decorated spire marks the headquarters of F.W. Woolworth's empire. It is still the finest "cathedral of commerce" ever built *(see p93).*

Maritime Crafts Center
At Pier 15, craftspeople demonstrate traditional seafaring skills such as woodcarving and model-making.

Titanic Memorial
The lighthouse on Fulton Street commemorates the sinking of the Titanic, the largest steam ship ever built.

Police Plaza
Five in One (1971–4), in
Police Plaza, is a sculpture
by Bernard Rosenthal. It
represents the five boroughs
of New York.

Municipal Building
Among the offices of this vast
building is the Marriage Chapel,
where weddings "at City Hall"
actually take place. The copper
statue on the skyline is *Civic Fame*
by *Adolph Weinman (see p87).*

**Surrogate's Court
and Hall of Records**
Archives dating back to 1664
are stored and displayed here
(see p87).

United States Courthouse
The Civic Center is marked on the
skyline by the golden pyramid of
architect Cass Gilbert's courthouse
(see p87).

Con Edison Mural
In 1975, artist Richard
Haas re-created the
Brooklyn Bridge on the
side wall of a former
electrical substation.

Brooklyn Bridge
Views of, and from, the bridge have made it one of
New York's best-loved landmarks *(see pp88–91).*

Midtown Manhattan

The skyline of Midtown Manhattan is graced with some of the city's most spectacular towers and spires – from the familiar beauty of the Empire State Building's Art Deco pinnacle to the dramatic wedge shape of Citicorp's modern headquarters. As the shoreline progresses uptown, so the architecture becomes more varied; the United Nations complex dominates a long stretch, and then Beekman Place begins a strand of exclusive residential enclaves that offer the rich and famous some seclusion in this busy part of the city.

Locator Map
▢ Midtown

Empire State Building
At 1,250 ft (381 m), this was the tallest building in the world for many years *(see pp138–9).*

Grand Central Terminal
Now dwarfed by its neighbors, this landmark building is full of period details, such as this fine clock *(see pp158–9).*

Chrysler Building
Glinting in the sun by day or lit up by night, this stainless-steel spire is, for many, the ultimate New York skyscraper *(see p157).*

United Nations
Works of art from member countries include this Barbara Hepworth sculpture, a gift from Britain *(see pp162–5).*

Tudor City
Built in the 1920s, this complex is mock Tudor on a grand scale, with over 3,000 apartments *(see p160).*

1 and 2 UN Plaza
Angular glass towers house offices and the UN Millennium Plaza Hotel *(see p160).*

General Electric Building
Built of brick in 1931, this Art Deco building has a tall spiked crown that resembles radio waves. *(see p178)*.

KEY
① The Highpoint
② MetLife Building
③ Trump World Tower
④ 100 UN Plaza
⑤ General Electric Building
⑥ 866 Plaza
⑦ Citigroup Center

Rockefeller Center
The outdoor skating rink and walkways of this complex of office buildings, shops, and eateries are a great place to people watch *(see p146)*.

Waldorf–Astoria
The splendid interior of one of the city's finest hotels lies beneath twin copper-capped towers *(see p179)*.

The Nail
This exterior cross designed by Arnaldo Pomodoro, resides in St. Peter's Church, which is located in one corner of the Citigroup Center *(see p179)*.

St. Mary's Garden
The garden at Holy Family Church is a peaceful haven.

Japan Society
Japanese culture, from avant-garde plays to ancient art, can be seen here *(see pp160–61)*.

Beekman Tower
Now an all-suite hotel, this Art Deco tower was built in 1928 as a hotel for women who were members of US college sororities.

Queensboro Bridge and Midtown Manhattan skyline at dusk ▶

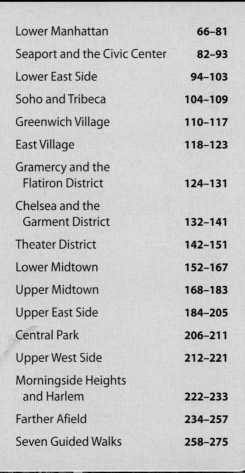

NEW YORK CITY AREA BY AREA

LOWER MANHATTAN

The old and the new converge at Lower Manhattan, where Colonial churches and early American monuments stand in the shadow of skyscrapers. New York was born here, and this was the site of the nation's first capitol. Commerce has also flourished here since 1626, when Dutchman Peter Minuit purchased the island of Man-a-hatt-ta from the Algonquian Indians for goods valued at $24 *(see p21)*. Several buildings are under development around the National September 11 Memorial *(see p56)*. Two skyscrapers are now complete, including One World Trade Center, which is the third tallest building in the world soaring to 1,776 ft (541 m). Visitors should call all sights to check opening times.

Sights at a Glance

Historic Buildings and Important Sites
1. Federal Reserve Bank
2. Federal Hall
3. New York Stock Exchange *pp72–3*
6. National September 11 Memorial & Museum
13. Fraunces Tavern Museum
16. Battery Maritime Building

Museums and Galleries
8. Skyscraper Museum
11. US Custom House
18. Ellis Island *pp80–81*
20. Castle Clinton National Monument
21. Museum of Jewish Heritage

Monuments and Statues
9. Charging Bull
17. Statue of Liberty *pp76–7*

Parks and Squares
10. Bowling Green
14. Vietnam Veterans' Plaza
19. Battery Park

Boat Trips
15. Staten Island Ferry

Churches
4. Trinity Church
12. Saint Elizabeth Ann Seton Shrine

Modern Architecture
5. World Financial Center
7. Battery Park City

☐ **Restaurants** *see pp292–97*
1. Adrienne's Pizza Bar
2. Battery Gardens
3. Fraunces Tavern
4. Les Halles

See also Street Finder maps 1, 2

◄ Statue of Liberty monument, Liberty Island

For keys to map symbols *see back flap*

Street by Street: Wall Street

No intersection has been of greater importance to the city, past or present, than the corners of Wall and Broad streets. Three important sites are located here. Federal Hall National Monument marks the place where, in 1789, George Washington was sworn in as president. Trinity Church is one of the nation's oldest Anglican parishes. The New York Stock Exchange, founded in 1817, is to this day a financial nerve center whose ups and downs cause tremors around the globe. The surrounding buildings are the very heart of New York's famous financial district.

The Marine Midland Bank rises straight up 55 stories. This dark, glass tower occupies only 40% of its site. The other 60% is a plaza in which a large red sculpture by Isamu Noguchi, *Cube*, balances on one of its points.

Trinity Building, an early 20th-century Gothic skyscraper, was designed to complement nearby Trinity Church.

The Equitable Building (1915) deprived its neighbors of light, prompting a change in the law: skyscrapers had to be set back from the street.

❹ ★ Trinity Church
Built in 1846 in a Gothic style, this is the third church on this site. Once the tallest structure in the city, the bell tower is now dwarfed by the skyscrapers that surround it. Many famous early New Yorkers are buried in the churchyard.

Wall Street subway (lines 4, 5)

BROADWAY

EXCHANGE PLACE

NEW STREET

BROAD STREET

The Irving Trust Company, built in 1932, has an outer wall patterned to look like fabric. In the lobby is an Art Deco mosaic in shades of flame and gold.

26 Broadway was built as the home of the Standard Oil Trust. An oil lamp rests on top of it.

❸ ★ New York Stock Exchange
The hub of the world's financial markets is housed in a 17-story building constructed in 1903.

The Liberty Tower is clad in white terra-cotta and is in the Gothic style. It was later turned into apartments.

The Chamber of Commerce is a fine Beaux Arts building of 1901.

Chase Manhattan Bank and Plaza has the famous Jean Dubuffet sculpture, *Four Trees*, located in the plaza.

Locator Map
See Manhattan Map pp16–17

Key

— Suggested route

```
0 meters          100
0 yards           100
```

❶ ★ Federal Reserve Bank
In the style of a Renaissance palace, this is a bank for banks. US currency is issued here.

Louise Nevelson Plaza is a park containing Nevelson's sculpture *Shadows and Flags*.

Wall Street is named for the wall that kept enemies and warring Indians out of Manhattan – the street is now the heart of the city's business center.

❷ ★ Federal Hall
Built as the US Custom House in 1842, this classical building houses a fascinating exhibit about the Constitution.

Wall Street in the 1920s

Entrance to Federal Reserve Bank

❶ Federal Reserve Bank

33 Liberty St. **Map** 1 C2. **Tel** (212) 720-6130. Ⓜ Fulton St–Broadway Nassau. 🎟 **Open** 10am–3pm Mon–Fri on the hour. Free (register in advance). **Closed** pub hols. 🖂 ♿ 🆆 **newyorkfed.org**

This is a government bank *for* banks – it is one of the 12 Federal Reserve banks, and therefore issues US currency. You can identify bank notes originating from this branch by the letter B in the Federal Reserve seal on each note.

Five stories below ground is one of the largest storehouses for international gold. Each nation's hoard is stored in its own compartment within the subterranean vault, guarded by 90-ton doors. Payments between nations used to be made by physical transfers of gold. An exhibition of "The History of Money," with 800

items, runs from 10am to 4pm. Designed by York & Sawyer in the Italian Renaissance style, the 1924 building occupies a full block and is adorned with fine wrought-iron grillwork.

❷ Federal Hall

26 Wall St. **Map** 1 C3. **Tel** (212) 825-6888. Ⓜ Wall St. **Open** 9am–5pm Mon–Fri. **Closed** public hols. ♿ 🎟 10am, 11am, 1–3pm Mon–Fri. 🏠 🆆 **nps.gov/feha**

A bronze statue of George Washington on the steps of Federal Hall marks the site where the nation's first president took his oath of office in 1789. Thousands of New Yorkers jammed Wall and Broad Streets for the occasion. They roared their approval when the Chancellor of the State of New York shouted, "Long live George Washington, President of the United States."

The present structure, renovated in 2006, was built between 1834 and 1842 as the US Customs House. It is one of the finest Classical designs in the city. Display rooms off the Rotunda include the Bill of Rights Room and an interactive computer exhibit about the Constitution.

❸ New York Stock Exchange

See pp72–3.

Trinity Churchyard

❹ Trinity Church

Broadway at Wall St. **Map** 1 C3. **Tel** (212) 602-0800. Ⓜ Wall St, Rector St. **Open** 7am–6pm Mon–Fri, 8am–4pm Sat, 7am–4pm Sun (church); 7am–4pm Mon–Fri, 8am–3pm Sat & pub hols, 7am–3pm Sun (churchyard). 🚹 12:05pm Mon–Fri, 9am & 11:15am Sun. except during services. 🎟 2pm daily; also Sun after 11:15am service. Concerts see details online. 🏠 ⬜ 🆆 **trinitywallstreet.org**

This square-towered Episcopal church at the head of Wall Street is the third one on this site. Designed in 1846 by Richard Upjohn, it was among the grandest churches of its day, marking the beginning of the best period of Gothic Revival architecture in America. Richard Morris Hunt's design for the sculpted brass doors was inspired by Lorenzo Ghiberti's *Doors of Paradise* at the Baptistery in Florence.

Restoration has uncovered the original rosy sandstone, long buried beneath layers of city grime. The 280-ft (86-m) steeple, the tallest structure in New York until the 1860s, still commands respect despite its towering neighbors.

Many prominent early New Yorkers are buried in the graveyard: statesman Alexander Hamilton; steamboat inventor Robert Fulton; and William Bradford, founder of New York's first newspaper in 1725.

Marble-columned rotunda within Federal Hall

5 World Financial Center

West St. **Map** 1 A2. **Tel** (212) 945-2600. M Fulton St, WTC Station, Cortlandt St, Rector St.
W **worldfinancialcenter.com**

A model of urban design by Cesar Pelli & Associates, this development is a vital part of the revival of Lower Manhattan, and its damage in the World Trade Center attack was attended to as a matter of urgency. Four office towers soar skyward, housing the headquarters of some of the world's most important financial companies, including Dow Jones and American Express. At the heart of the complex lies the dazzling Winter Garden, a vast glass-and-steel public space (all 2,000 panes of glass had to be replaced), flanked by 45 restaurants and shops, opening onto a lively piazza and marina on the Hudson River. The sweeping marble staircase leading down to the Winter Garden often doubles as seating for free events, varying from classical to contemporary in music, dance, and theater. Sixteen *Washingtonia robusta* palm trees, 40 ft (15 m) high, have been replaced in this contemporary version of the "palm court" of yesteryear.

Inaugurated in 1988, the building has been hailed as the Rockefeller Center of the 21st century.

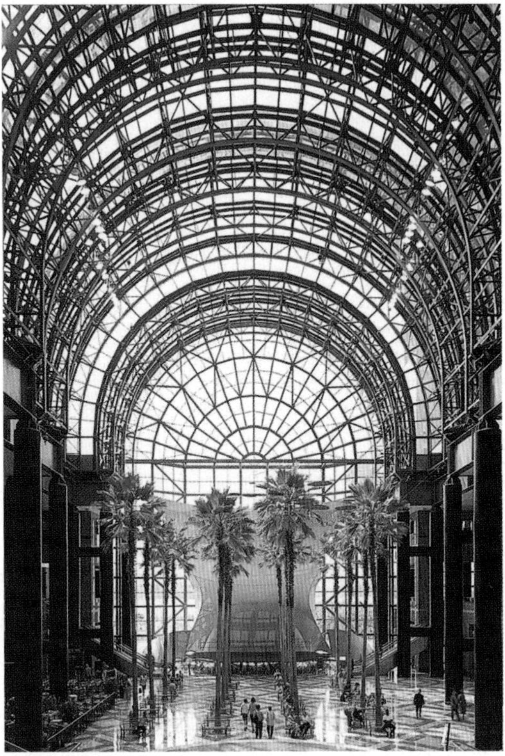
Main floor of the Winter Garden

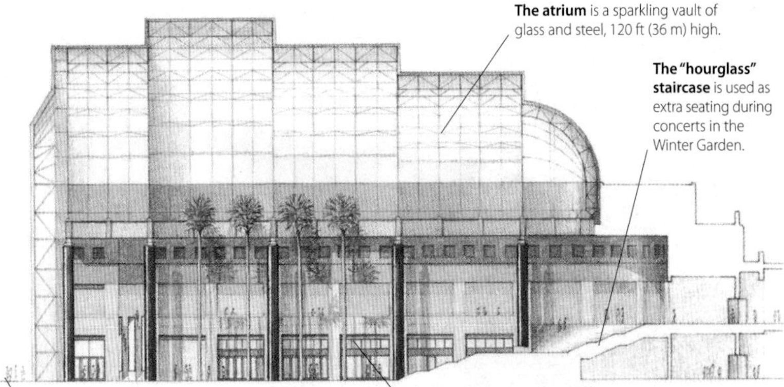
The atrium is a sparkling vault of glass and steel, 120 ft (36 m) high.
The "hourglass" staircase is used as extra seating during concerts in the Winter Garden.
An esplanade borders the Hudson.
Cafés and shops line the atrium.

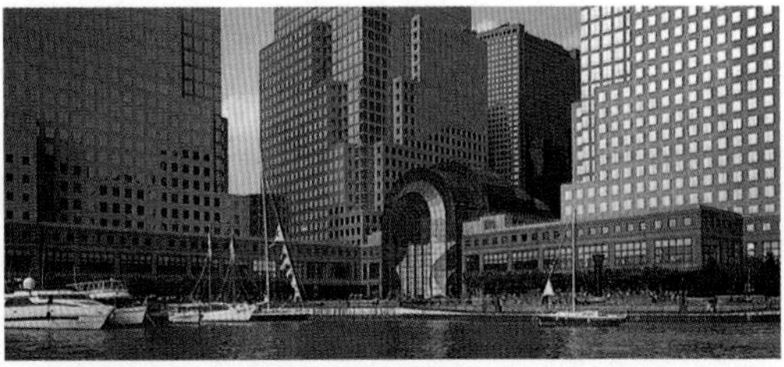
World Financial Center viewed from the Hudson River

❸ New York Stock Exchange

In 1790, trading in stocks and shares took place haphazardly on or around Wall Street, but in 1792, 24 brokers who traded at 68 Wall Street signed an agreement to deal only with one another: the basis of the New York Stock Exchange (NYSE) was formed. The NYSE has weathered a succession of alternating slumps ("bear markets") and booms ("bull markets"), growing from a local market-place into a financial center of global importance. Membership is strictly limited. In 1817, a "seat" cost $25; in the "bullish" years of the late 1990s, the prices ran as high as $4 million. In 2006, the NYSE became a for-profit public company, and all the seats were exchanged for cash and stock settlements. Traders now buy one-year licenses.

What a Trading Post Does

The 17 trading posts each consist of 22 groups, or "sections," of traders and technology, each trading the stock of up to 10 listed companies. Commission brokers work for brokerage firms, and rush between booth and trading post, buying and selling securities (stocks and bonds) for the public. A specialist trades in just one stock at a time, quoting bids to other brokers, and independent floor brokers handle orders for busy brokerage firms. Clerks process the orders that come into the trading post via SuperDOT computer into the Exchange's Market Data System. The pages help on the busy exchange floor, bringing orders from the booths to the brokers and specialists. Post display units show stock prices, and flat screens show prices and trades for the specialist. As of January 24, 2007, all NYSE stocks have been traded via an electronic hybrid market.

Trading post

KEY

① **Computerized stock tickers,** flash a steady stream of prices as fast as the human eye is able to read them.

② **Public viewing gallery**

③ **Trading post**

Ticker-tape Machine
Introduced in the 1870s, these machines printed out up-to-the-minute details of purchase prices on ribbons of paper tape.

The 48-Hour Day
During the 1929 Crash, stock exchange clerks worked nonstop for 48 hours. Their mood stayed cheerful despite the panic outside.

Trading Floor
On a typical day, some 3.5 billion shares are traded for more than 2,000 listed companies. The advanced electronics that support the Designated Order Turnaround (SuperDOT) computer are carried above the chaos of the trading floor in a web of gold piping.

Great Crash of 1929
On Tuesday, October 29, over 16 million shares changed hands as the stock market crashed. Investors thronged Wall Street in bewilderment but, contrary to popular myth, traders did not leap from windows in panic.

Members' entrance, Wall Street

1792 Buttonwood Agreement signed on May 17

1844 Invention of the telegraph allows trading nationwide

1867 Ticker-tape machines introduced

1903 Present Stock Exchange building opens

1987 "Black Monday" crash, October 19. Dow Jones Index drops 508 points

2007 Dow Jones Index hits 14,169, an all-time peak

1750	1800	1850	1900	1950	2000	2050

1817 New York Stock & Exchange Board created

1865 New Exchange Building opens at Wall and Broad Streets

1869 "Black Friday" gold crash, September 24

1929 Wall St. Crash, October 29

2001 After 8 years of bull markets, economy falters after September 11

2006 The NYSE merges with Archipelago Holdings to become a for-profit public company

2009 Dow Jones Index hits 6,547, a 12-year low

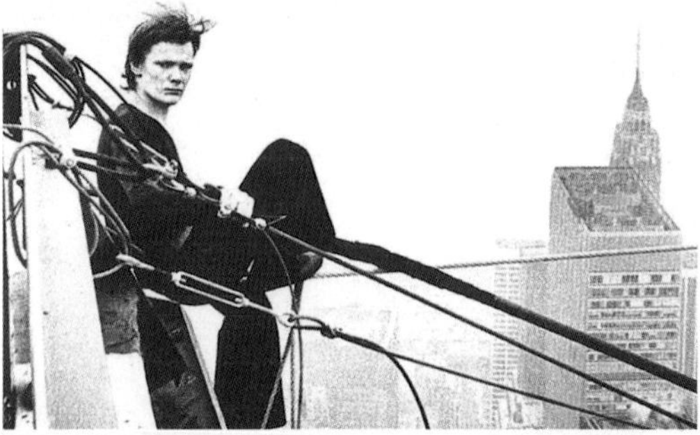

Philippe Petit about to step out between the two towers in 1974

❻ National September 11 Memorial and Museum

Map 1 B2. Ⓜ Chambers St, Rector St. Tribute WTC Visitor Center 120 Liberty St. **Tel** 1-866-737-1184. **Open** 10am–6pm Mon–Sat, till 5pm Sun (varies by season). Ⓦ **911memorial.org**

The twin towers of the World Trade Center dominated the skyline of Lower Manhattan for 27 years, until they were destroyed in a terrorist attack *(see p56)*. When the towers opened, in 1973, they were the tallest buildings in the world and soon became an iconic part of New York's history. One particularly memorable incident occured on August 7, 1974, when Philippe Petit stepped onto a tightrope between the towers and entertained crowds of office workers for almost an hour.

Today, the former World Trade Center site consists of a moving memorial to those who lost their lives during the terrorist attacks of February 26, 1993 and September 11, 2001. The memorial opened to the public soon after the tenth anniversary of the latter attacks, in 2011. A museum, located 70 ft (21 m) below ground with views of the "trident" installations and walls that remained untouched after the attack, will be completed in 2014.

The design, by Israeli-American architect Michael Arad of Handel Architects and landscape architecture firm Peter Walker and Partners, features two square pools in the center, where the twin towers once stood. The largest manmade waterfalls in the US cascade down the sides of the pools; together they symbolize the loss of life and the physical void left by the terrorist attacks. The names of the 2,977 who were killed in the September 11 attacks in New York City, Arlington, VA, and Shanksville, PA, and the names of the six victims killed in the 1993 World Trade Center bombing are inscribed in bronze around the edges of the pools. The sound of the waterfalls drowns out the noise of the city, making the site a contemplative sanctuary. A forest of roughly 400 trees fills the rest of the Memorial Plaza, furthering the reflective nature of the site.

❼ Battery Park City

Map 1 A3. Ⓜ Rector St. Ⓦ **batteryparkcity.org**

Governor Mario Cuomo set the tone for this project in 1983 when he urged the developers, "Give it a social purpose – give it a soul." The ambitious

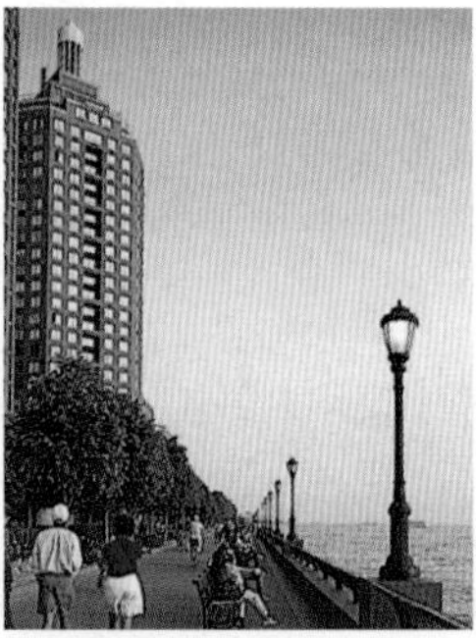

Battery Park City esplanade

neighborhood is on 92 reclaimed acres (37 ha) along the Hudson River. The restaurants, apartments, sculptures, and gardens are built on a human scale.

Battery Park City is designed to house more than 25,000 people. The most visible part of it is the World Financial Center *(see p71)* and total costs are estimated at $4 billion.

The 1.2-mile (2-km) walk along the river offers unobstructed views of the Statue of Liberty.

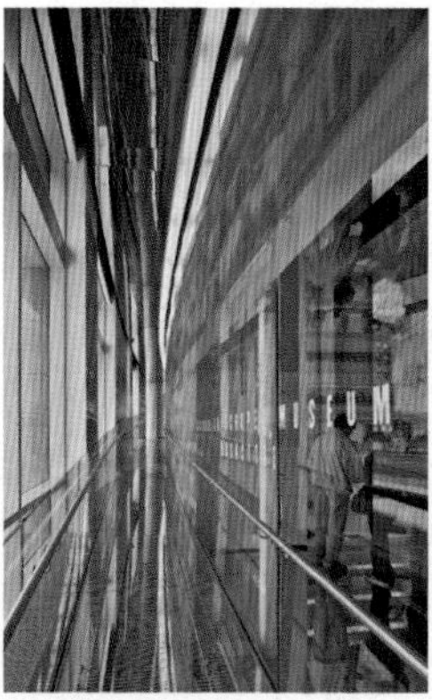

The airy Skyscraper Museum

❽ Skyscraper Museum

39 Battery Pl. **Map** 1 A3. **Tel** (212) 968-1961. Ⓜ Bowling Green, Rector St. **Open** noon–6pm Wed–Sun. Ⓦ **skyscraper.org**

Adjacent to the Ritz Carlton hotel, this museum celebrates New York's architectural heritage and examines the historical forces and individuals that shaped the city's skyline. There is a permanent exhibition on the World Trade Center and a digital reconstruction of how Manhattan has changed over time, as well as temporary exhibitions that analyze the various definitions of tall buildings: as objects of design, products of technology, sites of construction, real-estate investments, and places of work and residence.

Arturo Di Modica's iconic bull statue, at the southern end of Broadway

❾ Charging Bull

Broadway at Bowling Green.
Map 1 C4. Ⓜ Bowling Green.

At 1am on December 15, 1989, sculptor Arturo Di Modica and 30 friends unloaded his 7,000-lb (3,200-kg) *Charging Bull* bronze statue in front of the New York Stock Exchange. The group had eight minutes between police patrols to place the sculpture, but they managed to carry out the deed in just five. The bull was later taken away for obstructing traffic and lacking a permit. Due to the large outcry, however, the Parks Department gave it a "temporary" stomping ground on Broadway, just north of Bowling Green, where it remains to this day, the unofficial mascot of Wall Street.

Di Modica created the sculpture after the 1987 stock-market crash, to symbolize the "strength, power, and hope of the American people for the future." It took him two years to complete at a personal cost of $350,000.

❿ Bowling Green

Map 1 C4. Ⓜ Bowling Green.

This triangular plot north of Battery Park was the city's earliest park, used first as a cattle market and later as a bowling ground. A statue of King George III stood here until the signing of the Declaration of Independence, when, as a symbol of British rule, the statue was hacked to pieces and smelted for ammunition *(see pp24–5)*. The wife of the governor of Connecticut is said to have melted down enough pieces to mold 42,000 bullets.

The fence, erected in 1771, is still standing, but minus the royal crowns that once adorned it. They met the same fate as the statue. The Green was once surrounded by elegant homes. Beyond it is the start of Broadway, which runs the length of Manhattan and, under its formal name of Route 9, all the way north to the State capital in Albany.

Top of a column at the
US Custom House

Fountain at Bowling Green

⓫ US Custom House

1 Bowling Green. **Map** 1 C4.
Ⓜ Bowling Green. National Museum of the American Indian. **Tel** (212) 514-3700. **Open** 10am–5pm daily (to 8pm Thu). **Closed** Dec 25. Ⓖ 🅿
🆆 nmai.si.edu

One of New York's finest Beaux Arts designs, this 1907 granite palace by Cass Gilbert is a fitting monument to the city's role as a great seaport, decorated by the best sculptors and artists of the time. Forty-four Ionic columns stand guard, with an ornate frieze. Heroic sculptures by Daniel Chester French depict four continents as seated women: Asia (contemplative), America (facing optimistically forward), Europe (surrounded by symbols of past glories) and Africa (still sleeping). Inside, murals by Reginald Marsh decorate the fine marble rotunda, showing the progress of ships into the harbor. Opposite the entrance is a portrait of movie star Greta Garbo giving a press conference on board ship. In 1973 the US Customs Service moved out, leaving the building empty but for a small bankruptcy court.

The Custom House took on a different function in 1994, when the George Gustav Heye Center of the **Smithsonian National Museum of the American Indian** was unveiled on three floors of the building. The museum's outstanding collection of about a million artifacts along with an archive of many thousands of photographs, spans the breadth of the native cultures of North, Central and South America.

Exhibitions include works by contemporary Native American artists as well as changing displays drawn from the permanent collection.

⓱ Statue of Liberty

A gift from the French to the American people, the statue was the brainchild of sculptor Frédéric-Auguste Bartholdi and has become a symbol of freedom throughout the world. In Emma Lazarus's poem, which is engraved on the base, Lady Liberty says: "Give me your tired, your poor,/ Your huddled masses yearning to breathe free." Unveiled by President Grover Cleveland on October 28, 1886, the statue was restored in time for its 100th anniversary in 1986. Public access to the balcony surrounding the torch has been barred for safety reasons since 1916.

★ Golden Torch
In 1986, a new torch replaced the corroded original. The replica's flame is coated in 24-carat gold leaf.

The Statue
With a height of 305 ft (93 m) from ground to torch, the Statue of Liberty dominates New York harbor.

From Her Toes to Her Torch
Three hundred molded copper sheets riveted together make up Lady Liberty.

KEY

① **The original torch**, now stands in the main lobby.

② **Museum**

③ **The pedestal** is set within the walls of an army fort. It was the largest concrete mass ever poured.

④ **354 steps** lead from the entrance to the crown.

⑤ **Observation deck**

⑥ **A central pylon** anchors the 200-ton statue to its base.

⑦ **The frame** was designed by Gustave Eiffel, who later built the Eiffel Tower. The copper shell hangs on bars from a central iron pylon.

⑧ **The crown**'s seven rays represent the world's seas and continents.

★ Statue of Liberty Museum
Posters featuring the statue are among the items on display.

★ **Ferries to Liberty Island**
Ferries cross New York Harbor to Liberty Island, where the Statue offers some of the city's finest views.

Portrait of Liberty
Bartholdi's mother was the model for Liberty. The seven rays of her crown represent the seven seas and seven continents.

Making the Hand
To mold the copper shell, the hand was made first in plaster, then wood.

A Model Figure
A series of graduated scale models enabled Bartholdi to build the largest metal statue ever constructed.

Frederic-Auguste Bartholdi

The French sculptor who designed the Statue of Liberty intended it as a monument to the freedom he found lacking in his own country. He said "I will try to glorify the Republic and Liberty over there, in the hope that someday I will find it again here." Bartholdi devoted 21 years of his life to making the statue a reality, even traveling to America in 1871 to talk President Ulysses S. Grant and others into funding it and installing it in New York's harbor.

Restoration Celebration
On July 3, 1986, after a $100-million restoration, the statue was unveiled. The $2-million fireworks display was the largest ever seen in America.

Elizabeth
Ann Seton

⓬ Saint Elizabeth Ann Seton Shrine

7 State St. **Map** 1 C4. **Tel** (212) 269-6865. Ⓜ Whitehall, South Ferry. **Open** 10am–4:30pm daily. 🕆 8:05am, 12:15pm Mon–Fri; 11am Sun. 🅦 setonshrine.com

Elizabeth Ann Seton (1774–1821), the first native-born American to be canonized by the Catholic Church, lived here from 1801 to 1803. Mother Seton founded the American Sisters of Charity, the first order of nuns in the

United States. After the Civil War, the Mission of Our Lady of the Rosary turned the building into a shelter for homeless Irish immigrant women – 170,000 passed through on their way to a new life in America. The adjoining church was built in 1883. The Mission established and maintains the shrine to Mother Seton.

⓭ Fraunces Tavern Museum

54 Pearl St. **Map** 1 C4. **Tel** (212) 425-1778. Ⓜ Wall St, Broad St, Bowling Green. **Open** noon–5pm daily. **Closed** public hols. 🖂 🎦 groups only. Lectures, films. 🖉 🏛 🅦 fraunces tavernmuseum.org
NYC Police Museum
100 Old Slip, South St.
Map 1 D3. **Tel** (212) 480-3100. **Open** noon–5pm daily. Donation suggested. 🎦 groups only.
🅦 nycpm.org

New York's only remaining block of 18th-century commercial buildings contains an exact replica of the 1719 Fraunces Tavern where George Washington said farewell to his officers in 1783. The tavern had been an early casualty of the Revolution: the British ship *Asia* shot a cannonball through its roof in August 1775. The building was bought in 1904 by the Sons of the Revolution.

Its restoration in 1907 was one of the first efforts to preserve the nation's heritage. The ground floor restaurant has wood-burning fires and great charm. An upstairs museum has changing exhibits interpreting the history and culture of early America.

The **New York City Police Museum** (see p86) is at South Street. Exhibits include NYPD artifacts, interactive displays, seminars, and special events. Visit the Hall of Heroes and try your hand at the firearms training simulator.

⓮ Vietnam Veterans' Plaza

Between Water St and South St.
Map 2 D4. Ⓜ Whitehall, South Ferry.

This multilevel brick plaza features, in its center, an enormous wall of translucent green glass, engraved with excerpts from speeches, news stories, and moving letters to families from servicemen and women who died in the Vietnam war between 1959 and 1975.

Staten Island Ferry – one of the city's best bargains

⓯ Staten Island Ferry

Whitehall St. **Map** 2 D5. **Tel** 311.
Ⓜ South Ferry. **Open** 24 hrs. Free. ♿
🅦 siferry.com

The first business venture of a promising Staten Island boy named Cornelius Vanderbilt, who later became the railroad magnate, the ferry has operated since 1810, carrying island commuters to and from the city and offering visitors an unforgettable close-up of the harbor, the Statue of Liberty,

The 18th-century Fraunces Tavern Museum and restaurant

Ellis Island and lower Manhattan's incredible sky-line. The fare is still the city's best bargain: it's free.

⑯ Battery Maritime Building

11 South St. **Map** 2 D4. Ⓜ South Ferry. **Closed** to the public.

From 1909 to 1938, the municipal terminal for ferries to Brooklyn operated here on the site of a small wharf known as Schreijers Hoek, from which Dutch Colonial ships once set sail for the mother country. At the height of the ferry era, 17 lines made regular runs from these bustling piers, which are used now only by the Coast Guard service for Governors Island.

The building was designed in 1907. Arriving boats face 300-ft (91-m) arched openings guarded by tall, ornately scrolled columns and adorned with latticework, molding, and rosettes typical of the Beaux Arts period. This is actually a false front of sheet metal and steel, painted green to resemble copper.

Ironwork railing on the Battery Maritime Building

⑰ Statue of Liberty

See pp76–7.

⑱ Ellis Island

See pp80–81.

Castle Clinton National Monument in Battery Park

⑲ Battery Park

Map 1 B4. Ⓜ South Ferry, Bowling Green.

Named for the cannons that once protected the harbor, the park is one of the best places in the city for gazing out to sea. Over the years, landfill has extended the greenery far beyond its original State Street boundary.

The park is rimmed with statues and monuments, such as the Netherlands Memorial Monument and memorials to New York's first Jewish immi-grants and the Coast Guard. Fritz Koenig's *The Sphere*, a sculpture that once stood in the World Trade Center Plaza, is now here, serving as a memorial to those who died in the 9/11 terrorist attack.

Beaux Arts subway entrance at the corner of Battery Park

⑳ Castle Clinton National Monument

Battery Park. **Map** 1 B4. **Tel** (212) 344-7220. Ⓜ Bowling Green, South Ferry. **Open** 8:30am–5pm daily. **Closed** Dec 25. Concerts. Ⓦ nps.gov/cacl

Castle Clinton was built in 1811 as an artillery defense post 300 ft (91 m) offshore, connected to Battery Park by a causeway; but landfill gradually linked it to the mainland. None of its 28 guns was ever used in battle.

The fort was enclosed in 1824 to become a fashionable theater, where Phineas T. Barnum introduced "Swedish nightingale" Jenny Lind in 1850. In 1855 it preceded Ellis Island as the city's immigration point, processing over 8 million newcomers. In 1896, it became the New York Aquarium, which moved to Coney Island in 1941 *(see p251)*.

Now it is a monument and visitors' center for Manhattan's National Park Service sites, with historical panoramas of the city. The complex is the departure point for the Statue of Liberty–Ellis Island ferry *(see p378)*.

㉑ Museum of Jewish Heritage

36 Battery Place. **Map** 1 B4. **Tel** (646) 437-4200. Ⓜ Bowling Green, South Ferry. M5, M15, M20. **Open** 10am–5:45pm Sun–Thu (to 8pm Wed), 10am–3pm Fri and eve of Jewish holidays. **Closed** Sat, Jewish holidays, Thanksgiving. Lectures. Ⓦ mjhnyc.org

The museum has a core exhibition of more than 2,000 photographs, 800 artifacts, and 25 documentary films about Jewish life, before, during, and after the Holocaust. It also contains a state-of-the-art theater for films, lectures and performances; a memorial garden; classrooms; a resource center and library; a family history center; expanded gallery space for temporary exhibitions; offices; a café and event hall.

⑱ Ellis Island

Half of America's population can trace its roots to Ellis Island, which served as the country's immigration depot from 1892 until 1954. Nearly 12 million people passed through its gates and dispersed across the country in the greatest wave of migration the world has ever known. Centered on the Great Hall or Registry Room, the site today houses the three-story *Ellis Island Immigration Museum*. Much of this story is told with photos and the voices of actual immigrants, and an electronic database traces ancestors. Outside, the *American Immigrant Wall of Honor* is the largest wall of names in the world. No other place explains so well the "melting pot" that formed the character of the nation. Visit early to avoid the crowds.

Main building

★ Baggage Room The immigrants' meager possessions were checked here on arrival.

Rail Ticket
A special fare for emigrants led many on to California.

★ Dormitory
There were separate sleeping quarters for male and female detainees.

★ Great Hall
Immigrant families were made to wait for "processing" in the Registry Room. The old metal railings were replaced with wooden benches in 1911.

KEY

① **The ferry office** sold tickets to New Jersey.

② **The railroad office** sold tickets onward to the final destination.

③ **The metal and glass awning** is a re-creation of the original.

The Restoration

In 1990 a $156-million project by the Statue of Liberty-Ellis Island Foundation, Inc., renewed several ruined buildings, replacing the copper domes and restoring the interior with original fixtures.

Main entrance

③

Arrival
Steerage passengers
crowd the deck as the
ship approaches Ellis

Immigrant Family
An Italian mother and her
children arrive in 1905.

Medical Examining Rooms
Immigrants with contagious
diseases could be refused
entry and sent back home.

SEAPORT AND THE CIVIC CENTER

Manhattan's busy Civic Center is the hub of the city and the state, of the federal governments' court systems and the city's police department. In the 1880s it was the heart of the newspaper publishing business as well. The area is still a handsome enclave of imposing architecture with fine landmarks from every period in the city's history, from the 20th-century Woolworth Building to 19th-century City Hall and 18th-century St. Paul's Chapel, New York's oldest building in continuous use. Nearby is South Street Seaport. Called the "street of sails" in the 19th century because of the many ships that were moored there, the seaport underwent a decline when sailing ships became unprofitable. The area has been restored and is home to a museum and many shops and restaurants. The Brooklyn Bridge, once the largest suspension bridge in the world, lies to the north.

Sights at a Glance

Historic Streets and Buildings
1 South Street Seaport
2 Schermerhorn Row
3 *Brooklyn Bridge pp88–91*
4 Criminal Courts Building
5 New York County Courthouse
6 United States Courthouse
7 Municipal Building
8 Surrogate's Court, Hall of Records
9 Old New York County Courthouse
10 City Hall
12 Woolworth Building
14 AT&T Building

Churches
13 St. Paul's Chapel

Parks and Squares
11 City Hall Park and Park Row

See also Street Finder maps 1, 2, 4

☐ **Restaurants** *see p297*
1 SUteiShi

0 meters 400
0 yards 400

East River

PIER 18
PIER 17
PIER 15

◀ Brooklyn Bridge, the world's first steel suspension bridge

For keys to map symbols *see back flap*

Street by Street: South Street Seaport

Part commercial and part historical, the development of South Street Seaport has transformed the former heart of the 19th-century port of New York, which had long been neglected, into a lively and pleasant part of the city. Tall ships are moored here, and shops, restaurants, and cafés abound. The South Street Seaport Museum, currently closed due to Hurricane Sandy, tells the story of the city's maritime past through craft demonstrations, ship tours, and river cruises.

❶ ★ South Street Seaport
Once full of sailors and sailing ships, the seaport is now a lively complex of shops, restaurants, and museums.

Cannon's Walk is a 19th- and 20th-century block of buildings, with an outdoor café, shops, and a very lively marketplace.

The Titanic Memorial is a lighthouse built in 1913 in memory of those who died on the *Titanic*. It now stands on Fulton Street.

To Fulton St. subway (4 blocks)

❷ Schermerhorn Row
Built as counting houses in 1811, the Row contains the South Street Seaport Museum (closed due to Hurricane Sandy), as well as shops and restaurants.

The Boat-Building Shop lets you watch as skilled crafts-people build and restore small wooden vessels.

At the Maritime Crafts Center woodcarvers and painters can be seen at work on models, ship carvings, and figureheads.

The Pilothouse was originally from a steam tugboat built in 1923 by New York Central. The Seaport's admission and information center is to be found here.

The Consolidated Edison
electrical substation, built in 1975, has an illusionistic mural of the Brooklyn Bridge by Richard Haas on one side to help it blend in with its historic neighbors.

Locator Map
See Manhattan Map pp16–17

Key

— Suggested route

| 0 meters | 100 |
| 0 yards | 100 |

Meyer's Hotel,
built in 1873, became a hotel in 1881. Now a café, it retains a feel of days gone by when markswoman Annie Oakley stayed here.

❸ ★ Brooklyn Bridge
An engineering wonder when it was built in 1883, the bridge is still remarkable. From the pedestrian walkway there are fine views of the city and the bridge itself.

Pier 17 is currently undergoing extensive renovations, which are due to be completed in 2015. When open, there are great views from the pier's top floor of the Brooklyn Bridge and historic ships moored in the harbor.

The schooner *Pioneer* is used for river cruises from the Seaport. The 1908 *Ambrose* lightship, which guided ships into port, is also moored here.

The Ambrose lightship at a South Street Seaport pier on the East River

❶ South Street Seaport

Fulton St. **Map** 2 E2. **Tel** (212) SEA-PORT. Ⓜ Fulton St. **Open** Apr–Oct: 10am–9pm Mon–Sat, 11am–8pm Sun; Nov–Mar: 10am–7pm Mon–Fri, 11am–6pm Sun. ♿ 🎵 Concerts. ⬛
🏛 South Street Seaport Museum 12 Fulton St. **Tel** (212) 748-8600.
Closed expected to reopen in 2014.
⬛ ♿ 🎵 Lectures, exhibits, films. ⬛
🏛 🆆 seany.org

The heart of New York's 19th-century seaport has been given an imaginative new lease on life. In addition to several stores and restaurants, visitors will find seafaring craft, historic buildings, and museums, along with spectacular views of Brooklyn Bridge and the East River from the cobble-stone streets. Historic ships berthed here range from the little tugboat *W.O. Decker* to the great four-masted sailing ship *Peking*. Mini-trips on the schooner *Pioneer* are a great way to see the river.

The **Museum** covers 12 blocks of what was once America's leading port. Not only is it home to the largest fleet of privately

maintained historic vessels in the US, but there are also artifacts, artworks, and documents from the 19th- and early 20th-century. The museum is currently closed due to damage caused by Hurricane Sandy.

The New York City Police Museum *(see p78)* chronicles the history of law enforcement. Exhibits include weapons, the art of fingerprinting and forensics, and the arrest records of famous criminals.

Fulton Fish Market, a popular attraction at Seaport for more than 150 years, moved to the Bronx in 2006.

❷ Schermerhorn Row

Fulton and South Sts. **Map** 2 D3.
Ⓜ Fulton St.

This is Seaport's architectural showpiece. Constructed in 1811 by shipowner and chandler Peter Schermerhorn on land reclaimed from the river, the buildings were originally warehouses and counting-houses. With the opening of the Brooklyn Ferry terminus in 1814 and of Fulton Market in 1822, the block became desirable property.

The Row has been restored as part of the South Street development, and it now houses museum galleries, as well as shops, and restaurants.

Restored buildings on Schermerhorn Row

❸ Brooklyn Bridge

See pp88–91.

❹ Criminal Courts Building

100 Centre St. **Map** 4 F5. Ⓜ Canal St.
Open 9am–5pm Mon–Fri.
Closed public hols. ♿

This 1939 building is Art Moderne in style, with towers reminiscent of a Babylonian temple. The three-story-high entrance is set back in a court, behind two huge, square, free-standing granite columns – an intimidating sight for the accused. The building also houses the Manhattan Detention Center for Men, which was formerly across the street in a building known as "The Tombs" because of its Egyptian-style architecture. The nickname has stuck, although the original is long gone. An aerial walkway, or "bridge of sighs," links the courts with the correctional facility across Centre Street.

The building also houses the night courts, where cases are generally heard from 5pm to 1am on weekdays.

Entrance to the Criminal Courts Building

❺ New York County Courthouse

60 Centre St. **Map** 2 D1.
Ⓜ Brooklyn Br-City Hall.
Open 9am–5pm Mon–Fri.
Closed public hols. ♿

Built to replace the Tweed Courthouse *(see p92)*, this county supreme courthouse was completed in 1926. The fluted Corinthian portico at the top of a wide staircase is the main feature of the hexagonal building. The austere exterior is offset by a circular-columned interior rotunda featuring Tiffany lighting fixtures and a series of rich marble and ceiling murals by Attilio Pusterla on themes of law and justice. Six wings radiate from the rotunda, each housing a single court and its facilities.

The courtroom drama *Twelve Angry Men*, starring Henry Fonda, was filmed here.

New York County Courthouse

❻ United States Courthouse

40 Centre St. **Map** 2 D1. Ⓜ Brooklyn Br-City Hall. **Open** 9am–5pm Mon–Fri. **Closed** public hols. ♿

This courthouse was the last project undertaken by noted architect Cass Gilbert, designer of the Woolworth Building *(see p93)*. Begun in 1933, the year before his death, it was finished by his son. The 31-story structure is a pyramid-topped tower set on a classical temple

United States Courthouse

base. The bronzework on the doors is handsome, but the interior lacks the colorful decoration Gilbert had outlined in his sketchbooks. Aerial walkways link the building with its Police Plaza Annex.

❼ Municipal Building

1 Centre St. **Map** 1 C1. Ⓜ Brooklyn Br-City Hall. ♿

The Municipal Building, constructed in 1914, dominates the Civic Center and straddles Chambers Street. It was McKim, Mead & White's first skyscraper and houses government offices and a marriage chapel. The exterior, in harmony with City Hall, has no excess detail to detract from the earlier building. The most notable feature is the top, a fantasy of towers capped by Adolph Wienman's statue *Civic Fame*.

A railway passage (no longer in use) through the base, and the plaza joining the Municipal Building to the entrance of the IRT subway station were built as concessions to modern transportation needs. The building has had a far-reaching influence on architectural style; the main building at Moscow University is said to have been modeled on its design.

❽ Surrogate's Court, Hall of Records

31 Chambers St. **Map** 1 C1. Ⓜ City Hall. **Open** 9am–5pm Mon–Fri. **Closed** public hols. ♿ 📷

A Beaux Arts triumph, the original Hall of Records was begun in 1899 and completed in 1911. The elaborate columned facade is of white Maine granite, with a high mansard roof. The figures by Henry K. Bush-Brown in the roof area represent life's stages from childhood to old age; the statues by Philip Martiny over the colonnade are of notable New Yorkers such as Peter Stuyvesant.

Municipal Building

Martiny also made the representations of New York in its infancy and New York in revolutionary times at the Chambers Street entrance.

The Paris Opéra Garnier was the inspiration for the twin marble stairways and painted ceiling of the dazzling central hall. The ceiling mosaic by William de Leftwich Dodge features the signs of the zodiac and symbols of record keeping.

The Hall of Records holds public records dating back to 1664. A permanent exhibition, *Windows on the Archives*, features historical papers, drawings, letters, and photographs illustrating what life was like in New York from 1626 to the present.

Surrogate's Court

❸ Brooklyn Bridge

Completed in 1883, the Brooklyn Bridge was the largest suspension bridge and the first to be constructed of steel. Engineer John A. Roebling conceived of a bridge spanning the East River while ice-bound on a ferry to Brooklyn. The bridge took 16 years to build, required 600 workers and claimed over 20 lives, including Roebling's. Most died of caisson disease (known as "the bends") after coming up from the underwater excavation chambers. When finished, the bridge linked Manhattan and Brooklyn, then two separate cities.

Souvenir medal cast for the opening of the bridge

Brooklyn Bridge
From making the wire to sinking the supports, the bridge was built using new techniques.

Anchorage
The ends of the bridge's four steel cables are fastened to a series of anchor bars held in place by anchor plates. These are held down by giant granite vaults up to three stories high. Their vast interiors, once used for storage, are now used for summer art displays.

Caisson
The towers rose up above caissons, each the size of four tennis courts, which provided a dry area for underwater excavation. As work went on, they sank deeper beneath the river.

Shaft

Granite vault

Cable to tower

Anchor bar

Anchor Plates
Each of the four cast-iron anchor plates holds one cable. The masonry was built up around them after they were placed in position.

Anchor plates

Vault

Anchor plate

Central span is 1,595 ft (486 m) long

Vault

Roadway from anchorage to anchorage is 3,579 ft (1,091 m)

First Crossing
Master mechanic E.F. Farrington in 1876 was the first to cross the river on the bridge-in-progress, using a steam-driven traveler rope. His journey took 22 minutes.

Steel Cable Wire
Each cable contains 3,515 miles (5,657 km) of wire, galvanized with zinc for protection from the wind, rain, and snow.

Brooklyn Tower (1875)
Two Gothic double arches, each 271 ft (83 m) high, one in Brooklyn, the other in Manhattan, were meant to be the portals of the cities.

John A. Roebling

The German-born Roebling designed the bridge. In 1869, just before construction started, his foot was crushed between an incoming ferry and the ferry slip. He died three weeks later. His son, Washington Roebling, finished the bridge, but in 1872 he was taken from a caisson suffering from the bends and became partly paralyzed. His wife, under his tutelage, then took over.

Inside the Caisson
Immigrant workers broke up rocks in the riverbed.

Making the Cables

Thickness of steel wire (actual size)

End of wire

How the Cables Were Made
Each of the four main cables has 19 strands, each made of 278 steel wires. The wires were not twisted, but laid parallel.

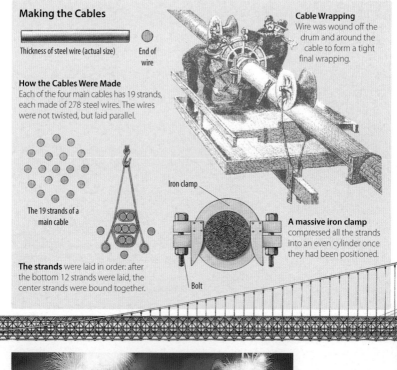

Cable Wrapping
Wire was wound off the drum and around the cable to form a tight final wrapping.

The 19 strands of a main cable

Iron clamp

Bolt

The strands were laid in order: after the bottom 12 strands were laid, the center strands were bound together.

A massive iron clamp compressed all the strands into an even cylinder once they had been positioned.

1983 Centennial Fireworks over the Brooklyn Bridge
Celebrating the bridge's 100th year, this display was awesome.

Bustling Bridge
This 1883 view from the Manhattan side shows the original two outer lanes for horse-drawn carriages, two middle lanes for cable cars, and the elevated center walkway.

Panic of May 30, 1883
After a woman tripped on the bridge, panic broke out. Of the estimated 20,000 people on the bridge, 12 were crushed to death.

Holding the Cables
Saddle plates anchor the cables at the top of each of the two towers.

Cable

Diagonal stays

Suspender wires

Nearing Completion (1883)
Vertical suspender wires lashed to diagonal stays hold the floor beams in place.

Floor Beams
The steel floor beams weigh 4 tons each.

Odlum's Jump
Robert Odlum was the first to jump off the bridge, on a bet, in May 1885. He later died from internal bleeding.

Elevated Walkway
Poet Walt Whitman said that the view from the walkway –18 ft (5.5 m) above the road – was "the best, most effective medicine my soul has yet partaken."

9 Old New York County Courthouse

52 Chambers St. **Map** 1 C1.
M Chambers St-City Hall. 🏛
included in City Hall tour.

This building is best known for the scandal it caused. It is nicknamed the "Tweed Courthouse" for the political boss who spent 20 times the budget for the building and pocketed $9 million of the total $14 million cost. "Boss" Tweed even bought a marble quarry and sold materials to the city at huge profit. Public outrage eventually led to his downfall in 1871 – ironically, he was tried in his own courthouse and died in a New York jail *(see p29)*.

After an $85 million restoration, including the 85-ft (26-m) rotunda and the grand staircase, this vibrant 19th-century landmark became the home of the Department of Education.

City Hall's magnificent early 19th-century facade

10 City Hall

City Hall Park. **Map** 1 C1. **Tel** 311.
M Brooklyn Br-City Hall Park Pl.
Open for prearranged tours only. ♿
📷 (212) 788-2656.

City Hall has been the seat of the New York city government since 1812, and is one of the finest examples of early 19th-century American architecture. A stately Federal-style building (with some influences from the French Renaissance), it was designed by John McComb, Jr.,

P.T. Barnum's museum blazes in 1865 as crowds watch from City Hall Park

the first prominent American-born architect, and the French emigré Joseph Mangin.

Marble cladding was not used for the building's rear, since it was not expected that the city would ever develop farther to the north. In 1954, a program of restoration remedied this and the interior was refurbished.

Mangin is usually given credit for designing the exterior, and McComb for the beautiful interior with its fine domed rotunda encircled by 10 columns. The space beneath it opens onto an elegant marble stairway, leading to the splendid second-floor City Council chambers and the Governor's Room, which houses a portrait gallery of early New York leaders. This magnificent entrance has welcomed rulers and heroes for nearly 200 years. In 1865 Abraham Lincoln's body lay in state in this hall.

Stand on the steps and look to your right to see a statue of Nathan Hale, a US soldier hanged by the British as a spy in September 1776 during the Revolutionary War. His last words – "My only regret is that I have not more lives than one to offer in the service of my country" – won him a permanent place in the history books and hearts of America.

11 City Hall Park and Park Row

Map 1 C2.
M Brooklyn Br-City Hall Park Plc.

This was New York's village green 250 years ago, complete with stocks and whipping post. It was the scene of pre-Revolution protests against English rule, and there is a memorial to the "Liberty Poles" (symbols of revolt) on City Hall's west lawn. The Declaration of Independence was read to George Washington and his troops here on July 9, 1776.

Later, Phineas T. Barnum's American Museum at the park's southern tip drew crowds from 1842 until it burned down in 1865. The Park Row building was the site of the Park Theater. From 1798 to 1848, the best actors of the day, such as Edmund Kean and Fanny Kemble, performed there. Park Row runs along the east side of City Hall Park. Once called "Newspaper Row," it was lined with the lofty offices of the *Sun*, *World*, *Tribune*, and other papers.

Statue of Benjamin Franklin in Printing House Square

Printing House Square has a statue of Benjamin Franklin with his *Pennsylvania Gazette*.

City Hall Park is a green space, used by those working nearby as a peaceful place to sit and relax.

Bas-relief caricature of architect Gilbert in the Woolworth lobby

⑫ Woolworth Building

233 Broadway. **Map** 1 C2. **Closed** to the public. Ⓜ City Hall Park Pl.

In 1879, salesclerk Frank W. Woolworth opened a new kind of store, where shoppers could see and touch the goods, and everything cost five cents. The chain of stores that followed made him a fortune and changed retailing forever.

The 1913 Gothic headquarters of his empire was New York's tallest building until 1930. It set the standard for the great skyscrapers. Architect Cass Gilbert's soaring two-tiered design, adorned with gargoyles of bats and other wildlife, is topped with a pyramid roof, flying buttresses, pinnacles, and four small towers. The marble interior is rich with filigree, sculptured reliefs, and painted decoration, and has a high glass-tile mosaic ceiling that almost seems to glow. The lobby is one of the city's treasures. Gilbert showed his sense of humor here, in bas-relief caricatures of the founder counting out his fortune in nickels and dimes; of the real-estate broker closing a deal; and of Cass Gilbert himself cradling a large model of the building. Paid for with $13.5 million in cash, the building has never had a mortgage. Woolworth's went out of business in 1997. The building is now owned by the Witkoff Group.

⑬ St. Paul's Chapel

209–211 Broadway. **Map** 1 C2. **Tel** (212) 233-4164. Ⓜ Fulton St. **Open** 10am–6pm Mon–Fri, 10am–4pm Sat, 7am–9pm Sun. **Closed** most public hols. 🕿 12:30pm Wed; 8am, 10am Sun. 🎵 by appt. Concerts 1pm Mon. 🌐 saintpaulschapel.org

Miraculously untouched when the World Trade Center towers collapsed in 2001, St. Paul's is Manhattan's only extant church built before the Revolutionary War. It is a Georgian gem. The colorful interior, lit by Waterford chandeliers, is the setting for free concerts. The pew where newly inaugurated

The Georgian interior of St. Paul's Chapel

George Washington prayed has been preserved. In the churchyard, the Actor's Monument commemorates George F. Cooke, who played many great roles at the Park Theater; he drank himself to death at the Shakespeare Tavern on Fulton Street. The chapel's "Unwavering Spirit" exhibition chronicles the volunteer efforts after September 11.

⑭ AT&T Building

195 Broadway. **Map** 1 C2. Ⓜ Broadway-Nassau Fulton St. **Open** office hours.

This former headquarters was designed by Welles Bosworth from 1915 to 1922. The facade is said to have more columns than any other building in the world, and the interior of the building is a forest of marble pillars. The whole edifice looks like a gigantic square-topped layer cake.

A sea sprite above the door of the AT&T (American Telephone and Telegraph) Building

LOWER EAST SIDE

Nowhere does the strong ethnic flavor of New York come through more tangibly than in Lower Manhattan, where immigrants began to settle in the late 19th century. Here Italians, Chinese and Jews established distinct neighborhoods, preserving their languages, customs, foods and religions in the midst of a strange land. This neighborhood of low-rise buildings is steadily becoming gentrified, but the old flavor remains. The area brims with restaurants, bars, and trendy stores, but still offers some of the city's greatest bargains and has a spirit found nowhere else. The composer Irving Berlin, who grew up here, famously said: "Everybody ought to have a Lower East Side in their life."

Sights at a Glance

Historic Streets and Buildings
① Home Savings of America
② Police Headquarters Building
③ Little Italy
④ Chinatown
⑧ Orchard Street
⑩ Delancey Street
⑪ East Houston Street
⑫ Puck Building
⑭ Engine Company No. 31

Parks and Squares
⑤ Columbus Park

Museums and Galleries
⑦ Lower East Side Tenement Museum
⑯ New Museum of Contemporary Art
⑲ FusionArts Museum

Shops and Markets
⑮ The Pickle Guys
⑰ Economy Candy
⑳ Essex Street Market

Churches and Synagogues
⑥ Eldridge Street Synagogue
⑨ Bialystoker Synagogue
⑬ Old St. Patrick's Cathedral
⑱ Angel Orensanz Center

☐ **Restaurants** see pp292–97
1 Beauty & Essex
2 Congee Village
3 Freemans
4 Il Palazzo
5 'inoteca
6 Joe's Shanghai
7 Katz Delicatessen
8 Lombardi's
9 Pho Pasteur
10 Public
11 Sammy's Roumanian
12 Stanton Social

0 meters 500
0 yards 500

See also Street Finder maps 4, 5

◀ Striking facade of the New Museum of Contemporary Art

For keys to map symbols see back flap

Street by Street: Little Italy and Chinatown

New York's largest and most colorful ethnic neighborhood is Chinatown, which is growing so rapidly that it is overrunning nearby Little Italy as well as the Lower East Side. Streets here teem with grocery stores, gift shops and hundreds of Chinese restaurants; even the plainest offer good food. What is left of Little Italy can be found at Mulberry and Grand streets, where old-world flavor abounds.

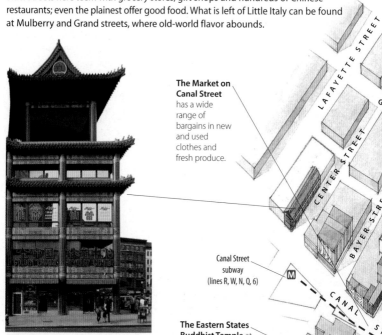

The Market on Canal Street has a wide range of bargains in new and used clothes and fresh produce.

Canal Street subway (lines R, W, N, Q, 6)

The Eastern States Buddhist Temple at 64b Mott Street contains over 100 golden Buddhas.

❹ ★ **Chinatown**
Home to a thriving – and still expanding – community of Chinese immigrants, this area is famous for its restaurants and hectic street life. The area truly comes alive around the Chinese New Year in January or February.

The Wall of Democracy on Bayard Street is covered with newspapers and posters describing the situation in China.

❺ **Columbus Park**
Once a slum, this park now fills with residents playing mahjong.

Bloody Angle, where Doyers Street turns sharply, was the gruesome site of many gangland ambushes during the 1920s.

Chatham Square has a memorial to Chinese-American war dead.

❷ Police Headquarters Building
The dome of this Baroque civic building towers over the City Hall area. In 1973, the police moved out; ten years later the building was turned into apartments.

Locator Map
See Manhattan Map pp16–17

❸ ★ Little Italy
The scents of Italy still waft from the restaurants and bakeries of this area, once home to thousands of immigrants.

Umbertos Clam House, known as the place where Mafia boss Joey Gallo was shot in 1972, once occupied this location on Mulberry Street.

❶ Home Savings of America
Stanford White designed this in1894 for the old Bowery Savings Bank.

STREET

MOTT STREET

HESTER STREET

BOWERY

CHRYSTIE STREET

ELDRIDGE STREET

Confucius Plaza is marked by sculptor Liu Shih's monument to the Oriental philosopher.

Key

— Suggested route

0 meters   100
0 yards   100

❻ ★ Eldridge Street Synagogue
Built in 1887, this was the first large temple built in the US by European Jews.

❶ Home Savings of America

130 Bowery. **Map** 4 F4.
Ⓜ Grand St, Bowery.

Imposing inside and out, this Classical Revival building was built for the Bowery Savings Bank in 1894. Architect Stanford White designed the ornamented lime-stone facade to wrap around the rival Butchers' and Drovers' Bank, which refused to sell the corner plot. The interior is decorated with marble pillars and a ceiling scattered with gilded rosettes.

Detail from Home Savings of America building

By the mid-20th century, the bank was a contrast to the Bowery with its vagrants and flophouses. It is now the site of opulent Capitale, and open only for private functions.

❷ Police Headquarters Building

240 Centre St. **Map** 4 F4. Ⓜ Canal St. **Closed** to the public.

Completed in 1909, this was a fitting home for the city's new professional police force. The main portico and end pavilions have Corinthian columns and the dome dominates the sky-line. However, lack of space meant the headquarters had to fit into a wedge-shaped site in the midst of Little Italy.

For nearly three-quarters of a century, this was where "New York's finest" came to work. During Prohibition, Grand Street from here to the Bowery was known as "Bootleggers' Row," and alcohol was easily obtained except when a police raid was due. The liquor merchants paid handsomely for a tip-off from inside police headquarters.

The police moved to different head-quarters in 1973, and in 1985 the building was converted into a luxury cooperative apartment project.

A street scene in Little Italy

❸ Little Italy

Streets around Mulberry St. **Map** 4 F4.
Ⓜ Canal St. Ⓦ littleitalynyc.com

The southern Italians who came to New York in the late 19th century found themselves living in the squalor of "dumbbell" apartments. These were built so close together that sunlight never reached the lower windows or backyards. With over 40,000 people living in 17 small, unsanitary blocks, diseases such as tuberculosis were rife.

Despite the privations of life on the Lower East Side, the community that grew up around Mulberry Street was lively with the colors, flavors, and atmosphere of Italy. These have lingered on, though the Italian population has dwindled to 5,000 and Chinatown has encroached on the traditional "Little Italy."

The most exciting time to visit is during the Feast of San Gennaro around September 19 *(see p54)*. For nine days Mulberry Street is renamed Via San Gennaro. On the saint's day, his shrine and relics are paraded through the streets. Throughout the feast there is music, dancing, and sideshows, and stalls selling Italian food and drink, as well as other ethnic cuisines.

Little Italy's restaurants offer simple, rustic food served in friendly surroundings at reasonable prices. NoLIta, North of Little Italy, is filled with boutiques, shops, and cafés. The fashionable flock here for the coolest small labels.

❹ Chinatown

Streets around Mott St. **Map** 4 F5.
Ⓜ Canal St. Eastern States Buddhist Temple 64b Mott St. **Open** 9am–6pm daily. Ⓦ explorechinatown.com

The Chinatown of the early 20th century was primarily a male community, made up of immigrants who had first gone to California. Wages were sent home to their families in China, who were prevented from joining them by US immigration laws. The men relaxed by gambling at mahjong. The community remained isolated from the rest of the city, financed and controlled by its own secret organizations, the Tongs.

Some of the Tongs were simply family associations who provided loans. Others, such as the On Leong and the Hip Sing, who were at war with one another, were criminal fraternities. Tiny, crooked Doyers Street was called "Bloody Angle"; enemies were lured there and

Stonework figures adorning the Police Headquarters Building

A Chinese grocer tending his shop on Canal Street

set upon by gang members waiting around the bend.

A truce between the Tongs in 1933 brought peace to Chinatown. By 1940 it was home to many middle-class families. Immigrants and businesses from Hong Kong also brought postwar prosperity to the community. Today over 80,000 Chinese-Americans live here.

Many visit the neighborhood to sample the cuisine, but there is more to do here than eat. There are galleries, antiques and curio shops, and Oriental festivals (see p55). To glimpse another side of Chinatown, step into the incense-scented Eastern States Buddhist Temple

Window, Eldridge Street Synagogue

at 64b Mott Street, where offerings are piled up and over 100 golden Buddhas gleam in the candlelight.

❺ Columbus Park

Map 4 F5. Ⓜ Canal St.

The tranquillity of Columbus Park today could not be further removed from the scene near this site in the early 1800s. The area, known as Mulberry Bend, was a red-light district, part of the infamous Five Points slum. Gangs with names like the Dead Rabbits and the Plug Uglies roamed the streets. A murder a day was common-place; even the police were afraid to pass through. Partly as a result of the writings of reformer Jacob Riis (see p51), the slum was taken down in 1892. The park is now the only open space in Chinatown.

❻ Eldridge Street Synagogue

12 Eldridge St. **Map** 5 A5. **Tel** (212) 219-0888. Ⓜ East Broadway. **Open** 10am–5pm Sun–Thu, 10am–3pm Fri. 🕿 🖂 ⓓ Every half hour from 10am until 3pm. 🏠 Ⓦ eldridgestreet.org

When this house of worship was built by the Orthodox Ashkenazi from Eastern Europe in 1887, it was the most flamboyant temple in the neighborhood. But many immigrant Jews saw the Lower East Side as just the beginning

of a new life, and later moved out of this massive synagogue. In the 1930s, the huge sanctuary, rich with stained glass, brass chandeliers, marbleized wood paneling, and fine carving, was closed. Much later a group of citizens raised funds for preservation, and the main sanctuary was reopened in 2007. The synagogue has become a vibrant cultural center, with concerts and other special programs.

Even after years of neglect, the facade, with touches of Romanesque, Gothic and Moorish designs, is impressive. Inside, the Italian hand-carved ark and sculpted wooden balcony show why this building was the pride of the area.

Street vendor's pushcart (1890s), Lower East Side Tenement Museum

❼ Lower East Side Tenement Museum

108 Orchard St. **Map** 5 A4. **Tel** (212) 431-0233. Ⓜ Delancey, Grand St. **Open** 10am–6pm daily. 🗗 compulsory (book ahead). First tour: 10:30am; last tour: 5pm. **Closed** Jan 1, Thanksgiving, Dec 25. 🕿 🖂 Lectures, films, videos. 🏠 (daily). Ⓦ tenement.org

The interior of this building was restored to re-create apartments as they appeared in the late 1870s, in 1916, 1918, and 1935. There were no regulations on tenement living conditions until 1879. Many rooms had no windows, and indoor plumbing was rare. The rooms give a sense of the cramped and deplorable conditions in which so many lived. The program includes the exhibit "Piecing It Together," about the area's garment history. The museum also offers superb walking tours.

8 Orchard Street

Map 5 A3. **M** Delancey, Grand St.
See Shopping p312.
W lowereastsideny.com

Jewish immigrants founded the New York garment industry on this street, named for the orchards that once stood here on James De Lancey's Colonial estate. For years the street was filled with pushcarts loaded with goods for sale. The pushcarts are long gone, and not all the shopkeepers are Jewish, but the flavor remains. On Sunday there is an outdoor market, and shoppers fill the street from Houston to Canal, looking for clothing bargains.

Orchard Street is also at the heart of the Lower East Side's gentrification. Boutiques and vintage stores nestle alongside bars, clubs, restaurants, and the boutique Blue Moon Hotel, formerly a tenement.

Vegetable stall at an outdoor market in Canal Street

Mural representing the zodiac sign Cancer in Bialystoker Synagogue

9 Bialystoker Synagogue

7–11 Willett St. **Map** 5 C4. **Tel** (212) 475-0165. **M** Essex St. **✪** frequent services. **📷** prearranged only.
W bialystoker.org

This 1826 Federal-style building was originally the Willett Street Methodist Church. It was bought in 1905 by Jewish immigrants from the Bialystok province of Poland, who converted it into a synagogue. For this reason, it faces west in the tradition of Christian churches instead of east.

The synagogue has a beautiful interior, with lovely stained-glass windows, a three-story carved wooden ark, and murals representing views of the Holy Land and the signs of the zodiac, including an interesting oddity: a lobster meant to represent Cancer, the crab.

10 Delancey Street

Map 5 C4. **M** Essex St. *See Shopping p312.* **Bowery Ballroom** 6 Delancey St. **Tel** (212) 533-2111. See website for shows schedule. **♿**
W boweryballroom.com

Once a majestic boulevard, Delancey Street these days is little more than an obligatory entrance to the Williamsburg Bridge. The street was named for James De Lancey, whose farm was situated here in Colonial days. During the American Revolution *(see pp24–5)*, De Lancey remained loyal to King George III. After the war, he fled to England, and his land was seized.

At 6 Delancey sits the **Bowery Ballroom**, a three-story theater completed only weeks before the stock market crash of 1929 *(see p33)*. Throughout the Great Depression and World War II, the building was deserted. Later, it served as a retail space, housing a haberdashery, a jeweler's boutique, and Treemark Shoes, until its resurrection as a live-music venue in the late 1990s. Much of the theater's original structure is still in place, including such decorative details as the brass rails, the copper-vaulted plaster ceiling of the mezzanine bar, and the brass and iron exterior metalwork.

Live music at the Bowery Ballroom, a stylish 1920s theater

Trays of bagels at a traditional Jewish bakery in East Houston Street

⓫ East Houston Street

East Houston St. **Map** 4 F3, 5A3.
Ⓜ Second Ave.

The dividing line between the Lower East Side and the East Village, East Houston between Forsyth and Ludlow streets clearly demonstrates the changing mix of old and new in the area. Between Forsyth and Eldridge streets is the Yonah Schimmel Knish Bakery, a fixture since 1890, still with its original showcases. Further down the block is the Sunshine Theater, constructed as a Dutch Church in the 1840s and later used as a boxing arena and a Yiddish vaudeville theater. Today it shows art films.

While much of the Jewish flavor of the Lower East Side has disappeared, there are two survivors farther along East Houston. Russ and Daughters is a culinary landmark, a third-generation family business that began on a pushcart, circa 1907. At this location since 1920, the store has seen its fortunes change with the neighborhood. It is famed for traditional smoked fish and herring, and has an impressive stock of caviar.

At the corner of Ludlow Street is perhaps the best-known survivor, the bustling Katz's Delicatessen (see p293), well past its 100th birthday

and still packing them in for pastrami and corned beef sandwiches.

⓬ Puck Building

295–309 Lafayette St. **Map** 4 F3.
Ⓜ Lafayette. **Open** to the public during business hours. **Tel** (212) 274-8900.

This block-square architectural curiosity was built in 1885 by Albert and Herman Wagner. It is an adaptation of the German *Rundbogenstil*, a mid-19th-century style characterized by horizontal bands of arched windows and the skillful use of molded red brick.

From 1887 to 1916 the building housed the satirical magazine *Puck*, and at the turn of the century it was the largest building in the world devoted to lithography and publishing.

Today it is the site of some of New York's most stylish parties and artiest fashion-photography shoots. The only connection remaining to the mythical Puck is the gold-leaf statue on the corner of Mulberry and Houston, and the smaller version over the entrance on Lafayette Street.

Statue of Puck on the northeast corner of the Puck Building

Facade of Old St. Patrick's Cathedral, now a parish church

⓭ Old St. Patrick's Cathedral

263 Mulberry St. **Map** 4 F3.
Tel (212) 226-8075. Ⓜ Prince St.
Open 8am–12:30pm & 3:30–6pm Thu–Tue. ✝ 9am, noon Mon–Fri; 5:30pm Sat; 9:15am, 12:45pm Sun; Spanish: 11:30am Sun.
Ⓦ oldsaintpatricks.com

The first St. Patrick's was begun in 1809, and it is one of the oldest churches in the city. When fire destroyed the original in the 1860s, it was rebuilt much as it is today. When the archdiocese transferred the see to the new St. Patrick's Cathedral uptown (see pp180–81), Old St. Patrick's became the local parish church, and it has flourished despite a constantly changing ethnic congregation.

Below the church are vaults containing the remains of, among others, one of New York's most famous families of restaurateurs, the Delmonicos. Pierre Toussaint was also buried here, but in 1990 his remains were moved from the old graveyard beside the church to a more prestigious burial place in a crypt in the new St. Patrick's Cathedral. Born a slave in Haiti in 1766, Toussaint was brought to New York, where he lived as a free man and became a prosperous wig-maker. He later devoted himself to caring for the city's poor, also tending cholera victims and using his money to build an orphanage. The Vatican is now considering the philanthropic Toussaint for sainthood.

⓮ Engine Company No. 31

87 Lafayette St. **Map** 4 F5.
Tel (212) 966-4510. Ⓜ Canal St.
Closed to the public.

In the 19th century, fire stations were considered important enough to merit a building of architectural importance and the Le Brun firm was the acknowledged master of the art. This 1895 station is one of their best. The building resembles a Loire château, with its steep roof, dormers and towers, seeming almost fairy tale-like in this location.

The present-day tenant is the Downtown Community Television Center, which offers courses and workshops to members. However, the building is no longer open to the public.

⓯ The Pickle Guys

49 Essex St. **Map** 5 B4. **Tel** (212) 656-9739. Ⓜ Grand St. **Open** 9am–6pm Sun–Thu, 9am–4pm Fri.
Ⓦ pickleguys.com

The scent of pickles permeates this little section of Essex Street, just as it did in the early 1900s when Jewish pickle shops filled the area. True to the old Eastern European recipe, The Pickle Guys store their pickles in barrels filled with brine, garlic and spices; this mixture preserves the pickles for months on end. Pickle varieties include full sour, three-quarters sour, half sour, new, and hot. No chemicals or preservatives

Facade of Engine Company No. 31, in the style of a French château

are added and the shop operates to strict Kosher rules.

The store also carries pickled tomatoes, pickled celery, olives, mushrooms, hot peppers, sun-dried tomatoes, sweet kraut, sauerkraut, and herring. It is run like a family business, with a friendly, chatty atmosphere, which perpetuates the neighborhood's traditions.

⓰ New Museum of Contemporary Art

235 Bowery St. **Map** 4 E3. **Tel** (212) 219-1222. Ⓜ Spring St, Bowery.
Open 11am–6pm Wed–Sun (to 9pm Thu). 🎟 free 7–9pm Thu. ♿🚫📷
Lectures, readings, music. 📱
Ⓦ newmuseum.org

Marcia Tucker left her post as the Whitney Museum's Curator of Painting and Sculpture in 1977 to found this museum. Her aim was to exhibit the kind of work she felt was missing from more traditional museums. She created one of New York's most cutting-edge exhibition spaces, which includes an innovative Media Lounge for digital art, video installations, and sound works.

The rotating collection features a wide range of art, from large-scale photographs of 1960s America to geometric abstracts. The museum takes an inclusive approach, showcasing both emerging and established

artists, including Mark Rothko and Roy Lichtenstein.

The striking seven-story building, designed by Tokyo-based architects Sejima & Nishizawa, is a notable addition to this Manhattan street. It rises like a sculptural stack of glowing cubes and is the first art museum to be built in downtown Manhattan in over a century. It has 60,000 sq ft (5,574 sq m) of exhibition space, a theater, store, café, and a rooftop terrace offering stunning views of the city.

Sweets on the densely packed shelves at Economy Candy

⓱ Economy Candy

108 Rivington St. **Map** 5 B3. **Tel** 1-800 352-4544. Ⓜ Second Ave–Houston St. **Open** 10am–6pm Mon, 9am–6pm Tue–Fri & Sun, 10am–5pm Sat.
Ⓦ economycandy.com

A Lower East Side landmark since 1937, this family-owned candy store stocks hundreds of varieties of candy, nuts, and dried fruit. Lined with floor-to-ceiling shelves packed with old-fashioned dispensers, the store

THE PICKLE GUYS
49 ESSEX ST TEL:(212)656-9739
WE SHIP NATIONWIDE

Entrance to The Pickle Guys' store, with traditional pickling barrels is one of the few businesses on Lower East Side that has remained almost unchanged in name and specialty throughout the neighborhood's fluctuating fortunes over 50 years.

This is due in no small part to Jerry Cohen's enterprise in transforming his father's "Nosher's Paradise" from a penny candy store to a national company. The shop carries sweets and treats from all over the world, as well as numerous food items dipped in chocolate and 21 colors of candy-covered chocolate buttons.

Interior of the Angel Orensanz Center, once a large synagogue

⑱ Angel Orensanz Center

172 Norfolk St. **Map** 5 B3. **Tel** (212) 529-7194. Ⓜ Essex St, Delancey St. **Open** 10am–5pm Mon–Fri and by appt. ♿ Ⓦ orensanz.org

Built in 1849, this cherry-red Neo-Gothic structure was once the oldest synagogue in New York. With ceilings 54 ft (15 m) high and seating for 1500, it was also the largest in the United States at the time. It was designed by the Berlin architect Alexander Saelzer in the tradition of the German Reform movement, and closely resembles Cologne Cathedral and the Friederichwerdeschekirche in the Mitte in Berlin.

After World War II and the decline of Lower East Side's Yiddish population, the synagogue was one of many to close. In 1986, the building was acquired by the Spanish sculptor Angel Orensanz, who turned it into an art studio. It now serves as a spiritual and cultural center with a program of artistic, musical, and literary events.

⑲ FusionArts Museum

57 Stanton St. **Map** 5 A3. **Tel** (212) 995-5290. Ⓜ Second Ave-Houston St. **Open** noon–6pm Tue–Fri & Sun. ♿ 🏠 Ⓦ fusionartsmuseum.org

With psychedelic metal sculptures that give a foretaste of the pieces displayed inside, the entrance to this museum is hard to miss. It is dedicated to showing "fusion art", defined as art in which various artistic disciplines, such as painting, sculpture, photography, and video, meld to form a distinct genre in themselves. The museum's location gives it access to an underground art scene that uptown contemporary art museums often neglect, and it also offers lesser-known artists the opportunity to exhibit their work in a reputable gallery.

Many New York City artists who have been creating fusion art on the Lower East Side for more than two decades have already shown their work in group exhibitions here.

Metal sculptures at the entrance of the FusionArts Museum

⑳ Essex Street Market

120 Essex St. **Map** 5 B3. **Tel** (212) 312-3603/388-0449. Ⓜ Essex St, Delancey St. **Open** 8am–7pm Mon–Sat, 10am–6pm Sun. ⊘ 🏠 Ⓦ essexstreetmarket.com

The market was created in 1938 by Mayor Fiorello H. La Guardia to bring pushcart vendors together and out of the way of traffic, especially police cars and fire trucks that used the narrow streets.

Two dozen meat, cheese, produce, and spice stalls fill the market. One of the oldest vendors is Jeffrey's butcher store, which has been at the market since 1939. Also here are the Essex Restaurant, which servies Latin/Jewish fare, and Cuchifritos, an art gallery showing the work of the neighborhood's artists.

Cuts of meat on a butcher's display at the indoor Essex Street Market

SOHO AND TRIBECA

Art and architecture are the twin lures that have transformed these formerly industrial districts. SoHo (south of Houston) was threatened with demolition in the 1960s until preservationists drew attention to the rare historic cast-iron architecture. The district was saved, and artists began to move into the loft spaces. Galleries, cafés,

shops, and then boutiques followed. Brunch and gallery-hopping in SoHo is now a favorite weekend outing. As rents rose, many artists were priced out of SoHo and moved to TriBeCa (Triangle Below Canal). Now, trendy TriBeCa has galleries, many restaurants, and the Tribeca Film Festival in spring.

Sights at a Glance

Historic Streets and Buildings
1. Haughwout Building
2. St. Nicholas Hotel
3. Greene Street
4. Singer Building
8. Harrison Street
9. White Street

Museums and Galleries
5. Children's Museum of the Arts
6. New York Earth Room
7. New York City Fire Museum

☐ **Restaurants** *see pp292–97*

1. Aquagrill
2. Balthazar
3. Boqueria
4. Bouley
5. Bubby's
6. Dos Caminos
7. The Dutch
8. L'Ecole
9. The Harrison
10. Hundred Acres
11. Kittichai
12. Locanda Verde
13. Megu
14. Nobu
15. Odeon
16. Petite Abeille
17. Spring Street Natural

| 0 meters | | 500 |
| 0 yards | | 500 |

See also Street Finder map 4

◀ Cast-iron facades in Tribeca with Art Deco tower in the background

For keys to map symbols *see back flap*

Street by Street: SoHo Cast-Iron Historic District

The largest concentration of cast-iron architecture in the world (see p44) survives in the area between West Houston and Canal streets. The heart of the district is Greene Street, where 50 buildings erected between 1869 and 1895 are found on five cobblestoned blocks. Most of their intricately designed cast-iron facades are in the Neo-Classical Revival style, with Corinthian columns and pediments. Mass-produced in a foundry, they were relatively inexpensive, and easy to erect and maintain. Now they are rare works of industrial art, well suited to the present character of this district.

West Broadway, as it passes through SoHo, combines striking architecture with a string of art galleries, shoe shops, designer boutiques, and small restaurants.

The Broken Kilometer, at 393 West Broadway, is an installation by Walter De Maria (see p109). Its 500 brass rods are arranged to play tricks with perspective. Laid end to end, the rods would measure 1 km.

72–76 Greene Street, the "King of Greene Street," is a splendid Corinthian-columned building. It was the creation of Isaac F. Duckworth, one of the masters of cast-iron design.

Performing Garage is a tiny experimental theater that pioneers the work of avant-garde artists.

WEST BROADWAY

WOOSTER STREET

BROOME STREET

GREENE STREET

GRAND STREET

Canal Street-Broadway subway (2 blocks)

❸ ★ **Greene Street**
Of all Greene Street's fine cast-iron architecture, one of the best is 28–30, the "Queen," which was built by Duckworth in 1872, and has a tall mansard roof.

10–14 Greene Street dates from 1869. Note the glass circles in the risers of the iron stoop, which allowed daylight to reach the basement.

15–17 Greene Street is a late addition dating from 1895, in a simple Corinthian style.

❹ ★ Singer Building
This terra-cotta beauty was built in 1904 for the famous sewing machine company.

Richard Haas, the prolific muralist, has transformed a blank wall into a convincing cast-iron frontage.

Locator Map
See Manhattan Map pp16–17

Key

— Suggested route

Prince Street subway station (lines N, R)

Dean & DeLuca
is one of the best gourmet food stores in New York. Its range includes a global choice of coffee beans (see p328).

M

101 Spring Street, with its simple, geometric facade and large windows, is a fine example of the style that led to the skyscraper.

Spring Street subway station

❷ St. Nicholas Hotel
During the Civil War, this former luxury hotel was used as a headquarters for the Union Army.

0 meters	100
0 yards	100

❶ Haughwout Building
In 1857 this was an elegant store, featuring the first Otis safety elevator.

Haughwout Building facade

❶ Haughwout Building

488–492 Broadway. **Map** 4 E4.
Ⓜ Canal St, Spring St.

This cast-iron building was erected in 1857 for the E.V. Haughwout china and glassware company, which once supplied the White House. Beneath the grime, the design is superb: rows of windows are framed by arches set on columns flanked by taller columns. Mass-produced sections repeat the pattern over and over. The building was the first to use a steam-driven Otis safety elevator, an innovation that made the skyscraper a possibility.

❷ St. Nicholas Hotel

521–523 Broadway. **Map** 4 E4.
Ⓜ Prince St, Spring St.

English parliamentarian W. E. Baxter, visiting New York in 1854, reported of the recently opened St. Nicholas Hotel: "Every carpet is of velvet pile; chair covers and curtains are made of silk or satin damask … and the embroidery on the mosquito nettings itself might be exhibited to royalty." It

St. Nicholas Hotel in its heyday in the mid-19th century

is small wonder, then, that it cost over $1 million to build – and with profits of over $50,000 for that year it must have seemed money well spent. Its glory was short-lived, however. In the Civil War it served as a Union Army headquarters. Afterward, the better hotels followed the entertainment district uptown, and by the mid-1870s the St. Nicholas had closed. There is little left on the ground floor to attest to its former opulence, but look up to the remains of its once-stunning marble facade.

Haas mural on Greene Street

❸ Greene Street

Map 4 E4. Ⓜ Canal St.

This is the heart of SoHo's Cast-Iron District. Along five cobblestoned blocks are 50 cast-iron buildings dating from 1869 to 1895. The block between Broome and Spring streets has 13 full cast-iron facades and from 8–34 is the longest row of cast-iron buildings anywhere. Those at 72–76 are known as the "King of Greene Street," but 28–30, the "Queen," is considered to be the finest. The architecture is best appreciated as a streetscape, with row upon row of columned facades. Walk into any of the

galleries housed within to see the spacious interior lofts. At the corner of Greene and Prince streets, the illusionistic muralist Richard Haas has created an eye-catching work, disguising a plain brick side wall as a cast-iron frontage. Look for the detail of the little gray cat, which sits primly in an "open window."

❹ Singer Building

561–563 Broadway. **Map** 4 E3.
Ⓜ Prince St.

The "little" Singer Building built by Ernest Flagg in 1904 is the second and smaller Flagg structure by this name, and many critics think it superior to the 41-story tower on lower Broadway that was torn down in 1967. The charmingly ornate building is adorned with wrought-iron balconies and graceful arches painted in striking dark green. The 12-story facade of terra-cotta, glass and steel was advanced for its day, a forerunner of the metal and glass walls to come in the 1940s and 1950s. The building was an office and warehouse for the Singer sewing machine company, and the original Singer name can be seen cast in iron above the entrance to the store on Prince Street.

Early electric-powered Singer sewing machine

❺ Children's Museum of the Arts

103 Charlton St. **Map** 3 C4. **Tel** (212) 274-0986. Ⓜ Houston St. 🚍 M20, M21. **Open** noon–5pm Mon & Wed, noon–6pm Thu & Fri, 10am–5pm Sat & Sun. 🅿 ♿ 🆆 **cmany.org**

Founded in 1988, this innovative museum aims to make the most of children's artistic potential by providing plenty of hands-on activities, sing-alongs, workshops, and performances. Children aged 1–12 can busy themselves with paint, glue, paper and other messy materials to create their own drawings and sculptures. For inspiration, displays of work by local artists are exhibited alongside examples of children's art from around the world. Kids can play around in the dressing-up room and the ball pond, and the museum also hosts a varied program of events appealing to children and families.

Brightly colored exhibition space at the Children's Museum of the Arts

❻ New York Earth Room

141 Wooster St. **Map** 4 E3. **Tel** (212) 989-5566. Ⓜ Prince St. **Open** noon–3pm & 3:30–6pm Wed–Sun. **Closed** mid-Jun–mid-Sep. ♿ 🆇 🆆 **earthroom.org**

Of the three Earth Rooms created by conceptual artist Walter De Maria, this is the only one still in existence. Commissioned by the Dia Art Foundation in 1977, the interior earth sculpture consists of 280,000 lbs (127,000 kg) of dirt piled 22 in (56 cm) deep in a 3,600 sq ft (335 sq m) room. *The Broken Kilometer*, another sculpture by De Maria, can be seen at 393 West Broadway *(see p106)*. It is composed of 500 solid brass rods arranged in five parallel rows.

1901 La France horse-drawn steam pumper in the City Fire Museum

❼ New York City Fire Museum

278 Spring St. **Map** 4 D4. **Tel** (212) 691-1303. Ⓜ Spring St. **Open** 10am–5pm daily. **Closed** public hols. 🅿 ♿ 🏠 🆆 **nycfiremuseum.org**

This museum is housed in a Beaux Arts–style 1904 firehouse. New York City's unsurpassed collection of fire-fighting equipment and memorabilia from the 18th century to 1917 includes scale models, bells, and hydrants. Upstairs, fire engines are neatly lined up for an 1890 parade. An interactive fire simulation, available for groups, gives an insight into fire-fighting.

The museum's first floor features an exhibition on 9/11, filled with tributes.

❽ Harrison Street

Map 4 D5. Ⓜ Chambers St.

Surrounded by modern high-rise blocks, this rare row of eight beautifully restored Federal town houses, with their pitched roofs and distinctive dormer windows, almost seems like a stage set. The houses were constructed in the late 1700s and early 1800s. Two of the buildings were designed by John McComb, Jr., New York's first major native-born architect, and were moved from Washington Street, their original site, for preservation purposes. The houses had previously been used as warehouses and were about to be razed to the ground, when, in 1969, the Landmarks Preservation Commission intervened to secure the necessary funding to enable them to be restored. They are now privately owned.

On the other side of the high-rise complex is Washington Market Park. This area was formerly the site of New York City's wholesale produce center. The market relocated to the Bronx in the 1970s.

❾ White Street

Map 4 E5. Ⓜ Franklin St.

While not as fine and intricate as some of the SoHo blocks, this sampling of TriBeCa cast-iron architecture shows a considerably wide range of styles. The house at No. 2 has carefully balanced Federal features and a rare gambrel roof, in contrast with the mansard roof of No. 17. Numbers 8 to 10 White, designed by Silesian-born Henry Fernbach, in 1869, have impressive Tuscan columns and arches, with Neo-Renaissance shorter upper stories to give an illusion of height. In contrast, 38 White is the home of neon artist Rudi Stern's gallery, Let There Be Neon.

Rudi Stern's Let There Be Neon gallery in White Street

GREENWICH VILLAGE

New Yorkers call it "the Village," and it began as a country village, an escape for city dwellers during the 1822 yellow fever epidemic. The random pattern of streets, reflecting early farm boundaries or streams, makes it a natural enclave that has been a bohemian haven and home to many artists and writers. A popular gay district is here, but the area has become mainstream and expensive. Near Washington Square, it is dominated by New York University students. Once cheaper, the East Village attracts a trendy crowd from all over the city. The Meatpacking District, which still has a few meatpackers, has become overwhelmed with smart boutiques and restaurants.

Sights at a Glance

Historic Streets and Buildings

1 St. Luke's Place
2 75½ Bedford Street
3 Grove Court
4 Isaacs-Hendricks House
5 Meatpacking District
7 Jefferson Market Courthouse
8 Patchin Place
10 Salmagundi Club
13 Washington Mews
14 New York University

Museums and Galleries

9 Forbes Magazine Building

Churches

11 First Presbyterian Church
12 Church of the Ascension
15 Judson Memorial Church

Parks and Squares

6 Sheridan Square
16 Washington Square

See also Street Finder maps 3, 4

Restaurants see pp292–97

1 Babbo
2 Blue Hill
3 Blue Ribbon Bakery
4 Corner Bistro
5 Da Silvano
6 Fatty Crab
7 Gotham Bar & Grill
8 Jane
9 Kesté
10 The Little Owl
11 Lupa
12 Minetta Tavern
13 Moustache
14 One if by Land, Two if by Sea
15 Otto
16 Pearl Oyster Bar
17 Spice Market
18 The Spotted Pig
19 The Standard Grill
20 Strip House
21 Tertulia
22 Waverly Inn & Garden
23 Westville

◄ Entrance to a charming, old-fashioned house in Greenwich Village

For keys to map symbols see back flap

Street by Street: Greenwich Village

A stroll through historic Greenwich Village is a feast of unexpected small pleasures – charming row houses, hidden alleys, and leafy courtyards. The often quirky architecture suits the bohemian air of the Village. Many famous people, particularly artists and writers, such as playwright Eugene O'Neill and actor Dustin Hoffman, have made their homes in the houses and apartments that line these old-fashioned narrow streets. By night, the Village really comes alive. Late-night coffeehouses and cafés, experimental theaters and music clubs, including some of the city's best jazz venues, beckon you at every turn.

Christopher Street, popular with New York's gay community, is lined with all kinds of shops, bookstores, and bars.

The Lucille Lortel Theater is at No. 121 Christopher Street; it opened in 1955 with *The Threepenny Opera*.

Twin Peaks at No. 102 Bedford Street began life in 1830 as an ordinary house. It was rebuilt in 1926 by architect Clifford Daily to house artists, writers, and actors. Daily believed that the quirky house would help their creativity flourish.

❸ Grove Court
Six houses dating from 1853–4 are set at the back of a quiet leafy courtyard.

The building on the corner of Bedford and Grove streets was used as the characters' apartment block in the TV sitcom *Friends*.

Christopher St subway

❷ No. 75½ Bedford Street
Built in 1873 in an alley, this is the city's narrowest house.

To Houston Street subway (2 blocks)

The Cherry Lane Theatre was founded in 1924. Originally a brewery, it was one of the first of the Off-Broadway theaters.

❶ ★ St. Luke's Place
This beautiful row of Italianate houses was built in the 1850s.

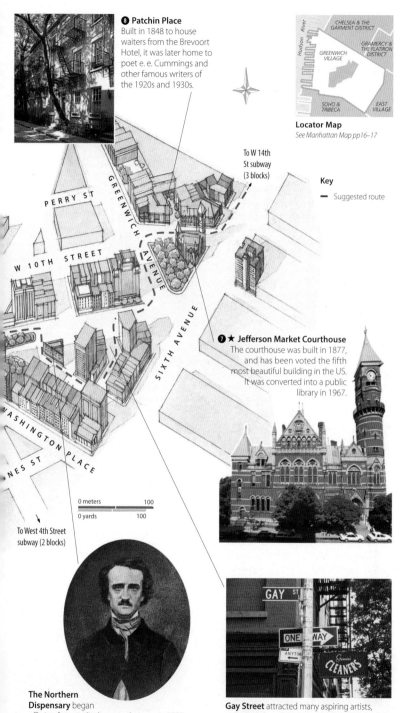

❽ Patchin Place
Built in 1848 to house waiters from the Brevoort Hotel, it was later home to poet e. e. Cummings and other famous writers of the 1920s and 1930s.

Locator Map
See Manhattan Map pp16–17

To W 14th St subway (3 blocks)

Key
— Suggested route

PERRY ST

GREENWICH AVENUE

W 10TH STREET

SIXTH AVENUE

WASHINGTON PLACE

NES ST

0 meters 100
0 yards 100

To West 4th Street subway (2 blocks)

❼ ★ Jefferson Market Courthouse
The courthouse was built in 1877, and has been voted the fifth most beautiful building in the US. It was converted into a public library in 1967.

The Northern Dispensary began offering free medical care to the poor in 1827. Edgar Allan Poe was treated here for a cold in 1837. It is now a hostel for the disabled.

Gay Street attracted many aspiring artists, writers, and musicians during the 1920s. It was the setting for Ruth McKenney's novel, *My Sister Eileen*, and the film *Carlito's Way*.

Row houses on St. Luke's Place, a street with literary associations

❶ St. Luke's Place

Map 3 C3. Ⓜ Houston St.

Fifteen attractive row houses, dating from the 1850s, line the north side of this street. The park opposite is named for a previous resident of St. Luke's Place, Mayor Jimmy Walker, the popular dandy who ran the city from 1926 until he was forced to resign after a financial scandal in 1932. In front of the house at No. 6 are the tall lamps that always identify a mayor's home in New York. The most recognizable house on the block is probably No. 10, the exterior of the Huxtable family home in *The Cosby Show* (although the series places it in Brooklyn). This is also the block where *Wait Until Dark* was filmed, starring Audrey Hepburn as a blind woman living at No. 4. Theodore Dreiser and the poet Marianne Moore are just two of the several writers who have lived here. Dreiser wrote *An American Tragedy* while living at No. 16. One block north, the corner of Hudson and Morton Streets marked the edge of the Hudson River in the 18th century.

Mayor's lamp at No. 6

❷ 75½ Bedford Street

Map 3 C2. Ⓜ Houston St. **Closed** to the public. Ⓦ cherrylanetheatre.com

New York's narrowest home, just 9½ ft (2.9 m) wide, was built in 1893 in a former passageway. The poet Edna St. Vincent Millay lived here briefly, followed by the actor John Barrymore, and later Cary Grant. The three-story building, now renovated, is marked by a plaque.

Just around the corner, at 38 Commerce Street, Miss Millay founded the Cherry Lane Theater in 1924 as a site for avant-garde drama. It still premieres new works. Its biggest hit was the 1960s musical *Godspell*.

❸ Grove Court

Map 3 C2. Ⓜ Christopher St/ Sheridan Sq.

An enterprising grocer named Samuel Cocks built the six town houses here, in an area formed by a bend in the street. (The bends in this part of the Village originally marked divisions between colonial properties.) Cocks reckoned that having residents in the empty passage between 10 and 12 Grove Street would help his business at No. 18.

But residential courts, now highly prized, were not considered respectable in 1854, and the lowbrow residents attracted to the area earned it the nickname "Mixed Ale Alley." O. Henry later chose this block as the setting for his 1902 work *The Last Leaf*.

Isaacs-Hendricks House

❹ Isaacs-Hendricks House

77 Bedford St. **Map** 3 C2. Ⓜ Houston St. **Closed** to the public.

This is the oldest surviving home in the Village, built in 1799. The old clapboard walls are visible on the sides and rear; the brickwork and third floor came later. The first owner, John Isaacs, bought the land for $295 in 1794. Next came Harmon Hendricks, a copper dealer and associate of revolutionary Paul Revere. Robert Fulton, who used copper for the boilers in his steamboat, was one of Hendricks's customers.

❺ Meatpacking District

Map 3 B1 Ⓜ 14th St (on lines A, C, E); 8th Av L.

Once the domain of butchers in blood-stained aprons hacking at sides of beef, these days (and particularly nights) the Meatpacking District is very different. Squeezed into an area south of 14th Street and west of 9th Avenue, the neighborhood is now dotted with trendy clubs, lounges, and boutique hotels that swell with New Yorkers out for a good time.

The mid-19th-century town houses at Grove Court

The neighborhood's hipness quotient rose when Soho House, the New York branch of the London private members' club, moved in, followed by the classy Hotel Gansevoort, with its rooftop swimming pool. Hip clothiers, including Stella McCartney and Marc Jacobs, have outlets here; upscale restaurants have opened; and new nightclubs and bars pop up every month.

The great allure of the Meatpacking District is, of course, that chic urbanites like some edginess to their nighttime recreation, and this is where the district delivers. The face of the neighborhood may be forever changed, but club-hoppers might still catch the occasional whiff of the meat-processing business that gave the area its name.

❻ Sheridan Square

Map 3 C2. Ⓜ Christopher St-Sheridan Sq.

This square, where seven streets converge, is the heart of the Village. It was named for the Civil War General Philip Sheridan who became commander in chief of the US Army in 1883. His statue stands in nearby Christopher Park.

The Draft Riots of 1863 took place here. Over a century later, another famous disturbance rocked the square. The Stonewall Inn on Christopher Street was a gay bar that had stayed in business (it was then illegal for gays to gather in bars) by paying off the police. However, on June 28, 1969, the patrons rebelled, and in the pitched battle that ensued police officers were barricaded inside the bar. It was a landmark moral victory for the budding gay rights movement. The inn that stands today is not the original. The Village remains a focus for the city's gay community.

"Old Jeff," the pointed tower of Jefferson Market Courthouse

❼ Jefferson Market Courthouse

425 Ave of the Americas. **Map** 4 D1. **Tel** (212) 243-4334. Ⓜ W 4th St-Washington Sq. **Open** 10am–8pm Mon & Wed, 11am–6pm Tue & Thu, 10am–5pm Fri & Sat. **Closed** public hols. ♿ 🖥 nypl.org

This treasured Village landmark was saved from the wrecking ball and converted into a branch of the New York Public Library through a spirited preservation campaign that began at a Christmas party in the late 1950s.

The site became a market in 1833, named after former president Thomas Jefferson. Its fire lookout tower had a giant bell that was rung to alert the neighborhood's volunteer fire fighters. In 1865, the founding of the municipal fire department made the bell obsolete, and the Third Judicial District, or Jefferson Market, Courthouse was built. With its Venetian Gothic-style spires and turrets, it was named one of the 10 most beautiful buildings in the country when it opened in 1877.

The old fire bell was installed in the tower. Here, in 1906, Harry Thaw was tried for Stanford White's murder (see p128).

Statue of General Sheridan in Christopher Park

By 1945, the market had moved, court sessions had been discontinued, the four-sided clock had stopped and the building was threatened with demolition. In the 1950s, preservationists campaigned first to restore the clock and then the whole building. Its renovation was undertaken by architect Giorgio Cavaglieri, who preserved many of the original details, including the stained glass and a spiral staircase that now leads to the library's dungeonlike reference room.

Facade and an ailanthus tree at Patchin Place

❽ Patchin Place

W 10th St. **Map** 4 D1. Ⓜ W 4th St-Washington Sq.

One of many delightful and unexpected pockets in the Village is this tiny block of small residences. It is lined with ailanthus trees that were planted in order to "absorb the bad air." The houses were built in the mid-19th century for Basque waiters working at the Brevoort Hotel on Fifth Avenue.

Later the houses became fashionable addresses, with many writers living here. The poet e. e. Cummings lived at No. 4 from 1923 until his death in 1962. The English poet laureate John Masefield also lived on the block, as did the playwright Eugene O'Neill and John Reed, whose eyewitness account of the Russian Revolution, *Ten Days That Shook The World* was made into a film, *Reds*, directed by Warren Beatty.

Toy battleship from the Forbes
Magazine Collection

❾ Forbes Magazine Building

60 5th Ave. **Map** 4 E1. **Tel** (212) 206-
5548. **M** 14th St-Union Sq. **Galleries
Open** 10am–4pm Tue–Wed, Fri–Sat
(times may vary). No strollers. 📷 Thu:
groups only. ♿ **Closed** public hols.

Some architectural critics
have called this 1925
limestone cube by Carrère
& Hastings pompous. It was
originally the headquarters
of the Macmillan Publishing
Company. When Macmillan
moved uptown, the late
Malcolm Forbes moved in with
his financial magazine, *Forbes*.
The Forbes Magazine Galleries
here show Forbes's diverse
tastes, with over 500 antique
toy boats; Monopoly games;
trophies; 12,000 toy soldiers;
and a signed copy of Abraham
Lincoln's Gettysburg Address,
among other historical
memorabilia. Paintings, from
French to American Military
works, are also on display.

❿ Salmagundi Club

47 5th Ave **Map** 4 E1. **Tel** (212) 255-
7740. **M** 14th St-Union Sq. **Open**
1–6pm Mon–Fri, 1–5pm Sat & Sun. 📷
W salmagundi.org

America's oldest artists club
resides in the last remaining
mansion on lower Fifth Avenue.
Built in 1853 for Irad Hawley, it
now houses the American
Artists' Professional League, the
American Watercolor Society
and the Greenwich Village

Society for Historic
Preservation. Washing-
ton Irving's satiric
periodical, *The Salmagundi
Papers*, gave the club its name.
Founded in 1871, the club
moved here in 1917. Periodic
art exhibits open the late 19th-
century interior to the public.

Exterior of the Salmagundi Club

⓫ First Presbyterian Church

5th Ave at 12th St. **Map** 4 D1. **Tel** (212)
675-6150. **M** 14th St-Union Sq.
Open 11:45am–12:30pm Mon, Wed,
Fri, 11am–12:30pm Sun. ✝ 6pm Wed
in chapel. **W** fpcnyc.org

Designed by Joseph C. Wells
in 1846, this Gothic church
was modeled on the Church
of St Saviour in Bath, England.
The church is noteworthy for
its brownstone tower. The
carved wooden plaques on
the altar list every pastor since
1716. The south transept by
McKim, Mead & White was
added in 1893. The fence of
iron and wood was built in
1844 and restored in 1981.

⓬ Church of the Ascension

5th Ave at 10th St. **Map** 4 E1.
Tel (212) 254-8620. **M** 14th St-Union
Sq. **Open** noon–2pm, 5–7pm daily.
✝ 6pm Mon–Fri, 9am, 11am Sun.
(except during services).
W ascensionnyc.org

This English Gothic Revival
church was designed in
1840–41 by Richard Upjohn,
architect of Trinity Church.
The interior was redone in
1888 by Stanford White, with
an altar relief by Augustus Saint-
Gaudens. Above the altar hangs
The Ascension, a mural by John
La Farge, who also designed
some of the stained glass.
The belfry tower is lit at
night to show off the colors.
In 1844 President John Tyler
married Julia Gardiner here;
she lived in nearby Colonnade
Row (*see p122*).

Church of the Ascension

⓭ Washington Mews

Between Washington Sq N and E 8th
St. **Map** 4 E2. **M** W 4th St.

Built originally as stables, this
hidden enclave was turned
into carriage houses around
1900. The south side was
added in 1939. Gertrude
Vanderbilt Whitney, founder
of the Whitney Museum (*see
pp202–203*), once lived here.
At No. 16 is NYU's French
House, remodeled in a French
style. Movies, lectures, and
classes in French are held here.

Bust of Sylvette by Picasso, between Bleecker and West Houston streets

⓮ New York University

Washington Sq. **Map** 4 E2. **Tel** (212) 998-1212, (212) 998-4636.
Ⓜ W 4th St. Ⓦ nyu.edu

Originally called the University of the City of New York, NYU was founded in 1831 as an alternative to Episcopalian Columbia University. It is now the largest private university in the US and extends for blocks around Washington Square. The visitor center is on West 4th St.

Construction of the school's first building on Waverly Place sparked the Stonecutters' Guild Riot of 1833: contractors protested the use of inmates from a state prison to cut stone. The National Guard restored order. The original building no longer exists, but a memorial with a piece of the original tower is on a pedestal set into the pavement on Washington Square South. Samuel Morse's telegraph, John W. Draper's first-ever photographic portrait, and Samuel Colt's six-shooter were invented here.

The Brown Building, on Washington Place near Greene Street, was the site of the Triangle Shirtwaist Company. In 1911, 146 factory workers died in a fire here, leading to new fire safety and labor laws.

A 36-ft (11-m) enlargement of Picasso's *Bust of Sylvette* is in University Village.

⓯ Judson Memorial Church

55 Washington Sq S. **Map** 4 D2.
Tel (212) 477-0351. Ⓜ W 4th St.
Open 10am–1pm, 2–6pm Mon–Fri.
🕇 11am Sun. Ⓦ judson.org

Built in 1892, this McKim, Mead & White church is an impressive Romanesque building with stained glass by John La Farge. Designed by Stanford White, it is named after the first American missionary sent to foreign soil, Adoniram Judson, who served in Burma in 1811. A copy of his Burmese translation of the Bible was put in the cornerstone when the building was dedicated.

It is the unique spirit of this church, not the architecture, that makes it stand out. Judson Memorial has played an active role in local and world concerns and has been the site of activism on issues ranging from AIDS to the arms race. It is also home to avant-garde art exhibitions and Off-Off Broadway plays.

Arch on the north side of Washington Square

⓰ Washington Square

Map 4 D2. Ⓜ W 4th St.

This vibrant open space was once marshland through which the quiet Minetta Brook flowed. By the late 1700s, the area had been turned into a public cemetery – when excavation began for the park, some 10,000 skeletal remains were exhumed. The

square was used as a dueling ground for a time, then as a site for public hangings until 1819. The "hanging elm" in the northwest corner remains. In 1826 the marsh was filled in and the brook diverted underground, where it still flows; a small sign on a fountain at the entrance to Two Fifth Avenue marks its course.

The magnificent marble arch by Stanford White, was completed in 1895 and replaced an earlier wooden arch that spanned lower Fifth Avenue to mark the centenary of George Washington's inauguration. A stairway is hidden in the right side of the arch. In 1916, a group of artists led by Marcel Duchamp and John Sloan broke in, climbed atop the arch, and declared the "free and independent republic of Washington Square, the state of New Bohemia."

Across the street is "the Row." Now part of NYU, this block was once home to New York's most prominent families. The Delano family, writers Edith Wharton, Henry James and John dos Passos, and artist Edward Hopper all lived here. Number 8 was once the mayor's official home.

Today students, families and free spirits mingle and enjoy the park side by side. A few drug dealers frequent the park, but it is safe by day.

Window on the corner of West 4th Street and Washington Square

EAST VILLAGE

Peter Stuyvesant had a country estate in the East Village, and in the 19th century, the Astors and Vanderbilts lived here. But around 1900, high society moved uptown, and immigrants moved in. The Irish, Germans, Jews, Poles, Ukrainians, and Puerto Ricans all left their mark in the area's churches and landmarks, and the city's most varied and least expensive ethnic restaurants. In the 1950s, low rents attracted the "beat generation." Later, hippies were followed by punks, and experimental music clubs and theaters still abound. Astor Place buzzes with students. To the east are Avenues A, B, C, and D, an area known as "Alphabet City," which, despite being somewhat gritty, has become one of the city's social hotspots.

Sights at a Glance

Historic Streets and Buildings
1. Cooper Union
3. Colonnade Row
8. Bayard-Condict Building

Museums and Galleries
4. Merchant's House Museum

Churches
5. St. Mark's-in-the-Bowery Church
6. Grace Church

Parks and Squares
7. Tompkins Square

Famous Theaters
2. Public Theater

Restaurants see pp292–97
1. Angelica Kitchen
2. Il Bagatto
3. Caracas Arepa
4. Casimir
5. Dirt Candy
6. Dumpling Man
7. Edi & the Wolf
8. Empellon Cocina
9. Great Jones Cafe
10. Hearth
11. Jewel Bako
12. Lil Frankies
13. The Mermaid Inn
14. Momofuku Noodle Bar
15. La Palapa
16. Prune
17. Zum Schneider

Gothic bas-relief on the facade of Grace Church

0 meters 400
0 yards 400

See also Street Finder maps 4, 5

◄ People relaxing in Tompkins Square Park

For keys to map symbols see back flap

Street by Street: East Village

At the spot where Tenth and Stuyvesant streets now intersect, Peter Stuyvesant's country house once stood. His grandson, also named Peter, inherited most of the property and had it divided into streets in 1787. Among the prize sites of the St. Mark's Historic District are the St. Mark's-in-the-Bowery Church, the Stuyvesant-Fish house and the 1795 home of Nicholas Stuyvesant, both on Stuyvesant Street. Many other homes in the district were built between 1871 and 1890 and still have their original stoops, lintels and other architectural details.

Astor Place subway (line 6

Alamo is the title of the 15-ft (4.5-m) black steel cube in Astor Place designed by Bernard Rosenthal. It revolves when pushed.

E 8TH ST

ASTOR PLACE

LAFAYETTE STREET

STABLE COURT

FOURTH AVENUE

BOWERY

Astor Place saw rioting in 1849. English actor William Macready, playing Hamlet at the Astor Place Opera House, criticized American actor Edwin Forrest. Forrest's fans revolted and there were 34 deaths.

❸ Colonnade Row
Now in shabby disrepair, these buildings were once expensive town houses. The houses, of which only four are left, are unified by one facade in the European style. The marble was quarried by Sing Sing prisoners.

❷ Public Theater
In 1965 the late Joseph Papp convinced the city to buy the Astor Library (1849) as a home for the theater. Now restored, it sees the opening of many famous plays.

❹ ★ Merchant's House Museum
This museum displays Federal, American Empire, and Victorian furniture.

❶ ★ Cooper Union
This institution, known for its art and engineering programs, provides a free education to its students

❺ St. Mark's-in-the-Bowery-Church
The church was built in 1799 and the steeple added in 1828.

Locator Map
See Manhattan Map pp16–17

Key
— Suggested route

The Stuyvesant-Fish House
(1803–04) was constructed out of brick. It is a classic example of a Federal-style house.

Renwick Triangle is a group of 16 houses built in the Italianate style in 1861.

Stuyvesant Polyclinic was founded in 1857 as the German Dispensary, and it is still a health clinic. The facade is decorated with the busts of many famous physicians and scientists.

St. Mark's Place was once the main street of hippie life. It is still the hub of the East Village youth scene. Funky shops now occupy many of the basements.

E 10TH STREET
STUYVESANT ST
THIRD AVENUE
ST MARK'S PLACE
SECOND AVENUE
E 9TH STREET
E 7TH STREET
E 6TH STREET

0 meters 100
0 yards 100

Little India, the row of Indian eateries on the south side of East Sixth Street, offers a taste of India at budget prices.

McSorley's Old Ale House still brews its own ale and serves it in surroundings virtually unchanged since it opened in 1854 (see p309).

Little Ukraine is home to around 25,000 Ukrainians. The hub is St. George's Ukrainian Catholic Church.

Great Hall at Cooper Union, where Abraham Lincoln spoke

● Cooper Union

7 East 7th St. **Map** 4 F2. **Tel** (212) 353-4000. **M** Astor Pl. **Open** 11am–7pm Mon–Fri, 11am–5pm Sat, and for lectures and concerts in Great Hall. **Closed** Jun–Aug, public hols. 🅿 ♿ **W** cooper.edu

Peter Cooper, the wealthy industrialist who built the first US steam locomotive, made the first steel rails and was a partner in the first transatlantic cable venture, had no formal schooling. In 1859 he founded New York's first free, non-sectarian coeducational college specializing in design, engineering, and architecture. Still free, the school inspires intense competition for places. The six-story building, renovated in 1973–4, was the first with a steel frame, made of Cooper's own rails. The Great Hall was inaugurated in 1859 by Mark Twain, and Lincoln delivered his "Right Makes Might" speech there in 1860. Cooper Union still sponsors a Public Forum.

● Public Theater

425 Lafayette St. **Map** 4 F2. **Tel** (212) 967-7555 (tickets). Admin (212) 539-8500. **M** Astor Pl. *See also Entertainment p336.* **W** publictheater.org

This large redbrick and brownstone building began its life in 1849 as the Astor Library,

The Public Theater on Lafayette Street

the city's first free library, now part of the New York Public Library. It is a prime American example of German Romanesque Revival style.

When the building was threatened with demolition in 1965, Joseph Papp, founder of the New York Shakespeare Festival, which became The Public Theater, persuaded New York City to buy it as a home for the company. Renovation began in 1967, and much of the handsome interior was preserved during conversion into six theaters. Although much of the work shown is experimental, The Public Theater was the original home of hit musicals *Hair* and *A Chorus Line* and hosts the popular Shakespeare in the Park (in Central Park) every summer.

● Colonnade Row

428–434 Lafayette St. **Map** 4 F2. **M** Astor Pl. **Closed** to the public.

The Corinthian columns across these four buildings are all that remain of a once-magnificent row of nine Greek Revival town houses. They were completed in 1833 by developer Seth Geer and were known as "Geer's Folly" by skeptics who thought no one would live so far east. They were proved very wrong when the houses were taken by

such eminent citizens as John Jacob Astor and Cornelius Vanderbilt. Washington Irving, author of *Rip Van Winkle* and other classic American tales, lived here for a time, as did two English novelists, William Makepeace Thackeray and Charles Dickens. Five of the houses were lost when the John Wanamaker Department Store razed them in the early 20th century to make room for a garage. The remaining buildings are falling to ruin.

The original 19th-century iron stove in the kitchen of the Merchant's House Museum

● Merchant's House Museum

29 E 4th St. **Map** 4 F2. **Tel** (212) 777-1089. **M** Astor Pl., Bleecker St. **Open** noon–5pm Mon, Thu–Sun and by appt. 🅿 🅿 📷 📷 **W** merchantshouse.com

This remarkable Greek Revival brick town house, improbably tucked away on an East Village block, is a time capsule of a vanished way of life. It still has both its original fixtures and its kitchen, and is filled with the actual furniture, ornaments, and utensils of the family that lived here for almost 100 years. Built in 1832, it was bought in 1835 by Seabury Tredwell, a wealthy merchant, and stayed in the family until Gertrude Tredwell, the last member, died in 1933. She had maintained her father's home just as he would have liked it, and a relative opened the house as a museum in 1936. The first-floor parlors are very grand, a sign of how well New York's merchant class lived in the 1800s.

❺ St. Mark's-in-the-Bowery Church

131 E 10th St. **Map** 4 F1. **Tel** (212) 674-6377. Ⓜ Astor Pl. **Open** 8:30am–4pm Mon–Fri (hours may vary). ✝ 6:30pm Wed, 11am Sun; in Spanish 5:30pm Sat.

One of New York's oldest churches, this 1799 building replaced a 1660 church on the *bouwerie* (farm) of Governor Peter Stuyvesant. He is buried here, along with several generations of his descendants and many other prominent early New Yorkers. Poet W.H. Auden was a parishioner and is also commemorated here.

In 1878, a grisly kidnapping took place when the remains of department store magnate A.T. Stewart were removed from the site and held for $20,000 ransom.

The church rectory at 232 East 11th Street dates from 1900 and is by Ernest Flagg, who achieved renown for his Singer Building (*see p108*).

❻ Grace Church

802 Broadway. **Map** 4 F1. **Tel** (212) 254-2000. Ⓜ Astor Pl, Union Sq. 🚌 M1–3, M8, M101–3. ✝ Jul–Aug: 10am, 6pm Sun; Sep–Jun: 9am, 11am, 6pm Sun. 📽 ♿ **Concerts.** 🆆 gracechurchnyc.org

James Renwick, Jr., the architect of St. Patrick's Cathedral, was only 23 when he designed this church, yet many consider it his finest achievement. Its delicate early Gothic lines have a grace befitting the church's name. The interior is just as beautiful, with Pre-Raphaelite stained glass and a handsome mosaic floor.

The church's peace and serenity were briefly shattered in 1863, when Phineas T. Barnum staged the wedding

of midget General Tom Thumb here; the crowds turned the event into complete chaos.

The marble spire replaced a wooden steeple in 1888 amid fears that it might prove too heavy for the church – and it has since developed a distinct lean. The church is visible from afar, because it is on a bend on Broadway. Henry Brevoort forced the city to bend Broadway to divert it around his apple orchard.

Grace Church altar and window

❼ Tompkins Square

Map 5 B1. Ⓜ 2nd Ave, 1st Ave. 🚌 M8, M9, M14A.

This English-style park has the makings of a peaceful spot, but its past has more often been dominated by strife. It was the site of America's first organized labor demonstration in 1874, the main gathering place during the neighborhood's hippie era of the 1960s and, in 1991, an arena for violent riots when the police tried to evict homeless people who had taken over the grounds.

The square also contains a poignant monument to the

Tom Thumb and his bride at Grace Church

neighborhood's greatest tragedy. A small statue of a boy and a girl looking at a steamboat commemorates the deaths of over 1,000 local residents in the *General Slocum* steamer disaster. On June 15, 1904, the boat caught fire during a pleasure cruise on the East River. The boat was crowded with women and children from this then-German neighborhood. Many local men lost their entire families and moved away, leaving the area and its memories behind.

❽ Bayard-Condict Building

65 Bleecker St. **Map** 4 F3. Ⓜ Bleecker St.

The graceful columns, elegant filigreed terra-cotta facade and magnificent cornice on this 1898 building mark the only New York work by Louis Sullivan, the great Chicago architect who taught Frank Lloyd Wright. He died in poverty and obscurity in Chicago in 1924.

Sullivan is said to have objected vigorously to the sentimental angels supporting the Bayard-Condict Building's cornice, but he eventually gave in to the wishes of Silas Alden Condict, the owner.

Because this building is squeezed into a commercial block, it is better appreciated from a distance. Cross the street and walk a little way down Crosby Street for the best view.

The Bayard-Condict Building

GRAMERCY AND THE FLATIRON DISTRICT

Four squares were laid out in this area by real estate developers in the 19th century to emulate the quiet, private residential areas in many European cities. Gramercy Park, still mainly residential, was one of them. The townhouses around this square were designed by some of the country's best architects, such as Calvert Vaux and Stanford White, and occupied by some of New York's most prominent citizens. Today, not far away, boutiques, trendy cafés, and high-rise apartments have taken over the stretch of lower Fifth Avenue just south of the famous Flatiron Building.

Sights at a Glance

Historic Streets and Buildings

2 New York Life Insurance Company
3 Appellate Division of the Supreme Court of the State of New York
4 Metropolitan Life Insurance Company
5 Flatiron Building
6 Ladies' Mile
8 National Arts Club
9 The Library at the Players
11 Block Beautiful
12 Gramercy Park Hotel
14 Con Edison Headquarters

Museums and Galleries

7 Theodore Roosevelt Birthplace

Churches

16 The Little Church Around the Corner

Parks and Squares

1 Madison Square
10 Gramercy Park
13 Stuyvesant Square
15 Union Square

Restaurants see pp292–300

1 Aldea
2 Artisinal
3 Bamiyan
4 Blue Smoke
5 Chat 'n' Chew
6 Craft
7 Devi
8 Eataly
9 Eleven Madison Park
10 Gramercy Tavern
11 Hill Country
12 Pure Food and Wine
13 Saravanaa Bhavan
14 Shake Shack
15 Tamarind
16 Tocqueville
17 I Trulli
18 Union Square Café

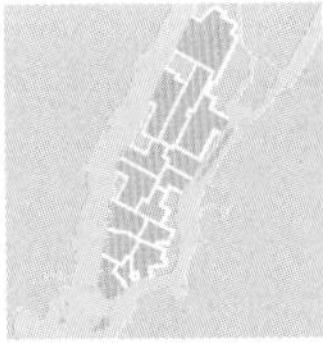

See also Street Finder maps 8, 9

◄ Pete's Tavern, a popular neighborhood bar in Gramercy Park District

For keys to map symbols see back flap

Street by Street: Gramercy Park

Gramercy Park and nearby Madison Square tell a tale of two cities. Madison Square is ringed by offices and traffic and is used mainly by those who work nearby, but the fine surrounding commercial architecture and statues make it well worth visiting. It was once the home of Stanford White's famous pleasure palace, the old Madison Square Garden, a place where revelers always thronged. Gramercy Park, however, retains the air of dignified tranquility it has become known for. Here, the residences and clubs remain, set around New York's last private park, for which only those who live on the square have a key.

❶ ★ Madison Square
The Knickerbocker Club played baseball here in the 1840s and was the first to codify the game's rules. Today office workers enjoy the park's many statues of 19th-century figures, among them Admiral David Farragut.

Statue of Diana atop the old Madison Square Garden

23rd Street subway (lines N, R)

❺ ★ Flatiron Building
The triangle made by Fifth Avenue, Broadway, and 22nd Street is the site of one of New York's most famous early skyscrapers. When it was built in 1903, it was the world's tallest building.

A sidewalk clock found in front of 200 Fifth Avenue marks the very end of the once-fashionable shopping area, known as Ladies' Mile.

❻ Ladies' Mile
Broadway from Union Square to Madison Square was once New York's finest shopping area.

❼ Theodore Roosevelt Birthplace
The house is a replica of the one in which the 26th American president was born.

0 meters 100
0 yards 100

❽ National Arts Club
This is a private club for the arts, on the south side of the park.

Locator Map
See Manhattan Map pp16–17

Key

— Suggested route

❸ Appellate Court
This small marble palace is said to be the world's busiest courthouse.

❷ New York Life Insurance Company
This spectacular building by Cass Gilbert bears his trademark pyramid-shaped top.

❹ Metropolitan Life Insurance Company Vast vaulted entrances mark each corner.

MADISON AVENUE

23rd Street subway (line 6)

Ⓜ

PARK AVENUE

❿ Gramercy Park
Only residents can use the park itself, but all can enjoy the peace and charm of the area around it.

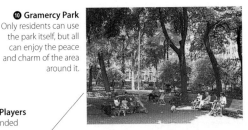

❾ The Library at the Players
Actor Edwin Booth founded this club in 1888.

The Brotherhood Synagogue was a Friends' Meeting House from 1859 to 1975, when it became a synagogue.

⓫ The Block Beautiful
This is a tree-lined stretch of East 19th Street. No particular house is outstanding, but the street as a whole is lovely.

IRVING PLACE

THRID AVENUE

Pete's Tavern
has been here since 1864. Short story writer O. Henry, a well-known chronicler of the city, wrote "The Gift of the Magi" in the second booth.

Farragut's statue, Madison Square

❶ Madison Square

Map 8 F4. Ⓜ 23rd St.

Planned as the center of a fashionable residential district, this square became a popular entertainment center after the Civil War. It was bordered by the elegant Fifth Avenue Hotel, the Madison Square Theater, and Stanford White's Madison Square Garden. The torch-bearing arm of the Statue of Liberty was exhibited here in 1884.

The Shake Shack is a top lunchtime spot for neighbor-hood office workers, while the surrounding park makes for a leisurely stroll to admire the sculptures. The 1880 statue of Admiral David Farragut is by Augustus Saint-Gaudens, with a pedestal by Stanford White. Farragut was the hero of a Civil War sea battle; figures representing Courage and Loyalty are carved on the base. The statue of Roscoe Conkling commemorates a US senator who died during the great blizzard of 1888. The Eternal Light flagpole, by Carrère & Hastings, honors the soldiers who fell during World War I.

❷ New York Life Insurance Company

51 Madison Ave. **Map** 9 A3.
Ⓜ 28th St. **Open** office hours.

This imposing building was designed in 1928 by Cass Gilbert of Woolworth Building fame. The interior is a master-piece, adorned with enormous hanging lamps, bronze doors and paneling, and a grand staircase leading, of all places, to the subway station.

Other famous buildings have stood on this site. Barnum's

Hippodrome was here in 1874, then the first Madison Square Garden opened in 1879. A wide range of entertainments were put on, including the prizefights of heavyweight boxing hero John L. Sullivan in the 1880s. The next Madison Square Garden – Stanford White's legendary pleasure palace – opened on the same site in 1890. Lavish musical shows and social events were attended by New York's elite, who paid over $500 for a box at the prestigious annual horse show.

The building had street-level arcades and a tower modeled on the Giralda in Seville. A gold statue of the goddess Diana stood atop the tower. Her nudity was shocking, but far more scandalous was the decadent life and death of White himself. In 1906, while watching a revue in the roof garden, he was shot dead by millionaire Harry K. Thaw, the husband of White's former mistress, showgirl Evelyn Nesbit. The headline in the journal *Vanity Fair* summed up popular feeling: "Stanford White, Voluptuary and Pervert, Dies the Death of a Dog." The ensuing trial's revelations about decadent Broadway high society leave modern soap operas far behind.

New York Life Insurance Company's golden pyramid roof

Statues of *Justice* and *Study* above the Appellate Court

❸ Appellate Division of the Supreme Court of the State of New York

E. 25th St. at Madison Ave. **Map** 9 A4
Ⓜ 23rd St. **Open** 9am–5pm Mon–Fri (court in session from 2pm Tue–Thu, from 10am Fri). **Closed** public hols. ✉

Appeals relating to civil and criminal cases for New York and the Bronx are heard here, in what is widely considered to be the busiest court of its kind in the world. James Brown Lord designed the small yet noble Palladian Revival building in 1900. It is decorated with more than a dozen handsome sculptures, including Daniel Chester French's Justice flanked by Power and Study. During the week, the public is invited to step inside to admire the fine interior, designed by the Herter brothers, including the courtroom when it is not in session. Among the elegant details worth looking for are the fine stained-glass windows and dome, the murals, and the striking cabinetwork.

Displays in the lobby often feature some of the more famous and infamous – cases that have been heard in this court. Among the celebrity names that have been involved in appeals settled here are Babe Ruth, Charlie Chaplin, Fred Astaire, Harry Houdini, Theodore Dreiser, and Edgar Allan Poe.

Clock tower of the Metropolitan Life Insurance Company building

❹ Metropolitan Life Insurance Company

1 Madison Ave. **Map** 9 A4. Ⓜ 23rd St. **Open** banking hours. ✉

In 1909, the addition of a 700-ft (210-m) tower to this 1893 building ousted the Flatiron as the tallest in the world. The huge four-sided clock has minute hands said to weigh 1000 lb (454 kg) each. The building is lit up at night, and is a familiar part of the evening skyline. It served as the company symbol "the light that never fails." A series of historical murals by N.C. Wyeth, the famed illustrator of such classics as *Robin Hood*, *Treasure Island* and *Robinson Crusoe* (and the father of painter Andrew Wyeth), once graced the walls of the cafeteria. The building now houses First-Boston Crédit-Suisse.

❺ Flatiron Building

175 5th Ave. **Map** 8 F4. Ⓜ 23rd St. **Open** office hours.

Originally named the Fuller Building after the construction company that owned it, this building by Chicago architect Daniel Burnham was the tallest in the world when it was completed in 1902. One of the first buildings to use a steel frame, it heralded the era of the skyscrapers.

It soon became known as the Flatiron for its unusual triangular shape, but some called it "Burnham's folly," predicting that the winds created by the building's shape would knock it down. It has withstood the test of time, but the winds along 23rd Street did have one notable effect. In the building's early days, they drew crowds of males hoping to get a peek at women's ankles as their long skirts got blown about. Police officers had to keep people moving along, and their call, "23-skidoo" became slang for "scram."

The stretch of Fifth Avenue to the south of the building, formerly rather run down, has come to life with chic shops such as Emporio Armani and Paul Smith, giving the area new cachet and a new name, "the Flatiron District."

Flatiron Building during its construction

Arnold Constable store

❻ Ladies' Mile

Broadway (Union Sq. to Madison Sq.). **Map** 8 F4–5, 9 A5. Ⓜ 14th St, 23rd St.

In the 19th century, the "carriage trade" came here in shiny traps from their town houses nearby to shop at stores such as Arnold Constable (Nos. 881–887) and Lord & Taylor (No. 901). The ground floor exteriors have changed beyond recognition; look up to see the remains of once-grand facades.

President Teddy Roosevelt

❼ Theodore Roosevelt Birthplace

28 E. 20th St. **Map** 9 A5. **Tel** (212) 260-1616. Ⓜ 14th St-Union Sq- 23rd St. **Open** 9am–5pm Tue–Sat (last adm: 4pm). **Closed** pub hols. 🅿 🎫 hourly. Lectures, concerts, films, videos. 📷 🌐 nps.gov/thrb

The reconstructed boyhood home of the colorful 26th president displays everything from the toys with which the young Teddy played to campaign buttons and emblems of the trademark "Rough Rider" hat that Roosevelt wore in the Spanish-American War. One exhibit features his explorations and interests; the other covers his political career.

Bas-relief faces of great writers at the National Arts Club

❽ National Arts Club

15 Gramercy Pk S. **Map** 9 A5. **Tel** (212) 475-3424. Ⓜ 23rd St. **Open** noon–5pm Mon–Fri during exhibitions.
Ⓦ nationalartsclub.org

This brownstone was the residence of New York governor Samuel Tilden, who condemned "Boss" Tweed *(see p29)* and established a free public library. He had the facade redesigned by Calvert Vaux in 1881–4. In 1906 the National Arts Club bought the home and kept the original high ceilings and stained glass by John La Farge. Members have included most leading American artists of the late 19th and early 20th century, who were asked to donate a painting or sculpture in return for life membership; these gifts form the permanent collection. The club is open to the public for exhibitions only.

❾ The Library at the Players

18 Gramercy Pk S. **Map** 9 A5. **Tel** (212) 228-7610. Ⓜ 23rd St. **Closed** except for pre-booked group tours.

This two-story brownstone was the home of actor Edwin Booth, brother of John Wilkes Booth, President Lincoln's assassin. Architect Stanford White remodeled the building as a club in 1888. Although intended primarily

for actors, members have included White himself, author Mark Twain, publisher Thomas Nast and Winston Churchill, whose mother, Jennie Jerome, was born nearby. A statue of Booth playing Hamlet is across the street in Gramercy Park.

Decorative grille at The Players club

❿ Gramercy Park

Map 9 A4. Ⓜ 23rd St, 14th St–Union Sq.

Gramercy Park is one of four squares (with Union, Stuyvesant and Madison) laid out in the 1830s and 1840s to attract society residences. It is the city's only private park, and residents in the surrounding buildings have keys to the park gate as the original owners once did. Look through the railings at the southeast corner to see Greg Wyatt's fountain, with giraffes leaping around a smiling sun.

The buildings around the square were designed by some of the city's most famous architects, including Stanford White, whose house was

Fountain with sun and giraffes by Greg Wyatt in Gramercy Park

located on the site of today's Gramercy Park Hotel.

Particularly fine are 3 and 4, with graceful cast-iron gates and porches. The lanterns in front of 4 serve as symbols marking the house of a former mayor of the city, James Harper. Number 34 (1883) has been the home of the sculptor Daniel Chester French, the actor James Cagney and circus impresario John Ringling (who had a massive pipe organ installed in his apartment).

House facade on the Block Beautiful on East 19th Street

⓫ Block Beautiful

E 19th St. **Map** 9 A5. Ⓜ 14th St–Union Sq, 23rd St.

This is a serene, tree-lined block of 1920s residences, beautifully restored. None of them is exceptional on its own, but together they create a wonderfully harmonious whole. Number 132 had two famous theatrical tenants: Theda Bara, silent movie star and Hollywood's first sex symbol, and the fine Shakespearean actress Mrs. Patrick Campbell, who originated the role of Eliza Doolittle in George Bernard Shaw's *Pygmalion* in 1914. The hitching posts outside 141 and the ceramic relief of giraffes outside 147–149 are two of the many details to look for as you walk along the block.

⓬ Gramercy Park Hotel

2 Lexington Ave at 21st St.
Map 9 B4. **Tel** (212) 920-3300.
Ⓜ 14th St-Union Sq, 23rd St.
Ⓦ gramercyparkhotel.com

Located on the site of Stanford White's house, this hotel has, for more than 60 years, been a home away from home for many international visitors and New Yorkers alike. It is also right next to the only private park in Manhattan.

The shabby-chic hotel drew all types, from old matrons, to wealthy young rock stars. Then Ian Schrager, of Studio 54 fame, began a $200-million renovation, in which the 185-room hotel was given an "eclectic-Bohemian" look by artist Julian Schnabel. The conversion included 23 condominiums that range in price from $5 million to $10 million. The elegant Rose and Jade bars and a Chinese restaurant are open to the public.

⓭ Stuyvesant Square

Map 9 B5. Ⓜ 3rd Ave, 1st Ave.

This oasis, in the form of a pair of parks divided by Second Avenue, was part of Peter Stuyvesant's original farm in the 1600s. It was still in the Stuyvesant family when the park was designed in 1836; Peter G. Stuyvesant sold the land to the city for the nominal sum of $5 (much to the delight of those living nearby, who saw real estate values jump). A statue of Stuyvesant by Gertrude Vanderbilt Whitney stands in the park. The park separated the Stuyvesant area from the poorer Gas House district.

⓮ Con Edison Headquarters

145 E 14th St. **Map** 9 A5.
Ⓜ 3rd Ave, 14th St-Union Sq.
Closed to the public.

The clock tower of this building, which dates from 1911, is a local landmark. Originally conceived

The towers of Con Edison (right), Metropolitan Life and the Empire State

by Henry Hardenbergh, the architect best known for such buildings as the Dakota (see p220) and the Plaza (see p183). The 26-story tower was built by the same firm who designed Grand Central Terminal. Near the top of the tower, a 38-ft (11.6-m) bronze lantern was built as a memorial to Con Ed's employees who died in World War I. The tower itself is not as tall as nearby Empire State Building, but when it is lit up at night, it makes an attractive show-piece, in addition to a potent symbol of the company that keeps Manhattan and the other four boroughs shining.

Greenmarket day at Union Square

⓯ Union Square

Map 9 A5. Ⓜ 14th St-Union Sq.
Farmers' Market **Open** 8am–6pm Mon, Wed, Fri, Sat.

Opened in 1839, this park joined Bloomingdale Road (now Broadway) with the Bowery Road (Fourth Avenue or Park), and hence its name. Later, the center of the square was lifted

up for a subway to run beneath it. The park became popular with soapbox orators. During the Depression in 1930, more than 35,000 unemployed people rallied here, before marching on to City Hall to demand jobs. The square hosts a greenmarket and is ringed by various shops from discount department stores to gourmet supermarkets.

⓰ The Little Church Around the Corner

1 E 29th St. **Map** 8 F3. **Tel** (212) 684-6770. Ⓜ 28th St. **Open** 8am–6pm daily. ✝ 12:10pm Mon–Fri; 8:30am, 11am Sun. For lectures & concerts, see website. ♿ 📷 Sun, after 11am service. Ⓦ littlechurch.org

Built from 1849 to 1856, the Episcopal Church of the Transfiguration is a tranquil retreat. It has been known by its nickname since 1870 when Joseph Jefferson tried to arrange the funeral of fellow actor George Holland. The pastor at a nearby church refused to bury a person of so lowly a profession. Instead, he suggested "the little church around the corner." The name stuck and the church has had special ties with the theater ever since. Sarah Bernhardt attended services here.

The south transept window, by John La Farge, shows Edwin Booth playing Hamlet. Jefferson's cry of "God bless the little church around the corner" is commemorated in a window in the south aisle.

CHELSEA AND THE GARMENT DISTRICT

This was open farmland in 1750. By the 1830s it was a suburb, and in the 1870s, with the coming of the elevated railroads *(see pp26–7)*, it had become commercial. Music halls and theaters lined 23rd Street. Fashion Row grew in the shadow of the El, with department stores serving middle-class New York. As fashion moved uptown, Chelsea drifted downhill. It became a warehouse district, until the Els were removed and New Yorkers rediscovered its town houses. When Macy's arrived at Herald Square to the north, the retailing and garment districts grew around it, along with the flower district. Today Chelsea is filled with art galleries and antique shops and has a large gay community.

Sights at a Glance

Historic Streets and Buildings
2 Empire State Building pp138–9
7 General Post Office
11 Chelsea Art Galleries
12 General Theological Seminary
13 Chelsea Historic District
15 Hugh O'Neill Dry Goods Store

Churches
1 Marble Collegiate Reformed Church
5 St. John the Baptist Church

Modern Architecture
6 Madison Square Garden
8 Jacob K. Javits Convention Center
10 Chelsea Piers Complex

Monuments
16 Worth Monument

Parks and Squares
3 Herald Square
9 High Line

Markets
14 Chelsea Market

Landmark Stores
4 Macy's

☐ **Restaurants** *see pp292–300*
1 Bottino
2 Buddakan
3 Morimoto
4 Suenos
5 Tia Pol
6 Trestle on Tenth
7 The Red Cat

0 meters 500
0 yards 500

See also Street Finder maps 7, 8

◀ Empire State Building, an enduring symbol of New York

For keys to map symbols *see back flap*

Street by Street: Herald Square

Herald Square is named for the New York *Herald*, which had its office here from 1894 to 1921. Today full of shoppers, the area was once one of the raunchiest parts of New York. During the 1880s and '90s, it was known as the Tenderloin District and was filled with dance halls and bordellos. When Macy's opened in 1901, the focus moved from flesh to fashion. New York's Garment District now fills the streets near Macy's around Seventh Avenue, also known as Fashion Avenue. To the east on Fifth Avenue is the Empire State Building, with the city's best eagle's-eye views from the observation deck.

Manhattan Mall is on the former site of Gimbel's, once Macy's archrival. It holds dozens of stores, including a massive J.C. Penney.

Fashion Avenue is another name for the stretch of Seventh Avenue around 34th Street. This area is the heart of New York's garment industry. The streets are full of men pushing racks of clothes.

The Hotel Pennsylvania was a center for the 1930s big bands – Glenn Miller's song "Pennsylvania 6-5000" made its telephone number famous.

34th Street subway (1, 2, 3)

❺ St. John the Baptist Church
A beautiful set of carved Stations of the Cross is hung on the walls of the white marble interior of this church.

SEVENTH AVENUE

W 31ST STREET

The SJM Building is at 130 West 30th Street. Mesopotamian-style friezes aadorn the outside of the building.

The Fur District is at the southern end of the Garment District. Furriers ply their trade between West 27th and 30th streets.

W 28TH STREET

SIXTH AVENUE

The Flower District, around Sixth Avenue and West 28th Street, hums with activity in the early part of the day as florists pack their vans with their highly scented, brightly colored wares.

28th Street subway (lines N, R)

❹ ★ Macy's
One of the biggest department stores in the world has something for everyone.

The Greenwich Savings Bank (now the HSBC) is a Greek temple to banking with huge columns on three sides.

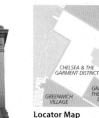

❸ Herald Square
The New York Herald Building's clock now is situated where Broadway meets Sixth Avenue.

Locator Map
See Manhattan Map pp16–17

Key

— Suggested route

| 0 meters | 100 |
| 0 yards | 100 |

34th Street subway (lines B, D, F, M, N, Q, R)

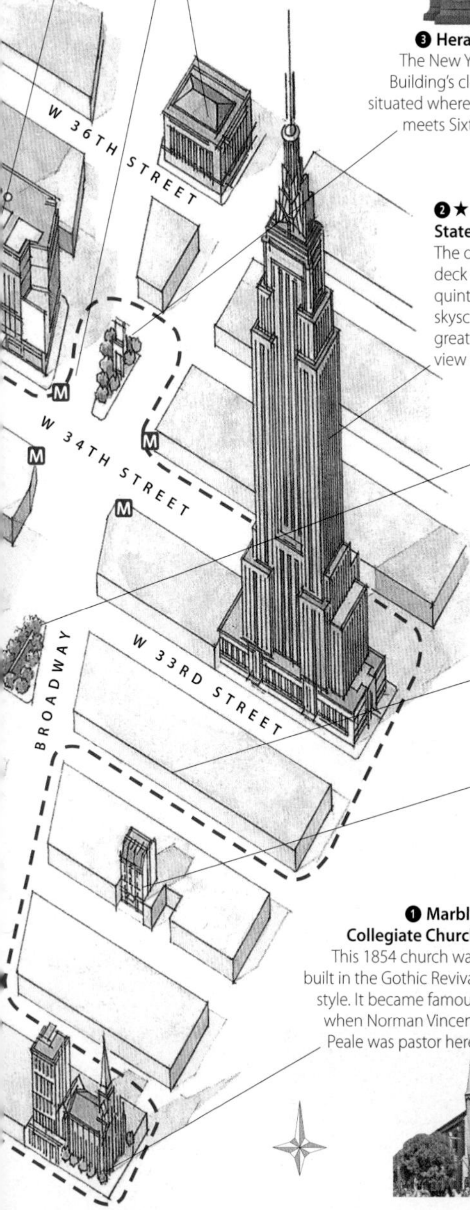

❷ ★ Empire State Building
The observation deck of this quintessential skyscraper is a great place to view the city.

Greeley Square is more of a traffic island than a square, but it does have a fine statue of Horace Greeley, founder of the New York *Tribune*.

Little Korea is an area of Korean businesses. In addition to shops, there are restaurants nearby on West 31st and 32nd streets.

❶ Marble Collegiate Church
This 1854 church was built in the Gothic Revival style. It became famous when Norman Vincent Peale was pastor here.

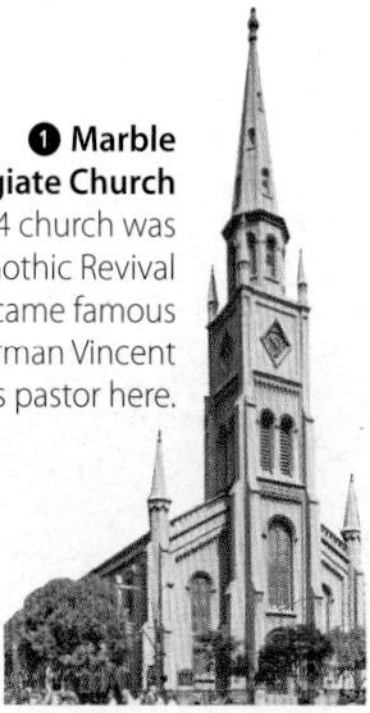

The Life Building at 19 West 31st Street housed *Life* magazine when it was a satirical weekly. Carrère & Hastings designed the building in 1894. It is now a hotel.

W 36TH STREET

W 34TH STREET

BROADWAY

W 33RD STREET

Marble Collegiate's Tiffany stained-glass windows

❶ Marble Collegiate Reformed Church

1 W. 29th St. **Map** 8 F3.
Tel (212) 686-2770. Ⓜ 28th St.
Open 8:30am–8:30pm Mon–Fri,
9am–4pm Sat, 8am–3pm Sun. **Closed**
public hols. 🛈 11:15am Sun. ♿
during services. ♿ Sanctuary 3 W
29th St. **Open** 10am–noon, 2–4pm
Mon–Fri. ⓦ **marblechurch.org**

This church is best known for its former pastor Norman Vincent Peale, who wrote *The Power of*

Positive Thinking. Another positive thinker, future US president Richard M. Nixon, attended services here when he was a lawyer in his pre-White House days.

The church was built in 1854 using the marble blocks that give it its name. Fifth Avenue was then no more than a dusty country road, and the cast-iron fence was there to keep livestock out.

The original white and gold interior walls were replaced with a stenciled gold *fleur-de-lis* design on a soft rust back-ground. Two stained-glass Tiffany windows, depicting Old Testament scenes, were placed in the south wall in 1893.

❷ Empire State Building

See pp138–9.

❸ Herald Square

6th Ave. **Map** 8 E2. Ⓜ 34th St-Penn
Station. *See Shopping p313.*

Named after the New York *Herald*, which occupied a fine arcaded, Italianate Stanford

White building here from 1893 to 1921, the square was the hub of the rowdy Tenderloin district in the 1870s and 1880s. Theaters such as the Manhattan Opera House, dance halls, hotels, and restaurants kept the area humming with life until reformers clamped down on sleaze in the 1890s. The ornamental Bennett clock, named for James Gordon Bennett Jr., publisher of the *Herald*, is now all that is left of the Herald Building.

The Opera House was razed in 1901 to make way for Macy's and, soon after, other department stores followed, making Herald Square a mecca for shoppers. One such store was the now-defunct Gimbel Brothers Department Store, once archrival to Macy's. (The rivalry was affectionately portrayed in the New York Christmas movie *A Miracle on 34th Street*.) In 1988 the store was converted into a vertical mall with a glittery neon front. Most of the old names have gone, but Herald Square is still a key shopping district packed with chain stores. It also features a pedestrian plaza.

❹ Macy's

151 W. 34th St. **Map** 8 E2. **Tel** (212)
695-4400. Ⓜ 34th St- Penn Station.
Open 9am–9:30pm Mon–Fri, 10am–
9:30pm Sat, 11am–8:30pm Sun.
Closed public hols. *See Shopping p311.*
ⓦ **macys.com**

The "world's largest store" covers a square block, and the merchandise inside includes any item you could imagine in every price range.

Macy's was founded by a former whaler named Rowland Hussey Macy, who opened a small store on West 14th Street in 1857. The store's red star logo came from Macy's tattoo, a souvenir of his sailing days.

By the time Macy died in 1877, his little store had grown to a row of 11 buildings. By 1902 Macy's had outgrown its 14th Street premises, and the firm acquired its present site, which covers about 2 million square feet (186,000 sq m) of floor

Macy's 34th Street facade

The nave of St. John the Baptist Church

space. The eastern facade has a modern entrance but still bears the bay windows and Corinthian pillars of the 1902 design. The 34th Street facade even has its original caryatids guarding the entrance, along with the clock, canopy, and lettering. Inside, many of the early wooden escalators are still in good working order. Unsurprisingly, Macy's is a designated National Historic Landmark.

Macy's sponsors New York's renowned Thanksgiving Day parade (see p54) and the Fourth of July fireworks (see p53). The store's popular Spring Flower Show draws thousands of visitors.

❺ St. John the Baptist Church

210 W 31st St. **Map** 8 E3. **Tel** (212) 564-9070. Ⓜ 34th St-Penn Station. **Open** 6:15am–6pm daily. ✝ 8:45am, 10:30am, 5:15pm daily. ♿ 📷

Founded in 1840 to serve a congregation of newly arrived immigrants, today this small Roman Catholic church is almost lost in the heart of the Fur District. The exterior

has a single spire. Although the brown-stone facade on 30th Street is dark with city soot, many treasures lie within this dull exterior. The entrance is through the modern Friary on 31st Street.

The sanctuary by Napoleon Le Brun is a marvel of Gothic arches in glowing white marble surmounted by gilded capitals. Painted reliefs of religious scenes line the walls; sunlight streams through the stained-glass windows. Also off the Friary is the Prayer Garden, a small, green and peaceful oasis with religious statuary, a fountain and stone benches.

❻ Madison Square Garden

4 Pennsylvania Plaza. **Map** 8 D2. **Tel** (212) 465-6741. Ⓜ 34th St-Penn Station. **Open** Mon–Sun, times vary according to shows. 🎭 See Entertainment p352. 📷 daily except during shows. ⓦ thegarden.com

There's only one good thing to be said for the razing of the extraordinarily lovely McKim, Mead & White Pennsylvania Station building in favor of this undistinguished 1968 complex: it so enraged city preservationists that they formed an alliance to ensure that such a thing would never be allowed to happen again.

Madison Square Garden itself, which sits atop underground Pennsylvania Station, is a cylinder of precast concrete, functional enough as a 20,000-seat, centrally located home for the NBA's famous New York

Knicks (basketball), Liberty (women's basketball), and New York Rangers (hockey) teams. It offers a packed calendar of other events: rock concerts, championship tennis and boxing, outrageously staged wrestling, an antiques show, a dog show and more. There is also a 5,600-seat theater. Tours are available daily.

Despite extensive renovations, Madison Square Garden lacks the panache of its earlier location, which combined a stunning Stanford White building with extravagant entertainment (see p128).

The massive interior of Madison Square Garden

❼ General Post Office

421 8th Ave. **Map** 8 D2. **Tel** (800) ASK-USPS. Ⓜ 34th St-Penn Station. **Open** 24 hrs a day, every day (incl public hols). See Practical Information p369.

Designed by McKim, Mead & White in 1913, in a style to complement their 1910 Pennsylvania Station across the street, the General Post Office is a perfect example of a public building of the Beaux Arts period. The imposing, two-block-long structure has a broad staircase leading to a facade with 20 Corinthian columns and a pavilion at each end. The 280-ft (85-m) inscription across it is based on a description of the Persian Empire's postal service, from around 520 BC: "Neither snow nor rain nor heat nor gloom of night stays these couriers from the swift completion of their appointed rounds."

The Corinthian colonnade of the General Post Office

❷ Empire State Building

The Empire State Building is one of the tallest skyscrapers in New York. Named after the state's nickname, it has become an enduring symbol of the city. Construction began in March 1930, not long after the Wall Street Crash, and by the time it opened in 1931, space was so difficult to rent that it was nicknamed "the Empty State Building." Only the immediate popularity of the observatories saved the building from bankruptcy; the observatories still attract more than 3.5 million visitors a year.

Symbols of the modern age are depicted on these bronze Art Deco medallions placed throughout the lobby.

Empire State Building

Construction

The building was designed for ease and speed of construction. Everything possible was prefabricated and slotted into place at a rate of about four stories per week.

KEY

① **Over 200 steel** and concrete piles support the 365,000-ton building.

② **Nine minutes 33 seconds** is the record for racing up the 1,576 steps from the lobby to the 86th-floor observatory, in the annual Empire State Run-Up.

③ **Sandwich space** between the floors houses the wiring, pipes and cables.

④ **Ten million bricks** were used to line the whole building.

⑤ **Aluminum panels** were used instead of stone around the 6,514 windows. The steel trim masks rough edges on the facing.

⑥ **The framework** is made from 60,000 tons of steel and was built in 23 weeks.

⑦ **High-speed** elevators travel at up to 1,000 ft (305 m) a minute.

⑧ **Colored floodlighting** of the top 30 floors marks special and seasonal events.

⑨ **The Empire State** was planned to be 86 stories high, but a then 150 ft (46 m) mooring mast for zeppelins was added. The mast, now 204 ft (62 m), transmits TV and radio to the city and four states.

⑩ **102nd-floor observatory**

★ Views from the Observatories
The 86th-floor observatory offers superb views, both from its indoor galleries and its 360-degree outdoor deck. The 102nd-floor observatory, 1,250 ft (381 m) high, requires an extra fee, payable at the second-floor Visitors' Center or online.

A Head for Heights
As the building took shape, construction workers often showed great bravery. Here, a worker clings to a crane hook. The Chrysler Building and other skyscrapers in the background appear surprisingly small.

Lightning Strikes
The Empire State Building is a natural lightning conductor, struck up to 100 times a year. The observation deck is open even during unfavorable weather.

Pecking Order
New Yorkers are justly proud of their city's symbol, which towers above the icons of other countries.

Empire State
1454 ft (443 m)
with mast

Eiffel Tower
1045 ft
(319 m)

Great Pyramid
350 ft (107 m)

Big Ben 220 ft
(67 m)

★ Fifth Avenue Entrance Lobby
A relief image of the skyscraper is superimposed on a map of New York State in the marble-lined lobby.

Encounters in the Sky
The Empire State Building has been seen in many films. However, the finale from the 1933 classic *King Kong* is easily its most famous guest appearance, as the giant ape straddles the spire to do battle with army aircraft. In 1945 a B-25 bomber flew too low over Manhattan in fog and struck the building just above the 78th floor. The luckiest escape was that of a young elevator operator whose cabin plunged 79 floors. The emergency brakes saved her life.

The Javits Center, New York's largest convention space

❽ Jacob K. Javits Convention Center

655 W. 34th St. **Map** 7 B2. **Tel** (212) 216-2000. Ⓜ 34th St-Penn Station, 42nd St. 🚌 M34, M42. **Open** only on show days – times vary. ♿ ♿ ♿ ♿ Ⓦ **javitscenter.com**

Strikingly modernistic in appearance, this glass building facing the Hudson River opened in 1986. It was designed by the Chinese-American architect I.M. Pei to give New York a new space for large-scale expositions, conventions, and trade shows. The 18-story building is constructed of 16,000 panes of glass, the two main halls can accommodate thousands of delegates, and the lobby is high enough to hold the Statue of Liberty.

In 1989 the construction of the Galleria River Pavilion provided an additional 40,000 sq ft (3,750 sq m) of open space to the building, and two outdoor terraces overlooking the river.

❾ High Line

Access at Gansevoort St, 14th St, 16th St, 18th St, and every two or three blocks to 30th St. **Map** 3 B1. **Tel** (212) 500-6035. Ⓜ 23rd St; 14th St (on lines A, C, E); 8th Av L; Christopher St/Sheridan Sq. **Open** 7am–10pm daily (to 8pm in winter). Ⓦ **thehighline.org**

This once-disused 1930s elevated railbed has been transformed into a slender city park. In 1999, local residents created the organization Friends of the High Line with the aim of saving the structure from demolition. Now extending from Gansevoort Street up Tenth Avenue to 30th Street, the park has played an important role in the gentrification of this neighborhood. The garden is planted with grasses, trees, and shrubs, and each section has different features – a mini-lawn, a sundeck, a steel flyover walkway – providing a totally unique experience.

❿ Chelsea Piers Complex

11th Ave (17th to 23rd Sts) **Map** 7 B5. **Tel** (212) 336-6666. Ⓜ 14th St, 18th St, 23rd St. 🚌 M14, M23. **Open** daily. Ⓦ **chelseapiers.com**

This mammoth complex converted four neglected piers into a center for a vast range of sports and leisure activities (see p35). The facilities include skating rinks, running tracks, a rock-climbing wall, a golf driving range, a marina, and TV and film production sound stages.

⓫ Chelsea Art Galleries

Between W 21st St and W 27th St, around 10th and 11th Aves. **Map** 7 C4. Ⓜ 23rd St. **Open** usually 10am–6pm Tue–Sat. Ⓦ **nygallerytours.com**

Attracted by cheap rents, the many galleries that set up shop in Chelsea during the 1990s were a driving force in this area's resurgence. Between 150 and 200 venues are here, exhibiting work from up-and-coming artists in all manner of media. Check out P.P.O.W. or David Zwirner, which have a reputation for intriguing or provocative work. Try to avoid Saturdays, when art-crawler traffic is at its heaviest.

A 15th-century music manuscript in the General Theological Seminary

⓬ General Theological Seminary

175 9th Ave. **Map** 7 C4. **Tel** (212) 243-5150. Ⓜ 23rd St. **Open** noon–3pm Mon–Fri, 11am–3pm Sat. ✝ 11:45am Mon, Wed–Fri, 6pm Tue, Sun. ✉ ♿ Ⓦ **gts.edu**

Founded in 1817, this block-square campus accepts 150 students at a time to train for the Episcopal priesthood. Clement Clarke Moore, a professor of Oriental Languages at what is today Columbia University (see p226), donated the site, officially known as Chelsea Square. The earliest remaining building dates from 1836; the most modern, St. Mark's Library, was built in 1960 and holds the largest collection of Latin Bibles in the world.

The campus can be entered from Ninth Avenue only. Inside, the garden is laid out in two quadrangles like an English cathedral close: it is especially lovely in the spring.

Aerial view of the Chelsea Piers Complex

⓭ Chelsea Historic District

W. 20th St from 9th to 10th Aves. **Map** 8 D5. Ⓜ 18th St. 🚌 M11.

Although he is better known as the author of the poem "A Visit from St. Nicholas" than as an urban planner, Clement Clarke Moore owned an estate here and divided it into lots in the 1830s, creating handsome rows of town houses. Restoration has since rescued many of the original buildings here.

Of these, the finest are seven houses known as Cushman Row, running from 406–418 West 20th Street, which were built from 1839–40 for Don Alonzo Cushman. He was a merchant who also founded the Greenwich Savings Bank. He joined Moore and James N. Wells in the development of Chelsea. Rich in detail and intricate ironwork, Cushman Row is ranked with Washington Square North as a supreme example of Greek Revival architecture. Look for cast-iron wreaths around attic windows and the pineapples on the newel posts of two of the houses – old symbols of hospitality.

Farther along West 20th Street, from 446–450, there are fine examples of the Italianate style for which Chelsea is also renowned. The detailed brickwork arches of windows and fanlights subtly implied the wealth of the owner, being able to afford this expensive effect.

Hugh O'Neill Dry Goods Store

⓮ Chelsea Market

75 9th Ave (between 15th and 16th sts). **Map** 7 C5. Ⓜ 14th St. **Open** 7am–10pm Mon–Sat, 8am–9pm Sun. 🌐 chelseamarket.com

This enclosed food court and shopping mall is one of New York's unmissable destinations for foodies. Visitors can pick up a

Enjoying a snack in the inviting Chelsea Market

range of gourmet ingredients, exotic foodstuffs, and charming gifts here. The retail options include Lucy's Whey, for artisanal US cheeses; Chelsea Wine Vault, for a global selection of wines; and Bowery Kitchen Supply, for professional-quality equipment. Several high-end purveyors maintain bakeries and kitchens, ensuring only the freshest, highest-quality snacks and meals. Chelsea Market also houses the TV production facilities for the Food Network.

⓯ Hugh O'Neill Dry Goods Store

655–671 6th Avenue. **Map** 8 E4. Ⓜ 23rd St.

Though the store is long gone, the 1876 cast-iron columned and pilastered facade clearly shows the scale and grandeur of the emporiums that once lined Sixth Avenue from 18th to 23rd streets, the area known as Fashion Row. O'Neill, whose sign can still be seen on the facade, was a showman and super-salesman whose trademark was a fleet of shiny delivery wagons. His customers came in droves via the conveniently close Sixth Avenue El. They were not the "carriage trade" enjoyed by Ladies' Mile (see p129), but their numbers allowed the Row to flourish until the turn of the century, when the retailing district continued its move uptown. Now mostly restored, the buildings have turned into superstores and bargain places like T. J. Maxx.

⓰ Worth Monument

5th Ave and Broadway. **Map** 8 F4. Ⓜ 23rd St-Broadway.

Hidden away behind a water meter on a triangle amid city traffic is an obelisk erected in 1857 to mark the grave of the one public figure to be buried under the streets of Manhattan. That honor belongs to General William J. Worth, a hero of the Mexican wars of the mid-1800s. A cast-iron fence of swords embedded in the ground surrounds the monument.

The Worth Monument

A house on Cushman Row

THEATER DISTRICT

It was the move of the Metropolitan Opera House to Broadway at 40th Street in 1883 that first drew lavish theaters and restaurants to this area. In the 1920s, movie palaces added the glamour of neon to Broadway, the signs getting bigger and brighter until eventually the street became known as the "Great White Way." After World War II, the pull of the movies waned, and the glitter was replaced by grime. However, a redevelopment program has brought the public and the bright lights back. Pockets of calm also exist away from the bustle: explore the Public Library or relax in Bryant Park. For the best of both worlds, though, visit the landmark Rockefeller Center.

Sights at a Glance

Historic Streets and Buildings
5 New York Yacht Club
8 New York Public Library
10 Times Square
12 Group Health Insurance Building
13 Paramount Building
14 Shubert Alley
18 Alwyn Court Apartments

Museums and Galleries
9 International Center of Photography
19 *Intrepid* Sea-Air-Space Museum
20 Museum of Arts and Design

Modern Architecture
1 Rockefeller Center
15 MONY Tower

Parks and Squares
6 Bryant Park

Famous Theaters
3 Lyceum Theater
11 New Amsterdam Theater
17 Carnegie Hall
16 City Center of Music and Dance

Landmark Hotels and Restaurants
4 Algonquin Hotel
7 Bryant Park Hotel

Landmark Stores
2 Diamond District

0 meters 500
0 yards 500

☐ **Restaurants** *see pp298–300*

1 Aureole
2 Becco
3 Le Bernardin
4 Blue Fin
5 Burger Joint at Le Parker Meridien
6 Carnegie Deli
7 DB Bistro Moderne
8 Esca
9 Estiatorioa Milos
10 Gordon Ramsay
11 Marea
12 Marseille
13 Molyvos
14 Norma's
15 Osteria al Doge
16 The Sea Grill
17 Taboon
18 Virgil's Real Barbecue

See also Street Finder maps 8, 11, 12

◀ Grand chandelier hanging from the ceiling of the New York Public Library

For keys to map symbols *see back flap*

Street by Street: Times Square

Named for the 25-story New York Times Tower, which opened in 1906, Times Square has been at the heart of the city's theater district since 1899, when Oscar Hammerstein built the Victoria and Republic theaters. Since the 1920s, the glowing neon of theater billboards has combined with the *Times'* illuminated newswire and other advertising to create a spectacular lightshow. After a period of decline starting in the 1930s, which saw sex shows taking over many of the grand theaters, rejuvenation of the district began in the 1990s. Old-style Broadway glamour again rubs shoulders with modern entertainment in this part of the city.

Paramount Hotel Designed by Philippe Starck, this hotel is the hip haunt of the theater crowd who drink in the late-night Paramount Bar *(see p308)*.

Sardi's In Times Square since 1921, Sardi's walls are lined with caricatures of Broadway stars of yesterday and today.

Westin Hotel This striking 45-story hotel consists of a prism split by a curving beam of light. Stun- ning views over the city.

E Walk This entertainment and retail complex has a multiplex cinema, restaurants, a hotel, and the BB King Blues Club.

W 48

W 47TH

W 45TH ST

W 43RD ST

Ⓜ

42nd St.–Port Auth. Bus Terminal subway (Lines A, C & E)

W 41ST ST

SEVENTH AV

Times Sq.–42nd St. subway (Lines N, Q, R, S, 1, 2, 3, 7)

❿ ★ **One Times Square**
Every New Year's Eve at midnight, the famed crystal ball drops from the top of One Times Square. There are great views from the front of this New York landmark.

★ **New Victory Theater**
This classic Broadway theater is used as a young people's performance space.

Electronic Ticker Tape
The figures on the Morgan Stanley LED tickertape are 10 feet (3 m) high. It is one of the many eye-catching lighting displays that illuminate Times Square day and night. City ordinances require office buildings to carry neon advertising.

Locator Map
See Manhattan Map pp16–17

Key

— Suggested route

McGraw-Hill Building

J.P. Stevens Tower

Celanese Building

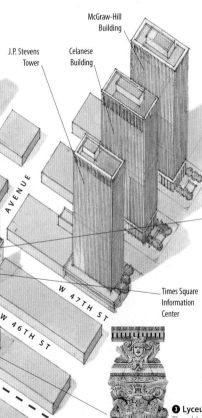

BROADWAY

AVENUE

SEVENTH

W 47TH ST

W 46TH ST

Times Square Information Center

43RD ST

Duffy Square A statue of actor, composer, and writer George M Cohan, responsible for many of Broadway's hits, stands proud in this small square. Duffy Square is named for World War I hero, "Fighting" Father Duffy, immortalized in a statue. It is also home to the **TKTS** *(see p322)* booth, where cut-price theater tickets are sold daily.

❸ Lyceum Theater
The oldest Broadway theater, the Lyceum has a beautifully ornate Baroque facade.

| 0 meters | | 100 |
| 0 yards | | 100 |

Belasco Theater Built in 1907 by producer David Belasco, it was the most technically advanced theater of its time. Original Tiffany glass and Everett Shinn murals decorate the interior. It is rumored that Belasco's ghost still treads the boards some nights.

A Christmas tree stands above the Rockefeller Plaza skating rink for the holiday season

❶ Rockefeller Center

Map 12 F5. Ⓜ 47th–50th Sts. **Tel** (212) 332-6868 (information). ♿ ⌀ 🄿 🄲 NBC, Rockefeller Center, daily. **Tel** (212) 664-7174 (reservations advised). Radio City Music Hall, daily. **Tel** (212) 247-4777. Top of the Rock, daily. **Tel** (212) 698-2000. Ⓦ **rockefellercenter.com** Ⓦ **nbc.com** Ⓦ **radiocity.com** Ⓦ **topoftherocknyc.com**

When the New York City Landmarks Preservation Commission unanimously voted to declare Rockefeller Center a landmark in 1985, they rightly called it "the heart of New York . . . a great unifying presence in the chaotic core of midtown Manhattan."

It is the largest privately owned complex of its kind. The Art Deco design was by a team of top architects headed by Raymond Hood. Works by 30 artists can be found in foyers, on facades, and in the gardens. The site, once a botanic garden owned by Columbia University, was leased in 1928 by John D. Rockefeller, Jr., as an ideal central home for an opera house. When the 1929 Depression scuttled these plans, Rockefeller, stuck with a long lease, went ahead with his own development. The 14 buildings erected between 1931 and 1940 provided jobs for up to 225,000 people during the Depression; by 1973 there were 19 buildings.

In December 1932, Radio City Music Hall opened within the complex. It still hosts its famous

Wisdom by Lee Lawrie, on the GE Building

Christmas and Easter shows here. Later, NBC opened its TV studios here. Rockefeller Plaza is home to a well-known ice-skating rink in winter; it is also the site of a famous Christmas tree.

The Top of the Rock, an observatory on the 67th–70th floors of the center, offers a dizzying 360° panoramic view of the city. On the 67th and 69th floors, the outdoor terraces feature transparent safely glass for stunning views downwards.

❷ Diamond District

47th St, between 5th and 6th Aves. **Map** 12 F5. Ⓜ 47th–50th Sts. *See Shopping p320.* Ⓦ **diamond district.org**

Most shop windows on 47th Street glitter with gold and diamonds. The buildings are filled with booths and workshops where jewelers vie for customers while, upstairs, vast sums of money change hands. The Diamond District was born in the 1930s, when the Jewish diamond cutters of Antwerp and Amsterdam fled to the US to escape Nazism. Today, Jewish dealers still predominate. Although mainly a wholesale district, individual customers are welcome. Bring cash, compare prices, haggle, and stay away if you know nothing about the value of diamonds.

❸ Lyceum Theater

149 W 45th St. **Map** 12 E5. **Tel** Telecharge (212) 239-6200. Ⓜ 42nd, 47th St, 49th St. *See Entertainment p337.* Ⓦ **lyceumtheater.com**

The oldest active New York theater is a frilly, Baroque-style bandbox. This 1903 triumph was the first theater by Herts and Tallant, later renowned for their extravagant style. The Lyceum made history with a record run of 1,600 performances of the comedy *Born Yesterday*. It was the first theater to be designated a historic landmark, and though the Theater District has shifted westward, there are still many shows here.

The Lobby in the Algonquin Hotel

❹ Algonquin Hotel

59 W 44th St. **Map** 12 F5. **Tel** (212) 840-6800. Ⓜ 42nd St. *See Where to Stay p283.* Ⓦ algonquinhotel.com

No other hotel captures the city's formidable literary history quite like the Algonquin Hotel. For more than a century it has played host to home-grown talent and international luminaries. In the 1920s, the Rose Room was home to America's best-known luncheon club, the Round Table, with literary lights such as Alexander Woollcott, Franklin P. Adams, Dorothy Parker, Robert Benchley, and Harold Ross. All were associated with the *New Yorker* (Ross was the founding editor), whose 25 West 43rd Street headquarters had a back door opening into the hotel.

Renovations have preserved the old-fashioned, civilized feel of the cozy, paneled lobby, where publishing types and theater-goers still like to gather for drinks, settling into comfortable armchairs and ringing a brass bell to summon the waiters.

❺ New York Yacht Club

37 W 44th St. **Map** 12 F5. **Tel** (212) 382-1000. Ⓜ 42nd St. *Closed* to the public (members only). Ⓦ nyyc.org

A whimsical 1899 creation, this private club has the carved sterns of 16th-century Dutch galleons in the three bay windows. The prows of the ships are borne up by sculpted dolphins and waves that spill over the window-sills and splash down to the pavement. This is the birthplace of the Americas Cup yacht race, which was based in the US from 1857 to 1983. That was the year the much coveted prize was taken from the table where it had stood for more than a century, when the *Australia II* sailed to a historic victory.

The Americas Cup, the coveted yachting prize

❻ Bryant Park

Map 8 F1. Ⓜ 42nd St. Ⓦ bryantpark.org

In 1853, with the New York Public Library site still occupied by Croton Reservoir, Bryant Park (then Reservoir Park) housed a dazzling Crystal Palace, built for the World's Fair of that year *(see p27)*.

In the 1960s the park was a hangout for drug dealers and other undesirables. In 1989 the city renovated the park, reclaiming it for workers and visitors to relax in. In spring and fall, world-famous fashion shows take place here; in the summer, classic movies are screened. Over seven million books lie in storage stacks beneath the park.

Statue of poet William Cullen Bryant in Bryant Park

❼ Bryant Park Hotel

40 W 40th St. **Map** 8 F1. **Tel** (212) 869-0100. Ⓜ 42nd St. Ⓦ bryantparkhotel.com

The American Radiator building (now the Bryant Park Hotel) was the first major New York work by Raymond Hood and John Howells, who went on to design the Daily News Building *(see p157)*, the McGraw-Hill building, and Rockefeller Center. The 1924 structure is reminiscent of one of Hood's best-known Gothic buildings, Chicago's Tribune Tower. Here, the design is sleeker, giving the building the illusion of being taller than its actual 23 stories. The black brick facade is set off by gold terra-cotta trim, evoking images of flaming coals: a comparison that would have suited its original owners well, since they made heating equipment. The building is now a luxury hotel *(see p284)* across the street from Bryant Park and boasts the New York outpost of trendy LA eatery Koi.

The Bryant Park Hotel, formerly the American Radiator Building

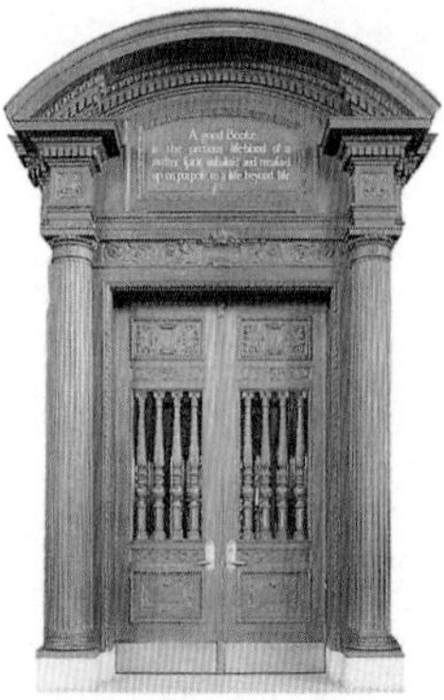

Doorway leading to New York Public Library's Main Reading Room

Barrel vaults of carved white marble over the stairs in the Astor Hall

❽ New York Public Library

5th Ave & 42nd St. **Map** 8 F1. **Tel** (212) 930-0830. Ⓜ 42nd St-Grand Central, 42nd St-5th Ave. **Open** 10am–6pm Mon & Thu–Sat, till 8pm Tue & Wed, 1–5pm Sun. **Closed** public hols. Lectures. **nypl.org**

In 1897 the coveted job of designing New York's main public library was awarded to architects Carrère & Hastings. The library's first director envisaged a light, quiet, airy place for study, where millions of books could be stored and yet be available to readers as promptly as possible. In the hands of Carrère & Hastings, his vision came true, in what is considered the epitome of New York's Beaux Arts period.

Built on the site of the former Croton Reservoir *(see p26)*, it opened in 1911 to immediate acclaim, despite having cost the city $9 million. The vast, paneled Main Reading Room stretches two full blocks and is suffused with daylight from the two interior courtyards. Below it are 88 miles (140 km) of shelves, holding over seven million volumes. A staff of over 100 and a computerized dumbwaiter can supply any book within 10 minutes.

The Periodicals Room holds 10,000 current periodicals from 128 countries. On its walls are murals by Richard Haas, honoring New York's great publishing houses. The original library combined the collections of John Jacob Astor and James Lenox. Its collections today range from Thomas Jefferson's handwritten copy of the Declaration of Independence to T.S. Eliot's typed copy of "The Waste Land." More than 1,000 queries are answered daily, using the vast database of the CATNYP and LEO computer catalogs.

This library is the hub of a network of 82 branches, with nearly seven million users. Some branches are very well known, such as the New York Public Library for the Performing Arts at the Lincoln Center *(see p214)* and the Schomburg Center in Harlem *(see p231)*.

The Main Reading Room, with its original bronze reading lamps

One of the library's two stone lions, named Patience and Fortitude by Mayor LaGuardia

❾ International Center of Photography

1133 Avenue of the Americas (43rd St). **Map** 8 F1. **Tel** (212) 857-0000. Ⓜ 42nd St. **Open** 10am–6pm Tue, Wed, Sat & Sun; 10am–8pm Thu & Fri. **Closed** major hols. 🅿 ⚞ ▣ 10am–5pm Tue–Sun. ⓦ icp.org

This museum was founded by Cornell Capa in 1974 to conserve the work of such photojournalists as his brother Robert, who was killed on assignment in 1954. The collection of 12,500 original prints contains work by top photographers such as Ansel Adams, Henri Cartier-Bresson, and W. Eugene Smith. Special exhibitions are organized from the ICP'S archive as well as from outside sources. There are also films, lectures, and classes.

❿ Times Square

Map 8 E1. Ⓜ 42nd St-Times Sq. ℹ Times Square Visitor Center, 1560 Broadway (46th St), 8am–8pm daily. 🎟 noon Fri, (212) 869-1890. ⓦ timessquarenyc.org

The 1990s saw a transformation in Times Square, reversing a decline that began during the Depression. The square is now a safe and vibrant place where Broadway traditions comfortably coexist with modern innovations.

Although the *New York Times* has moved on from its original headquarters at the south end of the square, the glistening ball (now of Waterford crystal) still drops at midnight on New Year's Eve, as it has since the building opened with fanfare and fireworks in 1906. New buildings, such as the Bertelsmann and the fashionably minimalist Condé Nast offices, sit comfortably alongside the classic Broadway theaters.

Broadway's fortunes have also revived. Many theaters have been renovated and are again housing new, more contemporary

productions; theatergoers throng the area's bars and restaurants each evening.

One of the area's landmarks is the 57-story skyscraper designed by Miami architects Arquitectonica, that tops the E Walk entertainment and retail complex at 42nd Street and Eighth Avenue *(see p144)*. Other attractions include an outpost of Madame Tussaud's Wax Museum at 42nd Street, between Seventh and Eighth Avenues; a massive Disney Store; Bowlmor Lanes bowling alley; a pedestrian plaza; and Toys 'R' Us at 1514 Broadway.

W.C. Fields (far left) and Eddie Cantor (holding top hat, right) in the 1918 *Ziegfeld Follies* at the New Amsterdam Theater

⓫ New Amsterdam Theater

214 W 42nd St. **Map** 8 E1. **Tel** (212) 282-2900. Ⓜ 42nd St-Times Sq. 🎟 10am–3pm Mon–Tue, 10am–11am Thu–Sat, 10am Sun; (212) 282-2907.

This was the most opulent theater in the United States when it opened in 1903, and the first to have an Art Nouveau interior. It was owned for a time by Florenz Ziegfeld, who produced his famous *Follies* revue here between 1914 and 1918 – with Broadway's first $5 ticket price. He remodeled the roof garden into another theater, the Aerial Gardens. This is one of the fine early theaters on 42nd Street that fell on hard times. With the rehabilitation of Times Square its fortunes rose again and it is once more in Show Business.

Art Deco top of the Paramount Building

⓬ Group Health Insurance Building

330 W 42nd St. **Map** 8 D1. Ⓜ 42nd St-8th Ave. **Open** office hours.

This 1931 design by Raymond Hood was the only New York building selected for the influential International Style survey of 1932 *(see p45)*. Its unusual design gives it a stepped profile seen from east and west, but a slab effect viewed from the north or south. The exterior's horizontal bands of blue-green terra-cotta have earned it the nickname "jolly green giant." Step inside to see the classic Art Deco lobby of opaque glass and stainless steel.

One block west is Theater Row, a pleasant group of Off-Broadway theaters and cafés.

⓭ Paramount Building

1501 Broadway. **Map** 8 E1. Ⓜ 34th St.

The fabulous ground-floor movie theater where bobby-soxers stood in line in the 1940s to hear Frank Sinatra perform is gone, but there's still a theatrical feel to the massive building designed by Rapp & Rapp in 1927. On each side 14 symmetrical setbacks rise to an Art Deco crown – a tower, clock, and globe. In the heyday of the "Great White Way," the tower was lit, with an observation deck at the top. The Hard Rock Cafe is now here, along with a retail store and a concert area.

⑭ Shubert Alley

Between W 44th and W 45th St.
Map 12 E5. **M** 42nd St-Times Sq.
See Entertainment p334.

The playhouses on the streets west of Broadway are rich in theater lore – and in notable architecture. Two classic theaters built in 1913 are the Booth (222 West 45th Street), named after actor Edwin Booth, and the Shubert (225 West 44th), after theater baron Sam S. Shubert. They form the west wall of Shubert Alley, where aspiring actors lined up, hoping for a casting in a Shubert play.

A Chorus Line ran at the Shubert until 1990, for a record 6,137 performances; Katharine Hepburn starred earlier in *The Philadelphia Story.* Across from the 44th Street end of the alley is the St. James, where Rodgers and Hammerstein made their debut with *Oklahoma!* in 1941, followed by *The King and I.* Nearby is Sardi's, the restaurant where actors waited for opening-night reviews. Irving Berlin staged *The Music Box Revue* opposite the other end of the alley in 1921. His Music Box Theater has since housed many famous shows.

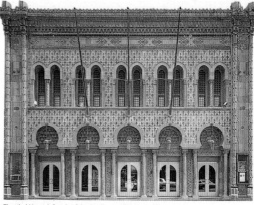
The tiled Moorish facade of the City Center of Music and Dance

⑮ MONY Tower

1740 Broadway. **Map** 12 E4. **M** 57th St-Seventh Ave. **Closed** to the public.

Built in 1950, the head office of the Mutual of New York insurance company (now MONY Financial Services) has a weather vane that tells you everything except the wind direction. The mast turns green for fair, orange for cloudy, flashing orange for rain and white for snow. Lights moving up the mast mean warmer weather; lights going down mean get out your overcoat!

⑯ City Center of Music and Dance

131 W 55th St. **Map** 12 E4. **Tel** (212) 581-1212. **M** 57th St-Seventh Ave. 🚻 ♿ *See Entertainment p338.*
W **citycenter.org**

This highly ornate Moorish structure with its dome of Spanish tiles was designed in 1924 as a Masonic Shriners' Temple. It was saved from the developers by Mayor LaGuardia, becoming home to the New York City Opera wand Ballet in 1943. When the troupes moved to Lincoln Center, City Center lived on as a major venue for dance. Renovation work has preserved the delightful excesses of the architecture.

⑰ Carnegie Hall

154 W 57th Street. **Map** 12 E3. **Tel** (212) 247-7800. **M** 57th St-Seventh Ave. **Open** 11am–4:30pm daily & during concert intermissions. **Closed** Wed. 🚻 ♿ 📷 11:30am, 12:30pm, 2pm & 3pm Mon–Fri; 11:30am & 12:30pm Sat; 12:30pm Sun. 📷 *See Entertainment p342.*
W **carnegiehall.org**

Financed by millionaire philanthropist Andrew Carnegie, New York's first great concert hall opened in 1891. The terra-cotta and brick Renaissance-style building has among the best acoustics in the world. On opening night, Tchaikovsky was a guest

Auditorium of the Shubert Theater, built by Henry Herts in 1913

Carnegie Hall offering some of the best acoustics in the world

conductor and New York's finest families attended. For many years Carnegie Hall was home to the New York Philharmonic, under conductors such as Arturo Toscanini, Bruno Walter, and Leonard Bernstein. Playing Carnegie Hall quickly became an international symbol of success for both classical and popular musicians.

In the 1950s, a campaign by violinist Isaac Stern saved the site from redevelopment, and in 1964 it was made a national landmark. Renovation in 1986 brought the bronze balconies and the ornamental plaster back to their original splendor. In 1991, a museum opened next to the first-tier level, telling the story of the first 100 years of "The House that Music Built." In 2003, the Judy and Arthur Zankel Hall re-established the lower level as a performance venue.

Millionaire Andrew Carnegie

Top orchestras and performers from around the world still fill Carnegie Hall, and the corridors are lined with memorabilia of artists who have performed here.

⑱ Alwyn Court Apartments

180 W 58th St. **Map** 12 E3. Ⓜ 57th St-Seventh Ave. **Closed** to the public.

You can't miss it – not with the fanciful crowns, dragons, and other French Renaissance-style terra-cotta carvings covering the exterior of this 1909 Harde and Short apartment building. The ground floor has lost its cornice, but the rest of the building is intact, and it's one of a kind in the city.

The facade follows the style of François I, whose symbol, a crowned salamander, can be seen above the entrance to the building.

The interior courtyard features a dazzling display of the illusionistic skills of artist Richard Haas, in which plain walls are transformed into "carved" stonework.

The crowned salamander, symbol of François I, on Alwyn Court

⑲ Intrepid Sea-Air-Space Museum

Pier 86, W 46th St. **Map** 11 A5. **Tel** (877) 957-SHIP. 🚌 M42, M50. **Open** Apr–Oct: 10am–5pm Mon–Fri; 10am–6pm Sat, Sun and hols; Nov–Mar: 10am–5pm daily. 🏛 📷 🅦 intrepidmuseum.org

Exhibits on board this World War II aircraft carrier include fighter planes from the 1940s, the A-12, the world's fastest spy plane, and the *Growler*, a guided-missile submarine.

The workings of today's super-carriers are traced in Stern Hall, while Technologies Hall looks at the rockets of the future and includes two flight simulators. Mission Control offers live coverage of NASA shuttle missions.

In 2012, the museum introduced the Space Shuttle Pavilion, that houses the historic space shuttle, *Enterprise*.

The flight deck of the Intrepid with fighter and spy planes on display

⑳ Museum of Arts and Design

2 Columbus Circle. **Map** 12 D3. **Tel** (212) 956-3535. Ⓜ 59th St-Columbus Circle. **Open** 10am–6pm Tue–Sun (to 9pm Thu & Fri). **Closed** public hols. 🏛 📷 ♿ 🛍 Lectures, films: 📷 🅦 madmuseum.org

The leading American cultural institution of its kind, this museum housed in a modern, bold, eye-catching building is dedicated to contemporary objects in an array of media, from clay and wood to metal and fiber. The collection has over 2,000 artifacts by international craftsmen and designers. Items by top-class American craftsmen are also on sale.

LOWER MIDTOWN

From Beaux Arts to Art Deco, this section of Midtown boasts some fine architecture. Quiet, residential Murray Hill was named for a country estate that once occupied the site. By the turn of the century, it was home to many of New York's first families, including the financier J.P. Morgan, whose library, now a museum, reveals the grandeur of the age. The commercial pace quickens at 42nd Street, near Grand Central Terminal, where tall office buildings line the streets. However, few of the newer buildings have equaled the Beaux Arts Terminal itself or such Art Deco beauties as the Chrysler Building.

Sights at a Glance

Historic Streets and Buildings
2 Grand Central Terminal pp158–9
3 Home Savings of America
4 Chanin Building
5 Chrysler Building
6 Daily News Building
7 Tudor City
8 Helmsley Building
12 Fred F. French Building
15 Sniffen Court

Museums and Galleries
11 Japan Society
14 Morgan Library & Museum pp166–7

Modern Architecture
1 MetLife Building
9 Nos. 1 and 2 United Nations Plaza
10 United Nations pp162–5

Churches
13 Church of the Incarnation

See also Street Finder maps 9, 12, 13

0 meters 400
0 yards 400

◀ Terraced arches with triangular windows on the spire of the Chrysler Building

For keys to map symbols see back flap

Street by Street: Lower Midtown

A walk in the neighborhood allows you to see an eclectic mix of New York's architectural styles. Step back to appreciate the contours of the tallest skyscrapers, and step inside to experience the many fine interiors, from modern atriums such as those in the Philip Morris Building and Ford Foundation buildings to the ornate details of the Home Savings Bank and the soaring spaces of Grand Central Terminal.

❶ MetLife Building
This skyscraper, built by Pan Am in 1963, towers above Park Avenue.

❷ ★ Grand Central Terminal
The vast, vaulted interior is a splendid reminder of the heyday of train travel. This historic building also features specialty shops and gourmet restaurants.

Grand Central-42nd St. subway (lines S, 4, 5, 6, 7)

❹ Chanin Building
Built for self-made real estate mogul Irwin Chanin in the 1920s, this building has a fine Art Deco lobby.

PARK AVENUE

E 41ST ST

LEXINGTON AVENUE

❸ ★ Home Savings of America
Formerly the headquarters of the Bowery Savings Bank, this is one of the finest bank buildings in New York. Architects York & Sawyer designed it to resemble a Romanesque palace.

The Mobil Building has a self-cleaning stainless steel facade that is embossed in geometric patterns to prevent it from warping. It was built in 1955.

8 Helmsley Building
Straddling Park Avenue between 45th and 46th, its ornate entrance symbolized the wealth of its first occupants, New York Central Railroad.

THE HELMSLEY BUILDING

Mailbox in the Chrysler Building

5 ★ Chrysler Building
Ornamented with automotive motifs, this Art Deco delight was built in 1930 for the Chrysler car company.

Locator Map
See Manhattan Map pp16–17

THEATER DISTRICT
UPPER MIDTOWN
LOWER MIDTOWN
GRAMERCY & THE FLATIRON DISTRICT
East Side
East River

Key
— Suggested route

Worker resting during construction of the Chrysler Building

The Ford Foundation Building
is the headquarters of Ford's philanthropic arm. It has a lovely interior garden surrounded by a cube-shaped building made of pinkish gray granite, glass, and steel.

THIRD AVENUE

E 43RD STREET

E 42ND STREET

SECOND AVENUE

FIRST AVENUE

Ralph J. Bunche Park

| 0 meters | 100 |
| 0 yards | 100 |

6 ★ Daily News Building
The Art Deco former home of the newspaper has a revolving globe in the lobby.

7 Tudor City
This 1928 private residential complex has 3,000 apartments. Built in the Tudor style, it features fine stonework details.

Lobby of the MetLife Building

❶ MetLife Building

200 Park Ave. **Map** 13 A5. **M** 42nd
St-Grand Central. **Open** office hours.

Once, the sculptures atop the
Grand Central Terminal stood
out against the sky. Then this
colossus, formerly called the Pan
Am Building and designed by
Walter Gropius, Emery Roth and
Sons, and Pietro Belluschi, rose
up in 1963 to block the Park
Avenue view. It dwarfed the
terminal and aroused universal
dislike. At the time it was the
largest commercial building in
the world, and the dismay over
its scale helped thwart a later
plan to build a tower over the
terminal itself.

It is ironic that the New York
skies were blocked by Pan Am,
a company that had opened
up the skies as a means of
travel for millions of
people. When the
company began in 1927,
Charles Lindbergh,
fresh from his solo transatlantic flight, was one of
their pilots and an adviser on
new routes. By 1936, Pan Am
managed to introduce the first
trans-Pacific passenger route,
and in 1947 they introduced the
first round-the-world route.

The building's famous roof-top
heliport was abandoned in 1977
after a freak accident showered
debris on to the surrounding
streets. Now Pan Am itself has
gone, too, and in 1981 the
entire building was sold to the
Metropolitan Life organization.

❷ Grand Central Terminal

See pp158–9.

❸ Home Savings of America

110 E 42nd St. **Map** 9 A1. **M** 42nd
St-Grand Central. **Open** by appt only.
Cipriani **Tel** (646) 723-0826.

Many consider this 1923 building
the best work of bank
architects York &
Sawyer, who chose the
style of a Romanesque
basilica for the offices of
the venerable Bowery
Savings Bank (now
Home Savings of
America). An arched
entry leads into the vast
banking room, with a
high beamed ceiling,
marble mosaic floors, and marble
columns that support the stone
arches that soar overhead.

Facade of Home Savings
of America building

Between the columns are
unpolished mosaic panels of
marble from France and Italy.
The building is also home to
Cipriani restaurant, whose
opulent decor lures high
rollers for celebratory dinners.

Stonework detail on the Chanin Building

❹ Chanin Building

122 E 42nd St. **Map** 9 A1. **M** 42nd
St-Grand Central. **Open** office hours.

Once the headquarters of Irwin
S. Chanin, one of New York's
leading real estate developers,
the 56-story tower was the first
skyscraper in the Grand Central
area, a harbinger of things to
come. It was
designed by Sloan &
Robertson in 1929
and is one of the best
examples of the Art
Deco period. A wide
bronze band,
patterned with birds
and fish, runs the full
length of the facade;
the terra-cotta base is
decorated with a
luxuriant tangle of stylized
leaves and flowers. Inside,
Radio City's sculptor René
Chambellan worked on the
reliefs and the bronze grills,
elevator doors, mailboxes,
clocks, and pattern of waves in
the floor. The vestibule reliefs
chart the career of Chanin,
who was a self-made man.

Carved detail in the banking hall of Home Savings of America

Stainless-steel gargoyle on the Chrysler Building

❺ Chrysler Building

405 Lexington Ave. **Map** 9 A1. **Tel** (212) 682-3070. Ⓜ 42nd St-Grand Central. **Open** office hours (7am–6pm), lobby only. ♿

Walter P. Chrysler began his career in a Union Pacific Railroad machine shop, but his passion for the motor car helped him rise swiftly to the top of this industry, to found, in 1925, the corporation bearing his name. His wish for a headquarters in New York that symbolized his company led to a building that will always be linked with the golden age of motoring. Following Chrysler's wishes, the stainless-steel Art Deco spire resembles a car radiator grill; the building's series of stepped setbacks are emblazoned with winged radiator caps, wheels and stylized automobiles; and there are gargoyles modeled on hood ornaments from the 1929 Chrysler Plymouth.

It stands at 1,046ft (320 m) but it lost the title of tallest building in the world to the Empire State Building a few months after its completion in 1930. William Van Alen's 77-story Chrysler Building and its shining crown are still among the city's best-known and most-loved landmarks.

The crowning spire was kept a secret until the last moment, when, having been built in the fire shaft, it was raised into position through the roof, ensuring that the building would be higher than the Bank of Manhattan, then just completed downtown by Van Alen's great rival, H. Craig Severance.

Van Alen was poorly rewarded for his labors. Chrysler accused him of accepting bribes from contractors and refused to pay him. Van Alen's career never recovered from the slur.

The stunning lobby, once used as a showroom for Chrysler cars, was perfectly restored in 1978. It is lavishly decorated with patterned marbles and granite from around the world and has chromed steel trim. A vast painted ceiling by Edward Trumball shows transportation scenes of the late 1920s.

Although the Chrysler Corporation never occupied the building as their headquarters, their name remains, as firm a fixture as the gargoyles.

Elevator door at the Chrysler Building

Entrance to the Daily News Building

❻ Daily News Building

220 E 42nd St. **Map** 9 B1. Ⓜ 42nd St-Grand Central. **Open** 8am–6pm Mon–Fri.

The *Daily News* was founded in 1919, and by 1925 it was a million-seller. It was known, rather scathingly, as "the servant girl's bible," for its concentration on scandals, celebrities, and murders, its readable style and heavy use of illustration. Over the years it has stuck to what it does best, and the formula paid off handsomely. It revealed stories such as the romance of Edward VIII and Mrs. Simpson, and has become renowned for its punchy headlines. Its circulation figures are still among the highest in the United States.

Its headquarters, designed by Raymond Hood in 1930, has rows of brown and black brick alternating with windows to create a vertical striped effect. Hood's lobby is familiar to many as that of the *Daily Planet* in the 1980s *Superman* movies. It includes the world's largest interior globe, and bronze lines on the floor indicate the direction of world cities and the position of the planets. At night, the intricate detail over the front entrance of the building is lit from within by neon. The newspaper's offices are now on West 33rd Street, but this building has been designated as a national historic landmark.

❷ Grand Central Terminal

In 1871 Cornelius Vanderbilt opened a railway station on 42nd Street. Although often revamped, it was never large enough and was finally demolished. The present station opened in 1913. This Beaux Arts gem has been a gateway to and symbol of the city ever since. Its glory is the soaring main concourse and the way it separates pedestrian and train traffic. The building has a steel frame covered with plaster and marble. Reed & Stern were in charge of the logistical planning; Warren & Wetmore for the overall design. The restoration by architects Beyer Blinder Belle is outstanding.

42nd Street colonnaded facade

Statuary on the 42nd Street Facade
Jules-Alexis Coutans sculptures of Mercury, Hercules, and Minerva crown the main entrance.

Cornelius Vanderbilt
The railroad magnate was known as the "Commodore."

KEY

① **Subway**

② **Circumferential Road**

③ **As many as 750,000 people** pass through the terminal each day. An escalator leads up into the MetLife Building, where there are specialty shops and restaurants.

④ **Main Concourse Level**

⑤ **Vanderbilt Hall**, adjacent to the Main Concourse, is a good example of Beaux Arts architecture. It is decorated with gold chandeliers and pink marble.

⑥ **The Lower Level** is linked to the other levels by stairways, ramps, and escalators.

Grand Central Oyster Bar
This popular spot *(see p299)*, with its yellow Guastavino tiles, is one of the many eateries in the station. The dining concourse is enormous, with food, snacks, and drinks to suit all tastes.

★ Main Concourse
This vast area with its vaulted ceiling is dominated
by three great arched windows on each side.

VISITORS' CHECKLIST

Practical Information
E 42nd St at Park Ave.
Map 13 A5.
Tel (212) 340-2583.
Open 5:30am–2am daily. ♿ 🚹
⏰ 12:30pm daily, sold online
and in the Main Concourse, (212)
935-3960; self-guided tours are
also available, see Grand Central
Terminal website for details.
🍴 💻 📷 Lost & found: (212)
340-2555.
W grandcentralterminal.com

Transport
Ⓜ 4, 5, 6, 7, S to Grand Central.
🚌 M1–5, M42, M50,
M101–103, Q32.

Vaulted Ceiling
A medieval manuscript
provided the basis
for French artist Paul
Helleu's zodiac design
containing over 2,500
stars. Lights pinpoint
the major constellations.

Grand Staircase
There are now two of
these double flights of
marble steps, styled
after the staircase in
Paris' Opera House, and
a vivid reminder of the
glamorous days of
early rail travel.

★ Central Information
This four-faced clock tops the
travel information booth on
the Main Concourse.

❼ Tudor City

E 41st–43rd St between 1st and 2nd
Aves. **Map** 9 B1. Ⓜ 42nd St- Grand
Central. 🚌 M15, M42, M50.

Dating from 1925–8, this early
urban renewal effort by the
Fred F. French Company was
designed as a middle-class
city within the city. Rents were
modest, thanks to the "large-
scale production." There are
12 buildings containing
apartments, a hotel, shops,
restaurants, a post office, and
two small private parks, all
built in the Tudor Gothic style.

In the mid-19th century the
area was the haunt of gangs and
criminals and was known as
Corcoran's Roost, after Paddy
Corcoran, the leader of the
notorious "Rag Gang." The East
River shore was lined with glue
factories, slaughterhouses,
breweries, and a gasworks. Some
were still there when Tudor City
was planned, so its buildings
have only a few outward-facing
windows from which residents
might enjoy what is now a great
view of the river.

Upper stories of Tudor City

❽ Helmsley Building

230 Park Ave. **Map** 13 A5.
Ⓜ 42nd St-Grand Central.
Open office hours.

One of the great New York
views looks south down Park
Avenue to the Helmsley
Building straddling the busy
traffic flow beneath. There is
just one flaw – the monolithic
MetLife Building (which was
built by Pan Am as its corporate
headquarters in 1963) that

Performance at the Japan Society

towers behind it, replacing
the building's former
backdrop, the sky.

Built by Warren & Wetmore
in 1929, the Helmsley Building
was originally the headquarters
of the New York Central Railroad
Company. Its namesake, the late
Harry Helmsley, was a
billionaire who
began his career
as a New York
office boy for
$12 per week.
His wife Leona,
who passed
away in 2007,
was a prominent
feature in
all the
advertise-
ments for their hotel chain –
until her imprisonment in 1989
for tax evasion on a grand scale.
Many observers believe that
the extravagant glitter of the
building's face-lift is due to
Leona's over-blown
taste in decor.

Roman gods reclining against the Helmsley Building clock

❾ 1 & 2 United Nations Plaza

Map 13 B5. Ⓜ 42nd St-
Grand Central. 🚌 M15,
M42, M50.

These two great
columns of blue-
green mirrored glass
are set at an angle to
each other; the play of light and
reflections on their gleaming
sides and sloping setbacks
make them seem a giant,
ever-changing, work of
modern art. The marble
and mirrored interiors
are also stunning. They
house streamlined
modern offices and,
in No. 1, the
Millennium
United
Nations Plaza Hotel. Here, the
guest list frequently includes
many UN delegates from all over
the world as well as a number
of visiting heads of state. Even
the stresses of international
diplomacy must ease when one
is floating lazily in the glassed-in
swimming pool, enjoying the
bird's-eye views of the city and
the United Nations itself.

❿ United Nations

See pp162–5.

⓫ Japan Society

333 E 47th St. **Map** 13 B5.
Tel (212) 832-1155. Ⓜ 42nd St- Grand
Central. 🚌 M15, M50. Gallery **Open**
11am–6pm Tue–Thu, 11am–9pm Fri,
11am–5pm Sat–Sun. 🚫 ♿ 📷
🌐 japansociety.org

The headquarters of the Japan
Society, founded in 1907 to
foster understanding and
cultural exchange
between Japan
and the US,
was built with

the help of John D. Rockefeller III, who underwrote costs of some $4.3 million. The striking black building with its delicate sun grilles was designed by Tokyo architects Junzo Yoshimura and George Shimamoto in 1971. It includes an auditorium, a language center, a research library, a museum gallery, and traditional Oriental gardens.

Changing exhibits include a variety of Japanese arts, from swords to kimonos to scrolls. The society offers programs of Japanese performing arts, lectures, language classes, and many business workshops for American and Japanese executives and managers.

⑫ Fred F. French Building

521 5th Ave. **Map** 12 F5. Ⓜ 42nd St-Grand Central. **Open** office hours.

Built in 1927 to house the best-known real estate firm of the day, this is a fabulously opulent creation.

It was designed by French's chief architect, H. Douglas Ives, in collaboration with Sloan & Robertson, whose other work

Lobby of the Fred F. French Building

Tiffany stained-glass window in the Church of the Incarnation

included the Chanin Building (see p156). They handsomely blended Near Eastern, ancient Egyptian and Greek styles with early Art Deco forms.

Multicolored faïence ornaments decorate the upper facade, and the water tower is hidden in a false top level of the building. Its disguise is an elaborate one, with reliefs showing a rising sun flanked by griffins and bees and symbols of virtues such as integrity and industry. Winged Assyrian beasts ride on a bronze frieze over the entrance. These exotic themes continue into the vaulted lobby, with its elaborate poly-chrome ceiling decoration and 25 gilt-bronze doors.

This was the first building project to employ members of the Native Canadian Caughnawaga tribe as construction workers. They did not fear heights and soon became highly sought-after as scaffolders for many of the city's most famous skyscrapers.

⑬ Church of the Incarnation

209 Madison Ave. **Map** 9 A2. **Tel** (212) 689-6350. Ⓜ 42nd St-Grand Central, 33rd St. **Open** 11:30am–2pm Mon–Fri (also 4–7pm Tue, 5–7pm Wed), 1–4pm Sat, 8:15am–12:30pm Sun. ✝ 12:15pm & 6:30pm Wed, 12:45pm Fri, 8:30am & 11am Sun. ♿ 🄳 By appointment. 🅦 churchoftheincarnation.org

This Episcopal church dates from 1864, when Madison Avenue was home to the elite. Its patterned sandstone and brownstone exterior is typical of the period. The interior has an oak communion rail by Daniel Chester French; a chancel mural by John La Farge; and stained-glass windows by La Farge, Tiffany, William Morris and Edward Burne-Jones.

⑭ Morgan Library & Museum

See pp166–7.

⑮ Sniffen Court

150–158 E 36th St. **Map** 9 A2. Ⓜ 33rd St.

Here is a delightful, intimate courtyard of ten brick Romanesque revival carriage houses, built by John Sniffen in the 1850s. They are perfectly and improbably preserved off a busy block in modern New York. The house at the south end was used as a studio by the American sculptor Malvina Hoffman, whose plaques of Greek horsemen decorate the exterior wall.

Malvina Hoffman's studio

⑩ United Nations

Founded in 1945 with 51 members, the United Nations now numbers 193 nations. Its aims are to preserve world peace, to promote self-determination, and to aid economic and social well-being around the globe. New York was chosen as the UN headquarters, and John D. Rockefeller, Jr. donated $8.5 million for the purchase of the site. The chief architect was American Wallace Harrison, who worked with an international Board of Design Consultants. The 18-acre (7-ha) site is an international zone, with its own stamps and post office. In 2006, the UN's General Assembly approved a $1.6-billion renovation of the complex that is due for completion in 2015; visitors should phone ahead to check access.

United Nations headquarters

★ **Security Council**
Delegates and their assistants confer around the horseshoe-shaped table while verbatim reporters and other UN staff members sit at the long table in the center.

KEY

① **Economic and Social Council**

② **Trusteeship Council**

③ **The Conference Building** houses meeting rooms for the Security Council, the Trusteeship Council and the Economic and Social Council.

④ **Secretariat building**

⑤ **The statue of peace** was a gift from Yugoslavia.

★ **Peace Bell**
Cast from the coins of 60 nations, this gift from Japan hangs on a cypress pagoda shaped like a Shinto shrine.

Rose Garden
Twenty-five varieties of roses adorn the manicured gardens on the East River.

★ **Reclining Figure** *(1982)*
This bronze statue was a gift from the
Henry Moore Foundation.

Colors of the World
Flags of member nations fly in
front of the UN complex.

VISITORS' CHECKLIST

Practical Information
1st Ave at 46th St.
Map 13 C5.
Tel (212) 963-8687.
Open 9:30am–5:30pm Mon–Fri,
10am–4:15pm Sat & Sun (last adm
45 mins before closing). **Closed**
Jan 1, Presidents' Day, Memorial
Day, Independence Day, Labor
Day, Eid, Thanksgiving, Dec 25
(limited hours during year-end
hols).   Mon–Fri; must book
in advance; no children under 5.
un.org/tours

Transport
M 4, 5, 6, 7 and S to 42nd
St-Grand Central. M15,
M42, M50.

★ **General Assembly**
This is the only UN organ in which
all member states are represented.
One regular, three-month session
is held each year

Non-Violence *(1988)*
Luxembourg donated
this peace sculpture by
Karl Fredrik Reutersward.

Visitors'
entrance

⑤

Let Us Beat Swords Into Plowshares
This bronze statue *(1958)* by Soviet
sculptor Evgeny Vuchetich
symbolizes the main goal of the
United Nations.

The Work of the United Nations

The goals of the United Nations are pursued by three UN councils and a General Assembly comprising all of its member nations. The Secretariat carries out the administrative work of the organization. Guided tours allow visitors to see the Security Council Chamber. Often there is a chance to briefly observe a meeting.

Secretary General

Translators interpret debates in Arabic, Chinese, French, Russian, Spanish, or English.

Reporters

Public gallery

Public entrance

Nation delegates sit in alphabetical order by country, but who sits at the front is decided before every session by drawing lots.

General Assembly Hall

General Assembly

The General Assembly is the governing body of the UN and has regular sessions each year from mid-September to mid-December. Special sessions are also held when the Security Council or a majority of members request one. All member states are represented with an equal vote, regardless of size. The General Assembly may discuss any international problem raised by the members or by other UN bodies. Although it cannot enact laws, recommen-dations strongly influence world opinion; these require a two-thirds majority vote.

Lots are drawn before each session to determine the seating in the chamber for the delegations. All 1,898 seats in the chamber are equipped with earphones that offer simultaneous translations in several languages. The General Assembly also appoints the Secretary General (on the recommendation of the Security Council), approves the UN budgets and elects the non-permanent members of the Councils. Together with the

Foucault's Pendulum (Holland); its slowly rotating swing is proof of the earth's rotation on its axis

Security Council, it also appoints the judges of the International Court of Justice, based in the Netherlands.

Mural symbolizing peace and freedom by Per Krohg (Norway)

Security Council

The most powerful part of the UN is the Security Council. It strives to achieve international peace and security and intervenes in crises such as the fighting in Iraq and Afghanistan. It is the only body whose decisions member states are obliged to obey as well as the only one in continuous session.

Five of its members – China, France, the Russian Federation, the United Kingdom, and the United States – are permanent. The other nations are elected by the General Assembly to serve two-year terms.

When international conflicts arise, the Council first tries to seek agreement by mediation. If fighting breaks out, it may issue cease-fire orders and impose military or economic sanctions. It could also decide to send UN peace-keeping missions into troubled areas to separate opposing factions until issues can be resolved through diplomatic channels.

Military intervention is the Council's last resort. UN forces may be deployed, and peace-keeping forces are resident in such places as Cyprus and the Middle East.

Trusteeship Council

The smallest of the councils, this is the only UN body whose workload is decreasing. The council was established in 1945 with the goal of fostering peaceful independence for non-self-governing territories or colonies. Since then, more than 80 colonies have gained self-rule, and the number of people living in dependent territories has been reduced from 750 million to about 3 million. The Trusteeship Council consists of the five permanent members of the Security Council.

Trusteeship Council Chamber

Economic and Social Council

The 54 members of this Council work to improve the standard of living and social welfare around the world, goals that consume 80% of the UN's resources. It makes recommendations to the General Assembly, to each member nation and to the UN's specialized agencies. The Council is assisted by commissions dealing with regional economic problems, human rights abuses, population, narcotics, and women's rights. It also works with the International Labor Organization, the World Health Organization, UNICEF, and other global welfare organizations.

Secretariat

An international staff of 16,000 works for the Secretariat to carry out the day-to-day work of the United Nations. The Secretariat is headed by the Secretary General, who plays a key role as a spokesperson in the organization's peace-keeping efforts. The Secretary General is appointed by the General Assembly for a five-year term. On January 1, 2007, Ban Ki-moon of South Korea became the latest Secretary General.

Zanetti mural (Dominican Republic) in the Conference Building depicting the struggle for peace

Important Events in UN History

The UN depends on voluntary compliance and military support from its members to keep the peace in the event of disputes. In 1948, the UN declared South Korea the legitimate government of Korea; two years later, it played a major role in defending South Korea against North Korea. In 1949, the UN helped negotiate a cease-fire between Indonesia and the Netherlands and set up a conference that led to the Dutch granting independence to Indonesia.

In 1964 a UN military force was sent to Cyprus to keep peace between the Greeks and Turks, and still remains. Persistent issues in the Middle East have kept UN forces in the area since 1974, the year that China – long refused membership in favor of Taiwan – gained UN membership. In the 1990s, the UN was involved in the break-up of Yugoslavia, and more recently in the conflicts in Afghanistan and Libya. A 2004 UN mission to Congo was plagued by accusations of sexual abuse by UN peace-keepers. In 2006–7 there were arrests over kickbacks in the UN oil-for-food program to Iraq.

At any given time at least half a dozen missions are active somewhere in the world. The UN was awarded the Nobel Peace Prize in 1988 and 2001.

Soviet premier Krushchev speaking to the General Assembly in 1960

Works of Art at the UN

The UN Building has acquired numerous works of art and reproductions by major artists; many have been gifts from member nations. Most of them have either a peace or international friendship theme. The legend on Norman Rockwell's *The Golden Rule* reads "Do unto others as you would have them do unto you." Marc Chagall designed a large stained-glass window as a memorial to former Secretary General Dag Hammarskjöld, who was accidentally killed while on a peace mission in 1961. There is a Henry Moore sculpture in the grounds (limited access) and many other sculptures and paintings by the artists of many nations.

The Golden Rule (1985), a large mosaic by Norman Rockwell

⑭ Morgan Library & Museum

The Morgan Library's collection, accumulated by banker Pierpont Morgan, is housed in a magnificent palazzo-style 1906 building by architects McKim, Mead & White. Morgan's son, J. P. Morgan, Jr., made it a public institution in 1924. One of the world's finest collections of rare manuscripts, drawings, prints, books, and bindings is on display in a complex that includes the original library and the home of Pierpont Morgan himself.

Exterior of the original library building

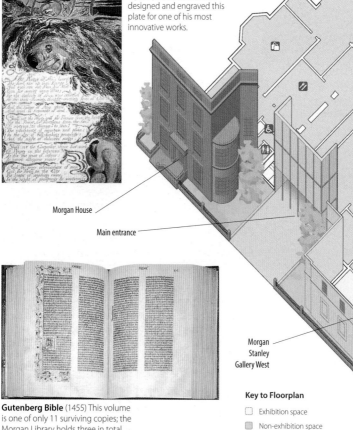

The Song of Los (1795)
Mystic poet William Blake designed and engraved this plate for one of his most innovative works.

Morgan House

Main entrance

Morgan Stanley Gallery West

Gutenberg Bible (1455) This volume is one of only 11 surviving copies; the Morgan Library holds three in total.

Key to Floorplan

☐ Exhibition space

☐ Non-exhibition space

Mozart's Horn Concerto in E-flat Major
The six surviving leaves of this score are written in different colored inks.

Library Guide

*Mr. Morgan's Study and the
original library contain some
of his favorite paintings, objets
d'art and rare acquisitions.
Changing exhibitions feature
a wide variety of impressive
cultural artifacts.*

★ Mr. Morgan's Study
Renaissance art and an
antique, Florentine wooden
ceiling adorn this room.

First floor

Clare Eddy
Thaw Gallery

Morgan Stanley
Gallery East

★ Mr. Morgan's Library
The walls are lined from
floor to ceiling with triple
tiers of bookcases. Murals
show historical figures
and their muses, and
signs of the zodiac.

★ The Rotunda (1504)
The entrance foyer of the
Library has marble columns
and pilasters; the marble floor
is modeled on the floor in Villa
Pia in the Vatican gardens.

The Nursery Alice
Lewis Carroll's
characters are
immortalized in
John Tenniel's
classic illus-
trations
(c. 1865).

Pierpont Morgan

Pierpont Morgan (1837–1913) was
not only a leading financier but
also one of the great collectors of
his time. Rare books and original
manuscripts were his passion,
and inclusion in his collection
was an honor. In 1909, when
Morgan requested the donation
of the manuscript of *Pudd'nhead
Wilson*, Mark Twain responded,
"One of my high ambitions is gratified."

UPPER MIDTOWN

Upscale New York in all its diversity is here, in this district of churches and synagogues, clubs and museums, grand hotels and famous stores, as well as trend-setting skyscrapers and pockets of luxury living. For almost 30 years from 1833, Upper Midtown was home to society names such as Astor and Vanderbilt. In the 1950s, architectural history was made when the Lever and Seagram buildings were erected. These first great modern towers marked Midtown Park Avenue's change from a residential street to a prestigious office address.

Sights at a Glance

Historic Streets and Buildings
- **9** Villard Houses
- **11** General Electric Building
- **17** Sutton Place
- **18** Beekman Place
- **19** Roosevelt Island
- **21** Fuller Building

Modern Architecture
- **2** Trump Tower
- **3** IBM Building
- **13** Lever House
- **14** Seagram Building
- **15** Citigroup Center

Museums and Galleries
- **5** Museum of Modern Art (MoMA) pp174–7
- **6** American Folk Art Museum
- **7** The Paley Center for Media

Churches and Synagogues
- **4** St. Thomas Church
- **8** St. Patrick's Cathedral pp180–81
- **10** St. Bartholomew's Church
- **16** Central Synagogue

Landmark Hotels
- **12** Waldorf–Astoria
- **22** Plaza Hotel

Landmark Stores
- **1** Fifth Avenue
- **20** Bloomingdale's

0 meters 500
0 yards 500

☐ **Restaurants** *see pp298–300*

1 Aquavit
2 BLT Steak
3 Dawat
4 Felidia
5 Four Seasons
6 La Grenouille
7 Pampano
8 Rue 57
9 Shun Lee Palace
10 Smith & Wollensky

See also Street Finder maps 12, 13, 14

◀ Beautiful stained-glass windows inside St. Patrick's Cathedral

For keys to map symbols *see back flap*

Street by Street: Upper Midtown

The luxury stores that are synonymous with Fifth Avenue first blossomed as society moved on uptown. In 1917, Cartier's acquired the mansion of banker Morton F. Plant in exchange for a string of pearls, setting the style for other retailers to follow. But this stretch of Midtown is not simply for shoppers. There are three distinctive museums and an equally diverse assembly of architectural styles to enjoy, too.

❶ Fifth Avenue
The popular carriage rides offer tourists a taste of past elegance and a leisurely way to view some of the main sights around this thoroughfare.

The University Club was built in 1899 as an elite club for gentlemen.

❹ St. Thomas Church
Much of the interior carving was designed by sculptor Lee Lawrie.

❺ ★ Museum of Modern Art
One of the world's finest collections of modern art.

❼ The Paley Center for Media
Exhibitions, seasons of special screenings, live events and a vast library of historic broadcasts are offered at this media museum.

Fifth Avenue subway (lines E, V)

Saks Fifth Avenue has offered goods in impeccable taste to generations of New Yorkers. *(See p311.)*

❽ ★ St. Patrick's Cathedral
This, one of the largest Catholic cathedrals in the United States, is a magnificent Gothic Revival building.

Olympic Tower combines offices, apartments and a skylit atrium within its sleek walls.

❾ Villard Houses
Five handsome brownstone houses now form part of the New York Palace Hotel.

Paley Park
is a tiny
green oasis,
known as a
"vest-pocket"
park.

2 Trump Tower
Donald Trump's
tower contains
luxury residences.

3 IBM Building
A restful atrium is to be found
at the base of this polished
black granite building.

Sony Building has a very
distinctive "Chippendale" top.

Locator Map
See Manhattan Map pp16–17

Key

— Suggested route

0 meters   100
0 yards   100

Tiffany & Company is
renowned for its discreet
luxury. The store contains
many precious jewels.
(See p321.)

13 Lever House
This building is one of
the most prominent
"glass-box" buildings
in New York.

11 General Electric Building
The spiky pinnacle of
this building, built in 1931,
is meant to symbolize
electrical waves.

Park Avenue Plaza is a
bulky glass prism containing
an airy atrium.

Racquet Club, a Renaissance palazzo–
style building, provides squash and
tennis courts for its members.

**10 St. Bartholomew's
Church**
A Byzantine dome sets this
place apart from other
Midtown churches.

Ⓜ
51st Street
subway (line 6)

12 Waldorf-Astoria
Old-world elegance has attracted many
famous guests to this hotel, including
the late Duke and Duchess of Windsor.

Window display at Bergdorf Goodman *(see p311)*

❶ Fifth Avenue

Map 12 F3–F4. Ⓜ 5th Ave-53rd St, 5th Ave-59th St.

In 1883, when William Henry Vanderbilt built his mansion at Fifth Avenue and 51st Street, he started a trend that resulted in palatial residences stretching as far as Central Park, built for top families such as the Astors, Belmonts, and Goulds. Only a few remain to attest to the grandeur of the era.

One of these is the Cartier store at 651 Fifth Avenue, once the home of Morton F. Plant, millionaire and commodore of the New York Yacht Club. As retailers swept north up the avenue – a trend that began in 1906 – society gradually moved uptown. In 1917, Plant moved to a mansion at 86th Street, and legend has it that he traded his old home to Pierre Cartier for a perfectly matched string of pearls.

Fifth Avenue has been synonymous with luxury goods ever since. From Cartier at 52nd Street to Henri Bendel at 56th and Tiffany and Bergdorf Goodman at 57th, you will find many brands symbolizing wealth and social standing today, just as Astor and Vanderbilt did over a century ago.

❷ Trump Tower

725 5th Ave. **Map** 12 F3. **Tel** (212) 832-2000. Ⓜ 5th Ave-53rd St, 5th Ave–59th St. Garden level **Open** 10am–6pm Mon–Sat, noon–5pm Sun. Building **Open** 8am–10pm daily.
♿ ⬭ ▯ ▨

This glittering, exorbitantly expensive apartment and office tower rises above a lavish six-story atrium. Designed in 1983 by Der Scutt of Swanke, Hayden, Connell & Partners, the public space has pink marble, mirrors and glitz throughout. There is an impressive 80-ft (24-m) high indoor waterfall, while the exterior is lined with hanging gardens. The tower is a flamboyant monument to affluence by the developer Donald Trump, a symbol of the excesses and grandeur of the 1980s *(see p35)*.

Next door, 727 Fifth Avenue is a complete contrast: the location of Tiffany & Co., the prestigious jewelers founded in 1837. Famed for exquisite window displays, the store uses understated but elegant blue packaging as a status symbol in itself. Tiffany's was immortalized by Truman Capote in his 1958 novel *Breakfast at Tiffany's*.

Entrance to Tiffany & Co., the exclusive jewelry emporium

❸ IBM Building

590 Madison Ave. **Map** 12 F3. Ⓜ 5th Ave. Garden Plaza **Open** 8am–10pm daily. ♿

Completed in 1983, this 43-story tower was designed by Edward Larrabee Barnes. It is a sleek, five-sided prism of gray-green polished granite, with a cantilevered corner at 57th Street. The **Garden Plaza**, with its bamboo trees, is open to the public and has been redubbed "The Sculpture Garden." Eight new works, which change four times a year, are on view at any one time. Near the atrium is a work by American sculptor Michael Heizer, entitled *Levitated Mass*. Inside a low, stainless-steel tank is a huge slab of granite that seems to float on air.

On the corner of 57th Street and Madison Avenue is *Saurien*, a bright-orange abstract sculpture by Alexander Calder.

Interior of the Trump Tower atrium

❹ St. Thomas Church

1 W 53rd St. **Map** 12 F4. **Tel** (212) 757-7013. **M** 5th Ave-53rd St. **Open** 7am–6pm daily. ✝ frequent. ✉ ♿ 🎵 after 11am service & concerts. 🌐 saintthomaschurch.org

This is the fourth home for this parish and the second on this site. Today's church was built between 1909 and 1914 to replace an earlier structure destroyed in a fire in 1905. The previous building had provided the setting for many of the glittering high-society weddings of the late 19th century. The most lavish of these was in 1895 when heiress Consuelo Vanderbilt married the English Duke of Marlborough.

The limestone building, in French–Gothic style, has a single asymmetrical tower and an off-center nave, novel solutions to the architectural problems posed by its corner position. The richly carved, shimmering white screens behind the altar were designed by architect Bertram Goodhue and sculptor Lee Lawrie. Carvings in the choir stalls, dating from the 1920s, include modern inventions such as the telephone, Presidents Roosevelt and Wilson, and Lee Lawrie himself.

❺ Museum of Modern Art

See pp174–7.

❻ American Folk Art Museum

45 W 53rd St. **Map** 12 F4. **Tel** (212) 265-1040. **M** 5th Ave- 53rd St. **Open** noon–7:30pm Tue–Sat, noon–6pm Sun. ✉ ♿ 🛗 💻 🏛 🌐 folkartmuseum.org

The permanent home for the appreciation and study of American folk art is here, in the first free-standing art museum built in New York since 1966. Designed by the innovative architectural firm of Tod Williams Billie Tsien & Associates and built in 2001, the structure is

Beatles Paul, Ringo and John on the "Ed Sullivan Show" in 1964

clad in panels of white tombasil, a white bronze alloy. The museum has 30,000 sq ft (2,787 sq m) of exhibition space on eight levels. The museum still retains the Eva and Morris Feld Gallery at the Lincoln Square location *(see p216)*.

The American Folk Art Museum

❼ The Paley Center for Media

25 W 52nd St. **Map** 12 F4. **Tel** (212) 621-6800. **M** 5th Ave-53rd St. **Open** noon–6pm Wed–Sun (to 8pm Thu). **Closed** publichols. ♿ ✉ 🛗 🏛 🌐 paleycenter.org

In this one-of-a-kind repository museum, visitors can watch and listen to news and a collection of entertainment and sports documentaries from radio and television's earliest days to the present. Pop fans can see the early

Beatles or a young Elvis Presley making his television debut. Sports enthusiasts can relive classic Olympic competitions. World War II footage might be chosen by students of history or by those who lived through the war. Six choices at any one time can be selected from a computer catalogue that covers a library of over 50,000 programs. The selections are then played on small private areas. There are larger screening areas and a theater for 200, where retrospectives of artists and directors are shown. There are also photo exhibits and memorabilia.

The museum was the brain-child of William S. Paley, a former head of the CBS TV network. It opened in 1975 as the Museum of Broadcasting on East 53rd Street. It proved so popular that in 1991 it moved into this hi-tech $50 million home in a building reminiscent of an antique radio set.

1960s television star Lucille Ball

❺ The Museum of Modern Art

MoMA contains one of the world's most comprehensive collections of modern art. Founded in 1929, it set the standard for museums of its kind. Following an expansion program, MoMA in Midtown reopened in 2004. The renovated building provides gallery space over six floors, almost twice that of the old museum. Expanses of glass allow abundant natural light both to penetrate inside the building and to bathe the sculpture garden.

Museum facade on 54th Street

Christina's World (1948)
Andrew Wyeth contrasts an overwhelming horizon with the minutely-studied surroundings of his handicapped neighbor.

Gallery Guide

The sculpture garden is on the first floor. The contemporary art, print, and media galleries are on the second floor. Painting and sculpture are exhibited on the second, fourth, and fifth floors. Architecture and design, photography, and drawings are all on the third floor. Changing exhibitions are displayed on the third and sixth floors. Films are shown on the lower level.

Sculpture Garden
The Abby A. Rockefeller Sculpture Garden has a peaceful atmosphere.

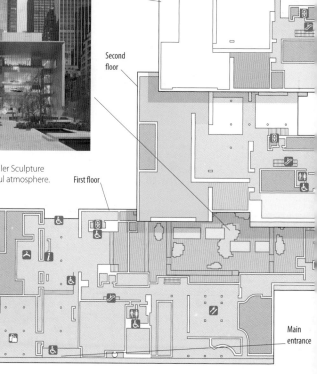
Third floor

Second floor

First floor

Main entrance

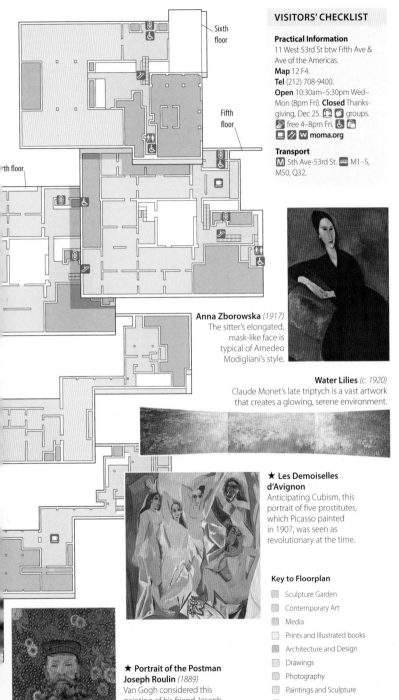

Sixth floor

Fifth floor

th floor

VISITORS' CHECKLIST

Practical Information
11 West 53rd St btw Fifth Ave &
Ave of the Americas.
Map 12 F4.
Tel (212) 708-9400.
Open 10:30am–5:30pm Wed–
Mon (8pm Fri). **Closed** Thanks-
giving, Dec 25. 🎧 📷 groups.
🎟 free 4–8pm Fri. ♿ 📷
📷 ✏ ⓦ moma.org

Transport
Ⓜ 5th Ave-53rd St. 🚌 M1–5,
M50, Q32.

Anna Zborowska *(1917)*
The sitter's elongated,
mask-like face is
typical of Amedeo
Modigliani's style.

Water Lilies *(c. 1920)*
Claude Monet's late triptych is a vast artwork
that creates a glowing, serene environment.

★ **Les Demoiselles
d'Avignon**
Anticipating Cubism, this
portrait of five prostitutes,
which Picasso painted
in 1907, was seen as
revolutionary at the time.

Key to Floorplan

▢ Sculpture Garden
▢ Contemporary Art
▢ Media
▢ Prints and Illustrated books
▢ Architecture and Design
▢ Drawings
▢ Photography
▢ Paintings and Sculpture
▢ Special exhibitions
▢ Non-exhibition space
▢ Non-accessible space

★ **Portrait of the Postman
Joseph Roulin** *(1889)*
Van Gogh considered this
painting of his friend Joseph
Roulin to be a "modern
portrait" that used color to
best represent the sitter.

Exploring the Collection

The Museum of Modern Art has approximately 150,000 works of art ranging from Post-Impressionist classics to an unrivaled collection of modern and contemporary art, from fine examples of design to early masterpieces of photography and film.

The Persistence of Memory by the Surrealist Salvador Dalí (1931)

1880s to 1940s Painting and Sculpture

Paul Cézanne's monumental *The Bather* and Vincent Van Gogh's *Portrait of the Postman Joseph Roulin* are two of the seminal works in the museum's collection of late-19th-century painting. Both Fauvism and Expressionism are well represented with works by Matisse, Derain, Kirchner, and others, while Pablo Picasso's *Les Demoiselles d'Avignon* marks a transition to the Cubist style of painting.

The collection also has an unparalleled number of Cubist paintings, providing an overview of a movement that radically challenged our perception of the world. Among the vast range are Picasso's *Girl with a Mandolin*, Georges Braque's *Man with a Guitar* and *Soda*, and *Guitar and Flowers* by Juan Gris. Works by the Futurists, who brought color and movement to Cubism to depict the dynamic modern world, include *Dynamism of a Soccer Player* by Umberto Boccioni, plus works by Balla, Carrà, and Villon. The geometric abstract art of the Constructivists

is included in a strong representation of Lissitzky, Malevich, and Rodchenko: De Stijl's influence is seen in paintings by Piet Mondrian, such as *Broadway Boogie Woogie*. There is a large body of work by Matisse, such as *Dance I* and *The Red Studio*. Dalí, Miró, and Ernst feature among the bizarre, strangely beautiful Surrealist works.

Postwar Painting and Sculpture

The extensive collection of postwar art includes works by Bacon and Dubuffet, and has a particularly strong representation of American artists. The collection of Abstract Expressionist art, for example, includes Jackson Pollock's *One [Number 31, 1950]*, Willem de Kooning's *Women, I*, Arshile Gorky's *Agony*, and *Red, Brown, and Black* by Mark Rothko.

The Bather, an oil painting by French Impressionist Paul Cézanne

Other notable works include Jasper Johns' *Flag*, Robert Rauschenberg's *First Landing Jump*, composed of urban refuse, and *Bed*, which consists of bed linen. The Pop Art collection includes Roy Lichtenstein's *Girl with Ball* and *Drowning Girl*, Andy Warhol's famous *Gold Marilyn Monroe*, and Claes Oldenburg's *Giant Soft Fan*.

Works after about 1965 include pieces by Judd, Flavin, Serra, and Beuys, among many others.

Man with a Hat by Pablo Picasso (1912), a collage with charcoal

Drawings and Other Works on Paper

More than 7,000 artworks ranging in size from tiny preparatory pieces to large mural-sized works are among MoMA's holdings. Many drawings use conventional materials, such as pencil, charcoal, pen and ink, pastel, and watercolor. However, there are also collages and mixed-media works composed of paper ephemera, natural products, and man-made goods.

The collection provides an overview of Modernism, from the late 19th century to the present day, including movements such as Cubism, Dadaism, and Surrealism. Drawings by famous and well-established artists, such as Picasso, Miró, and Johns, are exhibited alongside a growing number of works by talented emerging artists.

American Indian Theme II by Roy Lichtenstein (1980)

Prints and Illustrated Books

All significant art movements from the 1880s onward are represented in this extensive collection, which provides a fascinating overview of printed art. With more than 50,000 items in the department's holdings, there are wide-ranging examples of historical and contemporary printmaking. Works created in such traditional media as etchings, lithographic prints, screenprints, and woodcuts are displayed alongside pieces created using more experimental techniques.

There are some particularly fine examples of works by Andy Warhol, who is widely considered to be the most important printmaker of the 20th century. There are also many illustrations and prints by other artists including Redon, Munch, Matisse, Dubuffet, Johns, Lichtenstein, Freud, and Picasso.

Photography

The photography collection begins with the invention of the medium around 1840. It includes pictures by fine artists, journalists, scientists, and entrepreneurs, as well as amateur photographers.

Among the highlights of the collection are some of the best-known works by American and European photographers including Atget, Stieglitz, Lange, Arbus, Steichen, Cartier-Bresson, and Kertesz. There is also a range of contemporary practitioners, most notably Friedlander, Sherman, and Nixon.

The photographers have covered an extensive variety of subject matter in both colour and black and white–delicate landscapes, scenes of urban desolation, abstract imagery, and stylish portraiture, including some beautiful silver-gelatin print nudes by the French Surrealist Man Ray. Together, they form a complete history of photographic art and represent one of the finest collections in existence.

Film Department

With a collection of over 22,000 films and four million stills, the collection can offer a wide range of programs, including retrospectives of individual directors and actors, films in specific genres and experimental work, as well as a broad range of other exhibitions. Film conservation is a key part of the department's work. Today's top directors are donating copies of their films to help fund this expensive but vital work.

Film still of Charlie Chaplin and Jackie Coogan in *The Kid* (1921)

Sunday on the Banks of the Marne, photographed by Henri Cartier-Bresson in 1939

Architecture and Design

The Museum of Modern Art was the first art museum to include utilitarian objects in its collection. These range from household appliances such as stereo equipment, furniture, lighting, textiles, and glassware to industrial ball bearings and silicon chips. Architecture is represented in the collection through photo-graphs, scale models, and drawings of buildings that have been or might have been built.

Graphic design is shown in typography and posters. Larger exhibits that look as if they belong in a museum of transportation include Willys-Overland Jeep and the Bell helicopter, which dates from 1945.

Reclining rocking chair of steam-bent beech and cane by Gebrüder Thonet (c. 1880)

❽ St. Patrick's Cathedral

See pp180–81.

❾ Villard Houses

457 Madison Ave (New York Palace Hotel). **Map** 13 A4. **Tel** (800) NY PALACE. Ⓜ 51st St. Ⓦ **newyork palace.com** Municipal Art Sociey Urban Center: **Open** 10am–7pm Mon–Thu, 10am–6pm Fri, 10am–5:30pm Sat. **Tel** (212) 935 3960. ♿ 🏠 Ⓦ **mas.org**

Henry Villard was a Bavarian immigrant who became publisher of the *New York Evening Post* and founder of the Northern Pacific Railroad. In 1881, he bought the land opposite St. Patrick's Cathedral and hired McKim, Mead & White to design town houses on the site. The inspired result has six four-story houses set round a central court opening to the street and the church, though financial difficulties forced Villard to sell and ownership passed to the Roman Catholic archdiocese. When the church outgrew its space in the 1970s the houses were saved when the Helmsley chain purchased air rights for the 51-story Helmsley (now New York) Palace Hotel.

The center wing comprises the hotel's formal entrance and the Villard Bar & Lounge. The **Municipal Art Society Urban Center** occupies the north wing, and its bookshop is the best place in New York for architectural books on the city. The Municipal Art Society also organizes excellent architectural tours, from Harlem to Brooklyn and Staten Island.

St. Bartholomew's Church

❿ St. Bartholomew's Church

109 E 50th St. **Map** 13 A4. **Tel** (212) 378-0222. Ⓜ 51st St. **Open** 8am–6pm daily (to 7:30pm Thu & 8:30pm Sun). 🚌 frequent. ♿ Lectures, concerts. 🏠 📷 after 11am Sunday services. 🎵 (212) 888-2664. Ⓦ **stbarts.org**

Known fondly to New Yorkers as "St. Bart's," this Byzantine structure with its ornate detail, pinkish brick, open terrace and a polychromed gold dome brought color and variety to Park Avenue in 1919.

Architect Bertram Goodhue incorporated into the design the Romanesque entrance portico created by Stanford White for the original 1903 St. Bartholomew's on Madison Avenue, and marble columns from the earlier church were used in the chapel.

St. Bartholomew's program of concerts is well known, as is its theater group, which mounts three productions here each year.

⓫ General Electric Building

570 Lexington Ave. **Map** 13 A4. Ⓜ Lexington Ave. **Closed** to the public.

In 1931 architects Cross & Cross were commissioned to design a skyscraper that would be in keeping with its neighbor, St. Bartholomew's Church. Not an easy task, but the result won unanimous acclaim. The colors were chosen to blend and contrast, and the design of the tower complemented the church's polychrome

The General Electric Building on Lexington Avenue

dome. View the pair from the corner of Park and 50th to see how well it works. However, the General Electric is no mere backdrop but a work of art in its own right and a favorite part of the city skyline. It is an Art Deco gem from its chrome and marble lobby to its spiky "radio waves" crown.

Walk one block north on Lexington Avenue to find a place much cherished by movie fans. It is right at this spot that Marilyn Monroe, in a billowing white frock, stood so memorably in the breeze from the Lexington Avenue subway grating in the movie *The Seven-Year Itch*.

Villard Houses, now the entrance to the New York Palace Hotel

⑫ Waldorf–Astoria

301 Park Ave. **Map** 13 A5. **Tel** (212) 355-3000. Ⓜ Lexington Ave, 53rd St. *See Where to Stay p287.*
Ⓦ **waldorf.com**

This Art Deco classic, which covers an entire city block, was designed by Schultze & Weaver in 1931. The original Hotel at 34th Street was demolished to make way for the Empire State Building. Still deservedly one of New York's most prestigious hotels, the Waldorf–Astoria serves, too, as a reminder of a more glamorous era in the city's history. The 625-ft (190-m) twin towers, where the Duke and Duchess of Windsor lived, have hosted numerous celebrities, including every US president since 1931. The giant lobby clock, executed for the Chicago World's Fair of 1893, is from the original hotel, and the piano in the Peacock Alley cocktail lounge belonged to Cole Porter when he was a resident of the hotel's exclusive Towers.

Winston Churchill and New York philanthropist Grover Whalen at the Waldorf–Astoria in 1946

⑬ Lever House

390 Park Ave. **Map** 13 A4. Ⓜ 5th Ave-53rd St. Lobby and building: **Closed** to the public. ♿

Imagine a Park Avenue lined with sturdy, residential buildings – and then imagine the sensation when they were suddenly reflected here in the first of the city's glass-walled skyscrapers, one of the most influential buildings of the modern era. The design, by Skidmore, Owings & Merrill, is simply two rectangular slabs of stainless steel and glass, one laid horizontally, the other

Lever House on Park Avenue

stacked to stand tall above it, to allow light in from every side. The crisp and bright design was intended to symbolize many of the Lever Brothers' products – they make soaps and other cleaning products.

Revolutionary though it was in 1952, Lever House is now dwarfed by its many imitators, but its importance as an architectural pacesetter remains undiminished. The Casa Lever restaurant is a VIP scene.

⑭ Seagram Building

375 Park Ave. **Map** 13 A4. Ⓜ 5th Ave-53rd St. **Open** 9am–5pm Mon–Fri. ♿ *See Where to Eat p300.*

Samuel Bronfman, the late head of Seagram distillers, was prepared to put up an ordinary commercial building until his architect daughter, Phyllis Lambert, intervened and persuaded him to go to the best – Mies van der Rohe. The result, which is widely considered the finest of the

The pool at the Four Seasons in the Seagram Building

many Modernist buildings of the 1950s, consists of two rectangles of bronze and glass that let the light pour in.

Within is the exclusive Four Seasons Restaurant *(see p300)*, a landmark in its own right. Designer Philip Johnson has created a remarkable space, with the centerpiece of one room a pool, and another a bar topped by a quivering Richard Lippold sculpture.

Office workers at lunch in the spacious Citigroup Center atrium

⑮ Citigroup Center

153 E 53rd St. **Map** 13 A4. Ⓜ 53rd St-Lexington Ave. **Open** 7am–11pm daily. ♿ 🏛 St. Peter's Lutheran Church 619 Lexington Ave. **Tel** (212) 935-2200. **Open** 9am–9pm daily. ✝ 12:15pm Mon–Fri, 6pm Wed, 8:45am & 11am Sun. Jazz vespers 5pm Sun. Concerts noon Wed. York Theater at St. Peter's; **Tel** (212) 935-5820.
Ⓦ **saintpeters.org**

An aluminum-clad spire built on ten-story stilts with a sliced-off roof, Citigroup Center is unique; it caused a sensation when it was completed in 1978. The unusual base design had to incorporate St. Peter's Lutheran Church. The church is separate both in space and design, a granite sculpture below a corner of the tower. Step inside to see the striking interior and the Erol Beker Chapel by sculptor Louise Nevelson. The church is well known for its organ concerts, jazz vespers, and theater presentations. Citigroup's slanting top never functioned as a solar panel as intended, but it is an unmistakable landmark on the skyline.

❽ St. Patrick's Cathedral

The Roman Catholic Church originally intended this site for use as a cemetery, but in 1850 Archbishop John Hughes decided to build a cathedral instead. Many thought that it was foolish to build so far beyond the (then) city limits, but Hughes went ahead anyway. Architect James Renwick built New York's finest Gothic Revival building, one of the largest Catholic cathedrals in the US. The cathedral, which seats 2,500 people, was completed in 1878, though the spires were added between 1885 and 1888.

★ **Lady Chapel**
This chapel honors the Blessed Virgin. The stained-glass windows portray the mysteries of the rosary.

Pietà
American sculptor William O. Partridge created this *Pietà* in 1906. The statue stands at the side of the Lady Chapel.

The cathedral's Fifth Avenue facade

★ **Baldachin**
The great baldachin rising over the high altar is made entirely of bronze. Statues of the saints and prophets adorn the four piers supporting the canopy.

Stations of the Cross
Carved of Caen stone in Holland, these reliefs won first prize in the field of religious art at the Chicago World's Fair in 1893.

Saint Elizabeth Ann Seton Shrine
The bronze statue and screen depict the life of the first American to be canonized a saint. She founded the Sisters of Charity *(see p78)*.

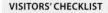

★ Great Organ and Rose Window
Measuring 26 ft (8 m) in diameter, the rose window shines above the great organ, which has more than 7,000 pipes.

★ Great Bronze Doors
The massive doors weigh 20,000 lb (9,000 kg) and are adorned with important religious figures.

Main entrance

KEY

① **The Cathedral Facade's** exterior wall is built of white marble. The spires rise 330 ft (101 m) above the pavement.
② **Crypt**
③ **Lady of Guadalupe**

⑯ Central Synagogue

652 Lexington Ave. **Map** 13 A4.
Tel (212) 838–5122. Ⓜ Lexington
Ave-53rd St. **Open** noon–2pm
Tue–Wed. 🕐 12:45pm Wed. ♿ ✿
6pm Fri, also 10am Sat (Jul–Aug),
10.30am Sat (Sep–Jun).
Ⓦ centralsynagogue.org

This is New York's oldest building in continuous use as a synagogue. It was designed in 1870 by Silesian-born Henry Fernbach, America's first prominent Jewish architect. He also designed some of SoHo's finest cast-iron buildings. Restored after a 1999 fire, the Synagogue is considered the city's best example of Moorish-Islamic Revival architecture. The congregation was founded in 1846 as Ahawath Chesed (Love of Mercy) by 18 immigrants, most of them from Bohemia, on Ludlow Street on the Lower East Side.

The stenciled interior is a colorful mix of red, blue, ocher, and gilt and was inspired by Victorian prints of a Moorish palace in Spain called the Alhambra.

Banded "horseshoe" arches are an Hispano-Mooresque design.

The ark holds the sacred scrolls of the Jewish Holy Book, The Torah.

The facade is an understated Moorish design in local brownstone.

The twin towers represent the two columns that stood outside Solomon's Temple. The domed minarets, which rise 122 ft (37 m), are onion-shaped and made of green copper.

⑰ Sutton Place

Map 13 C3. Ⓜ 59th St, 51st St.
🚌 M15, M31, M57.

Sutton Place is a posh and pleasant neighborhood, delightfully devoid of busy traffic, made up of elegant low-rise apartment houses and town houses designed by noted architects. The arrival of New York society in the 1920s transformed an area that had once been the province of factories and tenements. Three Sutton Square is the residence of the secretary-general of the United Nations. Look beyond Sutton Square and 59th Street for a glimpse of Riverview Terrace, a private street of five ivy-covered brownstones fronting the river. The tiny parks at the end of 55th Street and jutting out at 57th Street offer views of the river and the Queensboro Bridge.

After much neighborhood opposition, Bridgemarket opened in 2000. Located between the huge vaults under the Queensboro Bridge, there is an upscale Terence Conran's for housewares and a Food Emporium supermarket.

Park at Sutton Place, looking toward Queensboro Bridge and Roosevelt Island

⑱ Beekman Place

Map 13 C5. Ⓜ 59th St, 51st St. 🚌 M15, M50.

Smaller than Sutton Place, and even more tranquil, is Beekman Place, a virtually private two-block enclave of 1920s town houses and small-scale apartments. Famous residents here have included Gloria Vanderbilt, Rex Harrison, Irving Berlin and members of the large Rockefeller family.

At Turtle Bay Gardens, restored brownstone houses dating from the 1860s hide a charming Italianate garden. Among the residents enticed by this privacy have been the film stars Tyrone Power and Katharine Hepburn, composer Stephen Sondheim, and writer E.B. White.

⑲ Roosevelt Island

Map 14 D2. Ⓜ 59th St. Tram, Roosevelt Island station (F).
Ⓦ **rioc.com**

Since 1976 a Swiss cable car departing from Second Avenue at 60th Street has offered a quick, thrilling ride across the East River to Roosevelt Island, with eagle-eye views of the city and the Queensboro Bridge. The island is now also serviced by the F subway line.

Near the tram station are the remains of the Blackwell farmhouse, which stood from 1796 to 1804 and gave the island its name until real estate development began in the 1920s. From then until the 1970s, the island housed a succession of hospitals, an almshouse, a jail, a workhouse, and an insane asylum, and became known as Welfare Island. In 1927, Mae West was held in the penitentiary here after a "lewd performance." The ruins of 19th-century hospitals still remain, as does an 1872 lighthouse built by an asylum inmate.

Bloomingdale's store sign

⑳ Bloomingdale's

1000 3rd Ave. **Map** 13 A3. **Tel** (212) 705-2000. Ⓜ 59th St. **Open** 10am–8:30pm Mon–Fri, 10am–7pm Sat, 11am–7pm Sun. See Shopping p311.
Ⓦ **bloomingdales.com**

For a while in the booming 1980s, "Bloomies" was synonymous with the good life. Founded by Joseph and Lyman Bloomingdale in 1872, this famous department store had a bargain-basement image until the 3rd Avenue El was taken down in the 1960s. Then came the store's transformation to the epitome of trendy, sophisticated shopping. But the late 1980s brought new ownership and eventual bankruptcy. While not as flashy as in the past, Bloomingdale's is open every day and remains one of the city's best-stocked stores. Downtown shoppers can head to the SoHo location, at 504 Broadway.

㉑ Fuller Building

41 E 57th St. **Map** 13 A3. Peter Findlay Gallery. **Tel** (212) 644-4433; James Goodman Gallery. **Tel** (212) 593-3737. **Open** 10am–6pm Tue–Sat. Ⓜ 59th St.

This slim-towered black, gray and white 1929 beauty by Walker & Gillette is a prime example of geometric Art Deco design. The striking statues on either side of the clock above the entrance are by Elie Nadelman. Step inside to admire the intricate mosaic tile floors; one panel shows the Fuller Company's former home in the famous Flatiron Building on

Fifth Avenue (see 129). The Fuller Building is a hive of exclusive art galleries, most of which are open to the public daily.

French Renaissance-style facade of the Plaza Hotel

㉒ Plaza Hotel

5th Ave & Central Park South. **Map** 12 F3. Ⓜ Fifth Ave-59th St.
Ⓦ **theplaza.com**

The city's grande dame of hotels was designed by Henry J. Hardenbergh, known for the Dakota (see p220) and the original Waldorf–Astoria. Completed in 1907 at the exorbitant cost of $12.5 million, the Plaza was proclaimed "the best hotel in the world," with 800 rooms, 500 baths, a two-story ballroom, five marble staircases, and 14- to 17-room apartments for such families as the Vanderbilts and the Goulds (see p51).

The 18-story cast-iron structure resembles a French Renaissance château. Much of the interior decoration came from Europe. The Palm Court still has mirrored walls and Italian carvings of the four seasons, and is a lovely place for afternoon tea.

Already lavishly restored by its former owner Donald Trump, the building underwent a $400-million conversion into a mix of apartments, hotel condo-miniums, and a 282-room hotel. There are also six floors of luxury retail and upscale dining, including a gourmet food hall.

The clock statues above the Fuller Building entrance

UPPER EAST SIDE

At the turn of the century, New York society moved to the Upper East Side – and stayed. Many of the Beaux-Arts mansions in this district are now museums and embassies, but the well-to-do still occupy the grand apartment buildings on Fifth and Park avenues. Chic shops and galleries line Madison Avenue. Farther east, the area includes what is left of German Yorkville in the East 80s, Hungarian Yorkville to the south, and little Bohemia, with its Czech population, below 78th Street. Although many of these ethnic groups no longer inhabit the area, their churches, restaurants, and shops still remain.

Sights at a Glance

Historic Streets and Buildings
- ⑩ Park Avenue Armory
- ⑭ Henderson Place
- ⑯ Gracie Mansion

Museums and Galleries
- ❶ Neue Galerie New York
- ❷ Jewish Museum
- ❸ Cooper-Hewitt National Design Museum
- ❹ National Academy Museum
- ❺ *Solomon R. Guggenheim Museum pp190–91*
- ❻ *Metropolitan Museum of Art pp192–9*
- ❼ *Whitney Museum of American Art pp202–3*
- ❽ *Frick Collection pp204–5*
- ❾ Asia Society
- ⑫ Society of Illustrators
- ⑬ Mount Vernon Hotel Museum and Garden
- ⑲ Museum of the City of New York

Churches and Synagogues
- ⑪ Temple Emanu-El
- ⑰ Church of the Holy Trinity
- ⑱ St. Nicholas Russian Orthodox Cathedral

Parks and Squares
- ⑮ Carl Schurz Park

☐ Restaurants *see pp300–1*
1 Beyoglu
2 Brother Jimmy's BBQ
3 Café Boulud
4 Café d'Alsace
5 Café Sabarsky
6 Daniel
7 David Burke Townhouse
8 Flex Mussels
9 Maya
10 Sasabune
11 Sfoglia
12 Shanghai Pavilion

0 meters   500
0 yards   500

See also Street Finder maps 12, 13, 16–18, 21

◀ Brightly lit facade of the Solomon R. Guggenheim Museum

For keys to map symbols *see back flap*

Street by Street: Museum Mile

Many of New York's museums are clustered on the Upper East Side, in homes ranging from the former Frick and Carnegie mansions to the modernistic Guggenheim, designed by Frank Lloyd Wright. The displays are as varied as the architecture, running the gamut from Old Masters to photographs to decorative arts. Presiding over the scene is the vast Metropolitan Museum of Art, New York's answer to Paris's Louvre. Some of the museums stay open late one day a week.

2 Jewish Museum
The most extensive collection of Judaica in the world is housed here. It includes coins, archaeological objects, and ceremonial and religious artifacts.

3 ★ Cooper-Hewitt National Design Museum
Ceramics, glass, furniture and textiles are well represented here.

The Church of the Heavenly Rest was built in 1929 in the Gothic style. The madonna in the pulpit is by sculptor Malvina Hoffman.

4 National Academy Museum
The Academy, founded in 1825, moved here in 1940. Its fine collection includes paintings and sculptures by its members.

Graham House is an apartment building with a splendid Beaux Arts entrance. It was built in 1892.

5 ★ Solomon R. Guggenheim Museum
Architect Frank Lloyd Wright's building, which is in the form of a spiral, is floodlit at dusk. The best way to see one of the world's premier collections of modern art is to take the elevator to the top and walk down.

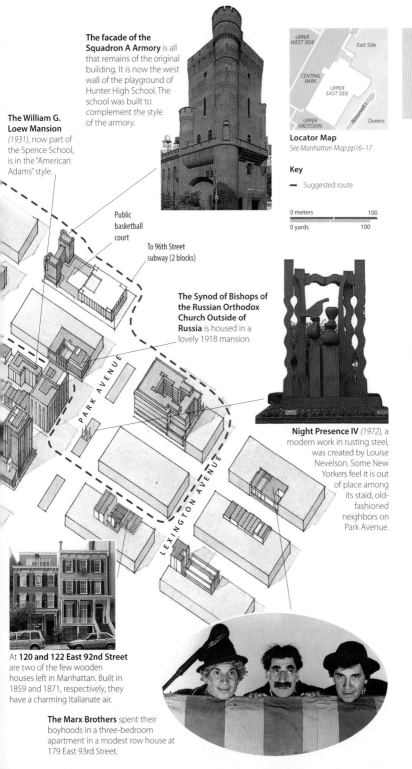

The facade of the Squadron A Armory is all that remains of the original building. It is now the west wall of the playground of Hunter High School. The school was built to complement the style of the armory.

The William G. Loew Mansion *(1931),* now part of the Spence School, is in the "American Adams" style.

Locator Map
See Manhattan Map pp16–17

Key

— Suggested route

| 0 meters | 100 |
| 0 yards | 100 |

Public basketball court

To 96th Street subway (2 blocks)

The Synod of Bishops of the Russian Orthodox Church Outside of Russia is housed in a lovely 1918 mansion.

PARK AVENUE

LEXINGTON AVENUE

Night Presence IV *(1972),* a modern work in rusting steel, was created by Louise Nevelson. Some New Yorkers feel it is out of place among its staid, old-fashioned neighbors on Park Avenue.

At **120 and 122 East 92nd Street** are two of the few wooden houses left in Manhattan. Built in 1859 and 1871, respectively, they have a charming Italianate air.

The Marx Brothers spent their boyhoods in a three-bedroom apartment in a modest row house at 179 East 93rd Street.

❶ Neue Galerie New York

1048 5th Ave at E 86th St. **Map** 16 F3. **Tel** (212) 628-6200. **M** 86th St. ▦ M1–4. **Open** 11am–6pm Thu–Mon. **Closed** public hols. ▦ ▣ ▨ ⊘ Café 9am–6pm daily (to 9pm Thu–Sun). ▦ ♿ **w** neuegalerie.org

This museum was founded by art dealer Serge Sabarsky and philanthropist Ronald Lauder. Its objective is to collect, research, and exhibit the fine and decorative arts of Germany and Austria from the early 20th century.

The Louis XIII-style Beaux-Arts structure was completed in 1914 by Carrère & Hastings, who also designed the New York Public Library (see p148). The building, a designated landmark, is considered one of the most distinguished buildings on Fifth Avenue. Once occupied by Mrs. Cornelius Vanderbilt III, the mansion was purchased by Lauder and Sabarsky in 1994. The ground floor houses the entrance, a bookshop, and the Café Sabarsky, which draws its inspiration from the Viennese cafés of old and also plays host to chamber, cabaret, and classical music concerts. The second floor is devoted to the works of Klimt, Schiele, and Wiener Werkstätte objects. The upper floors feature works from Der Blaue Reiter (artists such as Klee, Kandinsky), the Bauhaus (Feininger, Schlemmer), and Die Brücke (Mies van der Rohe, Breuer).

❷ Jewish Museum

1109 5th Ave. **Map** 16 F2. **Tel** (212) 423-3200. **M** 86th St, 96th St. ▦ M1–4. **Open** 11am–5:45pm Thu–Tue (to 8pm Thu, to 4pm Fri). **Closed** public & Jewish hols. ▨ ▨ ♿ ⊘ ▣ ▦ **w** thejewishmuseum.org

The exquisite château-like residence of Felix M. Warburg, financier and leader of the Jewish community, was designed by C. P. H. Gilbert in 1908. It now houses one of the world's largest collections of Jewish fine and ceremonial art, and historical Judaica. The stonework in an extension is by the stonemasons of St. John the Divine (see pp228–9).

Objects have been brought here from all over the world, some at great risk of persecution to the donors. Covering 4,000 years, artifacts include Torah crowns, candelabras, kiddush cups, plates, scrolls, and silver ceremonial objects.

There is a Torah ark from the Benguiat Collection, the exquisite faience entrance wall of a 16th-century Persian synagogue, and the powerful *Holocaust* by sculptor George Segal. Changing exhibitions reflect Jewish life and experience around the world.

19th-century ewer and basin from Istanbul at the Jewish Museum

❸ Cooper-Hewitt National Design Museum

2 E 91st St. **Map** 16 F2. **Tel** (212) 849-8400. **M** 86th St, 96th St. ▦ M1–4. **Open** 10am–5pm Mon–Sat (to 6pm Sat), 11am–6pm Sun. **Closed** Jan 1, Thksg, Dec 25. ▨ ▨ ♿ ⊘ ▣ ▦ ▢ **w** cooperhewitt.org

One of the largest design collections in the world, this museum occupies the former home of industrialist Andrew Carnegie. The collection was amassed by the Hewitt sisters, Amy, Eleanor, and Sarah. The museum opened in 1897 at Cooper Union (see p122); the Smithsonian Institution acquired the collections in 1967, and the Carnegie Corporation offered the mansion.

Carnegie asked for "the most modest, plainest, and most roomy house in New York," but

Cooper-Hewitt Museum entrance

the house set new trends with central heating, private elevator, and air-conditioning. Note the wooden staircase, rich paneling and carving, and the sunny solarium.

The museum is due to reopen in 2014 after renovations.

❹ National Academy Museum

1083 5th Ave. **Map** 16 F3. **Tel** (212) 369-4880. **M** 86th St. ▦ M1–4. **Open** 11am–6pm Wed–Sun. **Closed** public hols. ▨ ▨ ♿ ⊘ ▣ **w** nationalacademy.org

Over 6,000 paintings, drawings, and sculptures, including works by Thomas Eakins, Winslow Homer, and Frank Lloyd Wright, comprise the collection of the National Academy Museum, founded in 1825 by a group of artists. The group's mission was (and is) to train artists and exhibit their work.

In 1940, Archer Huntington, an art patron and philanthropist, donated his house, an attractive building with patterned marble floors. The grand entrance foyer has a statue of Diana by sculptor Anna Hyatt Huntington.

Statue of Diana in the National Academy Museum entrance foyer

❺ Solomon R. Guggenheim Museum

See pp190–91.

❻ Metropolitan Museum of Art

See pp192–9.

❼ Whitney Museum of American Art

See pp202–3.

❽ Frick Collection

See pp204–5.

❾ Asia Society

725 Park Ave. **Map** 13 A1. **Tel** (212) 288-6400. Events: (212) 517-ASIA. Ⓜ 68th St. **Open** 11am–6pm Tue–Sun (to 9pm Fri). **Closed** public hols. 🎫 📷 2pm Tue–Sat, 6:30pm Fri. 🚻 ♿ 🛍 📷
Ⓦ asiasociety.org

Founded by John D. Rockefeller III in 1956 to increase understanding of Asian culture, the society is a forum for 30 countries from Japan to Iran, Central Asia to Australia.

South Asian sculpture at the Asia Society

The 1981 eight-story building was designed by Edward Larrabee Barnes and is made of red granite. After a renovation in 2001, the museum has increased gallery space. One gallery is permanently devoted to Rockefeller's own collection of Asian sculptures, amassed by him and his wife on frequent trips to the East.

Changing exhibits show a wide variety of Asian arts, and the society has a full program of films, dance, concerts, and lectures and a well-stocked bookshop.

Entrance hall of the Park Avenue Armory

❿ Park Avenue Armory

643 Park Ave. **Map** 13 A2. **Tel** (212) 616-3930. Ⓜ 68th St. 📷 10am Tue & Thu (excluding holidays). 🎫 ♿
Ⓦ armoryonpark.org

From the War of 1812 through two world wars, the Seventh Regiment, an elite corps of "gentlemen soldiers" from prominent families, has played a vital role. Within the fortresslike exterior of their armory are extraordinary rooms filled with lavish Victorian furnishings, *objets d'art*, and regimental memorabilia.

The design by Charles W. Clinton, a veteran of the regiment, had offices facing Park Avenue, with a vast drill hall stretching behind to Lexington Ave. The reception rooms include the Veterans' Room and the Library by Louis Comfort Tiffany. The drill hall is now the site of the Winter Antiques Show *(see p55)* and a favorite venue for charity balls. The Armory hosts many cultural performances, from modern dance to concerts by the New York Philharmonic Orchestra.

⓫ Temple Emanu-El

1 E 65th St. **Map** 12 F2. **Tel** (212) 744-1400. Ⓜ 68th St, 63rd St. **Open** 10am–5pm Sun–Fri (last adm on Fri 3:30pm), 12:30–4:45pm Sat. **Closed** Jewish hols. ✡ 5:30pm Sun–Thu, 5:15pm Fri, 10:30am Sat. ♿ 📷 📷
Ⓦ emanuelnyc.org

This impressive limestone edifice of 1929 is the largest synagogue in the world, with seating for 2,500 in the main sanctuary alone. It is home to the oldest Reform congregation in New York, and the wealthiest members of Jewish society worship here.

Among the synagogue's many fine details are the bronze doors of the Ark, which represent an open Torah scroll. The Ark also has stained glass depicting biblical scenes and showing the tribal signs of the houses of Israel. These signs also appear on a great recessed arch that frames a magnificent wheel window, the dominant feature of the Fifth Avenue facade.

The synagogue stands on the site of the palatial home of Mrs. William Astor, the legendary society hostess. Lady Astor moved to the Upper East Side after a feud with her nephew, who lived next door. Her wine cellar and three marble fireplaces still remain at the synagogue.

The Ark at Temple Emanu-El

❺ Solomon R. Guggenheim Museum

Home to one of the world's finest collections of modern and contemporary art, the building itself is perhaps the museum's greatest masterpiece. The exterior of the museum was beautifully restored in celebration of the 50th anniversary of the building in 2009. Designed by Frank Lloyd Wright, the shell-like facade is a veritable New York landmark. The spiral ramp curves down and inward from the dome, passing works by major 19th-, 20th-, and 21st-century artists along the way.

Paris Through the Window
The vibrant colors of Marc Chagall's 1913 masterpiece illumine the canvas, conjuring up images of a magical and mysterious city where nothing is quite what it appears to be.

Woman Ironing *(1904)*
A work from Pablo Picasso's Blue Period, this painting is his quintessential image of hard work and fatigue.

Main entrance

KEY

① Sackler Center for Arts Education
② Small Rotunda
③ Tower
④ Great Rotunda
⑤ Café

Yellow Cow *(1911)*
Franz Marc's late work focused on nature and color.

Nude *(1917)*
This sleeping figure is typical of Amedeo Modigliani's stylized work.

Museum Guide

The Great Rotunda features special exhibitions. The Small Rotunda shows some of the museum's Impressionist and Post-Impressionist holdings. The Tower galleries (also known as The Annex) hold exhibitions of work from the permanent collection, as well as contemporary pieces. The permanent collection is shown on a rotating basis, and only parts of it are on display at any one time.

Before the Mirror *(1876)*
In trying to capture the flavor of 19th-century society, Edouard Manet often used the image of the courtesan.

VISITORS' CHECKLIST

Practical Information
1071 5th Ave at 89th St. **Map** 16
F3. **Tel** (212) 423-3500. **Open**
10am–5:45pm Fri–Wed (7:45pm
Sat). **Closed** Thksgv, Dec 25. 🖼
donation. 🚹 📷 📱 Lectures,
performing arts, concerts. 📺 📷
W **guggenheim.org**

Transport
Ⓜ 4, 5, 6 to 86th St. 🚌 M1–4.

Woman Holding a Vase
Fernand Léger incorporated elements of Cubism into this work from 1927.

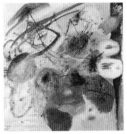

Black Lines *(1913)*
This is one of Vasily Kandinsky's earliest examples of his work in "non-objective" art.

Woman with Yellow Hair
(1931) The gentle, voluptuous figure of Picasso's mistress often appears in his work.

Frank Lloyd Wright

During his lifetime, Wright was considered the great innovator of American architecture. Characteristic of his work are Prairie-style homes and office buildings of concrete slabs, glass bricks, and tubing. Wright received the Guggenheim commission in 1942 and it was completed after his death in 1959, his only New York building.

Interior of the Guggenheim's Great Rotunda

❻ Metropolitan Museum of Art

Founded in 1870 by a group of artists and philanthropists who dreamed of an American art institution to rival those of Europe, this collection is thought to be the most comprehensive in the Western world. Works date from prehistoric times to the present. The museum opened here in 1880 and houses collections from all continents. The Greek and Roman galleries on the first floor are especially popular.

The entrance of the Metropolitan Museum of Art

Ground floor

★ Jeanne Hébuterne (1919)
Amedeo Modigliani's mistress, Hébuterne, appears in over 20 of his works. She killed herself the day after he died in 1920.

Pendant Mask
The kingdom of Benin (now part of Nigeria) was renowned for its art. This mask was made in the 16th century.

Mezzanine floor

Gallery Guide

Most of the collections are housed on the two main floors. Works from 19 curatorial areas are in the permanent galleries, with designated sections for temporary exhibitions. Central on the first and second floors are European painting, sculpture, and decorative art. The Costume Institute is situated on the ground level, directly below the Egyptian galleries on the first floor.

Seated Man with Harp
This statuette was made in the Cyclades c. 2,800 BC.

Key to Floorplan
- The American wing
- Art of Africa, Oceania, and the Americas
- Arms and armor
- Egyptian art
- European sculpture and decorative arts
- Greek and Roman art
- Medieval art
- Modern and Contemporary art
- Robert Lehman Collection
- Special exhibitions
- Non-exhibition space

★ Portrait of the Princesse de Broglie
This portrait, painted in 1853, was J.A.D. Ingres' last.

First floor

VISITORS' CHECKLIST

Practical Information
1000 Fifth Ave. **Map** 16 F4.
Tel (212) 535-7710. **Open**
10am–5:30pm Mon–Thu & Sun,
10am–9pm Fri–Sat. **Closed** Jan 1,
Thanksgiving, Dec 25.

Concerts, lectures, classes, seminars, film & video presentations.
W **metmuseum.org**

Transport
M 4, 5, 6 to 86th St. M1–4.

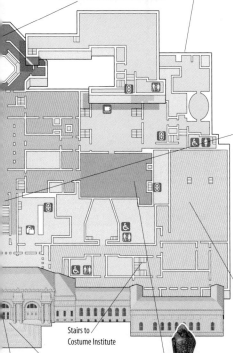

★ Byzantine Galleries
This marble panel with a griffin is from Greece or the Balkans (c.1250). It is just one of the pieces on display in the Byzantine Galleries.

Stairs to
Costume Institute

Main entrance

The Marriage Feast at Cana
This rare 16th-century panel painting by Juan de Flandes is part of the Linsky Collection.

English Armor
This was made for Sir George Clifford around 1580.

★ Temple of Dendur (15 BC)
The Roman emperor Augustus built this three-room temple, which is located in the Egyptian Art section.

Metropolitan Museum of Art: Upper Levels

Sculpture Garden
These modern sculptures, on the roof of the Modern Art wing, are changed annually.

Card Players (1890)
Paul Cézanne departed here from his traditional landscapes, still lifes, and portraits to paint this scene of peasants intently playing cards.

Roof Garden

Gertrude Stein (1905–6)
This portrait of the American writer is by Pablo Picasso. The masklike face is evidence of his debt to African and Roman art.

First floor   Second floor

★ Cypresses (1889)
Vincent Van Gogh painted this the year before he died. The heavy brushstrokes and the swirling style mark his later work.

★ Diptych (1425–30)
Flemish painter Jan van Eyck was one of the earliest masters of oil painting. These scenes of the Crucifixion and Last Judgment show him to be a forerunner of realism, too.

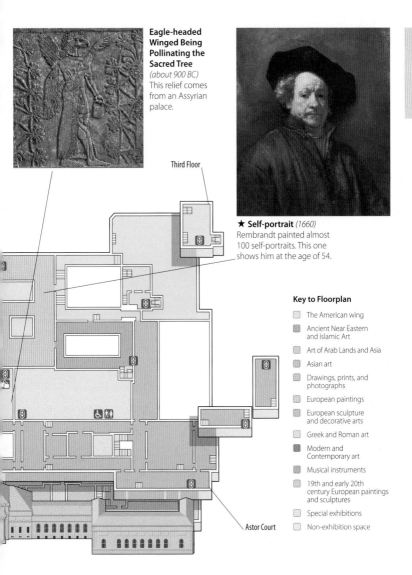

Eagle-headed Winged Being Pollinating the Sacred Tree *(about 900 BC)* This relief comes from an Assyrian palace.

Third Floor

★ **Self-portrait** *(1660)* Rembrandt painted almost 100 self-portraits. This one shows him at the age of 54.

Key to Floorplan

- The American wing
- Ancient Near Eastern and Islamic Art
- Art of Arab Lands and Asia
- Asian art
- Drawings, prints, and photographs
- European paintings
- European sculpture and decorative arts
- Greek and Roman art
- Modern and Contemporary art
- Musical instruments
- 19th and early 20th century European paintings and sculptures
- Special exhibitions
- Non-exhibition space

Astor Court

The Astor Court

In 1979, 27 crafts-people from China, responsible for the care of Souzhou's historic gardens, came to New York to replicate a Ming-style scholar's garden in the Metropolitan Museum. They used centuries-old techniques and handmade tools that had been passed down for generations. It was the first cultural exchange between the United States and the People's Republic of China. The result is a quiet garden for meditation, a Western parallel to Souzhou's Garden of the Master of the Fishing Nets.

Exploring the Metropolitan

The treasures of the "Met" include a vast collection of American art and more than 2,500 European paintings, including masterpieces by Rembrandt and Vermeer. There are also many Islamic exhibits, plus the greatest collection of Egyptian art outside Cairo.

A painted gold funerary mask (10th–14th century) from the necropolis of Batán Grande, Peru

Mysterious in identity and origin, a rare 5,000-year-old copper head from the Near East

It holds not only one of the world's finest collections of American painting and sculpture but also of decorative arts from Colonial times to the beginning of the 20th century. Highlights range from elegant Neo-Classical silver vessels made by Paul Revere to innovative glassware by Tiffany & Co. In the furniture section are settees, dining chairs, tables, bookcases, and desks from major centers of American cabinetmaking such as Boston, Newport, and Philadelphia.

Period rooms, with their original decorative woodwork and furnishings, range from the saloon hall in which George Washington celebrated his last birthday to the elegant prairie-style living room from the house that Frank Lloyd Wright designed for Francis W. Little in Wayzata, Minnesota, in 1912.

The Charles Engelhard Court is an indoor sculpture garden with large-scale architectural elements, including the lovely stained-glass and mosaic loggia from Louis Comfort Tiffany's Long Island estate and the facade of an 1824 United States Branch Bank that once stood on Wall Street.

Art of Africa, Oceania, and the Americas

Nelson Rockefeller built the Michael C. Rockefeller Wing in 1982 in memory of his son, who lost his life on an art-finding expedition in New Guinea. The wing showcases a superb collection of over 1,600 objects from Africa, the islands of the Pacific and the Americas.

Among the African works, the ivory and bronze sculptures from the royal kingdom of Benin (Nigeria) are outstanding, as is the wooden sculpture by the Dogon, Bamana and Senufo peoples of Mali. From the Pacific come carvings by the Asmat people of New Guinea and decorations and masks from the Melanesian and Polynesian islands. From Mexico and Central and South America come pre-Columbian gold, ceramics and stonework. The wing also contains fine Native American artifacts by the Inuit and other groups.

The American Wing

Gilbert Stuart's portrait of George Washington, George Caleb Bingham's *Fur Traders Descending the Missouri*, John SingerSargent's notorious portrait of *Madame X*, and the monumental *Washington Crossing the Delaware* by Emanuel Leutze are among the icons in the American Wing.

Ancient Near Eastern and Islamic Art

Massive stone sculptures of winged, human-headed animals, once the guardians of the 9th-century BC Assyrian palace of Ashurnasirpal II, stand at the entrance to the Ancient Near Eastern galleries. Inside is a collection spanning 8,000 years, rich in Iranian bronzes, Anatolian ivories and Sumerian sculptures, and Achaemenian and Sassanian silver and gold. An adjacent area contains Islamic art of the 7th to the 19th centuries; glass and metalwork from Egypt, Syria and Meso-potamia; royal miniatures from Persia and Mughal India; 16th- and 17th-century rugs; and an 18th-century room from Syria.

Arms and Armor

Mounted knights in full armor charge at each other across the equestrian court here. These galleries are a favorite with children and anyone moved by medieval romance or thrilled by power.

There are suits of armor, rapiers and sabers with hilts of precious stones and gold, firearms inlaid with ivory and mother-of-pearl, plus colorful

The pistol of Holy Roman Emperor Charles V (16th century)

heraldic banners and shields. Highlights include the armor of gentleman-pirate Sir George Clifford, a favorite of Queen Elizabeth I. The rainbow-colored armor of a 14th-century Japanese shogun and a collection of Wild West revolvers that once belonged to gunmaker Samuel Colt are also exhibited here.

The Old Plum, a Japanese paper screen from the early Edo period (about 1650)

Asian Art

Many outstanding galleries contain masterpieces of Chinese, Japanese, Korean, Indian, and Southeast Asian art, dating from the second millennium BC to the 20th century. A full-scale Ming-style Chinese scholar's garden was built by craftspeople from Souzhou as part of the first cultural exchange between the United States and the People's Republic of China. The museum also has one of the finest collections of Sung and Yuan paintings in the world, Chinese Buddhist monumental sculptures, fine Chinese ceramics and jade, and an important display of the arts of ancient China.

The full range of Japanese arts is represented in a breath-taking suite of 11 galleries featuring chronological and thematic displays of Japanese lacquer, ceramics, painting, sculpture, textiles, and screens. Indian, Southeast Asian, and Korean galleries display superb sculptures and other arts from these regions.

Costume Institute

The 31,000-piece collection of costumes and accessories has expanded by over 23,000 items under an agreement with the Brooklyn Museum *(see pp252–55).* There is no permanent display due to the fragility of the objects, but there are two special exhibitions a year.

The collection spans five centuries from the 17th century to the present and is a definitive compendium of fashionable dress, from the elaborately embroidered dresses of the late 1600s to gowns from the Napoleonic era. The designs of Elsa Schiaparelli, Worth, and Balenciaga are also included, along with Ballets Russes costumes and even David Bowie's sequined jockstrap.

The *Art of Dress* audio tour, narrated by actress Sarah Jessica Parker, focuses on how artists have used clothing to express identity and power.

The Institute is sophisticated in its understanding of conservation techniques, with a state-of-the-art laboratory.

A 17th-century European silk-and-satin doublet

Drawings, Prints, and Photographs

This eclectic gallery regularly displays selections from the museum's incredible holdings of drawings, prints, etchings, and photographs. The drawings collection is especially rich in Italian and French art from

Michelangelo's studies of a Libyan Sibyl for the ceiling of the Sistine Chapel (1508)

the 15th to the 19th century. Specific exhibits of the drawings in this collection are shown on a rotating basis because of the light-sensitive nature of works on paper.

Highlights among the 11,000 drawings include works by Michelangelo, Leonardo da Vinci, Raphael, Ingres, Goya, Rubens, Rembrandt, Tiepolo, and Seurat.

The encyclopedic print collection of nearly 1.5 million images and over 14,000 illustrated books includes major works by virtually every master printmaker, from an early German woodcut called *Virgin and Child* to some of Dürer's most accomplished works and Goya's *The Giant.* Influential gallery-owner Alfred Stieglitz's donation of his own extensive collection of photographs brought here such gems as Edward Steichen's *The Flatiron.* It formed the core of a photography collection that is now also particularly strong in Modernist works dating from between the wars.

Ephemera such as posters and advertisements form another part of this collection.

Egyptian Art

One of the museum's best-loved areas is the ancient Egyptian wing, which displays every one of its thousands of holdings – from the prehistoric period to the 8th century AD. Objects range from the fragmented jasper lips of a 15th-century BC queen to the massive Temple of Dendur. Other amazing archaeological finds, most of them originating from museum-sponsored expeditions undertaken early in the 20th century, include sculptures of the notorious Queen Hatshepsut, who seized the Theban throne in the 16th century BC; 100 carved reliefs of Amenhotep IV's reign; and tomb figures like the blue faïence hippo that has become the museum's mascot.

Fragment of the
head of a pharoah's queen

European Paintings

The heart of the museum is its awe-inspiring collection of over 3,000 European paintings. The Italian works include Botticelli's *Last Communion of Saint Jerome* and Bronzino's *Portrait of a Young Man*. The Dutch and Flemish canvases are among the world's finest, with

Young Woman with a Water Jug (1660) by Johannes Vermeer

Brueghel's *The Harvesters*, several works by Rubens, Van Dyck, and Rembrandt, and more Vermeers than any other museum. The collection also has masterpieces by Spanish artists El Greco, Velázquez, and Goya, and by French artists Poussin and Watteau. Some of the finest Impressionist and Post-Impressionist canvases reside here: 34 Monets, including *Terrace at Sainte-Adresse;* 18 Cézannes; and several Van Goghs, including *Cypresses*.

European Sculpture, and Decorative Arts

In the Kravis wing and adjacent galleries are works from the impressive 60,000-object collection of European sculpture and decorative arts. The galleries include exquisite pieces such as Tullio Lombardo's marble statue of Adam; a bronze statuette of a rearing horse, after a model by Leonardo; and dozens of works by Degas and Rodin. Period settings include the patio from a 16th-century Spanish castle and a series of ornate

18th-century French domestic interiors known as the Wrightsman Rooms. The Petrie European Sculpture Court features French and Italian sculpture in a beautiful garden setting reminiscent of Versailles in France.

Greek and Roman Arts

A Roman sarcophagus from Tarsus, donated in 1870, was the first work of art in the Met's collections. It can still be seen in the museum's Greek and Roman galleries, along with breath-taking wall panels from a villa that was buried under the lava of Vesuvius in AD 79, Etruscan mirrors, Roman portrait busts, exquisite objects in glass and silver, and hundreds of Greek vases. A monumental 7th-century BC statue of a youth shows the movement toward naturalism in sculpture, and the Hellenistic *Old Market Woman* demonstrates how the Greeks had mastered realism by the 2nd century BC.

An amphora by Exekias, showing
a wedding (6th century BC)

Lehman Collection

What had been one of the the finest private art collections in the world, that of investment banker Robert Lehman, came to the museum in 1969. The Lehman Wing is a dramatic glass pyramid housing an extraordinarily varied collection rich in Old Masters and 19th-century French paintings, drawings, bronzes,

Egyptian Tomb Models

In 1920, a Met researcher's light illuminated a room, which had been closed for 2,000 years, in the tomb of the nobleman Meketre. Within were 24 tiny, perfect replicas of his daily life: his house and garden, fleet of ships and herd of cattle. Meketre is there, too, on his boat, inhaling a lotus's scent and enjoying the music of his singer and harpist. The museum has 13 of these delightful replicas.

A panel from the stained-glass *Death of the Virgin* window, from the 12th-century cathedral of Saint Pierre in Troyes, France

Renaissance majolica, Venetian glass, furniture, and enamels. Among the canvases are works by north-European masters; Dutch and Spanish paintings, French masterworks, Post-Impressionists and Fauves.

Medieval Art

The Metropolitan's medieval collection includes works dating from the 4th to the 16th century, roughly from the fall of Rome to the beginning of the Renaissance. The collection is split between the main museum and its uptown branch, the Cloisters *(see pp238–41).* In the main building are a chalice once thought to be the Holy Grail, six silver Byzantine plates showing scenes from the life of David, a 1301 pulpit by Giovanni Pisano in the shape of an eagle, and several monumental sculptures of the Virgin and Child. Other exhibits include Migration jewelry, liturgical vessels, stained glass, ivories, and 14th- and 15th-century tapestries.

Muscial Instruments

The world's oldest piano, Andrés Segovia's guitars and a sitar shaped like a peacock are some of the features of a broad and sometimes quirky collection of musical instruments that spans six continents and dates from prehistory to the present. The instruments illustrate the history of music and performance, and most of them are conserved to remain in playable condition. Worth particular mention are instruments from the European courts of the Middle Ages and the Renaissance; rare violins; harpsichords; instruments inlaid with precious materials; and a fully equipped traditional violin-maker's workshop; there are also African drums, Asian *pi-pas,* or lutes; and Native American flutes. Visitors can use audio equipment to hear many of the instruments playing the music of their day.

Stradivari violin from Cremona, Italy (1691)

Modern and Contemporary Art

Since its foundation in 1870, the museum has been acquiring contemporary art, but it was not until 1987 that a permanent home for 20th- century art was built – the Lila Acheson Wallace Wing. Other museums in New York have larger collections of modern art, but this display space is considered among the finest. European and American works from 1900 onward are featured on three levels, starting with Europeans such as Picasso, Kandinsky, Braque, and Bonnard. The collection's greatest strength lies in its col-lection of modern American art, with works by New York school "The Eight," including John Sloan; such Modernists as Charles Demuth and Georgia O'Keeffe; American Regionalist Grant Wood; Abstract Expressionists Willem de Kooning; and such Color Field painters as Clyfford Still. Special areas of the wing house Art Nouveau and Art Deco furniture and metalwork; a large collection of works on paper by Paul Klee; and the Sculpture Gallery, with its large-scale sculptures and canvases.

Gems of the collection include Picasso's portrait of Gertrude Stein, Matisse's *Nasturtiums* and *"Dance, 1"* Demuth's *I Saw the Figure 5 in Gold,* Jackson Pollock's *Autumn Rhythm,* and Andy Warhol's last self-portrait.

Each year the Cantor Roof Garden at the top of the wing features a new installation of contemporary sculpture, especially dramatic against the backdrop of the New York skyline and Central Park.

Grant Wood's view of *The Midnight Ride of Paul Revere* (1931)

Book cover (1916) by illustrator N. C. Wyeth

⓬ Society of Illustrators

128 E 63rd St. **Map** 13 A2. **Tel** (212) 838-2560. Ⓜ Lexington Ave. **Open** 10am–8pm Tue, 10am–5pm Wed–Fri, noon–4pm Sat. **Closed** public hols. ♿ restricted. 📷 📷
🆆 **societyillustrators.org**

Established in 1901, this society was formed to promote the illustrator's art. Its notable roster included Charles Dana Gibson, N. C. Wyeth, and Howard Pyle. It was at first concerned with education and public service, and still holds monthly lectures. In 1981, the Museum of American Illustration opened in two galleries. Changing thematic exhibitions show the history of book and magazine illustration, with an annual exhibition of the year's finest American illustrations.

⓭ Mount Vernon Hotel Museum

421 E 61st St. **Map** 13 C3. **Tel** (212) 838-6878. Ⓜ Lexington Ave, 59th St. **Open** 11am–4pm Tue–Sun. **Closed** Aug, public hols. 📷 📷 📷
📷 🆆 **mvhm.org**

Built in 1799, the Mount Vernon Hotel Museum and Garden was once a country day hotel for New Yorkers who needed to escape from the crowded city, then only at the south end of the island. The stone building sits on land once owned by Abigail Adams Smith, daughter of President John Adams.

It was acquired by the Colonial Dames of America, a women's patriotic society, in 1924 and turned into a charming re-creation of a Federal home. Costumed guides show visitors through eight rooms, which exhibit Chinese porcelain, Sheraton chests, and a Duncan Phyfe sofa. One bedroom even contains a baby's cradle and children's toys. An 18th-century-style garden has been planted around the house.

Queen Anne row houses at Henderson Place

⓮ Henderson Place

Map 18 D3. Ⓜ 86th St.
🚌 M31, M79, M86.

Now surrounded by modern apartment blocks, this enclave of 24 red-brick Queen Anne row houses was built in 1882. The row houses were commissioned by John C. Henderson, a hat-maker, as a self-contained community. The elegant Lamb & Rich design has gray slate roof gables, pediments, parapets, chimneys and dormer windows forming patterns, and a turret marking the corner of each block.

Carl Schurz Park promenade

⓯ Carl Schurz Park

Map 18 D3. Ⓜ 86th St.
🚌 M31, M79, M86.

Laid out in 1891, this park along the East River has a wide promenade over the East River Drive. It offers fine vistas of the river and the turbulent waters of Hell Gate, where the river meets Long Island Sound. It is named after Carl Schurz, a native who became Secretary of the Interior (1869–75). The first part of the promenade is the John Finlay Walk, named for an editor of the *New York Times* known for his hiking prowess. One of the city's most pleasant green escapes, the park's grassy areas are filled with basking New Yorkers on sunny days.

⓰ Gracie Mansion

East End Ave at 88th St. **Map** 18 D3. **Tel** (212) 639-9675. Ⓜ 86th St. 🚌 M31, M79, M86. **Open** 10am, 11am, 1pm, 2pm most Weds for prebooked guided tours only. 📷 📷
📷 📷 🆆 **nyc.gov/gracie**

This gracious, balconied wooden 1799 country home is the official mayor's residence. Built by wealthy merchant Archibald Gracie, it is one of the best Federal houses left in New York.

Acquired by the city in 1887, it was the first home of the Museum of the City of New York. In 1942 it became the official Mayoral Residence.

Front view of Gracie Mansion

When Fiorello LaGuardia moved in after nine years in office, preferring it to a 75-room palace on Riverside Drive, he said that even the modest Gracie Mansion was too fancy for him. "The Little Flower" (from Fiorello) had fought corruption in the city.

Arched doorway of the Church of the Holy Trinity

⓱ Church of the Holy Trinity

316 E 88th St. **Map** 17 B3. **Tel** (212) 289-4100. Ⓜ 86th St. **Open** 9am–5pm Mon–Fri, 7:30am–2pm Sun. ✝ 8:45am Tue & Thu; 8am, 10:30am, 6pm Sun. Ⓦ holytrinity-nyc.org

Delightfully placed in a serene garden setting, this church was constructed in 1889 of glowing golden brick and terra-cotta in French Renaissance style. It boasts one of New York's best bell towers, which holds a handsome wrought-iron clock with brass hands. The arched doorway is richly decorated with carved images of the saints and prophets.

The complex was donated by Serena Rhinelander in memory of her father and grandfather. The land was part of the Rhinelander farm, which the family had owned for 100 years.

Farther down at 350 E. 88th Street is the Rhinelander Children's Center, also a gift, and the headquarters of the Children's Aid Society.

⓲ St. Nicholas Russian Orthodox Cathedral

15 E 97th St. **Map** 16 F1. **Tel** (212) 876-2190. Ⓜ 96 St. **Open** by appt. ✝ throughout the week, including 10am & 6pm Wed & Sun. Ⓦ russianchurchusa.org

Built in Muscovite Baroque style in 1902, this church has five onion domes crowned with crosses, and blue and yellow tiles on a red brick and white stone facade. Among the early worshipers were White Russians who had fled the first uprisings at home, mostly intellectuals and aristocrats who soon became a part of New York society. Later, there were more waves of refugees, dissidents, and defectors.

The cathedral now serves a scattered community, and the congregation is small. Mass is celebrated in Russian with great pomp and dignity.

The cathedral is filled with the scent of incense. The high central sanctuary has marble columns with blue and white trim above. Ornate wooden screens trimmed with gold enclose the altar. It is unique, an unexpected find on a side street in this staid part of Manhattan.

Facade and domes of St. Nicholas Russian Cathedral

Facade of the Museum of the City of New York

⓳ Museum of the City of New York

1220 5th Ave at 103rd St. **Map** 21 C5. **Tel** (212) 534-1672. Ⓜ 103rd St. **Open** 10am–6pm daily (to 8:30pm Sat). **Closed** Jan 1, Thanksgiving, Dec 25. ♿ ♨ �🖥 📷 📷 Ⓦ mcny.org

Founded in 1923 and at first housed in Gracie Mansion, this museum is dedicated to New York's development from its earliest beginnings up to the present and on to the future.

Housed in a handsome Georgian Colonial building since 1932, the museum has expanded its public space, with special exhibitions throughout the year. These cover subjects such as fashion, architecture, theater, social and political history, and photography. In addition there is a collection of toys, including the famed Stettheimer Dollhouse, with original works of art in miniature, painted by such luminaries as Marcel Duchamp and Albert Gleizes.

A core exhibition of the museum is the film *Timescapes: A Multimedia Portrait of New York* (every 30 mins, 10:15am–4:45pm). It uses images from the museum's collection and historic maps to chart the growth of New York, from its early days as a tiny settlement to its current status as one of the largest cities in the world.

⓿ Whitney Museum of American Art

The Whitney Museum is the foremost showcase for American art of the 20th and 21st centuries. It was founded in 1930 by sculptor Gertrude Vanderbilt Whitney after the Metropolitan Museum of Art turned down her collection of works by living artists such as Bellows and Hopper. In 1966 the museum moved to the present inverted-pyramid building designed by Marcel Breuer. The Whitney Biennial, held in even years, is the most significant survey of new trends in American art.

The cantilevered facade of the Whitney Museum

Green Coca-Cola Bottles
Andy Warhol's 1962 work is a commentary on mass production and monopoly.

Children Meeting *(1978)*
This painting by Elizabeth Murray reveals her interest in the use of color and form.

Little Big Painting
The 1965 work by Roy Lichtenstein is a comic critique of Abstract Expressionist painting.

Early Sunday Morning (1930)
Edward Hopper's paintings often convey the emptiness of American city life.

Museum Guide

The second and fifth floors showcase exhibitions from the permanent collection, which may include works by the likes of Calder, O'Keeffe, and Hopper. Changing exhibitions occupy the third and fourth floors.

Dempsey and Firpo
In 1924, George Bellows depicted one of the most famous prizefights of the century.

Three Flags (1958)
Jasper Johns's use of familiar objects in an abstract form was influential in the development of Pop Art.

Painting Number 5
The early modernist artist MarsdenHartley painted this oil on canvas between 1914 and 1915.

Circus (1926–31)
Alexander Calder's fanciful creation is usually on display.

Tango (1919)
This is considered Polish-born Elie Nadelman's greatest work of wood sculpture.

Gertrude Vanderbilt Whitney (1916)
Robert Henri's oil shows the Whitney Museum's founder.

❶ Frick Collection

The art collection of steel magnate Henry Clay Frick (1849–1919) is exhibited in a residential setting amid the furnishings of his opulent mansion, which provides a rare glimpse of how the extremely wealthy lived in New York's gilded age. Henry Frick intended the collection to be a memorial to himself, and on his death he bequeathed the entire house to the nation. The collection includes important Old Master paintings, major works of sculpture, French furniture, rare Limoges enamels, and beautiful Oriental rugs.

The Harbor of Dieppe (1826)
J.M.W. Turner was criticized by some skeptical contemporaries for depicting this northern European port suffused with light.

Garden Court

Library

West Gallery

The Polish Rider
The identity of the rider in this equestrian portrait, painted by Rembrandt in 1655, is unknown. The somber, rocky landscape creates an eerie atmosphere of unknown danger.

★ **Sir Thomas More** (1527)
Holbein's portrait of Henry VIII's Lord Chancellor was painted eight years before More's execution for treason.

Living Hall

Gallery Guide

Of special interest are the West Gallery, with oils by Vermeer, Hals, and Rembrandt; the East Gallery, featuring Van Dyck and Whistler; the Oval Room, featuring Gainsborough; the Library and Dining Room, with English works; and the Living Hall, with works by Titian and Holbein.

★ **Officer and Laughing Girl**
(1655–60)
Johannes Vermeer is unique
among 17th-century Dutch
painters for his bold use of
light and shadow.

VISITORS' CHECKLIST

Practical Information
1 E 70th St.
Map 12 F1.
Tel (212) 288-0700.
Open 10am–6pm Tue–Sat,
11am–5pm Sun.
Closed most public hols. 🚫 (no
children under 10). 📷 ♿ 📱 📹 🔔
Concerts, lectures, film & video.
🅦 frick.org

Transport
Ⓜ 6 to 68th St. 🚌 M1–M4.

Key to Floorplan

☐ Exhibition space

▨ Nonexhibition space

East
Gallery

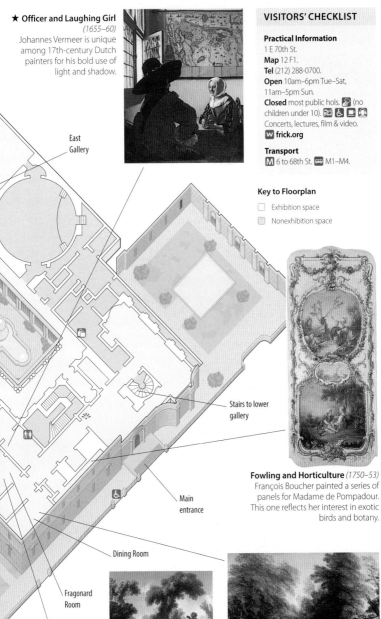

Stairs to lower
gallery

Main
entrance

Dining Room

Fragonard
Room

Fowling and Horticulture *(1750–53)*
François Boucher painted a series of
panels for Madame de Pompadour.
This one reflects her interest in exotic
birds and botany.

The Pursuit
This is part of *The
Progress of Love* (1771–3
and 1790–91), by Jean-
Honoré Fragonard. The
series of paintings
depicts the events of
an idealized courtship.

★ **Mall in St. James's Park** *(1783)*
The three central figures in Thomas
Gainsborough's London landscape
may be the daughters of George III.

CENTRAL PARK

The city's "backyard" was created in 1858 by Frederick Law Olmsted and Calvert Vaux on an unpromising site of quarries, pig farms, swampland, and shacks. Five million cubic yards of stone, earth, and topsoil turned it into the lush 843-acre (340-ha) park of today. There are scenic hills, lakes and lush meadows, dotted throughout with outcrops of Manhattan bedrock, and planted with more than 500,000 trees and shrubs. Over the years the park has blossomed, with playgrounds, skating rinks, ball fields, and spaces for every other activity, from chess and croquet to concerts and events. Cars are not allowed on weekends, giving bicyclists, in-line skaters, and joggers the right-of-way.

Sights at a Glance

Historic Buildings
1 The Dairy
3 Belvedere Castle

Monuments and Statues
2 Strawberry Fields
4 Bow Bridge
5 Bethesda Fountain and Terrace

Lakes and Gardens
6 Conservatory Water
7 Central Park Zoo
8 Conservatory Garden

☐ **Restaurants** *see p302*
1 Loeb Boathouse Restaurant

See also Street Finder maps 12, 16, 21

◀ New York's most treasured green space, Central Park

For keys to symbols *see back flap*

A Tour of Central Park

On a short visit, a walking tour from 59th to 79th streets takes in some of Central Park's loveliest features, from the dense, wooded Ramble to the open formal spaces of Bethesda Terrace. Along the way are man-made lakes and more than 30 graceful bridges and arches that link around 68 miles (109 km) of footpaths, bridle paths, and roads in the park. In summer the park is often several degrees cooler than the city streets around it, and thus is a favorite retreat.

➋ ★ Strawberry Fields
One of the park's most visited spots, this peaceful area was created in memory of John Lennon, who lived nearby.

➎ ★ Bethesda Fountain and Terrace
The richly ornamented formal terrace overlooks the Lake and the wooded shores of the Ramble.

Wollman Rink was restored in the 1980s for future generations of skaters by tycoon Donald Trump.

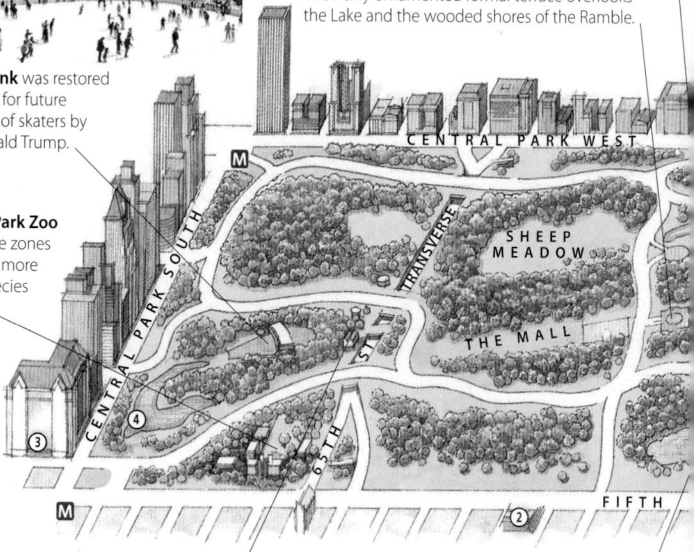

➐ Central Park Zoo
Three climate zones are home to more than 150 species of animals.

CENTRAL PARK WEST

CENTRAL PARK SOUTH

TRANSVERSE

SHEEP MEADOW

THE MALL

65TH ST.

FIFTH

➊ ★ The Dairy
This Victorian Gothic building houses one of the park's visitor centers. Make it your first stop and pick up a calendar of park events.

➏ ★ Conservatory Water
From March to November, this is the scene of model boat races. Many of the tiny craft are stored in the boathouse that adjoins the Lake.

④ Bow Bridge
This cast-iron bridge links the Ramble with Cherry Hill by a graceful arch, 60 ft (18 m) above the Lake.

Locator Map
See Manhattan Map pp16–17

Alice in Wonderland is immortalized in bronze at the northern end of Conservatory Water, along with her friends the Cheshire Cat, the Mad Hatter and the Dormouse. Children love to slide down her toadstool seat.

KEY

① **Hans Christian Andersen's** statue is a favorite Central Park landmark for children. It is on the west side of Conservatory Water and is a popular site for story-telling in the summer.

② **Frick Collection** *(see pp204–5)*

③ **Plaza Hotel** *(see p183)*

④ **The Pond**

⑤ **Dakota Building** *(see p220)*

⑥ **San Remo Apartments** *(see p216)*

⑦ **American Museum of Natural History** *(see pp218–19)*

⑧ **Reservoir**

⑨ **Obelisk**

⑩ **The Ramble** is a wooded area of 37 acres (15 ha), crisscrossed by paths and streams. It is a paradise for birdwatchers. More than 275 species of birds have been spotted in the park, which is on the Atlantic migration flyway.

⑪ **Metropolitan Museum** *(see pp192–9)*

⑫ **Guggenheim Museum** *(see pp190–91)*

③ ★ Belvedere Castle
From the terraces, there are unequaled views of the city and surrounding park. Within the stone walls is a visitor center.

The Carousel, part of the park's Children's District

❶ The Dairy

Map 12 F2. **Tel** (212) 794-6564.
🅼 Fifth Ave. **Open** 10am–5pm daily.
Slide show. 📷
🅦 centralparknyc.org

Now used as Central Park's Visitor Center, this charming building of natural stone was planned as part of the "Children's District" of the park, which included a playground, the Carousel, a Children's Cottage, and stable. In 1873, there were cows grazing on the meadows in front of the Dairy, a ewe and her lambs feeding nearby, and chickens, guinea fowl, and peacocks roaming the lawn. City children could get fresh milk and other refreshments here. Over the years, the Dairy deteriorated, being used as a shed until restoration in 1979, done according to original photographs and drawings. The Dairy is the place to begin exploring the lush and leafy park; maps and details of events can be obtained here. The less energetic can rent chess and checkers sets for use on the pretty inlaid boards of the *kinderberg*, the charming little "children's hill" nearby.

❷ Strawberry Fields

Map 12 E1. 🅼 72nd St.

The restoration of this teardrop-shaped section of the park was Yoko Ono's tribute in memory of her slain husband, John Lennon. They lived in the Dakota apartments overlooking this spot *(see p220)*. Gifts for the garden came from all over the world. A mosaic set in the pathway, inscribed with the word *Imagine* (named for Lennon's famous song), was a gift from the city of Naples in Italy.

This broad expanse of the park's landscape was designed by Vaux and Olmsted. Now it is an international peace garden, with 161 species of plants (one from every country of the world), including jetbead, roses, witch hazel, birches – and strawberries.

❸ Belvedere Castle

Map 16 E4. **Tel** (212) 772-0210.
🅼 81st St. **Open** 10am–5pm Tue–Sun. **Closed** Tue in winter.
♿ to main floor only.

This stone castle atop Vista Rock, complete with tower and turrets, offers one of the best views of the park and the city from its lookout on the rooftop. Inside is the Henry Luce Nature Observatory, with a delightful exhibit telling inquisitive young visitors about the surprising variety of wildlife to be found in the park.

The view to the north from the castle allows you to look down into the Delacorte Theater, home to the free productions of Shakespeare in the Park every summer, often featuring big-name stars *(see p339)*. The theater was the gift of George T. Delacorte. Publisher and founder of Dell paperbacks, Delacorte was a delightful philanthropist who was responsible for many of the park's pleasures.

Belvedere Castle with its lookout over the park

❹ Bow Bridge

Map 16 E5. 🅼 72nd St.

This is one of the park's seven original cast-iron bridges and is considered one of the finest. It was designed by Vaux as a bow tying together the two large sections of the Lake. In the 19th century, when the Lake was used for ice skating, a red ball was hoisted from a bell tower on Vista Rock to signal that the ice was safe. The bridge offers expansive views of the park and the buildings bordering it on both the east and west sides.

A tranquil scene in Central Park, overlooked by exclusive apartments

An 1864 print of Bethesda Fountain and Terrace

❺ Bethesda Fountain and Terrace

Map 12 E1. Ⓜ 72nd St.

Situated between the Lake and the Mall, this is the architectural heart of the park, a formal element in the naturalistic landscape. The fountain was dedicated in 1873. The statue, *Angel of the Waters*, marked the opening of the Croton Aqueduct system in 1842, bringing the city its first supply of pure water; its name refers to a biblical account of a healing angel at the pool of Bethesda in Jerusalem. The Spanish-style detailing, such as the sculptured double staircase, tiles, and friezes, is by Jacob Wrey Mould.

The terrace is one of the best spots to relax and take in some people-watching.

❻ Conservatory Water

Map 16 F5. Ⓜ 77th St.

Better known as the Model Boat Pond, this stretch of water is home to model yacht races every weekend.

At the north end of the lake, a sculpture of Alice in Wonderland is a delight for children. It was commissioned by George T. Delacorte in honor of his wife. He himself is immortalized in caricature as the Mad Hatter. On the west bank, free story hours are held at the Hans Christian Andersen statue. The author is portrayed reading from his own story, "The Ugly Duckling," while its hero waddles at his

feet. Children like to climb on the statue and snuggle in the author's lap. Conservatory Water's literary links continue into adolescence: it is here that J. D. Salinger's Holden Caulfield comes to tell the ducks his troubles in *The Catcher in the Rye*.

Each spring, birdwatchers gather at the pond to see the city's most famous red-tailed hawk, Pale Male, nest on the roof of 927 Fifth Avenue.

❼ Central Park Zoo

Map 12 F2. **Tel** (212) 439-6500. Ⓜ Fifth Ave between 63rd and 66th sts. **Open** 10am–5pm Mon–Fri, 10am–5:30pm Sat–Sun & hols; Nov–Mar: 10am–4:30pm daily. Last adm: 30 mins before closing. Ⓦ **centralparkzoo.com**

This imaginative zoo has won plaudits for its creative and humane use of small space. More than 150 species of animals are represented in three climate zones, the Tropics, the Polar Circle, and the California coast. An equatorial rain forest is home to monkeys and free-flying birds, while penguins and polar bears populate an Arctic landscape that allows views both above and under water.

At the Tisch Children's Zoo children can get close to goats, sheep, alpacas, cows, and pot-bellied pigs. By its entrance is the much-loved Delacorte Clock, which plays nursery rhymes every half hour, as bronze musical animals (such as a goat playing pan pipes) circle around it. Toward Willowdell Arch is another favorite – the memorial to Balto, leader of a team of huskies that made a heroic journey across Alaska with serum for a diphtheria epidemic.

Statue of Balto, the heroic husky dog, Central Park Wildlife Center

❽ Conservatory Garden

Map 21 B5. Ⓜ Central Pk N, 103rd St. **Tel** (212) 860-1382. **Open** 8am–dusk.

The Vanderbilt Gate on Fifth Avenue is the entry to a 6-acre (2.4-ha) park containing three formal gardens. Each one represents a different national landscape style. The Central Garden, with a large lawn, yew hedges, crabapple trees, and a wisteria pergola recreates an Italian style. The South Garden, spilling over with perennials, represents an English style, with a bronze statue in the reflecting pool of Mary and Dickon, from Frances Hodgson Burnett's *The Secret Garden*. Beyond is a slope with thousands of native wildflowers, spreading into the park beyond. The North Garden, in the French style, centers around the bronze *Fountain of the Three Dancing Maidens*. It puts on a brief but brilliant display of annuals each summer.

Polar bear in the Central Park Zoo

UPPER WEST SIDE

This district of New York became residential in the 1870s, when the Ninth Avenue elevated railroad (see pp28–9) made commuting to Midtown possible. The Dakota, the city's first luxury apartment house, was built here in 1884, and the streets were graded and leveled. Buildings sprang up on Broadway and Central Park West, and cross streets, dating from the 1890s, still retain fine brownstone row houses. The area is bustling and diverse, with many cultural institutions, including the American Museum of Natural History, Lincoln Center, and Columbus Circle complex for Time Warner and CNN.

Sights at a Glance

Historic Streets and Buildings
1 Twin Towers of Central Park West
7 Columbus Circle
8 Hotel des Artistes
9 The Dakota
13 Pomander Walk
14 Riverside Drive and Park
16 The Ansonia
17 The Dorilton

Museums and Galleries
10 New-York Historical Society
11 American Museum of Natural History pp218–19
12 Rose Center for Earth and Space
15 Children's Museum of Manhattan

Famous Theaters
2 Lincoln Center for the Performing Arts
3 New York State Theater
4 Metropolitan Opera House
5 Lincoln Center Theater
6 Avery Fisher Hall

Restaurants see pp301–2
1 Asiate
2 Bar Boulud
3 Café Fiorello
4 Café Frida
5 Café Luxembourg
6 Calle Ocho
7 Gennaro
8 Jean Georges
9 Masa
10 Ouest
11 Per Se
12 Picholine
13 Pio Pio
14 Rosa Mexicano
15 Telepan

0 meters 500
0 yards 500

See also Street Finder maps
11, 12, 15, 16

◄ The Rose Center for Earth and Space, part of the American Museum of Natural History   For keys to map symbols see back flap

Street by Street: Lincoln Center

Lincoln Center was conceived when both the Metropolitan Opera House and the New York Philharmonic required homes, and a large tract on Manhattan's west side was in dire need of revitalization. The notion of a single complex where different performing arts could exist side by side seems natural today, but in the 1950s it was considered both daring and risky. Today Lincoln Center has proved itself by drawing audiences of five million each year. Proximity to its halls prompts both performers and arts lovers to live nearby.

❷ ★ Lincoln Center for the Performing Arts
Dance, music, and theater come together in this fine contemporary complex. It is also a great place to sit around the fountain and people-watch.

❺ Lincoln Center Theater
The Vivian Beaumont and the Mitzi E. Newhouse theaters are both housed in this building.

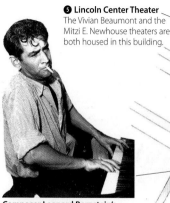

Composer Leonard Bernstein's famous musical *West Side Story*, which was based on the Romeo and Juliet theme, was set in the impoverished neighborhood that was razed to make room for Lincoln Center. Bernstein was later instrumental in setting up the large music complex.

The Guggenheim Bandshell in Damrosch Park is the site of free concerts.

❸ The New York State Theater
This is the home of the New York City Ballet, as well as an opera company.

❹ Metropolitan Opera House
Lincoln Center's focus is the Opera House. The café at the top of the lobby offers wonderful plaza views.

The College Board Building is an Art Deco delight that now houses condominiums and the administrative offices of the College Board, developers of the college entrance exam.

American Folk Art Museum
Quilting, pottery, and furniture are some of the arts displayed here.

Early American quilt

❽ ★ Hotel des Artistes
Artists Isadora Duncan, Noël Coward, and Norman Rockwell once lived here.

James Dean once lived in a one-room apartment on the top floor at 19 West 68th Street.

Locator Map
See Manhattan Map pp16–17

Key

— Suggested route

| 0 meters | 100 |
| 0 yards | 100 |

To 72nd Street subway
(4 blocks)

W 67TH STREET

W 65TH STREETT

CENTRAL PARK WEST

An ABC-TV sound stage for soap operas is housed in this castle-like building, formerly an armory.

55 Central Park West is the Art Deco apartment building that featured in the film *Ghostbusters*.

The Society for Ethical Culture was one of the city's first Art Nouveau buildings. It also houses a school.

To 59th Street subway
(2 blocks)

Central Park West
is home to many celebrities, who like the privacy of its exclusive apartments.

❶ Century Apartments
The Century's twin towers are visible from the park, making it a New York landmark.

The San Remo, a twin-towered apartment house designed by Emery Roth

❶ Twin Towers of Central Park West

Map 12 D1, 12 D2, 16 D3, 16 D5. Ⓜ 59th St-Columbus Circle, 72nd St, 81St, 86th St. **Open** to the public.

A familiar landmark on the New York skyline, the four twin-towered apartment houses on Central Park West were built between 1929 and 1931, before the Great Depression halted all luxury construction. They are among the most sought-after residences in New York.

Admired today for their grace and architectural detail, they were designed in response to a city planning law allowing taller apartments if set-backs and towers were used.

Emery Roth designed the San Remo (145 CPW), whose tenants have included Dustin Hoffman, Paul Simon, and Diane Keaton. Turned down by the residents' committee, Madonna went to live close by at 1 West 64th Street. The towers of the Eldorado (300 CPW), also by Roth, were home to

Groucho Marx, Marilyn Monroe, and Richard Dreyfuss. The Majestic (115 CPW) and the Century (25 CPW) are both sleek classics by Art Deco designer Irwin S. Chanin.

❷ Lincoln Center for the Performing Arts

Map 11 C2. **Tel** (212) 546-2656. Ⓜ 66th St. ♿ 🅿 (212) 875-5350. 🖉 🎧 *See Entertainment pp342–3.* 🌐 lincolncenter.org

In May 1959, President Eisenhower traveled to New York to turn a shovelful of earth, Leonard Bernstein lifted his baton, the New York Philharmonic and the Juilliard Choir broke into the Hallelujah Chorus – and the city's major cultural center was born. It soon covered 15 acres (6 ha) on the site of the slums that had been the setting for Bernstein's classic musical *West Side Story*. The plaza fountain is by Philip Johnson, and the sculpture, *Reclining Figure*, is by Henry Moore.

Jazz at the Lincoln Center has developed a state-of-the-art facility dedicated to a wide range of jazz performances. It forms part of a major complex at Columbus Circle *(see p217).*

❸ New York State Theater

Lincoln Center. **Map** 11 D2. **Tel** (212) 870-5570. Ⓜ 66th St. ♿ 🎧 🖉 🎧 *See Entertainment pp338–9.* 🌐 nycballet.com

The home base for the highly acclaimed New York City Ballet and the New York City Opera, a troupe devoted to presenting opera at popular prices, is a Philip Johnson design. It was inaugurated in 1964.

Gargantuan white marble sculptures by Elie Nadelman dominate the vast four-story foyer. The theater seats 2,800 people. Because of its rhinestone lights and chandeliers both inside and out, some have described the theater as "a little jewel box."

❹ Metropolitan Opera House

Lincoln Center. **Map** 11 D2. **Tel** (212) 362-6000. Ⓜ 66th St. ♿ 🎧 🖉 🎧 *See Entertainment pp342–3.* 🌐 metopera.org 🌐 abt.org

Home to the Metropolitan Opera Company and the American Ballet Theater, "the Met" is the most spectacular of Lincoln Center's buildings. Five great arched windows offer views of the opulent foyer and two murals by Marc Chagall. (You can't see them in the mornings when they are protected from

Central plaza at Lincoln Center

the sun.) Inside there are curved white marble stairs, red carpeting, and exquisite starburst crystal chandeliers that are raised to the ceiling just before each performance. All the greats have sung here, including Maria Callas, Jessye Norman, and Luciano Pavarotti. First nights are glittering, star-studded occasions.

The Guggenheim Bandshell, in Damrosch Park next to the Met, is a popular concert site. The high point of the season is the Lincoln Center Out-of-Doors Festival, which takes place in August and features global music, dance, and spoken-word performances.

Concert at Guggenheim Bandshell, Damrosh Park, near the Met

❺ Lincoln Center Theater

Lincoln Center. **Map** 11 C2. **Tel** (212) 362-7600 (Beaumont and Newhouse), (212) 870-1630 (Library). 800-432 7250 (tickets). Ⓜ 66th St. ♿ 🎫 🖊 🏛 *See Entertainment pp342–3.* Ⓦ lct.org

Two theaters make up this innovative complex, where eclectic and often experimental drama is presented.

The theaters are the 1,000-seat Vivian Beaumont and the more intimate 280-seat Mitzi E. Newhouse. Works by some of New York's best modern playwrights have featured at the Beaumont. Among these was Arthur Miller's *After the Fall*, the theater's inaugural performance in 1962.

The size of the Newhouse suits workshop-style plays, but it can still make the news with theatrical gems such as Robin Williams and Steve Martin in a

production of Samuel Beckett's *Waiting for Godot*. The complex also houses the New York Public Library for the Performing Arts, which has exhibits including audio cylinders of early Met performances and original scores and playbills.

❻ Avery Fisher Hall

Lincoln Center. **Map** 11 C2. **Tel** (212) 875-5030. Ⓜ 66th St. ♿ 🎫 🖊 🏛 *See Entertainment pp342–3.* Ⓦ nyphil.org

Located at the northern end of the Lincoln Center Plaza, Avery Fisher Hall is home to America's oldest orchestra, the New York Philharmonic. It also provides a stage for some of the Lincoln Center's own performers, and the Mostly Mozart Festival.

When the venue opened in 1962 as the Philharmonic Hall, critics initially complained about the acoustics. Several structural modifications, however, have rendered the hall an acoustic gem, comparing favorably with other great classical concert halls around the world. For a small fee, the public can attend rehearsals on Thursday mornings in the 2,738-seat auditorium.

❼ Columbus Circle

Columbus Circle, New York. **Map** 12 D3. Ⓜ 59th St. Concerts (212) 258-9800. Ⓦ jazzatlincolncenter.org

Presiding over this urban plaza at the corner of Central Park is a marble statue of explorer Christopher Columbus, perched on top of a tall granite column in the center of a fountain and plantings. The statue is one of the few remaining original features in this circle – it has become one of the largest building projects in New York's history.

Multi-use skyscrapers have been erected, attracting national and international businesses. Global

media company Time Warner has its headquarters in an 80-story skyscraper. The 2.8 million sq ft (260,000 sq m) building provides a retail, entertainment, and restaurant facility. Facilities include shops such as Hugo Boss, Williams-Sonoma, Borders Books, and Whole Foods Market; dining at Per Se and Masa; and a Mandarin Oriental hotel.

The Time Warner Center is also home to Jazz at the Lincoln Center. The two venues here – The Frederic P. Rose Concert Hall and The Allen Room – together with a jazz club and education center, comprise the world's first performing arts facility dedicated to jazz.

Other notable buildings in Columbus Circle include Hearst House, designed by British architect Norman Foster, Trump International Hotel, the Maine Monument, and the eye-catching Museum of Arts and Design, formerly the American Craft Museum.

❽ Hotel des Artistes

1 W 67th St. **Map** 12 D2. **Tel** (212) 877-3500 (café). Ⓜ 72nd St.

Built in 1918 by George Mort Pollard, these two-story apartments were intended to be working artists' studios, but they have attracted a variety of interesting tenants, including Alexander Woollcott, Norman Rockwell, Isadora Duncan, Rudolph Valentino, and Noël Coward. The base of the building's facade is decorated with figures of artists.

Decorative figure on the Hotel des Artistes

⑪ American Museum of Natural History

This is one of the world's largest natural history museums. Since the original building opened in 1877, the complex has grown to cover four city blocks, and today holds more than 30 million specimens and artifacts. The most popular areas are the dinosaurs and the Milstein Hall of Ocean Life. The Rose Center for Earth and Space includes the Hayden Planetarium *(see p220)*.

The facade on 77th Street

Gallery Guide

The museum houses 46 exhibition halls, research laboratories, and a library, spread over 25 interconnected buildings. Enter at Central Park West onto the second floor to view the Barosaurus exhibit, African, Asian, Central and South American peoples and animals. First floor exhibits include ocean life, meteors, minerals and gems, and the Hall of Biodiversity. North American Indians, birds, and reptiles occupy the third floor. Dinosaurs, fossil fishes, and early mammals are on the fourth floor.

★ Star of India
This 563-carat gem is the world's largest blue star sapphire. Found in Sri Lanka, it was given to the museum by J. P. Morgan in 1900.

★ Blue Whale
The blue whale is the largest animal, living or extinct. Its weight can exceed 100 tons. This replica is based on a female captured off South America in 1925.

★ Great Canoe
This 63-ft (19.2-m) seafaring war canoe from the Pacific Northwest was carved from the trunk of a single cedar. It stands in the Grand Gallery.

Entrance on W. 77th St

Dinosaurs

Fourth floor

Third floor

Second floor

Rose Center for Earth and Space
(see p218)

First floor

Central Park West entrance

VISITORS' CHECKLIST

Practical Information
Central Park West at 79th St.
Map 16 D5.
Tel (212) 769-5100.
Open 10am–5:45pm daily.
Closed Thanksgiving, 25 Dec.
w amnh.org

Transport
M B, C to 81st St. M7, M10, M11, M79, M104.

Komodo Dragons
The largest living lizards, which can grow to 10 ft (3 m), live on Komodo and other Indonesian islands.

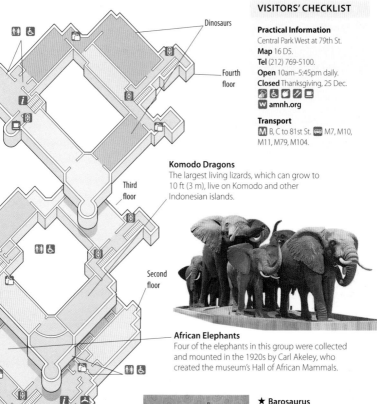

African Elephants
Four of the elephants in this group were collected and mounted in the 1920s by Carl Akeley, who created the museum's Hall of African Mammals.

★ Barosaurus
This exhibit shows a mother Barosaurus rearing up to protect her baby from an attacking predator. All three skeletons were cast from original fossils. The plant-eating dinosaur lived 140 million years ago.

Key to Floorplan

- Dinosaurs and other fossil vertebrates
- Birds
- Fishes
- Mammals
- Meteorites, minerals, and gems
- Human cultures
- Human origins
- Amphibians and reptiles
- Environment and ecology
- Rose Center for Earth and Space
- Special exhibitions
- Non-exhibition space

Giant Sequoia
Sequoias are among the world's longest-lived plants. This section has 1,342 annual rings and measures more than 16 ft (4.8 m) across.

❾ The Dakota

1 W 72nd St. **Map** 12 D1. Ⓜ 72nd St. **Closed** to the public.

The name and style reflect the fact that this apartment building was truly "way out West" when Henry J. Hardenbergh, the architect responsible for the Plaza Hotel, designed it in 1880–84. It was New York's first luxury apartment house and was originally surrounded by squatters' shacks and wandering farm animals. Commissioned by Edward S. Clark, heir to the Singer sewing machine fortune, it is one of the city's most prestigious addresses.

The Dakota's 65 luxurious apartments have had many famous owners, including Judy Garland, Lauren Bacall, Leonard Bernstein, and Boris Karloff, whose ghost is said to haunt the place. It was the setting for the film *Rosemary's Baby*, and the site of the tragic murder of former Beatle John Lennon. His widow, Yoko Ono, still lives here.

Carved Indian head over the entrance to the Dakota

❿ New York Historical Society

170 Central Park West. **Map** 16 D5. **Tel** (212) 873-3400. Ⓜ 81st St. Galleries **Open** 10am–6pm Tue–Sat (to 8pm Fri), 11am–5pm Sun. 📷 Library **Open** 9am–3pm Tue–Fri, 10am–1pm Sat (varies by season). **Closed** public hols. ✉ ♿ 📷 💻 📷 ⓦ nyhistory.org

Founded in 1804, this society houses a distinguished research library and the city's oldest museum. Its collections include historical material relating to

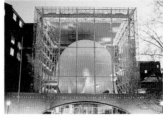

The Rose Center for Earth and Space

slavery and the Civil War, an outstanding collection of 18th-century newspapers, all 435 watercolors of Audubon's *Birds of America*, and the world's largest collection of Tiffany lamps and glasswork. There are also fine displays of American furniture and silver.

⓫ American Museum of Natural History

See pp218–19.

⓬ Rose Center for Earth and Space

Central Park West at 81st St. **Map** 16 D4. **Tel** (212) 769-5100. Ⓜ 81st St. **Open** 10am–5:45pm daily. IMAX show: every hour on the half-hour 10:30am–4:30pm; Space show: every half-hour 10:30am–4:30pm (from 11am Wed, to 5pm Sat & Sun). ⓦ amnh.org/rose

On the northern side of the American Museum of Natural History *(see pp218–19)* is the spectacular Rose Center for Earth and Space. Housed within an 87-ft (26-m) sphere, the center contains the technologically advanced Space Theater, the Cosmic Pathway, a 350-ft (107-m) spiral ramp with a timeline chronicling 13 billion years of evolution; and the Big Bang Theater, where the origins of the universe are explained.

The Hall of Planet Earth, centered around rock samples and using state-of-the-art computer and video displays explaining how the Earth works, explores our geologic history. Exhibits in the Hall of the Universe present the

discoveries of modern astrophysics. Four zones have hands-on interactive exhibits. Seen from the street at night, the Rose Center is breathtaking; the exhibits inside prove that, as Carl Sagan said, "We are starstuff."

⓭ Pomander Walk

261–7 W 94th St. **Map** 15 C2. Ⓜ 96th St.

Look through the gate for a delightful surprise – a double row of tiny town houses built in 1921 to look like the London mews setting of a popular play of the same name. It was much favored as a home by movie actors, including Rosalind Russell, Humphrey Bogart, and the Gish sisters.

Facade of a house on Pomander Walk

⓮ Riverside Drive and Park

Map 15 B1–B5, 20 D1–D5. Ⓜ 79th St, 86th St, 96th St.

Riverside Drive is one of the city's most attractive streets – broad, with shaded and lovely views of the Hudson River. It is lined with the opulent original town houses, as well as more modern apartment buildings. At 40–46, 74–77, 81–89, and 105–107 Riverside Drive are houses designed in the late 19th century by local architect Clarence F. True. The curved gables, bays, and arched windows seem to suit the curves of the road and the flow of the river.

The bizarrely named Cliff Dwellers' Apartments at 243 (between 96th and 97th streets) is a 1914 building with a frieze showing early Arizona cliff dwellers, complete with masks, buffalo skulls, mountain lions, and rattlesnakes.

Riverside Park was designed by Frederick Law Olmsted in 1880. He also laid out Central Park (see pp206–9).

Soldiers' and Sailors' monument in Riverside Park

⓯ Children's Museum of Manhattan

212 W 83rd St. **Map** 15 C4. **Tel** (212) 721-1223. Ⓜ 79th St, 81st St, 86th St. **Open** 10am–5pm Tue–Sun (to 7pm Sat). **Closed** Jan 1, Thanksgiving, Dec 25. ♨ ♿ ♫ Ⓦ **cmom.org**

This particularly imaginative participatory museum was founded in 1973 and is based on the premise that children learn best through play. The exhibit called "Eat, Sleep, Play" links food, the digestive system, and healthy living, while in "Block Party" children can build castles, towns, and bridges out of wooden blocks. Kids also delight in the exhibits on cartoon favorites Curious George and Dora the Explorer and her adventurous cousin Diego, where they learn about travel and cultures around the world.

Children's Museum entrance

On weekends and holidays there are guest performers, from puppeteers to storytellers, in the 150-seat theater. There is also a gallery for free events, like "Pajama Day," as well as lively, theme-based tours of the museum.

⓰ The Ansonia

2109 Broadway. **Map** 15 C5. Ⓜ 72nd St. **Closed** to the public.

This Beaux Arts gem was built in 1899 by William Earl Dodge Stokes, heir to the Phelps Dodge Company fortune, who brought French architect Paul E.M. Duboy to design a building to rival the Dakota. The hotel was converted to a condominium in 1992. The most prominent features are the round corner tower and the two-story mansard roof adorned with single and double dormers. The building had a roof garden (complete with Dodge's menagerie: ducks, chickens, and a tame bear) and two swimming pools.

Distinctive rounded turret of the Ansonia Hotel

The hotel's thick, sound-muffling walls soon made it a favorite with the musical stars of yesteryear. Florenz Ziegfeld, Arturo Toscanini, Enrico Caruso, Igor Stravinsky, and Lily Pons were once regular guests there.

Balcony on the Dorilton, supported by groaning figures

⓱ The Dorilton

171 W 71st St. **Map** 11 C1. Ⓜ 72nd St. **Closed** to the public.

Opulent detail and an impressive high mansard roof adorn this apartment house. On the West 71st Street side of the building is a nine-story-high gateway. To the modern eye, the Dorilton is gloriously elaborate, but when it was first built in 1902 it provoked this reaction, reported by the Architectural Record: "The sight of it makes strong men swear and weak women shrink affrighted."

What would the critics have made of the Alexandria Condominium, at 135 West 70th Street, just a block away? Built in 1927 as the Pythian Temple, its current name stems from the lavish Egyptian-style motifs that adorned this former Masonic lodge. Many were stripped away when the building was converted to a condominium, but you can still see what the polychrome designs were like. There are lotus leaves, hieroglyphics, ornately carved columns, mythical beasts, and, in majestic splendor on the roof, two seated pharaohs.

MORNINGSIDE HEIGHTS AND HARLEM

Morningside Heights, near the Hudson River, is home to Columbia University and two of the city's finest churches. Farther east is Hamilton Heights, situated on the border of Harlem, America's most famous black community. One way to see the district's highlights, which are spread over a large area, is by taking one of the tours offered, including a Sunday morning tour. Many tours start in Hamilton Heights, move east to the St. Nicholas Historic District, stop to enjoy the gospel choir at the Abyssinian Baptist Church, and end with a Southern-style brunch at Sylvia's, Harlem's best-known restaurant.

Sights at a Glance

Historic Streets and Buildings
1. Columbia University
2. St. Paul's Chapel
3. Low Library
6. Grant's Tomb
7. City College of the City University of New York
8. Hamilton Grange National Memorial
9. Hamilton Heights Historic District
10. St. Nicholas Historic District

Museums and Galleries
12. Schomburg Center for Research into Black Culture
16. Studio Museum in Harlem
17. Mount Morris Historic District
19. Museo del Barrio

Famous Theaters
13. Harlem YMCA
15. Apollo Theater

Churches
4. Cathedral of St. John the Divine pp228–9
5. Riverside Church
11. Abyssinian Baptist Church

Parks and Squares
18. Marcus Garvey Park

Landmark Restaurants
14. Sylvia's

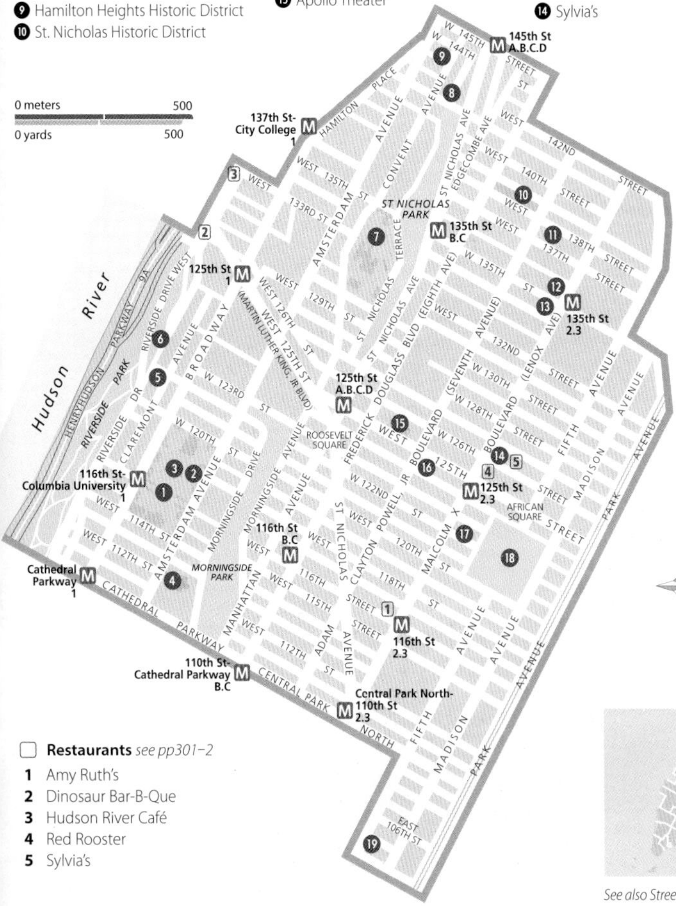

Restaurants see pp301–2
1. Amy Ruth's
2. Dinosaur Bar-B-Que
3. Hudson River Café
4. Red Rooster
5. Sylvia's

See also Street Finder maps 19–21

◄ Harlem's most famous landmark, the Apollo Theater

For keys to map symbols see back flap

Street by Street: Columbia University

A great university is as much spirit as buildings. After admiring the architecture, linger awhile on Columbia's central quadrangle in front of the Low Library, where you will see the jeans-clad future leaders of America meeting and mingling between classes. Across from the campus on both Broadway and Amsterdam Avenue are the coffeehouses and cafés where students engage in lengthy philosophical arguments, debate the topics of the day or simply unwind.

ALMA MATER

Alma Mater was sculpted by Daniel Chester French in 1903 and survived a bomb blast in the 1968 student demonstrations.

116th St/ Columbia University subway (line 1)

Ⓜ

BROADWAY

The School of Journalism is one of Columbia's many McKim, Mead & White buildings. Founded in 1912 by publisher Joseph Pulitzer, it is the home of the Pulitzer Prize awarded for the best in letters and music.

114TH ST

❸ Low Library
With its imposing facade and high dome, the library dominates the main quadrangle. McKim, Mead & White designed it in 1895–97.

Butler Library is Columbia's main library.

AMSTERDAM AVENUE

W 113TH

❶ ★ Central Quadrangle
Columbia's first buildings were designed by McKim, Mead & White and built around a central quadrangle. This view looks across the quad toward Butler Library.

❷ St. Paul's Chapel
Designed by the architects Howells & Stokes in 1907, this church is known for its fine woodwork and magnificent vaulted interior. It is full of light and has fine acoustics.

The Sherman Fairchild Center was built in 1977 to house the university's life sciences departments.

Locator Map
See Manhattan Map pp16–17

Key

— Suggested route

0 meters	500
0 yards	500

Student demonstrations put Columbia University in the news in 1968. The demonstrations were sparked by the university's plan to build a gymnasium in nearby Morningside Park. The protests forced the university to build elsewhere.

W 116TH ST

MORNINGSIDE DRIVE

The Église de Notre Dame was built for a French-speaking congregation. Behind the altar is a replica of the grotto at Lourdes, France, the gift of a woman who believed her son was healed there.

Carved stonework decorates the facade of the Cathedral.

❹ ★ Cathedral of St. John the Divine
If this Neo-Gothic cathedral is ever finished, it will be the largest in the world. Although one third of the structure has not yet been built, it can hold 10,000 parishioners.

Alma Mater statue at the Low Library, Columbia University

❶ Columbia University

Main entrance at W 116th St and Broadway. **Map** 20 E3. **Tel** (212) 854-1754. Ⓜ 116th St-Columbia University. Visitors' Center: **Open** 9am–5pm Mon–Fri. 📷 1pm Mon–Fri. Ⓦ columbia.edu

This is the third location of one of America's oldest universities. Founded in 1754 as King's College, it was first situated close to where the World Trade Center stood.

In 1814, when a move uptown was proposed, the university approached the authorities for funding but was instead given a plot of land valued at $75,000, on which to build a new home. The university never built on the land itself, but leased it out and spent the years from 1857 to 1897 in buildings nearby. It finally sold the plot in 1985 to the leaseholders, Rockefeller Center Inc., for $400 million.

The present campus was begun in 1897 on the site of the Bloomingdale Insane Asylum.

Charles McKim, the architect, placed the university on a terrace, serenely above street level. Its spacious lawns and plazas still create a sense of contrast in the busy city.

Columbia is noted for its law, medicine, and journalism schools. Its distinguished faculty and alumni, past and present, include over 50 Nobel laureates. Famous alumni include Isaac Asimov, J.D. Salinger, James Cagney, and Joan Rivers. Across the street is the affiliated Barnard College, a highly selective liberal arts college for women.

Interior brick vaulting of St. Paul's Chapel dome

❷ St. Paul's Chapel

Columbia University. **Map** 20 E3. **Tel** (212) 854-1487, for concert info. Ⓜ 116th St-Columbia Univ. **Open** 10am–11pm Mon–Sat (term time), 10am–4pm (breaks). 🕙 Sun. ♿

Columbia's most outstanding building, built in 1904, is a mix of Italian Renaissance, Byzantine, and Gothic. The interior Guastavino vaulting is of intricate patterns of aged red brick; the whole chapel is bathed in light from above.

The free organ concerts are an exceptionally fine way to appreciate the beauty and acoustics of this church. The Aeolian-Skinner pipe organ is renowned for its fine tone.

Facade of St. Paul's Chapel

❸ Low Library

Columbia University. **Map** 20 E3. Ⓜ 116th St-Columbia University.

A Classical, columned building atop three flights of stone stairs, the library was donated by Seth Low, a former mayor and college president. The statue in front of it, *Alma Mater* by Daniel Chester French, became familiar as the backdrop to the many 1968 anti-Vietnam War student demonstrations. The building is now used as offices, and its rotunda for a variety of academic and ceremonial purposes. The books were moved in 1932 to the Butler Library, across the quadrangle. The university's library collections total more than six million volumes.

❹ Cathedral of St. John the Divine

See pp228–9.

❺ Riverside Church

490 Riverside Dr at 122nd St. **Map** 20 D2. **Tel** (212) 870-6700. Ⓜ 116th St-Columbia Univ. **Open** 7am–10pm daily. 🕙 10:45am Sun. ♿ 📷 Carillon bell concerts; (212) 870-6784; 10:30am, 12:30pm & 3pm Sun. Theater; (212) 870-6784. 🖥 Ⓦ theriversidechurchny.org

A 21-story steel frame with a Gothic exterior, the church design was inspired by the cathedral at Chartres. It was lavishly funded by John D. Rockefeller, Jr., in 1930. The Laura Spelman Rockefeller Memorial Carillon (in honor of

Columbia University's main courtyard and the Low Library

Rockefeller's mother) is the largest in the world, with 74 bells. The 20-ton Bourdon, or hour bell, is the largest and heaviest tuned carillon bell ever cast. The organ, with its 22,000 pipes, is among the largest in the world.

At the rear of the second gallery is a figure by Jacob Epstein, *Christ in Majesty*, cast in plaster and covered in gold leaf. Another Epstein statue, *Madonna and Child*, stands in the court next to the cloister. The panels of the chancel screen honor eight men and women whose lives have exemplified the teachings of Christ. They range from Socrates and Michelangelo to Florence Nightingale and Booker T. Washington.

For quiet reflection, enter the small, secluded Christ Chapel, patterned after an 11th-century Romanesque church in France.

The church is particularly welcoming during the holiday season, as the public is invited to a host of festive activities such as candlelight caroling.

Mosaic mural in Grant's Tomb showing Grant (right) and Robert E. Lee

❻ Grant's Tomb

W 122nd St and Riverside Dr.
Map 20 D2. **Tel** (212) 666-1640.
Ⓜ 116th St-Columbia Univ.
M5. **Open** 9am–5pm Thu–Mon.
Closed in bad weather (call ahead),
Jan 1, Thanksgiving, Dec 25.
Ⓦ nps.gov/gegr

This grandiose monument honors America's 18th president, Ulysses S. Grant, the commanding general of the Union forces in the Civil War.

The mausoleum contains the coffins of General Grant and his wife, in accordance with the president's last wish that they be buried together. After Grant's death in 1885, more than 90,000 Americans contributed $600,000 to build the sepulcher, which was inspired by Mausoleus's tomb at Halicarnassus, one of the Seven Wonders of the Ancient World.

General Grant on a Civil War campaign

The tomb was dedicated on what would have been Grant's 75th birthday, April 27, 1897. The parade of 50,000 people, along with a flotilla of 10 American and 5 European warships, took more than seven hours to pass in review.

The interior was inspired by Napoleon's tomb at Les Invalides in Paris. Each sarcophagus weighs 8.5 tons. Two exhibit rooms feature displays on Grant's personal life and his presidential and military career. Surrounding the north and east sides of the building are 17 sinuously curved mosaic benches that seem totally out of keeping with the formal architecture of the tomb. They were designed in the early 1970s by the Chilean-born Brooklyn artist Pedro Silva and were built by 1,200 local volunteers, who worked under his supervision. The benches were inspired by the work of Spanish architect Antonio Gaudi in Barcelona. The mosaics depict subjects ranging from the Inuit to New York taxis to Donald Duck.

A short walk north of Grant's Tomb is another monument. An unadorned urn on a pedestal marks the resting place of a young child who fell from the riverbank and drowned. His grieving father placed a marker that simply reads: "Erected to the memory of an amiable child, St. Clair Pollock, died 15 July 1797 in his fifth year of his age."

The 21-story Riverside Church, from the north

❹ Cathedral of St. John the Divine

Started in 1892 and still only two-thirds finished, this will be the largest cathedral in the world. The interior is over 600 ft (180 m) long and 146 ft (45 m) wide. It was originally designed in Romanesque style by Heins and LaFarge; Ralph Adams Cram took over the project in 1911, devising a Gothic nave and west front. Medieval construction methods, such as stone-on-stone supporting buttresses, continue to be used to complete the cathedral, which also serves as a venue for theater, music, and avant-garde art.

★ **Peace Fountain**
The sculpture is the creation of Greg Wyatt and represents nature in its many forms. It stands within a granite basin on the Great Lawn, south of the cathedral.

Nave
Rising to a height of over 100 ft (30 m), the piers of the nave are topped by graceful stone arches.

★ **West Front Entrance**
The portals of the cathedral's west front are adorned with many fine stone carvings. Some are recreations of medieval religious sculpture, but others have modern themes. This apocalyptic vision of New York's skyline, by local stonemason Joe Kincannon, seems almost to predict the events of September 11, 2001 *(see p56)*.

KEY

① Pulpit

② **The Bishop's Chair** is a copy from the Henry VII chapel in Westminster Abbey.

★ **Rose Window**
Completed in 1933, the stylized motif of the Great Rose is symbolic of the many facets of the Christian Church.

Baptistry
The Gothic Baptistry has Italian, French, and Spanish influences.

Choir
Each of the choir's columns is 55 ft (17 m) tall and made of polished gray granite.

St. Ambrose Chapel
Named after a 4th-century Italian bishop, the chapel is decorated with Renaissance-style ironwork.

The Finished Design

The north and south transepts, the crossing tower, and the west towers have yet to be finished. When the money to fund their construction is raised, the proposed design will still take at least another 50 years to complete.

Crossing tower

West towers

South transept

★ **Bay Altars**
The bay altar windows are devoted to human endeavor. The sports window shows feats of skill and strength.

1823 Cathedral planned for Washington Square	1891 Site chosen and designated Cathedral Parkway	1909 Pulpit designed by Henry Vaughan	2001 Major fire destroys interior and roof of north transept	2008 Cathedral reopens after seven-year closure for renovations
		1911 Cram design replaces earlier ones		

1800	**1850**	**1900**	**1950**	**2000**	**2050**

1873 Charter granted		1916 Ground broken for nave	1941 Work halted by World War II and does not resume until 1978	1978–89 Third phase of building. Stonemasons' Yard opened and south tower heightened
1888 Competition to design cathedral won by Heins & LaFarge	1892 December 27 (St. John's Day), cornerstone laid			

❼ City College of the City University of New York

Main entrance at W 138th St and Convent Ave. **Map** 19 A2. **Tel** (212) 650-7000. Ⓜ 137th St-City College. Ⓦ ccny.cuny.edu

Set high on a hill adjoining Hamilton Heights, the original Gothic quadrangle of this college, built between 1903 and 1907, is very impressive. The material used for the buildings is Manhattan schist, a stone that had been excavated in building the IRT subway. Later, contemporary buildings were added to the school, which enrolls nearly 15,000 students.

Once free to all residents of New York, City College still offers an education at low tuition rates. Three-quarters of the students are from minority groups, and a large number of them are the first in their families to attend college.

Shepard Archway at City College of the City University of New York

❽ Hamilton Grange National Memorial

Saint Nicholas Park, 414 W 141st St. **Map** 19 A1. **Tel** (212) 283-5154. Ⓜ 137th St-City College. **Open** 9am–5pm Wed–Sun. **Closed** Thanksgiving & Dec 25. 🎧 hourly. Ⓦ nps.gov/hagr

Squeezed between a church and apartments is the 1802 country home of Alexander Hamilton. He was one of the architects of the federal government system, First Secretary of the treasury and founder of the National Bank. His face is on the $10 bill.

Statue of Alexander Hamilton at Hamilton Grange

Hamilton lived in The Grange for the last two years of his life. He was killed in a duel with political rival Aaron Burr in 1804.

In 1889, St. Luke's Episcopal Church acquired the site, and the building was moved four blocks west. A second relocation in 2006–2011 moved the building to its current site in St. Nicholas Park.

❾ Hamilton Heights Historic District

W 141st–W 145th St and Convent Ave. **Map** 19 A1. Ⓜ 137th St- City College.

Originally this was a setting for the impressive country estates of the wealthy. Also known as Harlem Heights, it was developed during the 1880s following the extension of the El line *(see p28)* into the neighborhood. The privacy of the enclave, on a high hill above Harlem, made it a very desirable location.

The section of Hamilton Heights known as Sugar Hill was highly favored by Harlem's elite – US Supreme Court Justice Thurgood Marshall, notable jazz musicians Count Basie, Duke Ellington, wand

Cab Calloway, and world champion boxer Sugar Ray Robinson have all lived there.

The handsome three- and four story stone row houses were built between 1886 and 1906 mixing Flemish, Romanesque and Tudor influences. In fine condition, many are used as residences by the faculty of City College.

Row houses in Hamilton Heights

❿ St. Nicholas Historic District

202–250 W 138th & W 139th St. **Map** 19 B2. Ⓜ 135th St (B, C).

A startling contrast to the rundown surroundings, the two blocks here, known as the King Model Houses, were built in 1891 when Harlem was considered a neighborhood for New York's gentry. They till comprise one of the city's most distinctive examples of row townhouses.

The developer, David King, chose three leading architects, who succeeded in blending their different styles to create a harmonious whole. The most famous of these was the firm

Houses in St. Nicholas district

Adam Clayton Powell, Jr. addressing a civil rights campaign

of McKim, Mead & White, designers of the Pierpont Morgan Library *(see pp166–7)* and Villard Houses *(see p178)*, who were responsible for the northernmost row of solid brick Renaissance palaces. Their homes featured ground floor entrances rather than the typical New York brownstone stoops. Also, the elaborate parlor floors have ornate wrought-iron balconies below, as well as carved decorative medallions above their windows.

The Georgian buildings designed by Price and Luce are built of buff brick with white stone trim. James Brown Lord's section of buildings, also Georgian in architectural style, feels much closer to Victorian, with outstanding red-brick facades and bases constructed of brownstone.

Successful blacks were attracted here in the 1920s and 1930s, giving it the nickname Strivers' Row. Among them were celebrated musicians W. C. Handy and Eubie Blake.

⑩ Abyssinian Baptist Church

132 W 138th St. **Map** 19 C2. **Tel** (212) 862-7474. Ⓜ 135th St (B, C, 2, 3). ⛪ 11am Sun. Groups of 10 or more need reservations. Ⓦ abyssinian.org

Founded in 1808, New York's oldest black church became famous through its charismatic pastor Adam Clayton Powell, Jr. (1908–72), a congressman

and civil rights leader. Under his leadership it became the most powerful black church in America. A room in the church houses memorabilia from his life.

The church, a fine 1923 Gothic building, welcomes properly dressed visitors to Sunday services and to hear its superb gospel choir.

⑫ Schomburg Center for Research into Black Culture

515 Malcolm X Blvd. **Map** 19 C2. Ⓜ 135th St (2, 3). **Tel** (212) 491-2200. **Open** noon–8pm Tue–Thu, 10am–6pm Fri & Sat. **Closed** public hols. 📷 (212) 491-2207. ♿ 📷 Ⓦ schomburgcenter.org

Housed in a sleek contemporary complex opened in 1991, this is the largest research center of black and African culture in the United States. The immense collection was assembled by the late Arthur Schomburg, a black man of Puerto Rican descent, who was told by a teacher that there was no such thing as "black history." The Carnegie Corporation bought

Kurt Weill, Elmer Rice, and Langston Hughes at the Schomburg Center

the collection in 1926 and gave it to the New York Public Library; Schomburg was made curator in 1932.

The library was the unofficial meeting place for writers involved in what later became known as the Harlem Renaissance of the 1920s, including Langston Hughes, W.E.B. Du Bois, and Zora Neale Hurston. It also hosted many poetry readings and literary gatherings.

The Schomburg Library has excellent facilities for conserving and making available the archive's treasures, which include rare books, photos, movies, art, and recordings. The library was planned and designed to double as a cultural center and includes a theater and two art galleries, which feature changing shows of art and photography.

Sociologist W. E. B. Du Bois

⑬ Harlem YMCA

180 W 135th St. **Map** 19 C3. **Tel** (212) 281-4100. Ⓜ 135th St (2, 3).

Paul Robeson and many others made their first stage appearances here in the early 1920s. The Krigwa Players, organized by W.E.B. Du Bois in the basement in 1928, was founded to counter the derogatory images of blacks often presented in Broadway reviews of the time. The "Y" also provided temporary lodgings for some notable new arrivals in Harlem, including writer Ralph Ellison.

Gospel singers performing at Sylvia's during Sunday brunch

⑭ Sylvia's

328 Lenox Ave. **Map** 21 B1. **Tel** (212) 996-0660. **Ⓜ** 125th St (2, 3). **Ⓦ** sylviassoulfood.com

Harlem's best-known soul food restaurant serves up Southern-fried or smothered chicken, spicy ribs, black-eyed peas, collard greens, candied yams, sweet potato pie, and other comforting Southern delicacies. Sunday brunch here is served to the accompaniment of Gospel singers.

Take some time to explore the market at the corner of 125th Street and Lenox Avenue (opposite Sylvia's), extending for a block or more in either direction. Vendors sell African clothing, jewelry, and art of varying quality.

⑮ Apollo Theater

253 W 125th St. **Map** 21 A1. **Tel** (212) 531-5300 **Ⓜ** 125th St. **Open** at showtimes. **Ⓖ** Groups only. **Ⓐ Ⓐ** See Entertainment p345. **Ⓦ** apollotheater.com

The Apollo opened in 1913 as a whites-only opera house. Its great fame came when Frank Schiffman, a white entrepreneur, took over in 1934. He then opened the theater to all races and turned it into Harlem's best-known showcase, with great artists such as Bessie Smith, Billie Holiday, Duke Ellington, and Dinah Washington.

Wednesday Amateur Nights, (begun in 1935) with winners determined by audience applause, were famous, and there was a long waiting list for performers. These amateur nights launched the careers of Sarah Vaughan, Pearl Bailey, James Brown, and Gladys Knight, among others, and they still attract hopefuls.

Apollo Theater

The Apollo was *the* place during the swing band era; following World War II, a new generation of musicians, such as Charlie "Bird" Parker, Dizzy Gillespie, Thelonius Monk, and Aretha Franklin, continued the tradition.

Rescued from decline and refurbished in the 1980s, the Apollo once again features top black entertainers and hosts Amateur Nights.

⑯ Studio Museum in Harlem

144 W 125th St. **Map** 21 B2. **Tel** (212) 864-4500. **Ⓜ** 125th St (2, 3). **Open** noon–9pm Thu & Fri, 10am–6pm Sat, noon–6pm Sun. **Closed** public hols. **Ⓐ** Donations; free Sun. **Ⓐ Ⓐ Ⓐ** Lectures, films, children's programs, video presentations. **Ⓐ Ⓐ** **Ⓦ** studiomuseum.org

The museum was founded in 1967 in a loft on upper Fifth Avenue with the mission of becoming the premier center for the collection and exhibition of the art and artifacts of African-Americans.

The present premises, a five-story building on Harlem's main commercial street, was donated to the museum by the New York Bank for Savings in 1979. There are galleries on two levels for changing exhibitions featuring artists and cultural themes, and three galleries are devoted to the permanent collection of works by major black artists.

The photographic archives comprise one of the most complete records in existence of Harlem in its heyday. A side door opens onto a small sculpture garden.

Exhibition space at the Studio Museum in Harlem

In addition to its excellent exhibitions, the Studio Museum also maintains a national artist-in-residence program, and offers regular lectures, seminars, children's programs, and film festivals. An excellent shop sells a range of books, unique prints, and various African crafts.

⓱ Mount Morris Historical District

W 119th–W 124th Sts. **Map** 21 B2. Ⓜ 125th St (2, 3).

You can plainly see that the late 19th-century Victorian-style town houses near Marcus Garvey Park were once grand. This was a favorite neighborhood of German Jews moving up in the world from the Lower East Side. Time has not been kind, and this district shows how the area has deteriorated.

A few impressive churches, such as St. Martin's Episcopal Church, remain. There are also some interesting juxtapositions of faiths to be seen: the columned Mount Olivet Baptist Church, at 201 Lenox Avenue, was once Temple Israel, one of the most imposing synagogues in the city; and at the Ethiopian Hebrew Congregation, 1 West 123rd Street, housed in a former mansion, the choir sings in Hebrew on Saturdays.

St. Martin's Episcopal Church on Lenox Avenue

The flamboyant black nationalist leader Marcus Garvey

⓲ Marcus Garvey Park

120th–124th Sts. **Map** 21 B2 Ⓜ 125th St (2, 3). Ⓦ nycgovparks.org

This hilly, rocky, two-block square of green is the site of New York's last fire watchtower, an open cast-iron structure built in 1856, with spiral stairs leading to the observation deck. The bell below the deck sounded the alarm. It may be best to view it from a distance, however, if you have any doubts about your safety.

Previously known as Mount Morris Park, it was renamed in 1973 in honor of Marcus Garvey. He came to Harlem from Jamaica in 1916 and founded the Universal Negro Improvement Association, which promoted self-help, racial pride and a back-to-Africa movement.

⓳ Museo del Barrio

1230 5th Ave. **Map** 21 C5. **Tel** (212) 831-7272. Ⓜ 103rd St, 110th St. **Open** 11am–6pm Wed–Sat. **Closed** Jan 1, Jul 4, Thanksgiving, Dec 25. 🎫 ♿ 🛗 📷 Ⓦ elmuseo.org

Founded in 1969, this was North America's first museum devoted to Latin American art. It specializes in the culture of Puerto Rico. Exhibitions feature contemporary painting and sculpture, folk art, and historical artifacts. The stars of the collection are about 240 wooden Santos (carved figures of saints) and a reconstructed *bodega*, or Latino corner grocery. Exhibits change often, but some of the Santos are often on display. The Pre-Columbian collection contains rare artifacts from the Caribbean. Situated at the far end of Museum Mile, this unusual museum attempts to bridge the gap between the lofty Upper East Side and Spanish Harlem. A store sells eye-catching objects by artists from all over Latin America.

Folk art at the Museo del Barrio: one of the Three Wise Men (left) and the Omnipotent Hand

FARTHER AFIELD

Though officially part of New York City, the boroughs outside Manhattan are quite different in feel. They are residential and don't have the famous skyscrapers that are associated with New York. The difference is evident even in the way residents describe a trip to Manhattan as "going into the city." Yet the outlying areas boast many attractions, including the city's biggest zoo, botanical gardens, museums, beaches, and sports arenas. For a guided walk around Brooklyn, see pages 268–9.

Sights at a Glance

Historic Streets and Buildings
2 Morris-Jumel Mansion
3 George Washington Bridge
5 Wave Hill
10 Yankee Stadium
18 Grand Army Plaza
19 Park Slope Historic District
24 Historic Richmond Town
27 Alice Austen House

Museums and Galleries
1 Audubon Terrace
4 *The Cloisters Museum pp236–9*
6 Van Cortlandt House Museum
13 New York Hall of Science
14 Museum of the Moving Image and Kaufman Astoria Studio
15 MoMA PS1, Queens

16 Brooklyn Children's Museum
21 *Brooklyn Museum pp252–5*
25 Jacques Marchais Museum of Tibetan Art
26 Snug Harbor Cultural Center

Parks and Gardens
8 *New York Botanical Garden pp244–5*
9 *Bronx Zoo pp246–7*
12 Flushing Meadow-Corona Park
20 Prospect Park
22 Brooklyn Botanic Garden

Famous Theaters
17 Brooklyn Academy of Music

Cemeteries
7 Woodlawn Cemetery

Beaches
11 City Island
23 Coney Island
28 Jamaica Bay Wildlife Refuge Center
29 Jones Beach State Park

Key
= Freeway
— Major Road
=== Other Road
▨ Main sightseeing areas

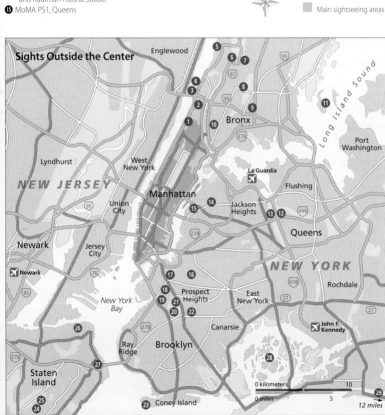

Sights Outside the Center

◀ Orchids in bloom at the New York Botanical Garden

For keys to map symbols *see back flap*

Upper Manhattan

It was in Upper Manhattan that the 18th-century Dutch settlers established their farms. Now a suburban area with little of the bustle of downtown Manhattan, it is a good place to escape the inner city for some relaxed museum and landmark sightseeing. The Cloisters *(see pp238–41)* displays a magnificent collection of medieval art, housed within original European buildings of the period. A piece of New York history is found at the Morris-Jumel Mansion in north Harlem: from his headquarters here, George Washington mounted the defense of Manhattan in 1776.

Facade of the American Academy of Arts and Letters

❶ Audubon Terrace

Broadway at 155th St. M 157th St. American Academy of Arts and Letters; (212) 368-5900. **Open** mid-Mar–mid-Apr, mid-May–mid-Jun: 1–4pm Thu–Sun. Hispanic Society of America; (212) 926-2234. **Open** 10am–4:30pm Tue–Sat, 1–4pm Sun. **Closed** public hols. Donations. 2pm Sat. W hispanicsociety.org

This 1908 complex of Classical Revival buildings by Charles Pratt Huntington is named for the great naturalist John James Audubon, whose estate once included this land. Audubon is buried in nearby Trinity Cemetery. His gravestone, a Celtic cross, bears the symbolic images of his adventurous career: the birds he painted, his palette and brushes, and his rifles. The complex was funded by the architect's cousin, civic benefactor Archer Milton Huntington. His dream was that it should be a center of culture and study. A central plaza contains statues by his wife, sculptress Anna Hyatt Huntington.

Audubon Terrace contains two themed museums that are worth seeking out. The American Academy of Arts and Letters was set up to honor American writers, artists, and composers, and 75 honorary members from overseas. On this illustrious roll are writers John Steinbeck and Mark Twain, painters Andrew Wyeth and Edward Hopper, and composer Aaron Copland. Exhibitions feature members' work. The library (for scholars, by appointment) has old manuscripts and first editions.

The Hispanic Society of America is a public museum and library based upon a personal collection amassed by Archer M. Huntington. The main gallery, in Spanish Renaissance style, holds works by Goya, El Greco, and Velázquez. There are also extensive collections of Spanish sculpture, decorative arts, prints, and

Bronze door, American Academy

photographs, with changing exhibits throughout the year.

Nearby, the Church of Our Lady of Esperanza stands on a knoll at 624 W 156th Street, which was once part of Audubon Park. It was built at the instigation of Señora de Barril, wife of the Spanish Consul-General in New York, as a church for the Spanish-speaking peoples of New York City. Built with funds provided by railroad magnate Archer Milton Huntington, the church was completed in 1912, and enlarged in the 1920s.

Statue of El Cid by Anna Hyatt Huntington at Audubon Terrace

❷ Morris-Jumel Mansion

Corner W 160th St and Edgecombe Ave. **Tel** (212) 923-8008. Ⓜ 163rd St. **Open** 10am–4pm Wed–Sun. **Closed** public hols. ♿ 🎫 noon Sat by appt. 📷 🌐 morrisjumel.org

This is one of New York's few pre-Revolutionary buildings. Now a museum with nine restored period rooms, it was built in 1765 for Roger Morris. His former military colleague George Washington used it as temporary headquarters while defending Manhattan in 1776. In 1810 it was bought and updated by Stephen Jumel, a merchant of French-Caribbean descent, and his wife Eliza.

The pair furnished the house with souvenirs of their many visits to France. Her boudoir has a "dolphin" chair, reputedly bought from Napoleon. Eliza's social climbing and love affairs scandalized New York society. It was rumored that she let her husband bleed to death in 1832 so she could inherit his fortune. She later married Aaron Burr, aged 77, and divorced him three years later on the day he died.

The exterior of the Palladian-style, wood-sided Georgian house with classical portico and octagonal wing has been restored. The museum exhibits include many original Jumel pieces.

The 3,500-ft (1,065-m) span of the George Washington Bridge

❸ George Washington Bridge

Ⓜ 175th St. 🌐 panynj.gov

French architect Le Corbusier called this "the only seat of grace in the disordered city." While not as famous a landmark as its Brooklyn equivalent, this bridge by engineer Othmar Ammann and his architect Cass Gilbert has its own character and history. Plans for a bridge linking Manhattan to New Jersey had been in the pipeline for more than 60 years before the Port of New York Authority raised the $59 million to fund the project. It was Ammann

The lighthouse under Washington Bridge

who suggested a road bridge rather than the more expensive rail link. Work began in 1927 and the bridge was opened in 1931: first across were two young roller skaters from the Bronx. Today it is a vital link for commuter traffic and is in constant use.

Cass Gilbert had plans to clad the two towers with masonry but funds did not permit it, leaving an elegant skeletal structure 600 ft (183 m) high and 3,500 ft (1,065 m) long. Ammann had also allowed for a second deck in his plan, and this lower deck was added in 1962, increasing the bridge's capacity enormously. Now the eastbound toll collection shows a traffic level of over 53 million cars per year.

Below the eastern tower is a lighthouse that was saved from possible demolition in 1951 by public pressure. Many thousands of young New Yorkers and children all around the world have loved the bedtime story *The Little Red Lighthouse and the Great Gray Bridge,* and wrote letters to save the lighthouse. Author Hildegarde Hoyt Swift wove the tale around her two favorite New York landmarks.

The bridge is also home to the world's largest free-flying American flag, which is hung out on major federal holidays.

Morris-Jumel Mansion, built in 1765, with its original colossal portico

❹ The Cloisters Museum

This world-famous museum of medieval art resides in a building constructed between 1934 and 1938, incorporating medieval cloisters, chapels, and halls. Sculptor George Grey Barnard founded the museum in 1914; John D. Rockefeller, Jr. funded the Metropolitan Museum of Art's 1925 purchase of the collection and donated the site at Fort Tryon Park and also the land on the New Jersey side of the Hudson River, directly across from The Cloisters.

Tomb Effigy of Jean d'Alluye
This tomb immortalizes the 13th-century crusader.

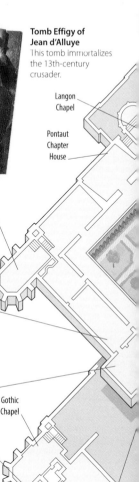

Langon Chapel

Pontaut Chapter House

Gothic Chapel

★ Unicorn Tapestries
The set of beautiful tapestries, woven in the Netherlands around 1500, depicts the quest and capture of the mythical unicorn.

Key to Floorplan

☐ Exhibition space
▨ Non-exhibition space

Gothic Chapel

Bonnefort Cloister

Glass Gallery

Boppard Stained-Glass Lancets *(1440–47)*
Below the lancet of St. Catherine, angels display the arms of the coopers' guild, of which Catherine was patron.

Trie Cloister

★ Annunciation Triptych *(c. 1425)*
The Campin Room is the location of this small Robert Campin of Tournai triptych, a magnificent example of early Netherlandish painting.

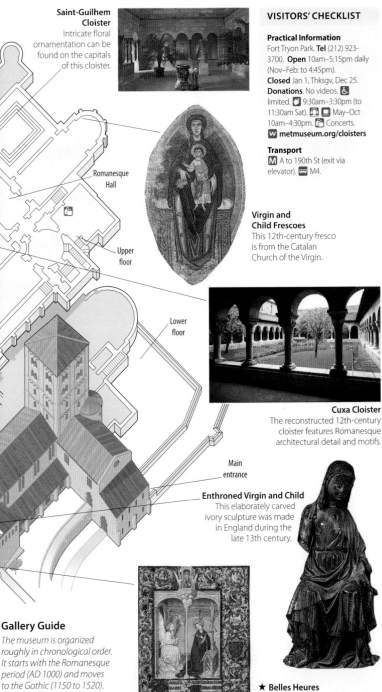

Saint-Guilhem Cloister
Intricate floral ornamentation can be found on the capitals of this cloister.

Romanesque Hall

Upper floor

Lower floor

Main entrance

Virgin and Child Frescoes
This 12th-century fresco is from the Catalan Church of the Virgin.

Cuxa Cloister
The reconstructed 12th-century cloister features Romanesque architectural detail and motifs.

Enthroned Virgin and Child
This elaborately carved ivory sculpture was made in England during the late 13th century.

Gallery Guide
The museum is organized roughly in chronological order. It starts with the Romanesque period (AD 1000) and moves to the Gothic (1150 to 1520). Sculptures, stained glass, paintings, and the gardens are on the lower floor. The Unicorn Tapestries are on the upper floor.

★ Belles Heures
This book of hours, commissioned by Jean, Duc de Berry, is among a rotating installation of exquisite illuminated books and folios.

Exploring the Cloisters Museum

Known particularly for its Romanesque and Gothic architectural sculpture, the Cloisters Museum's collection also includes illuminated manuscripts, stained glass, metalwork, enamels, ivories, and paintings. Among its tapestries is the renowned *Unicorn* series. The Cloisters' splendid medieval complex is unrivaled in North America.

A 16th-century Flemish boxwood rosary bead from the Treasury

A lifesized 12th-century Spanish crucifix portraying Christ as the King of Heaven

Romanesque Art

Fanciful beasts and people, acanthus blossoms and scrollwork top the columns around The Cloisters Museum. Many are in the Romanesque style that flourished in the 11th and 12th centuries. The museum has numerous masterpieces of Romanesque art and architecture, showing the style's powerful rounded arches and intricate details. Highly embellished capitals and warm, pink marble typify the 12th-century Cuxa Cloister from the Pyrenees in France. A griffin, a dragon, a centaur, and a basilisk are among the creatures parading over the Narbonne Arch nearby.

In a more solemn style, the apse from the church of Saint-Martín in Fuentidueña, Spain, is a massive rounded vault constructed from 3,300 blocks of limestone. It is decorated with a 12th-century fresco of the Virgin and Child and has a golden-crowned Christ depicted as triumphant over death.

More than 800 years ago, Benedictine and Cistercian monks sat on the cold stone benches in the Pontaut Chapter House. By the 19th century it had become so neglected that it was used as a stable. Its ribbed vaulting is a foretaste of the Gothic style to come.

Gothic Art

Where Romanesque art was solid, the Gothic style that followed (from 1150 to around 1520) was open, with pointed arches, glowing stained-glass windows, and three-dimensional sculpture. Gothic depictions of the Virgin and Child display exquisite craftsmanship.

The Gothic Chapel's brilliantly colored windows show scenes and figures from biblical stories. Lifesized tomb sculptures include the effigy of the Crusader knight Jean d'Alluye. During the 1790s, the statue's original home,

Vaulted ceiling of the Pontaut Chapter House

La Clarté-Dieu Abbey in France, was vandalized, and the statue was used to bridge a stream.

In the Boppard Room, the lives of the saints are told in marvelous late Gothic stained glass from Germany.

Robert Campin's Flemish masterwork, the *Annunciation* altarpiece, is the focus of the Campin Room. It is an intimate room with furnishings that might have belonged to a wealthy 15th-century family.

The Tapestries

The Cloisters' tapestries are full of rich imagery and symbolism, and are among the museum's most highly prized treasures. The four *Nine Heroes Tapestries* bear the coat of arms of Jean, Duc de Berry, who was a brother of the King of France and one of the greatest art patrons of the Middle Ages. These tapestries are one of only two sets that survived from the late 14th century; the other set belonged to Jean's brother, Louis, Duc d'Anjou.

Nine great heroes of the past – three pagan, three Hebrew, three Christian – are shown with members of the medieval court, from cardinals, knights, and damsels to musicians.

In an adjacent room is the magnificent *Hunt of the Unicorn*, a series of seven tapestries woven in the Netherlands around 1500. It depicts the symbolic hunt of the mythical unicorn and capture by a maiden.

Although they were misused in the 19th century to protect fruit trees from frost damage,

Medieval Gardens

More than 300 varieties of plants grown in the Middle Ages can be found in The Cloisters' gardens. The Bonnefont Cloister has many species of aromatic, magic, medicinal, and culinary herbs. The Trie Cloister features plants shown in the *Unicorn Tapestries* and reveals the use of flowers in medieval symbolism: roses (for the Virgin Mary), pansies (the Holy Trinity), and daisies (the eye of Christ).

Bonnefont Cloister

the tapestries are remarkably well preserved. They are also astonishing in detail, with

Julius Caesar, entertained by court musicians, in a *Nine Heroes* tapestry

literally hundreds of minutely observed plants and animals. Their story can be read as a tale of courtly love, but the series is also an allegory of the Crucifixion and the Resurrection of Christ.

The Treasury

In medieval times, precious objects were stored for safe-keeping in sanctuaries. At The Cloisters, they are found in the Treasury.

The collection includes several Gothic illuminated "books of hours." These were used for the private devotions of the nobility, such as the Limbourg brothers' *Belles Heures*, made for Jean, Duc de Berry, in 1410, and the tiny, palm-sized version by Gothic master Jean Pucelle for the Queen of France, around 1325.

Other religious artifacts range from a 13th-century English ivory Virgin to the 14th-century silver gilt and enamel reliquary shrine thought to have belonged to Queen Elizabeth of Hungary, along with censers, chalices, candlesticks, and crucifixes.

Curiosities here include the "Monkey Cup," an enameled beaker probably made for the 15th-century Burgundian court, showing mischievous monkeys robbing a sleeping peddler; an intricately carved rosary bead the size of a walnut; a 13th-century boat-shaped, jeweled saltcellar; and a full set of playing cards dating to the 15th century.

Hunting images and symbols depicted on a 15th-century deck of playing cards

The Bronx

Once a prosperous suburb with a famous Grand Concourse lined with apartment buildings for the wealthy, the Bronx has now become an unfortunate symbol of urban decay. Still, diverse ethnic communities and charming areas, such as Riverdale at the northern end, remain.

Two main attractions are the Bronx Zoo and New York Botanical Garden. There is also a golf course at Ferry Point Park, and Fulton Fish Market has relocated here. The much-loved Yankees baseball team's *(see p352)* state-of-the-art stadium is located in the Bronx.

The facade of Van Cortlandt House

❺ Wave Hill

W 249th St and Independence Ave, Riverdale. **Tel** (718) 549-3200. Ⓜ 231st St, then bus Bx7, 10, or museum shuttle bus hourly 9:10am–3:10pm. **Open** 9am–5:30pm Tue–Sun (to 4:30pm Nov–mid-Mar). 🎟 free Tue (Jul, Aug & Nov–Apr), 9am–noon Tue (May, Jun, Sep & Oct), 9am–noon Sat (all year). 📷 2pm Sun. 📷 Ⓦ **wavehill.org**

This 28-acre (11-ha) oasis of beauty boasts fine views over to the New Jersey Palisades across the Hudson River. The former estate of financier and conservationist George W. Perkins, Wave Hill has had many distinguished tenants, including Theodore Roosevelt, Mark Twain, and Arturo Toscanini. Perkins also owned neighboring estates, underneath which he built a recreation center complete with bowling alley, and a tunnel leading into the main building.

The house is frequently used for concerts. They often take place in the grand Armor Hall, designed in 1928 for Bashford

Dean, who was then the curator of the collection of arms and armor at the Metropolitan Museum of Art.

The gardens were originally designed by Viennese landscape gardener Albert Millard. There are also greenhouses, lawns, an herb garden, and woodlands. Exhibitions range from sculpture to horticulture.

The adjoining Riverdale Park, which is also open to the public, has attractive woodland and paths along the river.

The interior of the grand Armor Hall at Wave Hill

❻ Van Cortlandt House Museum

Van Cortlandt Park. **Tel** (718) 543-3344. Ⓜ 242nd St, Van Cortlandt Park. **Open** 10am–3pm Tue–Fri, 11am–4pm Sat, Sun (last adm: 30 mins before closing). **Closed** public hols & Nov 26. 🎟 free Wed. 📷 📷 *See The History of New York City pp22–3.* Ⓦ **vancortlandthouse.org**

A restored 1748 Georgian Colonial country manor built of rough stone, the Bronx's oldest building was the family home of Frederick Van Cortlandt, a New Yorker who inherited great wealth and was related to many influential families of his day.

The dining room was used as one of General George Washington's headquarters; the ground behind the house was once the scene of skirmishing during the Revolutionary War.

The interior has American period furnishings as well as a superb collection of delftware and a complete 17th-century Dutch bedroom.

On the exterior, look for the carved faces in the keystones over the windows.

The west parlor of the Van Cortlandt House Museum

❼ Woodlawn Cemetery

Webster Ave and E 233rd St.
Tel (718) 920-0500. Ⓜ Woodlawn.
Open 8:30am–5pm daily.
Closed public hols. 🅿 ♿ 🅲
Ⓦ thewoodlawncemetery.org

Established in 1863, Woodlawn Cemetery is the burial place of many a wealthy and distinguished New Yorker.

Memorials and tombstones are set in beautiful grounds. F.W. Woolworth and many members of his family are interred in a mausoleum only a little less ornate than the building that carries the family name. The pink marble vault of meat magnate Herman Armour is oddly reminiscent of a ham.

Entrance to the Woolworth mausoleum

Other New York notables buried here include Mayor Fiorello LaGuardia; Rowland Hussey Macy, the founder of the great department store; author Herman Melville; and jazz legend Duke Ellington.

❽ New York Botanical Garden

See pp244–5.

❾ Bronx Zoo/ Wildlife Conservation Park

See pp246–7.

❿ Yankee Stadium

E 161st St at River Ave, Highbridge.
Tel (718) 293-6000. Ⓜ 161st St. 🅲
noon–1:40pm daily (except on game afternoons); ticketed tours available.
See Sport p352. Ⓦ yankees.com

This has been the home of the New York Yankees baseball team since 1923. Among Yankee heroes are two of the greatest players of all time: Babe Ruth and Joe DiMaggio (who was also famous for marrying the actress Marilyn Monroe in 1954). In 1921 left-hander Babe Ruth, wearing the Yankees' distinctive pinstripes, hit the stadium's first home run – against the Boston Red Sox, his former team. The stadium was completed two years later by Jacob Ruppert, the owner of the Yankees, and became known as "the house that Ruth built".

Yankee Stadium had a facelift in the mid-1970s to seat up to 54,000 people. One of the largest annual gatherings has been that of the Jehovah's Witnesses, and in 1950, 123,707 people attended in a single day. In 1965 Pope Paul VI celebrated mass before a crowd of more than 80,000. It was the first visit to North America by a pope – the second was made in 1979 when John Paul II also visited the stadium.

In 2009, the Yankees moved to a new stadium located parallel to the old site. This stadium is one of the most expensive venues ever built, at a cost of around $1.5 billion.

The Yankees remain one of the top teams in the American League. There are five Yankee Clubhouse stores in New York, where tickets for tours and games can be purchased.

Joe DiMaggio in action at Yankee Stadium in 1941

⓫ City Island

Ⓜ 6 to Pelham Bay Park, then Bx29 to City Island. Museum 190 Fordham St.
Open 1–5pm Sat & Sun. **Tel** (718) 885-0008. Ⓦ cityislandmuseum.org

Situated off the northeast shore of the Bronx and surrounded by Long Island Sound, City Island is a small nautical outpost with a very New England feel and offers a refreshing change of pace. Its scenic marinas are filled with sailboats, and its seafood restaurants would satisfy any sailor's appetite. Several Americas Cup winners have been built in its boatyards.

The **City Island Museum** is in one of the island's most historic buildings, the old Public School 17, built on an Indian burial ground at a high point on the island. City Island is linked to the Bronx by bridge. To the north on the mainland is Orchard Beach, a crescent of white sand edged with bathing huts. The beach is popular with area residents, and it can be crowded.

An old tugboat moored at one of City Island's piers

⊙ The New York Botanical Garden

The New York Botanical Garden is 250 acres (100 ha) of dazzling beauty and hands-on enjoyment. From the nation's most glorious Victorian glasshouse to the 12-acre (5-ha) Everett Children's Adventure Garden, it is alive with things to discover. One of the oldest and largest botanical gardens in the world, it has 50 gardens and plant collections, and 50 acres (20 ha) of uncut forest. The spectacular Enid A. Haupt Conservatory houses a *A World of Plants*, with climates ranging from misty tropical rain forests to dramatic deserts.

Entrance to Enid A. Haupt Conservatory

Seasonal Exhibition Galleries

Deserts of Africa

④ **Rock Garden**
Rock outcroppings, streams, a waterfall, and a flower-rimmed pond create an alpine habitat for plants from around the world.

⑤ **Historic Forest**
One of New York City's last surviving natural forest areas includes red oak, white ash, tulip trees, and birch.

Deserts of the Americas

⑧ **Everett Children's Adventure Garden**
Kids can discover the wonders of ecology and plants.

Entrance

⑥

①② ③④
   ⑨ ⑤
  ⑧
      ⑦

Entrance

Locator Map

⑦ **Peggy Rockefeller Rose Garden**
Over 2,700 rose bushes have been planted in the Rose Garden, laid out in 1988 according to the 1916 design.

Palms of the Americas Gallery
100 majestic palms soar into a 90-ft (27-m) glass dome. A tranquil reflecting pool is surrounded by tropical plants.

① **The Enid A. Haupt Conservatory** consists of 11 interconnecting glass galleries housing *A World of Plants*, including rain forests, deserts, aquatic plants, and seasonal exhibitions.

⑥ **Garden Cafe**
This is a delightful spot to enjoy a meal. You can eat outside on terraces overlooking beautiful gardens.

VISITORS' CHECKLIST

Practical Information
Kazimiroff Blvd, Bronx River Parkway (Exit 7W).
Tel (718) 817-8700.
Open 10am–6pm Tue–Sun (until 5pm mid-Jan–Feb).
Closed pub hols. 🖼 Free all day Wed & 10am–noon Sat (grounds only). ♿ 📷 💻 📷 Lectures.
W nybg.org

Transport
Ⓜ 4, B, D to Bedford Park Blvd.
🚌 Bx26.

② **Jane Watson Irwin Perennial Garden**
Flowering perennials are arranged in dramatic patterns according to height, shade, color and blooming time

Conservatory

Tropical Lowland Rain Forest Gallery

Courtyard Pool

Aquatic Plants and Vines Gallery

⑨ **Leon Levy Visitor Center**
This modern pavilion has a shop, a café, and a visitor orientation facility.

Tropical Upland Rainforest Gallery

③ **Tram**
The half-hour tour of the gardens provides information about horticultural, educational, and botanical research programs. Passengers can alight at a number of stops to explore the gardens before reboarding.

⑨ Bronx Zoo

Opened in 1899, the Bronx Zoo is the largest urban zoo in the United States. It is home to more than 4,000 animals of 500 species, which live in realistic representations of their natural habitats. The zoo is a leader in the perpetuation of endangered species, such as the Indian rhinoceros and the snow leopard. Its 265 acres of woods, streams, and parklands include, in season, a children's zoo, the Butterfly Garden, the Wild Asia Monorail, and camel rides. Other attractions include daily sea lion feedings, primate training at the Monkey House, a one-of-a-kind bug carousel, and a 4-D theater experience.

★ **The Congo Gorilla Forest**
This award-winning replica of a central African rainforest is home to the largest population of Western Lowland gorillas in the US, as well as a family of pygmy marmosets, the world's smallest monkeys.

Baboon Reserve
Visitors walk along a dry riverbed to see wildlife in an Ethiopian mountain habitat.

Asia entrance

Camel Rides
Children enjoy such seasonal experiences as camel rides and other attractions.

★ **African Plains**
Wild dogs, zebras, lions, giraffes, and gazelles roam the African Plains. Predators and prey are separated by a moat.

★ **JungleWorld**
A climate-controlled tropical rain forest harbors mammals, birds, and reptiles from South Asia. The animals are kept apart from visitors by ravines, streams and cliffs.

Monkeys in JungleWorld

Children's Zoo
Kids can crawl through a prairie dog tunnel, try on a turtle shell, and pet and feed the animals.

Great
hornbill

★ World of Birds
Exotic birds soar free in the lush surroundings of a rain forest. An artificial waterfall rushes down a 50-ft (15-m) fiberglass cliff in this walk-through habitat.

Southern Boulevard entrance

VISITORS' CHECKLIST

Practical Information
Fordham Rd/Bronx River Pkwy.
Tel (718) 367-1010.
Open 10am–5pm Mon–Fri,
10am–5:30pm Sat & Sun (Nov–
Mar: 4:30pm daily). 🖼 by
donation Wed; separate fees may
apply to some exhibits. 🚹 📷
🚻 📷
Children's Zoo
Open Apr–Oct.
🆆 bronxzoo.com

Transport
Ⓜ 2, 5 to E Tremont Ave. 🚆 to
Fordham. 🚌 Bx9, Bx12, Bx19,
Bx22, Bx39, BxM11, Q44.

KEY

① 4-D Theater
② Wild Asia Monorail
③ Carter Giraffe Building
④ Wildfowl Marsh
⑤ World of Reptiles
⑥ Butterfly Garden
⑦ The Zoo Center
⑧ Madagascar!
⑨ Aquatic Bird House
⑩ Sea Bird Colony
⑪ Monkey House
⑫ Mouse-House
⑬ **Himalayan Highlands**,
Endangered species, such as snow leopards and red pandas, are here.

Rainey Gate entrance

Bronx Parkway entrance

★ Wild Asia Monorail
From May to October, the monorail journeys through forests and meadows, where rhinos, tigers, and Mongolian wild horses roam free.

★ Tiger Mountain
Amur tigers are on view all year. Only one inch of glass separates visitors from these magnificent wild cats.

Queens

A big, sprawling borough, Queens has a wide variety of attractions in its residential and commercial areas, including Long Island City, where museums and restaurants are springing up all over. Development of the borough accelerated after 1909, when the construction of Queensboro Bridge made commuting easier. The city's main airports are here, and there are many different ethnic enclaves including the Greek neighborhood of Astoria and the various Asian communities in Flushing.

⓬ Flushing Meadow–Corona Park

Ⓜ Willets Point-Shea Stadium. *See Sports p353.*

The site of New York's two World's Fairs now offers expansive waterside picnic grounds and a multitude of attractions. These include the 41,000-seat Citi Field stadium, home of the New York Mets baseball team, and a popular site for rock concerts. Flushing Meadow is also home to the US Tennis Center, where the prestigious United States Open is played. The courts are open for would-be Nadals, Sharapovas, and Federers for the remainder of the year. In the 1920s this area was known

A 1900 Mutoscope at the Museum of the Moving Image

as the Corona Dump, a nightmarish place of salt marshes and great piles of smoldering trash. In *The Great Gatsby*, author F. Scott Fitzgerald dubbed it the "valley of ashes." It reeked of rotting garbage and glowed red at night. New York's Parks' Commissioner Robert Moses was the driving force behind its transformation. A whole mountain of trash was removed and the river was totally re-channeled. The marsh was drained, and sewage works were built, helping to restore the area. This site was to serve as the location for the 1939 World's Fair, at which a world on the brink of war saluted the elusive notion of world peace.

The Unisphere, symbol of the 1964 fair, still dominates the remains of the fairground. This giant hollow ball of green steel, built by the US Steel Corporation, is 12 stories high and weighs a massive 350 tons.

The 1964 World's Fair Unisphere at Flushing Meadow-Corona Park

⓭ New York Hall of Science

46th Ave and 111th St Flushing Meadow, Corona Park. **Tel** (718) 699-0005. Ⓜ 111th St. **Open** Jul–Aug: 9:30am–5pm Mon–Fri, 10am–6pm Sat & Sun; Sep–Jun: 9:30am–2pm Mon–Thu, 9:30am– 5pm Fri, 10am–6pm Sat & Sun. **Closed** Labor Day, Dec 25. 🚫 ♿ 📷 🔍 🅦 **nysci.org**

The science pavilion was built for the 1964 World's Fair, with stained glass set in concrete. It is now a hands-on museum of science and technology, with exhibits on color, light, and physics. Kids love the giant video screens and laser optical exhibits.

The concrete curtain wall of the New York Hall of Science

⓮ Museum of the Moving Image and Kaufman Astoria Studio

35th Ave at 36th St, Astoria. Museum (718) 784-0077. Ⓜ 36th St. Steinway Museum: **Open** 10:30am–5pm Tue–Sun (to 8pm Fri, to 7pm Sat & Sun). Screenings: 7:30pm Fri, afternoon and eves Sat & Sun. 🚫 (free 4–8pm Fri). 🎬 2pm Sat & Sun. **Closed** Memorial Day, Thnksgv, Dec 25. Studio: **Closed** to public. ♿ 🔲 📷 🅦 **movingimage.us**

In New York's filmmaking heyday, Rudolph Valentino, W.C. Fields, the Marx Brothers, and Gloria Swanson all made films in the Astoria Studio, which was opened in 1920 by Paramount Pictures. When the movies went west, the army took over, making training films from 1941 to 1971.

The complex stood empty until 1977 when Astoria Motion Picture and Television Foundation was created to preserve it. *The Wiz*, a musical starring Michael Jackson and Diana Ross, was

Poster at the Museum of the Moving Image

In 1981 one of the studio buildings was transformed into the Museum of the Moving Image, with interactive displays on production and theaters for the screening of movies and television, as well as a special lecture hall.

There is a lot of memorabilia on display, from Ben Hur's chariot to *Star Trek* costumes. The main gallery draws from the permanent collection of over 85,000 movie artifacts. A major expansion of the museum has created a state-of-the-art facility, with a 254-seat theater, a video-screening

made here, helping to pay for restoration. Today, the studios house the largest moviemaking facilities on the East Coast.

ampitheatre, and an educational 71-seat screening room. An airy café serves drinks, baked goods, and light meals.

⑮ MoMA PS1, Queens

22–25 Jackson at 46th Ave, Long Island City. **Tel** (718) 784-2084. Ⓜ E, M to 23rd St-Ely Ave; 7 to 45 Road-Courthouse Square; G to Court Sq or 21 St-Van Alst. 🚌 B61, Q67. **Open** noon–6pm Thu–Mon. **Closed** Jan 1, Dec 25. 🅿️ ⬤ 🖥️ 🆆 ps1.org

Housed in an elementary school, PS1 was founded in 1971 under a scheme to transform abandoned New York City buildings into exhibition, performance, and studio spaces for artists. The museum is affiliated to the Museum of Modern Art *(see pp174–7)* and is one of the oldest art organisations in the US devoted solely to modern art. Temporary exhibitions are hosted alongside permanent works and many pieces are interactive. In summer, music is performed in the courtyard.

Brooklyn

If Brooklyn were a separate city, it would be the country's fourth largest. It has a character all of its own. Many entertainment greats – Mel Brooks, Phil Silvers, Woody Allen, and Neil Simon among them – celebrate their birthplace with great affection and humor. Brooklyn is a veritable melting pot, with West Indians, Hasidic Jews, Russians, Italians, and Arabs living side by side. Among the diverse neighborhoods are the historic residential districts of Park Slope and Brooklyn Heights.

The bandstand at Prospect Park *(see p250)*

⑯ Brooklyn Children's Museum

145 Brooklyn Ave. **Tel** (718) 735-4400. Ⓜ Kingston (C, 3). **Open** 10am–5pm Tue–Sun. **Closed** public hols. Rooftop Theater: **Open** 6:30–8pm Fri, 10am–5pm Sat & Sun. **Closed** public hols. 🅿️ ⬤ 🖥️ 📷
🆆 bchildmus.org

The Brooklyn Children's Museum was the first to be designed especially for

children and was founded in 1899. Since then, it has been a model, inspiration, and consultant to the development of more than 250 museums for children across the country and all over the world. Housed in a high-tech, specially designed underground building dating from 1976, it is one of the most imaginative children's museums anywhere.

The layout of the building, which has doubled in size and is a maze of complex interconnected passageways running off the main "people tube" – a huge

drainage pipe that connects the four levels. The emphasis here is on involvement and hands-on exhibits and everywhere you look there are curiosities to be discovered, experienced, made, or played with. There is even a walk-on piano like the one in the film *Big* – children of every age find it quite irresistible. Special exhibitions and events are designed to help children learn about the planet, resolve their fears or problems, understand other cultures, and discover the past. The squeals of laughter that are always heard are a sign of this museum's success in teaching both children and the young at heart.

A mask at the Brooklyn Children's Museum

The facade of the Brooklyn Academy of Music

⑰ Brooklyn Academy of Music

30 Lafayette Ave. **Tel** (718) 636-4100.
Ⓜ Atlantic Ave, Nevins St (M, N, Q, R, 2, 3, 4, 5). 🅿 ♿ 🛗 📷 🅦 **bam. org** *See Classic and Contemporary Music p342.*

Home to the Brooklyn Phil-harmonic, the Academy of Music (BAM) is Brooklyn's leading cultural venue and the oldest, founded in 1858. It offers outstanding performances, often tending toward the innovative and avant-garde.

The classic 1908 building, designed by Herts & Tallant, was inaugurated with a production of Gounod's opera *Faust* featuring the Neapolitan tenor Enrico Caruso. Among the greats who have performed here are actress Sarah Bernhardt, ballerina Anna Pavlova, musicians Pablo Casals and Sergei Rachmaninoff, poets Edna St. Vincent Millay and Carl Sandburg, and statesman Winston Churchill. Many international touring groups have made appearances here, including Britain's Royal Shakespeare Company.

The BAM Next Wave Festival, which usually runs over the last three months of the year, has presented contemporary artists such as musicians David Byrne

and Philip Glass and choreographers Pina Bausch and Mark Morris. The BAM also runs the Harvey Theater nearby, a movie theater now used for dance, drama, and music events. BAM Rose Cinemas show first-run independent films and BAMcinématek has classics, retrospectives, festivals, and sneak previews.

The Soldiers' and Sailors' Arch at Grand Army Plaza

⑱ Grand Army Plaza

Plaza St at Flatbush Ave. Ⓜ Grand Army Plaza (2, 3). Arch: **Open** for occasional exhibitions.

Frederick Law Olmsted and Calvert Vaux laid out this grand oval in 1870 as a gateway to Prospect Park. The Soldiers' and Sailors' Arch and its sculptures were added in 1892 as a tribute to the Union Army. The bust of John F. Kennedy here is the only official New York monument to him.

In June, the plaza is the center of the Welcome Back to Brooklyn Festival for the famous – and not-so-famous – people born in Brooklyn.

Relief work on the Montauk Club

⑲ Park Slope Historic District

Streets from Prospect Park W below Flatbush Ave, to 8th/7th/5th Aves. Ⓜ Grand Army Plaza (2, 3), 7th Ave (F).

This wonderful enclave of beautiful Victorian town houses was developed on the edge of Prospect Park in the 1880s. It served the upper-middle-class professionals who were able to commute into Manhattan after the Brooklyn Bridge was opened in 1883. The shady streets are lined with two- to five- story houses in every architectural style popular in the late 19th century, some with the towers, turrets, and curlicues so representative of the era. Particularly fine examples are in Romanesque Revival style, with rounded entry arches.

The Montauk Club at 25 Eighth Avenue combines the style of Venice's Ca' d'Oro palazzo with the friezes and gargoyles of the Montauk Indians, for whom this popular 19th-century gathering place was named.

⑳ Prospect Park

Ⓜ Grand Army Plaza, Prospect Park (B, Q). 📷 ♿ & information (718) 287-3400. 📷 🅦 **prospectpark.org**

Olmsted and Vaux considered this park, opened in 1867, better than their earlier Central Park *(see pp205–211)*. The Long Meadow, a sweep of broad lawns and grand vistas, is the longest unbroken swath of green space in New York.

Olmsted's belief was that "a feeling of relief is experienced by entering them [the parks] on escaping from the cramped, confining and controlling circumstances of the streets of the town." That vision is still as true today as it was a century ago.

The facade of the Brooklyn Public Library on Grand Army Plaza

Among the many notable features are Stanford White's colonnaded Croquet Shelter, and the pools and weeping willows of the Vale of Cashmere. The Music Grove bandstand shows Japanese influences and hosts both jazz and classical music concerts throughout the summer.

A favorite feature of the park is the Camperdown Elm, an ancient and twisted tree planted in 1872. The Friends of Prospect Park raise money to keep it and all the park trees healthy. This old elm has inspired many poems and paintings. Prospect Park has a wide variety of landscapes, from classical gardens dotted with statues to rocky glens with running brooks. A guided tour with a ranger is the best way to see the park.

An Atlantic green turtle at the New York Aquarium, on Coney Island

Carousel horse in Prospect Park

㉑ Brooklyn Museum

See pp252–3.

㉒ Brooklyn Botanic Garden

900 Washington Ave. **Tel** (718) 623-7200. Ⓜ Prospect Pk (B, Q), Eastern Pkwy (2, 3). Grounds **Open** Apr–Sep: 8am–6pm Tue–Fri (10am Sat, Sun, & public hols); Oct–Mar: 8am–4:30pm (10am Sat, Sun, & public hols). **Closed** Jan 1, Labor Day, Thanksgiving, Dec 25. 🅿 Mar–mid-Nov: free Tue & 10am–noon Sat; mid-Nov–late Feb: free for under-16s Mon–Fri. ♿ 🅿 🖉 🏛 🅦 bbg.org

Though it is not vast, you will find that this 50-acre (20-ha) garden holds many delights. The area was designed by the Olmsted Brothers in 1910 and features an Elizabethan-style

"knot" herb garden and one of North America's largest collections of roses.

The central showpiece is a Japanese hill-and-pond garden, complete with a teahouse and Shinto shrine. In late April and early May the park promenade is aglow with delicate Japanese cherry blossoms, which have prompted an annual festival featuring typical Japanese culture, food, and music. April is also the time for tourists to appreciate Magnolia Plaza, where some 80 trees display their beautiful, creamy blossoms against a backdrop of daffodils on Boulder Hill.

The Fragrance Garden is planted in raised beds, where the heavily scented, textured and flavored plants are all labeled in Braille, giving blind visitors an opportunity to identify them as well.

The conservatory houses one of America's largest bonsai collections and some rare rain forest trees, whose extracts allow scientists to produce life-saving drugs.

Brooklyn Botanic Garden lily pond

㉓ Coney Island

Ⓜ Stillwell Ave (D, F, N, Q), W 8th St (F, Q). New York Aquarium Surf Ave and W 8th St. **Tel** (718) 265-FISH. **Open** 10am–5pm daily (to 5:30pm Sat, Sun, & hols). (Jun–Aug: to 6pm Mon–Fri & 7pm Sat, Sun & hols; Nov–Mar: to 4:30pm daily). 🅿 last adm: 45 mins before closing. 🅿 🅦 **nyaquarium. com** Coney Island Museum 1208 Surf Ave, nr W 12th St. **Tel** (718) 372-5159. **Open** noon–6pm Sat & Sun. 🅿 🅦 coneyislandusa.com

In the mid-1800s, Brooklyn poet Walt Whitman composed many of his works on Coney Island, at that time untamed Atlantic coastline. By the 1920s, Coney Island was billing itself as the "World's Largest Playground," with three huge fairgrounds providing hair-raising rides. The subway arrived in 1920, and the 1921 boardwalk ensured Coney Island's popularity throughout the Depression.

A major attraction is the **New York Aquarium**, with over 350 species. The **Coney Island Museum** has memorabilia, souvenirs, and relics of old rides. Coney Island is in the process of being modernized, much to the chagrin of local residents, who fear that its character will

be lost. However, the boardwalk still yields lovely ocean views, and the Cyclone roller coaster has been designated an official city landmark. The Mermaid Parade in June is a major annual event.

㉑ Brooklyn Museum

When it opened in 1897, the Brooklyn Museum building, designed to be the largest cultural edifice in the world, was the greatest achievement of New York architects McKim, Mead & White. Though only one-sixth completed, the museum is today one of the most impressive cultural institutions in the United States, with a permanent encyclopedic collection of some one million objects, housed in a grand structure covering 560,000 sq ft (41,805 sq m).

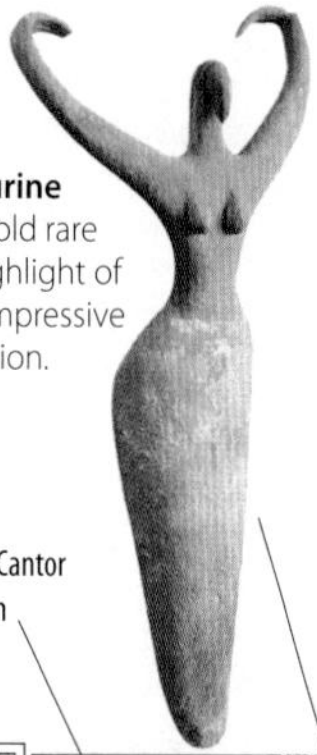

North facade, designed by McKim, Mead & White

Key to Floorplan

- Arts of Africa and the Americas
- Asian art
- Prints, drawings, and photographs
- Williamsburg Murals
- Egyptian and Classical art
- Decorative arts
- Painting and sculpture
- Special exhibitions
- Non-exhibition space

★ Female Figurine
This 5,000-year-old rare statuette is a highlight of the museum's impressive Egyptian collection.

Iris and B. Cantor Auditorium

Chinese Jar
Cobalt blue fishes and water plants adorn this 14th-century Yuan dynasty blue-and-white ceramic jar.

★ Beaded Crown
This 19th-century crown from Nigeria is the ultimate symbol of Yoruba kingship.

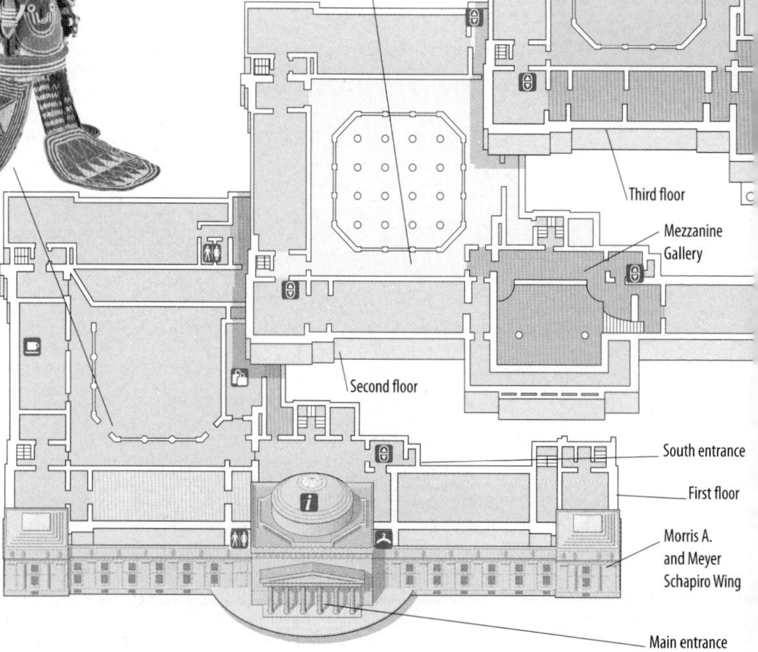

Third floor

Mezzanine
Gallery

Second floor

South entrance

First floor

Morris A. and Meyer Schapiro Wing

Main entrance

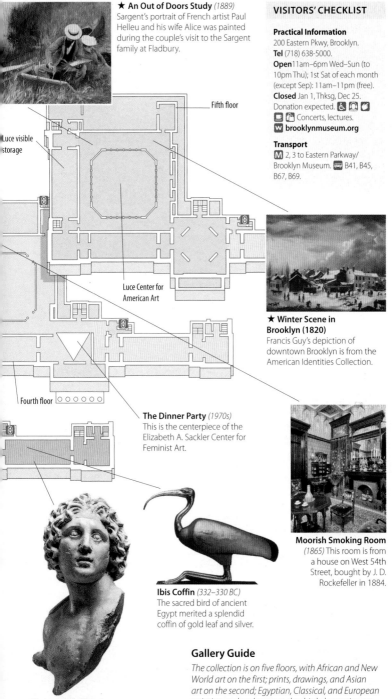

★ An Out of Doors Study (1889)
Sargent's portrait of French artist Paul Helleu and his wife Alice was painted during the couple's visit to the Sargent family at Fladbury.

Fifth floor

Luce visible storage

Luce Center for American Art

Fourth floor

★ Winter Scene in Brooklyn (1820)
Francis Guy's depiction of downtown Brooklyn is from the American Identities Collection.

The Dinner Party (1970s)
This is the centerpiece of the Elizabeth A. Sackler Center for Feminist Art.

Moorish Smoking Room
(1865) This room is from a house on West 54th Street, bought by J. D. Rockefeller in 1884.

Ibis Coffin (332–330 BC)
The sacred bird of ancient Egypt merited a splendid coffin of gold leaf and silver.

Alexander the Great
The military leader was portrayed in alabaster in the 1st century BC.

Gallery Guide

The collection is on five floors, with African and New World art on the first; prints, drawings, and Asian art on the second; Egyptian, Classical, and European painting and sculpture on the third; decorative art on the fourth; and American art on the fifth. There is special exhibition space on the first and fourth floors.

Exploring the Collection

The Brooklyn Museum houses one of the finest art collections in the United States. Its strengths include an outstanding collection of Native American art from the Southwest; American period rooms; exquisite pieces of ancient Egyptian and Islamic art; and important American and European paintings.

Seated Buddha torso in limestone, from India (late 3rd century AD)

Arts of Africa, The Pacific, and The Americas

The Brooklyn Museum set a precedent in the United States in 1923 by exhibiting African objects as works of art rather than artifacts. Since then, the African art collection has grown steadily in both importance and size.

Exhibits include a rare intricately carved ivory gong from the Benin kingdom of 16th-century Nigeria, one of only five in existence.

The museum also has a notable collection of Native American work, including totem poles, textiles, and pottery. A 19th-century deer-skin shirt, once worn by a chief of the Blackfoot tribe, depicts his brave and daring exploits in battle.

Ancient American artistic traditions are represented by Peruvian textiles, Central American gold, and Mexican sculpture. A beautifully preserved tunic from Peru, dating from AD 600, is so tightly woven that its vibrant symbolic designs appear to have been painted onto the cloth rather than woven in the traditional manner.

The Oceanic collection includes sculpture from the Solomon Islands, Papua New Guinea, and New Zealand.

Asian Art

Changing exhibitions from the museum's permanent collection of Chinese, Japanese, Korean, Indian, Southeast Asian, and Islamic art are always on display. Japanese and Chinese paintings, Indian miniatures, and Islamic calligraphy complement the Asian sculpture, textiles, and ceramics. The collections of Japanese folk art, Chinese cloisonné (enamel work), and Oriental carpets are of particular note. Good examples of Buddhist art range from a variety of Chinese, Indian, and Southeast Asian Buddhas to a mandala-patterned temple banner from 14th-century Tibet, painted in rich, luminous watercolors.

Blackfoot tribe deerskin shirt, decorated with porcupine quills and glass beads (19th century)

Decorative Arts

The decorative arts collection reflects changes in domestic life and design from the 17th century to the present.

The Moorish Smoking Room, from John D. Rockefeller's brownstone house, embodies elegant New York living in the 1880s. There is also a 1928–30 Art Deco study from a Park Avenue apartment, including a walk-in bar that was hidden behind paneling during the Prohibition era (see pp32–3).

More than 350 items from the museum's collection of silver, furniture, ceramics, and textiles are featured in the Luce Center for American Art. Although centered mostly on American art, the selection also includes pieces of Native American and Spanish colonial art.

Normandie chrome pitcher, by Peter Müller-Munk (1935)

The Luce galleries are arranged thematically and explore crucial moments and ideas in American visual culture over the past 300 years. Among the collection are pieces by John Singer Sargent, Frank Lloyd Wright, and Georgia O'Keeffe.

Egyptian, Classical, and Ancient Middle Eastern Art

Recognized as among the world's finest, the Egyptian collection holds many masterpieces. It begins with an early female figure dating from 3500 BC, and encompasses sculptures, statues, tomb paintings, and reliefs as well as funerary paraphernalia. Of the latter, the most unusual is the coffin of an ibis, probably recovered from the vast animal cemetery of Tuna el-Gebel in Middle Egypt. The ibis was a sacred bird representing the god Thoth, and this coffin is made of solid silver and wood overlaid with gold leaf, with rock crystal for the bird's eyes. These galleries have been renovated into a state-of-the-art, high-tech installation.

Among the artifacts from the Greek and Roman civilizations are statuary, pottery, bronzes, jewelry, and mosaics.

Among the Ancient Near and Middle Eastern exhibits are an extensive collection of pottery and 12 alabaster reliefs from the Assyrian palace of King Ashurnasirpal II. These date from around 883–859 BC and depict the king fighting, overseeing his crops, and purifying the "sacred tree," a major icon in Assyrian religion.

Pierre de Wiessant (about 1886) by Auguste Rodin, from his *Burghers of Calais* group

Painting and Sculpture

This section contains works from the 14th century to the present, including a well-known and outstanding 19th-century French art collection with works by Degas, Rodin, Monet, Cézanne, Matisse, and Pissarro. It also boasts one of the largest holdings of Spanish Colonial paintings and one of the best collections of North American paintings to be found in the United States. The museum's 20th-century American collection includes,

appropriately, *Brooklyn Bridge* by Georgia O1'Keeffe.

The Sculpture Garden holds architectural ornamentation taken from demolished New York buildings, including statues rescued from the original Penn Station, and a replica of the Statue of Liberty.

Rotherhithe, an etching by James McNeill Whistler (1860)

Prints, Drawings, and Photographs

The museum has an important collection of prints, drawings, and photographs that are constantly rotated for conservation purposes. The range includes a rare woodcut print by Dürer entitled *The Great Triumphal Chariot* and works by Piranesi. The Impressionist and Post-Impressionist collection includes works by Toulouse-Lautrec and Mary Cassatt, the only American woman associated with the Impressionist movement. There are lithographs by James McNeill Whistler, Winslow Homer engravings, and a superb selection of drawings by Fragonard, Paul Klee, Van Gogh, Picasso, and Gorky, among others, many of them in black and white.

The photography collection consists mainly of works by major 20th-century American photographers, including a 1924 portrait of Mary Pickford by Edward Steichen and work by Margaret Bourke-White, Berenice Abbott, and Robert Mapplethorpe.

Sandstone reliefs from Thebes in Egypt (c. 760–656 BC), depicting the great god Amun-Re and his consort Mut

Staten Island

Apart from the famous ferry ride, Staten Island and its attractions are not well known to New Yorkers in general. Residents feel so ignored, in fact, that they've talked about seceding from the city. Visitors who venture beyond the ferry terminal, however, will be pleasantly surprised to find hills, lakes, and greenery, with expanses of open space, amazing harbor views, and well-preserved early New York buildings. One of the biggest surprises here is a cache of Tibetan art that is hidden away in a replica of a Buddhist temple.

The Voorlezer House at Richmond Town

❷ Historic Richmond Town

441 Clarke Ave. **Tel** (718) 351-1611. S74 from ferry. **Open** 1–5pm Wed–Sun. **Closed** Jan 1, Easter Sun, Thanksgiving, Dec 25. 🅿️ ♿ 📷 📷 **historicrichmondtown.org**

There are now 29 buildings, 14 of which are open to the public, in New York's only restored village and outdoor museum. The village was first named Cocclestown, after the local shellfish, but was soon corrupted to "Cuckoldstown," much to the annoyance of the residents. By the end of the Revolutionary War, the alternative name of Richmondtown had been adopted. It was the county seat until Staten Island was made part of the city in 1898,

Cologne at the General Store

and has been preserved as an example of an early New York settlement.

The Voorlezer House, built in the Dutch era before 1696, is the oldest elementary school to be found in the country. The Stephens General Store, which opened in 1837, doubled as the local post office. It has been well restored, right down to the contents of the shelves. The complex, set on 100 acres (40 ha), includes wagon sheds, a courthouse built in 1837, houses, several shops, and a tavern. There are also seasonal workshops where traditional rural crafts are demonstrated to visitors. St. Andrew's Church, dating to 1708, and its old graveyard are just across the Mill Pond stream, and the Historical Society Museum is in the County Clerk's and Surrogate's Office. The toy room is a delight.

Sacred sculpture at the Jacques Marchais Center of Tibetan Art

❷ Jacques Marchais Museum of Tibetan Art

338 Lighthouse Ave. **Tel** (718) 987-3500. S74 from ferry. **Open** 1–5pm Wed–Sun (Dec–Mar: Fri–Sun only). **Closed** public hols. 📷 📷 📷 **tibetanmuseum.org**

A hilltop provides a tranquil setting for one of the largest collections of privately owned Tibetan art of the 15th to the 20th centuries outside Tibet. The main building is a replica of a mountain monastery with an authentic altar in three tiers, crowded with gold, silver, and bronze figures.

The second building is used as a library. The soothing garden has some stone sculptures, including life-size Buddhas. The museum was built in 1947 by Mrs. Jacques Marchais, a dealer in Asian art. The Dalai Lama paid his first visit here in 1991.

A gazebo at the Snug Harbor Cultural Center

❷ Snug Harbor Cultural Center

1000 Richmond Terrace. **Tel** (718) 448-2500. S40 from ferry to Snug Harbor Gate. Grounds: **Open** dawn–dusk daily. Art Gallery: **Open** 10am–5pm Tue–Sun. 📷 donation. Children's Museum **Open** noon–5pm (summer 11am–5pm) Tue–Sun. **Closed** Jan 1, Thanksgiving, Dec 25. ♿ limited. 📷 📷 **snug-harbor.org**

Founded in 1801 as a haven for aged sailors, Snug Harbor is now an arts center, with a complex of 28 buildings in various stages of restoration. There are five stately Greek Revival gems dating from 1831 to 1880, the finest such collection in the US. The oldest, the Main Hall, is the Visitors'

Center. This leads through to the **Newhouse Center for Contemporary Art**, but the ships in the stained-glass windows are a reminder of its origins. Other buildings house the award-winning **Staten Island Children's Museum** and Veterans Memorial Hall, used for indoor performances. A sculpture festival and summer shows are held on the lawns. The Staten Island Botanical Garden has a noted orchid collection and a beautiful rose garden.

Snug Harbor is the legacy of a Scottish sailor, Robert Richard Randall, who became rich in the Revolutionary War and bequeathed this property to be used by seamen, enabling them to enjoy its harbor views.

Clear Comfort, Alice Austen's lifetime residence

㉗ Alice Austen House

2 Hylan Blvd. **Tel** (718) 816-4506. 🚌 S 51 from ferry to Hylan Blvd. **Open** noon–5pm Thu–Sun; grounds: to dusk. **Closed** Jan, Feb, public hols. 🅿 Donation ♿ limited. 📷 📷
Ⓦ **aliceausten.org**

This small cottage built around 1690 has the delightful name of Clear Comfort. It was the home of the photographer Alice Austen, who was born in 1866

and who lived in this house for most of her life. She documented life on the island, in Manhattan, and also on trips to other parts of the country and on her travels to Europe. She lost all her money in the stock market crash of 1929, and her poverty forced her into a public poorhouse at the age of 84. One year later, her photographic talent was finally recognized by *Life* magazine, which published an article about her, earning her enough money to enter a nursing home. She left 3,500 negatives dating from 1880 to 1930. Today, the Friends of Alice Austen House mounts exhibitions of her best work.

Even Farther Afield

The village of Broad Channel at Jamaica Bay

㉘ Jamaica Bay Wildlife Refuge Center

Cross Bay Blvd at Broad Channel. **Tel** (718) 318-4340. Ⓜ Broad Channel (A). **Open** sunrise to sunset; visitor center: 8:30am–5pm daily. 🎫 seasonal (call ahead) Ⓦ **nps.gov/gate**

The marshes and uplands of the Refuge cover an area almost the size of Manhattan. Over 300 species of birds live here either seasonally or all year round. On the main Atlantic migratory path, the Refuge is at its best in spring and autumn, when the skies are filled with skeins of geese and ducks. The park rangers lead hikes and nature walks for

weekend visitors – wear suitable shoes and clothes, and take along a zoom-lens camera or binoculars to get the best from your visit.

㉙ Jones Beach State Park

Beaches. **Open** all year. 🏖 late May–Labor Day. **Tel** (516) 785-1600.
Ⓦ **nysparks.state.ny.us/parks**
🚆 Long Island Railroad: Penn Station to Jones Beach; train schedule (late May–Labor Day); (718) 217-5477. Jones Beach Theater; (516) 221-1000.
♿ Ⓦ **jonesbeach.com**

Jones Beach was the creation of Robert Moses, New York's Parks' Commissioner (*see p248*), who transformed this narrow spit of

land into Long Island's most accessible and popular beach in 1929. There are sand dunes, surf on the Atlantic side, and sheltered water in the bay. There is also miniature golf, swimming pools, restaurants, and the **Jones Beach Theater**, which hosts concerts in the summer.

Robert Moses State Park is on the next island to the east, Fire Island, which is over 30 miles (48 km) long, yet less than 900 yds (800 m) across. Areas of the island are totally unspoiled, with long stretches of white sands. Fire Island also has one of the few remaining forests on the Eastern Seaboard.

Fire Island's communities are small and varied. Some are favored by singles looking for the company of the opposite sex, others are sedate and family-orientated, and still others are favorites with New York's large gay community.

Sunbathers basking at Jones Beach

SEVEN GUIDED WALKS

Walking in New York is an excellent way to discover the human scale of the city. The following 16 pages explore the unique character and charm of New York through seven thematic walks. These range from an exploration of Greenwich Village and SoHo's literary and artistic connections *(see pp262–3)* to a trip across the Brooklyn Bridge for spectacular views and a glimpse of 19th-century New York *(see pp268–9)*.

In addition, each of the 15 areas of Manhattan described in the *Area by*

Area section of this book has a short walk on its *Street-by-Street* map, taking you past many of the interesting sights in that area. Various organizations run walking tours of the city. These range from serious appraisals of architectural history to a guide to the ghosts of Broadway. Details of tour organizers are listed on page 379. Although New York is generally a safe place to roam, as in any major city, take care of your personal belongings while walking *(see p364–5)*. Plan your route ahead and be extra cautious when exploring after dark.

The Chinese Garden Court at the Metropolitan Museum of Art, Upper East Side *(see pp266–7)*

Riverfront promenade, Brooklyn *(see pp268–9)*

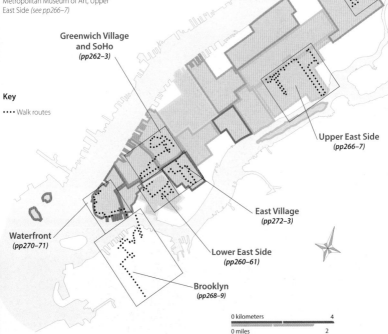

Harlem *(pp274–5)*

Greenwich Village and SoHo *(pp262–3)*

Key

•••• Walk routes

Upper East Side *(pp266–7)*

East Village *(pp272–3)*

Waterfront *(pp270–71)*

Lower East Side *(pp260–61)*

Brooklyn *(pp268–9)*

0 kilometers 4
0 miles 2

◀ Walking across Brooklyn Bridge, downtown Manhattan *(see pp88–91)*

A 90-Minute Walk in the Lower East Side

This walk is through old immigrant neighborhoods that have given New York its unique flavor, and illustrates the ever-changing texture of the city as neighborhoods are rediscovered and one set of newcomers replaces another. Along the way you can experience a variety of cultures and cuisines. Sunday is the most lively day. See more about Lower East Side on pages 94–103.

The Lower East Side

Begin on East Houston Street, the border between the Lower East Side (LES) and the East Village, where some of the best traditional Jewish cuisine can be found at Yonah Schimmel Knish Bakery ① (137). In the same location since 1920, Russ & Daughters, ② (179) is run by the great-grandson of the founder and famed for smoked fish and caviar. Katz's Delicatessen ③ (205) has been a fixture for over 100 years. Continue to Norfolk Street and turn right to see the Angel Orensanz Center ④ (172), housed in New York's oldest synagogue building. Turn right on Rivington Street for the Shaarai Shomoyim First

⑥ An 1885 iron from the Lower East Side Tenement Museum

Romanian-American Congregation ⑤ (89), a synagogue in a handsome 1890 brick building.

The LES has been discovered by hip young New Yorkers and is now home to cutting-edge boutiques, trendy clubs, and restaurants. On Rivington Street, cool fashion shops share the blocks with the old. Make a left onto Orchard Street, the traditional center of the Jewish LES. The sidewalk stands sell mostly cheap merchandise, but many stores offer discount designer leather and fashion. All are closed on Saturday, so Sunday is the busiest day.

A must stop for historians is the Lower East Side Tenement Museum ⑥ (108). An original tenement has been restored to show how three immigrant families lived from 1874 to the 1930s.

Take a short detour to the right down Broome Street for another unique survivor, the Kehila Kedosha Janina Synagogue and Museum ⑦ (280), a small but fascinating congregation with a little upstairs museum.

Return to Orchard Street, continuing along to the right. A left at Grand Street will bring you into New York's former "pickle district" on Essex. Step

into The Pickle Guys store ⑧ (49), where you can sample sour, half-sour, and hot pickles.

Head back along Grand Street, taking a left on Eldridge Street, which will take you, beyond Canal Street, to the grand Eldridge Street Synagogue ⑨ (12), the first Eastern European synagogue in New York, which also houses a museum on the Jewish community.

Key

··· Walk route

✹ Good viewing point

Ⓜ Subway station

Tips for Walkers

Starting point: East Houston St.
Length: 2 miles (3.2 km).
Getting there: Take the subway F or V to Second Avenue; exit East Houston at Eldridge. Other stops: F to Delancey; J, M, Z to Essex. The M15 bus stops on East Houston and on the corner of Delancey and Allen Streets; M14A and M9 run along Essex Street. Returning from Chinatown-Little Italy, Canal Street station is served by the J, N, Q, R, and 6 trains.
Stopping-off points: Little Italy's cafés are perfect for coffee and cakes. For more substantial fare, Hop Kee at 21 Mott Street is good for Chinese food, or for Italian on Mulberry Street, Il Cortile (125) or Il Palazzo (151). Il Laboratorio del Gelato, at 188 Ludlow Street, is a popular spot in summer, offering dozens of flavors of ice cream and sorbet.

Clothes vendors at Orchard Street market

Chinatown

Turn around and return to Canal Street, pausing to admire the spire of the Chrysler Building and the city skyline in view in the distance from Eldridge. Turn left and cross the Bowery, where many jewelry shops are found, remnants of the city's original Diamond District ⑩ (1). As you continue, the shops give way to stalls selling an exotic array of vegetables, and butcher shops with rows of roast ducks in the windows. At 200 Canal Street is Kam Man Food Products. One of the largest Chinese markets in the area, it is a fascinating place to explore. Turn left from Canal

② Russ & Daughters

decidedly unusual flavors such as black sesame, taro, and zen butter, as well as traditional ones. While still on Bayard, have a look at all the Chinese political posters and messages on the Wall of Democracy, then turn back and walk to Mulberry Street. The curve next to Columbus Park was Mulberry Bend ⑫, once notorious for gang murders and mayhem.

⑬ An Italian deli in Little Italy

Little Italy

Walk up Mulberry Street toward Grand Street, and you are suddenly in Little Italy ⑬. Small in area though it is, and encroached on by Chinatown, this is a colorful few blocks of Old-World restaurants, coffee shops, and stores selling home-made pasta, sausages, breads, and pastries.

The Italian population has dwindled over the years, but a staunch group of merchants remain, determined to retain the area's Italian atmosphere. Their stronghold is Mulberry Street, between Broome and Canal streets, with a few shops holding their own on Grand Street near Mulberry. If you continue to walk on Grand, however, you are quickly back into Chinatown.

The big event of the year is the Feast of San Gennaro, named for the patron saint of Naples. For 11 nights in September, Mulberry Street is jammed with locals and visitors enjoying the parades and the Italian food, with rows of sizzling sausages stalls.

Kam Man Food Products at 200 Canal Street

Pretzel seller on Orchard Street

to Mott Street, and you'll know you are right in the heart of Chinatown by all the Chinese neon signs. There are hundreds of restaurants here, from holes-in-the-wall to haute cuisine, all offering a chance to taste unusual fare. For spiritual sustenance. visit the Eastern States Buddhist Temple ⑪ in Mott Street (64b).

At Bayard Street, stop for an ice cream at the Chinatown Ice Cream Factory (65), which offers

A 90-Minute Walk in Greenwich Village and SoHo

A stroll through the patchwork quilt of streets in Greenwich Village takes you to where New York's best-known writers and artists have lived, worked, and played. It ends with a tour of SoHo's galleries and museums, where established artists show their work. For more details on sights in Greenwich Village, see *pages 110–17*, and for SoHo sights, *see pages 104–9*.

⑬ Facade in Washington Mews

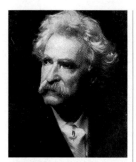

Author Mark Twain, who lived on 10th Street

West 10th Street

The junction of 8th Street and 6th Avenue ① has many book, music, and clothing stores nearby. Walk up Sixth to West Ninth Street to see (on the left at 425) Jefferson Market Courthouse ②.

Turn right at West 10th Street ③ to the Alexander Onassis Center for Hellenic Studies (58). A passageway at the front once led up to the Tile Club, a gathering place for the artists of the Tenth Street Studio, where Augustus Saint-

Gaudens, John LaFarge, and Winslow Homer lived. Mark Twain lived at 24 West 10th Street, and Edward Albee at 50 West 10th.

Back across Sixth Avenue is Milligan Place ④, with 19th-century houses, and Patchin Place ⑤, where the poets E. E. Cummings and John Masefield both lived. Farther on is the site of the Ninth Circle bar ⑥ which when it opened in 1898 was known as "Regnaneschi's." It was the subject of John Sloan's painting *Regnaneschi's Saturday Night*. Playwright Edward Albee first saw the question "Who's afraid of Virginia Woolf?" scrawled on a mirror here.

⑨ The unusual exterior of Twin Peaks

Greenwich Village

Turn left at Waverly Place past the Three Lives Bookstore (154 West 10th St), a typical literary gathering spot, to Christopher Street and the Northern Dispensary ⑦.

Follow Grove Street along Christopher Park to Sheridan Square, the busy hub of the Village. The Circle Repertory Theater ⑧, which premiered plays by Pulitzer Prizewinner Lanford Wilson, is now closed.

Cross Seventh Avenue and bear left on to Grove Street. At the corner of Bedford Street, you can't miss "Twin Peaks" ⑨ (102 Bedford), a home for artists in the 1920s. Turn back around to look at the northeast corner of Bedford and Grove streets ⑩: the exterior of this edifice had a recurring role in the TV sitcom *Friends* as the characters' apartment building. 75½ Bedford is the narrowest house in the Village, and was once the home of feminist poet Edna St. Vincent Millay. Walk up Carmine to Sixth Avenue and turn right at Waverly Place. At 116 Waverly ⑪, Anne Charlotte Lynch, an English teacher, held weekly gatherings in her town house for such eminent friends as Herman Melville and Edgar Allan Poe, who gave his first reading of *The Raven* here.

A detour left of just half a block will bring you to MacDougal Alley ⑫, a lane of carriage houses in which Gertrude Vanderbilt Whitney had her studio. She opened the first Whitney Museum here in 1932, just behind the studio.

Washington Square

Back on MacDougal, turn left to Washington Square North, to see the finest Greek Revival houses in the United States. Built of red brick, they have marble balustrades and entrances flanked by columns. Writer Henry James set his *Washington Square* in No. 18, his grandmother's home.

Washington Square Park and Arch

SoHo

Walk south on Thompson, a typical Village street lined with bars, cafés, and shops. Turn left at Houston, SoHo's northern limit, and right on West Broadway, lined with some of the city's most famous galleries along with a large number of chic and arty boutiques.

Turn left at Spring Street for yet more tempting shops, then right at Greene Street ⑮, which is the heart of the Cast-Iron Historic District. Many of these fine buildings now house art galleries.

Turn left at the end of Greene Street to Canal Street, the end of SoHo, to see how quickly the atmosphere of New York can change. This noisy street is full of hawkers and discount electronics stores. You can explore bargains for the next two blocks and then turn left up Broadway. Keen shoppers can turn right on Spring Street and head for the NoLita district, featuring clothes by trendy, aspiring designers.

Pause at Fifth Avenue to look back at Washington Square Park, with its famous Washington Square Arch. Go across to Two Fifth Avenue; opposite is Washington Mews ⑬, an elegant carriage house complex. John Dos Passos, Edward Hopper, and Rockwell Kent lived in the studio at No. 14a at various times.

Go back up Washington Square North, past some elegant houses. Writer Edith Wharton lived at 7 Washington Square North. Now walk beneath the arch and across Washington Square Park. On the left as you leave the park, is the fine Judson Memorial Church and Tower ⑭ by Stanford White and the NYU Loeb Student Center. The Center was once a boarding house, known as the "house of genius," and is where Theodore Dreiser wrote *An American Tragedy*.

Key

··· Walk route

✳ Good viewing point

Ⓜ Subway station

0 meters 500
0 yards 500

⑮ Cast-iron facade, Greene Street

Footbridge and colorful trees in Central Park ▶

A Two-Hour Walk in the Upper East Side

A promenade along upper Fifth Avenue and its environs will take you past the best remaining examples of New York's turn-of-the-century gilded age. A stroll through the old German district of Yorkville leads to Gracie Mansion, official residence of the city's mayor, dating from 1799. For details on Upper East Side sights, *see pages 184–205*.

From the Frick to the Met

Begin at the Frick mansion ①, built in 1913–14 for coal magnate Henry Clay Frick and home to an exquisite art collection *(pp204–5)*. Many such mansions were built as New York's first families outdid each other with miniature Versailles châteaux and Venetian palazzos. Most of those still standing have now become either institutions or museums. The apartment building opposite the Frick is typical of those where today's affluent New Yorkers live.

East on 70th is one of the city's top art galleries, Hirschl & Adler ② (21). Walk up Madison to the corner of 72nd Street, to the big Polo-Ralph Lauren store ③, the 1898 French Renaissance home of Gertrude Rhinelander Waldo. Wander inside to see the elegant restored interior.

Walk back toward Fifth on the north side of 72nd, past two limestone beauties that once housed the Lycée Français de New York ④. Continue along Fifth Avenue to 73rd Street. Turn east to 11, Joseph Pulitzer's former home ⑤.

A few blocks on, between Lexington and Third, is a fine row of town houses ⑥. Back on Fifth Avenue, walk to 75th Street, to

⑰ Church of the Holy Trinity

⑩ Ukrainian Institute of America

see No. 1, the former residence of Edward S. Harkness, son of a founder of Standard Oil. It is now the Commonwealth Fund ⑦. At 1 East 78th, the tobacco millionaire James B. Duke's 18th-century French-style château is now the New York University Institute of Fine Arts ⑧.

At 79th Street and Fifth, the former home of financier Payne Whitney, is the French Embassy ⑨, and 2 East 79th is the Ukrainian Institute of America ⑩. On the southeast corner of 82nd Street is Duke-Semans House ⑪, one of the few grand Fifth Avenue residences that are still privately owned. Save another full day for The Metropolitan Museum of Art ⑫ at 82nd.

0 meters 500
0 yards 500

Carl Schurz Park Promenade

Yorkville

Turn east on 86th Street for what is left of German Yorkville – Bremen House ⑬, cross Second Avenue, then turn right to the Heidelberg Café and German deli Schaller & Weber ⑭ for a break, or try Papaya King's hot dogs (179 East 86th Street).

East River and Gracie Mansion

Henderson Place ⑮ at East End Avenue is a cluster of 24 Queen Anne town houses. Carl Schurz Park opposite was named for the city's most prominent German immigrant, editor of *Harper's Weekly* and the *New York Post*. The park promenade atop East River Drive leads to a view of Hell Gate, where the Harlem River, Long Island Sound, and New York harbor meet. From the walkway you can see the back of Gracie Mansion ⑯, the mayor's official residence. Walk west on 88th Street past the Church of the Holy Trinity ⑰ and at Lexington Avenue go to 92nd Street and west past two of the few wooden houses left in Manhattan ⑱.

Key

··· Walk route

☀ Good viewing point

Ⓜ Subway station

⑱ Wooden houses on 92nd Street

⑳ The Cooper-Hewitt Museum

Carnegie Hill

Back on Fifth Avenue, turn downtown past the Felix Warburg Mansion of 1908, now the Jewish Museum ⑲, and continue to 91st Street and the huge Andrew Carnegie home, now the Cooper-Hewitt Museum ⑳. Built in 1902 in the style of an English country manor, it gave the area the unofficial name of Carnegie Hill. The James Burden House ㉑ at 7 East 91st Street, built for Vanderbilt heiress Adele Sloan in 1905, has a spiral staircase under a stained-glass skylight that was known in society as "the stairway to heaven." At 1 East 91st, the financier Otto Kahn's Italian Renaissance-style residence was a show-place with a drive-through porch and interior courtyard. It is now the Convent of the Sacred Heart School.

A Three-Hour Walk in Brooklyn

A trip across New York's most famous crossing leads to Brooklyn Heights, the city's first suburb. This neighborhood has a 19th-century feel, mixed with a hint of Middle Eastern cultures. The riverfront promenade has unrivaled views of Manhattan. For more details on sights in Brooklyn, *see pages 249–55*.

Fire Station on Old Fulton Street

Fulton Ferry Landing

About 3,580 ft (1 km) long, the Brooklyn Bridge span yields thrilling views of the lower New York skyline and prize photo opportunities. Take a taxi, or if you have time, walk across to Brooklyn.

On the far side, follow the Tillary Street sign to the right, turn right at the bottom of the stairs, then take the first path through the park and walk down Cadman Plaza West ① under the Brooklyn-Queens Expressway; here Cadman becomes Old Fulton Street. You can see the bridge on the right as you head to the river at Water Street and the Fulton Ferry landing ②. During the Revolutionary War, George

Washington's troops fled to Manhattan from here. In 1814, this was the depot for the ferry connecting Brooklyn and Manhattan Island. This transformed Brooklyn Heights from a predominantly farming area to a residential district. The area is full of character and is still a very popular place to live. To the right is the River Café ③. This restaurant's fine cuisine and spectacular views of the Manhattan skyline make it one of New York's most exceptional dining spots. Double back past the former Eagle Warehouse ④ of 1893.

④ Eagle Warehouse

Brooklyn Heights

From the landing, turn right to steep Everitt Street up Columbia Heights, on to Middagh Street, and along the streets of Brooklyn Heights. 24 Middagh ⑤ is one of the oldest, built in 1824.

Next turn right on Willow and left on Cranberry; here the town houses range from wooden clapboards to brick Federal-style to brownstones. Except for cars and a few modern buildings, you could be in the 19th century.

Many famous people have lived here. Truman Capote wrote *Breakfast at Tiffany's* and *In Cold Blood* in the basement of 70 Willow, and Arthur Miller once owned 155 Willow. Walt Whitman lived on

③ Entrance to the River Café

Cranberry Street when he was editor of the *Brooklyn Eagle*. He set the type for his *Leaves of Grass* at a print shop near the corner of Cranberry and Fulton. The town houses now on the site are called Whitman Close.

Turn right along Hicks. The Hicks family, local farmers, inspired the name "hick" for a yokel. Turn left on Orange Street to the Plymouth Church ⑥, home of Henry Ward Beecher, an antislavery preacher. His sister, Harriet Beecher Stowe, wrote *Uncle*

Truman Capote with feathered friend

Brooklyn Bridge-City M 4.5.6
550 yards/500m

Brooklyn Bridge

East River

BROOKLYN BRIDGE PARK

BROOKLYN QUEENS EXPRESSWAY

FURMAN STREET

COLUMBIA HEIGHTS

WILLOW STREET

HICKS STREET

PIERREPONT ST

MONTAGUE ST

REMSEN STREET

JORALEM

HENRY ST

STATE STREET

ATLANTIC AVE

Tom's Cabin. Meander along Henry and Pineapple streets. At Clark Street are marquees of once-luxurious hotels, such as the Towers. Follow Clark Street to 142 Columbia Heights, where Norman Mailer lived ⑦. Washington Roebling, architect of the Brooklyn Bridge, lived at 110.

anhattan Bridge

MPIRE-JLTON RY PARK

WATER STREET

FRONT STREET

① ⑥ Statue of preacher Henry Ward Beecher

M High Street
A.C

k Street

CADMAN PLAZA EAST

STREET

TILLARY STREET

ADAMS

M Court St
R

JAY STREET

⑫
M Borough Hall
2.3.4.5

Jay Street
Metro Tech M
A.C.F.R

FULTON STREET

STONE ST

BOERUM PLACE

SMITH STREET

LIVINGSTONE STREET

HOYT ST

STATE STREET

Hoyt-
Schermerhorn
Streets
A.C.G M

BOND STREET

STATE STREET

NEVINS STREET

ATLANTIC AVENUE

PACIFIC STREET

PACIFIC STREET

Atlantic Ave
2.3.4.5
M
⑭
3RD AVE

Key

••• Walk route

⚡ Good viewing point

M Subway station

0 meters 500
0 yards 500

The Promenade

At Montague, turn onto the riverfront Promenade ⑧. A tablet at the entrance marks the site of Four Chimneys, the house where George Washington lived during the Battle of Long Island. Walk a little farther for a stunning view of Lower Manhattan that will make you catch your breath in awe. Savor this scene, then turn inland again, on Montague. Here, make a quick detour right to 1 Montague Terrace ⑨ where the English poet W. H. Auden lived. Thomas Wolfe finished *Of Time and the River* while he was living at 5 Montague.

Tips for Walkers

Starting point: Brooklyn Bridge.
Length: 3½ miles (5.5 km).
Getting there: Take subway train 4, 5, or 6 on the Lexington Ave line to Brooklyn Bridge-City Hall (nearest stop to the bridge). The M15 Second Ave bus also stops at City Hall. Returning to Manhattan, take train 2, 3, 4, 5, M, N, or R from Borough Hall; or 2, 3, 4, 5, M, N, R, or Q from Atlantic Ave.
Stopping-off points: Teresa's, 80 Montague St, has Polish dishes at reasonable prices. Try Henry's End, 44 Henry St, for fine dining in Brooklyn Heights. For light meals visit acclaimed deli Mile End, 97A Hoyt St, or Iris Café, 20 Columbia Place.

The old Montague Street trolley, which led to the river and the ferry

Montague and Clinton Streets

Once back on Montague, walk to the heart of Brooklyn Heights, with its cafés and boutiques. The baseball team, the Brooklyn Dodgers, who relocated to Los Angeles in 1958, got their name from dodging the trolley cars that once ran down the street. Walk to the intersection of Montague and Clinton to see the stained glass of the 1834 Church of St. Ann and the Holy Trinity ⑩. Walk a block left on Clinton to Pierrepont Street for the Brooklyn Historical Society ⑪. A block farther, at Court Street, is the 1849 Borough Hall ⑫, and the subway back to Manhattan.

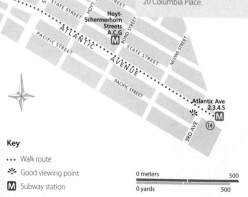

Brooklyn's Dodgers, who got their name from dodging trolley cars

Atlantic Avenue

Another option is to stay on Clinton Street and walk the five short blocks to Atlantic Avenue. A left turn here leads to a whole string of Middle Eastern emporia, such as Sahadi Imports ⑬ at 187 Atlantic Avenue, which stocks a huge selection of foods. The Damascus Bakery at 195 makes the most delicious filo pastries. Various other shops here sell Arabic books, tapes, DVDs, and CDs.

At Flatbush Avenue, look left to the Brooklyn Academy of Music ⑭ and the grand front of the Williamsburg Savings Bank. Watch for signs to the subway for your journey back to Manhattan.

A 90-Minute Waterfront Walk

From the breezy Battery Park City Esplanade with its sweeping river views and upscale condos to the magnificent schooners moored at South Street Seaport, this waterfront route introduces you to New York's formidable maritime legacy. The concrete jungle may lie just a few blocks inland, yet it seems worlds away, as the bleating horns and hiss of the crosstown buses are blessedly muffled. Stroll the green tip of Battery Park for a startling reminder that Manhattan is, in fact, an island. For more details on sights in Lower Manhattan, *see pp66–81.*

View of the Statue of Liberty from the waterfront promenade

⑤ The many photographs at the Museum of Jewish Heritage

Battery Park City

Begin your walk on the Esplanade ① near Rector Place Park, west of the Rector Street subway stop. Across the Hudson River looms the New Jersey skyline. Stroll toward the South Cove ②, where you'll catch sight, as did more than 100 million immigrants on their arrival, of Lady Liberty herself. Explore Robert F. Wagner, Jr. Park ③, named after a former New York City mayor. The leafy acres of grassy slopes, linden trees, and inviting pavilions are an important link in Lower Manhattan's waterfront

"greenbelt". Climb to the Wagner Park lookout point ④ for vistas of the Hudson River. Here, information panels chronicle New York City's seafaring history, when grand schooners and coastal packets plied these waters.

Battery Place

On Battery Place, visit the Museum of Jewish Heritage ⑤ *(see p79)* and its outdoor Garden of Stones, a calm, elegant space of dwarf oak saplings growing out of boulders. Since Manhattan is the undisputed king of tall buildings, pay homage at the sleek Skyscraper Museum ⑥, a marvel in stainless steel. Admire skyscraper history and contemporary designs from around the world, as well as the original model, created in 1971, of the former World Trade Center.

⑥ Shiny surfaces and sharp angles at the Skyscraper Museum

⑨ Castle Clinton, an early 19th century fort built to defend the harbor

Battery Park

On your way to nearby Battery Park, check out Pier A ⑦, which is all that remains of the 1886 grand marine firehouse. Important visitors who arrived by sea were once greeted with festive jets of water pumped into the sky by the fireboats. The clock on the pier tower used to keep time to the maritime system – eight bells and all's well. Continue along the waterfront, looking out for the American Merchant Mariners Memorial ⑧, a haunting sculpture of soldiers pulling a desperate comrade out of the waters, based on photographs of a World War II attack on an American ship.

Head past Castle Clinton monument ⑨, a fort

⑬ Enjoying a well-earned rest at a café, South Street Seaport

built during the War of 1812. It later became an opera house, theater, and aquarium, but is now a museum. Stroll through the park where you can relax on benches in the shade of trees. Continue on to State Street, turn right on Whitehall, and then left onto South Street, passing the graceful Beaux Arts Battery Maritime Building ⑩.

up the famed Wall Street ⑫ (see pp68–9) as you cross it, for a view of the spires of Trinity Church (see p70). Turn right at Maiden Lane, then left onto the quaint and cobblestoned Front Street, which feeds into South Street Seaport ⑬ (see pp84–7), marked by the wooden masts and sails of the tall ships in the harbor. Explore New York's seafaring history at the South Street Seaport Museum, and then wander the shop-lined Fulton Street to Water Street. Take a peek into Bowne & Co Stationers at 211 ⑭, a charming old-fashioned print shop with 19th-century antique hand presses. Amble toward Pier 16 for a further glimpse of the past at the Maritime Crafts Center ⑮ where painters and carvers work at figureheads. Continue on to Pier 17 ⑯, bustling with shops and cafés. As you walk the wooden pier, look back for a memorable view of Manhattan – the masts of ancient schooners against the city's towering skyscrapers. The pier is undergoing renovation so access may be limited. Finish up at the inviting Paris Café in the 1873 Meyer's Hotel (see p85).

Key

••• Walk route

⚡ Good viewing point

Ⓜ Subway station

```
0 meters        300
0 yards         300
```

South Street Seaport

Follow South Street, with the Brooklyn Bridge in the distance. Walk through the Vietnam Veterans Memorial Plaza ⑪ with its glass memorial etched with the poignant words from soldiers to their loved ones. Head north on Water Street, so named because it marks what was once the water's edge, and past Old Slip; all streets named "slip" are where boats used to dock between piers. Look west

Tips for Walkers

Starting point: The Esplanade near Rector Place.

Length: 2 miles (3.2 km).

Getting there: Take subway train 1 or R to Rector Street. Head west on Rector Street, cross the bridge over West Street to Rector Place, and walk to the Esplanade.

Stopping-off points: Gigino, on Wagner Park at 20 Battery Place, offers savory Italian fare outdoors.

A 90-Minute Walk in the East Village

Originally the farm or *bouwerie* of the Stuyvesant family, this historic area now has a different appeal thanks to its musical and artistic associations, as well as many of the city's buzzing and affordable ethnic bars and restaurants. It also manages to balance a peaceful residential area with business and creativity, which is reflected in the constantly changing funky record shops, vegan cafés, craft stores, and live music clubs. For more details on sights in the East Village, *see pp118–23.*

Astor Place

Adjacent to the Astor Place subway stop is a black steel cube called the *Alamo* ① – a meeting point for students and skateboarders. Walk towards Third Avenue through the large buildings that comprise Cooper Union ② *(see p122).* This scholarship college was founded in 1859 by Peter Cooper, an illiterate but successful businessman and proponent of free education. Across the street is the Continental ③, a live music venue that has hosted groups such as Iggy Pop and Guns N' Roses. In the East Village, 8th Street becomes St. Mark's Place ④, a former jazz, then hippie, then punk hangout. With so many sidewalk cafés and street vendors, this is one of the busiest pedestrian areas of Manhattan. St. Mark's Ale House ⑤ on the right, formerly The Five Spot, was where musicians and poets got together in the 1960s. A few steps down is Trash and Vaudeville ⑥, a punk/goth clothing store that was once the Bridge Theater. The venue was repeatedly shut down due to controversial acts, then reopened. Yoko Ono held

Locals enjoying celebrations on Ukrainian Day

"happenings," and the US flag was burned as an anti-war protest in 1967. At 19–25 St. Mark's Place ⑦, there was a Jewish hangout, then the Italian mafia ruled, until Andy Warhol turned the space into the infamous nightclub Electric Circus in the 1960s. The Velvet Underground was among the bands who played here.

Little Ukraine

Turn left onto Second Avenue, home to one of the largest and longest-standing Ukrainian populations in the US, with restaurants, bars, and centers such as the Ukrainian National Home ⑧ on the right (140), and the good-value, 24-hour Ukrainian eatery Veselka ⑨ on the corner. Farther up

Tips for Walkers

Starting point: The Alamo.
Length: 1.75 miles (2.8 km).
Getting there: Take the subway train 6 to Astor Place. Or take M101, M102, or M103 buses.
Stopping-off Points: Many good-value places on St. Mark's Place, but try Jules Bistro (French) between 1st and 2nd avenues, and Caracas Arepa Bar (cheap Venezuelan) at 93½ East 7th St.

⑥ Trash and Vaudeville store, once a venue known for controversial acts

⑪ The style and elegance of an earlier century at Veniero's

First Avenue Ⓜ

EAST 14TH STREET
EAST 13TH STREET
EAST 12TH STREET
EAST 11TH STREET
EAST 10TH STREET
EAST 9TH STREET
ST MARKS PLACE
AST 7TH STREET
9TH STREET

FIRST AVENUE
AVENUE A
AVENUE B

⑪
⑫
⑰
⑯

TOMPKINS SQUARE

⑬
⑮
⑭

⑭ Elm tree in Tomkins Square Park, a Hare Krishna memorial

Key

··· Walk route

Ⓜ Subway station

0 meters   200
0 yards   200

Second Avenue, at East 10th Street, sits the St. Mark's-in-the-Bowery Church ⑩ (see p123). Erected in 1795, this church was Dutch governor Peter Stuyvesant's private chapel and he is buried here. More recently, the Black Panthers and Young Lords gathered here, and Allen Ginsberg and other writers contributed to The Poetry Project that exists to this day. A right on 11th Street leads to Veniero's ⑪, a stylish Italian bakery that still has many of its original details, such as hand-stamped metal ceilings. Make a right and then a left onto 10th Street, past the three-story Russian and Turkish Bath House ⑫, to the northern edge of Tompkins Square Park ⑬ (see p123).

Tompkins Square Park
Built in 1834, this square has seen political activism of all kinds. It is also where a sacred elm tree in the middle of the park ⑭ commemorates the first Hare Krishna ceremony on American soil. Jazz great Charlie Parker lived across the street from the park from 1950 to 1955 ⑮. Walk to the southwestern corner on 7th Street where 7A ⑯ serves breakfast 24 hours a day. Down the block, Turntable Lab ⑰ sells DJ equipment and vinyl. If thirsty, continue west toward Second Avenue to McSorley's Old Ale House ⑱, one of the oldest bars in the city. Then get back onto Second Avenue and turn right to see where the old Fillmore East Auditorium ⑲ used to be (105). This classic rock scene featured such legends as The Doors, Jimi Hendrix, Janis Joplin, and Pink Floyd. The Who even premiered their rock opera *Tommy* here. Look left at 6th Street – "Indian Restaurant Row" ⑳ – where Bengali curry houses compete for business. Go down Second Avenue to number 80 ㉑; this was the home of Joe "The Boss" Masseria, head of the Italian mob in the 1920s. Turn right onto 4th Street where KGB bar ㉒, on the right, is a literary institution. Continue straight along 4th Street to Lafayette Street, and stop off at Other Music ㉓ to check out the city's hottest rock sounds. A right down Great Jones Street and a final left on Bowery lead to the former site (315) of CBGB & OMFUG ㉔, or Country, Bluegrass, Blues & Other Music For Uplifting Gormandizers, birthplace of American rock band Talking Heads.

⑳ "Indian Restaurant Row," lined with curry houses

A 90-Minute Walk in Harlem

Few neighborhoods in New York are as rich in cultural history as Harlem, a haven for African-American heritage. This walk starts in Strivers' Row, one of the few areas that provided affordable housing during the 1920s and 1930s when the area was bursting with creative and intellectual expression. It takes you past renowned gospel churches, jazz and blues clubs, and ends at the Apollo Theater, Harlem's famous showcase for new artists. For more details on sights in Harlem, *see pp222–33.*

⑭ Apollo Theater, famous for televised shows and legendary acts

Strivers' Row

The tree-lined area on 138th Street between Seventh and Eighth avenues is the St. Nicholas Historic District, commonly known as Strivers' Row ①. In the 1920s and 1930s wealthy and influential black professionals aiming for better lives moved into homes designed by such great architects as James Brown Lord and McKim, Mead & White. Signs on some of the gates still read "Private road walk your horses." A short detour left on Seventh Avenue (Adam Clayton Powell, Jr. Boulevard) and right on 139th Street leads to West 139th Street ②, where in 1932 16-year-old Billie Holiday moved into No. 108 shortly before landing her first singing job at a club in nearby "Jungle Alley."

① An ornate doorway in Strivers' Row

renowned for its magnificent Sunday gospel service. Founded in 1921 and named for the East African Americans of its first congregation, this church has hosted such notable pastors as Adam Clayton Powell, Jr. A stone's throw away on West 137th Street is the Mother Zion church ④, New York's first black church and one of America's oldest. While part of the Underground Railroad (an escape route for slaves), it acquired the nickname "Freedom Church." Continue to the Countee Cullen Regional Library where Madam C.J. Walker founded the Walker School of Hair ⑤. With her successful cosmetics line and hair-smoothing system, Walker was one of the first self-made female millionaires in the country. An active philanthropist, she donated to many African-American charities such as the National Association of Colored

Abyssinian Baptist Church

Turn right at Lenox Avenue and right back onto 138th Street toward the striking Abyssinian Baptist Church ③ *(see p237)*, which is internationally

People (NAACP) and Tuskegee Institute. After her death in 1919, her daughter A'Leila turned the salon into an intellectual center for artists, scholars, and activists. It was named "The Dark Tower" after Harlem writer Countee Cullen's protest poem. Around the corner on Lenox Avenue is the Schomburg Center for Research into Black Culture ⑥ *(see p231)*, a national research library named for the Puerto Rican-born black scholar who donated his personal collection to the library and served as its curator for six years. Down West 136th Street at No. 267 is "Niggerati Manor" ⑦, an artist's rooming house, so-named by Zora Neale Hurston, who lived here while collaborating with Wallace Thurman, Aaron Douglas, and Bruce Nugent on *Fire!!,* a magazine devoted to young black artists. Get back on Adam Clayton Powell, Jr. Boulevard

⑩ The famous Sylvia's restaurant, providing authentic soul food

and follow it down to "Jungle Alley" ⑧, the former highlight of Harlem nightlife, which once contained numerous bars, clubs, cabarets, and speakeasies. A detour across 131st Street will bring you to Marcus Garvey's house ⑨ (235), a major leader and fierce proponent of black unity, economic independence, and pride. Return to Adam Clayton Powell, Jr. Boulevard and make a left on 127th

⑥ Art displays at the Schomberg Center for Research into Black Culture

The great jazz singer Billie Holiday ②

and John Coltrane have all performed. Lenox Lounge is also home to the Zebra Room, a jazz spot that James Baldwin and Malcolm X frequented. In the middle of the next block is The Studio Museum in Harlem ⑬ (see pp232–3), with a variety of contemporary art exhibits, programs, lectures, and performances by artists of African descent. Its store is also worth a browse for its array of posters and books.

Apollo Theater

On West 125th Street is the famous Apollo Theater ⑭ (see p232), where since 1934, "stars are born and legends are made." These performers have ranged in style from Ella Fitzgerald to James Brown. Since 1987, "Amateur Night at the Apollo" has been televised nationwide and the theater has become the third-most popular tourist destination in Manhattan.

⑧ "Jungle Alley," where Billie Holiday first performed

0 meters 200
0 yards 200

Street until you reach Sylvia's Restaurant ⑩ (see p232), the self-proclaimed "Queen of Soul Food." Family-owned since 1962, Sylvia's serves authentic southern favorites, such as fried chicken, catfish, and BBQ ribs. Alternatively, stay on Lenox Avenue until 125th Street, where you'll find Red Rooster Harlem ⑪. Stop off here for a glimpse, as well as a taste, of modern, trendy Harlem before heading to Lenox Lounge ⑫, where Billie Holiday, Miles Davis,

Tips for Walkers

Starting point: Strivers' Row.
Length: 1.75 miles (2.8 km)
Getting there: Take subway train 2 or 3 to 135th St and Lenox Ave, then walk north to 138th St and west to Seventh Ave. Or take M2, M7, or M10 bus to 135th St and walk to Seventh Ave.
Stopping-off Points: Sylvia's on 127th and Lenox is the famous soul food place in Harlem. It is the perfect place to refuel.

Key

••• Walk route

Ⓜ Subway station

(Map labels: RIDGECOMBE AVENUE, WEST 141ST STREET, WEST 140TH STREET, WEST 139TH STREET, ① WEST 138TH STREET (STRIVERS' ROW), WEST 137TH STREET, ⑦ WEST 136TH ST, WEST 135TH STREET, WEST 134TH STREET, 133RD STREET, 135th Street Ⓜ 2,3, WEST 135TH STREET, (SEVENTH AVENUE), WEST 138TH STREET, ② ③ ④ ⑤ ⑥ ⑧, MALCOLM X BOULEVARD (LENOX AVE), ADAM CLAYTON POWELL JR BOULEVARD, WEST 132ND STREET, WEST 131ST STREET, WEST 130TH STREET, WEST 129TH STREET, WEST 128TH STREET, ⑩ ⑪ 125th Street Ⓜ 2,3, ⑬ ⑫, WEST 124TH STREET, AFRICAN SQUARE, WEST 123RD ST, MARCUS GARVEY PARK, FIFTH AVENUE)

TRAVELERS'
NEEDS

WHERE TO STAY

With over 90,000 hotel rooms available, New York offers something for everyone. The city's top hotels are the most expensive in the US, but the best news for visitors is the increase in budget and mid-priced hotels. While many of these are basic rather than charming, they offer good value. Other budget options are furnished apartments and studios, and bed and breakfasts, as well as youth hostels and YMCAs. The hotels listed in this guide have been selected for their value, location, and amenities. Entries are separated by theme and price, helping you choose accommodations that best suit your needs. Hotels highlighted as DK Choice offer something special such as beautiful interiors or remarkable service.

Rooftop terrace at the Peninsula New York *(see p287)*

Where to Look

The East Side, roughly between 59th and 77th Streets, is the traditional location for luxury hotels. The renovation of some landmark Midtown properties by famous hotel chains, however, such as the St. Regis by Starwood, and the former Gotham Hotel, which is now The Peninsula New York, has considerably increased the competition in this price range.

Business travelers tend to favor Midtown, especially the moderately priced hotels lining Lexington Avenue near Grand Central Terminal.

Those seeking relative quiet with access to Midtown should look in the Murray Hill area, while theater-lovers should note the revival of the Times Square area, where there are many hotels within walking distance of the bustling Theater District.

There are a number of good, inexpensive hotels around Herald Square, which is convenient for shopping. Trendy boutique hotels have flourished in SoHo and the Meatpacking District, where there are also plenty of good bars, restaurants, and upscale shops *(see pp312–13)* as well as trendy nightclubs.

New York City & Co. (the Convention & Visitors Bureau) publishes a free, annually updated leaflet called "The New York Hotel Guide," listing rates and toll-free numbers. This leaflet is available in the arrivals hall at JFK Airport. Staff will offer advice about hotels but do not make reservations.

Finding Bargains

Some hotels offer seasonal promotional rates and other off-peak reductions. For example, business travelers vacate hotels at the end of the working week, so you can take advantage of bargain weekend deals, even in luxury hotels, as prices drop *(see Special Rates p279).* There are a growing number of good value all-suite hotels available in every price category. Renting out a private home is also becoming increasingly popular and can often work out much cheaper than staying in a hotel.

Hidden Extras

When calculating the cost of hotels in New York, it is not enough simply to take into consideration the quoted room price. Hotel rooms are subject to a blanket 14.75% hotel tax, plus $2 per night per room fee.

Several hotels now include continental breakfast in the room price. This represents a big saving, since standard hotel continental breakfast prices, before tax and tip, start at about $10 and soar to $25 in some of the luxury hotels. To save money, head for the nearest deli or coffee shop and leave the hotel to business people having power breakfasts.

Hotel telephone charges are always high; it is much less expensive to use a cell phone, or Wi-Fi, if available.

Tips are expected. Staff who take your luggage to the room

Antique furnishings, Inn at Irving Place *(see p282)*

The Tribeca Grand lobby *(see p282)*

are usually tipped a minimum of $1 per bag – more in a luxury hotel. The concierge need not be tipped for normal services such as arranging transportation or making dinner reservations, but should be rewarded for exceptional services. When you order from room service, a service charge will usually be included in the bill; if not, a 15–20% tip is customary. Solo travelers will find that single room rates are usually at least 80% of the double rate and are sometimes the same as for two people.

Facilities

Television, radio, and at least one telephone are usually provided in every room, even in modest lodgings, and most hotel bedrooms have private bathrooms. In budget and mid-priced hotels, a shower, rather than a tub, is the norm. Many hotels offer Internet access (often with free Wi-Fi), a business center, and a health club or exercise room. Luxury facilities include minibars in the room, dual phones, private phone message systems, and electronic checkout.

Although you'd expect hotel rooms in New York City to be noisy, most windows are double- or even triple-glazed to keep out the noise. Air-conditioning is a standard feature, so there is no need to open the windows in hot weather. Even so, some rooms are obviously quieter than

others, especially if they are at the back of the hotel or overlooking a courtyard – check when reserving. Light sleepers may also want to request a room away from the elevator.

Most of the hotels listed here are within a few minutes' walk of shops and restaurants. Few hotels have their own parking, but valets may park your car in nearby garages. A reduced (but still expensive) daily parking fee is normally offered. If there is no concierge at the hotel, front desk staff will always help to answer any queries.

How to Reserve

It is advisable to make hotel reservations at least one month in advance, otherwise you may well find that the best rooms and suites have been taken. The busiest periods are at Easter, the New York Marathon week in late October or early November, Thanksgiving, and Christmas.

The easiest way to book a hotel room directly is through the hotel's website. You may be required to pay a deposit or provide a credit card number to secure the booking. Print out a copy of the booking confirmation to give to the hotel when you check in. Reservations through third party websites such as www.expedia.com and www.hotels.com can offer the best value for money.

Most hotels have a toll-free telephone number for use in the United States, but these numbers do not work from Europe and the

UK. If the hotel is part of an international chain, an affiliated hotel in your country should be able to reserve a room for you.

Special Rates

Hotels are busiest during the week, when business travelers are in the city, so most of them offer budget weekend packages. It's often possible to move from a standard to a luxury room for the weekend at the same rate. A lower corporate rate is usually available to employees of large companies. Quite often reservation clerks will grant corporate discounts on request without asking for a company affiliation. It is also worth checking a hotel website for special deals and promotions.

Some reservation agencies offer discount rates. A good travel agent should be able to get the best rates, but compare prices by contacting directly a discount reservation service such as **Quikbook** *(see p281)*, which offers discounts of 20–50%, depending on the time of year. You reserve by credit card and receive a voucher, which you present to the hotel. Sites such as www.kayak.com offer "private sales" of discounted hotel rooms.

Package tours can also provide savings. Their rates may not oblige you to stay with a tour group, only to use their air and hotel arrangements. They may also include airport transfers, an additional saving. Airlines frequently have special deals, particularly during slow

Understated elegance at the stylish Kitano *(see p287)*

travel seasons. A know-ledgeable travel agent should be able to tell you the current best deals, but searching online might be an easier and quicker way to find limited offers that can be booked directly. At off-peak times you may net even bigger savings than with the package plans.

Disabled Travelers

By law, new hotels must provide facilities for disabled visitors. Many older buildings have also been renovated so as to comply with this regulation.

To find out which hotels offer the best facilities, check their websites. These are provided for all the hotels listed on pp282–7. When booking, let the hotel know of any specific needs. Guide dogs are allowed in most hotels, but it is also advisable to check in advance.

The **Mayor's Office for People with Disabilities** produces the "Official Accessibility Guide", with useful information about hotels for disabled travelers.

Traveling with Children

American hotels are generally very welcoming toward children. Cots or cribs as well as lists of reliable baby-sitters are usually available, and most hotel restaurants will cater to young guests.

Traveling with children need not be expensive. Many hotels do not charge for children if they stay in their parents' room, or make only a small charge for an extra bed. There is usually a limit of one or two children per room in these cases, and most hotels stipulate that the children must be under a certain age, most often 12. Parents of older children are expected to pay the full price, although the age limit is occasionally extended to 18. Ask about family rates when you make your reservation.

Bed-and-Breakfast

A good number of bed-and-breakfast accommodations in private apartments is available in New York.

Lobby of the St. Regis Hotel *(see p287)*

Bed-and-breakfast lodgings can be found through many free booking services. Some booking agencies have a two-or-more-night minimum stay.

Rates for a double room typically start at $100 a night, depending on whether you have a private bathroom.

Private Homes

Increasingly, one of the most affordable ways to stay in New York is by renting out a private apartment or room. A number of services facilitate this, including the very popular – and well run – **AirBnB** (www.airbnb.com), which offers accommodation in a wide range of private homes and apartments in New York, from townhouses on the Upper East Side to student flats in the East Village and Brooklyn. Another source for budget lodging is **Couchsurfing** (www.couchsurfing.org), which has many member-hosts in New York. Rates for private apartments vary from about $100 to $300. Be aware that if the address is remote or inconveniently far from bus routes or subway stations, your costs will rise, as you will need frequent cabs. Ask about location and amenities when you reserve.

Youth and Budget Accommodations

New York's youth hostel and **YMCA** dormitories offer lodgings for those on a tight budget. For

the longer-term visitor, the **92nd Street Y**, a nonsectarian hostel in the Upper East Side, has good-value rooms, with prices starting from around $35 to $50 a night.

There are no campsites in Manhattan, and, sadly, youth hostels are not as prevalent in New York as they are in large European cities.

For budget-minded travelers looking for the bare essentials, inexpensive rooms are available in several areas of New York, particularly in Chelsea, the Garment District, and the Upper West Side, and to a lesser extent in such prime neighborhoods as Upper Midtown. Although some of these budget-price rooms are comfortable, with private baths or showers, others may be rather small, perhaps with no air-conditioning, and you may have to share a bathroom.

Suites

If you'd like extra space – or are planning on an extended stay in NYC – opt for an apartment or all-suite hotel, which feature sizeable kitchenettes. Suites offer extra space plus cooking facilities and a refrigerator. Most suites can accommodate up to four people, which makes them popular with families.

Beyond Manhattan

As Manhattan becomes more expensive – accommodation options are emerging in the outer boroughs for savvy travelers. Areas such as Williamsburg and Dumbo in Brooklyn have become destinations in their own right, thanks to a rising number of bars, good restaurants, and trendy stores.

For a little over $300, you can book a king room at the Best Western Gregory Hotel in Brooklyn *(see p285)*, or a room with flat-screen TV and wireless internet access at the four-star boutique hotel Le Bleu, in the up-and-coming area of Gowanus, close to Park Slope (www.hotellebleu.com).

As always, cheaper deals can often be negotiated or found on hotel websites.

Recommended Hotels

Our hotels are divided up into five categories: B&Bs, Boutique, Budget, Business, and Luxury. Boutique hotels are generally smaller, with high design elements. Luxury hotels encompass the finest of New York's upscale hotels, with many luxury amenities, from spas to celebrity-chef restaurants. New York City's B&Bs offer a friendly, personable experience, with cozy rooms and a hearty breakfast. Business hotels in New York feature sleek and contemporary rooms, and business amenities, from Wi-Fi and business centers to meeting rooms with audio and visual technology. Many business hotels offer good-value deals on the weekend.

Our hotels are divided into five geographical areas: Downtown is

Entrance to the Peninsula Hotel *(see p287)*

a richly varied area that encompasses Lower Manhattan, Seaport and the Civic Center, the Lower East Side, Soho and Tribeca, Greenwich Village, the East Village, and Gramercy and the Flatiron District. Midtown

covers both Lower and Upper Midtown, as well as Chelsea and the Theater District, which is popular with visitors who are in town to see Broadway shows. The Upper East Side features many of New York City's most upscale hotels, while the Upper West Side, which includes Morningside Heights and Harlem, features a broad range of hotels. Farther Afield includes hotels and B&Bs in Brooklyn and Queens.

Throughout our listings, we've marked recommended hotels as DK Choice. We've chosen these hotels because they offer a special experience – either for superlative service, beautiful interiors and rooms, top-notch amenities and gadgets, an excellent on-site restaurant or rooftop bar, or a combination of these.

DIRECTORY

Where to Look

New York City & Co.
810 7th Ave. **Map** 12 E4.
Tel (212) 484-1222.
W nycgo.com

Airport Reservations

Accommodations Plus
JFK International Airport.
Tel 1-800-733-7666.

Meegan Services
JFK International Airport.
Tel 1-800-441-1115.

Discount Reservation Services

Expedia
W expedia.co.uk

Hotel Rooms 365
Tel (212) 840-8686.
W hotelrooms365.com

Hotels.com
Tel 1-800-246-8357.
W hotels.com

Kayak
W kayak.co.uk

Quikbook
Tel (212) 779-7666.
W quikbook.com

Disabled Travelers

Mayor's Office for People with Disabilities
100 Gold St, 2nd floor,
NY, NY 10038.
Tel (212) 788-2830.
W nyc.gov/mopd

Bed & Breakfast

At Home in Brooklyn
15 Prospect Park W,
Brooklyn, NY 11215.
Tel (718) 622-5292.
W athomeinbrooklyn.
com

At Home in NY
Tel (212) 956-3125.
W athomeny.com

CountryInn The City
Tel (212) 580-4183.
W countryinnthecity.
com

Private Homes

Airbnb
W airbnb.co.uk

Couchsurfing
W couchsurfing.org

Youth Hostels and Budget Accommodations

Chelsea Hostel
251 W 20th St,
NY, NY 10011.
Map 8 D5.
Tel (212) 647-0010.
W chelseahostel.com

Hosteling International, NY
891 Amsterdam Ave at
W 103rd St, NY, NY 10025.
Map 20 E5.
Tel (212) 932-2300.
W hinewyork.org

New York's Jazz Hostels
W jazzhostels.com

92nd Street Y
1395 Lexington Ave, NY,
NY 10128. **Map** 17 A2.
Tel (212) 415-5650.
W 92y.org

YMCA– Vanderbilt
224 E 47th St,
NY, NY 10017.
Map 13 A5.
Tel (212) 912-2500.
W ymcanyc.org

YMCA– West Side
5 W 63rd St, NY, NY 10023.
Map 12 D2.
Tel (917) 441-8800.
W ymcanyc.org

Suite Hotels

Affinia Hotels
Reservations:
Tel (212) 465-3661.
Toll-free: 1-866-246 2203.
W affinia.com

Beekman Tower
3 Mitchell Pl.
Map 13 C5.
Tel 1-888-754-8044.
W thebeekmanhotel.
com

The Benjamin
125 E 50th St. **Map** 13 B4.
Tel (212) 715-2500.
W thebenjamin.com

Eastgate Tower
222 E 39th St. **Map** 9 B1.
W eastgate-tower-nyc.
hotel-rv.com.com

The Phillips Club
155 West 66th St.
Map 12 D2.
Tel 1-887-644-8900.
W phillipsclub.com

The Surrey
20 E 76th St. **Map** 17 A5.
Tel (212) 905-1477.
W thesurrey.com

Where to Stay

Bed and Breakfast

Downtown

DK Choice

East Village Bed & Coffee $
110 Avenue C, 10009
Tel (917) 816-0071   **Map** 5 B2
W bedandcoffee.com
Quirky inn with themed rooms,
from soothing Zen and bright
Mexican to earth-toned beach
decor. Each floor has shared
bathrooms and fully equipped
kitchens, while rooms feature
iPod docking stations.

Abingdon Guest House $$
13 Eighth Ave, 10014
Tel (212) 243-5384   **Map** 3 C1
W abingdonguesthouse.com
Unique guesthouse with inviting,
residential-style rooms.

Inn at Irving Place $$$
56 Irving Place, 10003
Tel (212) 533-4600   **Map** 9 A5
W innatirving.com
Exclusive, impeccable
guesthouse in two magnificent
adjoining brownstones.

Upper West Side

The Harlem Flophouse $
242 West 123rd St, 10027
Tel (347) 632-1960   **Map** 21 A2
W harlemflophouse.com
Cozy rooms, and shared bath-
rooms with antique brass fixtures.

Sugar Hill Harlem Inn $$
460 West 141st St, 10031
Tel (212) 234-5432   **Map** 19 A2
W sugarhillharleminn.com
Eco-friendly hotel in a lovely
Victorian townhouse.

Farther Afield

Bibi's Garden Bed & Breakfast $
762 Westminster Rd, Brooklyn, 11230
Tel (718) 434-3119
W bibisgarden.net
Victorian house with lovely rooms
decorated with antiques. Offers
continental breakfast spread.

The Sofia Inn $
288 Park Place, Brooklyn, 11238
Tel (917) 865-7428
W brooklynbedandbreakfast.net
Historic B&B with traditional
rooms and hardwood floors.
Check out the garden with its
private bath.

Boutique

Downtown

Duane Street Hotel $$
130 Duane St, 10013
Tel (212) 964-4600   **Map** 1 B1
W duanestreethotel.com
Intimate hotel with sleek, loft-
style rooms and smart urban
design; inviting restaurant.

Gershwin Hotel $$
7 East 27th St, 10016
Tel (212) 545-8000   **Map** 8 F3
W gershwinhotel.com
With a stylish and modern decor,
this hotel has a wide range of
accommodation options to suit
all budgets.

Gild Hall $$
15 Gold St, 10038
Tel (212) 232-7700   **Map** 2 D2
W thompsonhotels.com
Elegant, discreet hotel with a
classy wood-paneled library
and a Champagne bar. Its
proximity to Wall Street
attracts corporate travelers.

Price Guide
Prices are based on one night's stay in
high season for a standard double room,
inclusive of service charges and taxes.

$	under $200
$$	$200 to $400
$$$	over $400

DK Choice

Hotel Giraffe $$
365 Park Ave South, 10016
Tel (212) 685-7700   **Map** 9 A4
W hotelgiraffe.com
This hotel is the epitome of
boutique elegance, with a light-
filled lobby and a baby grand
piano. Impeccable rooms with
velveteen chairs and French
doors. There's a rooftop garden
bar. Complimentary breakfast.

Hotel on Rivington $$
107 Rivington St, 10002
Tel (212) 475-2600   **Map** 5 A3
W hotelonrivington.com
Fashionable hotel with spacious
rooms, plush decor, and great
floor-to-ceiling views.

Smyth Tribeca $$
85 West Broadway, 10007
Tel (212) 587-7000   **Map** 1 B1
W thompsonhotels.com
Modern hotel with classic
touches, sleek and sizeable
rooms, and marble bathrooms.

The Marcel at Gramercy $$–$$$
201 East 24th St, 10010
Tel (212) 696-3800   **Map** 9 B4
W marcelatgramercy.com
Chic rooms with rain showers
in bathrooms. Beds have
luxurious Italian linens.

The Roger New York $$
131 Madison Ave, 10016
Tel (212) 448-7000   **Map** 9 A3
W therogernewyork.com
Warm, inviting hotel with lots of
amenities. There are terrace
rooms with private balconies.

The Standard $$
25 Cooper Square, 10003
Tel (212) 475-5700   **Map** 4 F2
W standardhotels.com
Eye-catching hotel designed by
Carlos Zapata. Comfy rooms with
all modern amenities. Compli-
mentary continental breakfast.

Wall Street Inn $$
9 South William St, 10004
Tel (212) 747-1500   **Map** 1 C3
W thewallstreetinn.com
Business-friendly hotel with cozy
rooms and comfortable beds.

Chic interiors and classy lounge area at Hotel Giraffe

Washington Square Hotel $$
103 Waverly Place, 10011
Tel (212) 777-9515 **Map** 4 D2
W washingtonsquarehotel.com
A stylish marble lobby gives way
to comfy rooms, some with views
of lush Washington Square Park.

60 Thompson $$$
60 Thompson St, 10012
Tel (877) 431-0400 **Map** 4 D4
W 60thompson.com
Very elegant, minimalist rooms
with top-notch gadgets. There's
a fashionable rooftop bar.

Crosby Street Hotel $$$
79 Crosby St, 10012
Tel (212) 226-6400 **Map** 4 E3
W firmdalehotels.com
A slice of upscale London in the
heart of SoHo. Cheerful rooms
and afternoon tea.

Nolitan $$$
30 Kenmare St, 10012
Tel (212) 925-2555 **Map** 4 F4
W nolitanhotel.com
Charming and pet-friendly hotel.
Many rooms have private
balconies and rain showers.

SoHo Grand Hotel $$$
301 West Broadway, 10013
Tel (212) 965-3000 **Map** 4 E4
W sohogrand.com
Sophisticated hotel with
tastefully done up rooms. Great
views of downtown Manhattan.

The Bowery Hotel $$$
335 Bowery, 10003
Tel (212) 505-9100 **Map** 4 F3
W theboweryhotel.com
Luxurious, fashionable hotel with
earthy touches such as fireplaces
and wood-paneling.

The James $$$
27 Grand St, 10013
Tel (212) 465-2000 **Map** 4 E4
W jameshotels.com
Elegant rooms with natural linens,
and rain showers in bathrooms.
Rooftop bar with glittering
skyline views.

The Mercer Hotel $$$
147 Mercer St, 10012
Tel (212) 966-6060 **Map** 4 E3
W mercerhotel.com
Intimate hotel with loft-style
rooms and an excellent New
American restaurant.

Thompson LES $$$
190 Allen St, 10002
Tel (212) 460-5300 **Map** 5 A3
W thompsonhotels.com
Industrial-chic hotel decorated
with contemporary art. There is
a unique Andy Warhol filmstrip
pool on the roof.

Eye-catching art adorns the walls at the Ace Hotel

Tribeca Grand Hotel $$$
2 Sixth Ave, 10013
Tel (212) 519-6700 **Map** 3 E5
W tribecagrand.com
A grand atrium lobby leads to
well-appointed rooms. Enjoy top-
shelf cocktails at the Church Bar.

Midtown

Ace Hotel $$
20 West 29th St, 10001
Tel (212) 679-2222 **Map** 8 F3
W acehotel.com
A chic, rock-and-roll hotel that
offers more than 200 rooms,
most featuring art by local and
international artists.

Algonquin Hotel $$
59 West 44th St, 10036
Tel (212) 840-6800 **Map** 12 F5
W algonquinhotel.com
Home of the famous 1920s
literary "Round Table." Cozy,
refurbished rooms.

Andaz 5th Avenue $$
485 5th Ave, 10017
Tel (212) 601-1234 **Map** 8 F1
W newyork.5thavenue.andaz.hyatt.
com
Enjoy a charming experience at
this sleek hotel. Hypoallergenic
rooms with state-of-the-art air
purification system.

Casablanca Hotel $$
147 West 43rd St, 10036
Tel (212) 869-1212 **Map** 8 E1
W casablancahotel.com
Moroccan-themed hotel with
complimentary nightly wine-
and-cheese receptions.

Dylan $$
52 East 41st St, 10017
Tel (212) 338-0500 **Map** 9 A1
W dylanhotel.com
Set in a historic Beaux-Arts
building, with handsome
walnut furnishings and a
steakhouse restaurant.

Eventi Hotel $$
851 6th Ave, 10001
Tel (212) 564-4567 **Map** 8 E3
W eventihotel.com
Warm and colorful rooms,
floor-to-ceiling windows, and
superlative service.

Hotel Americano $$
518 West 27th St, 10001
Tel (212) 216-0000 **Map** 7 C3
W hotel-americano.com
Sleek, minimalist rooms. Lively
rooftop bar and pool.

Hotel Mela $$
120 West 44th St, 10036
Tel (877) 452-6352 **Map** 12 D5
W hotelmela.com
Stylish hotel with spacious and
modern rooms in earthy colors.

Ink 48 $$
653 11th Ave, 10036
Tel (212) 757-0088 **Map** 11 B5
W ink48.com
Brightly colored rooms with
skyline views. Sip cocktails under
the stars in the rooftop bar.

Kimberly Hotel $$
145 East 50th St, 10022
Tel (212) 755-0400 **Map** 13 A5
W kimberlyhotel.com
This low-profile hotel is great
value for money, with well-
appointed and spacious rooms.

Library Hotel $$
299 Madison Ave, 10017
Tel (212) 983-4500 **Map** 9 A1
W libraryhotel.com
A library theme drives the decor
of this charming hotel. There are
books in all the impeccable
rooms plus a poetry garden.

Michelangelo $$
152 West 51st St, 10019
Tel (212) 765-0505 **Map** 12 F4
W michelangelohotel.com
Step back into the Italian
Renaissance at this classic hotel.

For more information on types of hotels *see p281*

Comfortable outdoor seating with great views at The Standard High Line

Roger Smith Hotel $$
501 Lexington Ave, 10022
Tel (212) 755-1400   **Map** 13 A5
W rogersmith.com
Charming, arty hotel with
individually decorated rooms.
Clean and spacious. There is an
intimate rooftop bar.

St. Giles New York – The Court & The Tuscany $$
120–130 East 39th St, 10016
Tel (212) 686-1600   **Map** 9 A1
W stgilesnewyork.com
Matched set of well-appointed
hotels with elegant and
spacious rooms; trendy lounges.

The Benjamin $$
125 East 50th St, 10022
Tel (212) 715-2500   **Map** 13 A4
W thebenjamin.com
Classic hotel with a focus on
comfortable beds, including a
plush pillow menu.

The Maritime $$
363 West 16th St, 10011
Tel (212) 242-4300   **Map** 8 D5
W themaritimehotel.com
Upscale, trendy hotel with a
nautical theme. Porthole
windows in the rooms have
views of the Hudson River.

The Nomad Hotel $$
1170 Broadway, 10001
Tel (212) 796-1500   **Map** 8 F3
W thenomadhotel.com
Beautifully restored Beaux-Arts
hotel with a very popular bar
and lounge. Laptops and iPads
available on request.

The Standard High Line $$
848 Washington St, 10014
Tel (212) 645-4646   **Map** 3 B1
W standardhotels.com
Soaring, ultra-trendy hotel
with great views of the Hudson
River. Impeccable rooms, floor-
to-ceiling windows, and
exceptional service standards.

The Strand $$
33 West 37th St, 10018
Tel (212) 448-1024   **Map** 8 F2
W thestrandnyc.com
Fashionable hotel with vintage
Condé Nast prints on the walls
and a breezy rooftop bar.

70 Park $$$
70 Park Ave, 10016
Tel (212) 973-2400   **Map** 9 A1
W 70parkave.com
Pet-friendly, inviting hotel with
elegant rooms and a nightly
hosted wine hour. Offers eco-
friendly, in-room spa service.

Bryant Park $$$
40 West 40th St, 10018
Tel (212) 869-0100   **Map** 8 F1
W bryantparkhotel.com
Minimalist rooms with excellent
amenities, plus a huge
underground bar with live DJs.

Morgans $$$
237 Madison Ave, 10016
Tel (212) 686-0300   **Map** 9 A8
W morganshotel.com
Chic hotel with taxi-inspired
black-and-white checkered
pattern throughout. Complimentary continental breakfast.

The Chatwal $$$
130 West 44th St, 10036
Tel (212) 764-6200   **Map** 12 E5
W thechatwalny.com
Art Deco meets contemporary
decor in this sophisticated hotel
filled with eye-catching art. Plush
rooms and luxurious interiors.
Enjoy the spa services.

Upper East Side

Bentley Hotel $$
500 East 62nd St, 10065
Tel (212) 644-6000   **Map** 13 C2
W bentleyhotelnyc.com
Towering hotel with stellar views
of the East River. Rooms are handsome, with designer amenities.

Upper West Side

6 Columbus $$$
6 Columbus Circle, 10019
Tel (212) 204-3000   **Map** 12 D3
W thompsonhotels.com
Colorful 1960s Modernist decor,
original artwork, a rooftop lounge,
and an excellent sushi bar.

Budget
Downtown

Cosmopolitan Hotel $
95 West Broadway, 10007
Tel (212) 566-1900   **Map** 1 B1
W cosmohotel.com
Simple but well-maintained
rooms with luxury linens and
fragrant toiletries.

Hotel 17 $
225 East 17th St, 10003
Tel (212) 475-2845   **Map** 9 B5
W hotel17ny.com
Small but clean rooms with tidy
bathrooms. It was featured in a
Woody Allen movie in the 1990s.

Hotel 31 $
129 East 31st St, 10016
Tel (212) 685-3060   **Map** 9 A3
W hotel31.com
Sister property to Hotel 17, with
simple but well-kept rooms and
cable TV.

Off Soho Suites $
11 Rivington St, 10002
Tel (212) 979-9808   **Map** 5 A3
W offsoho.com
Well-maintained budget suites
with either private or shared
kitchen; fully stocked.

Union Square Inn $
209 East 14th St, 10003
Tel (212) 614-0500   **Map** 4 F1
W unionsquareinn.com
Basic but clean apartments and
rooms, most with kitchenettes.
Lower rates for extended stays.

Best Western Seaport Inn Downtown $$
33 Peck Slip, 10038
Tel (212) 766-6600   **Map** 2 D2
W seaportinn.com
Splendid views of Brooklyn
Bridge from the terrace rooms.
Traditional decor, and a 24-hour
fitness center.

Blue Moon Hotel $$
100 Orchard St, 10002
Tel (212) 533-9080   **Map** 5 A3
W bluemoon-nyc.com
A former tenement transformed
into a lovely hotel. Cozy rooms
with modern amenities.
Complimentary continental
breakfast included.

The Gem $$
135 East Houston St, 10002
Tel (212) 358-8844 **Map** 5 A3
W thegemhotel.com
Snug, clean, and well-maintained rooms with sturdy furnishings and flatscreen TVs.

Midtown

Americana Inn $
69 West 38th St, 10018
Tel (212) 840-6700 **Map** 8 F1
W theamericanainn.com
Basic rooms with shared bathrooms. Each floor has a communal kitchenette.

Chelsea International Hostel $
251 West 20th St, 10011
Tel (212) 647-0010 **Map** 8 D5
W chelseahostel.com
One of the city's best hostels – a variety of accommodations from dorms to private rooms.

Chelsea Lodge $
318 West 20th St, 10011
Tel (212) 243-4499 **Map** 8 D5
W chelsealodge.com
This restored townhouse has small rooms with wood floors and clean, shared bathrooms.

Chelsea Star Hotel $
300 West 30th St, 10011
Tel (212) 244-7827 **Map** 8 D3
W starhotelny.com
A life-size statue of Betty Boop greets guests at this colorful hotel. Dorms and private rooms.

Colonial House Inn $
318 West 22nd St, 10011
Tel (212) 243-9669 **Map** 8 D4
W colonialhouseinn.com
Gay-friendly townhouse inn with modern rooms, some with private bathrooms and fireplaces.

Comfort Inn Chelsea $
18 West 25th St, 10010
Tel (212) 645-3990 **Map** 8 F4
W comfortinn.com
Historic 1901 brick building with comfy rooms. Complimentary breakfast, and fitness room.

Herald Square Hotel $
19 West 31st St, 10001
Tel (212) 279-4017 **Map** 8 F3
W heraldsquarehotel.com
Family-run, inviting Beaux-Arts hotel with attractive rooms and wood floors.

Hotel NYMA $
6 West 32nd St, 10001
Tel (212) 643-7100 **Map** 8 E3
W applecorehotels.com
Tasteful rooms in shades of soothing brown and beige, with flatscreen TVs and coffeemakers.

Hotel Wolcott $
4 West 31st St, 10001
Tel (212) 268-2900 **Map** 8 F3
W wolcott.com
Simple, spacious, and clean rooms with cable TV and well-maintained bathrooms.

La Quinta Manhattan $
17 West 32nd St, 10001
Tel (212) 736-1600 **Map** 8 E3
W applecorehotels.com
Comfortable rooms with coffee machines. Complimentary breakfast; lovely rooftop bar.

Pod 39 $
145 East 39th St, 10016
Tel (877) 358-0617 **Map** 9 A1
W podhotel.com
Snug but smartly furnished rooms with flatscreen TVs and bathrooms with rain showers.

DK Choice

Pod 51 $
230 East 51st St, 10022
Tel (212) 355-0300 **Map** 13 B4
W podhotel.com
One of New York City's best budget hotels – rooms are small and "pod-like" but savvily outfitted with colorful furnishings, comfortable beds, and flatscreen TVs. The lobby features bright murals, communal tables, a friendly concierge, and a café/ bar with a daily happy hour. Relax on the rooftop, surrounded by the skyscrapers of Midtown.

Belvedere Hotel $$
319 West 48th St, 10036
Tel (212) 245-7000 **Map** 12 D5
W belvederehotelnyc.com
Family-friendly, spacious rooms in soothing earthy colors. Lively Brazilian restaurant.

Snug rooms and classy wooden flooring, Chelsea Lodge

Fitzpatrick Grand Central Hotel $$
141 East 44th St, 10017
Tel (212) 351-6800 **Map** 13 A5
W fitzpatrickhotels.com
Warm and inviting rooms, some with canopied beds. Check out the bustling on-site pub.

Yotel $$
570 10th Ave, 10036
Tel (646) 449-7700 **Map** 7 C1
W yotel.com
A massive hotel with snug rooms and jaunty, space-age decor. Automated check-in/ check out.

Upper West Side

Astor on the Park $
465 Central Park West, 10025
Tel (212) 866-1880 **Map** 21 A5
Snug, clean rooms with cable TV and marble bathrooms. Snack machines and laundry services are available.

Hostelling International New York $
891 Amsterdam Ave, 10025
Tel (212) 932-2300 **Map** 20 E5
W hinewyork.org
A vast building resembling a campus dorm, with a cafeteria, game room, and picnic tables.

Jazz on the Park $
36 West 106th St, 10025
Tel (212) 932-1600 **Map** 21 A5
W jazzonthepark.com
An arty, lively hostel with simple dorm rooms, complimentary breakfast, and a coffeehouse with live music.

Milburn $$
242 West 76th St, 10023
Tel (212) 362-1006 **Map** 15 C5
W milburnhotel.com
Comfortable, well-maintained suites, fitted with kitchenettes, microwaves, and refrigerators.

On the Avenue $$
2178 Broadway, 10024
Tel (212) 362-1100 **Map** 15 C5
W ontheave-nyc.com
Stylish rooms, many with balconies. Lovely breezy deck with skyline views. Two great restaurants on site to choose from.

Farther Afield

Best Western Gregory Hotel Brooklyn $$
8315 Fourth Ave, Brooklyn, 11201
Tel (718) 238-3737
W bestwestern.com
Comfortable, well-appointed rooms, complimentary breakfast, and an old-fashioned bar with reasonably priced cocktails.

For more information on types of hotels *see p281*

Business

Downtown

Holiday Inn Soho $$
138 Lafayette St, 10013
Tel (212) 966-8898 **Map** 4 F5
W hidowntown-nyc.com
Simple but comfortable rooms
with plush beds and ergonomic
desk chairs.

Marriott Downtown $$
85 West St, 10006
Tel (212) 385-4900 **Map** 1 B3
W marriott.com
Business-oriented hotel with
elegantly decorated rooms.
Some with great views of the
Statue of Liberty.

**Mariott New York City Financial
Center** $$
85 West St, 10006
Tel (212) 385-4900 **Map** 1 B3
W marriott.com
Contemporary rooms and all
modern amenities. Grand decor
and opulent interiors – has an
indoor pool, great views, and
excellent service.

Midtown

Affinia Dumont $$
150 East 34th St, 10016
Tel (212) 481-7600 **Map** 9 A2
W affinia.com
Upscale rooms that resemble
apartments, with full kitchenettes.
Get pampered in the spa or work
out in the fitness center.

Four Points by Sheraton $$
160 West 25th St, 10001
Tel (212) 627-1888 **Map** 8 42
W starwoodhotels.com
Plush, well-maintained rooms,
some with balconies. Cozy
restaurant and bar.

Hyatt 48 Lex $$
517 Lexington Ave, 10017
Tel (212) 838-1234 **Map** 13 A5
W 48lex.hyatt.com
Great for corporate travelers, this
high-end hotel has suites with
landscaped terraces. Great on-
site restaurant.

Metro Apartments $$
440 West 41st St, 10036
Tel (212) 706-2082 **Map** 7 C1
Comfortable aparthotel with
fully equipped kitchenettes.

Millennium Broadway $$
145 West 44th St, 10036
Tel (212) 768-4400 **Map** 12 E5
W millenniumhotels.com
Choose from over 700 spacious
and comfortable rooms at this
hotel; popular with corporates.

Murray Hill East Suites $$
149 East 39th St, 10016
Tel (212) 661-2100 **Map** 9 A1
Residential-style accommodations
with suites, each with a fully
equipped kitchenette.

Radio City Apartments $$
142 West 49th St, 10019
Tel (212) 730-0728 **Map** 12 E5
W radiocityapts.com
Cozy accommodations, from
studios to one-bedroom suites,
most with kitchenettes.
Penthouse options available.
There is a great on-site Italian
restaurant for guests.

**Radisson Martinique on
Broadway** $$
49 West 32nd St, 10001
Tel (212) 736-3800 **Map** 3 F3
W radisson.com
Historic French-Renaissance
building with an ornate lobby
and sophisticated rooms.
Sink into elegance and enjoy
superlative service at this
upscale hotel.

**Renaissance New York
Hotel 57** $$
130 East 57th St, 10022
Tel (212) 753-8841 **Map** 13 A3
W marriott.com
Trendy boutique hotel with
impeccably kept spacious
rooms, hardwood floors, and
spotless marble bathrooms.

Farther Afield

**Sheraton LaGuardia
East Hotel** $$
135–20 39th Ave, Queens, 11354
Tel (718) 460-6666
W starwoodhotels.com
This 16-story hotel features
simple but well-maintained
rooms with coffeemakers.

Facade of The Greenwich Hotel,
Downtown

Luxury

Downtown

Gansevoort Hotel $$$
18 Ninth Ave, 10014
Tel (212) 206-9700 **Map** 3 B1
W hotelgansevoort.com
Well-appointed rooms with plush
feather beds. The rooftop pool is
a popular draw.

Gramercy Park Hotel $$$
2 Lexington Ave, 10010
Tel (212) 920-3300 **Map** 9 A4
W gramercyparkhotel.com
Drawing heavily on its Bohemian
heritage, this opulent hotel is
filled with original artwork.

Ritz-Carlton Battery Park $$$
2 West St, 10004
Tel (212) 344-0800 **Map** 1 B4
W ritzcarlton.com
Elegant and modern rooms,
complete with telescopes for
views of the Statue of Liberty.

Soho House $$$
59 Ninth Ave, 10014
Tel (646) 253-6122 **Map** 3 B1
W sohohouseny.com
The New York branch of
London's exclusive private club.
Rooftop pool, library, and
spacious rooms.

The Greenwich Hotel $$$
377 Greenwich St, 10013
Tel (212) 941-8900 **Map** 1 B1
W thegreenwichhotel.com
Eclectic global style, from
Moroccan tiles to Tibetan rugs.
Snug rooms and inviting decor.

Trump SoHo $$$
246 Spring St, 10013
Tel (212) 842-5500 **Map** 4 D4
W trumphotelcollection.com
Rise above Manhattan in Trump's
looming luxury hotel. Handsome
rooms and a pool deck.

Midtown

DK Choice

Omni Berkshire $$
21 East 52nd St, 10022
Tel (212) 753-5800 **Map** 12 F4
W omnihotels.com
Superlative service and modern,
well-equipped rooms with
marble bathrooms make this
an ideal choice for business
travelers and families. Work out
in the fully equipped fitness
center with a sun deck,
followed by creative cocktails
and delicious cuisine in the
Fireside Restaurant.

Key to Prices *see p282*

Four Seasons New York $$$
57 East 57th St, 10022
Tel (212) 758-5700   **Map** 13 A3
W fourseasons.com
The crown jewel in the Four Seasons chain, this luxury masterpiece has stunning views of Central Park.

Hilton Times Square $$$
234 West 42nd St, 10036
Tel (212) 840-8222   **Map** 8 E1
W timessquare.hilton.com
Great service and elegant, well-equipped rooms offer a respite from the bustle of the city.

Kitano $$$
66 Park Ave, 10017
Tel (212) 885-7000   **Map** 13 A5
W kitano.com
Great for corporate guests. Superlative Japanese service and complimentary green tea.

Le Parker Meridien $$$
118 West 57th St, 10019
Tel (212) 245-5000   **Map** 12 E3
W parkermeridien.com
Spacious designer rooms, great service, and a rooftop pool. Serves some of the best burgers in town.

New York Palace $$$
455 Madison Ave, 10022
Tel (212) 888-7000   **Map** 13 A4
W newyorkpalace.com
A lavish hotel that lives up to its name. Set in an 1882 landmark building with a lovely courtyard.

Peninsula New York $$$
700 Fifth Ave, 10019
Tel (212) 956-2888   **Map** 12 F4
W peninsula.com
The Asian chain's Big Apple outpost offers well-appointed, plush rooms and an indulgent spa to unwind in after a long day.

DK Choice

Ritz-Carlton Central Park $$$
50 Central Park South, 10019
Tel (212) 308-9100   **Map** 12 F3
W ritzcarlton.com
This luxury hotel maximizes its proximity to Central Park at every turn – each floor features great views of the greenery. The stylish rooms and white-glove service are signature Ritz-Carlton – this hotel is among the very best in the city.

Sofitel $$$
45 West 44th St, 10036
Tel (212) 354-8844   **Map** 12 F5
W sofitel.com
A warm blend of the contemporary and classic fills this 30-story building. Rooms on higher floors feature splendid views.

Spacious outdoor seating area at The Surrey

St. Regis $$$
2 East 55th St, 10022
Tel (212) 753-4500   **Map** 12 F4
W stregis.com
A 1904 Beaux-Arts building, with a butler for every floor. Don't miss the Bloody Mary, a signature cocktail of the St. Regis group.

The London NYC $$$
151 West 54th St, 10019
Tel (212) 307-5000   **Map** 2 E4
W thelondonnyc.com
A mural of London's Hyde Park defines this grand hotel. Experience creative cuisine at Gordon Ramsay's on site restaurant.

The Plaza $$$
768 5th Ave, 10019
Tel (212) 759-3000   **Map** 12 F3
W theplaza.com
This magnificent 1907 grande dame effortlessly combines traditional decor with modern facilities. Exceptional service.

The Setai $$$
400 5th Ave, 10018
Tel (212) 695-4005   **Map** 8 F2
W capellahotels.com
A classy hotel with spacious suites filled with all modern amenities, including espresso machines and rain shower heads.

W Times Square $$$
1567 Broadway, 10036
Tel (212) 930-7400   **Map** 12 E5
W whotels.com
Upscale yet personable, with well-equipped rooms, a popular restaurant, and a lively bar scene.

Waldorf Astoria/Waldorf Towers $$$
301 Park Ave, 10022
Tel (212) 355-3000   **Map** 13 A5
W waldorfastoria.com
Presidents and heads of state have all graced this hotel. Come here to experience great sophistication. Gorgeous lobby.

Upper East Side

Carlyle $$$
35 East 76th St, 10021
Tel (212) 744-1600   **Map** 17 A5
W rosewoodhotels.com
Frequented by celebrities and royalty, this esteemed hotel – with sophisticated interiors and ultra-elegant decor – offers phenomenal service and afternoon tea.

Sherry-Netherland $$$
781 5th Ave, 10022
Tel (212) 355-2800   **Map** 12 F3
W sherrynetherland.com
An old-world hotel with enormous and well-appointed suites; indulge in luxury living and top-of-the-line service.

The Pierre $$$
2 East 61st St, 10021
Tel (212) 838-8000   **Map** 12 F3
W tajhotels.com
A grand lobby gives way to impeccable rooms with gracious interiors. Service is sophisticated and includes a special room service menu for pets.

The Surrey $$$
20 East 76th St, 10021
Tel (212) 288-3700   **Map** 17 A5
W thesurrey.com
Check into one of the suites at this luxurious hotel, many of which have kitchens. A roof garden and fitness center, and great, personalized service.

Upper West Side

Mandarin Oriental $$$
80 Columbus Circle, 10023
Tel (212) 805-8800   **Map** 12 D3
W mandarinoriental.com
A dramatic hotel with Asian-inspired opulence. Over 200 luxuriously appointed rooms and a trendy bar. Enjoy stellar views of Central Park and get pampered in the spa.

For more information on types of hotels *see p281*

WHERE TO EAT AND DRINK

New Yorkers love to eat well, and in the five boroughs there are more than 25,000 restaurants. City dwellers avidly read restaurant reviews in magazines and websites such as *New York* (www.nymag.com), to ensure that they are seen in the latest fashionable place. "In" restaurants and cuisines change with great regularity, while some haunts remain perennially popular. The restaurants cited in our listings have been selected as the best that New York can offer across a wide price range. While the information on pages 292–303 will help you to select a suitable restaurant, there are details of lighter refreshments on pages 304–306. *New York's Bars* on pages 307–309 suggests some of the city's best drinking spots.

Street-corner hot dog stand

Restaurant Menus

Meals in most of the better restaurants consist of three courses: an appetizer (starter), an entrée (the main course), and a dessert. In some fine restaurants you may be offered a complimentary appetizer. Appetizers at the better restaurants are often the chef's most creative dishes. Coffee or tea and a dessert ordinarily conclude the meal in restaurants above the coffee-shop level. Some establishments also offer a cheeseboard.

Traditional Italian menus offer antipasti (hot and cold appetizers), a first course – often a pasta dish, the main course – usually meat or fish, and a dessert. However, in many places pasta is served as a main course.

To get a sense of a restaurant's cuisine, visit www.menupages.com, which features the menus of many Manhattan eateries. Other local websites, including the weekly *New York* magazine's (www.nymag.com), often have links to restaurant menus.

Prices

You will always find a restaurant in New York to suit your budget. At inexpensive coffee shops, diners and fast-food chains, $10–$15 will buy you a filling meal. There are also many acceptable, even first-rate, restaurants where you can eat well at a moderate cost – around $25 per person for a decent, filling meal, not including drinks – in attractive surroundings.

For dinner at a trendy New American venue with a star chef, the bill could be upward of $80 to $100 per person, excluding drinks. Many top restaurants do, however, offer fixed-price (or, as they are known in New York, prix-fixe) meals. This is a cheaper way of enjoying a good meal than choosing dishes from the à la carte menu. Lunch is less expensive than dinner in such places and, because of the profusion of business diners, lunch is often the busiest period of the day.

Taxes and Tipping

New York City sales tax of 8.875% will be added to your bill. Service is not usually included. Tipping can run from 10% at a coffee shop to 20% at the fanciest places, with 15% an average fair tip. Many people just double the sales tax to work out a tip.

The bill is known as the "check" in the US. The most commonly accepted credit cards are VISA, MasterCard and American Express. Traveler's checks in US dollars are taken in some restaurants. Diners and coffee shops may accept cash only. In fast-food chains, you order at the counter and pay cash in advance.

The world-famous Carnegie Deli *(see p298)*

Dining on a Budget

Despite the tales of $200 business lunches, there are ways to stretch a meal budget in New York.

Order fewer courses than you would normally. American portions are huge, and an appetizer is often big enough for a light main course. You could share one with your companion or choose two appetizers and no entrée.

Ask your waiter if there is a prix-fixe menu. Many of the more expensive restaurants offer this at lunch and dinner – in the early evening it may be called the pre-theater menu. Or try a prix-fixe lunch buffet. These are popular in Indian restaurants and make for very reasonably priced meals.

Other options for a quick, tasty, and restorative meal are the less expensive Chinese, Thai, and Mexican restaurants. Italian pizzerias and French bistros, as well as places that serve hamburgers or sandwiches and desserts, also offer good value. Alternatively, go to bars featuring "happy hours." They often offer hors d'oeuvres,

McSorley's Old Ale House *(see p308)*

like Spanish tapas, which can make a meal in themselves.

If you simply want to see inside the restaurants every visitor has heard about such as Gotham Bar and Grill or Four Seasons, just go to have a drink and soak up the atmosphere. Many restaurants post their menus or will let you see them before you are seated, which is good for checking prices in advance. During Restaurant Week (held in Jan/Feb and Jun/Jul), you can dine in some of the city's restaurants for a fraction of the usual cost – visit www.nycgo.com.

Hours

Breakfast hours are usually from 7 to 10:30 or 11am. Sunday brunch, a popular meal, is served at many restaurants between about 11am and 3pm. Lunch runs from 11:30am or noon to 2:30pm at most places, but the busiest time of the day is 1pm. Dinner is usually served from 5:30 or 6pm onward. The most popular time is around 7:30 or 8pm.

Some restaurants stop serving at 10pm during the week, or 11pm on Friday and Saturday. Certain informal restaurants are open from 11:30am to 10pm. Coffee shops are open long hours, from 7am to midnight or even 24 hours.

Dress Codes

Few restaurants demand that male diners dress formally, though a jacket is required at classy restaurants, and a jacket and tie at the very best. At most restaurants, for both men and women, smart "business casual" suffices.

Women tend to dress up when dining at the more expensive restaurants. If you are unsure, check what the dress code is when you make your reservation.

Reservations

It is wise to make reservations at any restaurant above the diner/fast-food level, especially on weekends. Some of the trendiest restaurants won't accept bookings, or won't take them less than

Dining in style at the Oyster Bar in Grand Central Terminal *(see p298)*

two months in advance. Make reservations for lunch at a Midtown restaurant as places here are popular with business diners. Waits of an hour at the most popular spots are not unusual.

Smoking

Smoking is illegal in all bars and restaurants. The only exceptions are owner-operated bars that have special smoking rooms.

Children

When eating out with children, ask if there's a child's menu with half-portions. The prices are reduced, often by half. Dining out in the more formal New York restaurants is certainly not a family affair but children are accepted in more casual restaurants. Many family-friendly restaurants have facilities for babies or toddlers; others may not be so well equipped.

Wheelchair Access

While many restaurants may be able to accommodate a wheelchair, always mention your requirements when making your reservation. Many of the smaller places cannot cater to disabled customers due to lack of space.

Celebrity Chefs

New York City attracts top chefs from around the world, all of whom are determined to make their mark and win over the local diners and the *New York Times'* influential restaurant reviewer.

A meal in a top restaurant will not come cheaply, but it can be worth the splurge. Booking a table can be difficult, and reservations should be made as early as two months in advance. Some reservations can be made online through Opentable (www.opentable.com).

Recommended Restaurants

New York City offers an array of cuisines *(see Flavors of New York, pp290–91)*, from Spanish, Greek, and Italian to local New York fare. Our restaurants are divided into five geographical areas: Downtown encompasses Lower Manhattan, Seaport and the Civic Center, the Lower East Side, Soho and Tribeca, Greenwich Village, the East Village and Gramercy and the Flatiron District. Midtown covers both Lower and Upper Midtown, as well as Chelsea and the Theater District, which is filled with restaurants that offer theater menus for the Broadway-bound. The Upper East Side features many upscale restaurants, while the Upper West Side includes Morningside Heights and Harlem. Farther Afield includes restaurants in Brooklyn and Queens, which often have an international flavor.

Throughout our listings, we've marked recommended restaurants as DK Choice. We've chosen these restaurants because they offer a special experience – either for the superb cuisine, for enjoying a uniquely New York night out surrounded by locals, for the excellent value, or a combination of these.

The Flavors of New York

Few cities can match the diversity of New York's restaurants. Reflecting the city's melting pot of nationalities, foods range from the "hautest" of French and continental cuisine to the freshest sushi outside of Tokyo. Caribbean, Mexican, Thai, Vietnamese, Korean, Greek, Indian – all are well represented, and every block seems to have an Italian restaurant. The quality of the city's top restaurants is unsurpassed and their chefs are superstars, as well-known and revered as movie idols. Yet, because so many nationalities are represented in its culinary culture, only a few foods are native to the city itself.

Dim sum

Fresh, local produce on display at the Greenmarket

Deli Dining

A large Jewish population has given rise to some of New York's best known specialties, now enjoyed by all – overstuffed corned beef and pastrami sandwiches, dill pickles, matzo ball soup, herrings, blintzes, and bagels

served with cream cheese and smoked salmon. The bagel, once synonymous with New York, has become a universal American food, but a true New York bagel is nothing like the bready imitations found in the hinterlands. It is shaped by hand, and the dough is cooked briefly in boiling water before being baked, resulting in a unique firm and chewy texture. A relative, and another New York specialty, is the bialy,

a flat, chewy flour-dusted roll with a center indentation filed with toasted onions. The finest examples of each are to be found in the kosher bakeries of the Lower East Side *(see pp94–103)*.

The Greenmarket

You may well find yourself next to a well-known chef browsing at New York's greenmarkets, open-air markets where farmers

Pastrami on rye

Blintzes

Dill pickles

Bagels with smoked salmon and cream cheese

Pickled herrings

Selection of classic foods available at any New York deli

New York Specialties

While New York dining may span all nations, a few special dishes are closely associated with the city. Manhattan Clam Chowder, prepared with tomatoes rather than cream, has been popular ever since it was introduced at Coney Island beach stands in the 1880s. In the city's many steak houses, a prime selection is the "New York strip steak," a boneless sirloin cut from the short loin, the tenderest portion of beef. Italian cuisine has often been given a New York spin. Rich and creamy New York cheesecake is made with cream cheese rather the Italian ricotta. And, since traditional wood-burning ovens were impractical in New York, the first Italian immigrant chefs used coal ovens. Though these are rare today, purists still insist they are necessary for a true New York pizza.

Pretzels

Manhattan clam chowder This is a rich blend of potatoes, onions, tomatoes, oyster crackers crumbs and clams.

Fast food cart on a Manhattan street corner, selling hot dogs and sodas

from upstate New York sell fresh-picked fruits and vegetables, as well as meat, poultry and dairy products. Dozens of chefs patronize the greenmarkets, so you'll find ultra-fresh local produce on many menus in the city. As many as 70 vendors attend the biggest of the markets in Union Square on Monday, Wednesday, Friday, and Saturday *(see p131)*.

Street Food

Street food is a favorite choice in a fast-moving city. Hot dogs and oversize soft pretzels are classic New York choices, along with some surprisingly good food cart specialties, from falafel to soup to barbecue to Texas chili, all ready to eat on the run. In winter, vendors all over town offer hot roasted chestnuts.

Soul Food

Harlem is America's most famous African-American community, and restaurants here are the place to sample specialties from the Deep South, such as fried chicken, ribs, collard greens, yams, and cornbread. A popular Harlem dish, fried chicken and waffles,

An Asian produce store in New York's Chinatown

is said to have originated to serve musicians leaving jazz clubs in the wee hours.

Asian Food Rivals

Chinese restaurants and dim sum parlors have long been found throughout the city, but lately they have been challenged by the arrival of many excellent Thai and Vietnamese restaurants. All these, however, take second place to the multiplying sushi bars and high-profile, highly praised Japanese chefs.

DELICATESSEN CLASSICS

Babkas Slightly sweet, yeasted coffee cakes.

Blintzes Crêpes filled with sweetened soft white cheese and/or fruit and sautéed.

Chopped liver Chicken livers mashed with minced onion, hard-cooked eggs and *schmaltz* (chicken fat).

Gefilte fish Minced white fish dumplings poached in fish broth. A holiday dish.

Knishes Soft dough shells filled with oniony mashed potatoes.

Latkes Grated potato, onion and matzo-meal pancakes.

Rugelach Rich, cream-cheese-dough pastries filled with jam, chopped nuts and raisins

New York-style pizza Thick- or thin-crusted, a true New York pizza must be baked in a coal-fired oven.

New York Strip Steak Served with creamed spinach, fries or hash-browns, this tender steak is hard to beat.

New York cheesecake This is a dense, rich, baked cake with a crust of pastry or graham crackers (digestives).

Where to Eat and Drink

Modern decor at Dirt Candy, popular for its vegetarian fare

Downtown

Adrienne's Pizza Bar $
Pizza   Map 1 C4
87 Pearl St, 10004
Tel (212) 248-3838
Munch on thin-crust square pizzas at this neighborhood favorite. Also try the antipasti and lighten the meal with a fresh salad.

Angelica Kitchen $
Vegetarian   Map 5 A1
300 East 12th St, 10003
Tel (212) 228-2909
Try innovative vegetarian cuisine, from aromatic soups and fresh salads to creatively prepared pasta dishes, served in an airy setting. All ingredients in the menu are grown organically, and bottled beverages of any kind are not used.

Bamiyan $
Afghan   Map 9 B3
358 Third Ave, 10016
Tel (212) 481-3232
Bite into juicy charcoal-grilled kebabs or indulge in a delicious chicken stew at this authentic Afghan restaurant. Tribal rugs and low tables create a cozy ambience. Custom hookahs are also available, with a wide variety of flavors to choose from.

Bubby's $
American   Map 4 D5
120 Hudson St, 10013
Tel (212) 219-0666
Bubby's offers hearty traditional fare and famous pies that are rolled by hand and made with locally grown ingredients. Try the Arkansas red velvet cake or apple pie with creamy ice cream. The best place to sample established American recipes.

Caracas Arepa Bar $
Venezuelan   Map 5 A2
536 East 5th St, 10009
Tel (212) 228-5062
Small but perennially packed joint with flavorful Venezuelan fare. The specialty is *arepas* (corn cakes with a variety of savory fillings). Have them as a snack or a meal.

Casimir $
French   Map 5 B2
103 Avenue B, 10009
Tel (212) 358-9683
Hopping bistro with wholesome classics such as *bouillabaisse* (fish stew) and juicy *steak frites*. The small backyard here offers the chance to experience a relaxing dinner under the stars.

Chat 'n' Chew $
American   Map 8 F5
10 East 16th St, 10003
Tel (212) 243-1616
Kitschy comfort food, including meatloaf and year-round Thanksgiving turkey, in a bright setting. Don't miss dessert, from pies to chocolate cake.

Congee Village $
Chinese   Map 5 A4
100 Allen St, 10002
Tel (212) 941-1818
Massive, bustling restaurant specializing in congee, a hot rice porridge with meat or fish and spices. The fragrant noodle dishes are good too.

Corner Bistro $
American   Map 3 C1
331 West 4th St, 10014
Tel (212) 242-9502
Some of the best burgers in the city make this dive bar a cult favorite. After your meal, choose from the extensive menu of local beer.

Devi $
Indian   Map 8 F5
8 East 18th St, 10003
Tel (212) 691-1300
Relish regional Indian cuisine in a cozy setting of wood carvings and Indian textiles. Try the tandoor-grilled lamb chops or Manchurian cauliflower.

Dirt Candy $
Vegetarian   Map 5 B1
430 East 9th St, 10009
Tel (212) 228-7732   **Closed** *Sun & Mon*
High-concept vegetarian cuisine, from mint and tarragon zucchini pasta to portobello mushroom mousse. Everything on the menu can be made vegan on request.

Dumpling Man $
Chinese   Map 5 A1
100 St Mark's Place, 10009
Tel (212) 505-2121
Tiny eatery serving classic northern Asian-style dumplings: fried or steamed, stuffed with pork, chicken, tofu, or veggies.

Empellon Cocina $
Mexican   Map 5 A2
105 First Ave, 10003
Tel (212) 780-0999
Innovative, but rooted in authentic Mexican style, this restaurant blends the classic and contemporary. Try the lamb sweetbreads with pumpkin seeds.

Great Jones Café $
American   Map 4 F2
54 Great Jones St, 10012
Tel (212) 674-9304
An Elvis likeness draped with Mardis Gras beads sets the tone for this eatery. Enjoy the cocktails at the bar. Do sample the Cajun Mary, and play some vinyl, old-school style, on the jukebox.

Hearth $
Italian   Map 5 A1
403 East 12th St, 10009
Tel (212) 602-1300
Feast on Tuscan-American fare at this popular bohemian-chic restaurant. Signature dishes include marinated sardines, pan-seared skate, and stuffed cabbage. Top off the meal with olive-oil cake.

Il Bagatto $
Italian   Map 5 B2
192 East 2nd St, 10009
Tel (212) 228-0977   **Closed** *Mon*
Friendly eatery that draws the
crowds. There's a festive atmosphere at all times, with dim lights
and candles. The inexpensive red
wine is an added incentive.

Il Palazzo $
Italian   Map 4 F4
151 Mulberry St, 10013
Tel (212) 343-7000
Fresh pasta and risottos, a decent
wine list, and a glassed-in garden
make this one of Little Italy's best
eateries. The outdoor courtyard
simply adds to the charm.

Joe's Shanghai $
Chinese   Map 4 F5
9 Pell St, 10013
Tel (212) 233-8888
A downtown institution, this
bustling restaurant makes
delectable dumplings stuffed
with everything from pork to
vegetables. Be sure to try the
special soup dumplings.

Katz Delicatessen $
Deli   Map 5 A3
205 East Houston St, 10002
Tel (212) 254-2246
A New York institution, this Jewish
deli serves towering pastrami or
corned-beef sandwiches, and
other local delicacies. Vegetarians
can relish the fat *knishes* (potato,
meat and cabbage dumplings),
split pea soup, and potato latkes.

La Palapa $
Mexican   Map 5 A1
77 St Marks Place, 10003
Tel (212) 777-2537
Colorful restaurant with regional
Mexican cooking such as baked
catfish, plus tart margaritas, and
other tequila drinks. Expect rich,
spicy salsas and sauces.

Lil' Frankies $
American   Map 5 A2
19-21 First Ave, 10003
Tel (212) 420-4900
Hip neighborhood pizzeria with a
backyard garden for alfresco
dining. Pizzas are made in a
wood-fired brick oven.

Lombardi's $
American   Map 4 F4
32 Spring St, 10012
Tel (212) 941-7994
One of the top pizzerias in the
city, with thin, charred, brick-
oven-baked pizzas topped
with everything from eggplant
to pepperoni. Home-made
meatballs and clam pie are also
popular dishes.

Moustache $
Middle Eastern   Map 3 C2
90 Bedford St, 10014
Tel (212) 229-2220
Hugely popular, casual eatery
with flavorful grilled lamb and
chicken and delicious, crisp
Turkish "pitzas" – pizzas made
with *pita* dough.

Pho Pasteur $
Vietnamese   Map 4 F5
85 Baxter St, 10013
Tel (212) 608-3656
Sample excellent Vietnamese
rolls and hot noodle soup with
beef brisket or fish balls at this
tiny, but very popular, eatery.

Sammy's Roumanian $
Eastern European   Map 5 A4
157 Chrystie St, 10002
Tel (212) 673-0330
Feast on latkes, ruby-red
pastrami, and chopped liver at
this old-world restaurant. Try a
local beer to top off the meal.
There is a party room upstairs for
those looking to shake a leg.

Saravanaa Bhavan $
Indian/Vegetarian   Map 9 A4
81 Lexington Ave, 10016
Tel (212) 679-0204
Inexpensive, all-vegetarian menu,
which incorporates a dizzying
assortment of South Indian
specialties such as Rasam, a spicy
lentil soup. Good selection of
Indian desserts. Friendly service
matches the casual ambience.

Shake Shack $
American   Map 9 A4
*Southeast corner of Madison Square
Park, near Madison Ave and East
23rd St, 10010*
Tel (212) 889-6600
Sink your teeth into juicy burgers
and crinkle-cut fries at this
perennially popular shack where
guests can eat under the cool
shade of trees. Delicious shakes.

Tamarind $
Indian   Map 8 F4
41–43 East 22nd St, 10010
Tel (212) 674-7400
Feast on excellent curries
and succulent lamb at this
modern and vibrant restaurant.
Offers great value for money,
with generous portions and a
wide range of Indian dishes to
choose from.

Tia Pol $
Spanish tapas   Map 7 C4
205 Tenth Ave, 10011
Tel (212) 675-8805
An infectious spirit pervades this
tiny tapas bar; sample fried
chickpeas, squid in its own ink,
and fresh fruit jugs of sangria.
Check out the comprehensive
all-Spanish wine list.

Westville $
American   Map 3 C2
210 West 10th St, 10014
Tel (212) 741-7971
Hearty traditional fare, from
mac 'n' cheese to cod po'boys, at
this casual, narrow eatery. The
food is simple but wholesome,
and the domestic beer list is top-
notch too.

Zum Schneider $
German   Map 5 B2
107 Ave C, 10009
Tel (212) 598-1098
It's Oktoberfest all year round at
this boisterous beer garden with
super sausages. Traditional
Bavarian-German menu. Big
crowds on the weekend.

Aldea $$
Mediterranean   Map 8 F5
31 West 17th St, 10011
Tel (212) 675-7223   **Closed** *Sun*
Portuguese-American chef
George Mendes is at the helm of
this intimate Mediterranean-
inspired spot. Do not miss the
suckling pig with truffle puree.

Customers dining at Aldea restaurant

For more information on types of restaurants *see p289*

Fresh fish on display at the elegant Aquagrill

Aquagrill $$
Seafood   **Map** 4 D4
201 Spring St, 10012
Tel (212) 274-0505
Calling all seafood lovers: this
lovely restaurant, with an airy
outdoor patio, serves the freshest
fish and shellfish in town, accom-
panied by aromatic sauces.

DK Choice

Balthazar $$
French   **Map** 4 E4
80 Spring St, 10012
Tel (212) 965-414
This French bistro's hopping
atmosphere is hard to resist,
especially once you've caught a
glimpse of it through the large
picture windows overlooking
Spring Street. Restaurateur
Keith McNally's brasserie empire
is crowned by this stylish place,
which rolls out French favorites
– *steak frites*, oysters, and
Bordeaux wine – for a lively
crowd, from SoHo literati to
fashionistas in stilettos.

Battery Gardens $$
American   **Map** 1 C4
17 State St, 10004
Tel (212) 809-5508
This eatery's unique waterside
location makes it worth a visit.
The Mediterranean-influenced
American fare is decent, but come
also for the phenomenal views of
the Statue of Liberty.

Beauty & Essex $$
American   **Map** 5 B3
146 Essex St, 10002
Tel (212) 614-0146
Extremely elegant, sophisticated,
and spacious. Serves global
small plates and offers an
elaborate pre-selected menu
for large groups.

Blue Hill $$
American   **Map** 4 E4
75 Washington Place, 10011
Tel (212) 539-1776
New American restaurant that
uses the freshest ingredients
sourced from local farms. Try
the smoked salmon with beet
puree, and check out the
elaborate five-course "Farmer's
Feast" tasting menu, based on
the week's harvest.

Blue Ribbon Bakery $$
American   **Map** 4 D3
35 Downing St, 10014
Tel (212) 337-0404
A small plates menu of excellent
locavore cuisine, from barbecued
pork to organic salads. Wash
it down with the excellent
selection of local beers.

Blue Smoke $$
American   **Map** 9 A3
116 East 27th St, 10016
Tel (212) 447-7733
Esteemed restaurateur Danny
Meyer delivers authentic pit
BBQ at its finest. Try the ribs or

Place settings at Boqueria, a Barcelona-
style tapas bar

pulled-pork sandwiches, both
dripping with juices. There is an
excellent jazz club downstairs
with two sets every evening.

Boqueria $$
Spanish tapas   **Map** 4 D4
171 Spring St, 10012
Tel (212) 343-4255
Taste Barcelona-style tapas
along with sangria, in this lively,
vibrant place. Try grilled squid,
lamb meatballs, and creamy
croquettes with ham.
The restaurant works closely
with local farmers to get fresh,
local ingredients.

Craft $$
American   **Map** 9 A5
43 East 19th St, 10003
Tel (212) 780-0880
Creative chef Tom Colicchio
offers a "deconstructed" menu
that celebrates fresh ingredients.
Try the roasted swordfish or
rabbit loin, or braised beef
short ribs. Be sure to taste the
mouthwatering desserts.

Da Silvano $$
Italian   **Map** 4 D3
260 Sixth Ave, 10014
Tel (212) 982-2343
A Tuscan restaurant that's better
known for its celebrity clientele
than its cuisine. Coveted outdoor
tables and gently lit interiors
make for a great ambience.

Dos Caminos $$
Mexican   **Map** 4 F3
475 West Broadway, 10012
Tel (212) 277-4300
Fresh Mexican cuisine, such as
thick guacamole served with
warm tortilla chips and grilled
chicken, as well as potent
tequilas, draws daily crowds to
this rather boisterous restaurant.
Popular for brunch.

Edi & the Wolf $$
Austrian Map 5 B2
102 Ave C, 10009
Tel (212) 598-1040
This rustic restaurant is inspired by the casual neighborhood taverns in Austria. Feast on traditional fare such as pork schnitzel and delicious pastry desserts. Good choice of wine.

Fatty Crab $$
Malaysian Map 3 B1
643 Hudson St, 10014
Tel (212) 352-3590
Chef Zak Pelaccio delights tastebuds with fragrant, Malaysian-inspired cuisine. Try classics such as beef rendang, and do not miss the delicious cocktails flavored with elderflower, honey, and Thai basil.

Fraunces Tavern $$
American Map 1 C4
54 Pearl St, 10004
Tel (212) 968-1776 **Closed** *Sun*
Historic 18th-century tavern with classic American steak and fish dishes. Stop by the bar for happy hours. The place offers 18 craft beers on tap.

Freemans $$
American Map 5 A3
Freeman Alley, near Rivington, 10002
Tel (212) 420-0012
This fashionable restaurant, hiding at the end of an alley, has a menu reminiscent of a 1950s supper party, with rum-soaked ribs and stiff cocktails. Old-world American tavern-style decor.

Gotham Bar & Grill $$
American Map 4 E1
12 East 12th St, 10003
Tel (212) 620-4020
A stately restaurant that has become a respected New York institution. The Greenmarket fixed price lunch menu offers excellent value for money.

Low lighting and rustic decor at Da Silvano

Gramercy Tavern $$
American Map 9 A5
42 East 20th St, 10003
Tel (212) 477-0777
Acclaimed chef Michael Anthony creates superlative, market-fresh fare in this rustic yet elegant restaurant. Do not miss the chocolate bread pudding.

Hill Country $$
Barbecue Map 8 F4
30 W 26th St, 10010
Tel (212) 255-4544
This lively spot honors Texan barbecue by using a custom meat-smoking room to yield tender brisket, sausage, and ribs, which can be accompanied by an extensive choice of sides. Casual environs, featuring live music most nights.

Hundred Acres $$
American Map 4 D3
38 MacDougal St, 10012
Tel (212) 475-7500
Tuck into farm-to-fork cuisine, such as juicy lamb and fried green tomatoes, at this cozy spot. There is a lovely garden at the back of the restaurant.

I Trulli $$
Italian Map 9 A3
122 East 27th St, 10010
Tel (212) 481-7372
Romantic, upscale restaurant specializing in southern Italian cuisine. Strict policy of sourcing all ingredients locally. Dine outside in the garden in summer.

'inoteca $$
Italian Map 5 A3
98 Rivington St, 10002
Tel (212) 614-0473
One of the city's most distinguished wine bars. Enjoy panini, antipasti, and other dishes that draw from classic Italian wine bar cuisine.

Jane $$
American Map 4 E3
100 West Houston St, 10012
Tel (212) 254-7000
Casual neighborhood bistro with a loyal following thanks to unpretentious dishes made with fresh, local produce. Welcoming environs are packed for the popular weekend brunch service.

Jewel Bako $$
Japanese Map 4 F2
239 East 5th St, 10003
Tel (212) 979-1012 **Closed** *Sun*
This tiny but impeccable restaurant serves exquisite sushi. Also check out the wide range of sashimi on offer. Note that the prices of dishes can quickly add up – but it's well worth it.

Kesté $$
Pizza Map 4 D2
271 Bleecker St, 10014
Tel (212) 243-1500
Acclaimed Italian pizza-maker churns out some of the city's most delicious wood-fired, Neapolitan-style pizzas. Inventive toppings, as well as gluten free, vegetarian, and vegan options.

The bar area at Freemans restaurant

For more information on types of restaurants *see p289*

Stately red-brick entrance to One if by Land, Two if by Sea

Kittichai $$
Thai   **Map** 4 D4
60 Thompson St, 10012
Tel (212) 219-2000
Graceful orchids at the entrance are an apt introduction to this soothing Thai restaurant. Try the pan-seared tuna with toasted coconut red curry.

L'Ecole $$
French   **Map** 4 E4
462 Broadway, 10012
Tel (212) 219-3300
Delightful restaurant where students of the French Culinary Institute prepare all the exquisite meals for customers – from seared fish to rich meats.

Les Halles $$
French   **Map** 1 C2
15 John St, 10038
Tel (212) 285-8585
A friendly and lively brasserie with top-notch fare, from succulent steak with Béarnaise sauce to tasty grilled salmon to fresh salads with tangy dressings. There is a fine selection of French wine on the menu.

Locanda Verde $$
Italian   **Map** 4 D5
379 Greenwich St, 10013
Tel (212) 925-3797
Enjoy family-style, impeccably crafted Italian cuisine, from pasta to seafood, at this stylish restaurant in actor Robert De Niro's hotel. Try the specialty Italian beers and cocktails.

Lupa $$
Italian   **Map** 4 F3
170 Thompson St, 10012
Tel (212) 982-5089
Celebrity chef Mario Batali serves superb pasta and grilled meats at this Italian *trattoria*. It is busy most nights of the week, so book ahead. Enjoy a cocktail at the bar while waiting for your table.

Minetta Tavern $$
Italian   **Map** 4 D2
113 McDougal St, 10012
Tel (212) 475-3850
Sink your teeth into juicy steaks at this bistro that is both casual and celebrity-friendly. The dark-wood bar serves top-notch cocktails and bourbons.

Momofuku Noodle Bar $$
Asian   **Map** 5 A1
171 First Ave, 10003
Tel (212) 475-7899
Celebrated Korean-American chef David Chang offers innovative ramen and other Japanese classics. Try the pork buns and the fried chicken, which comes with pancakes. Don't miss the delectable desserts.

Odeon $$
French   **Map** 1 B1
145 West Broadway, 10013
Tel (212) 233-0507
This bistro offers great steak tartare and spicy chicken dumplings – plus people-watching. Enjoy the dessert wines and cocktails on offer. Online reservations only.

One if by Land, Two if by Sea $$
American   **Map** 3 C3
17 Barrow St, 10014
Tel (212) 228-0822
One of the most romantic restaurants in NYC, set in Aaron Burr's famous carriage house. Nightly three-course fixed price menu with live piano music. Try the seven-course tasting menu.

Otto $$
Italian   **Map** 4 E1
1 Fifth Ave, 10003
Tel (212) 995-9559
Buzzing, upscale pizzeria from chef Mario Batali; don't miss the lardo pizza. The creative wine list features excellent vintages from Italy.

Pearl Oyster Bar $$
Seafood   **Map** 4 D4
18 Cornelia St, 10014
Tel (212) 691-8211   **Closed** *Sun*
This longtime favorite serves up a raw oyster bar and sinfully tasty lobster rolls. Be prepared to wait – lines are long at peak times.

Petite Abeille $$
Belgian   **Map** 1 B1
134 West Broadway, 10013
Tel (212) 791-1360
Slurp on mussels and French fries at this inviting eatery decorated with the beloved cartoon character Tintin.

Prune $$
American   **Map** 5 A3
54 East 1st St, 10003
Tel (212) 677-6221
Small and rustic, this place does offshoots of American favorites such as bacon and eggs atop a tangle of peppery spaghetti.

Public $$
Australian   **Map** 4 F3
210 Elizabeth St, 10012
Tel (212) 343-7011
Experience cuisine from Down Under with a classy twist at this hip restaurant. Try the grilled kangaroo and the New Zealand wines.

Pure Food and Wine $$
Vegan   **Map** 9 A5
54 Irving Place, 10003
Tel (212) 477-1010
Unique and upscale restaurant dedicated to raw vegan cuisine, including coconut noodles and zucchini lasagne. Does not use any processed ingredients.

Spice Market $$
Southeast Asian   **Map** 3 B1
403 West 13th St, 10014
Tel (212) 675-2322
This sensuous restaurant serves Southeast Asian "street food" and fusion cocktails. Check out the vinegar-infused pork *vindaloo* (a spicy curried dish).

Spring Street Natural $$
Vegetarian   **Map** 4 F4
62 Spring St, 10012
Tel (212) 966-0290
Wholesome dishes made with fresh natural ingredients have been a neighborhood staple for decades. Choices include vegan macrobiotic plates.

Stanton Social $$
American   **Map** 5 A3
99 Stanton St, 10002
Tel (212) 995-0099
The party atmosphere and creative cocktails overshadow

the small plates designed for sharing at this trendy spot. There is a DJ on weekends.

Strip House $$
American **Map** 4 E1
13 East 12th St, 10003
Tel (212) 328-0000
A bordello-inspired steakhouse with plush banquettes. Opt for the dry-aged strip steak with goose-fat potatoes, and the 24-layer chocolate cake.

SUteiShi $$
Sushi **Map** 2 D2
24 Peck Slip, 10038
Tel (212) 766-2344
Top-notch sushi and straight-forward Japanese offerings in a stylish, high-ceilinged space. Creative, locally-themed rolls include the "King of NY" and "Peck's Peak."

Tertulia $$
Spanish tapas **Map** 4 D2
359 Sixth Ave, 10014
Tel (646) 559-9909
Sample smoked mussels and steaming paella heaped with shrimp at this vibrant tapas bar.

The Dutch $$
American **Map** 4 D3
131 Sullivan St, 10012
Tel (212) 677-6200
Oysters and traditional US-cuisine, like rabbit pot pie, are highlights at this trendy tavern. Also enjoy an American bourbon, straight up.

The Harrison $$
American **Map** 4 D5
355 Greenwich St, 10013
Tel (212) 274-9310
American classics with a twist, such as pork tenderloin with cherries, are served at this homey yet hip spot. Great selection of local and international beers.

The Little Owl $$
American **Map** 3 C2
90 Bedford St, 10014
Tel (212) 741-4695
Charming neighborhood joint with innovative, market-fresh, Mediterranean-style cuisine. Try their signature pork chops and gravy meatball sliders.

The Mermaid Inn $$
Seafood **Map** 5 A2
96 Second Ave, 10003
Tel (212) 674-5870
With its raw bar, New England-style chowder, and lobster sandwiches, this casual place draws a youthful, trendy crowd. Wash the seafood down with a Brooklyn beer.

The Spotted Pig $$
British **Map** 3 B2
314 West 11th St, 10014
Tel (212) 620-0393
Britons will feel at home in this upscale – and extremely trendy – pub. Excellent wine list plus, of course, plenty of stout and ale. Try the "5 veg" – a five-course vegetarian platter.

The Standard Grill $$
American **Map** 3 B1
848 Washington St, 10014
Tel (212) 645-4100
Bustling farmhouse-chic bistro with grilled steaks and burgers, locally sourced salads, and an excellent assortment of ales. The grilled Mayan shrimp is popular.

The Waverly Inn and Garden $$
American **Map** 3 C1
216 Bank St, 10014
Tel (212) 243-7900
The homespun name belies the scene within: celebrities and fashionistas dine on classic American fare such as juicy pork chops. Popular weekend brunch. Reservations are a must.

Babbo $$$
Italian **Map** 4 D2
110 Waverly Place, 10011
Tel (212) 777-0303
Famous chef Mario Batali's flagship restaurant, with superlative pasta, grilled meats, and offal. The wine list is extensive and bound to make wine lovers happy.

Bouley $$$
French **Map** 1 C1
163 Duane St, 10013
Tel (212) 66-5829 **Closed** *Sun*
A high-profile restaurant by chef Daniel Bouley; exquisite, pricey fare – but more than worth it. The emphasis is on both taste and nutritional value.

Eleven Madison Park $$$
American-French **Map** 9 A4
11 Madison Ave, 10010
Tel (212) 889-0905 **Closed** *Sun*
Contemporary cuisine is served in this beautiful Art Deco restaurant. The food is exquisite but it comes at a price. Don't forget your credit card.

Megu $$$
Japanese **Map** 1 B1
62 Thomas St, 10013
Tel (212) 964-7777
Fantastic Japanese fare, including the freshest fish, in this massive, trendy restaurant. The focus is on organic dining. Don't miss the kobe beef skewers.

Nobu $$$
Japanese **Map** 4 D5
105 Hudson St, 10013
Tel (212) 219-0500
One of NYC's best-known Japanese restaurants. Chef Nobu Matsuhisa has designed a super-lative menu but be prepared to splurge. Try the lobster with wasabi pepper sauce.

Tocqueville $$$
French **Map** 8 F5
1 East 15th St, 10003
Tel (212) 647-1515 **Closed** *Sun*
This inconspicuous gem offers French cuisine with a Japanese twist, including lavender Arctic char. Excellent wine list.

Union Square Café $$$
American **Map** 9 A5
21 East 16th St, 10003
Tel (212) 243-4020
Danny Meyer's flagship restaurant is one of NYC's most popular. This place uses the freshest ingredients from the local greenmarket. The elaborate chef's table menu can feed up to 12 guests.

Plush surroundings at the Union Square Café

For more information on types of restaurants *see p289*

Stylish decor at Buddakan, an Asian fusion eatery in Chelsea

Midtown

Burger Joint at Le Parker Meridien
American   **Map** 12 E3
119 West 57th St, 10019
Tel (212) 708-7414
Kitschy spot with mouth-watering burgers, shakes, and beers. It is tucked away behind the curtains in the lobby of Le Parker Meridien hotel.

Carnegie Deli
Deli   **$**
      Map 12 E4
854 Seventh Ave, 10019
Tel 800-334-5606
Huge pastrami and corned beef sandwiches are served at this New York deli. Also worth trying are the *knishes* (dumplings).

Eataly
Italian   **$–$$**
      Map 8 F4
200 Fifth Ave, 10010
Tel (212) 229-2560
Mario Batali's exuberant Italian market – fresh pasta, sausages, cheeses, multiple eateries and cafés, and a rooftop beer garden.

Sueños
Mexican   **$**
      Map 8 D5
311 West 17th St, 10011
Tel (212) 243-1333   **Closed** *Monday*
Tangy margaritas and filling Mexican cuisine. Try the chili tasting menu and don't miss the shredded beef mini tacos.

Taboon
Middle Eastern   **$**
      Map 11 C4
773 Tenth Ave, 10019
Tel (212) 713-0271
Middle Eastern meets Mediterranean at this inviting rustic eatery. Excellent wine list.

Ali Baba
Turkish   **$$**
      Map 9 B2
212 East 34th St, 10016
Tel (212) 683-92-6
Dine on babaganoush and stuffed grape leaves at this traditional eatery. Mouthwatering grilled meats are also on the menu.

Artisanal
French   **$$**
      Map 9 A2
2 Park Ave, 10016
Tel (212) 725-8585
Dashing bistro with elegant interiors. Try the elaborate cheese platter and the fondues.

Becco
Italian   **$$**
      Map 11 D5
355 West 46th St, 10036
Tel (212) 397-7597
Homely restaurant most famous for its pasta tasting menu and excellent Italian wine list.

BLT Steak
American   **$$**
      Map 13 A3
106 East 57th St, 10022
Tel (212) 752-7470
Trendy Bistro Laurent Tourondel serves up fat, succulent steaks with a variety of tangy sauces, including a creamy Béarnaise and a tart three-mustard. The signature warm popovers and oversized onion rings are great.

Blue Fin
Seafood   **$$**
      Map 12 E5
1567 Broadway, 10036
Tel (212) 918-1400
Spacious and sophisticated, this restaurant serves excellent seafood. One of the better dining experiences in fast food-packed Times Square. There is live jazz in the evenings.

Bottino
Italian   **$$**
      Map 7 C4
246 Tenth Ave, 10001
Tel (212) 206-6766
Housed in a century-old hardware shop, this northern Italian restaurant offers great food and a boutique wine list. It also has a beautiful patio and garden.

Buddakan
Asian fusion   **$$**
      Map 8 D5
75 Ninth Ave, 10011
Tel (212) 989-6699
Enjoy modern Asian cuisine and cocktails at Buddakan, with its soaring ceilings and incredible decor. The spacious dining room is ideal for large groups.

Dawat
Indian   **$$**
      Map 13 B3
210 East 58th St, 10022
Tel (212) 355-7555
Experience fragrant and delicious Indian fare here. Try the excellent salmon rubbed with coriander chutney, or go for the ever popular chicken tikka masala. The shrimp appetizer is a good bet, too.

Esca
Italian   **$$**
      Map 8 D1
402 West 43rd St, 10036
Tel (212) 564-7272
Chef Mario Batali achieves greatness again in this excellent southern Italian *trattoria*. Try the superb whole sea bass for two, cooked in sea salt.

Estiatorio Milos
Greek   **$$**
      Map 12 E4
125 West 55th St, 10019
Tel (212) 245-7400
Seafood palace with everything from grilled lobster to traditional Greek fish soup. Try the Mediterranean meze plate, or the grilled Canadian scallops, and sample the selection of Greek wines. The crab cakes are great.

Felidia
Italian   **$$**
      Map 13 B3
99 East 52nd St, 10022
Tel (212) 758-1479
TV star and chef Lidia Bastianich serves upscale Italian cuisine in this refined townhouse. The wine list is top-notch.

Entrance of Carnegie Deli, great for authentic New York fare

DK Choice

Grand Central Oyster Bar $$
Seafood · Map 9 A1
Lower Level, Grand Central Terminal, 89 East 42nd St, 10017
Tel (212) 490-6650
Sample fresh oysters at this seafood palace, which is crowned by grand, vaulted ceilings. The chefs opt for simple preparation – a squirt of lemon or a hand-plucked garnish – allowing the fresh fish and shellfish to shine on its own delectable merit.

Chic dining room at Pampano restaurant

La Grenouille $$
French · Map 12 F4
3 East 52nd St, 10022
Tel (212) 752-1495 · **Closed** *Mon*
A classic French restaurant, ideal for a romantic dinner. The intimacy factor is magnified by the soft banquettes and flickering candles.

Marseille $$
French-Moroccan · Map 12 D5
630 Ninth Ave, 10036
Tel (212) 333-2323
This inviting French-Moroccan restaurant with tiled floors features classic dishes such as duck cassoulet and tagines.

Michael Jordan's Steakhouse NYC $$
American
23 Vanderbilt Ave, Grand Central Terminal, 10017
Tel (212) 655-2300
The chances of seeing the celebrity basketball player are slim, but the steaks are perfectly charred. Ideal for a power lunch.

Molyvos $$
Greek · Map 12 E4
871 Seventh Ave, 10019
Tel (212) 582-7500
Superb Greek fare, from steaming moussaka to juicy lamb. There is

also a fish display showcasing what the kitchen has to offer. Dining rooms are spacious; great for large groups.

Norma's $$
American · Map 12 E3
119 West 56th St, 10019
Tel (212) 708-7460
One of Midtown's best-known brunch spots, serving massive omelets and pancakes. The dining room is sleek and inviting.

Osteria al Doge $$
Italian · Map 12 E5
142 West 44th St, 10036
Tel (212) 944-3643
Northern Italian specialties, from hearty grilled meats to fresh home-made pasta, are served at this friendly, rustic spot. Do not miss the thin-crust pizzas.

Pampano $$
Mexican · Map 13 B2
209 East 49th St, 10017
Tel (212) 751-4545
A chic restaurant from chef Richard Sandoval. Signature dishes include smoked swordfish,

grilled halibut, and chunky guacamole. Good selection of desserts. Lovely terrace.

Rue 57 $$
French fusion · Map 12 F3
60 West 57th St, 10019
Tel (212) 307-5656
The unlikely pairing of French cuisine and Japanese sushi draws the crowds here. Or enjoy authentic bistro cuisine – it also dishes out American classics.

Shun Lee Palace $$
Chinese · Map 13 A4
155 East 55th St, 10022
Tel (212) 371-8844
This upscale restaurant serves traditional Chinese mainland cooking. The Grand Marnier prawns are sinfully good.

Smith & Wollensky $$
American · Map 13 B5
797 Third Ave, 10022
Tel (212) 753-1530
Bite into quality steaks at this clubby steakhouse. Equally hearty are the appetizers, including split pea soup and seafood cocktails.

Dining in style at the glamorous Grand Central Oyster Bar, famed for its seafood

For more information on types of restaurants *see p289*

Lovely outdoor seating at Cafe Boulud

The Red Cat $$
American Map 7 C4
227 Tenth Ave, 10011
Tel (212) 242-1122
New England-style barnhouse setting, relaxed atmosphere, and professional service. Offers delectable dishes such as fried oysters. Sample the wild bass in white-wine butter. Great selection of wines too.

The Sea Grill $$
Seafood Map 12 F5
19 West 49th St, 10020
Tel (212) 332-7610 **Closed** Sun
An elegant temple to seafood, with superb grilled fish and shellfish. Modern setting with spectacular views. In the summer, enjoy breezy outdoor dining.

Trestle on Tenth $$
Swiss Map 7 C4
242 Tenth Ave, 10001
Tel (212) 645-5659
Dine on Swiss specialties, including rosti and pork, at this charming spot. In the summer, opt for the shaded garden. Especially popular with artists and art enthusiasts.

Virgil's Real Barbecue $$
American Map 12 E5
152 West 44th St, 10036
Tel (212) 921-9494
Fill up on juicy pork ribs, chicken wings, hunks of cornbread, and collard greens at this noisy BBQ joint. Offers a wide variety of authentic dishes, from Mexican to Creole and Cajun classics.

Aquavit $$$
Scandinavian Map 13 A4
65 East 55th St, 10022
Tel (212) 307-7311
Inventive cuisine in a sleek, minimalist dining room. Try classics such as Swedish

meatballs, gravlax, and toast skagen. Enjoy signature cocktails in the comfy bar lounge.

Aureole $$$
American Map 8 F1
135 West 42nd St, 10036
Tel (212) 319-1660
Chef Charlie Palmer offers inventive cuisine at this handsome restaurant, which also features a popular pre-theater menu and an excellent selection of wines.

DB Bistro Moderne $$$
French Map 8 F1
55 West 44th St, 10036
Tel (212) 391-2400
Famed chef Daniel Boulud is at the helm of this comfortably noisy bistro with excellent fare. There are two dining rooms, linked by a paneled wine bar. The French wine list is excellent.

Four Seasons $$$
American Map 13 A4
99 East 52nd St, 10022
Tel (212) 754-9494 **Closed** Sun
Thanks to its impressive longevity and stunning decor, this restaurant is one of New York's most famous. Experience a relaxing lunch by the poolside. There is a dedicated grill room and a wooden bar that is a popular draw. The art collection is excellent.

Gordon Ramsay $$$
French-Asian Map 12 E4
151 West 54th St, 10019
Tel (212) 468-8888
Closed Sun-Mon
British celebrity chef Gordon Ramsay performs his magic in the kitchen, with exquisite dishes such as lobster ravioli. For a true sampling, opt for the seven-course tasting menu, offered at lunch and dinner.

Le Bernardin $$$
French Map 12 E4
155 West 51st St, 10019
Tel (212) 554-1515
Chef Eric Ripert turns out French masterpieces at this elegant restaurant. Favorite dishes include red snapper with smoked paprika. Great for seafood lovers.

Marea $$$
Seafood Map 12 D3
240 Central Park South, 10019
Tel (212) 582-5100
Dine on razor clams and sea bass at this seafood oasis, or enjoy the wide variety of oysters and antipasti. Excellent weekend brunch.

Morimoto $$$
Japanese Map 7 C5
88 Tenth Ave, 10011
Tel (212)-989-8883
Choose anything from fresh sushi to "Kentucky Fried" blowfish. A sake sommelier will act as your guide to the exceptionally extensive sake menu.

Upper East Side

Beyoglu $
Turkish Map 17 B5
1431 Second Ave, 10028
Tel (212) 650-0850
This whimsically decorated place offers delicious, authentic meze, including stuffed grape leaves and *borek*, (filo pastry parcels stuffed with feta cheese).

Brother Jimmy's BBQ $
American Map 17 B5
1485 Second Ave, 10021
Tel (212) 288-0999
Carnivores will swoon at this rowdy restaurant with "finger-lickin'" BBQ. Thanks to the generous portions, it offers great value for money.

Shanghai Pavilion $
Chinese Map 17 B5
1378 Third Ave, 10021
Tel (212) 585-3388
Extensive menu of Shanghai specialties, including top-notch dim sum. Also offers unique seafood dishes, such as lobster tropicana. Great food overall.

Café Boulud $$
French Map 16 F5
20 East 76th St, 10021
Tel (212) 772-2600
Enjoy chef Daniel Boulud's impeccable creations in a casual setting. Seasonal dishes include duck breast with Brussels sprouts and apple cider.

Café d'Alsace $$
French   **Map** 17 B3
1695 Second Ave, 10128
Tel (212) 722-5133
A cheery slice of French Alsace, with tiled floors, flowing red wine, and crisp tartes. Opt for a sidewalk table to watch the crowds stream by.

Café Sabarsky $$
Austrian   **Map** 16 F3
1048 Fifth Ave, 10028
Tel (212) 288-0665   **Closed** *Tue*
Classsic Viennese café with aromatic coffees and hearty specialties from goulash to strudel. Lovely dining room lined with Austrian art.

David Burke Townhouse $$
American   **Map** 13 A3
133 East 61st St, 10021
Tel (212) 813-2121
Enjoy innovative New American cuisine in a sleek, lacquered setting. The restaurant is popular for its weekend brunch, with a unique array of egg dishes. For dinner, choose the pretzel-crusted crabcake followed by lobster steak.

Flex Mussels $$
Belgian   **Map** 17 A4
174 E 82nd St
Tel (212) 717-7772
Be charmed by this delightful seafood bistro. Delicious mussels in a rainbow of flavors, from prosciutto and caramelized onion to blue cheese and bacon. The wine list is good too.

Maya $$
Mexican   **Map** 13 C2
1191 First Ave, 10021
Tel (212) 585-1818
Come here for Mexican specialties – try the flavorsome guacamole and freshly made tortillas. Don't miss the drinks, from tangy margaritas to tequilas.

Sfoglia $$
Italian   **Map** 17 A2
1402 Lexington Ave, 10128
Tel (212) 831-1402
A small and rustic eatery with Italian farmhouse fare such as duck with apricots. The menu changes bi-monthly and the Italian wine list is excellent.

DK Choice

Daniel $$$
French   **Map** 13 A2
60 East 65th St, 10021
Tel (212) 288-0033   **Closed** *Sun*
If splurging in the city is the objective, this is the place for it. The opulent French restaurant of acclaimed chef Daniel Boulud offers a super-lative sensory experience, from the first step into the grand dining room and the rich forkful of foie gras to the final bite of the sinful chocolate mousse. Excellent wine list and seamless service make the Daniel experience truly worthwhile.

Sasabune $$$
Sushi   **Map** 13 C1
401 East 73rd St, 10021
Tel (212) 249-8583
At this outpost of the famed Los Angeles and Honolulu sushi shrines the only option is the nightly *omakase* (chef's tasting) menu, freshly prepared to order.

Upper West Side

Amy Ruth's $
Southern American **Map** 21 B3
113 West 116th St, 10026
Tel (212) 280-8779
Soul food at its most comforting, from delicious fried chicken to ham hocks.

Café Fiorello $
Italian   **Map** 12 D2
1800 Broadway, 10023
Tel (212) 595-5330
Tuck into an array of dishes from the antipasto bar at this cheerful joint. And don't miss the signa-ture thin-crust pizza. Sit outside in warm weather and watch the Lincoln Center crowds stream by.

Café Frida $
Mexican   **Map** 15 C1
368 Amsterdam Ave, 10025
Tel (212) 749-2929
Chomp on Mexican favorites such as fajitas and tacos at this lively spot, and wash them down with the tangy, potent margaritas.

Sylvia's $
Southern American **Map** 21 B1
328 Lenox Ave, 10027
Tel (212) 996-0660
Soul food at its finest, from fried chicken with waffles to Carolina-style catfish. The breakfast spread is quite elaborate. The Southern desserts are divine, including the peach cobbler.

Asiate $$
Asian   **Map** 12 D3
80 Columbus Circle, 10019
Tel (212) 805-8881
Stellar views are matched by the creative Asian cuisine. Popular dishes include Wagyu beef with oxtail sauce, pan-seared foie gras, and butter-poached lobster. Three-course fixed price brunch menu on weekends.

Bar Boulud $$
French   **Map** 12 D2
1900 Broadway, 10023
Tel (212) 595-0303
Famed chef Daniel Boulud opened this "peasant" restaurant with rustic French fare. The decor is sleek and modern, and there is an outdoor terrace area.

Stylish dining room at Daniel, a great place for delightful French cuisine

Café Luxembourg $$
French   **Map** 11 C1
446 Columbus Ave, 10024
Tel (212) 873-7411
Art Deco Parisian bistro popular
with business diners. Charmingly
traditional, with antique mirrors
and a zinc-topped bar.

Calle Ocho $$
Cuban   **Map** 16 D4
446 Columbus Ave, 10024
Tel (212) 873-5025
It's a never-ending party at this
colorful restaurant. Feast on a
range of spicy Latino dishes, from
ceviche to yucca fries, or try
the marinated Aji tuna and
cured salmon.

Dinosaur Bar-B-Que $$
American   **Map** 20 D1
700 West 125th St, 10027
Tel (212) 694-1777
Started by avid bike enthusiasts,
this rowdy BBQ joint dishes
out massive ribs, crispy chicken
wings, and American beers.
Come by on the weekends for
live jazz and comedy shows.

Gennaro $$
Italian   **Map** 15 C2
665 Amsterdam Ave, 10025
Tel (212) 665-5348
Delectable cuisine, and a
reasonably priced wine list. The
lamb shank braised in red wine
is quite a hit. There is a no-
reservation policy at this popular
restaurant, so be prepared to
wait during peak times.

Hudson River Café $$
Latin American
697 West 133rd St, 10027
Tel (212) 491-9111
Treat your tastebuds to global
cuisine at this spacious, airy
eatery. Sink into the chic and
relaxed ambience, and enjoy a
chilled local beer.

Loeb Boathouse Restaurant
Central Park $$
American   **Map** 12 E1
*East 72nd St and Park Drive North,
Central Park, 10023*
Tel (212) 515-2233
Lovely setting by Central Park's
lake. Popular with couples on a
romantic date. Decent American
fare and an outdoor bar area.

Ouest $$
American   **Map** 15 C4
2315 Broadway, 10024
Tel (212) 580-8700
An elegant eatery with unique
twists on American favorites. Try
the seared tuna with chickpea
puree. Great selection of desserts
to choose from.

Picholine $$
French   **Map** 12 D2
35 West 64th St, 10023
Tel (212) 724-8585   **Closed** *Sun*
Superb French-Mediterranean
cuisine and artisanal cheeses.
Popular with those attending
a concert at Lincoln Center.
Sample the diver sea scallops or
the steamed black sea bass.

Pio Pio $$
Peruvian   **Map** 15 C2
702 Amsterdam Ave, 10025
Tel (212) 665-3000
Try the signature crispy rotisserie
chicken here. Hearty combo
platters are a great way to save
money – they're easily big
enough to feed two.

DK Choice

Red Rooster $$
American   **Map** 21 B1
310 Lenox Ave, 10027
Tel (212) 792-9001
Clever, Southern-style comfort
food is on offer at Red Rooster.
Try the succulent steak with

---

fried green tomatoes, tasty
roast pork loin, fiery jerk
chicken, or the popular Red
Rooster burger. There is a large
dining room and a vibrant bar.
The restaurant's name pays
homage to the original Red
Rooster, a Harlem speakeasy
– a place where liquor was sold
illicitly during Prohibition.

Rosa Mexicano $$
Mexican   **Map** 12 D2
61 Columbus Ave, 10023
Tel (212) 977-7700
This trendy restaurant serves
sparkling sangrias and chunky
guacamole. Try signature dishes
such as tacos with achiote-
seasoned pork, or spicy enchiladas.
The grilled fish and chicken
breast – made skillet style – is
quite popular too. Gluten-free
lunch and dinner also on offer.

Telepan $$
American   **Map** 12 D1
72 West 69th St, 10023
Tel (212) 580-4300
Chef Bill Telepan sources local
ingredients to create innovative
dishes such as heirloom tomato
gazpacho salad. There is a prix
fixe brunch menu, as well as a
four-course tasting menu.
Do not miss the popular grass-
fed beef burger.

Jean Georges $$$
French   **Map** 12 D3
1 Central Park West, 10023
Tel (212) 299-3900   **Closed** *Sun*
The jewel in the crown of famed
French chef Jean-Georges
Vongerichten. For an optimal
overview, choose one of the
exquisite tasting menus. Emphasis
is on organic ingredients.

Masa $$$
Japanese   **Map** 12 D3
10 Columbus Circle, 10029
Tel (212) 823-9800   **Closed** *Sun*
Chef Masa breaks the record for
the most expensive tasting meal
ever at $450, but it is worth every
cent. Take a seat at the sushi bar
to watch the chefs in action.

Per Se $$$
American   **Map** 12 D3
10 Columbus Circle, 10019
Tel (212) 823-9335
Famed chef Thomas Keller has
introduced superlative
Californian-influenced cuisine
to New York. There are two
unique nine-course tasting
menus to indulge in, and a great
selection of wines. Spectacular
views of Central Park and
impeccable service.

Elegant interiors at the well-reviewed Per Se

Farther Afield

Al Di Là $
Italian
248 Fifth Ave, Brooklyn, 11215
Tel (718) 783-4565
Try the braised rabbit with black olives at this whimsical Venetian-inspired joint. Don't miss the mouthwatering desserts, including tangy gelato.

Elias Corner $
Greek
24–02 31st St, Queens, 11102
Tel (718) 932-1510
Hugely popular restaurant with the freshest fish in town. The large garden is perfect for groups.

Fette Sau $
American
354 Metropolitan Ave, Brooklyn, 11211
Tel (718) 963-3404
Juicy BBQ, from ribs to pork belly, served in a rustic former garage. Wash the meal down with robust beer or a glass of wine.

Jackson Diner $
Indian
37–47 74th St, Queens,11372
Tel (718) 672-1232
Spacious cafeteria with one of the best buffets in town. Classic North Indian appetizers; try the *tandoori* chicken (cooked in a clay oven), *samosas* (fried stuffed pastries), and thick *lassis* (yogurt-based drink).

Pies-N-Thighs $
American
166 South 4th St., Brooklyn, 11211
Tel (347) 529-6090
Classic American, from the dining to the decor. Try shrimp and grits, fried chicken, pulled pork, and butter biscuits. Delicious breakfast spread, and the weekend brunch menu is great.

Red Hook Lobster Pound $
Seafood
284 Van Brunt St, Brooklyn, 11231
Tel (646) 326-7650   **Closed** *Mon–Thu*
Fresh lobster meat is served every which way at this seafood shack. Choose a Maine lobster from the saltwater tank and have it cooked. The excellent and flexible catering service includes a specialized "lobster" truck that delivers door to door.

Sripraphai $
Thai
64-13 39th Ave, Queens, 11377
Tel (718) 899-9599   **Closed** *Wed*
Locals swear by this hole-in-the-wall place, said to serve the best Thai in the city. There is an elaborate menu dedicated to vegetarian food – try the sauteed drunken noodles with tofu, vegetables, chili, and basil leaves. Wash it down with some black Thai ice tea.

Agnanti Meze $$
Greek
1906 Ditmars Blvd, Queens, 11105
Tel (718) 545-4554
Lively place with filled grape leaves and filo pastry stuffed with cheese on the menu. There is an outdoor patio for the summer, and a fireplace for winter.

Frankie's 457 Spuntino $$
Italian
457 Court St, Brooklyn, 11231
Tel (718) 403-0033
Trendy neighborhood favorite with brick walls, hearty food, and stiff cocktails. Seasonal dishes include giant meatballs and eggplant crostini.

Grimaldi's $$
Italian
19 Old Fulton St, Brooklyn, 11201
Tel (718) 387-7400
One of New York's most famous pizzerias. The coal-fired oven pizzas, with creamy mozzarella and fresh tomato sauce, are worth the long lines.

Il Bambino $$
Italian
34–08 31st Ave, Queens, 11106
Tel (718) 626-0087
Solid Italian-American cuisine, such as fat paninis, and affordable wines on the extensive wine list. Try their popular peanut butter hot chocolate. Casual atmosphere and sharp service.

Marlow & Sons $$
American
81 Broadway, Brooklyn, 11211
Tel (718) 384-1441
Wonderfully eccentric, with communal tables and Med-influenced American fare. The menu leans towards organic, and includes delicacies such as a tart of goat cheese and wild leeks.

Prime Meats $$
American
465 Court St, Brooklyn, 11231
Tel (718) 254-0327
A delight for carnivores, this friendly restaurant offers all kinds of meat from pork schnitzel to grass-fed beef. There's also a strong domestic beer list and potent cocktails.

Rye $$
American
247 South 1st St, Brooklyn, 11211
Tel (718) 218-8047
Taste the succulent meatloaf sandwich and wash it down with creative cocktails at this former factory.

The Grocery $$
American
288 Smith St, Brooklyn, 11231
Tel (718) 596-3335   **Closed** *Sun & Mon*
Delightful restaurant with a summer garden. Try seasonal treats such as duck with bulghur wheat, or bite into grilled squid and seared scallops. Enjoy the excellent selection of local beers.

Peter Luger Steakhouse, a haven for meat lovers

DK Choice

Peter Luger Steakhouse $$$
American
178 Broadway, Brooklyn, 11211
Tel (718) 387-7400
For more than 125 years, this New York institution has been satisfying carnivores with massive juicy slabs, from porterhouse to prime rib and pot roast. The sauce is rather too delectable, and it can be taken home – it's bottled and for sale.

For more information on types of restaurants *see p289*

Light Meals and Snacks

You can get a snack almost anywhere and anytime in Manhattan. New Yorkers seem to eat endlessly – on street corners, in bars, luncheonettes, delis, before and after work, and long into the night. Casual eating in New York might include soft pretzels or char-roasted chestnuts from a corner stand; a huge sandwich from a deli; a Greek gyro sandwich (roasted lamb in pita bread) from street vendors; a pre-theater snack at a café or coffee bar; or a post-party binge at an all-night diner or bistro. While street fare is generally cheap, the quality and culinary skills vary greatly.

Delis

Delicatessens are a New York institution, not to mention a great source for a hefty lunchtime sandwich. Any visitor to the city should definitely try a deli's wonderful corned beef and pastrami sandwiches. While **Carnegie Delicatessen** in the Theater District is perhaps New York's most famous deli, **Katz's Deli** on the Lower East Side is much more authentic – and cheaper. Also deservedly popular is **Second Avenue Deli**, with its superb pastrami on rye and oozing blintzes.

Most deli business is takeout, and as a result, delis are bustling places serving huge sandwiches at relatively cheap prices. Counter staff are typically surly and impatient, and rudeness has almost become a trademark of the **Stage Deli**, which is now more of a tourist stop than the showbiz favorite it used to be.

For New York ethnic Jewish flavor, try **Barney Greengrass**, on the Upper West Side. In operation since 1929, the "Sturgeon King" serves up lox, salmon, pastrami, and, of course, sturgeon. **Zabar's** is a takeout heaven for yuppies who put up with the crowds for superb smoked fish, pickles, and salads.

Cafés, Bistros, and Brasseries

Cafés, bistros, and the larger brasseries have become "in" places in New York. Try the upscale **Balthazar** on Spring Street for "brilliantly faux" everything except the menu, which is stellar. In the Meatpacking District, **Kava Cafe**

serves gourmet sandwiches and expertly prepared coffees to a stylish crowd. The **Café Centro**, above Grand Central, is busy and noisy during lunchtime, and is a favorite with business types. The Centro's Provençal/Mediterranean fare includes fish soups and some succulent desserts. **Brasserie** on East 53rd, a longtime landmark, has had an elegant remodeling. **Benoit**, Alain Ducasse's casual bistro, is a classy destination offering familiar French fare to the midtown lunch crowd. Downtown, **Odeon** is a TriBeCa favorite for its brasserie menu and late hours. **Raoul's** in SoHo is a French bistro with a relaxed ambience that keeps artists and other habitués coming back for reliable, informal food. **Elephant and Castle**, a minimally decorated café, is a Greenwich Village standby for soup-salad-omelette lunches. Its real forte is breakfast and brunch, served in ample portions at modest prices. The bar scene is lively too. Tiny **Chez Jacqueline** is also a favored Village spot. Its French bistro fare and proximity to several off-Broadway theaters make it popular with the young, hip, and international crowd for a moderately priced dinner or late supper.

In the Theater District, try the Cuban **Victor's Café**. Large, lively, and Latin, it is known for authentic Cuban food served in giant portions at medium prices. **Chez Josephine** is an exuberant bistro-cabaret with live jazz piano playing. The scene is the main attraction here, and the French food is excellent.

La Boite en Bois, small but delightfully French, serves delicious French bistro food and is conveniently close to Lincoln Center. **P.J. Clarke's** is a welcoming bar famous for its burgers; it is also an affordable spot for a pre-theater meal.

Sarabeth's, on the Upper West Side, defies categorizing, but might best be dubbed a café. Breakfast or weekend brunch is the best time to try waffles, French toast, pancakes, and omelettes.

The Gramercy Park area's **Les Halles** is about as all-out French bistro as New York gets. At its late-night peak, the decibel level is high, but regulars think the *frites* and beef dishes are worth the noise and crowds.

Pizzerias

Pizza is available all over New York, from street stands and fast-food places that sell it by the slice to a traditional Neapolitan pizzeria.

Some pizzerias offer something more. **Arturo's Pizzeria** uses a coal oven for crisp, thin-crusted bases with the added inducement of live jazz. **Mezzogiorno** has a Tuscan menu and wonderful pizzas with unusual toppings. **Lombardi's** oven-baked pizzas are considered among the finest in Manhattan. The crowded **Mezzaluna** also specializes in brick-oven, thin-crusted pizza, as does **John's Pizzeria**, whose fans, including Woody Allen, consider it Manhattan's best. At **Two Boots**, specialty pies are named for characters in movies and TV shows, such as The Newman, from *Seinfeld*, and The Dude, from *The Big Lebowski*.

Brooklyn boasts a top pizzeria in Coney Island's **Totonno Pizzeria**, which is well worth the trip for real pizza aficionados, though it also has a Manhattan branch. **Joe's Pizza** has made a name for itself in Brooklyn and Manhattan. It's often busy, but the lines move quickly.

Generally, pizza parlors are good places to go for a cheap,

simple meal, particularly with children. Most places won't take reservations, so popular ones may have long lines.

Burger Joints

Apart from the hot dog stands on the street, New York has many places selling better quality burgers, even though prices for a top grade all-beef burger can go up to $20.

Burgers have even gone "upscale" with famed New York restaurateur Danny Meyer creating the **Shake Shack**, which has several locations around Manhattan, including one at Madison Square Park. It offers good-value eats all year round. In midtown, the stylish Le Parker Meridien Hotel houses the **Burger Joint**, which looks like a truck-stop, and has some of the best burgers in town.

Bright and basic, the five outlets of **Jackson Hole** offer fat, juicy, meaty burgers in 28 varieties popular with kids. Adults might prefer less glare and smarter decor, but they will like the low prices. Alternatively, sink your teeth into the juicy burgers on offer at the **Five Guys** chain.

The **Corner Bistro** in Greenwich Village offers New York's best burgers, tasty and reasonably priced. The beer selection is good, too, and the 4am closing makes this a great late-night stop.

Diners and Luncheonettes

Diners and luncheonettes, also called sandwich or coffee shops, can be found all over New York City. Food is mostly bland but served in huge, cheap platefuls. They are usually open from breakfast until evening, and you can stop in at almost any hour.

A favorite trend with diners has seen 1990s replicas of the old 1930s cheap-eats places. One such retro diner is **Chock Full o' Nuts**, a relaunch of a chain of coffee-branded cafés. A brighter, higher-energy option can be found near Carnegie Hall, in the **Brooklyn Diner**.

Theatergoers love **Junior's** diner in Brooklyn which is famous for its delicious cheesecake. **Big Nick's** on Broadway is the best place for a pizza, hamburger, or breakfast on the Upper West Side. The **Coffee Shop** in Union Square serves Brazilian-American fare and is open all night.

On the Upper East Side, Eli Zabar's **E.A.T.** sells excellent but pricey Jewish favorites – such as mushroom-barley soup and challah bread, as well as some sinful desserts. Another popular UES spot is **EJ's Luncheonette**, offering classic family meals in a retro 1950s setting.

Devotees swear by **Viand**, a spic-and-span East Side luncheonette, with cheap, ample American breakfasts, good burgers, egg creams, and the best turkey sandwiches in town. **Veselka**, not the usual New York sandwich shop, serves Polish/Ukrainian food at rock-bottom prices and also has a second outlet nearby, on the Bowery.

Tea Rooms

The only place you can be absolutely sure of getting a cup of real, brewed tea is at a formal, prix-fixe afternoon tea in a lounge at one of New York's pricier hotels, from 3pm to 5pm.

For an extra-stylish tea, on Chippendale furniture, visit **Carlyle** in the Upper East Side. Another good buy in hotel prix-fixe tea is **Hotel Pierre**. Tea at the **Waldorf-Astoria** comes with Devonshire cream, while the elegant tea at **The Plaza**'s Palm Court has been an NYC tradition for more than a century.

A variation on tea themes can be found in a chain of teahouses called **Saint's Alp**. These delightful spots, serving frothy, flavored, colorful tea drinks poured over crushed ice, can be found at 51 Mott Street near Chinatown and in the East Village and Times Square areas. Teatime can also be enjoyed at **Tea & Sympathy**, in the Village, on Greenwich Avenue.

Coffee and Cakes

You can get a decent cup of coffee for as little as 75 cents, with endless free refills, at most diners, luncheonettes, and coffee shops. There is a popular trend for coffee bars that serve a variety of specialty coffees, such as cappuccino, espresso, and caffè latte. Ice-cream parlors and patisseries also serve good coffee, along with sinfully luscious pastries.

People wait in lines out the door at **Magnolia Bakery's** original Greenwich Village location. There are also several other outposts across the city selling decadent cupcakes and delicious cookies. **Joe**, the self-proclaimed master of "the art of coffee," maintains numerous locations around the city, while **Ferrara Bakery and Café**, going strong since 1892, has moderately priced Italian pastries, good coffee, and outdoor seating.

The Hungarian Pastry Shop has a range of Austro-Hungarian delights and views of St. John the Divine. Located in the Hotel Edison, **Café Edison** offers reasonably priced food in an Art Nouveau setting. **Sant Ambroeus** is a luxurious outpost of the Milanese pasticceria selling sumptuous desserts. In addition to home delivery of pies or cakes, **Dessert Delivery** has a nifty café for tasting the pastries and coffee. Try **Serendipity 3**, famous for its Victoriana, ice-cream creations – if you're an ice-cream aficionado don't miss the frozen hot chocolate – as well as coffee, and mid-afternoon snacks.

Barnes & Noble Café is a happy refuge for coffee and a pastry while browsing the bookstore. **Mudspot** is the permanent counterpart to the mobile, bright orange "Mudtrack" van that sells potent coffee. And, like them or not, you can't ignore **Starbucks**, which has dozens of locations around town.

DIRECTORY

Lower East Side

Ferrara Bakery and Café
195 Grand St.
Map 4 F4.

Katz's Deli
205 E Houston St.
Map 5 A3.

Saint's Alp
51 Mott St.
Map 4 F4.

Two Boots
42 Avenue A.
Map 5 B2.

Soho and Tribeca

Lombardi's
32 Spring St.
Map 4 F4.

Mezzogiorno
195 Spring St.
Map 4 D4.

Odeon
145 W Broadway.
Map 1 B1.

Raoul's
180 Prince St.
Map 4 D3.

Greenwich Village

Arturo's Pizzeria
106 W Houston St.
Map 4 E3.

Balthazar
80 Spring St.
Map 4 E4.

Chez Jacqueline
72 MacDougal St.
Map 4 D2.

Corner Bistro
331 W 4th St.
Map 3 C1.

Elephant and Castle
68 Greenwich Ave.
Map 3 C1.

Five Guys
296 Bleecker St.
Map 3 C3.

Joe
141 Waverly Place.
Map 3 C1.

Joe's Pizza
7 Carmine St.
Map 4 D3.

Kava Cafe
803 Washington St.
Map 3 B1.

Magnolia Bakery
401 Bleecker St.
Map 3 C2.
200 Columbus Ave.
Map 12 D1.

Sant Ambroeus
259 W 4th St.
Map 3 C1.

Tea & Sympathy
108 Greenwich Ave.
Map 3 C1.

East Village

Mudspot
307 E 9th St.
Map 4 F1.

Veselka
144 2nd Ave. **Map** 4 F1.
9 E 1st St. **Map** 4 F3.

Gramercy and The Flatiron

The Coffee Shop
29 Union Square West.
Map 9 A5.

Les Halles
411 Park Ave South.
Map 9 A3.

Shake Shack
Madison Square Park.
Map 8 F4.

Chelsea and the Garment District

Chock Full o' Nuts
25 W 23rd St.
Map 8 F4.

Theater District

Café Edison
Edison Hotel,
228 W 47th St.
Map 12 D5.

Carnegie Delicatessen
854 7th Ave.
Map 12 E4.

Chez Josephine
414 W 42nd St.
Map 7 B1.

Junior's
Shubert Alley, enter on
45th St.
Map 12 E5.

Stage Deli
834 7th Ave.
Map 12 E4.

Victor's Café
236 W 52nd St.
Map 11 B4.

East Side Midtown

Second Avenue Deli
162 E 33rd St.
Map 9 B2.

Upper Midtown

Barnes & Noble Café
Citicorp Building,
160 E 54th St.
Map 13 A4.

Brasserie
100 E 53rd St.
Map 13 A4.

Brooklyn Diner
212 W 57th St.
Map 12 E3.

Burger Joint
Le Parker Meridien Hotel,
118 W 57th St.
Map 12 E3.

Waldorf-Astoria
301 Park Ave.
Map 13 A5.

Upper East Side

Benoit
60 W 55th St.
Map 12 F3.

Carlyle
35 E 76th St.
Map 17 A5.

Dessert Delivery
350 E 55th St.
Map 13 B4. Tel 838-5411.

E.A.T.
1064 Madison Ave.
Map 17 A4.

EJ's Luncheonette
1271 3rd Ave.
Map 13 B1.

Hotel Pierre
2 E 61st St.
Map 12 F3.

Jackson Hole
232 E 64th St.
Map 13 B2. *One of five branches.*

John's Pizzeria
408 E 64th St.
Map 13 C2. *One of three branches.*

Mezzaluna
1295 3rd Ave.
Map 17 B5.

The Plaza
768 5th Ave.
Map 12 F3.

Serendipity 3
225 E 60th St.
Map 13 B3.

Viand
1011 Madison Ave.
Map 17 A5. *One of four branches.*

Upper West Side

Barney Greengrass
541 Amsterdam Ave.
Map 15 C3.

Big Nick's
2175 Broadway at 77th St.
Map 15 C5.

La Boite en Bois
75 W 68th St.
Map 11 C1.

P.J. Clarke's
44 W 63rd St.
Map 12 D2.

Sarabeth's
423 Amsterdam Ave.
Map 15 C4.

Whitney Museum
945 Madison Ave.
Map 17 A5.

Zabar's
2245 Broadway.
Map 15 C2.

Morningside Heights and Harlem

The Hungarian Pastry Shop
Amsterdam & 109th St.
Map 20 E4.

Brooklyn

Totonno Pizzeria
1524 Neptune Ave.
Map 7 C5.

New York Bars

New York bars play a huge role in the life and culture of the city. Many New Yorkers spend the evening in a succession of bars, because each usually offers something more than just alcohol. There may be additional inducements, like excellent food, live music, dancing, or a particularly large selection of beers. Brew pubs, which serve meals and brew beer on the premises, are also popular. Bars suiting every taste and budget are to be found in every corner.

Rules and Conventions

Bars generally remain open from around 11am until 2am. Some stay open to 4am, when they must close by law. Many bars have a "happy hour" between 5pm and 7pm, when they offer twofers (two drinks for the price of one) and free snacks. Bartenders can refuse to serve anyone they consider having had too much to drink. Smoking is banned and is only allowed outside or in specially ventilated rooms.

The legal minimum drinking age is 21; if the bartender suspects you are younger, you'll be "carded," or asked for identification. Children aren't usually allowed in.

It is common to "run a tab" by giving the bartender a credit card and paying your bill just before you leave. Tipping the bartender is expected – 15 percent of the bill or about $1 per drink. Shots are not pre-measured, so if you want a bigger drink, it can help to "belly up" to the bar and tip the bartender accordingly for his or her generosity. You may even be poured a free drink if you tip handsomely. If you sit at a table, you'll be served there and charged more. A round of drinks can be expensive. Save money by buying a quart (95 cl) or a half gallon (190 cl) pitcher of beer.

Many bars have obtained liquor licenses under an oscure cabaret law that prohibits dancing. Bars are regularly closed down for ignoring this rule, so if staff ask you to refrain from dancing to music, they are serious and should be obeyed.

What to Drink

Mainstream bars serve standard beers from big producers, such as Budweiser, Coors, and Miller, as well as high-profile imports including Becks, Heineken, and draft Guinness. Old pubs and chic bars have a much wider variety of beers, imported and small domestics. These include flavorful beers, usually based on traditional European styles, made by some of New York's microbreweries. The locally brewed Brooklyn Lager is highly rated.

Other popular drinks include "designer," or "fusion," cocktails, rum and coke, vodka-and-tonic, gin-and-tonic, dry Martinis, and Scotch or bourbon – either "straight up" (without ice) or "on the rocks" (with ice). The "Cosmopolitan" is very New York: vodka, cranberry juice, triple sec, and lime. Most of the bars serve a range of Martinis made with vodka.

Wine is widely available at bars, and the "wine bar" concept has made a comeback, with options all over the city.

Food

Some bars serve food such as burgers, fries, salads, sandwiches, and spicy chicken wings throughout the day. If you are visiting the bar of a popular restaurant, you can often order bar snacks. Most bar kitchens stop serving food just before midnight.

Fashionable Bars

To get into a hip bar, you will need to look glamorous and be prepared to wait in line, unless you arrive early. The Meatpacking District is lined with lively bars, including **Cielo**, a strobe-lit bar and club with potent cocktails and a soundtrack with everything from 1980s pop to hip-hop. Hidden away in the trendy West Village is **Employees Only**, a stylish hangout that has won a cult-like following due to its expert cocktails and intense waitstaff. Many of its staff depart to run cocktail programs around the world, and its famed Bloody Mary mix can be purchased at fine specialty shops across the city. **Tao Bar**, located in a former theater next to the Four Seasons Hotel, is spread over three floors: the top two are devoted to pan-Asian cuisine and overlook the bar below. The nightlife in the Lower East Side (LES) is growing in leaps and bounds, with numerous bars and clubs opening their doors. Enjoy cocktails and conversation at the lively **Schiller's Liquor Bar**. Formerly the Bowery Bar, the **B-Bar** still attracts a stylish crowd, though some claim its glory days are over. In the summer, the enormous outdoor space can't be beaten. **Pravda** is another favorite in nearby NoLlta. Subdued lighting creates a degree of calm in this subterranean spot decorated in Soviet chic. **The Odeon** on Broadway captures the lively SoHo-TriBeCa scene.

Bars with Views

Top of the Tower, on the 26th floor of the Art Deco Beekman Tower, offers unsurpassed views of the city and great piano music. Also with great views are the **Rooftop Bar and Lounge** at the Empire Hotel, **Stone Rose Lounge** in the Time Warner Center, and, for views of the expanding World Trade Center skyline, the **Living Room Terrace** at the W Downtown. In warm weather, **Bryant Park Café** is a popular midtown scene, or you can sip cocktails and soak up the dazzling views on **230 Fifth**'s vast wrap-around terrace.

Historic and Literary Bars

If you sample only one New York bar, it should probably be **McSorley's Old Ale House**, an Irish saloon often dubbed "McSurly's" because of its staff. It opened in 1854, and is one of the city's oldest bars.

The Ear Inn dates from 1812 when the first tavern opened on this SoHo site. Its cramped interior and long wooden bar ooze authenticity. Another SoHo favorite is **Fanelli's Café**, a former speakeasy that opened its doors in 1922 (though locals have been visiting the watering hole on this site since 1847).

Greenwich Village has some of the city's oldest bars, such as Dylan Thomas's favorite, the **White Horse Tavern**, an 1880s landmark still crowded with literary and collegiate types. It also has an outdoor café for warm weather. **Peculier Pub** is a beer-lover's paradise, with over 360 varieties of beer.

A good, if touristy, place for a drink in the financial district is **Fraunces Tavern**, first built in 1719 (see p78).

Pete's Tavern in the Gramercy Park area dates to 1864. Busy until 2am, it is known for Victoriana and the house brew called Pete's Ale. The typical Irish pub **Old Town Bar** has been serving stout since 1892, and is now favored largely by advertising types. No longer the celebrity scene it once was, **Sardi's** still appeals to *New York Times* reporters, and serves generous portions.

Hidden away in the balcony of Grand Central Terminal is **The Campbell Apartment**, the former private office of 1920s tycoon John W. Campbell. The spectacular space resembles a 13th-century Florentine palace. On the Upper East Side, the **Uptown Lounge** offers potent cocktails, tasty nibbles, and lively dance tunes.

A bustling saloon with Irish bartenders, **P. J. Clarke's** has been New York's favorite since the 1890s. Dating back to 1930, the **21 Club** remains one of the city's most atmospheric haunts, complete with a ceiling crammed full of antique toys.

Near Carnegie Hall is **P. J. Carney's**, a watering hole for musicians and artists since 1927. It serves Irish ales and a good shepherd's pie.

Brew Pubs

Brew pubs, where the house beer is brewed on the premises, are all the rage with the 20- and 30-somethings, as are bars that stock a variety of microbrews and imported beers. The **Chelsea Brewing Company** is a large, fun-filled brew pub in the Chelsea Piers sports complex. In the Gramercy neighborhood, you will find the **Heartland Brewery**, a bustling brew pub with five beers, including the outstanding India Pale Ale, and many seasonals, such as pumpkin ale. The cozy bar at **The Room**, in SoHo, has a good selection of beers and wine.

Serious beer drinkers will enjoy the 170 draft and bottled Belgian beers on offer at **Burp Castle**, while homesick Brits will likely head to **Manchester Pub**. In a cozy, publike setting, you'll find Watneys or Newcastle Brown Ale on tap, just two of the 18 draft beers, and 40 bottled ones not widely available in New York.

In the East Village is bustling **d.b.a.**, which has 14 draft beers on tap, along with scores of microbrews and 50 single-malt whiskeys to choose from.

A popular beer stop uptown for the college-age crowd is the loud and noisy **Brother Jimmy's BBQ**, where you can snack on old-fashioned southern barbecued ribs.

Park Slope Ale House in Brooklyn is another brew pub favored by the young for its home brews and seasonal beers, as well as its decent pub grub and lively ambience.

Gay and Lesbian Bars

Gay bars can be found in Greenwich Village, Chelsea, and the East Village with a few on the Upper East and West Sides. Lesbian bars are mostly in Greenwich Village and East Village. For current listings, check the free weekly gay publication *Next* (www.nextmagazine.com).

Hotel Bars

Centrally located, the **Algonquin Hotel** (see p147) was a famous literary haunt in the 1920s and early 1930s. Its Lobby Lounge and Blue Bar are good places for a quiet pre-dinner or pre-theater drink.

The minimalist **Bar 44** in the lobby lounge of the Royalton Hotel is a perfect spot for a drink while watching the theatrical crowds drifting in and out. Also in the Theater District, the **Paramount Bar** has floor-to-ceiling windows and is usually frequented by fashion and theater types. In Upper Midtown there's the **Gilt Bar**, where you can recline on soft, plush red velvet seats.

The **Bull and Bear** in the Waldorf-Astoria, dating back to the Prohibition era, exudes comfort, charm, and a sense of history.

The stylish **King Cole Room** at St. Regis Hotel is named after a colorful mural behind the bar, by Maxfield Parrish.

Relax to downtempo tunes at the **Grand Bar**. One of New York's trendier nightspots, the Soho Grand's bar is a good place to people-watch. Its sister hotel, the Tribeca Grand, also draws a crowd to its **Church Lounge**.

With dark-wood panels, navy-blue color scheme, and a kitschy seafaring theme, the Maritime Hotel's **Lobby Bar** draws a young, trendy crowd. Special attractions include a roaring fire in winter and an outdoor terrace in summer.

The glass-floored **Hudson Bar** at Ian Schrager's trendy Hudson Hotel is a regular hotspot. The **Rose** and **Jade** bars, in Schrager's Gramercy Park Hotel, are filled with fashionistas drinking in the "eclectic-Bohemian" vibe. Equally popular are **Thom Bar** at the 60 Thompson Hotel and **Bookmarks** at the Library Hotel; both attract a sophisticated scene. For those interested in joining the *Sex and the City* crowd, there's Rande Gerber's **Whiskey Blue Bar** in one of the boutique W Hotels.

DIRECTORY

Lower Manhattan

Fraunces Tavern
54 Pearl St.
Map 1 C4.
🌐 fraucestavern.com

Living Room Terrace
W Downtown, 123
Washington St.
Map 1 B3.

Soho and Tribeca

Church Lounge
Tribeca Grand, 2 6th Ave.
Map 4 D4.
🌐 tribecagrand.com

The Ear Inn
326 Spring St.
Map 3 C4.
🌐 earinn.com

Fanelli's Café
94 Prince St.
Map 4 E3.

The Grand Bar
Soho Grand, 310
W Broadway.
Map 4 E4.
🌐 sohogrand.com

The Odeon
145 W Broadway.
Map 1 B1.
🌐 theodeonrestaurant.com

Pravda
281 Lafayette St.
Map 4 F3.
🌐 pravdany.com

The Room
144 Sullivan St.
Map 4 D3.

Thom Bar
60 Thompson Hotel, 60
Thompson St.
Map 4 D4.
🌐 60thompson.com

Greenwich Village

Cielo
18 Little W 12th St.
Map 3 B1.
🌐 cieloclub.com

Employees Only
510 Hudson St.
Map 3 C2.
🌐 employeesonly
nyc.com

Peculier Pub
145 Bleecker St.
Map 4 D3.
🌐 peculierpub.com

White Horse Tavern
567 Hudson St.
Map 3 C1.

East Village and Lower East Side

B-Bar
40 E 4th St.
Map 4 F2.
🌐 bbarandgrill.com

Burp Castle
41 E 7th St.
Map 4 F2.
🌐 burpcastlenyc.
wordpress.com

d.b.a.
41 1st Ave.
Map 5 A1.
🌐 drinkgoodstuff.com

McSorley's Old Ale House
15 E 7th St.
Map 4 F2.
🌐 mcsorleysnewyork.
com

Schiller's Liquor Bar
131 Rivington St.
Map 5 B3.

Gramercy

Heartland Brewery
35 Union Square W.
Map 9 A5.
🌐 heartlandbrewery.
com

Jade Bar
Gramercy Park Hotel,
2 Lexington Ave.
Map 9 A4.
🌐 gramercypark
hotel.com

Old Town Bar
45 E 18th St.
Map 8 F5.
🌐 oldtownbar.com

Pete's Tavern
129 E 18th St.
Map 9 A5.
🌐 petestavern.com

Rose Bar
Gramercy Park Hotel,
2 Lexington Ave.
Map 9 A4.
🌐 gramercypark
hotel.com

Chelsea and The Garment District

Chelsea Brewing Company
Pier 59, 11th Ave.
Map 7 B5.
🌐 chelsea
brewingco.com

Lobby Lounge
Maritime Hotel, 363 W
16th St.
Map 8 D5.
🌐 themaritimehotel.
com

Theater District

Bar 44
Royalton Hotel,
44 W 44th St.
Map 12 F5.

Bryant Park Café
Bryant Park.
Map 8 F1.
🌐 bryantpark.org

Hudson Bar
Hudson Hotel,
356 W 58th St.
Map 12 D3.
🌐 hudsonhotel.com

Paramount Bar
Paramount Hotel,
235 W 46th St.
Map 12 E5.

P. J. Carney's
906 7th Ave. Map 12 E3.
🌐 pjcarneys.com

Sardi's
234 W 44th St.
Map 12 F5.
🌐 sardis.com

Lower Midtown

230 Fifth
230 Fifth Ave. Map 8 F3.

Bookmarks
The Library Hotel, 299
Madison Ave. Map 9 A1.

The Campbell Apartment
Grand Central Terminal,
15 Vanderbilt Ave.
Map 9 A1.

Upper Midtown

Bull and Bear
Waldorf-Astoria Hotel,
Lexington Ave. Map 13 A5.
🌐 bullbearbar.com

Gilt Bar
New York Palace Hotel,
455 Madison Ave.
Map 13 A4.
🌐 giltnewyork.com

King Cole Room
St. Regis Hotel, 2 E 55th
St. Map 12 F5.

Manchester Pub
920 2nd Ave.
Map 13 B5.

P. J. Clarke's
915 3rd Ave.
Map 13 B4.

Stone Rose Lounge
10 Columbus Circle,
4th Floor.
Map 12 D3.
🌐 gerberbars.com

Tao Bar
42 E 58th St.
Map 13 A3.
🌐 taorestaurant.com

Top of the Tower
Beekman Tower, 3
Mitchell Place.
Map 13 C5.
🌐 thebeekman
hotel.com

Whiskey Blue Bar
541 Lexington Ave.
Map 13 A2.
🌐 gerberbars.com

Upper East Side

21 Club
21 W 52nd St. Map 12 F4.

Brother Jimmy's BBQ
1485 2nd Ave.
Map 17 B5.
🌐 brotherjimmys.com

Uptown Lounge
1576 Third Ave.
Map 17 B3.
🌐 uptownlounge
nyc.com

Upper West Side

Rooftop Bar and Lounge
Empire Hotel,
44 W 63rd St.
Map 12 D2.
🌐 empirehotelnyc.com

Brooklyn

Park Slope Ale House
356 6th Ave at 5th St.

SHOPPING

Visitors to New York inevitably include shopping in their plans. The city is the consumer capital of the world: a shopper's paradise and a constant source of entertainment, with dazzling window displays and a staggering variety of goods for sale. Anything can be found here, from high fashion to rare children's books, state-of-the-art electronics, and a mouthwatering array of exotic food. If you are looking for a personal Hovercraft, read-in-the-dark eyeglass attachments, a designer bed for your pet gerbil, or a Wurlitzer jukebox, this is the city of your dreams. Whether you have $50,000 or $5, New York is the place to spend it.

The 1920s-style Henri Bendel store *(see p311)*

Best Buys

New York is a bargain hunter's dream, with huge discounts on anything from household goods to designer clothes. Some of the best shops are on Orchard Street and Grand Street on the Lower East Side, where designer goods are sold at considerably lower than the retail price. You can find just about every imaginable item of clothing here, in addition to tableware, shoes, home furnishings, and electronics. Some shops in this area are closed on Saturday – the Jewish Sabbath – but are usually open all day Sunday.

Another great area for fashion bargain hunters is the Garment District, roughly between Sixth and Eighth avenues from 30th to 40th Street. The main hub, Seventh Avenue, was renamed Fashion Avenue in the early 1970s. Several designers and manu-facturers have showrooms here, some of which are open to the public. Many of their samples are put up for sales, announced on notices posted around the

area. The best time to visit them is just before one of the major gift-giving holidays. Top Button (www.topbutton.com) has comprehensive sales listings.

Sales

One word you'll come across all over the city, anytime of the year, is "sale." So check the sale goods before you pay full price for any purchase. The best sales are during New York's sale seasons, which generally run from June until end-July and from December 26 until February. Look up the local papers for ads. Along midtown Fifth Avenue you'll see signs announcing "Lost Our Lease" sales. Avoid them, as these signs have been up for years at many shops. Also keep your eyes peeled for "Sample Sales," where the top designers sell to the public the sample outfits they have created to show store buyers. Sample sales occur at different locations throughout the city, and are generally not advertised, so your best bet is to keep a look-out for signs announcing sample sales, particularly on Fifth Avenue and on Broadway.

Designer dress at a New York sale

The Bulgari entrance at Hotel Pierre *(see p287)*

How to Pay

Most shops accept major credit cards, although there will often be a minimum purchase price. If you want to use your traveler's checks, identification is needed. Personal checks drawn in another currency will be refused. Some stores only take cash, especially during sales.

Opening Hours

Most shops are open from 10am to 6pm, Monday to Saturday. Many department stores are open through Sunday, and until 9pm at least two nights a week. Lunch hours (noon to 2:30pm), Saturdays, sales, and holidays will be the most crowded times.

Taxes

The New York City sales tax is 8.875 percent, although clothing and shoes under $55 are exempt. However, sales tax will be waived if the goods are shipped home.

Shopping Tours

If you dread braving the stores alone, shopping tours are a good, reasonably priced option. Apart from the main department stores, you could visit private designer show-rooms, auction houses, or fashion shows. Some operators will customize tours to suit your requirements.

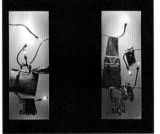

Window displays at Bloomingdale's *(see p183)*

Department Stores and Malls

Most of the large – and best – department stores are located in midtown Manhattan. Explore them at your leisure, since all these stores tend to be enormous, with a great range of goods. If possible, avoid weekends and vacation times, when the crowds can be overwhelming. Prices are often high, but it is possible to find some bargains during sales.

Stores such as Saks Fifth Avenue, Bloomingdale's, and Macy's provide a diverse and extraordinary range of shopping services, including actually shopping for you.

One of the biggest malls in Manhattan is the **Shops at Columbus Circle** in the Time Warner Center. Its stores include Williams-Sonoma, Coach, and Hugo Boss. **Century 21** is a legendary Downtown depart-ment store selling designer

clothes and gifts at discount prices.

Barney's New York, favored by young professionals, specializes in excellent, though expensive, designer clothes.

Luxurious, elegant, and understated, **Bergdorf Goodman** sells contemporary clothes by European designers at high prices. The men's store is across the street.

Bloomingdale's *(see p183)* is the Hollywood film star of the department stores, with many eye-catching displays and seductive goods. New Yorkers young and old come here to seek out the latest in fashion. The linen and fine china departments have a reputation for quality, and the gourmet food section features a shop devoted entirely to caviar. Extensive shopping services and amenities include a noted restaurant, Le Train Bleu, with its view of the Queensboro Bridge. There is also a SoHo branch on Broadway. Though much smaller than the main store, it stocks a similar selection of luxury goods.

At the exclusive **Henri Bendel**, everything from the Art Deco jewels to beautiful handmade shoes is displayed as a priceless work of art. The store, laid out in a series of 1920s-style boutiques, sells an excellent range of innovative women's fashions.

Lord & Taylor is renowned for its classic and much more conservative fashions for men and women, with an emphasis on US designers.

Macy's, the self-proclaimed largest store in the world *(see p136–7)*, has ten floors selling everything imaginable from can openers to antiques. **Saks Fifth Avenue**, known for style and elegance, has long been considered one of the city's best department stores,

A magnificent display offering household goods

with service to match. It sells stunning designerwear for adults as well as children.

New York's Best: Shopping

In a city where you can literally shop 24 hours a day, the best plan is to shop the way New Yorkers do, by neighborhood. Each has its own character and specialties. Here are highlights of the best shopping districts – where they are and what you will find in each. If time is very tight, head for one of the huge department stores *(see p311)*, or if window shopping is your preference, stroll along Fifth Avenue, home to Manhattan's most glittering stores *(see opposite)*. For great bargains in a truly ethnic area, try the Lower East Side.

Greenwich Village and the Meatpacking District
Quaint, eclectic, and antique choices in the Village, and gourmands will enjoy the myriad speciality food stores. Meander over to Meatpacking District for high fashion shopping *(see pp114–15)*.

SoHo
The area bordered by Sixth Avenue, Lafayette, Houston, and Canal streets is bustling with antiques, crafts, and clothes from designer flagships. Weekend brunchtime gallery-hopping is very popular. Cross Broadway to NoLIta for even trendier, cutting-edge fashion *(see pp106–7)*.

Chelsea and the Garment District

Gramercy and the Flatiron District

Hudson River

Greenwich Village

East Village

SoHo and TriBeCa

East Village and Lower East Side
Explore around St Mark's Place for shoes, avant-garde fashions, and ethnic goods *(see pp120–21)*. Bargains are becoming harder to find in the Lower East Side, but trendy options are increasing *(see pp96–7)*.

Seaport and the Civic Center

Lower East Side

Lower Manhattan

South Street Seaport
This is a browser's paradise of crafts, gifts, souvenirs, books, and antiques with a seafaring connection *(see pp84–5)*.

Herald Square and the Garment District
Here you will find Macy's, a store that occupies an entire block. The surrounding area (especially Seventh Avenue) is the fashion wholesale center with major discounts during sales – but some stores accept only cash *(see pp134–5)*.

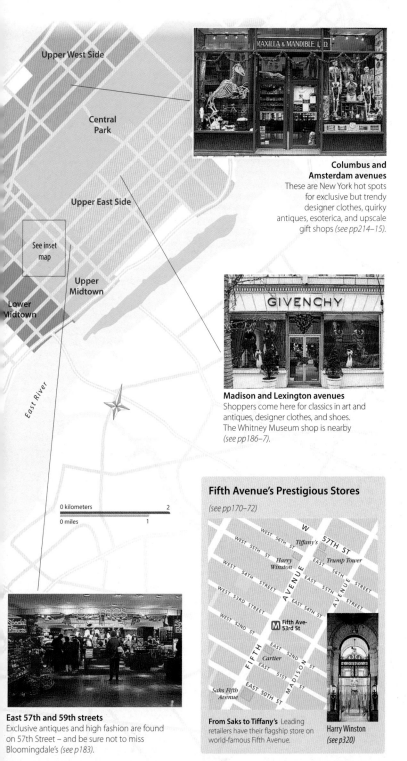

Columbus and Amsterdam avenues
These are New York hot spots for exclusive but trendy designer clothes, quirky antiques, esoterica, and upscale gift shops *(see pp214–15)*.

Madison and Lexington avenues
Shoppers come here for classics in art and antiques, designer clothes, and shoes. The Whitney Museum shop is nearby *(see pp186–7)*.

Upper West Side

Central Park

Upper East Side

See inset map

Upper Midtown

Lower Midtown

East River

0 kilometers   2
0 miles   1

Fifth Avenue's Prestigious Stores
(see pp170–72)

WEST 56TH ST   W 57TH ST
WEST 55TH ST   Tiffany's
WEST 54TH STREET   Harry Winston   EAST 56TH   Trump Tower
WEST 53RD STREET   EAST 55TH STREET
WEST 52ND STREET   EAST 54TH STREET

AVENUE

Fifth Ave-53rd St

EAST 53RD STREET

FIFTH

MADISON

Cartier
EAST 52ND ST
EAST 51ST ST

Saks Fifth Avenue

EAST 50TH STREET

From Saks to Tiffany's Leading retailers have their flagship store on world-famous Fifth Avenue.

Harry Winston
(see p320)

East 57th and 59th streets
Exclusive antiques and high fashion are found on 57th Street – and be sure not to miss Bloomingdale's *(see p183)*.

New York Originals

New York is a city where just about any kind of shop, no matter how esoteric, will always attract customers. Dozens of tiny shops scattered around the city specialize in unusual merchandise, from butterflies and bones to traditional Tibetan treasures and shamrock sprigs from Ireland. Coming across these in some tucked-away corner is what makes shopping in New York such an entertaining and invigorating experience.

Specialty Shops

For beautiful brass, onyx, and pewter chess sets, and the opportunity to play a decent game, make a move to the **Chess Shop**. For every type of pen **Arthur Brown & Bros.** stocks an enormous range, including such names as Mont Blanc and Schaeffer. For those with a bit more energy, **Blades** sells and rents out skates and also the trendiest skateboards plus all the safety equipment.

If you're looking for different or unusual buttons, a visit to **Tender Buttons**, which stocks millions, is a must. Whether you want enamel, wood, or Navajo silver buttons – or perhaps want your own buttons made into cuff links or earrings – here you'll find just what you want – and more. **Trash & Vaudeville** has been supplying punk and goth gear to New Yorkers for decades and is the HQ of Astor Place fashion.

Leo Kaplan Ltd. is the place to go if you are a keen collector of paperweights, while **Rita Ford's Music Boxes**, a 19th-century style shop, stocks a tuneful and extensive range of music boxes.

The **New York Firefighter's Friend** sells an intriguing range of items related to fire-fighting, including toy fire engines, firemen's jackets, badges, stuffed toy dalmatians (a breed of dogs historically associated with the fire-fighting service), and a wide selection of T-shirts, including a popular one with FDNY (Fire Department New York) on one side and "Keep back 200 feet" on the other.

For the true romantic who wants to impress, everything sold by **Only Hearts** is heart-shaped, including pillows, soap,

and jewelry. If you are artistic, or if you wish to buy a present for someone who is, visit **Pearl Paint**, which stocks everything you could need, from easels and brushes to modeling clay. **Forbidden Planet** is a science-fiction megastore with everything from comics to models for the true fan.

Cologne made especially for George Washington and the official soap of the White House during the Eisenhower era are just some of the many fascinating items for sale at **Caswell-Massey Ltd.**, which is the oldest pharmacy in the city.

Guitar gurus will want to visit **Rudy's**, Manny's, or Sam Ash's guitar shop. Not only is there a chance you'll bump into Eric Clapton or Lou Reed – both have their guitars made in this area – but you'll find the widest and best choice of musical instruments in the city.

Bibliophiles will find a range of gifts in both the **New York Public Library Shop** (see p148) (such as bookends of the lions guarding the main entrance) and the **Morgan Library Shop** (see pp166–7), including bookmarks and writing paper.

University logos and college colors dominate the many knickknacks and accessories for sale at **The Yale Club** gift shop and **The Princeton Club**.

Weisburg Religious Articles carries one of the largest selections of Jewish religious items in the city.

The Cathedral Shop at the Cathedral of St. John the Divine on Amsterdam Avenue is a large store selling books, artworks, herbs, jewelry, and religious items made locally.

Memorabilia

At Lincoln Center, the **Metropolitan Opera Shop** has records, cards, librettos, small binoculars, and many other opera-related items. For theater fans, everything from scripts and vocal scores to CDs can be found at **One Shubert Alley**. For thousands of rare and classic film stills and posters visit **Jerry Ohlinger's Movie Material Store** on 242 W 14th Street.

The **Carnegie Hall Shop** carries musically themed cards, T-shirts, games, posters, tote bags, and much more. For something truly original and very American, be sure to visit **Lost City Arts** and **Urban Archaeology** in SoHo. Between these two shops, you'll unearth all sorts of relics from America's past, from Barbie Doll lunch boxes to salvaged furniture, including antique, claw footed bath tubs.

Toys, Games, and Gadgets

For children's gifts, don't miss the legendary **F.A.O. Schwarz**. This is a massive store crammed with luxury toy cars, enormous stuffed animals and every kind of electronic toy imaginable. There are shoulder-to-shoulder crowds at Christmas, when you might have to line up to get in.

The **Children's General Store** is one of the city's smarter toy stores, with a focus on educational and classic goods, while a trip to **American Girl Place** doll store could entertain a young girl all day, with options such as a café, photo studio, and hair salon.

Myplasticheart is a quirky shop selling a dizzying assortment of designer toys and limited-edition collectibles. **Red Caboose** is for fans of model railways. On three floors, the **Toys 'R' Us** flagship glass building on Broadway is the largest toy store in the world, with a 60-ft (20-m) ferris wheel.

Dinosaur Hill on Second Avenue offers handmade

puppets and toys, mobiles, and beautifully made children's clothes. It's expensive but worth it. Since 1848, **Hammacher Schlemmer** have been encouraging shoppers to buy gadgets for home, office, and recreation that they didn't know they wanted. The quirky **Kidrobot** in SoHo draws both kids and collectors for its urban, cartoony action figures and memorabilia.

Museum Shops

Some of New York's best souvenirs can be found in the city's many museum shops. In addition to the usual range of books, posters, and cards, there are reproductions of the exhibits on display, including jewelry and sculpture. The **Museum of Arts & Design** (see p151) has an excellent selection of American crafts as well as original works for sale. In addition to realistic model dinosaurs, rubber animals, minerals, and rocks, the **American Museum of Natural History** (see pp218–19) has a variety of recycled products and earth-awareness gifts, which

include posters, bags, and T-shirts with environmental messages, and a large selection of Native American handicrafts. There is also a kids' shop with reasonably priced items such as shell sets, magnets, and toys.

The **Asia Society Bookstore and Gift Shop** (see p189) has a striking selection of Oriental prints, posters, art books, toys, and jewelry. Items related to interior design are offered at the **Cooper-Hewitt** (see p188). One of New York's largest collections of Jewish ceremonial objects, including menorahs and Kiddush cups, books, and jewelry, is found in the small shop at the **Jewish Museum** (see p188).

For reproduction prints of famous paintings and other exquisite gifts a visit to the **Metropolitan Museum of Art** (see pp192–9) gift shop is a must. There is also an enormous book department and a children's gift shop. The traditional **American Folk Art Museum** (see p173) prides itself on its American country crafts, including wooden toys, quilts, and weathervanes, which are mostly original. Works by

craftspeople who currently have pieces on display in the museum are also sold.

The **Museum of the City of New York** (see p201), specializes in pictures of old New York as well as books and unique prints and posters. The **Museum of Modern Art/MoMA Design Store** (see pp174–7) has a highly praised selection of innovative home furnishings, toys, and kitchenware inspired by international designers such as Frank Lloyd Wright and Le Corbusier.

For a selection of nautical items, including charts, maps, model ships, and scrimshaw, go to the **South Street Seaport Museum Shops** (see pp84–7). The **Whitney Museum's Shop** (see pp202–3) stocks American-made items, including jewelry, wooden toys, books, and posters complementing current exhibitions. The **Museum of Jewish Heritage** (see p79) has a gift shop with an unusual array of gifts, souvenirs, and educational material about Jewish life. Open to ticketed visitors only.

The Best of the Imports

New York is a massive melting pot of ethnic groups, nationalities, and cultures. Many ethnic shops specialize in food or goods of a particular group. **Alaska on Madison** has a collection of Eskimo art and Northwest prints and hangings, as does **Alaska House** in SoHo. The **Chinese Porcelain Company** sells exquisite Chinese decorative arts and furniture. **Pearl River Mart** has been a staple for Asian goods for thirty years, from novelty items to tea and tote-bags, and **Himalayan Crafts and Tours** stocks everything from paintings to Tibetan rugs. **Sweet Life**, on the Lower East Side, is a tiny, old-fashioned candy shop with delicacies from around the world. **Things Japanese** has beautifully made crafts and unusual books. **Surma** is a Ukrainian general store

that sells hand-painted eggs and linens. **Common Ground** sells Native American arts, and **Astro Gems** has a large collection of jewelry and mineral specimens from Africa and Asia. Nearby, Chinatown is packed with shops selling everything from souvenirs to leather goods, all at low prices.

Addresses

Alaska House
109 Mercer St. **Map** 4 E3.
Tel (212) 431-1580.

Alaska on Madison
937 Madison Ave. **Map** 17 A1.
Tel (212) 879-1782.

Astro Gems
185 Madison Ave. **Map** 9 A2.
Tel (212) 889-9000.

Chinese Porcelain Company
475 Park Ave. **Map** 13 A3.
Tel (212) 838-7744.

Common Ground
55 W 16th St. **Map** 8 F5.
Tel (212) 989-4178.

Himalayan Crafts and Tours
2007 Broadway. **Map** 11 C1.
Tel (212) 787-8500.

Pearl River Mart
477 Broadway. **Map** 4 E4.
Tel (212) 431-4770.

Sweet Life
63 Hester St. **Map** 5 B4.
Tel (212) 598-0092.

Surma
11 E 7th St. **Map** 4 F2.
Tel (212) 477-0729.

Things Japanese
127 E 60th St. **Map** 13 A3.
Tel (212) 371-4661.

DIRECTORY

Specialty Shops

Arthur Brown & Bros.
2 W 46th St.
Map 12 F5.
Tel (212) 575-5555.

Blades
120 W 72nd St.
Map 12 D1.
Tel (888) 552-5233.
One of two branches.

Caswell-Massey Ltd.
518 Lexington Ave.
Map 13 A5.
Tel (212) 755-2254.

The Cathedral Shop
Cathedral of St. John the
Divine, 1047 Amsterdam
Ave. **Map** 20 E4.
Tel (212) 316-7540.

Leo Kaplan Ltd.
114 E 57th St.
Map B A3.
Tel (212) 355-7212.

Morgan Library Shop
Madison Ave at 36th St.
Map 9 A2.
Tel (212) 685-0008.

**New York
Firefighter's Friend**
263 Lafayette St.
Map 4 F3.
Tel (212) 226-3142.

**New York Public
Library Shop**
5th Ave at 42nd St.
Map 8 F1.
Tel (212) 930-0869.

Only Hearts
386 Columbus Ave.
Map 15 D5.
Tel (212) 724-5608.

Pearl Paint
308 Canal St. **Map** 4 E5.
Tel (212) 431-7932.

The Princeton Club
15 W 43rd St. **Map** 8 F1.
Tel (212) 596-1200.

**Rita Ford's
Music Boxes**
19 E 65th St. **Map** 12 F2.
Tel (212) 535-6717.

Rudy's
169 W 48th St. **Map** 12 E5.
Tel (212) 391-1699.

Tender Buttons
143 E 62nd St. **Map** 13 A2.
Tel (212) 758-7004.

The Chess Shop
230 Thompson St.
Map 4 D3.
Tel (212) 475-9580.

Trash & Vaudeville
4 St. Mark's Pl. **Map** 5 A4.
Tel (212) 982-3590.

**Weisburg
Religious Articles**
45 Essex St. **Map** 5 B4.
Tel (212) 674-1770.

The Yale Club
50 Vanderbilt Ave.
Map 13 A5.
Tel (212) 661-2070.

Memorabilia

One Shubert Alley
1 Shubert Alley. **Map** 12
E5. **Tel** (212) 944-4133.

**The Carnegie
Hall Shop**
881 7th Ave. **Map** 12 E3.
Tel (212) 903-9610.

Forbidden Planet
840 Broadway.
Map 4 E1.
Tel (212) 473-1576.

**Jerry Ohlinger's
Movie Material Store**
253 W 35th St. **Map** 8 D2.
Tel (212) 989-0869.

Lost City Arts
18 Cooper Square.
Map 4 F2.
Tel (212) 375-0500.

**Metropolitan
Opera Shop**
Metropolitan Opera
House, Lincoln Center,
136 W 65th St.
Map 11 C2.
Tel (212) 580-4090.

Urban Archaeology
143 Franklin St. **Map** 4 D5.
Tel (212) 431-4646.

Toys, Games, And Gadgets

American Girl Place
609 Fifth Ave. **Map** 12 F5.
Tel (877) 247-5223.

**The Children's
General Store**
168 E 91st St. **Map** 17 A2.
Tel (212) 426-4479.

Dinosaur Hill
306 E 9th St, 2nd Ave.
Map 4 F1.
Tel (212) 473-5850.

F.A.O. Schwarz
767 5th Ave.
Map 12 F3.
Tel (212) 644-9400.

**Hammacher
Schlemmer**
147 E 57th St.
Map 13 A3.
Tel (212) 421-9000.
One of two branches.

Kidrobot
126 Prince St. **Map** 4 E3.
Tel (212) 966-6688.

Myplasticheart
210 Forsyth St.
Map 5 A3.
Tel (646) 290-6866.

Red Caboose
23 W 45th St.
Map 12 F5.
Tel (212) 575-0155.

Toys 'R' Us
1514 Broadway, Times
Square. **Map** 8 E2.
Tel (646) 366-8800.

Museum Shops

**Museum of
Arts & Design**
40 W 53rd St.
Map 12 F4.
Tel (212) 956-3535.

**American Folk
Art Museum**
45 W 53rd St. **Map** 12 F4.
Tel (212) 265-1040.

**American Museum
of Natural History**
W 79th St at Central Park
W. **Map** 16 D5.
Tel (212) 769-5100.

**Asia Society
Bookstore and
Gift Shop**
725 Park Ave. **Map** 13 A1.
Tel (212) 288-6400.

Cooper-Hewitt
2 E 91st St.
Map 16 F2.
Tel (212) 849-8400.

Jewish Museum
1109 5th Ave.
Map 16 F2.
Tel (212) 423-3200.

**Metropolitan
Museum of Art**
5th Ave at 82nd St.
Map 16 F4.
Tel (212) 535-7710.

**Museum of the
City of New York**
5th Ave at 103rd St.
Map 21 C5.
Tel (212) 534-1672.

**Museum of
Jewish Heritage**
18 1st Place, Battery Park
City. **Map** 1 B4.
Tel (646) 437-4200.

**Museum of
Modern Art/MoMA
Design Store**
44 W 53rd St.
Map 12 F4.
Tel (212) 767-1050.

**South St. Seaport
Museum Shops**
12 Fulton St.
Map 2 D2.
Tel (212) 748-8600.

**The Whitney
Museum's Store
Next Door**
943 Madison Ave.
Map 13 A1.
Tel (212) 570-3676.

Fashion

Whether you're looking for a secondhand pair of 501s or the kind of ballgown Ivana Trump would be proud to wear, you're sure to find it in New York. The city is the fashion capital of America and an important center of clothing manufacture and design. New York's clothing stores, like its restaurants, reflect the city's dramatically different styles and cultures. To save time it's probably best to visit one area at a time and wander from store to store. Alternatively, visit one of the major department stores for an excellent selection of fashion for everyone.

American Designers

Many American designers sell their creations in boutiques within the large department stores, or have exclusive shops of their own. One of the most famous is Michael Kors, known for sophisticated looks that are classic and comfortable.

The designs of Bill Blass, one of the kings of American fashion, feature an array of different colors, wild patterns, innovative shapes, and a lot of wit. Liz Claiborne's designs are always elegantly simple, casual, and reasonably priced, including everything you could possibly need from tennis whites to casual professional wear for women.

Marc Jacobs, known for his sportswear, has his own label and store in Greenwich Village. James Galanos is an exclusive designer for the rich and famous, making one-of-a-kind *couture* clothes, and Betsey Johnson is popular with women able to wear figure-hugging fashions in fabulous fabrics.

In the past two decades, Donna Karan has become a name that appears everywhere. Her simple, stylish, and great-looking designs work for everything from work-out clothes to black tie wear. Calvin Klein now has his name on place settings and sunglasses in addition to underwear, jeans, and a whole range of clothes. He is renowned for comfortable, sensuous, and well-fitting – as well as very hip – looks. Ralph Lauren is very well known for his aristocratic and expensive clothes, a "look" favored by the exclusive and posh Ivy League,

horsey set. For those with a taste for more experimental designs, Joan Vass specializes in moderately priced but exciting, colorful, and innovative knitwear.

Discount Designer Clothes

If you're on the lookout for discount designer clothes, **Designer Resale**, **Encore**, and **Michael's** sell a wide range. Oscar de la Renta, Ungaro, and Armani are just some of the leading labels available. Clothes are either new or worn but near-perfect.

The designer discount emporium **Century 21** in Lower Manhattan sells European and American designer fashions discounted up to an amazing 75 percent off regular retail prices. Bustling Union Square is flush with shopping options, including **Nordstrom Rack**, the discount offshoot of the famous Nordstrom department store. **Loehmann's** offers discounted clothes, and it's the place to shop if you want top-of-the-line fashions at unbelievable discounts.

Men's Clothes

In the center of midtown, you'll find two of the city's most highly regarded mens-wear stores: **Brooks Brothers** and **Paul Stuart**. Brooks Brothers is something of a New York institution, famous for its traditional, conservative clothing such as smart button-down shirts and Chinos. There's an ultra-conservative woman's line too. Paul Stuart prides itself

on its very British look and offers a stylish array of superbly tailored fashions. Go to the high-quality department store **Bergdorf Goodman Men** to find beautifully made Turnbull & Asser shirts and marvelous suits by Gianfranco Ferré or Hugo Boss.

Barney's New York has one of the most comprehensive men's departments in America, with a truly massive range of clothes and accessories.

Uniqlo, the hip Japanese chain known for its modern, well-made casual clothes, has a flagship store on Fifth Avenue. Go to **Burberry Limited** if you are looking for classic British trenchcoats and traditional outdoor wear.

J. Press sells classic, conservative yet elegant clothes while **John Varvatos** is famous for luxurious, sporty designs with superb detail. Uptown designer menswear boutiques include the renowned **Beau Brummel** with a selection of very stylish European clothes and **Thomas Pink** whose bright colors and fine fabrics make this store a celebrity favorite. Many of these men's stores also carry striking women's fashions. The **Hickey Freeman** store on Fifth Avenue sells a wide range of men's traditional clothing.

Children's Clothes

In addition to an excellent selection within the large department stores, there are several shops around the city that sell children's clothing exclusively. A good example is **Bonpoint**, which has a world of French-style charm. Also stocked with delightful outfits is **Bundle**, in SoHo.

GapKids and **BabyGap** shops, often in the **Gap** shops, have comfortable, long-lasting cotton overalls, sweat pants, denim jackets, sweatshirts, and leggings. Actress Phoebe Cates has opened a hip kids' clothing store on Madison Avenue called **Blue Tree**. **Space Kiddets** has everything from booties to Western wear.

Women's Clothes

Women's fashion is subject to design trends, and New York stores keep pace with them all. Most of the city's most fashionable shops are found in the midtown area around Madison and Fifth Avenues. These include some of the major department stores (see p319), which stock a range of American designers, including Donna Karan, Ralph Lauren and Bill Blass.

Leading international names such as **Chanel** and **Valentino** also have shops here, as does one of the outstanding American designers, **Michael Kors**. There is also a handful of popular ready-to-wear stores, including **Ann Taylor**, which is much favored by young, busy professionals looking for stylish, comfortable clothing. **Banana Republic** is a Fifth Avenue crowd-magnet that sells sleek, smart casualwear and blue jeans cut in the trendiest styles.

Right at the heart of this area stands the pink-marbled Trump Tower, which houses a selection of exclusive shops.

Madison Avenue is packed with designers for the smart set, who have everything you could ever need, including **Givenchy**, who sells show-stopping formal gowns at phenomenal prices; Valentino, who has classic Italian clothes; and **Missoni**, who is famous for richly textured sweaters in sumptuous wools and colorful patterns. **Yves St Laurent Rive Gauche** has evening gowns, one-of-a-kind jackets, silks and extravagant blouses, and beautifully cut pants suits.

Sophisticated Italian looks are also available from Italian style kings **Giorgio Armani** and **Gianni Versace**. **Dolce & Gabbana** sells unique, one-of-a-kind Italian clothing. **Gucci**, one of the oldest Italian shops in America, is only for the wealthy and status-conscious.

The Upper West Side has many shops competing for attention with contemporary fashions, including **Betsey Johnson**'s shop, with her whimsical, relatively inexpensive designs. **Calvin Klein** now has a store on the East Side, specializing in ultra-hip, casual fashions. **French Connection** is known for its affordable separates, both casual and for the office. **Scoop** is *the* place to get a little black dress.

The villages – the East Village in particular – are the best places to go for secondhand clothing and 1950s rock 'n' roll gear, with ever-changing interesting shops run by new and young designers and art school graduates. For a range of affordable, well-cut clothes from classic to casual, try **APC**.

Cheap Jack's carries a huge selection of secondhand Levi's as well as hundreds of denim and leather jackets. **Screaming Mimi's** is where you could unearth that pair of velvet bell-bottoms or go-go boots you've always dreamed of having. A more mainstream shop is **The Gap**, a chain store selling lots of moderately priced, casual and comfortable clothes for men, women, and children.

Sotto and Notto/Nolita rival Madison Avenue for designer boutiques specializing in expensive but interesting clothes – the fashions here are far more avant-garde. The playful boutique Kirna Zabete, for example, features a unique range of clothes as well as accessories. You'll also find **Yohji Yamamoto** in this area, among other exclusive stores. **Comme des Garçons** in the Garment District sells minimalist Japanese chic.

Cynthia Rowley is a prominent New York designer who sells flirty fashions for women and **What Comes Around Goes Around** on West Broadway is the place to go for vintage jeans.

Size Chart

For Australian sizes follow the British and American conversions.

Children's clothing

American	2–3	4–5	6–6x	7–8	10	12	14	16 (size)
British	2–3	4–5	6–7	8–9	10–11	12	14	14+ (years)
Continental	2–3	4–5	6–7	8–9	10–11	12	14	14+ (years)

Children's shoes

American	7½	8½	9½	10½	11½		12½	13½	1½	2½
British	7	8	9	10	11		12	13	1	2
Continental	24	25½	27	28	29		30	32	33	34

Women's dresses, coats and skirts

American	4	6	8	10	12	14	16	18
British	6	8	10	12	14	16	18	20
Continental	38	40	42	44	46	48	50	52

Women's blouses and sweaters

American	6	8	10	12	14	16	18
British	30	32	34	36	38	40	42
Continental	40	42	44	46	48	50	52

Women's shoes

American	5	6	7	8	9	10	11
British	3	4	5	6	7	8	9
Continental	36	37	38	39	40	41	44

Men's suits

American	34	36	38	40	42	44	46	48
British	34	36	38	40	42	44	46	48
Continental	44	46	48	50	52	54	56	58

Men's shirts

American	14	15	15½	16	16½	17	17½	18
British	14	15	15½	16	16½	17	17½	18
Continental	36	38	39	41	42	43	44	45

Men's shoes

American	7	7½	8	8½	9½	10½	11	11½
British	6	7	7½	8	9	10	11	12
Continental	39	40	41	42	43	44	45	46

DIRECTORY

Discount Designer Clothes

Century 21 Department Store
22 Cortland St.
Map 1 C2.
Tel (212) 227-9092.

Designer Resale
324 E 81st St.
Map 17 B4.
Tel (212) 734-3639.

Encore
1132 Madison Ave.
Map 17 A4.
Tel (212) 879-2850.

Loehmann's
101 7th Ave.
Map 8 E1.
Tel (212) 352-0856.

Michael's
1041 Madison Ave.
Map 17 A5.
Tel (212) 737-7273.

Nordstrom Rack
60 E 14th St.
Map 9 A5
Tel (212) 220-2080.

Men's Clothes

Barney's New York
660 Madison Ave.
Map 13 A3.
Tel (212) 826-8900.

Beau Brummel
347 W Broadway.
Map 4 E3.
Tel (212) 219-2666.
One of several branches.

Bergdorf Goodman Men
754 5th Ave.
Map 12 F3.
Tel (212) 753-7300.

Brooks Brothers
346 Madison Ave. **Map** 9
A1. **Tel** (212) 682-8800.

Burberry Limited
9 E 57th St.
Map 12 F3.
Tel (212) 757-3700.

Hickey Freeman
543 Madison Ave.
Map 13 A4.
Tel (212) 586-6481.

J. Press
7 E 44th St.
Map 12 F5.
Tel (212) 687-7642.

John Varvatos
122 Spring St. **Map** 4 E4.
Tel (212) 965-0700.

Paul Stuart
350 Madison Ave.
Map 13 A5.
Tel (212) 682-0320.

Polo/Ralph Lauren
Madison Ave at 72nd St.
Map 13 A1.
Tel (212) 606-2100.

Thomas Pink
520 Madison Ave.
Map 13 A4.
Tel (212) 838-1928.

Uniqlo
666 5th Ave.
Map 12 F4.
Tel (877) 486-4756.

Children's Clothes

Blue Tree
1283 Madison Ave.
Map 17 A2.
Tel (212) 369-2583.

Bonpoint
1269 Madison Ave.
Map 17 A3.
Tel (212) 722-7720.

Bundle
128 Thompson St.
Map 4 D3.
Tel (212) 982-9465.

GapKids
60 W 34th St. **Map** 8 F2.
Tel (212) 760-1268.
One of several branches.

Space Kiddets
26 E 22nd St.
Map 8 F4.
Tel (212) 420-9878.

Women's Clothes

Ann Taylor
645 Madison Ave.
Map 13 A3.
Tel (212) 832-2010.
One of several branches.

APC
131 Mercer St.
Map 4 E3.
Tel (212) 966-9685.

Banana Republic
626 5th Ave.
Map 12 F4.
Tel (212) 974-2350.

Betsey Johnson
248 Columbus Ave.
Map 16 D4.
Tel (212) 362-3364. One
of several branches.

Calvin Klein
654 Madison Ave.
Map 13 A3.
Tel (212) 292-9000.

Chanel
15 E 57th St.
Map 12 F3.
Tel (212) 355-5050.

Cheap Jack's
841 Broadway.
Map 4 E1.
Tel (212) 777-9564.

Comme des Garçons
520 W 22nd St.
Map 8 F3.
Tel (212) 604-9200.

Cynthia Rowley
376 Bleecker St.
Map 3 C2.
Tel (212) 242-3803.

Dolce & Gabbana
434 W Broadway.
Map 4 E3.
Tel (212) 965-8000.

French Connection
700 Broadway.
Map 4 E2.
Tel (212) 473-4486.
One of several branches.

The Gap
250 W 57th St.
ap 12 D3.
Tel (212) 315-2250.
One of many branches.

Gianni Versace
647 5th Ave.
Map 12 F4.
Tel (212) 317-0224.

Giorgio Armani
760 Madison Ave.
Map 13 A2.
Tel (212) 988-9191.
717 5th Ave.
Map 12 F3.
Tel (212) 207-1902.

Givenchy
710 Madison Ave.
Map 13 A1.
Tel (212) 688-4005.

Gucci
685 5th Ave.
Map 12 F4.
Tel (212) 826-2600.

Kirna Zabete
96 Greene St.
Map 4 E4.
Tel (212) 941-9656.

Michael Kors
790 Madison Ave.
Map 13 A2.
Tel (212) 452-4685.

Missoni
1009 Madison Ave.
Map 13 A1.
Tel (212) 517-9339.

Saks Fifth Avenue
611 5th Ave.
Map 12 F4.
Tel (212) 753-4000.

Scoop
532 Broadway (near
Spring St).
Map 4 E4.
Tel (212) 925-2886.
One of two branches.

Screaming Mimi's
382 Lafayette St.
Map 4 F2.
Tel (212) 677-6464.

Valentino
747 Madison Ave.
Map 13 A2.
Tel (212) 772-6969.

What Comes Around Goes Around
351 W Broadway.
Map 4 E4.
Tel (212) 343-9303.

Yohji Yamamoto
103 Grand St.
Map 4 E4.
Tel (212) 966-9066.

Yves St Laurent Rive Gauche
855 Madison Ave.
Map 13 A1.
Tel (212) 517-7400.

Accessories

In addition to the following shops, all of the major Manhattan department stores have extensive accessory departments stocking a range of hats, gloves, bags, jewelry, watches, scarves, shoes, and umbrellas.

Jewelry

Midtown Fifth Avenue is where to find the most dazzling jewelers. By day, windows glisten with gems from around the world; by night they are empty – the jewels safely locked away. The most sensational shops are all within a couple of blocks of one another and include the museum-like **Harry Winston**, which showcases its coveted jewels from around the world. **Buccellati** is well respected for its innovative Italian creations and excellent workmanship. **Bulgari** has an impressive collection that ranges in price from a couple of hundred to over a million dollars.

Housed in a Renaissance-style palazzo, **Cartier** is a jewel in itself and sells its beautiful baubles at unthinkable prices. **Tiffany & Co.** has ten floors of crystal, diamonds, and other jewels waiting to be packed up for you and taken away in the store's signature sky blue boxes.

The Diamond District, a one-block area on 47th Street (between Fifth and Sixth Avenues), is lined with shops displaying hundreds of thousands of dollars worth of diamonds, gold, pearls, and other exotic jewels from around the world. Try not to miss the **Jewelry Exchange**, a complex where 60 different crafts-people sell their ware direct to the public. Boisterous bargaining is very much alive here, so be prepared to play the game.

Hats

New York's oldest hat shop is **Worth & Worth**, which also has the largest collection of hats in the city. You can get anything here, from original Australian bush hats to silk toppers, to slouch hats and boaters. **Suzanne Millinery** is the hat-maker to the stars, as she has proved very popular with celebrities such as Ivana Trump and Whoopi Goldberg. **Lids** sells baseball caps in dozens of varieties, with logos ranging from sports teams to the evergreen "I HEART NY". For a wide range of fabulous headgear, stop by **The Hat Shop**, where you can find everything from classic to contemporary styles.

Umbrellas

The minute it starts to rain in New York, hundreds of street vendors selling umbrellas seem to sprout like mushrooms. Their umbrellas, which sell at just a few dollars, are without doubt the cheapest in the city, but unlikely to last much longer than the downpour itself. For good-quality umbrellas, you'll find a fine selection of Briggs of London at **Worth & Worth**. There is a wide range of different sizes, trendy patterns, and traditional tartans and stripes at **Barney's New York**, and there's always **Macy's** (see p311) for the usual sizes and styles. World-famous **Gucci** has umbrellas to match its ties. Subway-themed ones can be found at the **NY Transit Museum Store**.

Handbags and Briefcases

Twice a year, during the January and August sales, a serpentine line of buyers wraps around the corner of 48th Street and Madison Avenue waiting to get into **Crouch & Fitzgerald**, an old New York institution, selling handbags, briefcases, and luggage. All the well-known brands are sold here, including Judith Leiber, Ghurka, Dooney & Bourke, and Louis Vuitton, as well as the firm's own line. Elsewhere in the city are such exclusive shops as **Bottega Veneta**, and **Prada**, where handbags are displayed like precious art, with prices to match. Younger and trendier places include **Furla**, well-respected for its Italian designs, and the stylish **Il Bisonte**. Current must-have designer Rafé Totengco's soft suede pastel pouches are found at **TG-170**. **The Coach Store** is known for its simple, classic leather handbags. Designer **Kate Spade's** stylish yet practical rectangular handbags, in a plethora of prints and colors, have become modern classics, and add a chic touch to any woman's wardrobe. Jack Spade designs similarly unique bags for men.

For discount designer handbags try the legendary **Fine & Klein**, and for bargain briefcases from slim envelopes to thick lawyer's bags, a visit to the **Altman Luggage Company** is a must.

Shoes and Boots

Manhattan shoe stores are famous for their extensive selections of shoes and boots, and if you shop around, you are sure to find what you want at a reasonable price.

Most of the large department stores in New York also have shoe departments where you can find designer-label shoes in addition to other brands. **Bloomingdale's** (see p183) has wa huge women's footwear department, and **Brooks Brothers** has one of the best selections of tradi-tional men's shoes in the city.

For both men's and women's shoes, the most exclusive shops are around the midtown area. **Ferragamo** sells classic styles crafted in Florence. Go to **Botticelli** for whimsical shoe fashions. For stylish shoes at decent prices, head for **Sigerson Morrison** in Little Italy.

For cowboy boots, head for **Billy Martin's**. There's a huge selection of handmade boots, from basic, no-frills "ropers," which real American cowboys wear, to crocodile leather boots that sell for thousands of dollars. Billy Martin's stocks western garb and accessories, so you can dress in western gear from head to toe. For beautiful handcrafted boots, try **E. Vogel Custom Boots & Shoes**.

Sneaker collectors should make a stop at **Alife Rivington Club** on the Lower East Side, which stocks several hard-to-find styles.

For the best in children's shoes, **East Side Kids** stocks the trendiest fashions for kids, while **Shoofly** has imported shoes in all styles.

The **Jimmy Choo** boutique offers a plethora of sexy, stylish heels. Popular among Manhattan's chic set are the beautiful women's shoes, particularly the

flattering heels, at **Manolo Blahnik**. **Christian Louboutin** rounds out the stiletto heavyweights. Spain's most popular brand, **Camper**, has an airy SoHo store featuring their signature comfy, funky, and colorful shoes for women and men.

For discounted shoes, go to West 34th Street and West Eight Street between Fifth and Sixth Avenues, and Orchard Street on the Lower East Side. The **DSW** store, on the third floor of 40 E 14th Street, sells brand-name shoes and boots at a fraction of the regular price. There's also a branch near Battery Park.

Lingerie

Expensive imports from Europe, which are sexy yet elegant, can be found at **La Petite Coquette**.

More affordable is **Victoria's Secret** on 57th Street or SoHo, which offers beautifully made lingerie in satin, silk, and many other fine fabrics. **Henri Bendel's** lingerie department offers a sumptuous array of lingerie, from naughty to nice. The Italian **La Perla** features seductive lingerie and undergarments in sensual fabrics from tulle and chiffon to satin.

DIRECTORY

Jewelry

Buccellati
46 E 57th Ave. **Map** 12 F3.
Tel (212) 308-2900.

Bulgari
730 5th Ave. **Map** 12 F3.
Tel (212) 315-9000.

Cartier
653 5th Ave. **Map** 12 F4.
Tel (212) 753-0111.

Harry Winston
718 5th Ave. **Map** 12 F3.
Tel (212) 245-2000.

Jewelry Exchange
15 W 47th St. **Map** 12 F5.

Tiffany & Co
5th Ave. **Map** 12 F3.
Tel (212) 755-8000.

Hats

The Hat Shop
120 Thompson St. **Map** 4 D3. **Tel** (212) 219-1446.

Lids
243 W 42nd St. **Map** 8 E1.
Tel (212) 575-1717.

Suzanne Millinery
27 E 61st St. **Map** 13 A3.
Tel (212) 593-3232.

Worth & Worth
45 W 57th St, 6th floor,
Suite Le02. **Map** 12 F3.
Tel (212) 265-2887.

Umbrellas

Barney's New York
See p319.

Gucci
See p327.

NY Transit Museum Store
Grand Central Terminal.
Map 9 A1.
Tel (212) 878-0106.

Handbags and Briefcases

Altman Luggage Company
135 Orchard St. **Map** 5 A3.
Tel (212) 254-7275.

Il Bisonte
120 Sullivan St. **Map** 4 D4.
Tel (212) 966-8773.

Bottega Veneta
635 Madison Ave. **Map** 13 A3. **Tel** (212) 371-5511.

The Coach Store
595 Madison Ave. **Map** 13 A3. **Tel** (212) 754-0041.

Crouch & Fitzgerald
400 Madison Ave. **Map** 13 A5. **Tel** (212) 755-5888.

Fine & Klein
119 Orchard St. **Map** 5 A3.
Tel (212) 674-6720.

Furla
598 Madison Ave. **Map** 13 A3. **Tel** (212) 755-8986.
One of two branches.

Jack Spade
56 Greene St. **Map** 4 E4.
Tel (212) 625-1820.

Kate Spade
454 Broome St. **Map** 4 E4.
Tel (212) 274-1991.

Prada
49 E 57th St. **Map** 12 F3.
Tel (212) 308-2332.

TG-170
77 Ludlow St. **Map** 5 A3.
Tel (212) 995-8660.

Shoes and Boots

Alife Rivington Club
158 Rivington St. **Map** 5 B3. **Tel** (212) 375-8128.

Billy Martin's
220 E 60th St. **Map** 13 B3.
Tel (212) 861-3100.

Botticelli
620 5th Ave. **Map** 12 F4.
Tel (212) 582-6313.

Bloomingdale's
See p319.

Brooks Brothers
See p327.

Camper
125 Prince St. **Map** 4 E3.
Tel (212) 358-1842.

Christian Louboutin
941 Madison Ave. **Map** 17 A5. **Tel** (212) 396-1884.

DSW
40 E 14th St. **Map** 9 A5.
Tel (212) 674-2146.

E. Vogel Custom Boots & Shoes
19 Howard St. **Map** 4 E5.
Tel (212) 925-2460.

East Side Kids
1298 Madison Ave.
Map 17 A2.
Tel (212) 360-5000.

Ferragamo
655 5th Ave. **Map** 12 F3.
Tel (212) 759-3822.

Jimmy Choo
645 5th Ave. **Map** 12 F4.
Tel (212) 625-1820.

Manolo Blahnik
31 W 54th St. **Map** 12 F4.
Tel (212) 582-3007.

Shoofly
42 Hudson St. **Map** 1 B1.
Tel (212) 406-3270.

Sigerson Morrison
28 Prince St. **Map** 4 F3.
Tel (212) 219-3893.

Lingerie

Henri Bendel
See p319.

La Perla
93 Greene St. **Map** 4 E3.
Tel (212) 219-0999.

La Petite Coquette
51 University Place.
Map 4 E1.
Tel (212) 473-2478.

Victoria's Secret
34 E 57th St. **Map** 12 F3.
Tel (212) 758-5592.
591–593 Broadway.
Map 4 E3.
Tel (212) 219-3643.

Beauty, Manicures and Pedicures, and Hair Salons

You can shop 'til you drop in New York City – and when you do, rest assured that rejuvenation (and a heavenly foot massage) is just around the corner. There are plenty of well-stocked beauty stores, manicure and pedicure specialists, as well as sleek hair salons. Many of the manicurists and salons cater to New Yorkers and their hectic schedules, so they often accept same-day appointments that can easily fitted in between rounds of sightseeing and shopping. After a pamper session or two (or three…), you'll be ready to hit the shops again, this time with the prettiest toes and silkiest hair around.

Beauty Stores

The French-owned **Sephora** is a cosmetics megastore that offers its shoppers row upon row of beauty products, from skin cleansers to cosmetics and fragrances, and, thankfully, a no-pressure sales staff. For all-natural essences and products, try **Erbe** ("herbs" in Italian), a soothing sanctuary with a plethora of hypo-allergenic products, all made with fresh herbs and free from mineral oils, animal products, waxes, synthetic fragrances, or dyes. The royal jelly nutrient moisturizer and Pennywort exfoliating cream are popular choices.

The high-ceilinged **MAC Cosmetics** store is always busy. Their face powders, particularly the Studio Fix line, are unsurpassed. The promise of creamy Swedish skin (at a reasonable price) lures shoppers to **FACE Stockholm**, where they stock natural, botanical skin products plus lipstick and nail polish in a rainbow of colors. Since 1851, **Kiehl's** has been creating cleansers, toners, balms, and masques "in purposefully utilitarian" packaging as the natural ingredients speak for themselves.

The nature-friendly **Fresh** sells fragrant body creams and fruity perfume. **Sabon** sells a luxurious range of bath and beauty products that are 100 percent natural and irresistibly scented. Soaps can be bought by the pound here, and they are gift-wrapped for free.

For good quality makeup that stands the test of time, visit SoHo's stylish **Make Up for Ever**, which stocks everything from liquid face foundations and creamy lipsticks, to sparkling body powders. Head to earthy **Origins** and select from their plethora of plant-based lotions, an antioxidant moisturizer made with white tea, and body creams sensitive enough for a baby's skin. British beauty maven Nicky Kinnaird has opened her first outlet of **Space.NK** in SoHo. The shop also offers beauty services.

Most of New York's large department stores, including **Bloomingdale's**, **Lord & Taylor**, **Saks Fifth Avenue**, **Barney's New York**, and **Macy's** offer well-stocked makeup counters.

Manicures and Pedicures

Budget-minded Downtown trendsetters flock to the East Village's **Galleria Nail Salon**, one of the neighborhood's most popular destinations for inexpensive spa services. As well as manicures and pedicures, you can have waxing and browse hard-to-find makeup lines. **Eve's** may look somewhat bland and institutional, but appearances can be deceiving. Their long-lasting manicures and pedicures are top-notch. **Dashing Diva** not only offers excellent manicures and pedicures at a bargain price (starting at $10). The whole experience is made all the more alluring, however, as they offer treats with their treatments. On

Thursdays and Fridays, they serve Cosmopolitans and turn up the music.

Experience the ultimate in hand and nail care at **Sweet Lily Natural Nail Spa & Boutique**. The range includes an intoxicating blend of warm milk and almond oil for your hands, and a moisturizing honey walnut mask with a honey walnut manicure ($40). The hot lavender cream manicure includes a wonderful conditioning treatment for cuticles that contains tea tree and citrus oil. The boutique is not just for adults, as there is also a manicure for little girls: the Little Miss Mani includes a choice of nail art.

Hair Salons

If you're in the mood for a new hair do, or just want to refresh your current cut, try one of New York City's cutting-edge hair salons.

The stylists at the downtown **Arrojo Studio** will update your style, so that you walk out of the salon looking as hip as they do. Arrojo colorists are also top-notch, and the salon offers a wide range of exellent color treatments. Follow the celebrities, and get your hair cut, styled, and/or colored by stylist Frederic Fekkai or one of his associates at the chic **Frederic Fekkai Beaute de Provence**. This top salon is very much a cut above the rest.

Korean stylist Younghee Kim, formerly of Vidal Sassoon, offers hip cuts and colors, as well as "hair spa treatments" and thermal conditioning, starting at $110 at her eponymous nail salon, **Younghee Salon** in TriBeCa. Oprah Winfrey and Madonna are just two of the many celebs who have made the trek to **Garren Salon**, located in the suitably swish Sherry-Netherland Hotel. Set in a classy, sun-flooded loft, the **Aveda Institute** offers superb cuts, colors, and scalp massages. Pick up one of their plant-based beauty and bath products. The institute also offers the opportunity to receive a discount haircut by one of the trainee hairdressers. A great choice for men is **La Boite a Coupe**, whose clientele includes many advertising and media personalities. Moroccan-French stylist Laurent De Louya has been cutting hair here since 1972. The upscale, Asian-accented **Le Salon Chinois**, never fails to create a sleek cut that will turn heads. They also offer excellent scalp treatments, hair aromatherapy, and effective "Japanese straightening." Head

to the lovely **TwoDo Salon**, where you can get an expert cut and color amid a rustic, colorful decor of fresh flowers and brick walls hung with paintings by local artists.

Styling stalwart **Vidal Sassoon** is still going strong. Visit the elegant downtown salon on Fifth Avenue where accomplished stylists and colorists – all of whom have gone through the company's rigorous training – turn out impeccable, eye-catching cuts and colors. **Toni &**

Guy, a premiere hair salon from the UK, is renowned for its consistently good cuts. The NYC salon is the US training headquarters, where creative stylists offer the boldest cuts around. Toni & Guy colorists have also been lauded for their tinting and highlighting skill.

For more great cuts and colors, try the hip favorites **Antonio Prieto** and **Bumble & Bumble**, the refined **John Masters Organics**, and the elite **Oscar Blandi**.

DIRECTORY

Beauty Stores

Erbe
196 Prince St. **Map** 4 D3.**Tel** (212) 966-1445.

FACE Stockholm
10 Columbus Circle. **Map** 12 D3. **Tel** (212) 823-9415. 110 Prince St, SoHo. **Map** 4 E3. **Tel** (212) 966-9110.

Fresh
57 Spring St at Lafayette St. **Map** 4 F4. **Tel** (212) 925-0099. One of five branches.

John Masters Organics
77 Sullivan St near Broome St. **Map** 4 D4. **Tel** (212) 343-9590.

Kiehl's
109 3rd Ave. **Map** 9 B5. **Tel** (212) 677-3171.

MAC Cosmetics
113 Spring St. **Map** 4 E4. **Tel** (212) 334-4641.

Make Up for Ever
409 W Broadway at Spring St. **Map** 4 E4. **Tel** (212) 941-9337.

Origins
175 5th Ave at 23rd St. **Map** 8 F4. **Tel** (212) 677-9100.

Sabon
93 Spring St. **Map** 4 E4. **Tel** (212) 925-0742. One of three branches.

Sephora
555 Broadway. **Map** 4 E3. **Tel** (212) 625-1309. One of several branches.

Space.NK
99 Greene St, near Spring St. **Map** 4 E4.**Tel** (212) 941-9200.

Manicure and Pedicures

Barney's New York
660 Madison Ave. **Map** 13 A3. **Tel** (212) 826-8900.

Bloomingdale's
1000 3rd Ave. **Map** 13 B3. **Tel** (212) 705-2000.

Bloomingdale's SoHo
504 Broadway. **Map** 4 E4. **Tel** (212) 729-5900.

Dashing Diva
41 E 8th St. **Map** 4 E2. **Tel** (212) 673-9000.

Eve
400 Bleecker St. **Map** 3 C2. **Tel** (212) 807-8054.

Galleria Nail Salon
520 E 11th St #A. **Map** 5 B1. **Tel** (212) 387-8491.

Lord & Taylor
424 5th Ave. **Map** 8 F1. **Tel** (212) 391-3344.

Macy's
151 W 34th St. **Map** 8 E2. **Tel** (212) 695-4400.

Saks Fifth Avenue
611 5th Ave. **Map** 12 F4. **Tel** (212) 753-4000.

Sweet Lily Natural Nail Spa & Boutique
222 W Broadway, between N Moore & Franklin sts. **Map** 4 E5. **Tel** (212) 925-5441.

Hair Salons

Antonio Prieto
127 W 20th St. **Map** 8 F5. **Tel** (212) 255-3741.

Arrojo Studio
180 Varick St. **Map** 4 D3. **Tel** (212) 242-7786.

Aveda Institute
233 Spring St. **Map** 4 D4. **Tel** (212) 807-1492.

La Boite a Coupe
57 W 18th St, Suite 800. **Map** 12 F4. **Tel** (212) 246-2097.

Bumble & Bumble
415 13th St, near 9th Ave. **Map** 3 B1. **Tel** (212) 521-6500.

Frederic Fekkai Beaute de Provence
712 5th Ave, 4th Floor. **Map** 12 F3. **Tel** (212) 753-9500.

Garren Salon
781 5th Ave. **Map** 12 F3. **Tel** (212) 841-9400.

Oscar Blandi
545 Madison Ave. **Map** 13 A4. **Tel** (212) 421-9800.

Le Salon Chinois
44 W 55th St, 4th Floor. Between 5th & 6th aves. **Map** 12 F4. **Tel** (212) 956-1200.

Toni & Guy
673 Madison Ave, Suite 2 at 61st St. **Map** 13 A3. **Tel** (212) 702-9771.

TwoDo Salon
210 W 82nd St, between Broadway & Amsterdam. **Map** 15 C4. **Tel** (212) 787-1277.

Vidal Sassoon
32 W 18th St. **Map** 8 F5. **Tel** (212) 229-2200.

Younghee Salon
64 N Moore St. **Map** 4 D5. **Tel** (212) 334-3770.

Books and Music

As the publishing capital of America, it's not surprising that New York has the country's best selection of bookstores. These range from vast general interest stores to hundreds of esoteric bookstores specializing in everything from sci-fi to suspense, selling new books and old. Music lovers will also find sounds for all tastes at reasonable prices, plus thousands of rare recordings.

General Interest Bookstores

One of the best-known New York bookstores – for prices as well as selection of titles – is **Barnes & Noble** on Fifth Avenue, reputedly the world's largest bookstore and packed high with over three million books on every imaginable subject. There are branches all over the City, plus the sales annex across the street, with amazing bargains.

Several blocks away is the main branch of New York's famous **Strand Book Store**, with an astonishing two million copies of new and secondhand books spread out over several floors of crowded bookshelves and passageways. There is also a large rare book room for first editions.

Westsider Bookshop is as comprehensive as its music counterpart, as it stocks an enormous collection of used books and country/bluegrass LPs. **Powerhouse Arena**, an airy Dumbo space, frequently hosts events ranging from sedate author readings to wild literary-themed parties. Housing Works Bookstore Café is a lovely, high-ceilinged bookstore-café with a wide range of used books. The friendly McNally Jackson stocks classics and contemporary fiction, and also has a café.

Rizzoli has a big selection of photography, foreign language, music, and art books, plus children's books and videos. **Shakespeare & Co.** offers a sensational selection of titles and is open late every night.

Specialty Bookstores

Located in the bustling Williamsburg neighborhood of Brooklyn, **Spoonbill & Sugartown Booksellers** carries a wide variety of well-chosen titles focusing on art, design, and architecture. **Desert Island** draws Brooklyn's hipsters and artists with its range of independent 'zines, comics, and counter-culture titles. The city's largest selection of theatrical books and publications is found at **Drama Book Shop**. Jewish books and music abound at **J. Levine Judaica**. Rare books, out-of-print books, and old books about New York are the *raison d'être* of **JN Bartfield Books**. **Book Book** is the only midtown store specializing in diaries, letters, biographies, and autobiographies.

Books on murder and suspense are the focus of **Mysterious Bookshop**.

Try **Forbidden Planet** for old and new science-fiction books and comics. **Midtown Comics** has two spacious locations and offers a good range of comics at affordable prices, mostly from the late 1980s to the present. Vintage collectors might prefer **Jim Hanley's Universe**, across from the Empire State Building. Collectible merchandise here ranges from reasonable to "ask Santa" in price.

Bank Street Book Store has one of the best selections of current children's books; they also host storytime and other engaging events for kids. Visit **Books of Wonder** for a variety of hardcover and rare children's books.

The Complete Traveler stocks a wide selection of brand-new and antique travel books and guides for your trip. The staff is very knowledgeable and helpful.

The acclaimed publisher of art and architecture volumes **Taschen** maintains a handsome store in suitably stylish SoHo. Cookbooks are on the menu at **Kitchen Arts & Letters**, with

many out-of-print books and first editions. Radicals should head for **Revolution Books** or **St. Mark's Bookstore**, which also has an excellent selection of literary and art titles. **Idlewild** is a travel-centric bookstore where everything is arranged by destination.

Educational toys and their book tie-ins can be found in the airy and bright **Scholastic Store**, downstairs from the publisher's SoHo offices.

Records and Compact Discs

J&R Music World is a complete home-entertainment store with one of the best CD selections in the city.

For out-of-print records, go to **Westsider Records**, a treasure trove for collectors, with an excellent choice of classical, jazz, and opera recordings. **House of Oldies** has a massive stock of deleted and rare records to suit all tastes. **Bleecker Bob's Golden Oldies** record shop has everything from imports, rock, and punk to rare jazz. **Academy Records** is another excellent choice, with second-hand CDs, LPs, and DVDs.

DJs and vinyl lovers still have options for deep house, breakbeat, and electronica. Check out **Turntable Lab** in Manhattan, while in Brooklyn there is **Earwax** or the lively **Halcyon**. True music enthusiasts should head to **Other Music**, which stocks obscure gems, from hot electronica to 1970s free jazz. **Disc-O-Rama** has some of the cheapest CD prices around.

Sheet Music

The bookstore of the **Juilliard School**, one of the world's most respected music schools, sells sheet music, books, and recordings. The **Frank Music Company** has a huge collection of classical music scores. **Charles Colin Publications** specializes in jazz. For chart music and pop tunes try **Colony Music Center** in the Brill Building on Broadway.

DIRECTORY

General Interest Bookstores

Barnes & Noble
33 E 17th St.
Map 9 A5.
Tel (212) 253-0810.
One of several branches.

Housing Works Bookstore Café
126 Crosby St.
Map 4 F3.
Tel (212) 334-3324.

McNally Jackson
52 Prince St.
Map 4 F3.
Tel (212) 274-1160.

Powerhouse Arena
37 Main St, Brooklyn.
Tel (718) 222-1331.

Rizzoli
31 W 57th St.
Map 12 F3.
Tel (212) 759-2424.

Shakespeare & Co.
716 Broadway.
Map 4 E2.
Tel (212) 529-1330.
One of several branches.

Strand Book Store
828 Broadway.
Map 4 E1.
Tel (212) 473-1452.

Westsider Bookshop
2246 Broadway.
Map 15 C4.
Tel (212) 362-0706.

Specialty Bookstores

Bank Street Book Store
610 W 112th St.
Map 21 A4.
Tel (212) 678-1654.

Book Book
266 Bleecker St
Map 3 C2.
Tel (212) 807-0180.

Books of Wonder
18 W 18th St. **Map** 8 E5.
Tel (212) 989-3270.

The Complete Traveler
199 Madison Ave.
Map 9 A2.
Tel (212) 685-9007.

Desert Island
540 Metropolitan Ave, Brooklyn.
Tel (718) 388-5087.

Drama Book Shop
250 W 40th St.
Map 8 E1.
Tel (212) 944-0595.

Forbidden Planet
840 Broadway.
Map 4 E1.
Tel (212) 473-1576.

Idlewild
12 W 19th St.
Map 8 F5.
Tel (212) 414-8888.

Jim Hanley's Universe
4 W 33rd St.
Map 8 F2.
Tel (212) 268-7088.

J. Levine Judaica
5 W 30th St.
Map 8 F3.
Tel (212) 695-6888.

JN Bartfield Books
30 W 57th St.
Map 12 F3.
Tel (212) 245-8890.

Kitchen Arts & Letters
1435 Lexington Ave.
Map 17 A2.
Tel (212) 876-5550.

Midtown Comics
200 W 40th St. **Map** 8 E1.
459 Lexington Ave.
Map 13 A5.
Tel (212) 302-8192.

Mysterious Bookshop
58 Warren St.
Map 1 B1.
Tel (212) 582-1011.

Revolution Books
146 W 26th St.
Map 8 E4.
Tel (212) 691-3345.

St. Mark's Bookshop
31 3rd Ave.
Map 5 A2.
Tel (212) 260-7853.

The Scholastic Store
577 Broadway.
Map 4 E4.
Tel (212) 343-6166.

Spoonbill & Sugartown Booksellers
218 Bedford Ave, Brooklyn.
Tel (718) 387-7322.

Taschen Store
107 Greene St.
Map 4 E3.
Tel (212) 226-2212.

Records and Compact Discs

Academy Records
12 W 18th St.
Map 7 C5.
Tel (212) 242-3000.
One of several branches.

Bleecker Bob's Golden Oldies
118 W 3rd St.
Map 4 D2.
Tel (212) 475-9677.

Disc-O-Rama
186 W 4th St.
Map 4 D2.
Tel (212) 206-8417.

Earwax
218 Bedford Avenue, Brooklyn.
Tel (718) 486-3771.

Halcyon The Shop
57 Pearl St at Water St, Dumbo, Brooklyn.
Map 2 F2.
Tel (718) 260-WAXY.

House of Oldies
35 Carmine St.
Map 4 D3.
Tel (212) 243-0500.

J&R Music World
23 Park Row.
Map 1 C2.
Tel (800) 806-1115.

Other Music
15 E 4th St.
Map 4 F2.
Tel (212) 477-8150.

Turntable Lab
120 E 7th St.
Map 5 A2.
Tel (212) 677-0675.

West Sider Records
233 W 72nd St.
Map 11 D1.
Tel (212) 874-1588.

Sheet Music

Charles Colin Publications
315 W 53rd St.
Map 12 D4.
Tel (212) 581-1480.

Colony Music Center
1619 Broadway.
Map 12 E4.
Tel (212) 265-2050.

Frank Music Company
244 W 54th St.
Map 12 D4.
Tel (212) 582-1999.

The Juilliard Store
144 W 66th St.
Map 11 C2.
Tel (212) 799-5000.

Art and Antiques

Any art-loving visitor to New York could easily spend several days gallery-hopping around the several hundred galleries found throughout New York. Antique lovers can find an exciting variety of goods, including Americana and many bargains, at the many flea markets; or they can browse through European and American fine antiques in one of the more exclusive antiques centers. To find out what's happening, pick up the free monthly *Art Now Gallery Guide*, available at most galleries, or check the local papers.

Art Galleries

One of the city's best-known galleries is **Leo Castelli**, an important showcase for Pop Art during the early 1960s and now spotlighting new artists. **Mary Boone Gallery** features Neo-Expressionist artists such as Julian Schnabel. **Pace Gallery** exhibits current stars, especially painter-photographers. **Postmasters** features impressive changing shows of emerging artists. **Marian Goodman Gallery** focuses on the European avant-garde.

In Chelsea, the **Mathew Marks Gallery** and **Marianne Boesky Gallery** are worth a visit. **Paula Cooper** often hosts controversial shows in her beautiful loft space. The **Gagosian Gallery** exhibits paintings by modern masters, with great works by Johns and Lichtenstein. It has another outlet in the Upper East Side, where you can also find **L&M Arts**, with a good selection of European and American fine art. **Hirschl & Adler Galleries** in midtown is another option for high-profile exhibitions. **Meulensteen** is architecture-friendly, while **Lehmann Maupin Gallery** is the spot to see up-and-coming artists working in innovative forms. **Barbara Gladstone** is another heavy hitter in the art scene, and **Exit Art** is famed for its multimedia exhibitions. The airy **Agora Gallery** shows local and international works, including Art Nouveau pieces.

American Folk Art

The **American Primitive Gallery** sells a variety of curiosities, including vintage masks and arcade relics. Similar goods are at **Laura Fisher Quilts**, which sells everything from decoys to hooked rugs.

Antiques Centers and Secondhand Antiques

In addition to hundreds of small shops selling everything from tiger teeth to multimillion-dollar paintings, Manhattan is home to **The Manhattan Art & Antiques Center**, which has dozens of dealers under one roof. The **Showplace Antique and Design Center** in Chelsea, featuring four floors of antiques, retro furnishings, and memorabilia, is also well worth a visit.

American Furniture

For furniture from the 17th, 18th, and 19th centuries, try **Bernard & S. Dean Levy** or **Circa Antiques**. **Judith & James Milne** sell early American country furniture as well as a splendid collection of quilts. Alternatively, go to **Woodard & Greenstein American Antiques & Quilts** for a truly wonderful selection of Shaker pieces.

Collectors of Art Deco or Art Nouveau furniture should pay a visit to **Alan Moss**, which is full of furniture and decorative items of all kinds. **Macklowe Gallery** on Madison Avenue has a massive collection of fine Art Nouveau furniture. Just a few blocks away, **Lillian Nassau** has Tiffany lamps and many Art Nouveau and Art Deco pieces.

New York has a handful of retro shops, including **Adelaide**, which stocks treasures from the 1930s through to the 1960s.

International Antiques

If you're looking for English antiques, try **Florian Papp** and **Kentshire Galleries**. For European pieces, you'll have plenty of choices; try **Eileen Lane Antiques**, **Kurt Gluckselig Antiques**, **Linda Horn Antiques**, and **Center44**. **La Belle Epoque** stocks antique posters. Oriental dealers include luxury **Doris Leslie Blau**, **E. & J. Frankel**, and **Flying Cranes Antiques**.

Flea Markets

New York has a number of year-round weekend markets. Most flea markets officially open at 9 or 10am. If you arrive early, you could unearth some valuable piece of cultural Americana like a Barbie lunch box or a Soupy Sales record.

Avid collectors visit the **Hell's Kitchen Flea Market**, open year-round on weekends, for antiques, collectibles, vintage clothing, jewelry, and more. The **Greenflea Market** has new and second-hand clothing and furniture. For information on all street fairs and flea markets, check Friday's *The New York Times* or The Village Voice.

Auction Houses

Manhattan's two most celebrated auction houses are **Christie's** and **Sotheby's**, selling collectibles ranging from coins, jewels, and vintage wines to fine and decorative arts.

Also common is a try at **Doyle New York** and **Phillips de Pury & Co.** both well-respected names for fine art, jewelry, and antiques. Bear in mind that items for sale are previewed several days before the auctions, so check the Friday and Sunday *Times* beforehand to see what's coming up. The venerable **Swann Galleries** auctions prints, books, maps, posters, autographs, and photographs.

DIRECTORY

Art Galleries

Agora Gallery
530 W 25th St.
Map 7 C4.
Tel (212) 226-4151.

Barbara Gladstone
515 W 24th St.
Map 7 C4.
Tel (212) 206-9300.

Exit Art
475 10th Ave.
Map 7 C2.
Tel (212) 966-7745.

Gagosian Gallery
555 W 24th St.
Map 7 C4.
Tel (212) 741-1111.
One of several galleries.

Hirschl & Adler Galleries
730 5th Ave, 4th Floor.
Map 12 F3.
Tel (212) 535-8810.

L&M Arts
45 E 78th St.
Map 17 A5.
Tel (212) 861-0020.

Lehmann Maupin Gallery
540 W 26th St.
Map 7 C4.
Tel (212) 255-2923.

Leo Castelli
18 E 77th St.
Map 17 A5.
Tel (212) 249-4470.

Marian Goodman Gallery
24 W 57th St.
Map 12 F3.
Tel (212) 977-7160.

Marianne Boesky Gallery
509 W 24th St.
Map 7 C4.
Tel (212) 680-9889.

Mary Boone Gallery
745 5th Ave.
Map 12 F3.
Tel (212) 752-2929.
One of two galleries.

Mathew Marks Gallery
523 W 24th St.
Map 7 C4.
Tel (212) 243-0200.

Meulensteen
511 W 22nd St. Map 7 C4.
Tel (212) 633-6999.

Pace Gallery
534 W 25th St.
Map 7 C4.
Tel (212) 929-7000.
One of several galleries.

Paula Cooper
534 W 21st St.
Map 7 C4.
Tel (212) 255-1105.

Postmasters
459 W 19th St.
Map 7 C5.
Tel (212) 727-3323.

American Folk Art

American Primitive Gallery
49 E 78th St, Suite 2B.
Map 17 A5.
Tel (212) 628-1530.

Laura Fisher Quilts
Hayes Fine Arts
Warehouse, 305 E 61st St.
Map 13 B3.
Tel (212) 838-2596.

Antique Centers And Second-Hand Antiques

The Manhattan Arts & Antiques Center
1050 2nd Ave.
Map 13 A3.
Tel (212) 355-4400.

The Showplace Antique and Design Center
40 W 25th St.
Map 8 F4.
Tel (212) 633-6063.

American Furniture

Adelaide
702 Greenwich St.
Map 3 C2.
Tel (212) 627-0508.

Alan Moss
436 Lafayette St.
ap 4 F2.
Tel (212) 473-1310.

Bernard & S. Dean Levy
24 E 84th St. Map 16 F4.
Tel (212) 628-7088.

Circa Antiques
374 Atlantic Ave,
Brooklyn.
Tel (718) 596-1866.

Judith & James Milne
506 E 74th St.
Map 17 C5.
Tel (212) 472-0107.
By appointment only.

Lillian Nassau
220 E 57th St. Map 13 B3.
Tel (212) 759-6062.

Macklowe Gallery
667 Madison Ave.
Map 13 A3.
Tel (212) 644-6400.

Woodard & Greenstein American Antiques
506 E 74th St.
Map 17 A5.
Tel (212) 988-2906.

International Antiques

La Belle Epoque
115a Greenwich Ave.
Map 3 C1.
Tel (212) 362-1770.

Center44
222 E 44th St, 2nd Floor.
Map 13 B5.
Tel (212) 450-7988.

Doris Leslie Blau
306 E 61st St, 7th Floor.
Map 13 B3.
Tel (212) 586-5511.
By appointment only.

E. & J. Frankel
1040 Madison Ave.
Map 17 A5.
Tel (212) 879-5733.

Eileen Lane Antiques
236 E 60th St.
Map 13 B3.
Tel (212) 475-2988.

Florian Papp
962 Madison Ave.
Map 17 A5.
Tel (212) 288-6770.

Flying Cranes Antiques
1050 2nd Ave. Map 13 B4.
Tel (212) 223-4600.

Kentshire Galleries
37 E 12th St.
Map 4 E1.
Tel (212) 673-6644.

Kurt Gluckselig Antiques
200 E 58th St.
Map 13 B3.
Tel (212) 758-1805.

Linda Horn Antiques
1327 Madison Ave.
Map 17 A2.
Tel (212) 772-1122.

Flea Markets

Greenflea Market
Columbus Ave, between
76th and 77th sts.
Map 16 D5. Tel (212) 239-3025. Open Sun.

Hell's Kitchen Flea Market
39th St, between 9th &
10th aves. Map 7 C1.
Tel (212) 243-5343.
Open Sat & Sun.

Auction Houses

Christie's
20 Rockefeller Plaza.
Map 12 F5.
Tel (212) 636-2000.

Doyle New York
175 E 87th St.
Map 17 A3.
Tel (212) 427-2730.

Phillips de Pury & Co.
450 W 15th St.
Map 7 C5.
Tel (212) 940-1200.

Sotheby's
1334 York Ave.
Map 13 C1.
Tel (212) 606-7000.

Swann Galleries
104 E 25th St.
Map 9 A4.
Tel (212) 254-4710.

Gourmet Groceries, Specialty Food, and Wine Shops

New York's striking cultural and ethnic diversity is reflected in its food – the city's food shops provide a truly international feast. There is also a dazzling array of coffee stores and wine shops available almost everywhere you turn.

Gourmet Groceries

Scattered around town are several famous food emporiums that are tourist attractions in themselves. Remember, too, to visit the department stores, which often rival the specialty food stores.

At **Dean & DeLuca** on Broadway, a chic delicatessen, food has been elevated to an art form – don't miss the huge selection of take-out food. **Russ & Daughters** on Houston Street, one of the oldest gourmet shops, is known as an "appetizing" store, full of ethnic food and famous for smoked fish, cream cheese, chocolates, and bagels. The **Gourmet Garage** on Broome Street sells all kinds of delicious fresh food, in particular organic produce. **Zabar's** on Broadway is perhaps the finest food store in the world, with huge crowds jostling for the excellent smoked salmon, bagels, caviar, nuts and candies, cheese, and coffee.

William Poll on Lexington Avenue offers picnic hampers as well as a great variety of prepared dishes. For pâté de foie gras, Scottish smoked salmon, beluga, and caviar, go to **Caviarteria**.

Whole Foods, famed for their superb selection of natural, organic, wholesome foods, draws devoted shoppers throughout the city. The Whole Foods in Columbus Circle is one of the largest supermarkets in Manhattan, with row upon gleaming row of quality food "in its purest state" with no artificial additives. There's also a popular central Whole Foods on Union Square. **Fairway Market** on Broadway offers premium groceries from fresh produce to smoked fish and baked goods.

Specialty Food

Fabulous bread and cake shops abound, but one of the best is **Poseidon Greek Bakery**, renowned for its filo pastry. **Ess-a-Bagel** operates two locations, both of which churn out some of the city's highest-rated bagels. Try the delicious Chinese pastries at **Fung Wong Bakery**, or the pretzel croissants and great tarts at **City Bakery**. **Magnolia Bakery** is famed for its beautifully decorated and superb-tasting cupcakes. It has three locations in Manhattan.

Great confectionery shops include **Li-Lac** for handmade chocolates and **Mondel Chocolates** for chocolate animals. **Economy Candy** has a huge range of dried fruit but for a real treat go to **Teuscher Chocolates**, which has fresh champagne truffles flown in direct from Switzerland. **Myers of Keswick** imports English food. For something more exotic, **Kam Man Market** is a grocery store selling Chinese, Thai, and other Asian products. The sprawling **Eataly** has fine imported Italian goods; you can take their fine cheeses and pastas home or dine at one of the numerous eateries within the complex. Go to **Lobel's** (open since 1840) for fine cuts of meat and game, and **Citarella** for fine seafood. For exotic spices and teas, visit **Sullivan Street Tea & Spice Co.**, in Greenwich Village, or the Middle Eastern shop **Kalustyan's**.

For a wide choice of cheese, as well as olives and *charcuterie*, visit **Murray's Cheese Shop**. Named New York's Best Cheese Shop by many of the city's newspapers, it is heaven for cheese-lovers, with over 250 types of cheese from around the world, from bloomy rinds like Camembert to moist ricotta.

The friendly staff happily offers tastings from the mind-boggling selection. Make a picnic out of it, and pick up some of their fresh breads and olives to accompany your purchases.

If you are looking for true old Eastern European pickles, then **The Pickle Guys** is the right place. They also store pickled tomatoes, mushrooms, olives, hot peppers, sweet kraut, sauerkraut, herring, and sun-dried tomatoes.

For fruit and vegetables at reasonable prices, visit a farmers' green market, but get there early for the pick of the crop. Among the most popular are **79th Street Green Market**, **TriBeCa Greenmarket**, and **Union Square**. For information on the city's markets, phone: (212) 788-7476.

Coffee Stores

New York also has many fine coffee stores. Among the best are **Oren's Daily Roast** and **Porto Rico Importing Company**, each with a mouth-watering selection. **The Sensuous Bean** features a superb range of gourmet coffees and teas, as does the cozy **McNulty's Tea & Coffee Company**, one of the nation's oldest coffee stores.

Wine Shops

Acker, Merrall & Condit have been selling wines since 1820 and have an excellent selection. Go to **Garnet Wines & Liquors** for fine wines and champagnes at bargain prices. **Spring Street Wine Shop**, in the heart of SoHo, is a convenient, well-stocked spot to pop in for a bottle of fine wine. **Sherry-Lehmann** is New York's leading wine merchant. **Astor Wines & Spirits**, New York's largest wine store, features a massive selection of premium and discount wines and spirits. Every month they highlight their Top 10 choices under $10 – great for superb bargains. **Union Square Wines and Spirits** offers terrific a variety of wines, and features tastings every week.

DIRECTORY

Gourmet Groceries

Caviarteria
502 Park Ave.
Map 13 A3.
Tel (212) 759-7410.

Dean & DeLuca
560 Broadway.
Map 4 E3.
Tel (212) 226-6800.
One of several branches.

Fairway Market
2127 Broadway.
Map 15 C5.
Tel (212) 595-1888.
One of several branches.

Gourmet Garage
453 Broome St.
Map 4 E4.
Tel (212) 941-5850.
One of several branches.

Russ & Daughters
179 E Houston St.
Map 5 A3.
Tel (212) 475-4880.

Whole Foods
10 Columbus Circle.
Map 12 D3.
Tel (212) 823-9600.
One of several branches.

William Poll
1051 Lexington Ave.
Map 17 A5.
Tel (212) 288-0501.

Zabar's
2245 Broadway.
Map 15 C4.
Tel (212) 787-2000.

Specialty Food

79th Street Green Market
Columbus Ave between
78th & 81st sts.
Map 16 D5.
Open Sun.

Citarella
2135 Broadway.
Map 15 C5.
Tel (212) 874-0383.
One of several branches.

City Bakery
3 W 18th St.
Map 8 F5.
Tel (212) 366-1414.

Eataly
200 5th Ave.
Map 8 F4.
Tel (646) 398-5100.

Economy Candy
108 Rivington St.
Map 5 A3.
Tel (212) 254-1531.

Ess-a-Bagel
831 3rd Ave.
Map 13 B4.
Tel (212) 980-1010.
359 1st Ave.
Map 9 C4.
Tel (212) 260-2252.

Fung Wong Bakery
41 Mott St.
Map 4 F3.
Tel (212) 267-4037.

Kalustyan's
123 Lexington Ave.
Map 9 A3.
Tel (212) 685-3451.

Kam Man Market
200 Canal St.
Map 4 F5.
Tel (212) 571-0330.

Li-Lac
40 Eighth Ave.
Map 3 C1.
Tel (212) 924-2280.

Lobel's
1096 Madison Ave.
Map 17 A4.
Tel (212) 737-1372.

Magnolia Bakery
401 Bleecker St.
Map 3 C2.
Tel (212) 462-2572.
One of several branches.

Mondel Chocolates
2913 Broadway.
Map 20 E3.
Tel (212) 864-2111.

Murray's Cheese Shop
257 Bleecker St.
Map 4 D2.
Tel (212) 243-3289.
One of two branches.

Myers of Keswick
634 Hudson St.
Map 3 C2.
Tel (212) 691-4194.

The Pickle Guys
49 Essex St.
Map 5 B4.
Tel (212) 656-9739.

Poseidon Greek Bakery
629 9th Ave.
Map 12 D5.
Tel (212) 757-6173.

Sullivan Street Tea & Spice Co.
208 Sullivan St.
Map 4 D3.
Tel (212) 387-8702.

Teuscher Chocolates
25 E 61st St.
Map 12 F3. **Tel** (212) 751-8482.
620 5th Ave.
Map 12 F4.
Tel (212) 246-4416.

TriBeCa Greenmarket
Greenwich St, between
Chambers and Duane sts.
Map 1 B1.
Open Wed & Sat.

Union Square Greenmarket
E 17th St & Broadway.
Map 8 F5.
Open Mon, Wed, Fri,
and Sat.

Coffee Stores

McNulty's Tea & Coffee Company
109 Christopher St.
Map 3 C2.
Tel (212) 242-5351.

Oren's Daily Roast
1144 Lexington Ave.
Map 17 A4.
Tel (212) 472-6830.
One of several branches.

The Sensuous Bean
66 W 70th St.
Map 12 D1.
Tel (212) 724-7725.

Porto Rico Importing Company
201 Bleecker St.
Map 3 C2.
Tel (212) 477-5421.
One of several branches.

Wine Shops

Acker, Merrall & Condit
160 W 72nd St.
Map 11 C1.
Tel (212) 787-1700.

Astor Wines & Spirits
399 Lafayette St.
Map 4 F2.
Tel (212) 674-7500.

Garnet Wines & Liquors
929 Lexington Ave.
Map 13 A1.
Tel (212) 772-3211.

Sherry-Lehmann
505 Park Ave.
Map 13 A3.
Tel (212) 838-7500.

Spring Street Wine Shop
187 Spring St.
Map 4 D4.
Tel (212) 219-0521.

Union Square Wines and Spirits
140 4th Ave.
Map 4 F1.
Tel (212) 675-8100.

Electronics and Housewares

From flat-screen TVs and top-of-the-line sound systems to swanky designer home furnishings, New York City abounds with electronics and housewares stores. Perhaps the most competitive retailers in New York are the ones that sell electronics, so it pays to shop around. Be particularly careful with electronics stores on the heavily touristed streets and those around the major tourist sights, such as Fifth Avenue near the Empire State Building. Many of these stores sell mediocre, sometimes faulty equipment at inflated prices, and it's a hassle or near impossible to get a refund once you've returned home. If you're buying electronic goods to take to Europe, make sure they have compatible voltages and formats (many in the US are made to different standards).

Sound Systems and Equipment

For the latest in cutting-edge stereo equipment, head to **Sound by Singer**. **J&R Music World** sells competitively priced equipment and has the best jazz CD collection in the city. The Danish **Bang & Olufsen** showcases a range of sleek, minimalist sound systems that can dress up even the humblest flat. **Hammacher Schlemmer**, a New York mainstay since 1848, carries the "best, the only, and the unexpected" and has friendly, informative staff. Browse the quality systems at **Lyric Hi-Fi**, a longtime favorite that's been around since 1959. The perennially jam-packed **Sony Style** delivers on its wide range of top-shelf sound systems and plenty of impulse-buy gizmos. True to its name, the chain store **Best Buy** does offer some of the best buys on an assortment of stereo systems and home-entertainment products. For high-end stereo equipment and components, check out **Innovative Audio Video Showrooms**. Also stop to look around at the wide range of both used and new stereos at the friendly **Stereo Exchange**.

Photography

B & H Photo is where amateur and professional photographers can find everything they need. **Willoughby's** has decent sales on photographic equipment and supplies. The appropriately named **Olden Camera** on Broadway eschews anything digital offering instead quality, old-school cameras and gear. Head to Chelsea's **Foto Care** for a wide range of cameras and accoutrements. **Print Space Photo Lab** offers a variety of services, including digital rentals, film processing, and both color and black-and-white darkrooms. Make for **Adorama** in the Flatiron District, and browse the spectacular displays of digital cameras and accessories, point-and-shoots, and disposables, and also affordable prices on film developing and processing. Don't miss the quality, high-end cameras and equipment at the elegant **The Photo Village**.

Computers

There are several Macintosh meccas in Manhattan, including the immense, airy **Apple Store SoHo** and the gleaming cube of a store on Fifth Avenue, which is open 24 hours a day. Mac-philes flock to both to peruse and test-drive the latest models, plug in to iPods, and attend seminars geared to both novices and experts. If you brought your computer from home and find that you need a repair, head to the **Little Laptop Shop**, where a tech whiz should be able to fix whatever ails your computer. All brands and models are serviced, and the staff offers tips on new technologies, syncing services between devices, and even free advice via Facebook. The specialty at **Tekserve** is Mac repairs; you can also get a free estimate and browse for upgrades.

Kitchenware

Most of the department stores offer a wide range of household goods. For a specialized shop, try **Broadway Panhandler** on Eighth Street, a cook's heaven with outstanding baking and pastry-making equipment. **Bowery Restaurant Supply Co.** offers a wide range of kitchen essentials at great prices. **Williams-Sonoma** has kitchenware, utensils, and cookbooks. The East Village, particularly on and around Bowery Street, has long been the nucleus for restaurant supply stores, where you can find top-quality kitchenware at bargain prices. The **Japanese Culinary Center** sells professional Japanese cooking tools, from ceramics and high-end knives to soba-making machines and sushi supplies.

Housewares and Furnishings

Baccarat, **Lalique**, and **Villeroy & Boch** are where you'll find the finest crystal, china, and silverware. **Orrefors Kosta Boda** has beautiful glassware, from vases to candlesticks, and **Tiffany & Co.** is also a fashionable spot. Go to **Avventura** for crystal and china and, for the best of inexpensive, utilitarian china, visit **Fishs Eddy**. Try **Ceramica**, which stocks lovely handmade Italian pottery, and **La Terrine** and **Mackenzie-Childs** for hand-painted ceramics. Browse the hip SoHo showcase of designer **Jonathan Adler**, whose eye-catching pottery of natural shades and primitive and organic shapes will stand out from everything else in your living room. His collection includes a "family" of playful decanters in the shapes of man, woman, and child, plump vases of smiling suns and fish plates, and a menagerie of pottery animals, including bookends shaped like the front and back of a charging bull. **ABC Carpet & Home** on Broadway has an enviable reputation for home furnishings. For low prices on housewares, shop on **Grand Street** on the Lower East Side.

For elegant furniture, from soft leather sofas to luxurious beds, and sleek tableware, try Giorgio Armani's posh **Armani Casa**. **Dune** on Franklin Street in TriBeCa offers chic furniture by contemporary designers, including wool sofas and convertible lounges. **Design Within Reach** is the source for fully licensed classics, such as Saarinen, Eames, and Bertoia. If you lean toward retro, make a beeline for **Restoration Hardware** on Broadway, where you can choose from updated Art Deco furnishings, lighting fixtures, and patinated bronze accessories.

Linens

Linens can be found in most department stores, but for silk sheets and luxurious linens, visit **D. Porthault** and **Pratesi**. The Italian **Frette**, on Madison Avenue, sells thick towels and robes and wonderfully soft cotton sheets and bedding. **Bed, Bath & Beyond** offers a varied selection of bed linens, kitchen, and bath accessories.

DIRECTORY

Sound Systems and Equipment

Bang & Olufsen
927 Broadway. **Map** 8 F4.
Tel (212) 388-9792.

Best Buy
60 W 23rd St. **Map** 8 E4.
Tel (212) 366-1373.

Hammacher Schlemmer
147 E 57th St. **Map** 13 A3.
Tel (212) 421-9000.

Innovative Audio Video Showrooms
150 E 58th St. **Map** 13 A4.
Tel (212) 634-4444.

J & R Music World
23 Park Row. **Map** 1 C2.
Tel (212) 238-9000.

Lyric Hi-Fi
1221 Lexington Ave.
Map 17 A4.
Tel (212) 439-1900.

Sony Style
550 Madison Ave.
Map 13 A4.
Tel (212) 833-8800.

Sound by Singer
18 16th St. **Map** 8 F5.
Tel (212) 924-8600.

Stereo Exchange
627 Broadway. **Map** 4 E3.
Tel (212) 505-1111.

Photography

Adorama
42 W 18th St. **Map** 8 F5.
Tel (212) 741-0466.

B & H Photography
420 9th Ave. **Map** 8 D2.
Tel (212) 444-6615.

Foto Care
41 W 22nd St. **Map** 8 E4.
Tel (212) 741-2990.

Olden Camera
1263 Broadway, 4th floor.
Map 8 F3.
Tel (212) 725-1234.

The Photo Village
1133 Broadway, Suite 824.
Map 8 F4.
Tel (212) 989-1252.

Print Space Photo Lab
151 W 19th St, 8th Floor.
Map 8 E5.
Tel (212) 255-1919.

Willoughby's
298 5th Ave. **Map** 8 F3.
Tel (212) 564-1600.

Computers

Apple Store 5th Ave
767 5th Ave. **Map** 12 F3.
Tel (212) 336-1440.

Apple Store SoHo
103 Prince St. **Map** 4 E3.
Tel (212) 226-3126.

The Little Laptop Shop
7 Clinton St.
Map 5 B3.
Tel (212) 674-3111.

Tekserve
119 W 23rd St. **Map** 8 E4.
Tel (212) 929-3645.

Kitchenware

Bowery Restaurant Supply Co.
2 Delancey St. **Map** 5 A4.
Tel (212) 254-9720.

Broadway Panhandler
65 E 8th St. **Map** 4 E2.
Tel (212) 966-3434.

Japanese Culinary Center
711 3rd Ave. **Map** 13 B5.
Tel (212) 661-3333.

Williams-Sonoma
10 Columbus Circle.
Map 12 D3.
Tel (212) 823-9750.
One of several branches.

Housewares and Furnishings

ABC Carpet & Home
888 Broadway. **Map** 8 F5.
Tel (212) 473-3000.

Armani Casa
979 3rd Ave, Suite 1424.
Map 13 B3.
Tel (212) 334-1271.

Avventura
463 Amsterdam Ave.
Map 15 C4.
Tel (212) 769-2510.

Baccarat
625 Madison Ave.
Map 13 A3.
Tel (212) 826-4100.

Ceramica
59 Thompson St.
Map 4 D4.
Tel (212) 941-1307.

Design Within Reach
27 E 62nd St. **Map** 13 A2.
Tel (212) 888-4539.
One of several branches.

Dune
156 Wooster St. **Map** 4 E3.
Tel (212) 925-6171.

Fishs Eddy
889 Broadway. **Map** 8 F5.
Tel (212) 420-9020.

Grand Street
Lower East Side.
Map 4 E5.

Jonathan Adler
47 Greene St.
Map 4 E4.
Tel (212) 941-8950.

Lalique
609 Madison Ave.
Map 13 A3.
Tel (212) 355-6550.

Mackenzie-Childs
14 W 57th St.
Map 12 F3.
Tel (212) 570-6050.

Orrefors Kosta Boda
200 Lexington Ave.
Map 9 A2.
Tel (212) 684-5455.

Restoration Hardware
935 Broadway. **Map** 8 F4.
Tel (212) 260-9479.

La Terrine
1024 Lexington Ave.
Map 13 A1.
Tel (212) 988-3366.

Tiffany & Co.
See p329.

Villeroy & Boch
41 Madison Ave.
Map 9 A4.
Tel (212) 213-8149.

Linens

Bed, Bath & Beyond
620 Ave of the Americas.
Map 8 F5.
Tel (212) 255-3550.

D. Porthault
470 Park Ave.
Map 13 A3.
Tel (212) 688-1660.

Frette
799 Madison Ave.
Map 13 A1.
Tel (212) 988-5221.

Pratesi
829 Madison Ave.
Map 13 A2.
Tel (212) 288-2315.

ENTERTAINMENT IN NEW YORK CITY

New York City is a non-stop entertainment extravaganza, every day, all year round. Whatever your taste, you can be sure the city will satisfy it on both a grand and an intimate scale. The challenge is to take advantage of as many of the entertainments as possible. If it's theater, you can enjoy a mainstream success on Broadway or take a chance on an experimental production in a loft. If it's music, there's the magnificence of opera at the Met or a jazz group blowing in a club in the Village. You can catch a spectacle of avant-garde dance in a café or try your own avant-garde dancing in one of the city's warehouse-sized clubs. Movie theaters abound. But perhaps best of all is wandering and watching the vast show that is New York.

TKTS discount ticket booth

Practical Information

Find out what events there are to choose from in the arts and leisure listings of *The New York Times* and the *Village Voice* newspapers and in *Time Out New York*, *New York*, and *The New Yorker* magazines. Listings are updated on the websites of these magazines, such as www.nymag.com and www. newyork.timeout.com. At your hotel ask for *Where*, a free weekly magazine with maps and information on the many attractions.

Hotel staff may be able to answer some of your questions and should also carry a wide selection of brochures and leaflets. In addition, they may be willing to reserve tickets for you. Some hotel TVs have a New York visitor information channel.

At **NYC & Company**, touch-screen kiosks provide information and sell tickets to the city's top attractions. Multi-lingual counselors, discount coupons, free maps, brochures, tour information, and ATMs are available. **Broadway Inner Circle** gives brief descriptions of current

shows, schedules, and prices; **Moviefone** gives online information on all the films; and **ClubFone** has up-to-date information on nightlife.

Booking Tickets

Popular shows may be sold out for weeks ahead, so book early. Box offices are open daily, except Sundays, from 10am until one hour after the performance begins. Call in person, or phone the box office or a ticket agency and order your seats by credit card. The biggest agencies are **Telecharge**, **Ticketmaster**, and **Ticket Central**; they charge a small fee. An independent ticket agent may also be able to find seats for you – try **Prestige Entertainment**; others are listed in the Yellow Pages. Fees vary according to demand. Broadway Ticket Center in the Times Square Information Center (see p363) sells full-price tickets.

Discount Tickets

Established in 1973 to the advantage of theaters and theatergoers alike, the non-profit **TKTS** company sells unsold tickets on the day of the performance for all Broadway shows. Discounts range from 25 to 50 percent, but the price will include a small handling fee and must be paid for in cash or by traveler's check.

The **TKTS** booth in Times Square (at Duffy Square under the red steps) sells matinée tickets from 10am to 2pm every Wednesday and Saturday, and from 11am to 3pm on Sundays; evening tickets are sold from 3 to 8pm (from 2pm on Tuesdays). The booths at Front and John streets, where lines are often shorter, sell evening tickets from 11am to 6pm daily (until 4pm on Sundays; closed Sunday in winter). All matinée tickets are sold the day before. There is also a TKTS booth in downtown Brooklyn.

The **Broadway Ticket Center** in Times Square offers same-day and advance tickets for both Broadway and Off-Broadway shows. They also have seating charts and, occasionally, video previews to help you choose a show.

You can purchase day-of-performance tickets from **Ticketmaster** at discounts of 10 to 25 percent (with a small commission fee) by telephone. The **Hit Show Club** sells vouchers to its

A band playing at a cozy New York jazz club

The Booth Theater on Broadway *(see p337)*

members (it's free to join) that can be exchanged at box offices for discounted tickets. Some shows offer standing-room tickets on the day at a bargain price. It's often the only way to catch a sold-out show on short notice, but you might not get the best view. You can also get discount tickets for shows at **Best of Broadway**. StubHub! is the largest ticket resale site. Tickets for sports, music, and shows are FedExed to you.

"Scalpers" and Touts

If you buy from a "scalper" (a ticket tout), you risk getting tickets for the wrong day, counterfeit tickets, and paying outrageous prices. The police often monitor sports and theater venues for scalpers and their customers.

Free Tickets

Free tickets to TV shows, concerts, and special events are sometimes offered at **NYC & Co.** (New York Convention & Visitors Bureau), which is open from 8:30am to 6pm Monday to Friday and 9am to 5pm on weekends. Free or deeply discounted tickets to film or theater premieres are often advertised in *The New York Times*, *Daily News*, or *Time Out New York*. The "Cheap Thrills" section in the *Village Voice* lists

poetry readings, recitals, and experimental films. The Shakespeare Festival at the **Delacorte Theater** in Central Park offers free tickets – two per person – on a first-come, first-served basis (be prepared to queue).

Neon lights of theaters in the heart of Broadway

Disabled Access

Broadway theaters reserve a few spaces and cut-price tickets for the disabled. Call **Ticketmaster** or **Telecharge** well in advance for information and to reserve your tickets. For Off-Broadway theaters, call their box offices. Some theaters offer special equipment for their hearing-impaired patrons. **Tap** can arrange sign language for Broadway theaters.

USEFUL CONTACTS

Best of Broadway
226 W 47th St. **Map** 12 E5.
Tel (212) 398-8383, ext. 214.
w bestofbroadway.com

Broadway Inner Circle
Tel (212) 391-9621.
w broadwayinnercircle.com

Broadway Ticket Center
Times Square Information Center, 1560 Broadway.
Map 12 E5.

ClubFone
Tel (212) 777-2582.
w clubfone.com

Delacorte Theater
Entrance via 81st St at Central Park W. **Map** 16 E4.
Tel (212) 539-8500.
w publictheater.org
Summer time only.

Hit Show Club
Tel (212) 581-4211.
w hitshowclub.com

Movie Tickets Online
w movietickets.com
w fandango.com
w moviefone.com

NYC & Co.
810 7th Ave. **Map** 12 E4.
Tel (212) 484-1222.
w nycgo.com

Prestige Entertainment
Tel (203) 622-5151.

StubHub!
Tel (866) STUB-HUB.
w stubhub.com

Tap (Theatre Access Project)
Tel (212) 221-1103 (Voice).
w tdf.org

Telecharge
Tel (212) 239-6200,
1-800-432-7250.
w telecharge.com

Ticket Central
Tel (212) 279-4200.
w ticketcentral.org

Ticketmaster
Tel (212) 307-4100, 1-800-755-4000.
w ticketmaster.com

TKTS
Tel (212) 912-9770. Front & John Sts. **Map** 2 D2. Duffy Square, Times Square. 47th St & Broadway. **Map** 12 E5.
w tdf.org/TKTS

New York's Best: Entertainment

New York is one of the great entertainment capitals of the world. Top names in every branch of the arts are drawn here to perform and often to live and work. Major sports events are a huge attraction and live music, theater, and comedy can be found throughout the year. In terms of nightlife, New York truly lives up to its reputation as "the city that never sleeps." From the huge choice offered, there are some venues and events that stand out; this selection has been chosen from the listings on pages 336 to 355 as among those not to be missed. Even if you experience only one of them, you will have been part of something as essentially New York as the Empire State Building or the Brooklyn Bridge.

Madison Square Garden
Top sporting action is found at "the Garden," including home games for basketball's New York Knicks and ice hockey's Rangers, plus other sporting events and big-name concerts *(see p352).*

Village Vanguard
The jazz clubs of Greenwich Village have played host to all the great names in jazz. Fans can catch the stars of today and tomorrow at the world-famous Village Vanguard and the Blue Note *(see p344).*

Thea
Dist

Chelsea and
Garment Dis

Gramerc
the Flat
Distri

Hudson River

Greenwich
Village

East
Villag

SoHo and
TriBeCa

Film Forum
At New York's most stylish art-house movie theater you can see the latest foreign and American independent releases or catch up with a classic in a wide range of retrospectives *(see p341).*

Seaport and
the Civic
Center

Lower
Manhattan

Lower East
Side

Public Theater
Founded in 1954, the Public has a mandate to create theater for all New Yorkers. Its year-round Shakespeare Festival is part of a commitment to classical works, but new plays are also developed here *(see p122).*

Upper West Side

Upper East Side

Central Park

Upper Midtown

Lower Midtown

East River

Philharmonic Rehearsals
The Wednesday- and Thursday-morning rehearsals at Avery Fisher Hall are often open to the public at a fraction of the normal ticket price *(see p342)*.

0 kilometers — 2
0 miles — 1

Metropolitan Opera House
Reserve well ahead and prepare to pay high prices to see the giants of the opera world *(see p342)*.

Shakespeare in Central Park
If you are a summer visitor, set aside a time to get one of the rare free tickets for the Delacorte Theater's open-air Shakespeare featuring top Hollywood and Broadway names *(see p336)*.

Carnegie Hall
Conveniently situated in the Theater District, Carnegie Hall is famous the world over as a show-case for the best in the musical arts. A backstage tour gives a fascinating insight into "the house that music built" *(see p342)*.

The Nutcracker
The Christmas event for children of every age is performed each year at Lincoln Center by the New York City Ballet *(see p338)*.

Theater and Dance

New York is famous for its extravagant musicals and its ferocious critics. It is one of the world's greatest theater and dance centers, featuring every kind of production imaginable. Whether your preference is for the glitz and glamour of a Broadway blockbuster or something truly experimental, you'll find it here.

Broadway

Broadway has long been synonymous with New York's Theater District, but the majority of Broadway theaters are actually scattered between 41st and 53rd streets and from Sixth to Ninth Avenues, with a few around the much-improved Times Square. Most were built between 1910 and 1930, during the heyday of vaudeville and the famous Ziegfeld Follies. The **Lyceum** *(see p146)* is the oldest theater still in operation (1903), the **American Airlines Theater**, permanent home of the Roundabout Theater Co., is one of the newest (1918), and, in 2008, the historic **Biltmore Theater** was renamed the Samuel Friedman Theater.

Many Broadway theaters went through a slump in the 1980s but are now enjoying a revival, using big names to draw in the crowds. This is where you will find the "power productions" – the big, highly publicized dramas, musicals and revivals starring Hollywood luminaries in (it is hoped) sure-fire earners. Hits have included imports such as *Les Misérables*; New York originals such as *Cats* and *The Producers*; the popular children's favorite *The Lion King*; and great revivals like *42nd Street*. There have also been glitzy adaptations from popular movies, such as *Hairspray*; shows celebrating 60s and 70s pop favorites, such as ABBA in *Mamma Mia*! and Monty Python's *Spamalot*.

Off-Broadway and Off-Off-Broadway

There are about 20 Off-Broadway stages and 300 Off-Off-Broadway stages whose works will sometimes transfer to Broadway. Off-Broadway theaters have from 100 to 499 seats, and Off-Off-Broadway showplaces have fewer than 100. Both range from the well-appointed to the improvised, sited in lofts, churches, and even garages. Off-Broadway became very popular during the 1950s as a reaction to the commercialism of Broadway. It was also an ideal place for cautious producers to try out works considered too avant-garde for Broadway at lower operating costs. During the past two decades, Off-Off-Broadway theaters have staged more experimental pieces by these same producers.

Off-Broadway theaters are found all over Manhattan – from the **Douglas Fairbanks Theater**, where the irreverent *Forbidden Broadway* plays, to Central Park's open-air **Delacorte Theater**. Some are even in the Broadway district, such as the **Manhattan Theater Club**. Farther afield are the **Brooklyn Academy of Music (BAM)** *(see p250)*, and the **92nd Street Y**. In these venues you will find lively, unusual, and experimental showcases for new talent as well as lots of uninhibited productions.

The Off-Broadway theaters mounted the first productions in New York of the works of playwrights Eugene O'Neill, Tennessee Williams, Eugene Ionesco, Sean O'Casey, Jean Genet, and David Mamet. Samuel Beckett's *Happy Days* premiered at the **Cherry Lane Theatre** in 1961, a venue that still promotes cutting-edge writing. Off-Broadway theaters host modern and often irreverent treatments of the classics.

Sometimes a more intimate, smaller Off-Broadway stage suits a production better than a larger more established theater would, as proved by such long-running successes as *The Fantasticks* along with the *Threepenny Opera*, which has been shown at the **Lucille Lortel Theater** since 1955.

Performance Theaters

This extremely avant-garde art form can be found in several Off- and Off-Off-Broadway locations. Accurate descriptions and categorizations are almost impossible, but expect the bizarre and outlandish. The most likely venues to find this are **La MaMa Experimental Theatre Club**, **P.S. 122**, **HERE**, **Baruch Performing Arts Center**, **92nd Street Y**, **Symphony Space**, and the **Joseph Papp Public Theater** *(see p122)*. The latter is perhaps the most influential theater in New York. It was founded in the 1950s by the late director Joseph Papp, who introduced neighborhood tours to bring theater to people who had never seen it before.

The Public Theater created hits such as *A Chorus Line*; and *Hair*; it is most famous for its free summer performances of Shakespeare at the Delacorte Theater in Central Park *(see p208)*. It usually has several productions running, and at 6pm on the day of performance, "Quiktix" tickets (limited to two per person) are sold in the Public Theater lobby.

Theater Schools

New York is the best place in the country to see actors learning their trade. Foremost among the acting schools is **The Actors' Studio**. The late Lee Strasberg, the advocate of method acting – in which the actor aims for complete identification with the character being played – was its guru. His students included Dustin Hoffman, Al Pacino, and Marilyn Monroe. "In progress" productions feature trainees and are open to the public and free. Sandy Meisner trained many actors, including the late Lee Remick, at the **Neighborhood Playhouse School of the Theater**. Its plays are not open to the public. The **New Dramatists** began in 1949 to develop new playwrights, helping the careers of the likes of William Inge. Play readings are open to the public and free.

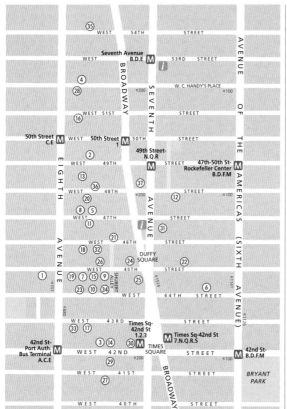

Broadway Theaters

① Al Hirschfield
302 W. 45th St.
Tel (212) 239-6200.

② Ambassador
219 W. 49th St.
Tel (212) 239-6200.

③ American Airlines Theater
227 W. 42nd St.
Tel (212) 719-1300.

④ August Wilson
245 W. 52nd St.
Tel (212) 239-6200.

⑤ Barrymore
243 W. 47th St.
Tel (212) 239-6200.

⑥ Belasco
111 W. 44th St.
Tel (212) 239-6200.

⑦ Bernard B Jacobs
242 W. 45th St.
Tel (212) 239-6200.

⑧ Biltmore
(Samuel Friedman Theater) 261 W. 47th St. **Tel** (212) 239-6200.

⑨ Booth
222 W. 45th St.
Tel (212) 239-6200.

⑩ Broadhurst
235 W. 44th St.
Tel (212) 239-6200.

⑪ Brooks Atkinson
256 W. 47th St.
Tel (212) 307-4100.

⑫ Cort
138 W. 48th St.
Tel (212) 239-6200.

⑬ Eugene O'Neill
230 W. 49th St.
Tel (212) 239-6200.

⑭ Foxwoods
213 W. 42nd St.
Tel (212) 556 4750.

⑮ Gerald Schoenfeld
236 W. 45th St.
Tel (212) 239-6200.

⑯ Gershwin
222 W. 51st St.
Tel (212) 307-4100.

⑰ Helen Hayes
240 W. 44th St.
Tel (212) 239-6200.

⑱ Imperial
249 W. 45th St.
Tel (212) 239-6200.

⑲ John Golden
252 W. 45th St.
Tel (212) 239-6200.

⑳ Longacre
220 W. 48th St.
Tel (212) 239-6200.

㉑ Lunt–Fontanne
205 W. 46th St.
Tel (212) 307-4747.

㉒ Lyceum
149 W. 45th St.
Tel (212) 239-6200.

㉓ Majestic
247 W. 44th St.
Tel (212) 239-6200.

㉔ Marquis
211 W. 45th St.
Tel (212) 307-4100.

㉕ Minskoff
200 W. 45th St.
Tel (212) 307-4100.

㉖ Music Box
239 W. 45th St.
Tel (212) 239-6200.

㉗ Nederlander
208 W. 41st St.
Tel (212) 307-4100.

㉘ Neil Simon
250 W. 52nd St.
Tel (212) 307-4100.

㉙ New Amsterdam
214 W. 42nd St.
Tel (212) 307 4100.

㉚ New Victory
209 W. 42nd St.
Tel (212) 239-6200.

㉛ Palace
1564 Broadway.
Tel (212) 307-4100.

㉜ Richard Rodgers
226 W. 46th St.
Tel (212) 307-4100.

㉝ St. James
246 W. 44th St.
Tel (212) 239-6200.

㉞ Shubert
225 W. 44th St.
Tel (212) 239-6200.

㉟ Studio 54
254 W. 54th St.
Tel (212) 719 3100.

㊱ Walter Kerr
219 W. 48th St.
Tel (212) 239-6200.

㊲ Winter Garden
1634 Broadway.
Tel (212) 239-6200.

For other theaters see p339.

Ballet

At the heart of the dance world is Lincoln Center *(see p216)*, where the New York City Ballet performs pieces in the **New York State Theater**. This company was created by the legendary brilliant choreographer George Balanchine *(see p51)* and is probably still the best in the world. The current director, Peter Martins, was one of Balanchine's best dancers and continues the strict policy of ensemble dancing rather than "star turns." The season runs from November to February and late April to early June. The ballet school at the **Juilliard Dance Theater** also presents a spring workshop every year, and this is a good chance to see budding stars.

The American Ballet Theater appears at the **Metropolitan Opera House**, which also hosts many visiting foreign companies, such as the Kirov, Bolshoi, and Royal ballets. Its repertoire includes 19th-century classics, such as *Swan Lake,* and works by modern choreographers such as Twyla Tharp and Paul Taylor.

Contemporary Dance

New York is the center of many of the most important movements in modern dance. The **Dance Theater of Harlem** is world famous for its modern, traditional, and ethnic productions. Other havens of experimental dance include the **92nd Street Y** and the **Merce Cunningham Studio** in Greenwich Village. The unique **Dance Theater Workshop** features contemporary dance and performance from around the world. **The Kitchen**, **La MaMa**, **Symphony Space**, and **P.S. 122** are all multimedia venues with the latest in contemporary dance, performance art and avant-garde music. Choreographer Mark Morris's company performs at the **Mark Morris Dance Center** in Brooklyn; **City Center** *(see p150)* is a favorite spot for dance fans. It used to house the New York City Ballet and the American Ballet Theater before Lincoln Center was built. As well as featuring the Joffrey Ballet, City Center has held performances by all the great contemporary artists, including Alvin Ailey's blend of modern, jazz, and blues, and the companies of modern dance masters Merce Cunningham and Paul Taylor. Avoid the mezzanine, as the view is restricted.

The city's single most active venue for dance is probably the **Joyce Theater**, where such well-established companies as the Feld Ballet, along with bold newcomers and visiting troupes, perform.

Each spring the Festival of Black Dance at the **Brooklyn Academy of Music (BAM)** *(see p250)* features everything from ethnic dance to hip-hop. During autumn the "Next Wave" festival of music and dance is held, celebrating international and American avant-garde dance and music. During winter, the American Ballet Festival is held here.

During June, **New York University** *(see p117)* holds a Summer Residency Festival with lecture-demonstrations, rehearsals, and performances, and **Dancing in the Streets** organizes summertime dance performances all over the city.

Throughout the month of August, **Lincoln Center Out of Doors** has a program of free dance events on the plaza, with such experimental groups as the American Tap Dance Orchestra.

The **Duke Theater** presents many contemporary dance companies and participates in events such as the New York Tap Festival.

At different times of the year, **Radio City Music Hall** holds several spectacular shows, with different companies from all over the world. At Christmas and Easter, it features the famously precise Rockettes dance troupe.

Choreographers and dance companies frequently present works-in-progress and recitals to the public. Among the most interesting venues for these is the **Joan Weill Center for Dance** , which is one of the country's largest dance facilities and was created by the Alvin Ailey American Dance Theater to promote black cultural expression. The **Hunter College Dance Company** performs new works by its student choreographers, and the **Isadora Duncan Dance Foundation** recreates Duncan's original dances. To see contemporary choreographers, the best place to go is **Juilliard Dance Theater**.

Prices

Theater is extremely expensive to produce, and ticket prices tend to reflect this. Even Off- and Off-Off-Broadway tickets are not cheap anymore. Preview tickets are easier to get hold of, though, and it's fun to see a show before the reviews are in so you're able to make up your own mind.

For a Broadway theater ticket you can expect to pay $80 or more; for musicals, up to $100; Off-Broadway, $25 to $60. For dance, $20 to $50 is the usual range, with up to $115 for the American Ballet Theater.

Times of Performance

The general rules for theater-hours are: closed on Mondays (except for most musicals), with matinees on Wednesdays, Saturdays, and sometimes Sundays. Matinees usually begin at 2pm, with evening performances at 8pm. Be sure to check the correct dates and times of the performance beforehand, as tickets are usually non-refundable if you fail to turn up at the correct time.

Backstage Tours and Lectures

For those interested in the mechanics and anecdotes of the theater, your best bet is to go on one of the theater tours. The **92nd Street Y** organizes insider's views of the theater, with famous directors, actors, and choreographers taking part. Writers are invited along to read or discuss their current works. **Radio City Music Hall** also holds tours.

DIRECTORY

Off-Broadway

92nd Street Y
1395 Lexington Ave.
Map 17 A2.
Tel (212) 415-5500.

Baruch Performing Arts Center
55 Lexington Ave. Map 9 A4. Tel (646) 312-4085.

Brooklyn Academy of Music
30 Lafayette Ave, Brooklyn.
Tel (718) 636-4100.

Cherry Lane Theatre
38 Commerce St. Map 3 C2. Tel (212) 239-6200.

HERE Art Center
145 6th Ave. Map 4 D4.
Tel (212) 647-0202.

Circle in the Square
1633 Broadway.
Map 12 E4.
Tel (212) 307-0388.

Delacorte Theater
Central Park. (81st St.)
Map 16 E4.
Tel (212) 539-8750.
Summer time only.

Douglas Fairbanks Theater
432 W 42nd St. Map 7 C1.
Tel (212) 239-6200.

Lambs Theater
130 W 44th St. Map 12 E5.
Tel (212) 575-0300.

Lucille Lortel Theater
121 Christopher St.
Map 3 C2.
Tel (212) 924-2817.

Manhattan Theater Club
311 W 43rd St.
Map 8 D1.
Tel (212) 399-3000.

New York Theater Workshop
79 E 4th St. Map 4 F2.
Tel (212) 460-5475.

Public Theater
425 Lafayette St.
Map 4 F2.
Tel (212) 539-8500.

Symphony Space
2537 Broadway.
Map 15 C2.
Tel (212) 864-5400.

Vivian Beaumont
Lincoln Center.
Map 11 C2.
Tel (212) 362-7600.

Off-Off-Broadway

Bouwerie Lane Theater
330 Bowery. Map 4 F2.
Tel (212) 677-0060.

The Kitchen
512 W 19th St. Map 7 C5. Tel (212) 255-5793.

Performing Garage
33 Wooster St. Map 4 E4.
Tel (212) 966-3651.

York Theater at St. Peter's Church
Citigroup Center, 619 Lexington Ave. Map 13 A4. Tel (212) 935-5820.

Performance Theater

La MaMa Experimental Theatre Club
74a E 4th St. Map 4 F2.
Tel (212) 475-7710.

P.S. 122
150 First Ave.
Map 5 A1.
Tel (212) 477-5288.

Public Theater
See Off-Broadway.

Theater Schools

The Actors' Studio
432 W 44th St.
Map 11 B5.
Tel (212) 757-0870.

New Dramatists
424 W 44th St.
Map 11 C5.
Tel (212) 757-6960.

Dance

92nd Street Y
See Off-Broadway.

Brooklyn Academy of Music

See Off-Broadway.

City Center
130 W 56th St. Map 12 E4.
Tel (212) 581-1212.

Dance Theater of Harlem
466 W 152nd St.
Tel (212) 690-2800.

Dance Theater Workshop
219 W 19th St. Map 8 E5.
Tel (212) 924-0077.

Dancing in the Streets
55 6th Ave (offices).
Tel (212) 625-3505.

Hunter College Dance Company
695 Park Ave. Map 13 A1.
Tel (212) 772-4490.

Isadora Duncan Dance Foundation
141 W 26th St.
Map 20 D2.
Tel (212) 691-5040.

Joan Weill Center for Dance
405 W 55th St. Map 11 D4. Tel (212) 405-9000.

Joyce Theater
175 Eighth Ave at 19th St.
Map 8 D5.
Tel (212) 242-0800.

Juilliard Dance Theater
60 Lincoln Center Plaza, W 65th St. Map 11 C2.
Tel (212) 769-7406.

Performance Venues

Duke Theater
229 W 42nd St. Map 8 E1.
Tel (646) 223-3000.

The Kitchen
See Off-Off-Broadway.

La MaMa Experimental Theatre Club
See Performance Theater.

Lincoln Center Out of Doors
Lincoln Center, Broadway at 64th St. Map 11 C2.
Tel (212) 362-6000.

Manhattan Center

311 W 34th St. Map 8 D2.
Tel (212) 279-7740.

Mark Morris
3 Lafayette Ave.
(Brooklyn)
Tel (718) 624-8400.

Merce Cunningham Studio
55 Bethune St. Map 3 B2.
Tel (212) 255-8240.

Metropolitan Opera House
Lincoln Center, Broadway at 65th St. Map 11 C2.
Tel (212) 362-6000.

New York State Theater
Lincoln Center, Broadway at 65th St. Map 11 C2.
Tel (212) 870-5570.

New York University
Tisch School of the Arts (TSOA), 111 2nd Ave.
Map 4 F1.
Tel (212) 998-1920.

P.S. 122
See Performance Theater.

Radio City Music Hall
50th St at Ave of the Americas. Map 12 F4.
Tel (212) 307-7171.

Symphony Space
See Off-Broadway.

Backstage Tours

92nd Street Y
See Off-Broadway.

Radio City Music Hall
Tel (212) 307-7171.

Events Guide
🔳 playbill.com
🔳 newyorkcitytheater.com

Movies

New York is a film buff's paradise. Apart from new US releases, which show months in advance of other countries, many classic and foreign films are screened here.

The city has always been the testing ground for new developments in films, and it continues to be a hotbed of young and innovative talent. Many of the movies' best known directors – Woody Allen, Martin Scorsese, and Spike Lee – were born and raised in New York, and the city's influence is perceptible in many of their films. They, and others, can often be seen filming on the streets of the city; many of New York's landmarks have become famous after appearing in films. Most of the TV networks based in New York offer free tickets to the recordings of their shows. Watching a show such as *The Late Show with David Letterman* is a popular activity for visitors.

First-Run Movies

New York reviews and box office returns are so vital to a film's success that most major American films have their pre-mieres in Manhattan's theaters. First-run films are shown mainly at the City Cinema chains, AMC Loews, United Artists, and Cineplex Odeon, which are scattered around the city. Some theaters have recorded information giving the names and duration of the different films showing, with starting times and ticket prices.

Programs start at 10am or 11am and are repeated every two to three hours until mid-night. You should expect to line up for most evening and weekend performances of the more popular films. Making reservations using a credit card is possible at some theaters for an additional charge of about $2 per ticket. Matinees (usually before 4pm) are easier to get into. Senior citizens pay a reduced price for tickets: the required age may be over 60, 62, or 65 depending on the policy of the theater.

New York Film Festival

A high point of the year for film buffs is the New York Film Festival, now in its third decade. Organized by the **Film Society of Lincoln Center**, the festival starts in late September and continues for two weeks at the many Lincoln Center theaters. Outstanding new films from the US and abroad are entered in a competition for the huge prestige of winning an award. Many of the films shown during the festival are later released and can usually be seen only in art houses.

The **TriBeCa Film Festival**, created in part by director and actor Robert De Niro, was launched in 2002 to celebrate New York City as a filmmaking capital and to contribute to the long-term recovery of Lower Manhattan. The festival show-cases a wide range of films, including classics, documentaries, and premieres, and usually takes place in late April and early May. Every spring, **Docfest** (the New York International Documentary Festival) presents five days of film and video documentaries from around the world, followed by panel discussions.

Film Ratings

Films in the United States are graded as follows:

G General audiences; all ages admitted.

PG Parental guidance suggested; some material unsuitable for children.

PG-13 Parents strongly cautioned; some material inappropriate for children under age 13.

R Restricted. Children under 17 need to be accompanied by a parent or an adult guardian.

NC-17 No children under 17 admitted.

On Location

Many New York locations have played starring roles in films. Here are a few:

The Brill Building (1141 Broadway) contained Burt Lancaster's penthouse in *Sweet Smell of Success*.

The Brooklyn Bridge was a great backdrop in Spike Lee's *Mo' Better Blues*.

Brooklyn Heights and the **Metropolitan Opera** appeared in *Moonstruck*.

Central Park has shown up in countless films, including *Love Story* and *Marathon Man*.

55 Central Park West will be remembered as Sigourney Weaver's home in *Ghostbusters*.

Chinatown played a major role in *Year of the Dragon*.

The Dakota was where Mia Farrow lived in the classic *Rosemary's Baby*.

The Empire State Building is still standing after *King Kong*'s last battle. The observation deck is where Cary Grant waited in vain in *An Affair to Remember*; here Meg Ryan finally met Tom Hanks in *Sleepless in Seattle*.

Grand Central Station is famous for Robert Walker's meeting with Judy Garland in *Under the Clock* and for the magical ballroom sequence in *The Fisher King*.

Harlem hosted the jazz musicians and dancers in *The Cotton Club*.

Katz's Deli was the setting for the café scene between Billy Crystal and Meg Ryan in *When Harry Met Sally…*

Little Italy appeared in *The Godfather I* and *II*.

Madison Square Garden was the setting for the dramatic climax of *The Manchurian Candidate*.

Tiffany & Co. was Audrey Hepburn's favorite shop in *Breakfast at Tiffany's*.

The United Nations Building featured in *North by Northwest* and *The Interpreter*.

Washington Square Park was where Robert Redford and Jane Fonda walked *Barefoot in the Park*.

Foreign Films and Art Houses

For the latest foreign and independent films, go to the **Angelika Film Center**, which also has an upscale coffee bar. Other good places are the **Rose Cinemas** at the BAM, the **Film Forum**, and **Lincoln Plaza Cinema**. The Plaza has a busy program of art and foreign films. For Asian, Indian, and Chinese films, you should visit the **Asia Society**. The **French Institute** screens many French films with English subtitles on Tuesdays. The **Quad Cinema** shows a wide selection of foreign films, often quite rare. **Cinema Village** runs special film events, such as the Festival of Animation.

The **Walter Reade Theater** houses the Film Society of the Lincoln Center, offering retrospectives of international movies as well as celebrations of contemporary works, such as the popular annual Spanish Cinema Now festival.

Classic Films and Museums

Retrospectives of films by particular directors or featuring specific actors are shown at the Public Theater and the Whitney Museum of American Art *(see pp202–3)*. The **Museum of the Moving Image** *(see p248)* screens old films and also has many exhibits of memorabilia from the film industry. The **Paley Center for Media** *(see p173)* has regular screenings of classic films; you can also see or hear specific television or radio programs. Students interested in classic, new and experimental movies will appreciate the collection of the **Anthology Film Archives**.

The shows at the **Rose Center for Earth and Space** at the **American Museum of Natural History** are well worth a whole day's visit.

On summer evenings in Bryant Park, you can watch free classic movies, and on Saturday mornings, the **Film Society of Lincoln Center,** where special children's shows are held.

Television Shows

A number of TV programs originate in New York. The popular *David Letterman* and *Saturday Night Live* shows are almost impossible to get tickets for, but tickets for many other shows can be obtained online, by calling the networks such as **NBC**, **ABC**, and **CBS**, or sometimes on standby.

Another good source of free tickets is the Times Square Information Bureau *(see p360)*. On weekday mornings on Fifth Avenue around **Rockefeller Plaza**, free tickets for a number of TV programs are sometimes distributed by the program's production staff. There's absolutely no way that you can plan for this. It's simply a matter of good luck and being in the right place at the right time.

For those who want to get a glimpse behind the scenes of TV, NBC organizes tours of the studios, from 8:30am to 5:30pm Mon–Thu, 8:30am to 6:30pm Fri–Sat, and 9:15am to 4:30pm on Sunday (depart every 15 mins).

Choosing What to See

If you feel bewildered by the huge range of films offered in New York, check the listings in *New York* magazine, the *New York Times*, the *Village Voice* and *The New Yorker*. The following Internet guides give show times and locations:
www.moviefone.com
www.movietickets.com

DIRECTORY

ABC
Tel (212) 580-5176.
w abc.com

American Museum of Natural History
Central Park W at 79th St.
Map 16 D5.
Tel (212) 769-5100.

Angelika Film Center
18 W Houston St.
Map 4 E3.
Tel (212) 995-2000.

Anthology Film Archives
32 2nd Ave at 2nd St.
Map 5 C2.
Tel (212) 505-5181.

Asia Society
725 Park Ave. Map 13 A1.
Tel (212) 517-2742.

CBS
Tel (212) 247-6497.

Cinema Village
22 E 12th St. Map 4 F1.
Tel (212) 924-3363.

Docfest
Tel (212) 668-1100.
w docfest.org

Film Forum
209 W Houston St.
Map 3 C3.
Tel (212) 727-8110.

French Institute
55 E 59th St. Map 12 F3.
Tel (212) 355-6160.

Lincoln Plaza Cinema
1886 Broadway.
Map 12 D2.
Tel (212) 757-2280.

Museum of Modern Art
11 W 53rd St.
Map 12 F4.
Tel (212) 708-9480.

Museum of the Moving Image
35th Ave & 36th St.
Astoria, Queens.
Tel (718) 784-0077.

NBC
30 Rockefeller Plaza at 49th St.
Tel (212) 664-3056.
w nbcstudiotour.com

The Paley Center for Media
25 W 52nd St. Map 12 F4.
Tel (212) 621-6600.

Public Theater
425 Lafayette St.
Map 4 F4.
Tel (212) 539-8500.

Quad Cinema
34 W 13th St.
Map 4 D1.
Tel (212) 255-8800.

Rockefeller Plaza
47th–50th St, 5th Ave.
Map 12 F5.

Rose Cinemas
Brooklyn Academy of Music (BAM), 30 Lafayette Ave, Brooklyn.
Tel (718) 636-4100.

TriBeCa Film Festival
Tel (212) 941-2400.
w tribecafilmfestival.org

Walter Reade Theater
70 Lincoln Center Plaza.
Map 12 D2.
Tel (212) 875-5600.

Whitney Museum of American Art
945 Madison Ave.
Map 13 A1.
Tel 1-800-WHITNEY.

Classical and Contemporary Music

New Yorkers have a voracious appetite for music. Live concerts by the world's most celebrated musical performers may be enjoyed at well-known halls throughout the year, and younger, newer artists, and exotic imports always find receptive audiences.

Tickets

Find out what you can choose from in New York by checking out the listings in the *New York Times* and the *Village Voice* and in *Time Out New York* and *The New Yorker* magazines.

Classical Music

The orchestra in residence at **Avery Fisher Hall** in Lincoln Center (*see p217*) is the New York Philharmonic. It is also the annual site for the popular "Mostly Mozart" series and Young People's Concerts. **Alice Tully Hall**, in Lincoln Center, is an acoustic gem and home to the Chamber Music Society.

One of the world's premier concert halls is the revamped **Carnegie Hall** (*see p150*). Upstairs in the Weill Recital Hall there are quality performances for reasonable prices.

The **Brooklyn Academy of Music (BAM)** (*see p250*) is the home of the Brooklyn Philharmonic. Classical music, dance, opera, jazz, and world music all find an audience at the **New Jersey Performance Arts Center** in Newark.

The **Merkin Concert Hall** is host to some top chamber ensembles and soloists. For really excellent acoustics, go to the **Town Hall**. The **92nd Street Y's** Kaufmann Concert Hall also offers a lively menu of music and dance. There's also the **Frick Collection** and **Symphony Space**, both of which offer a varied program

ranging from gospel to Gershwin, classical to ethnic. The beautiful Grace Rainey Rogers Auditorium at the **Metropolitan Museum of Art** is for chamber music and soloists, while the well-equipped **Florence Gould Hall**, at the Alliance Française, presents a varied program of chamber music, orchestral pieces, concerts, and even classic French films.

The **Juilliard School of Music** and the **Mannes College of Music** are both considered excellent. Their students and faculties give free recitals, and there are shows by leading orchestras, chamber music groups, and opera companies. The **Manhattan School of Music** offers an excellent program of over 400 events per year, from classical to jazz.

At 9:45am on the Thursdays of the New York Philharmonic concerts, the evening show is rehearsed at **Avery Fisher Hall** in Lincoln Center. Audiences are often admitted to listen, and rehearsal tickets are available at low prices. The **Kosciuszko Foundation** hosts the annual Chopin Competition. **Corpus Christi Church** has an active concert schedule, presenting such groups as the Tallis Scholars.

Opera

Dominating the city's operatic scene is **Lincoln Center** (*see p214*), home to the New York City Opera, and the **Metropolitan Opera House**, which has its own opera company. The Met is the jewel in the crown, offering top international performers. More accessible and dynamic is the New York City Opera. Its performances range from *Madame Butterfly* to *South Pacific*,

with subtitles above the stage to help the audience understand the plot. Lower-priced quality performances are staged by the up-and-coming singers at the **Village Light Opera Group**, the **Amato Opera Theater**, the **Kaye Playhouse** at Hunter College, and the students at the **Juilliard Opera Center** in Lincoln Center.

Contemporary Music

New York is one of the most important places in the world for contemporary music. Exotic, ethnic, and experimental music is played in many first-rate venues. The **Brooklyn Academy of Music (BAM)** is the standard-bearer of the avant-garde. Each autumn the Academy holds a festival of music and dance called "Next Wave," which has helped launch many musical careers.

An annual festival of serious modern music called "Bang on a Can" is performed at the **Ethical Culture Society Hall** and features works by Steve Reich, Pierre Boulez, and John Cage. Experimentalists, such as Davie Weinstein with his "audio-visual acid test" music – a mix of CD players, amplified instruments, keyboards, and sound effects – perform at the **Dance Theater Workshop**.

Other venues include the **Asia Society** (*see p189*), with its jewel of a theater for many visiting Asian performers, and **St. Peter's Church**.

Backstage Tours

Behind-the-scenes tours are offered by **Lincoln Center** and **Carnegie Hall**.

Religious Music

Few experiences are more moving than an Easter concert in the vast **Cathedral of St. John the Divine** (*see pp228–9*). Seasonal music is also offered at many of the city's museums and in almost every other available

Classical Radio

New York has three FM radio stations that broad-cast classical music: WQXR at 96.3, the National Public Radio station WNYC at 93.9 and WKCR 89.9.

space – from **Grand Central Terminal**'s main concourse (see pp158–9) to bank and hotel lobbies. For jazz vespers in a stunning modern building, visit **St. Peter's Church** (see p179). Most of these concerts are free, but you are encouraged to contribute.

Alfresco

Free outdoor summer concerts take place in **Bryant Park**, **Washington Square**, and **Lincoln Center's Damrosch Park**. The annual concerts on Central Park's Great Lawn and in Brooklyn's Prospect Park are performed by the New York Philharmonic and the Metropolitan Opera. In good weather, strolling musicians perform at South Street Seaport, on the steps of the **Metropolitan Museum of Art** (see pp192–9), and in the area around Washington Square.

Music for Free

Free musical performances are given at **The Cloisters** (see pp238–41) and the **Whitney Museum**'s Philip Morris Building (see p154). Sunday-afternoon recitals are held at Rumsey Playfield and the Naumburg Bandshell in Central Park (see p210), as well as the Summerstage. Call **The Dairy** for more information. You will also find music in the **Federal Hall** (see p170), while at **Lincoln Center**, don't miss the exciting free performances held in the **Juilliard School of Music**. Other venues include the **Greenwich House Music School** (free student recitals) and the **Winter Garden** at the World Financial Center (see p71). Numerous free concerts and talks take place in the city's churches, including **St. Paul's Chapel**, **Trinity Church** (see p70), and St. Thomas Church (see p173).

DIRECTORY

92nd Street Y
1395 Lexington Ave.
Map 17 A2.
Tel (212) 415-5500.

Amato Opera Theater
319 Bowery at 2nd St.
Map 4 F2.
Tel (212) 228-8200.

Asia Society
725 Park Ave. **Map** 13 A1.
Tel (212) 517-2742.

Brooklyn Academy of Music
30 Lafayette Ave,
Brooklyn.
Tel (718) 636-4100.

Bryant Park
Map 8 F1.
Tel (212) 768-4242.

Carnegie Hall
881 7th Ave. **Map** 12 E3.
Tel (212) 247-7800.

Cathedral of St. John the Divine
1047 Amsterdam Ave &
112th St.
Map 20 E4.
Tel (212) 316-7540.

The Cloisters
Fort Tryon Park.
Tel (212) 923-3700.

Corpus Christi Church
529 W 121st St.
Map 20 E2.
Tel (212) 666-9350.

The Dairy
Central Park at 65th St.
Map 12 F2.
Tel (212) 794-6564.

Dance Theater Workshop
See Dance p347.

Ethical Culture Society Hall
2 W 64th St. **Map** 12 D2.
Tel (212) 874-5210.

Federal Hall
26 Wall St. **Map** 1 C3.
Tel (212) 825-6888.

Florence Gould Hall (at the Alliance Française)
55 E 59th St. **Map** 13 A3.
Tel (212) 355-6160.

Frick Collection
1 E 70th St. **Map** 12 F1.
Tel (212) 288-0700.

Greenwich House Music School
46 Barrow St.
Map 3 C2.
Tel (212) 242-4770.

Internet Events Guide
W nymag.com
W nytoday.com
W newyork.city
search.com
W newyork.timeout.com

Kaye Playhouse (Hunter College)
695 Park Ave. **Map** 13 A1.
Tel (212) 772-4448.

Kosciuszko Foundation
15 E 65th St. **Map** 12 F2
Tel (212) 734-2130.

Lincoln Center
155 W 65th St. **Map** 11
C2. **Tel** (212) 546-2656.
Tours of various venues at
Lincoln Center can be
arranged by calling:
Tel (212) 875-5350.

Alice Tully Hall
Tel (212) 875-5050.

Avery Fisher Hall
Tel (212) 875-5030.

Damrosch Park
Tel (212) 875-5000.

Juilliard Opera Center
Tel (212) 769-7406.

Juilliard School of Music
Tel (212) 799-5000.

Metropolitan Opera House
Tel (212) 362-6000.

Manhattan School of Music
120 Claremont Ave.
Map 20 E2.
Tel (212) 749-2802.

Mannes College of Music
150 W 85th St. **Map** 15 D3.
Tel (212) 580-0210.

Merkin Hall
129 W 67th St.
Map 11 D2.
Tel (212) 501-3330.

Metropolitan Museum of Art
1000 5th Ave at 82nd St.
Map 16 F4.
Tel (212) 535-7710.

New Jersey Performance Arts Center
1 Center St, Newark, NJ.
Tel 1-888-466-5722.

St. Paul's Chapel
Broadway at Fulton St.
Map 1 C2.
Tel (212) 233-4164.

St. Peter's Church
619 Lexington Ave. **Map**
13 A4. **Tel** (212) 935-2200.
Symphony Space
2537 Broadway. **Map** 15
C2. **Tel** (212) 864-5400.

Town Hall
123 W 43rd St. **Map** 8 E1.
Tel (212) 997-1003.

Trinity Church
Broadway at Wall St.
Map 1 C3.
Tel (212) 602-0800.

Village Light Opera Group
Perform at: Schimmel
Center for the Arts at Pace
University, 3 Spruce St.
Map 1 C2.
Tel (212) 346-1715.

Washington Square
Map 4 D2.

Whitney Museum
Philip Morris Building, 120
Park Ave at 42nd St.
Map 9 A1.
Tel 1-800-944-8639.

Winter Garden
World Financial Center,
West St. **Map** 1 A2.
Tel (212) 945-2600.

Rock, Jazz, and World Music

There's every imaginable form of music in New York, from international stadium rock to the sounds of the 1960s, from Dixieland jazz or country blues, soul, and world music to talented street musicians. The city's music scene changes at a dizzying pace, with new arrivals (and departures) almost daily, so there's no way to predict what you may find when you arrive. Musical standards also vary.

Prices and Venues

At clubs, expect to pay a cover charge and possibly a one- or two-drink minimum (at $7 or more) requirement. The prices for concerts typically range from $50 to $150 for the major venues. Many of the smaller concert venues are arranged for seating in certain areas and dancing in others – often with different prices for each.

The top international bands are usually to be found in the huge stages at the **MetLife Stadium** or **Madison Square Garden** (see p137). Here the likes of Elton John, Bruce Springsteen, and Madonna perform. Tickets for these events sell out very fast, so buy as many as you need as soon as you hear of a concert, unless you don't mind paying a lot for them through an agent or a scalper (see p333). During the summer, big outdoor concerts are held at Jones Beach (see p257) and **Central Park SummerStage**.

Medium-sized venues for mainstream bands include the Art Deco palace of **Radio City Music Hall**, the **Manhattan Center** (formerly the Hammerstein Ballroom), and the **Beacon Theater**. Booking an impressive lineup of acts is the **Nokia Theater** in Times Square. This state-of-the-art venue is known for its top-notch acoustics. The most popular live-music venues are in the Upper West Side area.

Many leading rock venues are basically bars with music. They will often book different bands every night, so check the listings in the *New York Times, Village Voice,* or *Time Out New York* or phone the place to find out what's happening and at what time during that particular week.

Rock Music

Rock comes in many forms: gothic, industrial, techno, psychedelic, post-punk funk, indie, and alternative music are among the latest crazes. If you prefer to see more of a band than a giant video screen, the following venues have a much more intimate, friendly atmosphere.

The **Knitting Factory Brooklyn** has new music, while the **Mercury Lounge** is one of the most happening music spots, featuring hot new bands being groomed for MTV. **Irving Plaza** is where relatively unknown and sometimes known rock groups play, as do the occasional famous country and blues musicians.

The **Bowery Ballroom**, in the Lower East Side, boasts superior acoustics and sightlines and usually books well-known touring acts and local bands.

A converted bodega, **Arlene's Grocery** attracts a loyal crowd thanks to acts ranging from rock to country and comedy. Its Live Rock and Roll Karaoke on Monday nights is also popular. **Joe's Pub** draws those who appreciate the eclectic roster of rock, jazz, hip-hop, and lounge music. **Le Poisson Rouge**, a self-described "multimedia art cabaret," is one of Greenwich Village's hottest spots to catch up-and-coming international and independent music acts, and is a favorite of Downtown trend-spotters.

Jazz

The original Cotton Club and Connie's Inn, which were once crucibles of jazz, are long gone, as are the former speakeasies of West 52nd Street. However, many talented performers carry on the old traditions of Dave Brubeck, Les Paul, Duke Ellington, Count Basie, and other big bands. In Harlem, the stylish yet informal **Lenox Lounge** features contemporary jazz on the weekends.

In Greenwich Village, jazz temples from the 1930s survive and continue to foster great music. Foremost among them is the **Village Vanguard**, where some of the most highly revered jazz memories linger, and newer ones are being fashioned by such groups as the McCoy Tyner and Branford Marsalis trios. **Blue Note** hosts big bands at high prices but has a great atmosphere. **Smalls** offers cutting-edge jazz, with various acts every night often playing two or more sets each.

Smoke is an intimate nightspot offering a divergent roster of musicians, and **Birdland** features ex-Mingus alumni and musicians such as Bud Shank.

Café Carlyle, an East Side spot once famed for late jazz pianist and singer Bobby Short, now sometimes features clarinetist-filmmaker Woody Allen playing with Eddy Davis and his New Orleans Jazz Band. **Jazz Standard**, with an ample underground performance space, showcases top-notch jazz performers most nights of the week.

A sophisticated club and restaurant, **Iridium** features progressive jazz. If you're in New York in January, don't miss the annual **NYC Winter Jazzfest**, where famous jazz acts play at various clubs around Manhattan.

Jazz at Lincoln Center events are scheduled throughout the year, including concerts by the renowned Lincoln Center Jazz Orchestra under the direction of Wynton Marsalis. The music ranges from Duke Ellington's New York sounds to Johnny Dodds' traditional New Orleans-style jazz. Jazz at Lincoln Center now has its own home since it moved into the world's first performing arts center specifically for jazz. It is housed in the Time Warner Center – a multiroom facility on Columbus Circle, perched above Central Park, with bandstands posed against sparing walls of glass and a dance floor beneath the moon and stars (see p217). Finally, select Friday nights at the **Rose Center** offer cool parties "under the stars" featuring top live rock acts and DJs.

Folk and Country Music

Folk, rock music, and R&B (rhythm and blues) can be found at the rather faded **Bitter End**, which once showcased James Taylor and Joni Mitchell but now specializes in promising new talent, as does **Kenny's**

Castaways. Also worth checking out is the **Sidewalk Café**, with its wide range of emerging performers.

Blues, Soul, and World Music

For blues, soul, and world music, options include the **Apollo Theater** in Harlem (see p232). For more than 60 years the near-legendary Wednesday Amateur Nights have been responsible for discovering and launching stars, including James Brown and Dionne Warwick.

The **Cotton Club** is no longer located in its original spot, but the modern venue offers good blues, jazz, and a Sunday real Gospel brunch on Harlem's

main street. The **B.B. King's Blues Club** lineup often features legendary jazz and gospel performers. Food is also served, but can be pricy. Don't miss "Mambo Mondays" with Nestor Torres at **SOB's** (Sounds of Brazil), a world music club specializing in Afro-Latin rhythms.

Terra Blues's bar doubles as an interesting music venue. The blues artists that appear here range from authentic Chicago acoustic players to modern blues acts. In the East Village, **The Stone** showcases an eclectic range of artsy acts. Part community center and café, part jazz and experimental music space, the **5C Café** is a throwback to old New York and has a laidback vibe.

DIRECTORY

Music Venues

Beacon Theater
2124 Broadway.
Map 15 C5.
Tel (212) 465-6500.

Central Park SummerStage
Rumsey Playfield.
Map 12 F1.
Tel (212) 360-2777.

Madison Square Garden
7th Ave & 33rd St.
Map 8 E2.
Tel (212) 465-6741.

Manhattan Center
311 W 34th St. **Map** 8 D2.
Tel (212) 279-7740.

MetLife Stadium
1 MetLife Stadium Dr,
East Rutherford, NJ.
Tel (201) 559-1515.

Nokia Theater
1515 Broadway. **Map** 12 E5.
Tel (212) 930-1959.

Radio City Music Hall
See p339.

Rock Music

Arlene's Grocery
95 Stanton St. **Map** 5 A3.
Tel (212) 995-1652.

Bowery Ballroom
6 Delancey St. **Map** 4 F3.
Tel (212) 533-2111.

Irving Plaza
17 Irving Pl. **Map** 9 A5.
Tel (212) 777-6800.

Joe's Pub
Public Theater,
425 Lafayette St. **Map** 4 F2.
Tel (212) 539-8778.

Knitting Factory Brooklyn
361 Metropolitan Ave.
Tel (347) 529-6696.

Le Poisson Rouge
158 Bleecker St. **Map** 4 D3.
Tel (212) 505-3473.

Mercury Lounge
217 E Houston St.
Map 5 A3.
Tel (212) 260-4700.

Jazz

Birdland
315 W 44th St.
Map 12 D5.
Tel (212) 581-3080.

Blue Note
131 W 3rd St.
Map 4 D2.
Tel (212) 475-8592.

Café Carlyle
95 E 76th St. **Map** 17 A5.
Tel (212) 744-1600.

Iridium
1650 Broadway.
Map 12 D2.
Tel (212) 582-2121.

Jazz at Lincoln Center
150 W 65th St. **Map** 11 C2.
Tel (212) 258-9800
or 362-7600.

Jazz Standard
116 E 27th St. **Map** 9 A3
Tel (212) 576-2232.

Lenox Lounge
288 Malcolm X Blvd.
Map 21 B2.
Tel (212) 427-0253.

NYC Winter Jazzfest
w winterjazzfest.com

Rose Center
79th St at CPW.
Map 16 D5.
Tel (212) 769-5100.

Smalls
183 W 10th St.
Map 3 C2.
Tel (212) 252-5091.

Smoke
2751 Broadway.
Map 20 E5.
Tel (212) 864-6662.

Village Vanguard
178 7th Ave S.
Map 3 C1.
Tel (212) 255-4037.

Folk and Country

Bitter End
147 Bleecker St. **Map** 4 E3.
Tel (212) 673-7030.

Kenny's Castaways
157 Bleecker St. **Map** 4 E3.
Tel (212) 979-9762.

Sidewalk Café
94 Ave A. **Map** 5 B2.
Tel (212) 473-7373.

Blues, Soul, and World Music

5C Café
68 Avenue C. **Map** 5 C2.
Tel (212) 477-5993.

Apollo Theater
253 W 125 St. **Map** 19 A1.
Tel (212) 531-5305.

B.B. King's Blues Club
237 W 42nd St. **Map** 8 E1.
Tel (212) 997-4144.

Cotton Club
656 W 125th St. **Map** 22
F2. **Tel** (212) 663-7980.

SOB's
204 Varick St.
Map 4 D3.
Tel (212) 243-4940.

The Stone
Avenue C at 2nd St.
Map 5 C2.
w thestonenyc.com

Terra Blues
149 Bleecker St.
Map 4 E3.
Tel (212) 777-7776.

Clubs, Dance Halls, and Gay and Lesbian Venues

New York's nightlife and club scene is legendary, and deservedly so. Whatever your preference – be it a plush club with pricey bottle service, an old-school disco, or the soothing sounds and cocktails of a piano bar – you'll be amazed at the choice. There was a rash of big discos in the 1980s and 1990s, but few of these have survived and now the hip crowds tend to gravitate towards stylish, yet often casual, bars and lounges.

When and Where

The best and hippest time for clubbing is during the week – it's also a lot cheaper. Take a fair amount of money and some ID to prove that you're old enough to drink (which is over 21) – but beware, all the drinks are very expensive.

The trendiest clubs roll on until 4am or later. Fashions and club nights change all the time, so go to Tower Records on Broadway for all the latest leaflets, check club details in the listings magazines (see p332) and read the *Village Voice*. The most interesting places nowadays are often popularized by word of mouth. Your best bet is to go somewhere like Pacha and hope someone will tell you where to go on to. It's a well-known spot and often invitations to other clubs are given out there.

Dancing

New Yorkers thrive on music and dancing. The dance floors available all around the city range from the ever-popular **SOB's** – for jungle, reggae, soul, jazz, and salsa – to a few huge basketball-court-sized places, such as **Roseland**. This cavernous space hosts big-name acts and DJs, providing plenty of room in which to dance along to everything from classic soul and Latin funk to techno. It also has a good megasize, 700-seater, restaurant with a fully stocked bar.

The legendary club **Pacha**, which started out in Ibiza, has opened a swanky four-floor venue in the heart of Times Square and is consistently booking top international DJs to make the most of the colossal sound system installed here. This is the place for those who enjoy pounding music, sweaty dance floors, and a lively crowd. **Marquee** is another A-list spot in Chelsea, with a glass-enclosed VIP mezzanine that draws Hollywood starlets. Bring some models if you want to be sure of getting in.

The botanically themed **Greenhouse** has a spacious interior decorated and lit by thousands of tiny, colored bulbs. It is also eco-conscious and LEED- (Leadership in Energy and Environmental Design) certified. Fashion and film events are often held here, and savvy clubbers have made it one of their top destinations. Another venue that's always packed is **Webster Hall**, an elder statesman of NYC nightlife that offers four floors of R&B, pop, electro, or house (when it's not hosting a special event). By comparison, **Cielo** is embracing the 21st century. This sleek, upscale room aimed mostly at those who love electronica boasts a killer sound system that envelops dancers as they jostle in a sunken living-room dance floor.

Those who are seriously interested in music and dancing head to **The Sullivan Room**, which draws the cream of techno talent and boasts a top-notch sound system and plenty of seating; or **Santos Party House**, which is basically two large, square, and black-painted rooms, where people go to get wild. Santos is part-owned by rocker Andrew W.K.

Nightclubs

Nightclubs are the places to see a show. NY shows are less flashy than in the 1940s and 1950s but they still boast a wide variety of acts. Expect to pay a cover charge; many of the clubs also require that you have at least two drinks.

Marie's Crisis is a legendary Greenwich Village piano bar where patrons are invited and encouraged to sing cabaret standards and hit showtunes. **Uncle Charlie's** maintains a lively piano lounge, giving patrons of the nearby Theater District a chance to belt out their own versions of Broadway favorites after a show. **Joe's Pub** at the Public Theater has decent food and a wonderful array of performances and musical acts. **Feinstein's at the Regency** is the epitome of classic cabaret. Come here to enjoy everything from tinkling live piano shows to Broadway tributes and jazz trios.

Gay and Lesbian Venues

The past two decades have seen the arrival of clubs and restaurants specifically geared to gay and lesbian clientele. Popular gay cabarets include the **Duplex**, which has a mix of stand-up comics, comedy sketches and singers. Often adorned with year-round Christmas lights, the long-running **Pieces** heats up most nights of the week with everything from drag shows to karaoke.

The very fashionable night-clubs and bars for men include the trendy, older-skewing up-town **Town House**, a piano bar with restaurant, and **Don't Tell Mama**, a long-established gay bar that presents good musical revues and spoofs. The gay and lesbian crowd can enjoy VIP treatment and bottle service at the upscale **XL Nightclub**. This Midtown haunt provides an assortment of cabaret performances, as well as colorful themed parties and drag bingo.

Henrietta Hudson caters solely to women, as does the imaginatively decorated **Cubby Hole**, a cozy lesbian bar where regulars often sing along to the jukebox.

Magazines such as the *Village Voice* and *Next* have good listings of what's happening in the gay communities, and the *Gay Yellow Pages* covers the gay scene. If you need more information, phone the **Gay and Lesbian Switchboard**.

The Chelsea neighborhood, particularly around Eighth Avenue, is the bustling heart of New York's gay life. The Hell's Kitchen area, around the mid-40s between Eighth and 10th avenues, also thrums with gay nightlife – Barrage is a hopping bar featuring a popular Friday happy hour. The inviting and stylish **G Lounge** serves a potent selection of cocktails and flavored coffees, and is the perfect spot for a drink before hitting the clubs. Lively **Barracuda** features drag shows and draws a diverse crowd of regulars and newcomers, while **Gym** caters to those into sporting events. **Stonewall Inn**, the famed site of the Stonewall riots and birth of the modern gay movement, has undergone a multimillion-dollar refurbishment. The comfy neighborhood lounge **Posh** pulls in a friendly crowd for the popular happy hour 4–8pm, and no visit to NYC would be complete without the spectacle of loud and flashy **Splash nightclub**.

DIRECTORY

Dancing

Cielo
18 Little West 12th St.
Map 3 B1.
Tel (212) 645-5700.

Greenhouse
150 Varick St.
Map 4 D4.
Tel (212) 807-7000.

Marquee
289 10th Ave.
Map 7 C4.
Tel (646) 473-0202.

Pacha
618 W 46th St.
Map 12 E5.
Tel (212) 209-7500.

Roseland
239 W 52nd St.
Map 12 E4.
Tel (212) 247-0200.

Santos
Party House
96 Lafayette St.
Map 4 F5.
Tel (212) 714-4646.

SOB's
204 Varick St.
Map 4 D3.
Tel (212) 243-4940.

Sullivan
Room
218 Sullivan St.
Map 4 D2.
Tel (212) 252-2151.

Webster Hall
125 E 11th St.
Map 4 F1.
Tel (212) 353-1600.

Nightclubs

Feinstein's
at the Regency
540 Park Ave.
Map 13 A3.
Tel (212) 339-4095.

Joe's Pub
425 Lafayette St.
Map 4 F2.
Tel (212) 539-8778.

Marie's
Crisis
59 Grove St.
Map 3 C2.
Tel (212) 243-9323.

Uncle
Charlie's
139 E 45th St.
Map 13 A5.
Tel (212) 661-9097.

Gay and Lesbian Venues

Barracuda
275 W 22nd St.
Map 8 D4.
Tel (212) 645-8613.

Barrage
401 W 47th St.
Map 12 D5.
Tel (212) 586-9390.

The
Cubby Hole
281 W 12th St.
Map 3 C1.
Tel (212) 243-9041.

Don't
Tell Mama
343 W 46th St.
Map 12 D5.
Tel (212) 757-0788.

Duplex
61 Christopher St.
Map 3 C2.
Tel (212) 255-5438.

G Lounge
223 W 19th St.
Map 8 E5.
Tel (212) 929-1085.

Gay and
Lesbian
Switchboard
Tel (212) 989-0999.

Gym
167 Eighth Ave.
Map 8 D5.
Tel (212) 337-2439.

Henrietta
Hudson
438 Hudson St.
Map 3 C3.
Tel (212) 924-3347.

Pieces
8 Christopher St.
Map 4 D2.
Tel (212) 929-9291.

Posh
405 W 51st St.
Map 11 C4.
Tel (212) 957-2222.

Splash
50 W 17th St.
Map 8 F5.
Tel (212) 691-0073.

Stonewall Inn
53 Christopher St.
Map 3 C2.
Tel (212) 488-2705.

Town House
236 E 58th St.
Map 13 B4.
Tel (212) 754-4649.

XL Nightclub
512 West 42nd St.
Map 7 C1.
Tel (212) 239-2999.

Comedy, Cabaret, and Literary Events

From Jack Benny and Woody Allen to Chris Rock and Jerry Seinfeld, New York has spawned almost as many comics as it has jokes about itself, including the requisite quips: on crime – "In New York crime is getting worse. When I was there the other day, the Statue of Liberty had both hands up"; and on driving – "Always look both ways when running a red light." Comedy is a cut-throat business here. This is good news for punters, because it means that no matter what comedy club you walk into, you'll be crying with laughter. NYC is also a consummate romancer, judging by its plethora of classic cabarets and lounges. An unforgettable New York experience is to be serenaded by a lounge singer in a dusky piano bar. New York also boasts a booming literary scene, with superb weekly readings and lectures.

Comedy Showcases

Many of New York's best current comedy clubs or showcases have evolved from earlier "improvisational" comedy. Part of the allure of New York comedy clubs is that you never know who might get behind the mic to deliver their spiel. Anyone from Dennis Miller and Roseanne Barr to Robin Williams could show up. A word of caution: if you don't want to be singled out and made fun of, sit away from the stage. Many of the larger comedy clubs offer meals, and at the more popular clubs, it's always a good idea to make reservations to ensure admission.

Leading the comedy club pack is the **Broadway Comedy Club** in the Theater District, which has formed from a merger of Chicago City Limits |and NY Improv. As the city's largest club, it draws big names nightly. **Caroline's** also has big-name comics perform in elegant surroundings. The famous catchphrase of the bug-eyed New York comedian Roger Dangerfield was "I get no respect," but judging from the lasting fame of his **Dangerfield's Comedy Club**, which draws top acts from around the country, he seems to have gotten respect after all. The **Upright Citizens Brigade Theatre** has sassy, Chicago-style improvisation on various days of the week.

Many of the UCB's weekly late shows are free. The **Gotham Comedy Club** in the Flatiron District, presents a wide range of comics in a sophisticated setting. **Comic Strip Live**, on the East Side, has hosted a slew of top comics, including Eddie Murphy, and continues to introduce many new comics to the scene. The basement-level **Comedy Cellar** in Greenwich Village presents a nightly lineup of new and established comics. Also good are **Stand-Up NY**, **NY Comedy Club**, and **Laugh Lounge NYC**, which showcases two comedy shows a night, as well as offering nicely priced cocktails. **Underground Lounge** and **The Laugh Factory** are also good value.

Cabarets and Piano Bars

Cabarets have become a New York institution. Such cozy, just-for-listening places are often called "rooms" and are located in hotels. Most operate from Tuesday to Saturday (usually with a cover charge or a drink minimum), and most take credit cards.

Triad hosts a variety of shows, from stand-up comedy and burlesque to modern cabaret acts. For a classic piano lounge with a panoramic Manhattan view, visit the **Top of the Tower** at the Beekman Tower Hotel.

The "long-distance hummer" award goes to the late Bobby Short, who played his piano for over 25 years at the Café Carlyle in the **Carlyle Hotel**. Now Woody Allen plays there on Mondays with Eddy Davis's New Orleans Jazz Band.

Also in the Carlyle is **Bemelman's Bar**, with its whimsical murals; it attracts a relaxed crowd who enjoy first-class crooners.

The spirited cabaret **Don't Tell Mama** showcases emerging and established performers who belt out their songs with equal gusto. **Ars Nova**, in Hell's Kitchen, is an informal, anything-goes cabaret where you may see show tunes and experimental comedy, and has attracted the likes of Liza Minnelli and Tony Kushner.

For Manhattan's choicest cabaret, kick back and enjoy the show at lively **Duplex**, the longest-running cabaret venue in New York City. Relax to the tinkling of keys at the downstairs piano bar, or head upstairs for superlative classic cabaret shows, one-act plays, and top-notch comedy. A mixed crowd, including the talented staff, croons along at **Brandy's Piano Bar**. For a memorable evening of song and music, head to **Feinstein's at the Regency Hotel**, where top-of-the-line performers entertain an appreciative crowd. The **Metropolitan Room**'s intimate performance space hosts a wide range of shows, including cabaret acts and international jazz artists.

Literary Events and Poetry Slams

As the birthplace of some of the greatest American writers, from Herman Melville to Henry James, and the adopted home of countless others, New York has long been a writer's city. The literary tradition is celebrated throughout the year, with readings and talks that take place at bookstores, libraries, cafés, and community centers across the city. Readings are usually free, but expect long lines for the better known names. The **92nd Street Y** hosts readings by some of the greatest writers to pass through New York, including many Nobel- and Pulitzer-prize winning authors. Most NYC bookstores present a weekly or monthly reading series, including **Barnes & Noble** (the Fifth Avenue and Union Square branches usually attract high-profile authors). The **Mid-Manhattan Library** also presents readings, as does **Strand Bookstore**. Enjoy

spirited readings by playwrights at the **Drama Book Shop**. Check out *The New Yorker* magazine, available in bookstores and at many newsstands, for current listings of readings and talks.

Poetry slams (also known as Spoken Word), are just what the name implies – an evening of freeform poems, raps, and storytelling, usually raucous and entertaining, often unpredictable, and never boring. The **Nuyorican Poets Café** in Alphabet City, often heralded as the progenitor of spoken word in New York,

serves up a nightly mix of poetry slams, readings, and performances. Faculty and staff at Columbia and CUNY and writing professionals can be found at **KGB Bar**'s series of literary events. The **Bowery Poetry Club**, established as a performance space for spoken word in all its incarnations, presents an eclectic range of performances, from poetry jams to various performance arts. The **Poetry Project** at St. Mark's Church also hosts contemporary poetry readings, events, and workshops.

DIRECTORY

Comedy Showcases

Broadway Comedy Club
318 W 53rd St.
Map 12 E4.
Tel (212) 757-2323.

Caroline's
1626 Broadway.
Map 12 E5.
Tel (212) 757-4100.

Comedy Cellar
117 MacDougal St.
Map 4 D2.
Tel (212) 254-3480.

Comic Strip Live
1568 2nd Ave.
Map 17 B4.
Tel (212) 861-9386.

Dangerfield's
1118 1st Ave.
Map 13 C3.
Tel (212) 593-1650.

Gotham Comedy Club
208 W 23rd St.
Map 8 D4.
Tel (212) 367-9000.

The Laugh Factory
303 W 42 St.
Map 8 D1.
Tel (212) 586-7829.

Laugh Lounge NYC
151 Essex St.
Map 5 B3.
Tel (212) 614-2500.

NY Comedy Club
241 E 24th St.
Map 9 B4.
Tel (212) 696-5233.

Stand-up NY
236 W 78th St.
Map 15 C5.
Tel (212) 595-0850.

Underground Lounge
955 W End Ave.
Map 20 E5.
Tel (212) 531-4759.

Upright Citizens Brigade Theatre
307 W 26th St.
Map 8 D4.
Tel (212) 366-9176.

Cabarets and Piano Bars

Ars Nova
511 W 54th St.
Map 12 E4. **T el** (212) 489-9800.

Brandy's Piano Bar
235 E 84th St.
Map 17 B4.
Tel (212) 650-1944.

Carlyle Hotel
35 E 76th St.
Map 17 A5.
Tel (212) 744-1600.

Don't Tell Mama
343 W 46th St.
Map 12 D5.
Tel (212) 757-0788.

Duplex
61 Christopher St.
Map 3 C2.
Tel (212) 255-5438.

Feinstein's at the Regency Hotel
540 Park Ave. **Map** 13 A3.
Tel (212) 759-4100.

Metropolitan Room
34 W 22nd St.
Map 8 F4.
Tel (212) 206-0440.

Top of the Tower
Beekman Tower Hotel, 3 Mitchell Pl. **Map** 13 C5.
Tel (212) 355-7300.

Triad
158 W 72nd St, 2nd Floor.
Map 11 C1.
Tel (212) 362-2590.

Literary Events and Poetry Slams

92nd Street Y
1395 Lexington Ave.
Map 17 A2.
Tel (212) 415-5729.

Barnes & Noble
555 Fifth Ave.
Map 12 F5.
Tel (212) 697-3048.
33 E 17th St.
Map 9 A5.
Tel (212) 253-0810.

Bowery Poetry Club
308 Bowery.
Map 4 F3.
Tel (212) 614-0505.

Drama Book Shop
250 W 40th St.
Map 8 E1.
Tel (212) 944-0595.

KGB Bar
85 E 4th St.
Map 4 F2.
Tel (212) 505-3360.

Mid-Manhattan Library
455 Fifth Ave at 40th St.
Map 8 F1.
Tel (212) 340-0833.

Nuyorican Poets Café
236 E 3rd St.
Map 5 B2.
Tel (212) 505-8183.

Poetry Project
St. Mark's Church, 131 E 10th St.
Map 4 F1.
Tel (212) 674-0910.

Strand Bookstore
828 Broadway.
Map 4 E1.
Tel (212) 473-1452.

Late-Night New York

New York is indeed a city that never sleeps. If you wake up in the middle of the night – with a craving for fresh bread, a need to be entertained, or an urge to watch the sun rise over the Manhattan skyline – there are always plenty of options to choose from.

Bars

The best and friendliest bars are often the Irish ones. **O'Flanagan's** or **Scruffy Duffy's** are both loud, have late-night dancing, and cater to regulars. Go for a late-night dry martini at the **Temple Bar**. The best piano bars are in the hotels: try the Café Carlyle or, for a less expensive option, Bemelman's Bar, both in the **Carlyle Hotel**, or the legendary **Feinstein's at Loews Regency** (see p349).

For hot American jazz until 4am, go to **Joe's Pub** or the **Blue Note**. **Cornelia Street Café** is a lively nook for literary readings. Poetry, theater, and Latin music can be found at the **Nuyorican Poets Café**. If you're in midtown, stop in at **Rudy's** for an eclectic late-night scene and a free hot dog with each drink purchase.

Midnight Movies

Special midnight showings and a youthful crowd can be found the Angelika Film Center and the Film Forum (see p341). New multiplexes often show movies at midnight on weekends.

Shops

Shakespeare & Company Booksellers on Broadway and the St. Mark's Bookshop are open until late. The **Apple Store** on Fifth Ave is open 24 hours and well worth a visit at any time of the day. In the evening, DJs bring the store to life, while during the day, more than 300 Mac specialists are available for training and consultations. In SoHo, **H&M** sells affordable fashion until 9pm Monday to Saturday and until 8pm on Sundays.

Among the many Village clothing stores that stay open late is **Trash and Vaudeville** (open to 8pm Mon–Thu, to 8:30pm Fri, and to 9pm Sat);

Macy's at Herald Square is open daily until 9:30pm. For health essentials, many **Duane Reade**, **CVS**, and **Rite Aid** pharmacies are open 24 hours.

Take-Out Food and Groceries

A few take-out food stores are open 24 hours a day, including numerous **Gristedes** emporiums and the **West Side Supermarket**. Many Korean greengrocers also stay open all night. The **Food Emporium** is a supermarket chain usually open until midnight. Liquor stores are usually open until 10pm and many deliver.

For the best in bagels, go to **Ess-a-Bagel**, **Bagels On The Square**, and **Jumbo Bagels and Bialys**. Many pizzerias and Chinese restaurants stay open late.

Dining

The trendy set often frequent **Balthazar**, and **Les Halles** for good French dishes. Twentysomethings will seek out the **Coffee Shop** for late-night beer and Brazilian food. You'll find delicious and legendary sandwiches at the **Carnegie Deli**. **Caffè Reggio** in Greenwich Village has been a favorite for late-night coffee and desserts since 1927. Other good options include **Blue Ribbon** and **Odeon**. **The Dead Poet** is a real Upper West Side neighborhood hangout, with a jukebox, a lively bar, and late-night bar food. Downtown, the party crowds flock to **Bereket Turkish Kebab House** for excellent kebabs, or to the **Moonstruck Diner** in Chelsea. Both are open 24 hours a day.

Sports

There is late-night play at **Slate Billiards** until 4am on weekends.

Have late-night beers and burgers with the New York University crowd at **Bowlmor Lanes** bowling alley. Also popular is the Lucky Strike Lanes and Lounge, featuring cocktails, bowling, and music in a retro atmosphere. **24–7 Fitness Club** offers a no-frill gym around the clock.

Services

Midnight Express Cleaners picks up garments in Manhattan until midnight and has them ready the next day. Note that this service does not pick up or deliver to major hotels. On Thursdays hairdresser **George Michael of Madison Avenue/ Madora** is open until 9pm and will also make house calls. Primarily for women, the no-nonsense Korean spa **Juvenex** provides massages and saunas at any time. If you are locked out, try **Mr Locks Inc**. For stamps, head to the General Post Office, open 24 hours. Upscale grocer **Dean & DeLuca's** Kip's Bay branch is open till 10pm.

Tours and Views

One of New York's most enjoyable walks is along the Hudson River at the World Financial Center's **Battery Park City**, open (and safe) at all hours. Piers 16 and 17 at South Street Seaport attract strollers and revelers all night long and the **Harbour Lights** restaurant on Pier 17 is often open until 2am for a middle of the night pick-me-up. Enjoy the city lights by taking a **Circle Line** two-hour tour of the nighttime harbor.

Try the Riverview Terrace at Sutton Place: the benches offer a peaceful place to watch the sun rise over the East River, Roosevelt Island, and Queens. Two of the most sensational views with the Manhattan backdrop are (looking west) from the **River Café** and (looking east) from the **Chart House** restaurant.

Take a trip on the **Staten Island Ferry** (see p78) to see the Statue of Liberty and the Manhattan skyline in the dawn light, or take a taxi across Brooklyn Bridge *(see pp88–91)* to watch the sun rise over New York Harbor. Go to the **Beekman Tower Hotel**'s Top of the Tower for some panoramas of the city's East Side up to 1am. The ultimate view is from the **Empire State Building**: its observation decks *(see pp138–9)* stay open until 2am. **Top of the Rock**'s observation decks *(see p146)* are open until midnight. The **Living Room Terrace** at the W Downtown offers expansive views of the Downtown skyline.

Château Stables has rides in horse-drawn carriages and

Liberty Helicopters run flights over the city at sunset. If you want something a little bit different, try **New York Food Tours**' multicultural bar-hopping tour. And if you still can't sleep, stroll along the Upper West Side and grab a couple of hot dogs at the famous **Gray's Papaya**.

DIRECTORY

Bars

Blue Note
See p345.

Carlyle Hotel
See p349.

Cornelia Street Café
29 Cornelia St. **Map** 4 D2.
Tel (212) 989-9318.

Joe's Pub
See p345.

Nuyorican Poets Café
236 E 3rd St. **Map** 5 A2.
Tel (212) 505-8183.

O'Flanagan's
1215 1st Ave. **Map** 13 C2.
Tel (212) 439-0660.

Rudy's
627 9th Ave. **Map** 12 D5.
Tel (646) 707-0890.

Scruffy Duffy's
743 8th Ave. **Map** 12 D5.
Tel (212) 245-9126.

Temple Bar
332 Lafayette St. **Map** 4
F4. **Tel** (212) 925-4242.

Shops

Apple Store
767 5th Ave. **Map** 12 F3.
Tel (212) 336-1440.

CVS Pharmacy
158 Bleecker St. **Map** 4
D3. **Tel** (212) 982-3133.

Duane Reade Drugstores
224 W 57th (Broadway).
Map 12 D3.
Tel (212) 541-9708.
1279 3rd Ave at E 74th St.
Map 17 B5.
Tel (212) 744-2668.

H&M
558 Broadway. **Map** 4 E4.
Tel (212) 343-2722.

Macy's
See p136.

RiteAid Pharmacy
See p365.

Trash and Vaudeville
See p316.

Take-Out Food and Groceries

Bagels On The Square
7 Carmine St. **Map** 4 D3.
Tel (212) 691-3041.

Ess-a-Bagel
831 3rd Ave. **Map** 13 B4.
Tel (212) 980-1010.
359 1st Ave. **Map** 9 C4.
Tel (212) 260-2252.

Gristedes Food Emporium
262 W 96 St and
Broadway. **Map** 15 C2.
Tel (212) 663-5126.
One of many branches.

Jumbo Bagels and Bialys
1070 2nd Ave. **Map** 13 B3.
Tel (212) 355-6185.

West Side Market
2171 Broadway. **Map** 15
C5. **Tel** (212) 595-2536.

Dining

Balthazar
80 Spring St. **Map** 4 E4.
Tel (212) 965-1414.

Bereket Turkish Kebab House
187 E Houston St. **Map** 5
A3. **Tel** (212) 475-7700.

Blue Ribbon
See p294.

Caffè Reggio
119 MacDougal St. **Map** 4
D2. **Tel** (212) 475-9557.

Carnegie Deli
See p306.

Coffee Shop
See p306

The Dead Poet
450 Amsterdam Ave. **Map**
15 C4. **Tel** (212) 595-5670.

Gray's Papaya
Broadway at 72nd St.
Map 11 C1.
Tel (212) 260-3532.

Les Halles
See p306.

Moonstruck Diner
400 W 23rd St. **Map** 7 C4.
Tel (212) 752-1711.

Odeon
See p296.

Sports

24–7 Fitness Club
47 W 14th St. **Map** 4 D1.
Tel (212) 206-1504.

Bowlmor Lanes
110 University Pl. **Map** 4
E1. **Tel** (212) 255-8188.

Lucky Strike Lanes and Lounge
624–660 West 42nd St.
Map 7 B1.
Tel (646) 829-0170.

Slate Billiards
See p353.

Services

Dean & DeLuca
576 2nd Ave. **Map** 9 B3.
Tel (212) 696-1369.
One of several branches.

General Post Office
See p137.

George Michael of Madison Avenue/ Madora
422 Madison Ave. **Map** 13
A5. **Tel** (212) 752-1177.

Juvenex Spa
25 W 32nd St, Fifth Floor.
Map 8 F3.
Tel (646) 733-1330.

Midnight Express Cleaners
Tel (718) 392-9200.

Mr Locks Inc
Tel (866) 675-6257.

Tours and Views

Battery Park City
West St. **Map** 1 A3.

Beekman Tower Hotel
1st Ave & 49th St. **Map** 13
C5. **Tel** (212) 355-7300.

Chart House
Lincoln Harbor, Pier D-T,
Weehawken, NJ.
Tel (201) 348-6628.

Château Stables
608 W 48th St. **Map** 15 B3.
Tel (212) 246-0520.

Circle Line
W 42nd St. **Map** 15 B3.
Tel (212) 563-3200.

Harbour Lights
89 South St Seaport.
Pier 17. **Map** 2 D2.
Tel (212) 227-2800.

Liberty Helicopters
Tel (212) 487-4777.

Living Room Terrace
W Downtown, 123
Washington St. **Map** 1 B3.
Tel (646) 826-8600.

New York Food Tours
Tel (347) 559-0111.

River Café
See p311.

Staten Island Ferry
See p78.

Top of the Rock
See p146.

Sports

Many New Yorkers are ardent sports fans, and you'll find a range of sports events, both to watch and participate in, going on throughout the year. The city boasts two professional baseball teams, two hockey teams, a basketball team, and two football teams. Madison Square Garden plays host to an extraordinary variety of spectator sports, including basketball, hockey, boxing, and track and field events. Tennis fans can take in the US Open tournament every August and September in Queens, and those who follow track and field events swarm to the Millrose Games, where top runners and other athletes compete.

Tickets

The easiest way to get hold of tickets is through **Live Nation** or **Ticketmaster**. For the big games, you may need a ticket agent or an online ticketing reseller like **StubHub!**, which is far safer to use than a scalper outside the venue. You can also buy tickets at the stadium box office itself, though these tickets often sell out quickly. Finally, keep your eyes peeled for ticket offers in the free weeklies that are distributed throughout town.

Football

The city's two professional football teams are the New York Giants and the New York Jets. They both play their home games across the river at the **MetLife Stadium** in New Jersey, which will host the 2014 Super Bowl – the first time the NYC area has hosted the big game. Tickets for the Giants, a team with many NFL and Super Bowl championships under their belt, are very difficult to obtain, but they may be available for the Jets, seen by some as perpetual also-rans but no less beloved by their fans. Their last championship win was in 1969.

Baseball

To capture the essence of this American institution, baseball fans should try to see the famed New York Yankees, who play at **Yankee Stadium**. The team's legendary accomplishments include winning the most World Series titles and boasting such celebrated players as Joe DiMaggio and Jackie Robinson. The New York Mets, the other major baseball team, play at **Citi Field** in Queens. Catching a game of "America's favorite pastime" on a crisp summer day is a memorable event. If you can, try and catch a game when the Yankees are playing their archrivals, the Boston Red Sox. The baseball season runs April–October.

Basketball

The NBA season runs November–June. The New York Knicks play their home games at **Madison Square Garden**; tickets are pricey and difficult to attain, so reserve them far in advance through Ticketmaster or an online ticketing reseller. The Brooklyn Nets are the only major professional sports team in the borough; home matches are held at the gleaming **Barclays Center**. The ever-popular Harlem Globetrotters also play their games at The Garden.

Boxing

Professional boxing matches are more often seen on Paramount's wide TV screen than in the flesh at Madison Square Garden. Also at the Garden are the Daily News Golden Gloves in mid-April, the largest and oldest amateur boxing tournament in the US, with boxers from New York's five boroughs competing. Past Golden Glove winners, many of whom have gone on to become world champions, have included Sugar Ray Robinson and Floyd Patterson.

Horse Races

A day at the races may not be quite the lavish affair it once was, but the high-stakes races still draw the society crowd – hats, summer dresses and all – along with lively crowds who have come to cheer, jeer, and bet on their lucky horse. Harness racing, in which horses pull sulkies (small carts), takes place year-round at the **Yonkers Raceway**. Flat races are held daily, except Tuesday, October to May, at the **Aqueduct Race Track** in Queens, and May to October at the **Belmont Park Race Track** in Long Island.

Ice Hockey

Fists and ice fly when the New York Rangers meet their competition at Madison Square Garden. Two other National Hockey League teams call the metro area home: the New York Islanders play on Long Island at the **Nassau Coliseum**, and the New Jersey Devils play in the modern **Prudential Center** in Newark. The hockey season runs October–June, depending on playoffs.

Ice-Skating

There are a variety of good places to go ice skating out of doors. One is the **Rockefeller Plaza Rink**, which looks beautiful at Christmas. The others are in Central Park: **Wollman Memorial Rink** and **Lasker Ice Rink**. For indoor sites, try the Sky Rink at **Chelsea Piers**.

Marathon

To be one of the 45,000 who enter the New York Marathon, you have to sign up six months in advance. The race is held on the first Sunday in November. Phone (212) 423-2249 for information.

Tennis

The top tennis tournament in New York is the US Open, played each August at the **National**

Tennis Center. If you want to play tennis rather than watch it, look in the telephone directory under "Tennis Courts: Public and Private." For private courts, you can expect to pay about $50–70 an hour. The **Manhattan Plaza Racquet Club** offers both courts and lessons by the hour. For public courts, you will need a $50 permit, available from the **NY City Parks & Recreation Department**. You will also need an identity card and a reservation coupon.

Track and Field

The Millrose Games, which draws top athletes from around the world, are normally held in early February at **Madison Square Garden**. The 100-meter sprint, pole vault, and high jump competitions are particularly exciting. The Amateur Athletic Union (AAU) championships, where many renowned student athletes compete, are held in late February at the Garden. Chelsea Piers also has a complete track and field complex.

Sports Bars

New York City is crammed with sports bars, often unmissable for their big screens, sports banners, and cheering (or booing), beer-guzzling patrons. For a slice of American sports life, step into a sports bar when a big game is on, and you'll soon be whooping it up with the rest of them. Try **Mickey Mantle's**, which has a giant scoreboard. The **Village Pourhouse** in the East Village offers a plethora of screens so that you can follow the action no matter where you are. **Bounce**, on the Upper East Side, is a boisterous sports lounge with drinks specials through the week. **Bar None** and **Lunasa Bar** are also favorites, for soccer, try the amiable **Nevada Smith's** in the East Village, with friendly, Guinness-fueled crowds.

Other Activities

In Central Park, options include renting rowboats from **Loeb Boathouse** or playing chess – pick up the pieces from The Dairy *(see p208)*. Rent rollerblades at **Blades** and have a free lesson on stopping at Central Park before making a circuit. Bowling is available at **Chelsea Piers** and a few other lanes throughout the city. **Slate Billiards** and many bars offer pool and darts.

DIRECTORY

Aqueduct Race Track
Ozone Park, Queens.
Tel (718) 641-4700.

Bar None
98 3rd Ave.
Map 4 F1.
Tel (212) 777-6663.

Barclays Center
620 Atlantic Ave,
Brooklyn.
Tel (212) 359-6387.

Belmont Park Race Track
Hempstead Turnpike,
Long Island.
Tel (718) 641-4700.

Blades
156 W 72nd St.
Map 12 D1.
Tel (212) 787-3911.

Bounce
1403 Second Ave.
Map 13 B1.
Tel (212) 535-2183.

Chelsea Piers Sports & Entertainment Complex
Piers 59–62 at 23rd St & 11th Ave (Hudson River).
Map 7 B4–5.
Tel (212) 336-6000.
W chelseapiers.com

Citi Field
126th St at Roosevelt Ave,
Flushing, Queens.
Tel (718) 507-8499.

Lasker Ice Rink
Central Park Drive East at 108th St. Map 21 B4.
Tel (212) 534-7639.

Loeb Boathouse
Central Park.
Map 16 F5.
Tel (212) 517-2233.

Lunasa Bar
126 1st Ave.
Map 5 A2.
Tel (212) 228-8580.

Madison Square Garden
7th Ave at 33rd St.
Map 8 E2.
Tel (212) 465-6741.
W thegarden.com

Manhattan Plaza Racquet Club
450 W 43rd St.
Map 7 C1.
Tel (212) 594-0554.

MetLife Stadium
1 MetLife Stadium Dr, East Rutherford, NJ.
Tel (201) 559-1515.
W metlifestadium.com
Tel (516) 560-8200.
W newyorkjets.com

Mickey Mantle's
42 Central Park South.
Map 12 E3.
Tel (212) 688-7777.

Nassau Coliseum
1255 Hempstead Turnpike.
Tel (516) 794-9303.
W nassaucoliseum.com

National Tennis Center
Flushing Meadow Park,
Queens.
Tel (718) 595-2420.
W usta.com

Nevada Smith's
74 3rd Ave. Map 4 F1.
Tel (212) 982-2591.

NY City Parks & Recreation Department
Arsenal Building, 64th St & 5th Ave.
Map 12 F2.
Tel (212) 408-0100.
W nycgovparks.org

Plaza Rink
1 Rockefeller Plaza, 5th Ave.
Map 12 F5.
Tel (212) 332-7654.

Prudential Center
25 Lafayette St, Newark.
Tel (973) 757-6000.
W prucenter.com

Slate Billiards
54 W 21st St.
Map 8 E4.
Tel (212) 989-0096.

StubHub!
W stubhub.com

Ticketmaster
Tel (212) 307-4100.
W ticketmaster.com

Village Pourhouse
64 3rd Ave. Map 4 F1.
Tel (212) 979-2337.

Wollman Memorial Rink
Central Park, 5th Ave at 59th St.
Map 12 F2.
Tel (212) 439-6900.

Yankee Stadium
161st and 164th sts, The Bronx. Tel (718) 293-4300.

Yonkers Raceway
Yonkers, Westchester County.
Tel (914) 968-4200.

Fitness and Wellbeing

New York City may be (in)famous for its concrete, crowds, and cacophony, but the urban jungle is a boon for sports and fitness aficionados. A host of possibilities beckon, from pedaling on the sun-washed riverfront and jogging under the shadow of Manhattan's signature skyline at the Central Park Reservoir to scaling a soaring climbing wall at one of the city's many upscale gyms, indulging in a massage at gorgeous spa strewn with rose petals, and finding your inner Om in the lotus position at a yoga class.

Cycling

There's nothing like being stuck in midtown traffic to make you long for pedaling the open road. While Manhattan may be one of the most crowded islands on the planet, it offers a surprising 120 km (75 miles) of bike trails. At the last count, Manhattan boasted more than 110,000 everyday cyclists. One of the most pleasant places to cycle is in Central Park during the weekend, when it's closed to cars. Bikes may be rented from **Central Park Bike Rentals** on Columbus Circle. If you would like to feel the river breeze in your hair, pedal the well-maintained bike path along the West Side Highway that runs parallel to the Hudson River, or hit the bike trails in Riverside Park. On summer weekends, the paths can get exasperatingly congested, but if you go early or late in the day, or in the winter months, you can often coast solo.

The friendly folks at **Bicycle Habitat** on Lafayette Street rent bikes and dole out tips on getting around New York by bike.

Fitness Centers, Gyms, and Health Clubs

In New York, a weekly workout has become almost de rigueur for even the most extreme workaholics. Gyms and health clubs have sprouted across the city to accommodate the demand, and serious sweating goes on at all hours, day and night. The options are endless: Get your aggression out with a punch bag, increase your heart rate on the stairmaster, or pump iron. Most major hotels have fitness centers. Many commercial gyms and health clubs are open only to members, but an increasing number of gyms now offer day passes. Check out the **Chelsea Piers Sports & Entertainment Complex** on Piers 59–62 near Hudson River; there's something for everyone at this enormous facility. It's one-stop shopping at the multilevel **May Center for Health, Fitness, and Sport at the 92nd Street Y**, with exercise studios, weight-training, racquetball courts, a boxing room, and an indoor track. Day passes start at around $35. With its well-maintained gym along with an array of personal diet and exercise programs, the **Casa Spa & Fitness at the Regency Hotel** on Park Avenue lives up to its promise to be "your health and fitness oasis when you're away from home".

You can enjoy a wide range of activities at **YMCA** (one in West Side and the other on 47th Street) fitness centers. The state-of-the-art training equipment, a number of gymnasiums, swimming pools, aerobics studios, running/walking tracks, and various courts for different games, add to your enthusiasm of working out. The center also has special programs for elderly people designed to suit their physical stature for a healthy life.

Golf

Practice your swing at **Randalls Island Golf Center** on Randalls Island, **Chelsea Golf Club**, or play mini-golf at the **Wollman Memorial Rink** in Central Park. The city owns several courses in the boroughs, such as **Pelham Bay Park** in the Bronx and **Silver Lake** on Staten Island.

Jogging

Some parks are safe for joggers, others are not, so be guided by your concierge. None is safe after dark, at dusk or before dawn. The most popular and beautiful route is around the reservoir in Central Park. The **NY Road Runners** on 89th Street have weekly running clinics and races, as does **Chelsea Piers Sports & Entertainment Complex**.

Pilates

All you have to lose are your love handles. Work your abs and torso for lean, toned muscles at a Pilates class. The philosophy behind Pilates is based on the premise that the body's core is the "powerhouse" for the peripheral parts of the body. Challenge your muscles at a **Grasshopper Pilates** class, which is taught by a professionally trained dancer in a TriBeCa loft. **Power Pilates** also hold strengthening classes throughout the city.

Yoga

It's easier to get in touch your spiritual center when you can do it in a place like the airy **Exhale Mind Body Spa** on Madison Avenue, with its high ceilings and hard-wood floors. "Journey into the Core", "Ride the Vinyasa Wave", and "Dance into Trance" at a variety of yoga sessions, the ideal antidote to the city's madness. And, lest you should think yoga isn't enough of a workout, then you haven't tried the core fusion power pack abs session. **Fluid Fitness** on Sixth Avenue offers an introduction to Gyrotonic training, a workout that follows the principles of yoga while using fluid exercises and non-linear circular motion to strengthen the core.

Spas

Pamper yourself at one of New York City's choice spas and you'll emerge fresh as a daisy – and ready to take on the urban jungle once again. Most spas offer packages where you can enjoy several treatments at a lower price. If you're travelling with your significant other, bond over a couples' massage. The intoxicating wafts of incense that greet you at the front door of the fragrant, low-lit **Clay** are just a hint of the luxurious massage that awaits within.

At the comfy, casual **Oasis Day Spa**, on Park Avenue, select from six aromatherapy massages ($100) in aromas of uplift, refresh, balance, passion, calm, or relief. Men's specials include a Dead Sea salt scrub, an algae facial, or a muscle meltdown massage ($100 for an hour). For a slice of heaven, Bali style, disappear into the **Acqua Beauty Bar** on 14th Street and enjoy a botanical purifying facial ($115), orchid pedicure ($45), or Indonesian ritual of beauty ($170),

where your skin is scrubbed with ground rice and kneaded with fragrant oils. Enter **Bliss** on 57th Street and you'll soon discover that there's nothing a carrot and sesame body buff ($195) or fully loaded facial ($195) can't cure. Top it off with a decadent double chocolate pedicure, accompanied by a cup of creamy cocoa. Pure bliss.

Celebrities including Antonio Banderas and Kate Moss swear by **Mario Badescu** on 52nd Street whose facials and body scrubs, including the fresh fruit body scrub, with plump raspberries and strawberries, are as legendary as the beauty products, which are perfect to bring home as gifts.

Swimming

Many Manhattan hotels have pools with free access during your stay. It is also possible to purchase a day pass to use a hotel swimming pool and facilities – for example, at Le Parker Meridien (see p287).

You can also swim and surf at the Surfside 3 Maritime Center at **Chelsea Piers**. For a day trip, go to Jones Beach State Park (see p257) along Long Island's shoreline.

Indoor Sports

Chelsea Piers has it all: roller rinks, bowling, indoor soccer, basketball, rock-climbing walls, fitness centers, golf, a field house for gymnastics, sports medicine, spa centers, and of course, swimming pools. This huge complex, which is spread over four old West Side piers, is open to everyone.

Apart from providing fitness centers, gymnasium facilities, and indoor sports activities **YMCA** also offers exercise, balance, and flexibility classes; organizes day trips; special events; and sports and volunteer opportunities. If you are planning an adventurous day out for your children with fitness on the agenda or for burning extra calories then the club is worth a visit.

DIRECTORY

Acqua BeautyBar
7 E 14th St. **Map** 8 F5.
Tel (212) 620-4329.

Bicycle Habitat
244 Lafayette St.
Map 4 F3.
Tel (212) 431-3315.

Bliss
19 E 57th St. **Map** 12 F3.
Tel (212) 219-8970.
One of several locations.

Casa Spa & Fitness at the Regency Hotel
540 Park Ave. **Map** 13 A3.
Tel (212) 223-9280.

Central Park Bike Rental
348 W 57th St.
Map 12 D3.
Tel (212) 664-9600.

Chelsea Piers Sports & Entertainment Complex
Piers 59–62 at 23rd St &
11th Ave (Hudson River).
Map 7 B4–5.
Tel (212) 336-6000.
W chelseapiers.com

Clay
25 W 14th St.
Map 4 D1.
Tel (212) 206-9200.

Exhale Mind Body Spa
980 Madison Ave.
Map 17 A5.
Tel (212) 561-6400.

Fluid Fitness
1026 6th Ave.
Map 8 E1.
Tel (212) 278-8330.

Grasshopper Pilates
515 Broadway.
Map 4 E4.
Tel (212) 431-5225.

Mario Badescu
320 E 52nd St.
Map 13 B4.
Tel (800) 223-3728.

May Center for Health, Fitness, and Sport at the 92nd Street Y
1395 Lexington Ave.
Map 17 A2.
Tel (212) 415-5729.

NY Road Runners
9 E 89th St.
Map 17 A3.
Tel (212) 860-4455.

Oasis Day Spa
1 Park Ave.
Map 9 A2.
Tel (212) 254-7722.
One of two locations.

Pelham BayPark
The Bronx, 870 Shore Rd.
Tel (718) 885-1461.

Power Pilates
49 W 23rd St,10th floor.
Map 8 F4.
Tel (212) 627-5852.

Randalls Island Golf Center
Randalls Island.
Map 22 F2.
Tel (212) 427-5689.

YMCA West Side
1395 Lexington Ave.
Map 17 A2.
Tel (212) 415-5500.

Silver Lake
915 Victory Blvd. Staten
Island.
Tel (718) 447-5686.

Wollman Memorial Rink
Central Park, 5th Ave at
59th St.
Map 12 F2.
Tel (212) 439-6900.

YMCA 47th St
224 E 47th St.
Map 13 B5.
Tel (212) 756-9600.

CHILDREN'S NEW YORK CITY

Young visitors soon catch the contagious excitement in the air in New York. Attractions for all ages abound, and plenty are designed especially for children. More than a dozen theater companies, two zoos, and plenty of imaginative museums are aimed at the young, backed up with special events at many museums and parks. The chance to visit a TV studio is a treat, and New York's own Big Apple Circus is a perennial delight. With more to do than can ever be squeezed into a single visit, you'll never hear the cry "I'm bored!" Best of all, there's no need to spend a fortune to have fun.

A young visitor imitating the Statue of Liberty

Practical Advice

New York is family-friendly. Many of its hotels allow children in parents' rooms free, and will supply cots or cribs if needed. Most museums charge half price or less for children, while others are free. Children under 112 cm (44 in) also ride free on subways and buses when accompanied by an adult. Travel between 9am and 4pm to avoid rush hours.

Supplies such as diapers and medicines are readily available, and the Rite Aid Pharmacy (see p365) is open 24 hours a day. Finding changing tables in public toilets is less easy, but no one objects if a counter is used. Best bets are the facilities in libraries, hotels, and department stores. Most hotels will arrange babysitters; try **Baby Sitters' Guild** or **Pinch Sitters**.

To find out more about the range of current activities for children, get a copy of the free quarterly calendar of events,

available from the New York Convention and Visitors Bureau (see p360). Weekly listings can be found in *New York* magazine or *Time Out New York*.

New York Adventures

The city can seem like a giant amusement park for youngsters. Elevators whisk you sky-high for bird's-eye views from atop the world's highest buildings. You can set sail on the classic **Circle Line** tour around Manhattan; the sailboat **Pioneer** (see p86), or charter your own paddlewheeler from the marina at E. 23rd St; or the free round-trip on the Staten Island Ferry (see p78). The Roosevelt Island Tram (see p183) is a Swiss cable car offering an airborne ride over the East River. Central Park (see pp206–1) is a source of rides of every kind – from the oldfashioned charm of the carousel to real horseback and ponycart rides. Children who prefer a faster pace can join the skate-

Skating with Santa at Rockefeller Center

boarders and in-line skaters who cruise around the trafficfree park every weekend.

Cooling off in a playground in Central Park

Museums

While many of New York's museums appeal to all ages, some are designed just for the young. High on the list are the Children's Museum of Art (see p109), where kids can paint and sculpt, and the Children's Museum of Manhattan (see p221), a multimedia world in which children produce their own videos and newscasts. Farther afield are the **Staten Island Children's Museum**, where a huge climb-through anthill is one of the favorite items, and the Brooklyn Children's Museum (see p249). The *Intrepid* Sea-Air-Space Museum (see p151) is a real aircraft carrier. Finally, don't miss the dinosaur display at the American Museum of Natural History (see pp218–19).

Outdoor Fun

In summer, all of New York comes out to play. Central Park is a child's wonderland, from skating rinks to boating lakes, bicycle paths to miniature golf. The park offers free entertainment – such as guided walks by park rangers on Saturdays, toy sailboat races and summer storytelling. The Central Park Wildlife Center and the Tisch Children's Zoo are favorites.

Children of all ages will be fascinated by the Bronx Zoo/Wildlife Conservation Park which is home to over 500 species *(see pp246–7)*.

Coney Island *(see p251)* is just a subway ride away. Winter brings the chance to skate at Rockefeller Center *(see p146)* or in Central Park on a rink fringed with views of skyscrapers.

Indoor Fun

New York children's theater is of a quality and variety matching that for adults. Some favorite companies are the **Paper Bag Players** and **Theaterworks USA**, whose shows sell out fast; get schedules and reserve seats early.

The **Swedish Marionette Theater** in Central Park has shows at 10:30am and noon Tuesdays through Fridays, and Saturdays until 1pm.

The New York City Ballet's annual Christmas production of *The Nutcracker* at Lincoln Center *(see p214)* opens at the same time that the **Big Apple Circus** sets up its tent nearby. Ringling Brothers and Barnum & Bailey Circus is in action at Madison Square Garden *(see p137)* each spring.

Opportunities for youngsters to work off energy in winter are many, from indoor skating rinks to mini-golf and bowling alleys at **Chelsea Piers**. Kids can create video games, movies, and music for free at **Sony Wonder Technology Lab**.

Centerpiece clock at toy store F.A.O. Schwarz

Shopping

There will be no complaints about shopping trips if they include the huge **F.A.O. Schwarz** or **Toys 'R' Us** for a vast range of wonderful toys and other items. For more information on other toystores see New York Originals on pages 314–16. Youngsters are welcomed for storytelling sessions at **Books of Wonder**.

Eating Out

Hamburger-and-pasta joint **Ottomanelli's Café** is very popular with children, and even adults find it hard to finish their huge burgers. The colorful **S'Mac**, where the specialty is creamy macaroni and cheese, is also a hit with youngsters. The lively **Hard Rock Café** is also popular, and most children enjoy the foods sold around Chinatown and Little Italy. Drop into the **Chinatown Ice Cream Factory** for some strange and wonderful flavors. For a quick hot snack, try pizza-by-the-slice or pretzels and hot dogs from street vendors.

Storytelling session at South Street Seaport

SURVIVAL GUIDE

PRACTICAL INFORMATION

New York is one of the most diverse and exciting cities in the world. The fast pace of Manhattan may seem daunting at first, but there are many services to help tourists, and you will find the city is safe and easy to explore. Midtown streets are straight and mostly laid out in an easy-to-follow grid pattern. Buses and subway trains (see pp380–83)

are reliable and cheap; there are plenty of cash machines (see p366), and money can be easily exchanged at banks and hotels. The wide range of prices offered by the many hotels (see pp282–7), restaurants (see pp292–303), and entertainment venues (see pp332–57) in the city means that your New York trip can be both fun and affordable.

Skaters at an ice rink in Central Park

When to Go

September and October are the prize months in New York, offering warm days, cool nights, and colorful leaves in the city parks. Late spring is also appealing, when the city is less crowded and humid. Summers can be unpleasantly hot, but there are attractions such as outdoor concerts, plays, and sporting events to keep visitors busy. Christmas in the city is wonderful, although you will have to share your experience with thousands of other tourists. Weather-wise, any season can be unpredictable; always pack layers, and be prepared for changes.

Visas and Passports

All visitors to the United States require passports valid for at least six months after the dates of travel. Citizens of Great Britain, Australia, New Zealand, and 32 other countries, including most EU countries, do not need visas if they are staying in the US for 90 days or less. However, they must

apply and pay for entry online via the Electronic System for Travel Authorization (ESTA). The ESTA is valid for up to two years and can be used for multiple entries into the US (www.esta.cbp.dhs.gov/).

Canadians must show their passports when entering the US by air, and a passport or an enhanced driver's license proving citizenship when arriving by land or sea.

Those requiring a visa should apply in person at the nearest US embassy or consulate in their own country. It is vital to begin the process early, allowing sufficient time for processing the application. Some services will expedite the process for a fee. Visit www.travel.state.gov for more details.

Customs Information

Customs allowances per person when you enter the US are 200 cigarettes, 100 cigars, or 4.4 lb (2 kg) of tobacco; no more than 2 pints (1 liter) of alcohol; and gifts worth no more than $100. Many foods, including fruits and

vegetables, are prohibited from entering the United States. Baked items, candy, chocolate, and cured cheese are exceptions, as are canned goods (other than those containing meat or poultry products) if being imported for personal use.

Upon arrival at one of New York's airports, follow signs stating "other than American passports" to immigration counters, where your passport will be stamped. Next, reclaim your bags from the appropriate area and proceed to a customs officer, who will examine the customs declaration that you should have received and filled in on your flight.

New York tourist information office

Tourist Information

Advice on any aspect of life in New York City is available from the New York Convention & Visitors Bureau, known as **NYC & Co.** Its 24-hour touch-tone phone service (see p363) offers help outside office hours. New

York City has another free phone and Internet service, **311**, which provides government information and non-emergency general assistance. Calls are answered by a team 24 hours a day, with a translation service.

Smoking and Etiquette

It is illegal to smoke in any public place or building in New York, including restaurants, and this law is taken very seriously.

When boarding buses, New Yorkers generally form a line rather than pushing to enter. Subway boarders are not so polite at rush hours, but do stand aside to let passengers exit before rushing in. Turning off cell phones in theaters, cinemas, and museums is expected. Casual wear is accepted in many places in New York City, but some establishments may require formal dress; check when you make a reservation.

Many stores have late opening hours to accommodate workers

The New York Pass and CityPASS

The entrance to the Guggenheim Museum (see pp190–91)

Admission Prices

New York can be expensive for visitors, though you may often find a way to avoid high charges. Museum prices can run from $12 to $20, but some galleries, such as the Metropolitan Museum, call their charge a "suggested donation,"

leaving it to the visitor to decide what to pay. On Friday evenings (Saturdays for the Guggenheim), the Museum of Modern Art, Whitney Museum, and Folk Art Museum are open late and are free or have a "pay what you wish" policy. The Jewish Museum is free all day Saturday, while the Brooklyn Museum offers free art and entertainment on the first Saturday of the month (5–11pm). Consult local listings for museums of interest to you. The **New York Pass** and **CityPASS** *(see p362)*, offer discounted entry to some 50 attractions.

Opening Hours

Business hours are generally from 9am to 5pm, with no lunchtime closing. Many midtown stores stay open until 7pm to accommodate people in full-time jobs, and they may close even later on Thursdays, at 8:30 or 9pm. Most stores are also open rom noon to 6pm on Sundays.

Typical banking hours run from 9am to 6pm, Monday to Friday; some banks also open on Saturdays from 9am to 3pm. ATM machines are available 24 hours for credit and debit card cash withdrawals *(see p366)*.

Closing days vary for the major museums, as do the evenings they are open late, although most tend to be closed on a Monday. The Museum of Modern Art is closed on Tuesdays,

however, while the Guggenheim closes on Thursdays. Phone ahead of your visit, or check the website, before planning your itinerary.

New York's traffic rush hours extend roughly from 8 to 10am and 4:30 to 6:30pm, Monday to Friday. During these times, every form of public transportation will be crowded, as will pedestrian streets.

Public Bathrooms

New York City does not provide public bathrooms. Free restrooms can be found at city information centers, department stores, large bookstores (such as Barnes & Noble), and big restaurant chains (Starbucks, McDonald's), as well as at hotels. Bathrooms are also available in train and bus stations, but these are not always the most pleasant options.

Taxes and Tipping

Sales tax in New York is 8.875%, and it is added to all purchases (including meals), except for clothing and shoes under $110. Tipping is an integral part of New York life: taxi drivers expect 10–15%; cocktail waiters 15%; hotel room service 10% (when not added to the bill); coat check $1; hotel maids $1 or $2 per day after the first day; hotel bellhops about $1 per bag; hairstylists 15–20%, and barbers 10–20%. Waiters generally receive 15–20% of the bill, not including tax. A quick way to calculate restaurant tips is simply to double the tax, adding up to about 18%.

City bus with access ramp lowered for a disabled passenger

Travelers with Special Needs

All city buses have ramps for easy access. Subways, however, are a challenge for the disabled, as most stations are accessed via steps from the street. Only the busiest stops and stations, such as Grand Central and Penn stations and the Port Authority Bus Terminal, have elevators. A list of accessible stations is available on the Metropolitan Transit Authority website (www.mta.info).

Most hotels, restaurants, and attractions are equipped for disabled visitors, but do check in advance. It is also wise to ask about accessibility to the restrooms.

Some museums offer tours for deaf, blind, or disabled visitors, and all Broadway theaters have devices for the hearing-impaired. The *Official Accessibility Guide*, available free from the **Mayor's Office for People with Disabilities**, is a great resource, as is *Access for All*, published by **Hospital Audiences**. Both detail disabled access at public places such as museums, landmarks, theaters, and stadiums.

Senior Travelers

Seniors are welcomed in New York, and they are eligible for many offers. They travel half-fare on all subways and buses and get discounted prices at museums, movie theaters, and many sightseeing attractions. City buses can lower the entry steps to make it easier for older passengers to board.

Gay and Lesbian Travelers

New York has a large gay and lesbian population. Gay Pride Week in June brings celebrants from around the world for a big parade, and the Halloween parade in Greenwich Village also has a large gay following. The **Lesbian, Gay, Bisexual & Transgender Community Center** is a good first stop for general information. Christopher Street in Greenwich Village is the proud birthplace of New York's gay scene. Eighth Avenue around Chelsea is the epicenter of activity today, with Hell's Kitchen and the East Village increasingly popular; Park Slope in Brooklyn is a hotspot for the lesbian community. **Next** (www.next magazine.com) is a free weekly publication that can be found in these areas. The monthly **GO Magazine** (www.gomag.com) covers the lesbian scene, and *Time Out* New York *(see p369)* and the *New York* magazine website (www.nymag.com) have gay and lesbian listings.

Sign for the Lesbian, Gay, Bisexual & Transgender Community Center

Student Travelers

Many museums and theaters in New York offer discounted admission for students. To receive this, however, you will need to show proof of your student status. An **International Student Identity Card (ISIC)** can be purchased quite cheaply, provided you have the right credentials, from **STA Travel**, which has two branches in New York. At the same time, ask for a copy of the *ISIC Student Handbook*, which lists places and services that offer discounts to card-holders, including selected accommodations, various museums, tours, theaters, attractions, nightclubs, and restaurants.

Although it is very difficult to obtain permission to work in the US, students are eligible to work as part of exchange programs or as interns. Again, STA Travel can provide you with further details.

Note that the minimum age for drinking in New York is 21, and patrons may be asked for proof of age.

International Student Identity Card

Traveling on a Budget

There are many ways to take advantage of the best of New York while on a budget. The **TKTS** booth *(see p333)*, near Times Square, offers half-price admission to same-day Broadway shows, while pre-theater prix-fixe meals save on dining. The David Rubenstein Atrium, across from Lincoln Center *(see p216)*, offers discount tickets for same-day performances, in addition to a free concert in the Atrium itself on Thursdays at 8:30pm. The New York Philharmonic invites visitors to rehearsals for just $16, and the Juilliard School *(see p216)* also presents free concerts. In summer, free Shakespeare plays and music by the Philharmonic and the Metropolitan Opera are performed in Central Park. Many TV shows produced in the city are free to watch live if you request tickets in advance. The **New York Pass**, while not cheap, is good value for those who plan to do a lot of sightseeing. It offers free entry to over 50 attractions, from museums to the Empire State Building and river cruises. The **New York CityPASS** gives holders admission to six must-see sights in the city.

Time

New York is on Eastern Standard Time from early November to mid-March. Eastern Daylight

Time moves the American clock forward 1 hour the rest of the year.

Add 5 hours for the time in London, 8 hours for Moscow, 14 hours for Tokyo, and 16 hours for Sydney.

Electrical Appliances

All American electric current flows at a standardized 110 to 120 volts AC (alternating current). You will need to bring an adapter plug and a voltage convertor that fits standard US electrical outlets. US plugs have two flat prongs.

Most New York hotels provide wall-mounted electric hair dryers in bathrooms. In addition, some hotels have wall plugs capable of powering both 110- and 220-volt electric shavers, but little else – not even radios. It can, in fact, be dangerous to connect anything more powerful.

Some New York hotel rooms provide coffee-makers; however, most have radios and clocks, and a large number have iPod docking stations. If you require an iron and ironing board, but they are not in the room, ask room service.

Conversion Chart

Bear in mind that 1 US pint (0.5 liter) is a smaller measure than 1 UK pint (0.6 liter).

Imperial to Metric
1 inch = 2.5 centimeters
1 foot = 30 centimeters
1 mile = 1.6 kilometers
1 ounce = 28 grams
1 pound = 454 grams
1 US pint = 0.47 liter
1 US gallon = 3.8 liters

Metric to Imperial
1 millimeter = 0.04 inch
1 centimeter = 0.4 inch
1 meter = 3 feet 3 inches
1 kilometer = 0.6 mile
1 gram = 0.04 ounce

Responsible Tourism

New York is increasingly aware of "green issues." Proper recycling bins, with separate areas for paper and plastic, are widely available. Most hotels encourage guests to be ecologically aware and not request fresh towels every day. Shoppers tend to carry reusable cloth shopping bags, which are sold in almost every department store and super-

Fresh local produce for sale at one of New York's Greenmarkets

market. Most markets carry organic foods, and the city's many neighborhood Greenmarkets are popular sources of locally grown produce. The **Greenmarket at Union Square** (Mon, Wed, Fri, and Sat) is one of the best. Opening times vary.

You can contribute to these green efforts by patronizing restaurants that use locally grown produce. **5 Points** and **Gramercy Tavern** are two popular restaurants that have been given the **Slow Food NYC** seal of approval.

DIRECTORY

Embassies and Consulates

Australia
150 E 42nd St. **Map** 9 A1.
Tel (212) 351-6500.
australianyc.org

Britain
845 Third Ave. **Map** 13 B4.
Tel (212) 745-0200.
britainusa.com/ny

Canada
1251 Sixth Ave at 50th St.
Map 12 E4.
Tel (212) 596-1628.
canada-ny.org

Ireland
345 Park Ave. **Map** 13 A4.
Tel (212) 319-2555.
consulateofireland newyork.org

New Zealand
37 Observatory Circle, NW, Washington, DC, 20008. **Tel** (202) 328-4800.
nzembassy.org

Tourist Information

311
Tel 311. nyc.gov/311

NYC & Co.
810 Seventh Ave.
Map 12 E4.
Tel (212) 484-1222.
nycgo.com

New York CityPASS
citypass.com/city/ny

New York Pass
newyorkpass.com

Times Square Information Center
1560 Broadway.
Map 12 E5.
timessquarenyc.org

Travelers with Special Needs

Hospital Audiences
Tel (212) 575-7676.
hospitalaudiences.org

Mayor's Office for People with Disabilities
Tel (212) 788-2830.
nyc.gov/mopd

Gay and Lesbian Travelers

Lesbian, Gay, Bisexual & Transgender Community Center
208 West 13th St.
Map 3 C1.
Tel (212) 620-7310.
gaycenter.org

Student Travelers

International Student Identity Card (ISIC)
isic.org

STA Travel
30 Third Avenue.
Map 4 F1.
Tel (212) 473-6100.

Also at: 2871 Broadway.
Map 20 E4. **Tel** (212) 865-2700. statravel.com

Budget Travel
nycgo.com/free
nyc.gov/nyculture

Responsible Tourism

5 Points
31 Great Jones St. **Map** 4 F2. **Tel** (212) 253-5700.
fivepoints restaurant.com

Gramercy Tavern
42 East 20th St. **Map** 9 A5.
Tel (212) 477-6777.
gramercytavern.com

Greenmarket at Union Square
Union Square. **Map** 9 A5.
cenyc.org

Slow Food NYC
slowfoodnyc.org

Personal Security and Health

New York is one of the US's safest large cities. There is a good level of security in the city, the transportation system, and at airports, and the city's police force is very much in evidence around Manhattan. As in any major metropolis, there are places where travelers would be foolish to venture after dark alone, such as city parks and quiet streets. But if you keep your wits about you and stick to the following guidelines, you should enjoy a trouble-free and pleasant visit to New York City.

New York City police officers patrolling the streets

Police

The New York City Police Department has around-the-clock foot, horse, bike, and car patrols. These are concentrated in specific areas at critical times – for instance, the Theater District aftershow times. There is also a police presence on the subways and buses, and this is reflected in the dramatic drop in crime statistics.

Lost and Stolen Property

There is no city-wide lost-and-found service, but the Metropolitan Transit Authority (MTA) *(see p383)* has a lost-and-found department for city buses and subways, and the Taxi Commission *(see p379)* will assist passengers who have left their belongings in a cab. The lost-and-found rooms at Grand Central and Penn train stations are well managed, with helpful staff. If you don't know who to contact, phone 311 for guidance.

In the event of loss or theft of valuables, report all missing items to the police, or **Crime Victims Hot Line** and make sure you get a copy of the police report for your insurance claim. Keep the receipts of expensive items as proof of possession.

If your passport is stolen, report the theft immediately to your consulate *(see p363)*. Lost or stolen credit cards should also be reported promptly so that your account can be blocked. American Express *(see p367)* has offices in the city where new cards can be processed quickly, and other card companies can often provide replacements. It is always a good idea to separate your credit and debit cards so that if a wallet is lost, you have a backup card.

What to be Aware of

Manhattan has become quite a safe place to roam, but pickpockets do operate and common sense still rules, as in any big city. Be alert, and walk as if you know where you're going. Avoid eye contact and confrontations with down-and-outs. If someone asks you for money, be careful and do not be drawn into conversation.

It is better to avoid deserted locations late at night. Even if there is no actual danger, empty streets may make you feel uneasy. Neighborhoods such as parts of the Lower East Side, Chinatown, or midtown west of Broadway bustle through dinner hours but feel empty after 10pm or so. The Financial District is deserted after business hours, and even the very trendy TriBeCa and SoHo areas are empty late at night. Subways stay crowded until around 11pm, but many may not be advisable later. If you can't find or afford a taxi, try to travel with a group and keep to the main streets.

Parks are not recommended after dark, unless there is a concert or other event. If you want to go for a jog, ask your hotel concierge for a map of safe routes. In crowds, take precautions to avoid being pickpocketed.

When walking in the street, keep your wallet in an inconspicuous place, never in a back pocket, and have your MetroCard or change handy for bus fares – it's best not to have to dig into your purse or wallet while standing in line. Never stop to count your money on the street, and be aware of

It is best to travel in groups and stick to the main streets and avenues

Police car

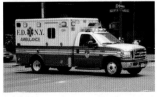
Ambulance

Fire engine

strangers watching at bank ATMs. Defeat purse snatchers by carrying your bag with the clasp facing toward you and the shoulder strap across your body.

Wise travelers always leave valuable jewelry at home or stored at the hotel. Do not allow anyone except hotel and airport personnel to carry your luggage or parcels, and stow your valuables and camera in a locked suitcase or a closet safe when you leave your hotel room.

In an Emergency

If you should be involved in a medical emergency, proceed at once to a hospital emergency room. Dial 411, and ask the operator to give you the number of the nearest hospital. Should you need an ambulance, telephone 911, and one will be sent. If you have time and a choice, avoid the crowded city-owned hospitals listed in the Blue Pages telephone book. Instead, choose one of the many private hospitals listed in the Yellow Pages (see

also Directory box). If your travel medical insurance is in order, you won't have to worry about costs, but remember that national insurance in other countries is not valid in the US.

If the situation is not urgent, ask your hotel to call a doctor or dentist to visit you in your room or to recommend one. You can find one yourself through the **NY Hotel Urgent Medical Services** or **NYU Dental Care**. The Beth Israel Medical Center has an excellent walk-in clinic, **DOCS**. For more general advice and information, call **Travelers' Aid**, a national organization geared to helping travelers. Note that the cost of prescriptions may be higher than in your home country.

Hospitals and Pharmacies

If you must visit a doctor or hospital, be prepared to undergo an expensive experience: some of the city's practitioners and facilities are among the best in the country, and they charge accordingly. The best way to protect yourself against large medical costs is with comprehensive travel insurance. Note that you will have to pay and then reclaim the money. Hospitals accept most credit cards, but physicians and dentists are more likely to want payment in cash. The city has many 24-hour pharmacies, some will often fill a prescription while you wait.

A 24-hour pharmacy, one of several in the city

Travel Insurance

Travel insurance is highly recommended, mainly because of the high cost of medical care. There are many types and levels of coverage, with prices dependent on the length of your trip and the number of people covered.

Among the most important features are emergency medical and dental care, trip cancellation, baggage and travel-document loss, and accidental dismemberment or death. Many policies will cover all of these items.

DIRECTORY
Police

All Emergency Services
Tel 911 (or 0).

Crime Victims Hot Line
Tel (212) 577-7777.

In an Emergency

DOCS
55 E 34th St. **Map** 8 F2.
Tel (212) 252-6000.
One of three branches.

NY Hotel Urgent Medical Services
Tel (212) 737-1212.

NYU Dental Care
345 E 24th St/First Ave. **Map** 9 B4.
Tel (212) 998-9800, (212) 998-9828 (weekends and after 9pm).

Travelers' Aid
JFK Airport, Terminal 410.
Tel (718) 656-4870.

Hospitals and Pharmacies

Duane Reade
4 Times Square, near Broadway.
Map 8 E1. **Tel** (646) 366-8047.

Midtown Hospital Emergency Rooms
11th St and Seventh Ave.
Map 3 C1. **Tel** (212) 604-7998.

NYU Medical Center
560 First Avenue at 33rd Street.
Map 9 C3. **Tel** (212) 263-5550.

Rite Aid
50th St/Eighth Ave. **Map** 12 D4.
Tel (212) 247-8384.

St. Luke's Roosevelt
58th St and Ninth Ave.
Map 12 D3. **Tel** (212) 523-6800.

Banks and Currency

New York is the nation's banking center. It has a wealth of local, regional, and major national banks, plus some retail branches of the leading foreign banks. HSBC and Barclays are well represented in the city; the banks of Australia, Canada, Ireland, Scotland, Japan, and Turkey also all have offices or branches. Exchange bureaux are located in airports, the major train stations, and in various locations throughout the city, though you will probably get a better rate of exchange from a bank.

American Express charge cards

Banking

New York banks are generally open weekdays from 9am to 6pm. Several banks open earlier or close later in the evening to suit commuters' needs, and many now stay open on Saturday 9am–3pm. Tellers are available to help customers inside the bank, or you can use a cash withdrawal machine (ATM). At most banks, all the tellers will cash traveler's checks and exchange your currency.

ATM (machine) for cash withdrawal

ATMs

Automated teller machines (ATMs) can be found in most bank lobbies. They enable you to obtain American currency 24 hours a day from your bank account using a debit card. ATMs usually issue American banknotes in $20 denominations. Among the many advantages of ATMs is the swift, secure exchange of your money at the wholesale rate used between the banks. Bank fees are generally much lower than those charged by money-exchange offices. Before you leave for New York, ask your bank which New York City banks

and ATM systems will accept your bank card and what fees and commissions will be charged on each transaction. Most ATMs are part of either the Cirrus or the Plus network. They accept various US bank cards, MasterCard and Visa cards, and certain others.

On a more cautionary note, always be aware of your surroundings when using an ATM. Make sure you shield your PIN, and, if available, use a machine located within the bank. Be careful when removing your card at the machine.

Credit Cards and Traveler's Checks

MasterCard, **American Express**, **Visa**, and **Diners Club** cards are widely accepted throughout the United States, regardless of which company or bank issued them. These cards can also be used for purchases, as well as to obtain cash advances from ATMs. Before you travel, it is a good idea to phone your card provider and inform them that you will be abroad, or you may find that your card gets blocked when you start using it in New York. Charges may be higher when using a credit card – check with your bank before you leave.

In the United States, you can use a credit card to pay for most purchases in store and online. Major expenses such as tours, travel packages, and expensive rentals are all best paid for by credit card. Using a card also means that you can avoid carrying large sums of money around with you.

Traveler's checks issued in dollars by American Express and

Thomas Cook are widely accepted without a fee by most department stores, shops, hotels, and restaurants in New York. Traveler's checks in other currencies, including sterling, are not universally accepted. Major hotels may have cashiers that will exchange traveler's checks, but more often than not you will need to visit a bank. Exchange rates for foreign currency are printed daily in *The New York Times* and *Wall Street Journal* and may be posted in bank windows. American Express checks may also be exchanged without a fee at American Express offices.

Among the most well-established foreign-exchange brokers are **Travelex Currency Services Inc.** and American Express. All brokers are listed in the Yellow Pages under **"Foreign Money Brokers."** When you use the services of a foreign-exchange broker, you will have to pay a fee, which will vary widely from one place to the next. There will also be a commission.

Banking company **Chase** has over 400 locations where you can exchange money, and there are scores of hole-in-the-wall check-cashing shops in Manhattan. **TD Bank** also has branches throughout Manhattan, many of which are open on Saturdays and until 8pm on weekdays. Both Chase and TD Bank are listed in the Yellow Pages.

Wiring Money

In emergencies, you can arrange to have money wired to you through **MoneyGram** or **Western Union**, though there is a considerable fee.

Coins

American coins come in 1-, 5-, 10-, 25- and 50-cent pieces. A gold-tone $1 coin is also in circulation, as are the State quarters, which feature a historical scene on one side. One-dollar coins are not popular, however, and you will receive them mainly as change from vending machines. Each value of coin has a popular name: 25-cent pieces are called quarters, 10-cent pieces are called dimes, 5-cent pieces are called nickels, and 1-cent pieces are called pennies.

1-cent coin
(a penny)

5-cent coin
(a nickel)

10-cent coin
(a dime)

25-cent coin
(a quarter)

1-dollar coin

Bank Notes (Bills)

The units of currency in the United States are dollars and cents. There are 100 cents to a dollar. Bank notes come in the following denominations: $1, $5, $10, $20, $50, and $100. Security features include subtle color hues and improved color-shifting ink in the lower right hand corner of the face of each note.

DIRECTORY

Credit Cards and Traveler's Checks

American Express
Tel (212) 758-6510.
W americanexpress.com

Chase
W chase.com

Diners Club
W dinersclubus.com

MasterCard
Tel (800) 424-7787 (ATM locator).
W mastercard.com

TD Bank
W tdbank.com

Thomas Cook
W thomascook.com/money

Travelex Currency Services Inc.
Tel (212) 265-6063.
W travelex.com

Visa
Tel (800) 843-7587. W visa.com

Wiring Money

MoneyGram
W moneygram.com

Western Union
W westernunion.com

1-dollar bill ($1)

5-dollar bill ($5)

10-dollar bill ($10)

20-dollar bill ($20)

50-dollar bill ($50)

100-dollar bill ($100)

Communications and Media

The wide use of cellular telephones and the Internet has changed the communications picture in most of the world, and New York is no exception. Though some public telephones may still be found in hotel lobbies, they have disappeared from city streets. Visitors will find the city is well supplied with mobile telephone stores, Internet cafés, and public access to computers and Wi-Fi. The variety of readily available local newspapers and magazines makes it easy for visitors to keep up with world news as well as the latest dining and entertainment options in the city. New York 1, the all-local TV outlet found at Channel 1, is a quick source for up-to-the minute weather reports and news.

Using a laptop in the New York Public Library

Reaching the Right Number

- Five area codes are used in New York: 212, 646, 917 (cell phones) are for Manhattan; the other boroughs use 718 and 347. Calls to 800, 888, 866, and 877 numbers are free.
- To call any number in Manhattan, even in your same area code, you must first dial 1.
- To make an international direct call, dial 011 followed by the country code (Australia: 61; New Zealand: 64; UK: 44), then the city or area code (minus the first 0) and the local number.
- International Directory Inquiries are on 00. International operator assistance is on 01.

Cell Phones

Visitors who wish to use their own cell phone in the US will need a tri-band phone and a SIM card that has been set up for "roaming." Ask your cell-phone provider if you are unsure whether your phone is ready to be used abroad.

Note that you are charged for the calls you receive as well as for the calls you make. However, some cell-phone companies offer "bundles" of calls to save costs while you are away.

If you are going to be in New York for some time, buy a sim card for better rates on local calls or rent a telephone. **Cellhire** offers rentals for $19 per week, with charges of 20 cents per minute and overseas rates from 49 cents.

Public Telephones

If you can find a public telephone, you will see that the setup is standard. Few use credit cards, but you can buy prepaid phone cards from newsstands for long-distance calls; they can be bought in $5, $10, and $25 amounts. The cards offer good savings compared to standard rates. Most phones are coin-operated and take 5-, 10-, and 25-cent coins. In some locations the pay phone may belong to an independent company. The independents are often more expensive and less reliable. Regulations require each public pay phone to post information about charges, toll-free numbers, and how to make calls using other carriers. Look for the Verizon logo on the box to be sure the phone will reach all numbers at standard rates. Within all boroughs of New York City, the standard charge, around 25 cents, buys 3 minutes' talking time. International rates for calls dialed from a land line vary.

US Postal Service logo

Internet

Visitors will find many ways to access the Internet in New York. The **Times Square Information Center** provides free use, as does the **New York Public Library** at its main facilities and all 85 branches. Almost all hotels offer the use of computers, but some hotel business centers can be expensive. Most hotels also have Wi-Fi, though you may have to pay. (In hotels' public areas, however, Wi-Fi is often complimentary.) **FedEx Office Center** locations around town have computer rentals at 30 cents per minute. Rates are better at Internet cafés. Some, such as the **Netzone Internet Café**, stay open late into the night; others, like **Cyber Café**, focus on the snacks and coffee. Expect to pay about $6 for 30 minutes. **The Village Copier** has computers for rent and offers printing and design services.

There is free Wi-Fi at all libraries, Barnes & Noble stores, and in most city parks and plazas below 59th Street, including Bryant Park and Union Square. Cafés such as Starbucks have Wi-Fi for around 10 cents per minute.

Postal Services

The city's main **General Post Office** is open 24 hours a day. Stamps can be bought here, from branch offices, and from some drugstores and news-stands. As well as at post offices, letters can be mailed at your hotel's concierge desk (which usually sells stamps too); in letter slots in office-building lobbies; and in street mailboxes. These are usually painted blue, or red, white, and blue. The mail is generally not picked up on Sundays. Post offices are shown on the Street Finder maps *(see pp386–7)*.

All letters are sent first class. The post office also offers several special-delivery services: Express Mail service, for next-day delivery; Global Express Guaranteed, which delivers overseas in one–three days; and Express Mail International, with delivery in 3–5 days. Private express services such as **FedEx**, **UPS**, or **DHL** can be arranged through hotels. Online services are available.

Newspapers and Magazines

New York has one major daily newspaper, *The New York Times*, and two colorful tabloids, *The Daily News* and the *New York Post*. Two free morning tabloids are also available, *AM New York* and *Metro*. Both are useful for local events and a brief run-down of the news. The best entertainment listings are found in the Friday and Sunday editions of *The New York Times* and in weekly magazines such as *Time Out New York*, *New York*, and *The New Yorker*. The *Village Voice*, a free weekly newspaper, also has entertainment listings, geared largely to a younger audience.

The free weekly *Where*, distributed through hotel con-cierges, lists major museums, their opening hours, locations, and any exhibitions. *Art Now/New York Gallery Guide*, also free, is released in art galleries monthly. It lists current exhibit-ions and has maps showing where they are located.

You can buy foreign newspapers at **Around the World**, **Hotalings**, **Barnes & Noble** bookstores, airports, and some hotels.

Television and Radio

TV program schedules for each day can be found in the local dailies. *The Daily News* on Sunday has a useful pull-out section of the next week's programs. The choice of TV stations in New York is vast. Major networks include CBS on channel 2, NBC on channel 4, ABC on channel 7, and WNYW (Fox) on channel 5. PBS offers cultural and educational fare on channel 13. Cable TV offers everything from the Arts & Entertainment Network (channel 46) to sports on ESPN (channel 28) and public-access programs.

AM radio stations include WCBS News (880AM), WINS News (1010AM), and WFAN Sports (660AM). Some FM stations are WWFS– contem-porary (102.7FM), WBGO– jazz (88.3FM), and WQXR– classical (105.9FM).

DIRECTORY

Useful Numbers

Directory Inquiries
Tel 411 or 10-10-9000.
w superpages.com
w yellowpages.com

Cell Phones

Cellhire
45 Broadway, 20th Floor.
Map 1 C3. **Tel** (888) 950-9391.
w cellhire.com

Internet

Cyber Café
250 W 49th St. **Map** 11 B5.
Tel (212) 333-4109.

FedEx Office Center
w fedex.com

**Library for
the Performing Arts**
40 Lincoln Center Plaza.
Map 11 C2. **Tel** (212) 870-1630.

Netzone Internet Café
28 W 32nd St, 5th Fl. **Map** 8 F3.

New York Public Library
5th Avenue and 42nd Street.
Map 8 F1. **Tel** (212) 939-0653.

**Times Square
Information Center**
1560 Broadway. **Map** 12 E5.
w timessquarenyc.org

The Village Copier
20 E 13th St. **Map** 4 F1.

Postal Services

DHL
Tel (800) 782-7892.

FedEx
Tel (800) 225-5345.

General Post Office
421 Eighth Ave. **Map** 8 D2.
Tel (800) ASK-USPS or (800) 222-1811. Priority and Express Mail:
Tel (800) 463-3339. w usps.com

UPS
Tel (800) 742-5877.

Newspapers and Magazines

Around the World
28 W 40th St. **Map** 8 F1.
148 W 37th St. **Map** 8 E2.

Barnes & Noble
1972 Broadway at 68th Street.
Map 11 C1.

Hotalings
630 W 52nd St. **Map** 11 B4.

Express Mail

Priority Mail

Standard Mail

GETTING TO NEW YORK CITY

A lot of global airlines run direct flights to New York. The city is also very well served by charter and domestic services. Price wars among airlines have reduced fares, and domestic flights are an affordable form of travel. Early reservation and seat selection are good ways to ensure a more comfortable flight. New York City is also a regular docking point for many cruise ships. The train network across the United States is not as extensive as that found in Europe, but Amtrak, the national carrier, has several comfortable and clean long-distance trains that run from New York. Interstate and long-distance buses are a cheaper way to travel and usually have air-conditioning and on-board toilets. For information on arriving in New York, see the map on *pages 374–5*.

Taxis heading into LaGuardia airport

Air Travel

New York can be reached by air direct from most major cities. The flight from London takes about 8 hours, however, there are no direct flights from Australia or New Zealand. Instead, the airlines fly to the West Coast or Asia, which takes around 10–14 hours, land, refuel, and then continue on to New York.

Allow extra time at the airport, for both arriving and departing, and for the careful passport and security checks in the United States.

Among the main airline carriers to New York are **Air Canada**, **Delta**, **British Airways**, **American Airlines**, **Virgin Atlantic**, and **United Airlines**. All international flights arrive at either JFK Newark airports.

Tickets and Fares

APEX (Advance Purchase Excursion) tickets for the scheduled airlines are usually the cheapest return fares apart from package tours. They must be bought at least 14 days in advance and are valid for a stay of 7–30 days. The least expensive international air fares to and from Europe are found from November to March, excluding holiday periods. Budget airlines flying within the US – such as **Southwest Airlines**, **JetBlue**, and **AirTran** – often have better fares than the major airlines.

Booking online can help save money. Websites such as wwwlastminute.com, www.priceline.com, and www.expedia.com have flight-and-hotel deals that tend to be cheaper than booking the two separately. Search engines like www.kayak.com are useful for comparing the costs of all the different airlines and online travel stores.

On Arrival

Be prepared for extra security precautions when you visit the United States. Make sure that you leave ample time for checking in – ask your flight carrier what time you need to arrive at the airport for your flight. They can also give you details about any restrictions on hand luggage.

The airline you are flying with will give you an I-94 form to fill out before you land. It asks simple questions such as your name, birth date, country of citizenship, passport number, and current address. Have this form and your passport ready for the Customs and Border Protection officer who will inspect your documents (get in the line that says "non-US passports"). The officer may ask you questions such as why you are visiting and how long and where you will stay. Your fingerprints will be taken, and you will be photographed with a digital camera. The I-94 is in two parts; one part will be for you to keep. This part must be returned on departing.

AirTrain en route to JFK

John F. Kennedy Airport (JFK)

Every year, over 40 million passengers pass through New York's main airport, JFK. It serves over 100 airlines in nine terminals and is the main New York entry for international flights. JFK lies 15 miles (24 km) southeast of Manhattan, in the borough of Queens, about 45–60 minutes from midtown. However, airport traffic is often heavy, so the trip can take longer.

Larger carriers like American Airlines, British Airways, Delta, and United Airlines have their own arrivals and departure terminals, which they may share with some of their partners. Terminal 4 is the main arrival area for over 50 international

Planes arriving at Newark airport

airlines, and Terminal 1 serves many foreign carriers, including Air China, Air France, Alitalia, and Japan Airlines.

Foreign-exchange offices and ATMs are located in all terminals, and each terminal has a service desk to help book hotels and answer any transportation questions. Courtesy phones are also provided by car-rental companies.

Dispatchers regulate the line for the yellow taxis waiting outside each terminal. There is a flat fee of $45, plus tolls and tip. New York Airport Service buses go to Grand Central, Penn Station, and the Port Authority; tickets start at $13. The Express Shuttle Service ($14) stops at many midtown hotels. **SuperShuttle** runs shared vans that will go to specific addresses for about $23 for the first guest and $10 for each additional passenger. Advance reservations are needed for the trip back to the airport. Air-Link has a similar service for $19. Round-trip fares are cheaper.

A light-rail system, **AirTrain JFK** connects to the A train at Howard Beach, and to the E, J, and Z trains and Long Island Rail Road (for Penn Station) at Jamaica. The AirTrain costs $5, the subway $2.25.

If you are feeling rich **Helicopter Flight Services** offer a 10-minute helicopter ride for $850 to East 34th Street.

Newark Liberty Airport (EWR)

Newark, New York's second-largest international airport, is about 16 miles (26 km) southwest of Manhattan, in New Jersey.

Most international flights into Newark arrive at Terminal B. Baggage trolleys are free for passengers arriving on international flights. Foreign-exchange desks and ATMs can also be found in the terminal, but there is no left-luggage room.

The Ground Transportation Services desk can help arrange private onward travel. Courtesy phones are provided by limousine and car-rental firms. Many of these have a free shuttle service to their rental offices.

As with JFK, there are taxi stands located outside most arrival areas, and uniformed taxi dispatchers will help you hail a cab. The taxi ride into Manhattan takes about 40–60 minutes and will cost you up to $50, plus tolls and tip.

Olympia Airport Express buses to Manhattan stop at the Port Authority Bus Terminal, 42nd Street near 5th Avenue, and Grand Central Station. The journey time is no longer than a cab, but the fare is only $15. Round-trip fares are cheaper.

AirTrain Newark takes approximately 10 minutes to link to NJ Transit and Amtrak trains, which then take around 25 minutes to arrive at Penn station. The total journey costs about $12 on NJ Transit, or $32 on Amtrak.

Hotels can be booked on arrival through courtesy phones in all terminals at Newark that link directly to various Manhattan hotels. Staff are on hand to help you make the best choice.

LaGuardia Airport (LGA)

LaGuardia is a busy airport serving domestic carriers from all over the US. It lies 8 miles (13 km) east of Manhattan, on the north side of Long Island, in Queens. The trip to Manhattan averages 30 minutes.

Upon arrival, you can rent luggage trolleys from the baggage-claim area next to the luggage carousels. Sky-caps, people who check in your luggage for you, are on hand to assist you. Baggage can also be left in the Tele-Trip business center on the departure level. A foreign-currency exchange desk and ATMs are located in the Central Terminal. A free bus service runs between each of the terminals and parking areas from 5am to 2am.

Buses and taxis into the city and its suburbs depart from the front of the terminal buildings. If you are approached by other taxis offering you transportation, do not accept. These drivers have no insurance, and you will be overcharged. A taxi fare starts at $2.50 and increases by $0.40 every fifth of a mile. A single bus ride is $2.25. The cost of tolls, plus a peak-hour surcharge of $1 (4–8pm) weekdays or a night surcharge of 50 cents (8pm–6am), will be added to the taxi fare s hown on the meter.

Terminal at LaGuardia airport

Ocean liner anchored in Manhattan

Arriving by Sea

Cruising past the Statue of Liberty into New York Harbor is a thrilling experience. The city's three cruise ports are popular stopping-off points for many major cruise lines sailing to the Caribbean, Bermuda, Canada, and Europe.

The main **New York Cruise Terminal**, on 12th Avenue between 46th and 54th streets, serves Carnival, Silversea, Holland America, MSC, and NCL lines. Taxis are available at the vehicle entrance, located at 55th Street and 12th Avenue. The M57 and M31 crosstown buses provide convenient, inexpensive access to Midtown, and it is only a 15–20-minute walk to the heart of Manhattan.

The state-of-the-art **Brooklyn Cruise Terminal** was opened in 2006 in Red Hook. It is the port of choice for Cunard and Princess Cruise lines and the home port of the *QM2*, which sails to New York from Southampton several times a year. You can also take the *QM2* from New York to Australia and New Zealand. Taxis from the terminal can drop you in Manhattan or at convenient subway stops into the city.

Royal Caribbean and Celebrity cruise ships use the **Cape Liberty Cruise Port** in Bayonne, on the New Jersey side of New York Harbor. It is 7 miles (11 km) from New York City and about 15 minutes from Newark International Airport. The Hudson–Bergen Light Rail station at 34th Street, an easy taxi ride just 2 miles (3 km) from the port, connects to PATH trains, New

Jersey Transit at Hoboken, and ferry services to and from New York. Visit www.njtransit.com for more information.

Passengers arriving by ship who remain in New York receive the same I-94 form as air passengers and go through the same procedures; *see p370.*

Arriving by Long-Distance Bus

Long-distance buses from all over the US arrive at the **Port Authority Bus Terminal**, on Eighth Avenue, between 40th and 42nd streets. The location is convenient to midtown, and many hotels are within walking distance. Taxis can be found on the Eighth Avenue side of the terminal; the A and C subway stops are located on the lower floors in the terminal; and a one-block-long tunnel leads to Times Square station and other subway connections. The M42 crosstown bus stops at the corner of Eighth Avenue and 42nd Street, and uptown buses are available on Eighth Avenue. Buses from the Port Authority connect with all three airports, and the terminal also serves many busy commuter bus lines to New Jersey. With over 6,000 buses arriving and departing daily, the atmosphere can be hectic at rush hour.

Buses can be an economical way to see the US. **Greyhound Lines** offer a Discovery Pass priced at $246 for seven days ($346 for 15 days). No advance reservations are necessary. Buses are comfortable and air-conditioned, and they have

reclining seats, ample legroom, and usually bathrooms. Greyhound **NeOn** buses – available from New York to Philadelphia (2 hours), Washington, DC (4 hours), Boston (4.5 hours), Toronto (11.5 hours), Montreal (8.5 hours), and other cities – offer free Wi-Fi and plug-ins for devices such as iPods.

Greyhound has a ticket office in the Port Authority Bus Terminal, but it is cheaper to buy tickets over the phone or online. APEX tickets save 25% off the regular price on shorter trips purchased at least 14 days in advance, and 10% (or more) for tickets bought seven days in advance. "Friends and family" rates offer savings of 50% for up to three companions with the purchase of a regular adult fare. Seniors, students, and military personnel have special discounts.

Arriving by Train

Amtrak, the US passenger rail service, connects New York with the rest of the country and Canada. Amtrak trains use **Penn Station** as their New York headquarters *(see p384).* The Metro-North train service and the daily commuter service from upstate New York and Connecticut arrive at Grand Central Terminal *(see p384).*

Amtrak has its own section in Penn Station for ticket sales and separate waiting rooms for coach and high-speed passengers. Tickets can be bought in advance by phone or online and picked up at the station at the ticket window or at automated kiosks. If you pick up tickets at the window, a photo ID will be requested.

Imposing entrance hall of Grand Central Terminal

Taxis are available from the station, and buses run downtown on Seventh Avenue and uptown on Eighth. The Lexington and Broadway lines also serve the station.

Amtrak trains are very comfortable, with ample legroom and snack-bar services, as well as dining cars on longer routes. Sleeping compartments are available on long-distance trips, some with showers and toilets ensuite.

Amtrak's USA Rail Pass allows eight journeys over a 15-day period for $429; children pay half-fare. The most used train service from New York is Amtrak's Northeast Corridor route between Boston, New York, Philadelphia, and Washington, DC. Most of the trains on this route have unreserved seating, but high-speed Acela Express trains offer an hourly service with reserved first-class and business-class seating plus electrical outlets for laptops.

Arriving by Car

Manhattan is an island, so it must be approached via bridge or tunnel. From the south, the

Traffic approaching the George Washington Bridge

entries are from New Jersey via the Holland Tunnel to the Financial District, or the Lincoln Tunnel to Midtown. A more scenic approach is the George Washington Bridge, which arrives at 178th Street to the north of the city.

The Robert Kennedy Bridge (formerly known as the Tri-borough Bridge) has branches from two boroughs connecting to Manhattan. The bridge from Queens, east of the city, is used by those arriving at LaGuardia or JFK airports. The second branch, from the Bronx, approaches Manhattan from the north. The

two bridges merge into one and offer a striking view of the city skyline on the approach.

Those driving in from Queens can avoid tolls by taking the 59th Street Bridge. Queens is also connected to Manhattan by the Midtown Tunnel, which feeds into the Long Island Expressway.

The most famous approach to New York is via the Brooklyn Bridge, with its vistas of the skyscrapers of the downtown Financial District. Brooklyn is also connected to the city by the Brooklyn Battery tunnel.

Bridge and Tunnel Tolls

Most of the major access routes in and out of New York City levy tolls. Tolls for the tunnels to and from Long Island and Brooklyn cost $6.50, as does the Robert Kennedy Bridge. The Lincoln Tunnel, Holland Tunnel, and the George Washington Bridge between New York and New Jersey are free for those leaving New York, but they charge $8 coming into the city. Tolls must be paid in cash. Avoid E-Z Pass lanes, marked with purple signs, which are only for holders of pre-paid passes.

DIRECTORY

Air Travel

Air Canada
Tel (888) 247-2262.
W aircanada.ca

Airport Information Service
Tel JFK: (718) 244-4444.
EWR: (973) 961-6000.
LGA (718) 533-3400.
W panynj.gov/airports

AirTran
Tel (800) 247-8726.
W airtran.com

American Airlines
Tel (800) 433-7300.
W aa.com

British Airways
Tel (800) AIRWAYS.
W british-airways.com

Delta
Tel (800) 241-4141.
W delta.com

Helicopter Flight Services
Tel (212) 355-0801.
W heliny.com

JetBlue
Tel (800) 538-2583.
W jetblue.com

Olympia Airport Express
Tel 877-863-9275.
W coachusa.com

Southwest Airlines
Tel (800) 435-9792.
W southwest.com

SuperShuttle
Tel (212) 209-7000.
W supershuttle.com

United Airlines
Tel (800) 241-6522.
W united.com

Virgin Atlantic
Tel (800) 862-8621.
W virgin-atlantic.com

Arriving by Sea

Brooklyn Cruise Terminal
Pier 12, Building 112,
Bowne Street,
Red Hook.
Tel (718) 246-2794.
W nycruise.com

Cape Liberty Cruise Port
14 Port Terminal Blvd,
Bayonne.
Tel (201) 823-3737.
W cruiseliberty.com

New York Cruise Terminal
Pier 90, 711
12th Avenue.
Map 11 B4.
Tel (212) 246-5450.
W nycruise.com

Arriving by Long-Distance Bus

Greyhound Lines
Tel (800) 231-2222.
W greyhound.com

NeOn
W neonbus.com

Port Authority Bus Terminal
Eighth Ave and
W 40th St.
Map 8 D1.
Tel (212) 564-8484.
W panynj.gov

Arriving by Train

Amtrak
Tel (800) 872-7245.
W amtrak.com

Penn Station
Eighth Ave and 31st St.
Map 8 E3.
W amtrak.com

Arriving in New York

This map shows the links between New York's three airports and the center of Manhattan. It also illustrates rail connections linking New York to the rest of the United States and Canada. Travel information, including times for bus and rail services, and connections to subway lines, is listed in each information box. The passenger ship terminal, New York's key point of arrival for the flood of post-war immigrants, is located on 55th Street. Port Authority Bus Terminal, on the West Side, provides services across the city.

Ships at the passenger terminal

🚢 Passenger Ship Terminal
Piers 88–92 for some cruise ships. Cunard and Princess services use Brooklyn Cruise Terminal.

Key

▬ New York Airport Service and Super Shuttle *see pp370–71*

▬ Long Island Rail Road *see pp384–5*

▬ New Jersey Transit buses *see p371*

▬ Olympia Airport Express *see p371*

▬ AirTrain *see p371*

▬ Subway A *see p381*

🚌 Port Authority Bus Terminal
All long-distance buses arrive and depart here; links to all city airports.

🚆 Penn Station
Long-distance trains serve the US and *Canada;* commuter trains to *Long Island* and *New Jersey;* AirTrain Newark to *Newark Airport.* 🚆 Amtrak, Long Island Rail Road and New Jersey Transit services. Ⓜ A, C, E, 1, 2, 3.

Passenger Ship Terminal 🚢

Theater District

Port Authority Bus Terminal 🚌

🚁 West 30th St Heliport

Chelsea and the Garment District

Penn Station

Super Shuttle buses take passengers to any point between Battery Park and 227th St.

Greenwich Village

East Village

SoHo and TriBeCa

Lower East Side

✈ Newark
🚌 Olympia Airport Express
4am–1am, every 15–30 mins to **Penn Station, Grand Central** and **Port Authority.**
🚌 New Jersey Transit Every 15–20 mins to **Port Authority.**
🚆 New Jersey Transit or Amtrak to Penn Station
5am–midnight, every 5–20 mins Mon–Fri; every 50 mins Sat & Sun.

Lower Manhattan

Seaport and the Civic Center

Pier 11

The Port Authority of New York and New Jersey, operator of JFK, Newark, and LaGuardia airports, has invested in the AirTrain, a rail link that connects JFK and Newark to the city subway system.

0 kilometers 2
0 miles 1

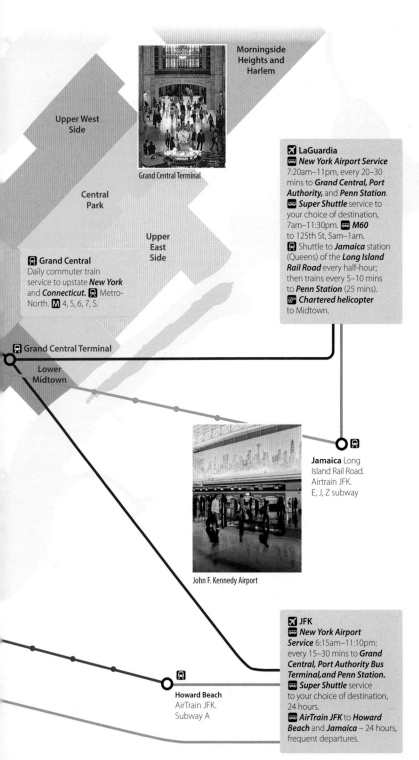

Morningside
Heights and
Harlem

Upper West
Side

Grand Central Terminal

Central
Park

Upper
East
Side

✈ LaGuardia
🚌 *New York Airport Service*
7:20am–11pm, every 20–30
mins to *Grand Central, Port
Authority,* and *Penn Station*.
🚌 *Super Shuttle* service to
your choice of destination,
7am–11:30pm. 🚌 *M60*
to 125th St, 5am–1am.
🚆 Shuttle to *Jamaica* station
(Queens) of the *Long Island
Rail Road* every half-hour;
then trains every 5–10 mins
to *Penn Station* (25 mins).
🚁 *Chartered helicopter*
to Midtown.

🚆 Grand Central
Daily commuter train
service to upstate *New York*
and *Connecticut*. 🚆 Metro-
North. Ⓜ 4, 5, 6, 7, S.

🚆 **Grand Central Terminal**

Lower
Midtown

Jamaica Long
Island Rail Road.
Airtrain JFK.
E, J, Z subway

John F. Kennedy Airport

✈ JFK
🚌 *New York Airport
Service* 6:15am–11:10pm;
every 15–30 mins to *Grand
Central, Port Authority Bus
Terminal,and Penn Station*.
🚌 *Super Shuttle* service
to your choice of destination,
24 hours.
🚆 *AirTrain JFK* to *Howard
Beach* and *Jamaica* – 24 hours,
frequent departures.

🚆 **Howard Beach**
AirTrain JFK.
Subway A

GETTING AROUND NEW YORK

With more than 6,000 miles (9,650 km) of streets, getting around New York might seem a problem, but the city is actually a network of small neighborhoods that are connected via subway or bus. Each one is also quite walkable or easy to get around on public transportation. Midtown Manhattan, for example, with many of the major sights, runs 25 blocks from 34th to 59th streets, and if you should tire, you can hop on a bus that goes down Fifth Avenue or up Sixth.

Subways are the quickest way to get around. Service is frequent, they are inexpensive and reliable, and they make stops throughout Manhattan. The city's bus service is also reliable and convenient but can be slow in traffic. Weekly or unlimited MetroCards, valid for all public transportation, provide excellent value. Taxis are the best option for door-to-door transit, but they can be expensive if you are held up by traffic.

Green Travel

New York is working hard to be more energy-efficient for those traveling around town. Back in the 1990s, the city was a pioneer in launching an alternative-fuel vehicle program aimed at cutting emissions and making its bus

Cyclist in Central Park

fleet one of the cleanest in the world. It was the first in the US to switch all diesel buses to ultra-low sulfur fuel. Cleaner-burning engines have been installed, and buses have been equipped with filters, cutting emissions by as much as 95 percent. The MTA currently has around 2,000 hybrid-electric buses in operation. Numerous bicycle lanes have also been added around town for those brave enough to use them amid the heavy city traffic.

When it comes to leaving the city, the US train system is quite limited, but New York has some of the better connections, especially Amtrak's East Coast Metroliner and Acela trains *(see pp373 and 385)*.

Finding your way Around New York

Manhattan's avenues run north to south; New Yorkers say "uptown" and "downtown." Streets (except in the older areas) run east to west, and are referred to as "cross-town." Fifth Avenue is the divider between East and West street addresses.

Most streets in midtown are one-way. In general, traffic is eastbound on even-numbered streets and westbound on odd-numbered streets. Avenues also tend to be one-way. First, Third (above 23rd Street), Madison, Avenue of the Americas (Sixth), Eighth, and Tenth avenues are northbound, while Second, Lexington, Fifth, Seventh, and Ninth avenues and Broadway below 59th Street are south-bound. There is two-way traffic

Finding an Address

A useful formula has been devised to help pinpoint any avenue address. By dropping the last digit of the address, dividing the remainder by 2, then adding or subtracting the key number given here, you will discover the nearest cross street. For example: to find No. 826 Lexington Avenue, you have to drop the 6; divide 82 by 2, which is 41; then add 22 (the key number). Therefore, the nearest cross street is 63rd Street.

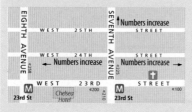

Avenue Address	Key Number	Avenue Address	Key Number
1st Ave	+3	9th Ave	+13
2nd Ave	+3	10th Ave	+14
3rd Ave	+10	Amsterdam Ave	+60
4th Ave	+8	Audubon Ave	+165
5th Ave, up to 200	+13	Broadway above	
5th Ave, up to 400	+16	23rd St	-30
5th Ave, up to 600	+18	Central Park W, divide	
5th Ave, up to 775	+20	full number by 10	+60
5th Ave 775–1286,	do	Columbus Ave	+60
not divide by 2	-18	Convent Ave	+127
5th Ave, up to 1500	+45	Lenox Ave	+110
5th Ave, up to 2000	+24	Lexington Ave	+22
(6th) Ave of		Madison Ave	+26
the Americas	-12	Park Ave	+35
7th Ave below 110th St		Park Ave South	+8
	+12	Riverside Drive, divide	
7th Ave above 110th St		full number by 10	+72
	+20	St Nicholas Ave	+110
8th Ave	+10	West End Ave	+60

Walking through Chelsea

on York, Park, 11th, and 12th avenues and on Broadway above 60th Street.

The grid of streets is rectangular rather than square, so crosstown blocks are longer than north–south avenue blocks. To gauge distances, 20 north–south city blocks equal about 1 mile (1.6 km); it takes only about five to eight crosstown (east–west) blocks to make up that distance.

Some streets have more than one name – for example, Avenue of the Americas is better known as Sixth Avenue. Park Avenue is called Park Avenue South below 34th Street and Fourth Avenue below 14th Street. The maps in this guide give the names most often used.

Planning your Journey

Buses and subways are busiest during the rush hours: 8–10am and 4:30–6:30pm, Monday to Friday. Through-out these periods, it may be easier to face the crowds on foot than attempt any journey by bus, taxi, or subway. At other times of day and during certain holiday periods (see p55), the traffic is often much lighter, and you should reach your destination quickly.

There are, of course, a few exceptions. When the president or other political celebrities visit, security measures can cause major disruption to the traffic. The area around Seventh Avenue, south of 42nd Street, is likely to be busy during the day with the truck and handcart traffic of New York's garment industry.

Avoid Fifth Avenue on parade days, which often take place in spring and fall. On these days, and during the New York Marathon, it is difficult to get across town as bus services are disrupted. If such events are scheduled during your visit, plan to see other areas of the city on that day. Subway traffic will not be affected, though trains may be more crowded than usual.

Driving in New York

Heavy traffic, lack of parking, and expensive rental cars make driving in New York a frustrating experience. If you decide to drive, you must wear a seat belt by law. Driving is on the right, and the speed limit is usually 30 mph (48 kmh) in midtown. Most streets are one-way, and there are traffic lights at almost every corner. Unlike the rest of New York State, you can never turn right on a red light unless there is a sign indicating otherwise.

To rent a car, you must be at least 25 years old. You will need a valid driver's license (foreign visitors need an International Driver's License), a passport, and a credit card.

Car Insurance

Unless you are adequately covered by your own insurance policy, you should take out damage and liability protection when renting a car. Check with your insurance company before you travel. Your car-rental agency will be able to provide you with a policy if necessary.

Parking

Parking in Manhattan is costly and difficult. You can use parking garages, or see if your hotel includes overnight parking, but both options are very expensive.

The busiest streets in midtown do not allow parking. Other streets may have curbside meters for short-term (20–60 minutes) parking. Yellow street and curb markings mean no parking.

"Alternate-side" parking applies on most of the city's side streets. Cars may usually be left all day and night, but they must be moved to the other side of the street before 8am the next day. For specific information, call 311.

Car-rental logos

Penalties

If you receive a parking ticket, you have seven days to pay the fine or to appeal. If you have any queries about your ticket, call the **Parking Violations Bureau**. If you cannot find your car, call 311 to find out if it has been towed. The **Traffic Department Tow Pound** is open 24 hours a day, Monday to Saturday. Redeeming your car will cost $185 towing fee, $70 execution fee, and $10–15 per day storage fee. Traveler's checks, certified checks, money orders, and cash are accepted. If you have rented the car, the contract must be produced, and only the authorized driver may redeem the vehicle.

Vibrant Times Square with its neon billboards

Taxis driving through an intersection in SoHo

Taxis

There are more than 12,000 yellow cabs in New York, easily identified by their color, the distinctive logo on the door, and the light on top. A taxi can carry up to four passengers, with a single fare covering everyone on board. All taxis are metered and can issue printed receipts. Taxis can be hailed anywhere on the street, but taxi stands are scarce. The best places to find waiting cabs are outside Penn and Grand Central stations. Cabs indicate that they are available by turning on the top light. This goes off if the cab is occupied or if the side lights indicate "off duty."

Licensed taxis undergo periodic inspections and are insured against accidents and losses. Non-licensed, or "gypsy," cabs are unlikely to have these safeguards. They will have no meters and charge what they please.

Once the cab driver accepts a passenger, the meter starts ticking at $2.50, plus a state tax surcharge of 50 cents. The fare increases 40 cents after each additional one-fifth of a mile (292 yards/267 meters) or every 60 seconds of waiting time. There is an additional 50-cent charge from 8pm to 6am, and a $1 extra charge from 4 to 8pm on weekdays. It is customary to tip the driver about 15%. Taxi drivers will accept credit cards.

Make sure your driver understands where you want to go before you start your ride. If you have a map of the area,

mark the locations you want. A driver should not ask you your destination until after you've sat down, and by law, they must take you anywhere in the city. They must follow your requests not to smoke or talk on a cell phone, to open or close a window, and to pick up or drop off passengers as you direct. Each yellow cab displays the driver's photograph and registered number next to the meter. If drivers don't comply with your requests, you can report them to the **Taxi & Limousine Commission**.

As an expensive alternative, radio-dispatched sedans can be hired for $40 per hour with a 2 hour minimum.

Walking

All intersections have lamp-posts with clearly marked street names; most have electric traffic signals. The lights show red (stop) and green (go) for vehicles, and "Walk/Don't Walk" signals for pedestrians. Crossing while the "Don't Walk" sign is showing is not recommended, nor is crossing mid-block, referred to in the US as "jay-walking."

Vehicles in the US drive on the right, and there are no markings on the road for pedestrians indicating the direction of traffic. It is best to look both ways before you cross, and beware of cars, trucks, and taxis turning the corner behind you as you start to cross the street.

Midtown has several small parks and plazas where visitors can rest. In the Broadway area you can have a rest with a Times Square view on the high tier of steps behind the TKTS booth (Broadway and 47th St). Some of the surrounding blocks are traffic-free and furnished with chairs. The traffic islands around the Lincoln Center also offer seating (as on p362).

Signs in Midtown

Ferries

The **Circle Line** runs several ferry services a day to the Statue of Liberty and Ellis Island from Battery Park, at the southern tip of Manhattan. The 24-hour **Staten Island Ferry**, also from Battery Park, travels the channel and offers splendid views of lower Manhattan, the Statue of Liberty, Ellis Island, the bridges, and Governors Island. The round trip is the best bargain in New York; it's free.

Water Taxis

The **New York Water Taxi** is mainly a commuter service, but it also offers various tours and a weekend hop-on/hop-off sightseeing boat (mid-Apr–mid-Oct). The route is around New York Harbor, between West 44th and East 34th streets, with stops including Chelsea Pier, World Financial Center, Battery Park, South Street Seaport, the Brooklyn riverfront, and Long Island City. In summer, water taxis provide a service to a couple of man-made beaches in Long Island City and on Governors Island.

A water taxi crossing New York Harbor

Guided Tours

Whichever way you choose to see New York – with the help of a knowledgeable guide, a photographer, a pre-recorded walk, or an exciting trip in a helicopter, boat, or horse-drawn carriage – organized sightseeing trips can save a lot of time and effort. Walking tours give in-depth background information about specific neighborhoods and the city's history and architecture that you might not get on your own. The **Municipal Art Society** is renowned for its knowledge-able guides. Fascinating behind-the-scenes tours are available for the New York Public Library, Metropolitan Opera, and Radio City Music Hall. Bus tours are also a great way to see the city, as you can hop on/hop off as you please *(see also p383)*.

Cycling

Hoping to cut down on auto traffic, the city is making a real effort to create bike paths, which cover over 90 miles (145 km) in Manhattan. It takes courage to travel beside heavy traffic on busy midtown streets; however, trails along the East River and far west side are pleasant and very popular, as are the many roads for bikers in Central Park, where auto traffic is banned on weekends. Visit www.nycbike maps.com for maps of bike routes. You can rent bikes at Columbus Circle or the Loeb Boathouse in Central Park *(see p354)*.

DIRECTORY

Car Rental Agencies

Avis
Tel (800) 331-1212.
ⓦ avis.com

Budget
Tel (800) 527-0700.
ⓦ drivebudget.com

Hertz
Tel (800) 654-3131.
ⓦ hertz.com

National
Tel (800) CAR RENT.
ⓦ nationalcar.com

Parking

Alternate Side Parking Information
Tel 311.

Parking Violations and Towing Information
Tel 311.

Parking Violations Bureau
Tel (718) 802-3636.

Police
Tel 911.

Traffic Department Tow Pound
Pier 76, W 38th St and 12th Ave. **Map** 7 B1.
Tel 311.

Taxis

Taxi & Limousine Commission
Tel 311.

Taxi Lost and Found
Tel 311.

Transportation Department
Tel 311.

Ferries

Circle Line
ⓦ circleline.com

Staten Island Ferry
ⓦ siferry.com

Water Taxis

New York Water Taxi
Tel (212) 742-1969.
ⓦ nywatertaxi.com

Guided Tours

Bicycle Tours: Bite of the Apple Tours
203 W 58th St. **Map** 12 D3.
Tel (212) 541-8759.

Boat Tours: Circle Line Sightseeing Yachts
Pier 83, W 42nd St. **Map** 7 A1. Tel (212) 563-3200.
ⓦ circleline42.com

Spirit of New York
W 23rd and Eighth Ave. **Map** 8 D4.
Tel (866) 211-3805.
ⓦ spiritofnewyork.com

World Yacht, Inc.
Pier 81, W 41st St. **Map** 7 A1. Tel (212) 630-8100.

Building Tours: Grand Central Terminal
E 42nd St at Park Ave. **Map** 13 A5.
Tel (212) 883-2420.
ⓦ grandcentralterminal. com

Heritage Trails
Federal Hall, 26 Wall St. **Map** 1 C3.
ⓦ nps.gov/feha/

Metropolitan Opera Tours
Lincoln Center. **Map** 11 C2. Tel (212) 769-7020.
ⓦ metoperafamily.org

NBC Studio Tour
30 Rockefeller Plaza. **Map** 12 F5. Tel (212) 664-7174.
ⓦ nbcstudiotour.com

New York Public Library
Fifth Ave and 42nd St. **Map** 8 F1. Tel (917) 275-6975. ⓦ nypl.org

Radio City Music Hall Stage Door Tours
Sixth Ave. **Map** 12 F4.
Tel (212) 247-4777.
ⓦ radiocity.com/tours

Walkin' Broadway
1619 Broadway. **Map** 12 E5. Tel (212) 997-5004.

Bus Tours: Gray Line of New York
42nd St and Eighth Ave. **Map** 8 D1.
Tel (212) 397-2620.

Carriage Tours
59th St at Fifth Ave and along Central Park S. **Map** 12 F3.

Helicopter Tours: Liberty
W 30th St and 12th Ave, South Ferry. **Map** 7 B3.
Tel (212) 967-6464.

Walking Tours: Adventures on a Shoestring
300 W 53rd St. **Map** 12 E4.
Tel (212) 265-2663.

Big Apple Greeters
1 Centre St, Suite 2035. **Map** 4 F4.
Tel (212) 669-8159.

Big Onion Walking Tours
76 13th St, Brooklyn.
Tel (212) 439-1090.
ⓦ bigonion.com

Eldridge Street Synagogue
12 Eldridge St. **Map** 5 A5.
Tel (212) 227-8780.

Harlem Spirituals, Inc.
690 Eighth Ave. **Map** 8 D1. Tel (212) 391-0900.

Lower East Side Tenement Museum
108 Orchard St. **Map** 5 A4.
Tel (212) 431-0233.
ⓦ tenement.org

Municipal Art Society
457 Madison Ave.
Map 13 A4. Tel (212) 980-1297. ⓦ mas.org

Wall Street Walks
Tel (212) 209-3379.
ⓦ wallstreetwalks.com

Cycling

Central Park Bike Rental
203 West 58th St. **Map** 12 E3. Tel (212) 541-8759.
ⓦ centralpark biketour.com

Traveling by Subway

The subway is the quickest and most reliable way to travel in the city. The vast system extends over 233 route miles (375 km) and has 468 stations. Most routes operate 24 hours a day throughout the year. The trains are air-conditioned, well lit, safe, and (unless you are riding at rush hour) comfortable. Since the 1980s, a portion of all station-improvement funds has gone to the Arts for Transit project, with some notable results. Keep an eye out for the mosaics, sculptures, and art that decorate many subway and commuter rail stations.

Entrance to Times Square 42nd Street Subway Station

Tickets and Fares

A MetroCard must be purchased to enter the subway. The fare is $2.50 no matter how far you travel; if you buy a single-use ticket, though, the price rises to $2.75. If you are making several trips, buy a weekly unlimited ticket, and the cost per journey will work out to be less. Or, if you get a Pay-Per-Ride MetroCard and put $5 or more on it, you will receive a 5 percent bonus credit. MetroCards, which can also be used on buses (see pp382–3), are sold at newsstands, drug-stores, and other locations around the city, as well as at all subway stations, where you can pay with cash. The machines take cash and debit and credit cards. One transfer per ride is allowed between the subway and bus; it must be used within 2 hours.

Using the Subway

Enter the subway by swiping your MetroCard at the turnstiles; the card is not needed to exit. Look for signs for uptown (northbound) and downtown (southbound) trains. Note that there are two types of trains: local trains stop at all stations, while faster express trains make fewer stops. Express lines have different letters or numbers than local ones; both types of stops are distinguished on every subway map.

Subway Stations

Many subway entrances are marked by illuminated spheres: green where the station booth is manned around the clock, red where there is restricted entry. Others are marked simply by a sign bearing the name of the station and the numbers or letters of the routes passing through it. Although the subway system runs 24 hours a day, not all routes operate at all times. The basic service is between 6am and midnight. The most crowded periods are the weekday rush hours (6–8:30am and 4:30–6:30pm); it is best to avoid these times if you can. If not, during crowded times the first and last cars are usually less busy.

New York City Subway

New York subway logo

Reading the Subway Map

Each route is identified on the subway map (see inside back cover) by color, by the names of the stations at each end of the line, and by a letter or number. Local and express stops and interchange points are also identified. The letters and numbers below the station names indicate which routes serve that particular station. A letter or number in heavy type indicates that trains on that route stop there between 6am and midnight; letters in lighter type mean that the route is served by a part-time service only; a boxed letter or number shows the last stop on the line. Express trains are indicated on subway maps with a white (rather than solid) circle. The maps posted in all the subway stations have a comprehensive guide that explains the trains and timetable of each route. Note that New Yorkers refer to subway lines by letter or number, not by color.

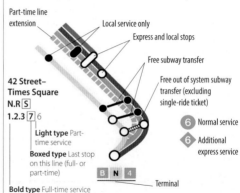

Part-time line extension

Local service only

Express and local stops

Free subway transfer

Free out of system subway transfer (excluding single-ride ticket)

42 Street–Times Square
N.R S
1.2.3 7 6

Light type Part-time service

Boxed type Last stop on this line (full- or part-time)

Bold type Full-time service

6 Normal service

6 Additional express service

B N 4

Terminal

Traveling by Subway

Subways run north–south up and down the city; the N, R, E and F trains run east–west from Midtown to Queens. See "Subway Lines" for the most useful routes.

1 There is a map of the subway system on the back inside cover of this book. Large-scale maps are also positioned in prominent areas in every station. Maps are also available at www.mta.info and at subway stations.

2 Buy a MetroCard from a station subway booth or MetroCard vending machine. The machines accept most credit and debit cards and bills up to $50, but no pennies. Vending machines can also be used to refill MetroCards.

3 Use MetroCard to pass through the turnstile onto the platform.

4 Follow the directions for the train you want. For safety, stay in sight of the booth as you wait for your train; at night, stay in one of the yellow off-hours waiting areas.

5 Each train displays its route number or letter in the appropriate color and the names of the terminal stations.

6 On every platform, you will find a line map, while on each train there is a system map next to the door on both sides of the car. Newer trains have electronic route maps for that line that light up overhead. Stops are announced on the public address system, and you will see station names at each platform. The doors are operated by the conductor.

7 After leaving the train, look for signs giving directions to the exit. If you need to change trains, just follow the signs to the connecting platforms.

The subway is generally quite safe, but visitors may feel more secure riding during the day and until around 10pm, when there are many other passengers around. If you feel unsure, stand in the "Off-Hours Waiting Area" on the platforms. In an emergency, contact either the station agent in the station booth or a member of the train crew, who are located in the first car and in the middle of the train.

Subway Lines

Subways run north–south on Lexington, Sixth Avenue, Seventh Avenue, Broadway, and Eighth Avenue. The #7 train runs west–east into Queens, while the E, F, M, N, Q, and R travel south–north until around midtown, and then east into Queens. A shuttle train connects Grand Central-42nd Street to Times Square-

42nd Street. Trains mostly run along one avenue, but some stations, such as those at Times Square, Union Square, and Columbus Circle, are convenient transfer points where several lines converge.

Each subway line has a distinct color, while the routes on each line are identified either by letter or number. For example, the Lexington Avenue line is green and the #6 is a local train, while #4 and #5 run express. The Eighth Avenue line is blue, and the A train is the express, while C and E are local trains. First and last stops are posted on track signs and on each car. Large system maps are posted in all stations. Free individual subway maps are usually available from booth attendants.

Some lines are especially useful for visitors. The Lexington Line is the only one serving the East Side and its many museums. The #6 train stops near the

Guggenheim, the Metropolitan Museum of Art, and the Frick Collection. The red #1 Broadway/Seventh Avenue line on the West Side takes you to Lincoln Center, MoMA, Times Square, Greenwich Village, SoHo, the Financial District, and South Ferry, where you can catch a ferry to the Statue of Liberty.

Track work at weekends can cause changes to the schedule. When you enter, ask the booth attendant about changes that may affect your journey.

DIRECTORY

MTA Automated Travel Planner

W tripplanner.mta.info

Subway Information

Tel 511.

W mta.info

Traveling by Bus

Traveling by bus is a good way to take in many of New York's sights. The city's 4,000-plus blue-and-white buses cover more than 200 routes in the five boroughs. Many run 24 hours a day, every day. The buses are modern, clean, air-conditioned, and energy-efficient. They are also quite safe and tend not to get crowded, except during rush hours. Smoking and eating are forbidden on all public buses, and only service animals (guide dogs) are allowed on board.

Bus stop in midtown Manhattan

Tickets and Fares

You can pay the $2.50 fare on a bus using a MetroCard (see p380), or exact change in coins. Bus drivers cannot make change, and fare boxes do not accept dollar bills, half-dollars, or pennies. You can buy a Metro-Card at any subway station booth or machine and at many other outlets around the city.

If you need to take more than one bus to reach your destination, you are eligible for a free transfer. If you pay your fare with a MetroCard, transfers to bus or subway are automatically placed electronically on the card. If you use cash, ask the driver for a transfer ticket when you pay. Transfers are good for 2 hours.

Senior citizens with proof of age and the disabled pay half-fare. All buses can "kneel," lowering the steps to help elderly people to board (see p362). They are also accessible to wheelchairs via a lift with ramp, at the rear or front depending on the bus design.

Bus Stops

Buses will stop only at designated bus stops. They follow north–south routes on the major avenues, stopping every two or three blocks. Crosstown buses run east–west and usually stop at every block, with the exception of Park Avenue, which is skipped by some lines. Many routes run a 24-hour daily service.

Bus stops are marked by red, white, and blue signs, and yellow paint along the curb. Most also have bus shelters; newer shelters provide seating and helpful signs giving the location. A route map and schedule is posted at each stop. Buses use letters to indicate the boroughs they serve: M for Manhattan, B for Brooklyn, Bx for the Bronx, and Q for Queens. Bus stops often serve several routes, so check the maps at the stop for your route, then look for that route number posted on the lighted strip above the windshield on the front of the bus.

Some buses will be marked "Limited," indicated by a flashing sign in the route number space and by a card in the front window. These buses are faster since they make fewer stops, but be sure the stops they do make are near your destination. Limited buses do stop at streets connecting to crosstown buses.

Free city bus maps are often available on board; ask the driver for a copy.

Using Buses

Most buses run every 3–5 minutes during the morning and evening rush hours, and every 7–15 minutes from noon to 4:30pm and from 7 to 10pm. Bad traffic or adverse weather conditions can cause delays. Service is reduced on weekends and holidays.

Enter the bus at the front door. If you are unsure of your route, ask the driver if they will be stopping at your destination or close to it. The majority of New York's bus drivers are helpful and will call out your stop if you ask when you board. Put your MetroCard in the slot or drop the correct coins in the fare box, then look for a seat.

To request a stop when traveling on the bus, press the yellow vertical call strip between the windows. Some newer buses also have stop buttons on center poles. A "Stop Requested" sign near the driver will then light up. If the bus is crowded, it is wise to start moving toward the exit door when you are a few blocks from your stop.

Leave through the double door located toward the rear of the bus. The driver will activate the door release as soon as the bus has stopped, and a green light will go on above the door. You then push the yellow stripe on the door, and the doors will open automatically; they will stay open long enough for everyone to leave. If the strip does not work properly, just push the door and then hold it open for the passenger behind you as you leave.

The M86 crosstown bus traveling through Central Park

Night Buses

Most lines run 24 hours, but be sure to check the schedule posted at your stop. After 10pm, many buses run every 20 minutes or so. From midnight to 6am, expect to wait 30–60 minutes for a bus.

Bus Tours

One of the most popular ways to see the sights is aboard a hop-on/hop-off bus tour that allows you to get off wherever you like, stay as long as you want, and catch another bus when you are ready. Gray Line *(see p379)* is the best-known company offering these tours aboard double-decker buses. Routes include a Downtown Loop, Uptown Loop, Brooklyn Loop, and Night/Holiday Lights Tour (not hop-on/hop-off). Buy a 48- or 72-hour pass, and you can see a great deal of New York. While you ride, narration is available in several languages through rented headsets.

MTA Trip Planner

The MTA website has a useful feature known as the Trip Planner, which provides a map and directions by bus and/or subway between any two points in New York. Enter your starting and ending points, the time you expect to travel, preferred mode of transportation, how far you are willing to walk, and whether you need accessible vehicles, and you will get clear directions. Visit http://travel.mtanyct.info to access the planner; www.hopstop.com offers a similar service.

DIRECTORY

MTA Travel Information

Tel 511. w mta.info

Route Maps

Available from MTA/NYCT,

Customer Service Center,

3 Stone Street, Lower Manhattan.

Map 1 C4.

Sightseeing Buses

For a pleasant and cheap alternative to a tour bus, hop on a city bus and see New York with the New Yorkers. Recommended bus routes include route M2, which runs down Fifth Avenue alongside Central Park and stops near the Guggenheim and the Metropolitan. It then returns north on Madison Avenue (via the Empire State Building and the Rockefeller Center), where it runs alongside the M5, which continues south to SoHo and Greenwich Village. From Broad Street, head north on the M15 to visit Brooklyn Bridge and the United Nations, or take route M7 or M20 along Eighth Avenue for Times Square and Madison Square Garden.

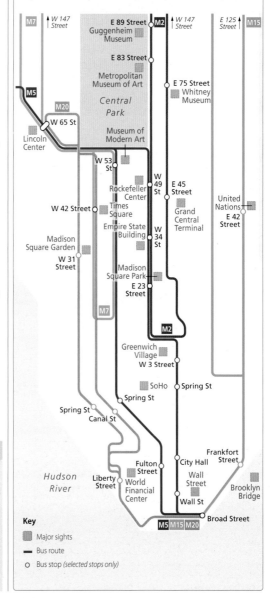

Key

- Major sights
- — Bus route
- O Bus stop *(selected stops only)*

Day Trips from New York

For a change of pace and some beautiful scenery, it is worth taking a day trip from New York City to the surrounding areas. Public transport links are excellent, and there are many convenient and easy ways to travel to nearby destinations (*see pp234–57*).

Departure board at Penn Station

Main Train Stations

New York has two main train stations, serving commuters as well as long-distance travelers.

Grand Central Terminal (*see pp158–9*), on Park Avenue at 42nd Street, is the main terminal for **Metro-North Railroad** trains (Hudson, New Haven, and Harlem lines), which run north of New York and serve southwest Connecticut and Westchester, Dutchess, and Putnam counties (*see pp372–3*). From Grand Central, you can travel by train to the Bronx Zoo (*see pp246–7*), the New York Botanical Garden, President Franklin D. Roosevelt's Hyde Park estate, and other mansions and towns overlooking the Hudson River.

The 4, 5, and 6 trains on the Lexington line and number 7 on the Flushing line serve Grand Central subway station. A shuttle train service links Grand Central to Times Square. Many bus lines stop near Grand Central, and taxis can usually be found in front of the station on 42nd Street or across from the side entrance on Vanderbilt Avenue at 43rd Street.

Penn Station, between Seventh and Eighth avenues and from 31st to 33rd streets, is a somewhat cramped underground terminal that was rebuilt in 1963 underneath the Madison Square Garden complex (*see p137*). **Long Island Rail Road** (LIRR) and **New Jersey Transit** commuter trains, plus **Amtrak** trains from Canada and other parts of the US, terminate at this station. There are no luggage trolleys, but redcap porters will help.

Taxis can be found at street level. Buses run downtown on Seventh Avenue and uptown on Eighth Avenue. The Eighth Avenue subway lines A, C, and E run on the Eighth Avenue side of the station; the Broadway lines 1, 2, and 3 run on the Seventh Avenue side of the station.

Commuter Rail Lines

Metro-North lines to upstate New York and Connecticut depart from Grand Central Station. These are mostly commuter trains but may be useful for trips to New Haven or Westchester County, or to destinations along the Hudson River. Long Island Rail Road and New Jersey Transit commuter rail lines depart from Penn Station. They can take you to New Jersey or Long Island beach resorts.

Long Island Rail Road logo

PATH trains are used mainly by commuters. They run around the clock between Newark, Jersey City and Hoboken stations and Manhattan. In the city they make stops at Christopher Street; the World Trade Center; Ninth, 14th, 23rd, and 33rd streets along Sixth Avenue.

Tickets and Fares

Train tickets are based on a one-way fare; a return fare is twice the single fare. Peak commuter fares are in operation on weekdays until 9am and between 4 and 8pm. All other hours and weekend days are considered off peak and cost much less.

The Long Island Rail Road has many One-Day Getaway packages, with discounted rail fares and admissions to places such as the Hamptons, vineyards, historic sites, and New York Mets baseball games.

Metro-North and LIRR cars are all one class and have no reserved seating, while Amtrak trains offer both services. The conductor will ask to see your ticket after the train has left the station.

Long Island Rail Road train

Booking Tickets

Ticketing offices at all train stations will accept most credit cards or cash. When there are lines for tickets, you can use the automated machines, which accept credit cards. Tickets can be purchased on board for payment in cash only. Note that there is a surcharge for buying tickets on board the train so it is advisable to purchase tickets in advance.

Yale University in New Haven, Connecticut

Day Trips by Train

Many destinations near New York are well worth a visit and easily reached by train. Below is a list of some recommended sights; for further details, call NYC & Co. *(see p363).*

Stony Brook is a peaceful North Shore village and the entrance to the Three Villages historic district. The journey takes 2 hours from Penn Station on a LIRR train.

The chic bars, clubs, and boutiques of the Hamptons are just under 3 hours from New York. Take a LIRR train from Penn Station.

Westbury House, John Phipps's 1906 re-creation of a Charles II mansion with English formal gardens, is 40 minutes from Manhattan. Take a LIRR train from Penn Station to Old Westbury.

Kykuit, the Rockefeller mansion; Washington Irving's home "Sunnyside;" and Jay Gould's mansion, "Lyndhurst", are all in Tarrytown. Take a Metro-North train from Grand Central Station, then a taxi. The journey should take 40–50 minutes.

Two hours outside of Manhattan is Hyde Park, where you can visit Franklin D. Roosevelt's Springwood estate and the Vanderbilt mansion. Take a Metro-North train from Grand Central to Poughkeepsie, then a bus.

Cold Spring, New York, is an antiquing mecca on the Hudson. The scenic riverside journey takes 70 minutes from Grand Central on the Metro-North Hudson Line.

New Haven, Connecticut, is home to the world-famous Yale University. The journey takes 1 hour and 45 minutes, again on a Metro-North train from Grand Central.

Day Trips by Bus

Many appealing destinations can be reached by bus from the Port Authority Bus Terminal *(see p373)* on Eighth Avenue. **Short Line Bus** offers popular day-out packages to the US Military Academy at West Point, Franklin D. Roosevelt's home at Hyde Park, and the Storm King Art Center. Also on offer is shopping at the Woodbury Common Outlet Center. Rates include round-trip bus fare and any admissions.

New Jersey Transit buses go to the casinos at Atlantic City; they also have stops on the Jersey shore. **Trans-Bridge Lines** has services to charming antiquing meccas such as Lambertville, New Jersey, and New Hope, Pennsylvania.

A number of budget bus lines have inexpensive fares to Philadelphia, a historic city with many attractions that is only 100 miles (160 km) from New York. Among the most reliable and comfortable of these are **Megabus** and **Bolt Bus**, both of which offer free Wi-Fi on board. For those with time to travel farther afield, these companies also serve Boston and Washington, DC.

Bus tickets are on sale in the main concourse of the Port Authority. The long-distance bus companies Greyhound *(see p373)*, **Peter Pan**, and **Adirondacks** and the Short Line, Trans-Bridge, and New Jersey Transit commuter lines have their own ticket counters. No reservations are taken on any of these bus lines.

Day Trips by Subway or City Bus

The outer boroughs, served by New York's subway and bus system, are also worth exploring. Head for the Coney Island beaches *(see p251)* and the New York Aquarium on the D, F, N or Q trains, or take the M4 bus to the last stop and visit The Cloisters *(see pp238–41)*, high above the Hudson River.

New York's ethnic neighbor-hoods are also easily reached by subway. At Grand Central Station, take the 7 Queens train to 74th Street in Jackson Heights, where you'll find a slice of India. Nearby, 37th Avenue is home to New York's Latin-American community. If you stay on the 7 train to the end of the line, you can explore a Chinatown that rivals the one in Manhattan, as well as the city's largest Korean neighbourhood.

In Brooklyn, the B train will take you to the Russian enclave of Brighton Beach, while the G train will let you sample a bit of Poland in Greenpoint. Take the N train to go Greek or Egyptian in Astoria, or the F train to the city's largest Orthodox Jewish community in Borough Park.

DIRECTORY

Train Information

Amtrak
Tel (800) USA-RAIL or (800) 872-7245. W amtrak.com

Long Island Rail Road (LIRR)
Tel (718) 217-LIRR. W mta.info

Metro-North Railroad
Tel (212) 532-4900. W mta.info

New Jersey Transit
Tel (973) 275-5555.
W njtransit.com

PATH
Tel (800) 234-7284.
W panynj.com

Bus Information

Adirondacks
Tel (518) 846-8016.
W visitadirondacks.com

Bolt Bus
Tel (877) 265-8287.
W boltbus.com

Megabus
Tel (877) 462-6342.
W megabus.com

Peter Pan
Tel (800) 343-9999.
W peterpanbus.com

Short Line Bus
Tel (201) 529-3666.
W coachusa.com/shortline

Trans-Bridge Lines
Tel (610) 868-6001.
W transbridgelines.com

STREET FINDER

The map references given with all sights, hotels, restaurants, bars, shops, and entertainment venues described in this book refer to the maps in this section *(see* How the Map References Work *opposite)*. These maps cover the whole of Manhattan. A complete index of street names and all the places of interest marked on the maps can be found on the following pages.

The key map *(below)* shows the areas covered by the *Street Finder*, within the various districts. The maps include all of Manhattan's sight-seeing areas (which are color-coded), with all the districts important for hotels, restaurants, bars, shops, theaters, and entertainment.

Browsing at South Street Seaport

0 kilometers — 2
0 miles — 1

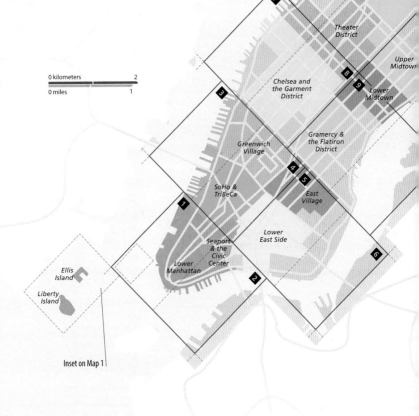

Upper West Side

Theater District

Upper Midtown

Chelsea and the Garment District

Lower Midtown

Greenwich Village

Gramercy & the Flatiron District

SoHo & TriBeCa

East Village

Lower East Side

Seaport & the Civic Center

Lower Manhattan

Ellis Island

Liberty Island

Inset on Map 1

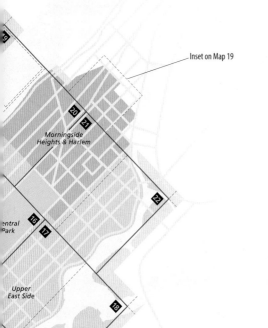

Inset on Map 19

Morningside
Heights & Harlem

entral
Park

Upper
East Side

Key to Streetfinder

- Major sight
- Other sight
- Railroad s tation
- M Subway station
- Heliport
- Ferry terminal
- Bus terminal
- Aerial tramway
- i Tourist information office
- Hospital with emergency room
- Police station
- Church
- Synagogue
- Railroad line
- Pedestrian street

Scale of map pages

0 meters	200	
0 yards	200	1:11,500

How the Map References Work

The first figure tells you which Street Finder map to turn to.

❼ Theodore Roosevelt Birthplace

28 E 20th St.
Map 9 A5. **Tel** 260-1616. M 14th St-Union Sq. **Open** 9am–5pm Wed–Sun (last adm: 4:30pm). **Closed** public hols. Lectures, concerts, films & video w nps.gov/thrb

A letter and number give the grid reference. Letters go across the map's top and bottom, numbers on its sides.

The map continues on map 5 of the *Street Finder*.

Street Finder Index

Each place name is followed by its borough (unless in Manhattan) and then by its Street Finder reference

Each place name is followed by its borough (unless in Manhattan) and then by its Street Finder reference

Each place name is followed by its borough (unless in Manhattan) and then by its Street Finder reference

Each place name is followed by its borough (unless in Manhattan) and then by its Street Finder reference

7

«460 «400 «484 «300 «200

WEST 13TH STREET

TENTH AVENUE

JACKSON SQUARE

St.Vincent's Hospital

SEVENTH AVENUE

ELEVENTH AVE

The Meatpacking District

HUDSON STREET

GREENWICH AVENUE

LITTLE HIGH LINE

WEST 12TH STREET

THE HIGH LINE

GANSEVOORT STREET

JANE STREET

EIGHTH AVENUE

WEST 12TH STREET

WAVERLY

MULRY SQUARE

1

PIER 54

Fire Boat Station

BLOOMFIELD STREET

HORATIO STREET

WASHINGTON STREET

GREENWICH STREET

STREET

WEST 11TH STREET

4TH STREET

STREET

McCARTHY SQUARE

PIER 53

JANE STREET

ABINGDON SQUARE

BANK STREET

WEST STREET

BLEECKER STREET

PERRY STREET

STREET

PIER 52

WEST 12TH STREET

BETHUNE STREET

STREET

STREET

CHARLES STREET

SOUTH

PIER 51

BANK STREET

STREET

Christopher St Sheridan Sq

WEST STREET

SHERID SQUAR

2

PIER 50

WEST 11TH STREET

PERRY STREET

WASHINGTON STREET

STREET

GREENWICH STREET

HUDSON STREET

WEST 10TH STREET

CHRISTOPHER STREET

GROVE STREET

BEDFORD STREET

COMMERCE ST

CHARLES LANE

CHARLES STREET

10TH ST

PIER 46

WEST STREET

WEEHAWKEN STREET

ST. LUKE'S GARDEN

PLACE

Grove Court

Isaacs-Hendricks House

75 Bed Stre

BARROW STREET

STREET

St Luke's Place

ST LUKE'S PLACE

3

PIER 45

MORTON STREET

STREET

JAMES J. WALKER PARK

LEROY STREET

«388

CLARKSON STREET

WEST STREET

HOUSTON

«363

HUDSON ST

HUDSON RIVER PARK

WASHINGTON STREET

WEST STREET

Children's Museum of the Arts

GREENWICH STREET

CHARLTON

PIER 40

VANDAM

4

WEST STREET

SPRING STREET

«301

CANAL STREET

GREENWICH STREET

STREET

PIER 34

WATTS STREET

Tunnel

Holland

STREET

DESBROSSE

PIER 32

VESTRY

LAIGHT

5

PIER 29

HUB

PIER 28

PIER 27

Manhat Commu Coll

PIER 26

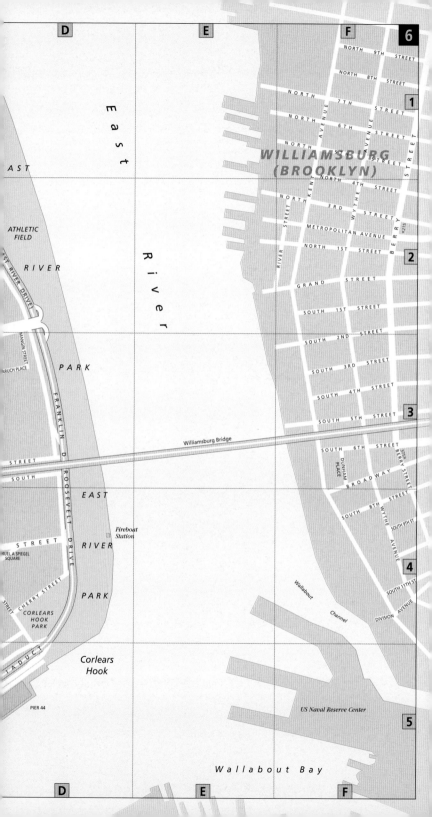

A **11** **B** **C**

1

PIER 83

*Circle Line
Boat Trip*

WEST 43RD STREET

WEST 42ND STREET (THEATER ROW

NYC Technical
College

PIER 81

WEST 41ST STREET

*Cardinal
Stepinac Plaza*

WEST 40TH STREET

West Midtown Ferry Terminal

Lincoln Tunnel

WEST 39TH STREET

WEST 38TH STREET

T
W
E
L
F
T
H

A
V
E
N
U
E

E
L
E
V
E
N
T
H

A
V
E
N
U
E

T
E
N
T
H

A
V
E
N
U
E

D
Y
E
R

A
V
E
N
U
E

WEST 37TH STREET

PIER 76

*Jacob K Javits
Convention Center*

WEST 36TH STREET

WEST 35TH STREET

WEST 34TH STREET

CALVIN AVENUE

WEST 33RD STREET

PIER 72

*Port Authority
West 30th Street Heliport*

WEST 30TH STREET

US Parcel Post Buildi

WEST 29TH STREET

WEST 28TH STREET

*CHELSEA
PARK*

WEST 27TH STREET

PIER 66

WEST 26TH STREET

WEST 25TH STREET

H
u
d
s
o
n

R
i
v
e
r

PIER 64

WEST 24TH STREET

*CHELSEA
WATERSIDE
PARK*

T
H
E

H
I
G
H

L
I
N
E

WEST 23RD STREET

Empire Diner

WEST 22ND STREET

i

WEST 21ST STREET

PIER 62

WEST 20TH STREET

*Chelsea Histo
District*

PIER 61

*Chelsea
Piers*

WEST 19TH STREET

WEST 18TH STREET

PIER 60

WEST 17TH STREE

PIER 59

WEST 16TH STREE

WEST 15TH STREE

A **B** PIER 57 **C**

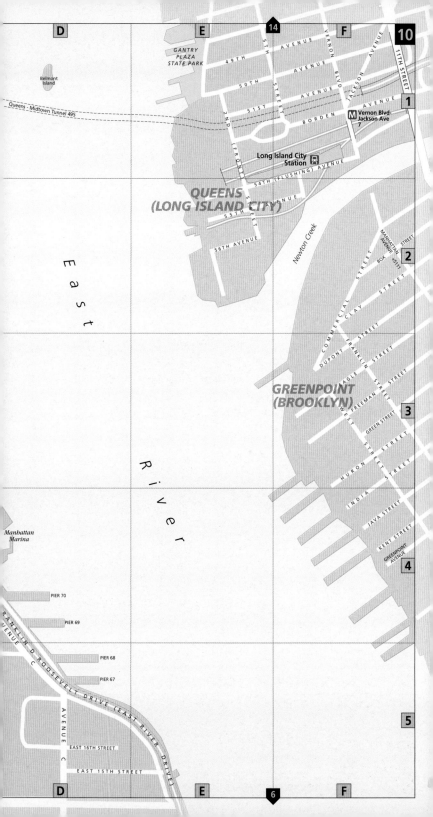

BLACKWELL
PARK

Roosevelt Island Bridge

FRANKLIN D ROOSEVELT DRIVE (EAST RIVER DRIVE)

36TH   AVENUE

9TH STREET

10TH STREET

11TH STREET

12TH STREET

13TH STREET

West   Channel

East   Channel

VERNON   BOULEVARD

37TH   AVENUE

38TH   AVENUE

MAIN STREET

LONG ISLAND
CITY

40TH   AVENUE

10TH STREET

12TH STREET

13TH STREET

Roosevelt Island **M**
F ST

ROOSEVELT
ISLAND

41ST   AVENUE

VERNON BOULEVARD
#4022

QUEENS
BRIDGE
PARK

QUEENS
COUNTY

41ST ROAD

AERIAL TRAMWAY
Queensboro Bridge

QUEENS   PLAZA   NORTH

Queensboro Bridge

QUEENS   PLAZA   SOUTH

West   Channel

East   Channel

WEST ROAD

EAST ROAD

VERNON BOULEVARD

9TH STREET

10TH STREET

11TH STREET

12TH STREET

13TH STREET

21ST ST

#4302

43RD   AVENUE

43RD   ROAD
#4302

WEST ROAD

EAST ROAD

AVENUE

44TH   ROAD

44TH DRIVE

44TH   DRIVE

45TH   AVENUE

5TH STREET

11TH   ROAD

45TH   ROAD

11TH   STREET

VERNON

46TH   AVENUE

46TH   ROAD

5TH STREET

47TH   AVENUE

47TH   ROAD

JACKSON AVENUE

48TH   AVENUE

1
2
3
4
5

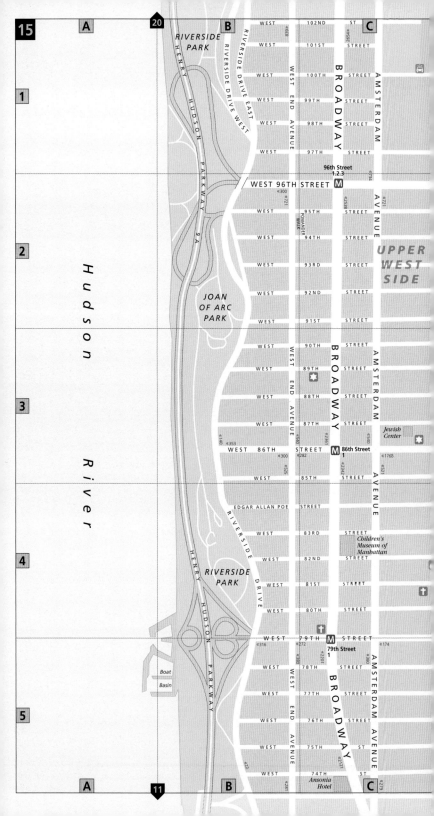

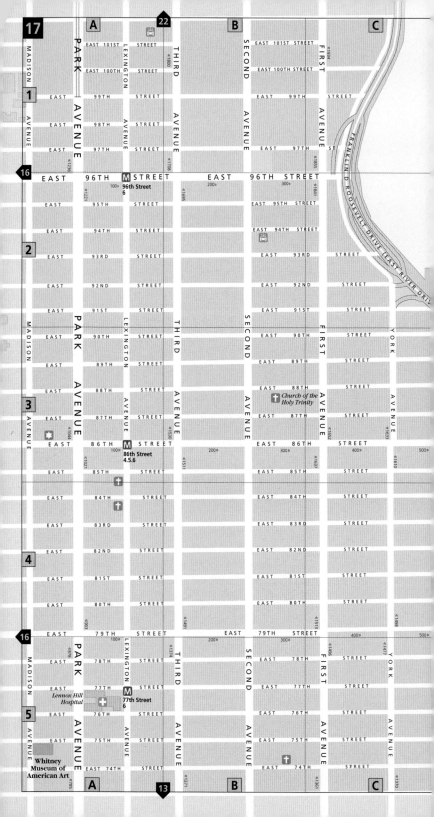

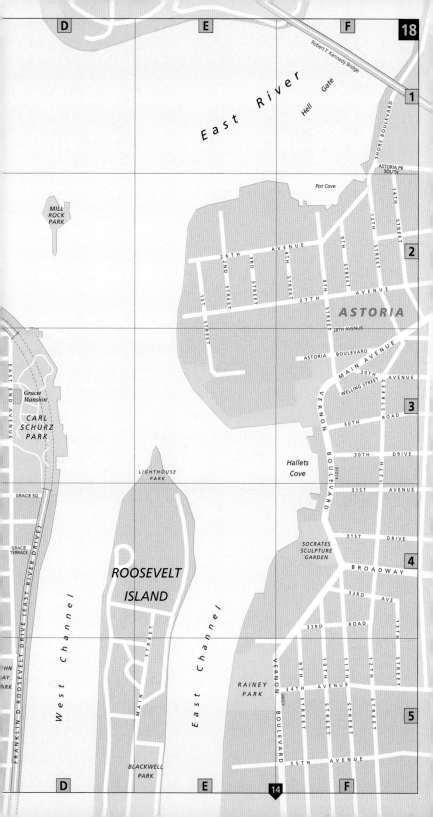

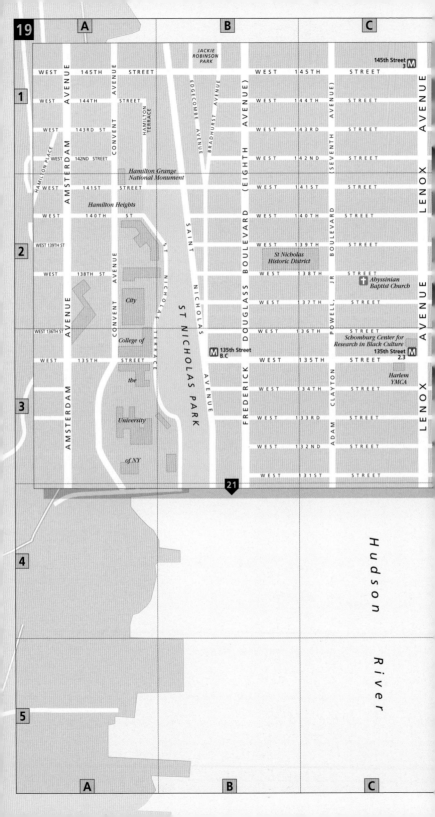

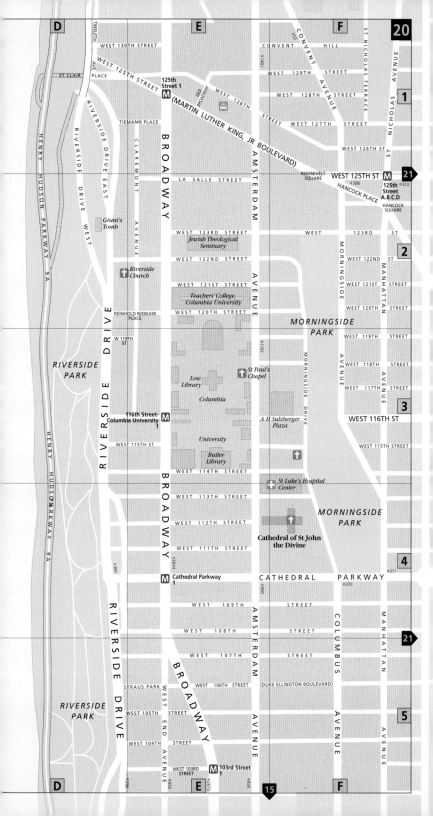

General Index

Acknowledgments

Dorling Kindersley would like to thank the many people whose help and assistance contributed to the preparation of this book.

Main Contributor
Eleanor Berman has lived in New York for around 40 years. Her travel articles are widely published and she is the author of *Away for the Weekend: New York*, a favorite since 1982. Her other books include *Away for the Weekend* guides for the Mid-Atlantic, New England and Northern California, *Travelling on Your Own* and *Reflections of Washington, DC*.

Museum Contributors
Michelle Menendez, Lucy O'Brien, Heidi Rosenau, Elyse Topalian, Sally Williams.

Dorling Kindersley wishes to thank editors and researchers at Websters International Publishers: Sandy Carr, Matthew Barrell, Sara Harper, Miriam Lloyd, Ava-Lee Tanner, Celia Woolfrey.

Additional Photography
Rebecca Carman, Rachel Feierman, Michelle Haimoff Andrew Holigan, Edward Hueber, Eliot Kaufman, Karen Kent, Dave King, Norman McGrath, Howard Millard, Ian O'Leary, Rough Guides/Nelson Hancock, Rough Guides/Angus Oborn, Susannah Sayler, Paul Solomon, Chuck Spang, Chris Stevens, Peter Wilson.

Additional Illustrations
Steve Gyapay, Arshad Khan, Kevin Jones, Dinwiddie MacLaren, Janos Marffy, Chris D. Orr, Nick Shewring, John Woodcock.

Cartography
Maps Uma Bhattacharya, Andrew Heritage, Suresh Kumar, James Mills-Hicks, Chez Picthall, John Plumer (Dorling Kindersley Cartography), Kunal Singh. Advanced Illustration (Cheshire), Contour Publishing (Derby), Europmap Ltd (Berkshire). Street Finder maps: ERA-Maptec Ltd (Dublin) adapted with permission from original survey and mapping by Shobunsha (Japan).

Cartographic Research
Roger Bullen, Tony Chambers, Ruth Duxbury, Ailsa Heritage, Jayne Parsons, Laura Porter, Donna Rispoli, Joan Russell, Jill Tinsley, Andrew Thompson.

Design and Editorial
Managing Editor Douglas Amrine
Managing Art Editors Stephen Knowlden, Geoff Manders
Senior Editor Georgina Matthews
Series Design Consultant Peter Luff
Editorial Director David Lamb
Art Director Anne-Marie Bulat
Production Controller Hilary Stephens
Picture Research Susan Mennell, Sarah Moule
Dtp Designer Andy Wilkinson
Revisions and Relaunch Team Keith Addison, Asad Ali, Emma Anacootee, Lydia Baillie, Eleanor Berman, Vandana Bhagra, Subhashree Bharati, Shruti Bahl, Jon Paul Buchmeyer, Ron Boudreau, Linda Cabasin, Rebecca Carman, Michelle Clark, Sherry Collins, Carey Combe, Diana Craig, Maggie Crowley, Guy Dimond, Vidushi Duggal, Nicola Erdpresser, Rhiannon

Furbear, Fay Franklin, Tom Fraser, Anna Freiberger, Jo Gardner, Camilla Gersh, Alex Gray, Eric Grossman, Michelle Haimoff, Marcus Hardy, Sasha Heseltine, Rose Hudson, Pippa Hurst, Kim Inglis, Jaqueline Jackson, Stuart James, Claire Jones, Bharti Karakoti, Priya Kukadia, Rakesh Kumar Pal, Mathew Kurien, Maite Lantaron, Jude Ledger, Shahid Mahmood, Nicola Malone, Susan Millership, Jane Middleton, Todd Obolsky, Helen Partington, Pollyanna Poulter, Leigh Priest, Pamposh Raina, Nicki Rawson, Alice Reese, Marisa Renzullo, Amir Reuveni, Ellen Root, Liz Rowe, Azeem Siddiqui, Sands Publishing Solutions, Anaïs Scott, Shailesh Sharma, Beverly Smart, Meredith Smith, AnneLise Sorensen, Anna Streiffert, Clare Sullivan, Andrew Szudek, Alka Thakur, Shawn Thomas, Conrad Van Dyk, Ajay Verma, Ros Walford, Catherine Waring, Lucilla Watson, Ed Wright.

Special Assistance
Beyer Blinder Belle, John Beatty at the Cotton Club, Peter Casey at the New York Public Library, Nicky Clifford, Linda Corcoran at the Bronx Zoo, Audrey Manley at the Morgan Library, Jane Fischer, Deborah Gaines at the New York Convention and Visitors Bureau, Dawn Geigerich at the Queens Museum of Art, Peggy Harrington at St. John the Divine, Pamela Herrick at the Van Cortlandt House, Marguerite Lavin at the Museum of the City of New York, Robert Makla at the Friends of Central Park, Gary Miller at the New York Stock Exchange, Laura Mogil at the American Museum of Natural History, Fred Olsson at the Shubert Organization, Dominique Palermo at the Police Academy Museum, Royal Canadian Pancake House, Lydia Ruth and Laura I. Fries at the Empire State Building, David Schwartz at the American Museum of the Moving Image, Joy Sienkiewicz at the South Street Seaport Museum, Barbara Orlando at the Metropolitan Transit Authority, the staff at the Lower East Side Tenement Museum, Msgr. Anthony Dalla Valla at St. Patrick's Cathedral.

Research Assistance
Christa Griffin, Bogdan Kaczorowski, Steve McClure, Sabra Moore, Jeff Mulligan, Marc Svensson, Vicky Weiner, Steven Weinstein.

Photographic Reference
Duncan Petersen Publishers Ltd.

Photography Permissions
Dorling Kindersley would like to thank the following for their kind permission to photograph at their establishments: American Craft Museum, American Museum of Natural History, Aunt Len's Doll and Toy Museum, Balducci's, Home Savings of America, Brooklyn Children's Museum, The Cloisters, Columbia University, Eldridge Street Project, Federal Hall, Rockefeller Group, Trump Tower.

Picture credits
a = above; b = below/bottom; c = center; f = far; l = left; r = right; t = top.

Works of art have been reproduced with the permission of the following copyright holders: © ADAGP, Paris and DACS, London 2011: April 1971–July 1972, by Jean Dubuffet 69tc, donated by the Norwegian Government, 1952 164tr, 190cla, 191cra, 191crb; © ARS, NY and DACS, London 2011:187cr, 203crb; Jose de Creeft ©DACS, London/VAGA,

New York 2011: 55cl, 209cla; © DACS, London 2011: 163crb, 165tc; Walter De Maria *Broken Kilometer* 1979 106cl; *Charging Bull* © Arturo Di Modica 1998 75tl; DK IMAGES: Judith Miller/Wallis & Wallis, Sussex 60br; © Kingdom of Spain, Gaia – Salvador Dali Foundation, DAC2S, London 2011: 176cla; © Marisol Escobar/DACS, London/VAGA, New York 2011: 57bc; Milton Hebald *Romeo and Juliet* 335cr. © Jasper Johns/DACS, London/VAGA, New York 2011: 203ca; ©The Estate of Roy Lichtenstein/DACS, London 2011: 177tl, 202clb; Georg John Lober *Hans Christian Andersen* 1956, 208br; By permission of E Jan Nadelman: 203br; © Succession Picasso/DACS, London 2011: 38tr, 117tl, 175cb, 176cra, 190clb, 191bl, 194cl; Printed by permission of the Norman Rockwell Family Trust © 1961 the Norman Rockwell Family Trust: 165br; © Licensed by The Andy Warhol Foundation for the Visual Arts, Inc/ARS, New York and DACS, London 2011: 202cla; © The Whitney Museum of American Art: 39br, 202bl; Yu Yu Yang: *Untitled*, 1973, 59br.

The Publishers are grateful to the following museums, companies and picture libraries for permission to reproduce their photographs:

Agence France Presse: Doug Kanter 35tr; **Alamy Images:** AA World Travel Library 141c; Ambient Images Inc./Joseph A. Rosen 173c; Sandra Baker 362tl; Patrick Batchelder 212; Peter Cavanagh 365cla; Comstock Images 291c; Wendy Connett 98ca, 118; Eye Ubiquitous/Jon Hicks 135cb; Kevin Foy 75tl; Jeff Greenberg 270cla; Bob Jones 113br; Richard Levine 373tc; Ian Marlow 365cl; Patti McConville 276-7; Ellen McKnight 370cla; PCL 291tl; Alex Segre 290cla; Lana Sundman 365tl; tbkmedia.de 332bc; Hugh Threlfall 364cla; **Ace Hotel:** Lyle Thompson 283tr; **Aldea Restaurant:** 293br; **American Museum-Hayden Planetarium, NY:** D. Finnin 220tc; **American Museum of the Moving Image:** Carson Collection © Bruce Polin 249tl; **American Museum of Natural History, NY:** 41clb, 218ca; D. Finnin 218bl; **Angel Orensanz Center:** Laszlo Regas 103cl; **Aquagrill:** 294tl; **Aquarius, UK:** 173tr; **The Asia Society, NY:** 189cl; **Attaché Communications:** 384crb; **Avery Fisher Hall:** © N McGrath 1976 335tr; **Avis Budget Group:** 377crb; © **The George Balanchine Trust:** *Apollo*, choreography by George Balanchine, photo by P Kolnik 5bl; George Balanchine's *The Nutcracker*, SM, photo by P Kolnik 335br; **The Bettmann Archive, NY:** 20clb, 21cla/cr/bl, 22cl, 24cb/bl, 24–5cb, 27br, 29cr, 30cla/cra/crb, 34cla, 35tl, 47br, 51c, 56–7b, 73tl, 76cla, 81crb, 81br, 113bl, 179cl, 187br, 211tl, 214cl, 227c, 233tc, 243tr, 269tr; **Bettmann/ UPI:** 31cra/bc, 32br, 33br, 34clb/bc, 48cl, 50cla, 51bl, 74tl, 80clb, 155ca, 165cr, 268br, 269cr; **Bloomingdale's:** 31crb; **British Film Institute:** © Roy Export Company Establishment 177tr; **The British Library, London:** 18; **Brooklyn Historical Society:** detail 91tl; **The Brooklyn Museum:** 40bl, 41c, 252-3 all, 254 -5 all; Lewis Wick Hine, *Climbing Into The Promised Land*, 1908 – 38clb; **Brown Brothers:** 69br, 92tr, 108br. **Camera Press:** 32crb/bl, 35clb, 129crb; R Open 50tr; **The Carlyle Hotel, NY:** 281tr; **Carnegie Hall:** © H. Grossman 335bl; **J Allan Cash:** 34br; **Cathedral of St. John The Divine:** Greg Wyatt Peace Fountain1985, 229tl; **CBS Entertainment/Desilu too:** "Vacation from Marriage" 173br; **Chelsea Lodge:** 285bc; **Chelsea Piers:** Fred George 35bl; **Children's Museum of the Arts:** 109cl; **CityPASS:** 361c; **Colorific!:** Colorific/Black Star: 81cr; T Cowell 225cr; R Fraser 76tr; D Moore 33bl; **Corbis:** Alan Schein Photography 222; Bettmann 139cl, 275ca; Jacques M. Chenet 274tl; Randy Duchaine 101tl; Kevin Fleming 273tl; Bob Krist 10cra; Todd Gipstein 77tl;

David Lehman: 140bl; Mascarucci 298tl; Gail Mooney 209bl, 271tr, 273br, 299b; Bill Ross 372tl; Michael Setboun 258, 270tr; Steven E. Sutton 53br; Ramin Talaie 37cra; VIEW/ Nathan Willock 94; Michael Yamashita 275cb; Bo Zaunders 368cl; **Culver Pictures, Inc:** (inset) 9, 21crb, 22clb, 23bl, 25tl/ br, 28cl, 31cb, 50br, 51tr, 76cb, 77cr/cb, 78tl, 81bl, 85c, 123bl, 126tc, 129bl, 139cr, 149c, 151clb, 231tl/bc/crb, 261cb; **Da Silvano:** Noah Fecks 295tr; **Daily Eagle:** (detail) 91clb; **The Dinex Group:** Eric Laignel 301b; B Milne 300tl; **Dirt Candy:** 292tl; Dollar Thrifty Automotive Group, Inc.: 377cra; **Dreamstime.com:** Alexpro9500 377br; Alexandre Fagundes De Fagundes 375cb; Tatiana Morozova 380cl; Rolf52 10bl; **Esto:** P Aaron 334clb; **Mary Evans Picture Library:** Library of Congress 8-9, 26br, 89br, 108bl; **The Forbes Magazine Collection, NY:** 116tl; **Four Seasons Hotel:** Peter Vitale 281cr; **Fraunces Tavern Museum, NY:** From the exhibit "Come All You Gallant Heroes" The World of the Revolutionary Soldier December 4, 1991 to August 14, 1992: 24cla; **Freemans:** S Freihon 295bl; **Copyright The Frick Collection, NY:** *St Francis In The Desert* by Giovanni Bellini 39bl, 204–5 all; **Garrard The Crown Jewellers:** 147c; **Getty Images:** AFP/Stan Honda 384cla; age fotostock 82, / JosÂ Fuste Raga 13br; AWL Images/Gavin Hellier 64–5, /Jon Arnold 2–3; FilmMagic 234; Mitchell Funk 333cb, 358–9; Glow Images, Inc 264–5; Michael Grimm 378tl; The Image Bank/Siegfried Layda 36, /Riou 13tl; Lonely Planet Images/ Angus Oborn 1; Neos Design – Cory Eastman 206; Photodisc/Thomas Northcut 142; Photolibrary/Barry Winiker 12br, 154clb; Stone/Hiroyuki Matsumoto 184; Vetta/S. Greg Panosian 66; Barry Winiker 147tl; **Greenmarket Farmers Market:** 363tr; **The Greenwich Hotel:** 286bc; **The Solomon R Guggenheim Museum, NY:** 190–91 all; **Robert Harding Picture Library:** Harpers New Monthly Magazine: 89tl; **The Image Bank:** 17clb, 91br; M Melford 385tl; P Miller 375tc; A Satterwhite 77bc; **Japan Society:** © Jack Vartoogian, NY 63bc, 160tc; **The Jewish Museum, NY:** 186tr, 188c; **The Kobal Collection:** 215tc; **Lebrecht Music:** Toby Wales 151tl; **The Leisure Pass Group:** 361cla; **The Lesbian, Gay, Bisexual, & Transgender Community Center:** 362c; **Frank Leslie's Illustrated Newspaper:** 88br, 89cra; **Library of Congress:** 22bc, 25cla, 29bl/br; **Library Hotel Collection:** 282bl; **Leonardo Media Ltd:** 278br/cla, 279br/tl; **The Lowell Hotel, NY:** 281cl; **Madison Square Garden:** 137cr, 334tr; **Magnum Photos:** © H Cartier-Bresson 177c; Erwitt 37cr; **Jacques Marchais Center of Tibetan Art:** 256bc; **Masterfile UK:** Gail Mooney 35br; **Metro-North Commuter Railroad:** F English 158tr/ca; **The Metropolitan Museum of Art, NY:** *Young Woman With A Waterjug* by Johannes Vermeer 37bl, *Figure of a Hippopotamus*, faience, Egypt, 12th Dynasty 39crb, 192cla/ clb/bc, 193 all, 194br/tr/c/bl/br, 195tl/tr, 196–7 all, 198–9 all, 238 all, 239ca/cr/bl/br, 240tl/tr, 241tr/c/b; **Metropolitan Transit Authority:** 380crc, 384bl; MTA/Patrick Cashin all 381, 382tr/bl; **Collection of The Morgan Library, NY:** *Blanche of Castille and King Louis IX of France, author dictating to a scribe*, moralized Bible, c1230 38cr, 167bl, *Song of Los* David A. Loggie (gift of Mrs Landon K Thorne) 166cla, *Biblia Latina* David A. Loggie 166clb, 166br, 167cb/tc/br; **Morris-Jumel Mansion, Inc NY:** 21tl; A Rosario 25crb; **The Museum of the City of New York:** 19b, 20cra, 20–1, 21tr, 22ca, photo J Parnell 23cb, 24cl, 26cla/clb, 27cb/crb/bc, 28cb, 29tc/crb/ cb, 30bl, 31tr, 32tc/c, 33tc/c, 39tr (silver porringer), 89crb (Talfour); **The Museum of Modern Art, NY:** 174ca, 175cr/ crb/cb/bl, 176cla/cr, 177tl/b; *The Bather*, c. 1885, Paul Cézanne 176bc; Lillie P. Bliss Collection 175cra; © 2004 Photo Elizabeth Felicella, architectural rendering Kohn Pedersen Fox Associates, digital composite Robert Bowen

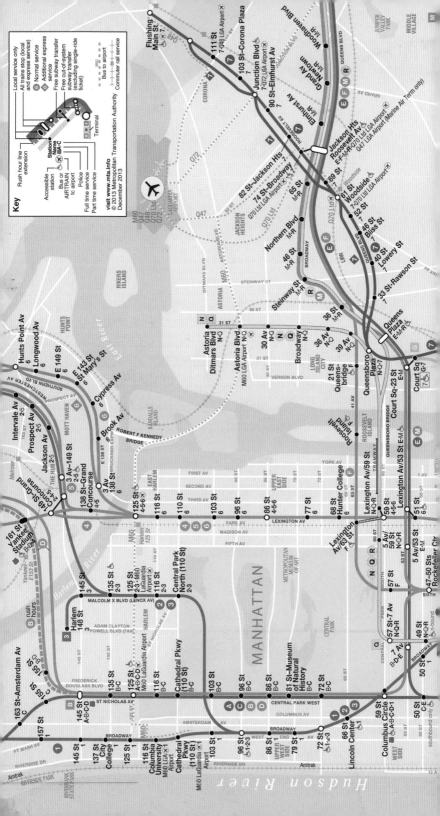